IC³ BASICS

Internet and Computing Core Certification

Ann Ambrose
Marly Bergerud
Dr. Donald Busche
Connie Morrison
Dolores Wells-Pusins

THOMSON
COURSE TECHNOLOGY

Australia • Canada • Mexico • Singapore • Spain • United Kingdom • United States

THOMSON

COURSE TECHNOLOGY

IC³ BASICS, Internet and Computing Core Certification

By Ann Ambrose, Marly Bergerud, Dr. Donald Busche, Connie Morrison, and Dolores Wells-Pusins

Senior Vice President
Chris Elkhill

Managing Editor
Chris Katsaropoulos

Senior Product Manager
Dave Lafferty

Product Manager
Robert Gaggin

Product Marketing Manager
Kim Ryttel

Associate Product Manager
Jodi Dreissig

Development Editor
Custom Editorial Productions Inc.

Production Editor
Custom Editorial Productions Inc.

Compositor
GEX Publishing Services

1 2 3 4 5 6 7 8 9 BM 04 03 02

For more information, contact Course Technology, 25 Thomson Place, Boston, Massachusetts, 02210.

Or find us on the World Wide Web at: www.course.com

ISBN 0-619-186038 (hard cover)
ISBN 0-619-183039 (soft cover)

Get Back to the Basics...

With these *exciting new products*

Our exciting new IC^3 BASICS text is part of a series of short, concepts and application suite books that provide everything needed to learn computing.

NEW! IC^3 BASICS, Internet and Computing Core Certification by Ambrose, Bergerud, Busche, Morrison & Wells-Pusins
75+ hours of instruction for capstone projects

0-619-18603-8 Textbook, Hard Bound Cover
0-619-18303-9 Textbook, Soft Bound Cover
0-619-18305-5 Instructor Resource Kit
0-619-18306-3 Review Pack (Data CD)

Computer Projects BASICS by Korb
35+ hours of instruction for additional projects on all software applications

0-619-05987-7 Textbook, Soft Spiral Bound Cover
0-619-05988-5 Instructor Resource Kit

Internet BASICS by Barksdale, Rutter, & Teeter
35+ hours of instruction for beginning through intermediate features

0-619-05905-2 Textbook, Soft Spiral Bound Cover
0-619-05906-0 Instructor Resource Kit

Web Design BASICS by Stubbs & Barksdale
35+ hours of instruction for beginning through intermediate features

0-619-05964-8 Textbook, Soft Spiral Bound Cover
0-619-05966-4 Instructor Resource Kit

Microsoft Office^{XP} BASICS by Morrison
35+ hours of instruction for beginning through intermediate features

0-619-05908-7 Textbook, Hard Spiral Bound Cover
0-619-05906-0 Instructor Resource Kit
0-619-05909-5 Activities Workbook
0-619-05907-9 Review Pack (Data CD)

Join Us On the Internet **http://www.course.com**

How to Use This Book

What makes a good computer instructional text? Sound pedagogy and the most current, complete materials. Not only will you find an inviting layout, but also many features to enhance learning.

Objectives—Objectives are listed at the beginning of each lesson, along with a suggested time for completion of the lesson. This allows you to look ahead to what you will be learning and to pace your work.

Step-by-Step Exercises—Preceded by a short topic discussion, these exercises are the "hands-on practice" part of the lesson. Simply follow the steps, either using a data file or creating a file from scratch. Each lesson is a series of these step-by-step exercises.

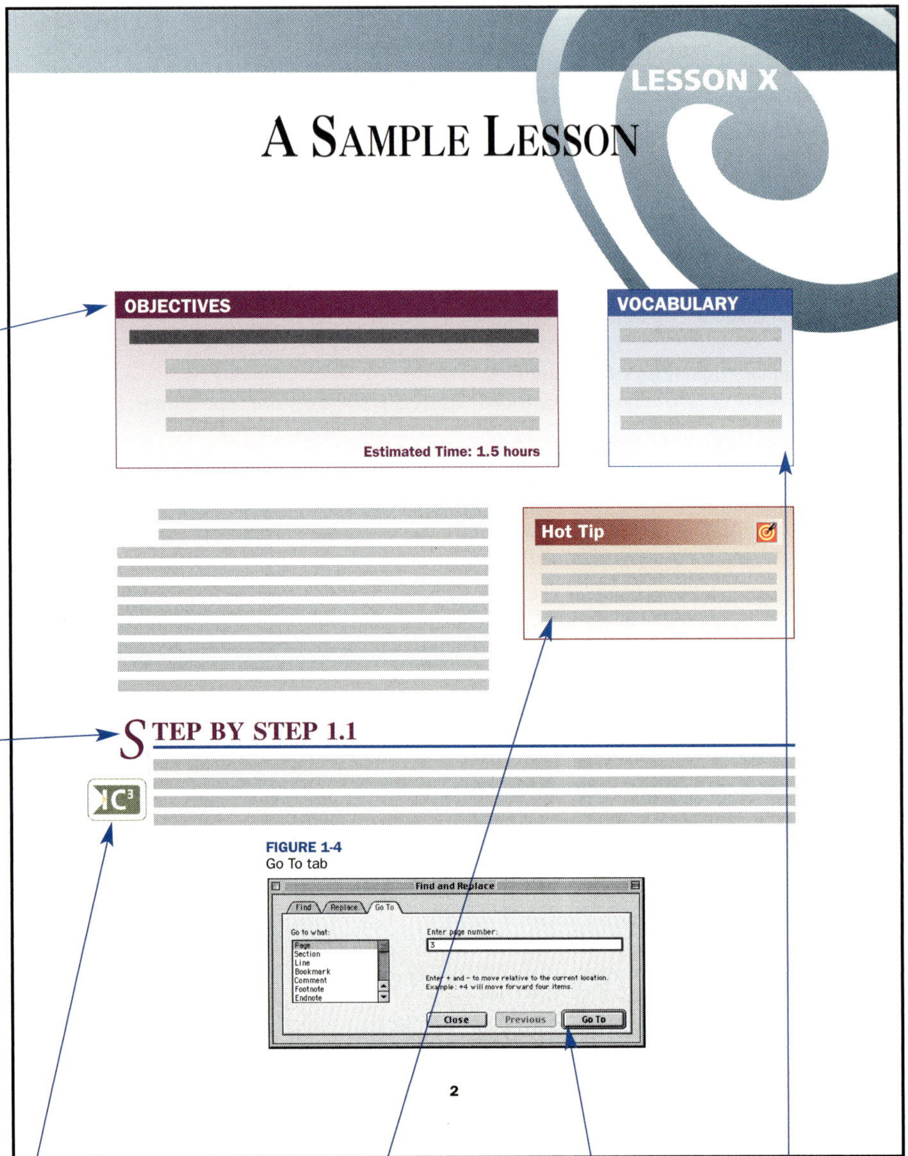

IC³—Internet and Computing Core Certification program skill

Marginal Boxes—These boxes provide additional information, such as Hot Tips, fun facts (Did You Know?), Computer Concepts, Internet Web sites, Extra Challenges activities, and Teamwork ideas.

Vocabulary—Terms identified in boldface throughout the lesson and summarized at the end.

Enhanced Screen Shots—Screen shots now come to life on each page with color and depth.

How to Use This Book

Summary—At the end of each lesson, you will find a summary to prepare you to complete the end-of-lesson activities.

Vocabulary/Review Questions—Review material at the end of each lesson and each unit enables you to prepare for assessment of the content presented.

Lesson Projects—End-of-lesson hands-on application of what has been learned in the lesson allows you to actually apply the techniques covered.

Critical Thinking Activities—Each lesson gives you an opportunity to apply creative analysis and use various resources to solve problems.

End-of-Unit Projects—End-of-unit hands-on application of concepts learned in the unit provides opportunity for a comprehensive review.

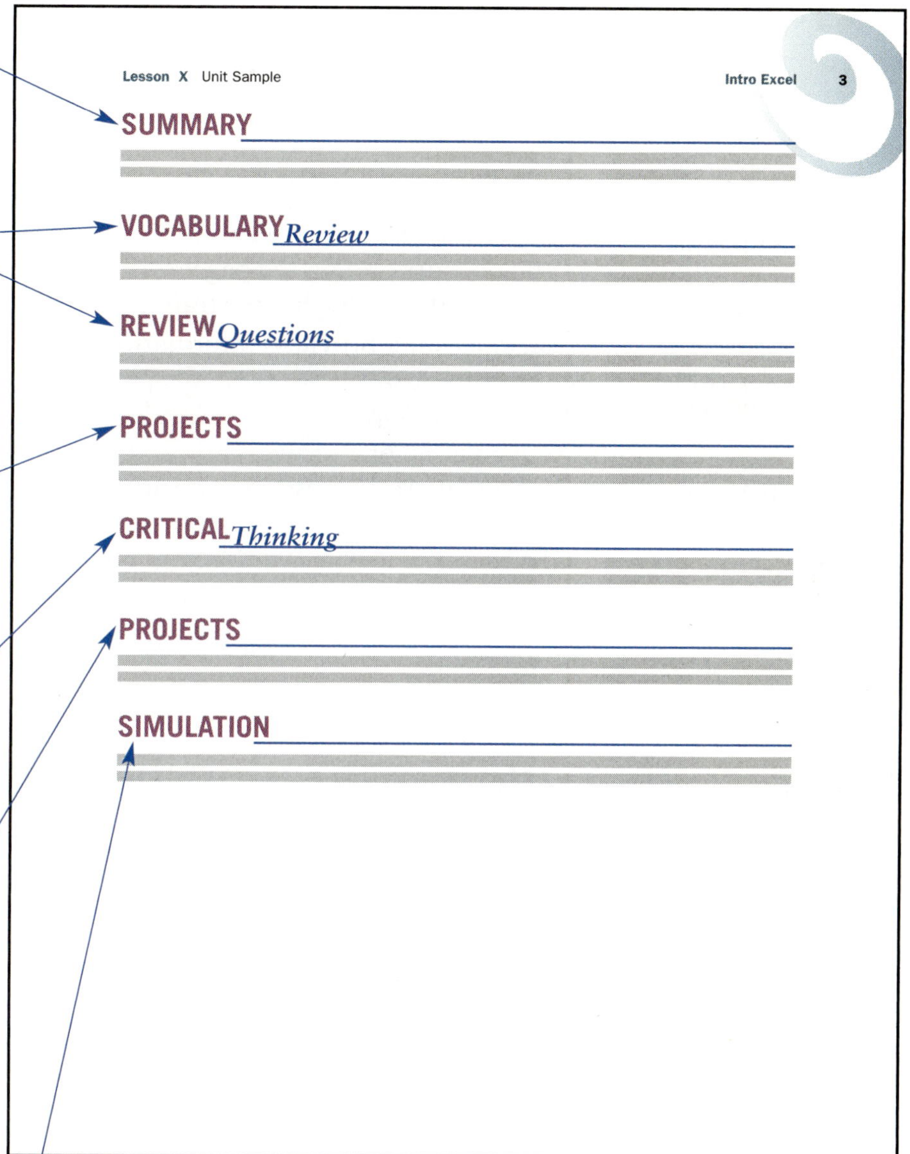

Simulation—Realistic simulation jobs are provided at the end of each unit, reinforcing the material covered in the unit.

PREFACE

IC^3 BASICS, Internet and Computing Core Certification provides complete coverage of topics of the new Internet and Computing Core Certification (IC^3) and is approved by Certiport Inc. IC^3 topics are correlated in an appendix and on the pages where they are discussed. All objectives from the three modules are presented to provide preparation for the IC^3 exams.

The *Computing Fundamentals* unit provides information on computing basics, including computer hardware and components, applications and operating system software, and social issues related to computing and technology.

The *Key Applications* unit focuses on software applications that learners use on a regular basis. Instruction is provided on word-processing, spreadsheet, database, presentations, and planning software.

The *Living Online* unit covers the concepts of computer networking, with comprehensive coverage of the Internet and the various services and resources it offers.

An appendix at the end of the text lists each exam's skills and objectives and where the objectives are covered in the text.

Organization and Features of the Text

The text is divided into three units that correlate to the three IC^3 exams. Lessons within each unit introduce concepts in a logical progression to build on previously learned concepts and features within the unit. Each lesson includes the following features:

- Lesson objectives that specify goals for the learner.
- Estimated time for completion of the lesson.
- Vocabulary list that summarizes the new terms introduced in the lesson.
- Step-by-step exercises that provide guidance for using the features.
- Screen illustrations that provide visual reinforcement of features and concepts.
- Sidebars with notes, tips, computer concepts, and other information related to the lesson topics.
- Special features that provide information about careers, computer ethics, and historical issues.

The end-of-lesson features focus on review and reinforcement of the skills and concepts presented in the lesson. They provide a comprehensive review of the lesson and a variety of ways to apply the newly learned skills. The end-of-lesson features include the following:

- Lesson summary.
- A vocabulary review listing the new terms presented in the lesson.

- Review questions to assess the comprehension of material.
- Lesson projects for applying the concepts and features.
- Web projects to encourage Internet access and Web research.
- Teamwork projects that suggest activities in which learners can work together.
- Critical thinking activities that require learners to analyze and process information or to do research.

Each unit is summarized in a unit review designed to check understanding. Each unit review includes the following:

- Review questions covering material from all lessons in the unit.
- Projects that provide integration of the skills and functions presented within the unit.
- Simulation jobs that propose real-world tasks.

Instructor Resource Kit and Review Pack CD-ROMs

All data files necessary for the Step-by-Step exercises, end-of-lesson projects, and end-of-unit projects and simulations are located on the *Review Pack* CD-ROM.

The *Instructor Resource Kit* CD-ROM contains a wealth of instructional material you can use to prepare for teaching this course. The CD-ROM stores the following information:

- ExamView® tests for each lesson. ExamView is a powerful testing software package that allows instructors to create and administer printed, computer (LAN-based), and Internet exams. ExamView includes hundreds of questions that correspond to the topics covered in this text, enabling learners to generate detailed study guides that include page references for further review. The computer-based and Internet testing components allow learners to take exams at their computers, and also save the instructor time by grading each exam automatically.
- Electronic *Instructor Manual* that includes lecture notes for each lesson.
- Answer keys that contain answers to the lesson and unit review questions, and suggested/sample solutions for some end-of-lesson activities and projects.
- Copies of the figures that appear in the learner text, which can be used to prepare transparencies.
- Suggested schedules for teaching the lessons in this course.
- Additional instructional information about individual learning strategies, portfolios, and career planning, and a sample Internet contract.
- PowerPoint presentations that illustrate objectives for each lesson in the text.

START-UP CHECKLIST

HARDWARE

- ✓ IBM or IBM-compatible PC
- ✓ 233-MHz or higher Pentium-compatible process (a 600-MHz or faster is preferred)
- ✓ 64 MB of RAM (256 MB of RAM is preferred)
- ✓ One hard disk (2 GB) with at least 650 MB of free hard disk space
- ✓ CD-ROM drive
- ✓ SVGA-capable video adapter and monitor (SVGA resolution of a minimum of 800 × 600 pixels with 256 or more colors)
- ✓ Enhanced keyboard
- ✓ Mouse or pen pointer
- ✓ 14,000 or higher baud modem (56,000 is preferred)
- ✓ Printer

SOFTWARE

- ✓ Windows 95 or later version (Windows XP for Part 2 of *Computing Fundamentals* unit)
- ✓ Microsoft Office recommended (Microsoft Office XP for *Key Applications* unit)
- ✓ Web browser

IC3 INTERNET AND COMPUTING CORE CERTIFICATION

SETTING THE STANDARD

IC³ . . . WHAT IS IT?

IC³, or the Internet and Computing Core Certification program, is a global training and certification program providing proof to the world that you are:

- **Equipped with the needed computer skills to excel in a digital world.**
- **Capable of using a broad range of computer technology - from basic hardware and software, to operating systems, applications and the Internet.**
- **Ready for what the work employers, colleges and universities want to throw your way.**
- **Positioned to advance your career through additional computer certifications such as CompTIA's A+, and other desktop application exams.**

IC³ . . . WHY DO YOU NEED IT?

Employers, Colleges and Universities now understand that exposure to computers does not equal understanding computers. So now, more than ever, basic computer and Internet skills are being considered prerequisites for employment and higher education.

THIS IS WHERE IC³ HELPS!

IC³ provides specific guidelines for the knowledge and skills required to be a functional user of computer hardware, software, networks, and the Internet. It does this through three exams:

- **Computing Fundamentals**
- **Key Applications**
- **Living Online**

By passing the three IC³ exams, you have initiated yourself into today's digital world. You have also given yourself a globally accepted and validated credential that provides the proof employers or higher education institutions need.

Earn your IC³ certification today - visit www.certiport.com/ic3 to learn how.

CERTIPORT™

Lifetime advancement through certification.

FM AXXXX 27938 PAGE IX 11/18/02 JO

TABLE OF CONTENTS

COMPUTING FUNDAMENTALS UNIT

KEY APPLICATIONS UNIT

LIVING ONLINE UNIT

Photo Credits

Computing Fundamentals

Lesson 1

Figure 1-1	©PhotoDisc
Figure 1-3	Courtesy of International Business Machines Corporation. Unauthorized use not permitted.
Figure 1-4	©PhotoDisc
Figure 1-5	Rapid Rental Software (1.800.263.0000)
Figure 1-6	Compaq Computer Corporation
Figure 1-7	Courtesy of International Business Machines Corporation. Unauthorized use not permitted.
Figure 1-9	Courtesy of International Business Machines Corporation. Unauthorized use not permitted.
Figure 1-10	Courtesy of Cray Research, a Silicon Graphics Company
Figure 1-11	©PhotoDisc

Lesson 2

Figure 2-3	©PhotoDisc
Figure 2-4	©PhotoDisc
Figure 2-7	©PhotoDisc

Lesson 3

Figure 3-2	©PhotoDisc
Figure 3-3	©PhotoDisc
Figure 3-4	©PhotoDisc
Figure 3-5	©PhotoDisc
Figure 3-6	©PhotoDisc
Figure 3-7	Lernout & Hauspie Speech Technology Products & Services
Figure 3-8	©PhotoDisc
Figure 3-9	©PhotoDisc
Figure 3-10	©PhotoDisc
Figure 3-16	©PhotoDisc

Lesson 6

Figure 6-1	©PhotoDisc
Figure 6-6	©PhotoDisc
Figure 6-7	©PhotoDisc

Lesson 7

Figure 7-4	©PhotoDisc

Living Online

Lesson 1

Figure 1-4	©PhotoDisc

Lesson 4

Figure 4-1	©PhotoDisc

Lesson 6

Figure 6-3	Courtesy of IriScan; IriScan's iris recognition technology identifies people by the patterns in the iris of the eye.

COMPUTING FUNDAMENTALS

Unit

Part 1 Computer Concepts

Lesson 1 — 1.5 hrs.
What Is a Computer?

Lesson 2 — 1.5 hrs.
How Does a Computer Process Data?

Lesson 3 — 1.5 hrs.
How Do I Input Data and Output and Store Information?

Lesson 4 — 1.5 hrs.
What Is Software?

Lesson 5 — 1.5 hrs.
What Basic Skills Do I Need to Use the Computer?

Lesson 6 — 1.5 hrs.
How Can I Use Technology to Solve a Problem?

Lesson 7 — 1.5 hrs.
How Is Technology Changing the Workplace and Society?

Part 2 Microsoft Windows XP

Lesson 8 — 1.5 hrs.
Introduction to Windows XP Professional

Lesson 9 — 1.5 hrs.
Manipulating Windows

Lesson 10 — 1.5 hrs.
Getting Help

Lesson 11 — 1 hr.
Customizing the Desktop

Lesson 12 — 1.5 hrs.
Introducing My Computer

Lesson 13 — 5 hrs.
Working with Disks, Folders, and Files

Lesson 14 — 2.5 hrs.
Using Shortcuts and Windows Explorer

Estimated Time for Unit: 25 hours

COMPUTING FUNDAMENTALS

Part 1 Computer Concepts

Lesson 1
What is a Computer?
1-1.1.1, 1-1.1.2, 1-1.1.6, 1-1.1.9, 1-1.1.10, 1-1.1.11, 1-1.4.1, 1-1.4.2, 1-1.4.3, 1-1.4.4, 1-1.4.5, 1-1.4.7, 1-1.4.8, 1-2.2.9

Lesson 2
How Does a Computer Process Data?
1-1.1.3, 1-1.1.5, 1-1.1.6, 1-1.1.7, 1-1.2.2, 1-1.2.7, 1-1.3.1, 1-1.3.2, 1-1.3.4

Lesson 3
How Do I Input Data and Output and Store Information?
1-1.1.5, 1-1.2.1, 1-1.2.3, 1-1.2.4, 1-1.2.5, 1-1.2.6, 1-1.3.3, 1-2.1.1, 1-2.1.2, 1-2.1.3

Lesson 4
What Is Software?
1-1.1.4, 1-1.1.7, 1-2.1.4, 1-2.1.5, 1-2.1.6, 1-2.2.1, 1-2.2.4, 1-2.2.6, 1-2.2.7, 1-2.2.10, 1-2.2.11, 1-2.2.13, 1-2.2.14, 1-3.1.2, 1-3.1.4, 1-3.1.5, 1-3.1.6, 1-3.3.5, 1-3.3.6, 1-3.3.7, 1-3.3.8, 1-3.3.9, 1-3.7.1

Lesson 5
What Basic Skills Do I Need to Use the Computer?
1-1.1.8, 1-3.1.3, 1-3.2.2, 1-3.2.3, 1-3.2.4, 1-3.2.7, 1-3.2.8, 1-3.2.13, 1-3.2.14

Lesson 6
How Can I Use Technology to Solve a Problem?
1-1.4.6, 1-2.2.2, 1-2.2.3, 1-2.2.5, 1-2.2.8, 1-2.2.9, 1-2.2.12

Part 2 Microsoft Windows XP

Lesson 8
Introduction to Windows XP Professional
1-1.2.3, 1-3.1.4, 1-3.2.1, 1-3.2.3, 1-3.2.4, 1-3.2.5, 1-3.2.6

Lesson 9
Manipulating Windows
1-3.2.2, 1-3.2.6, 1-3.3.2

Lesson 10
Getting Help
1-3.2.7

Lesson 11
Customizing the Desktop
1-3.2.2, 1-3.3.1, 1-3.3.2, 1-3.3.4

Lesson 13
Working with Disks, Folders, and Files
1-3.2.3, 1-3.2.15, 1-3.2.16, 1-3.2.17, 1-3.2.18, 1-3.2.19, 1-3.2.20, 1-3.3.3

Lesson 14
Using Shortcuts and Windows Explorer
1-3.2.5, 1-3.2.9, 1-3.2.10, 1-3.2.11, 1-3.2.12, 1-3.2.13, 1-3.2.15

LESSON 1

WHAT IS A COMPUTER?

OBJECTIVES

Upon completion of this lesson, you should be able to:

- Define a computer.
- Identify how computers are used in our daily lives.
- Compare the types of computers.
- List the parts of a computer system.
- Explain how the Internet, the World Wide Web, e-mail, and networks affect the use of computers.

Estimated Time: 1.5 hours

VOCABULARY

Channel
Computer
Computer system
Data
Data communications
E-mail
Extranet
Hardware
Internet
Intranet
Mainframe computers
Microcomputer
Minicomputers
Network
Notebook computer
People
Personal Digital Assistant (PDA)
Protocol
Receiver
Sender
Software
Supercomputers
Wide-area networks

The computer is probably the single most important invention of the twentieth century! It affects us not only individually but also as a society as a whole. You can see computers almost everywhere!

- In educational institutions they are used to enhance instruction.
- At arcades they can transport you to an imaginary world.
- At banks computers allow you to withdraw cash from your account without having to talk with a teller.
- While watching a football game on television, you can even see an instant replay of a tackle. The list could go on and on.

As technology produces more powerful computers, we will find more ways to use them to enhance our lives. See Figure 1-1.

FIGURE 1-1
One example of the wide variety of ways people use computer systems

1-1.1.9-1

What Is a Computer?

Just what is a ***computer***? What does it really do? It is an electronic device that receives data, processes data, stores data, and produces a result (output).

Let's see how this definition fits with the way the computer in a video store might be used.

- *Receives data:* Customers' names and the name of the video rented are entered into the computer.
- *Processes data:* The computer will change the data from what we entered into what we want the result to be.
- *Stores data:* The information is stored in the computer's memory or on disk.
- *Produces a result:* We will see a final display of the information we enter. See Figure 1-2.

FIGURE 1-2
The processing cycle of the computer

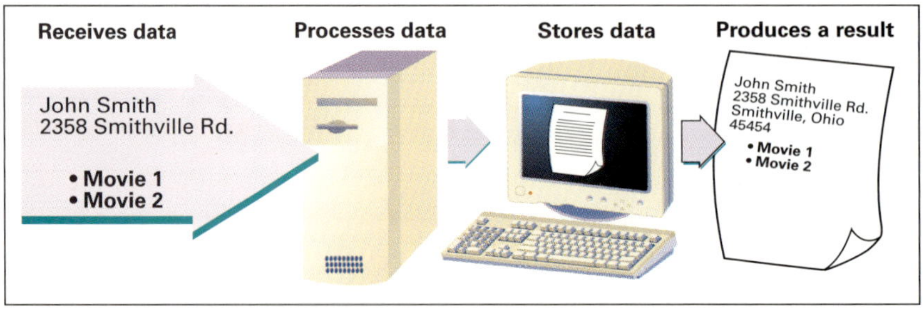

Why Are Computers So Popular?

OK, now you know what a computer is and what it does. But why has it become so popular? Basically, it performs only three operations:

- arithmetic operations (adding, subtracting, multiplying, and dividing)
- logical comparison of values (examples: equal to, greater than)
- storage and retrieval operations

However, what really makes the computer as widely used as it is? Is that it:

- performs these functions very quickly?
- produces accurate and reliable results?
- stores large amounts of data?
- provides versatility in its various applications?
- provides cost-effective applications?
- is becoming more and more powerful and more useful?

Did You Know?

Charles Babbage is the father of computers.

The History of the Computer

IC3 1-1.1.1-1

Can you remember a time when computers did not exist? You probably cannot. Computers in the 1950s, 1960s, and 1970s were larger and limited in what they could do. They were temperature sensitive and difficult to repair. Only large companies could afford them and only a few visionary people like Steve Jobs or Bill Gates saw a future for small home computers. See Figure 1-3.

FIGURE 1-3
Early generation computers

Small desktop computers are now the most popular type of computer today. They are much more powerful and less expensive. These home computers are called personal computers because they were designed to be used by one person at a time. The first personal computer was sold in 1977. Now they are in millions of homes and offices.

> **Internet**
>
> Visit the Computer Museum Network's site, *www.tcm.org*, to locate information about computer history.

How Computers Are Used

Computers have vastly impacted our lives. They have changed the way:

- we bank.
- we buy groceries.
- we shop for toys.
- we do homework.

They are so important in our lives today that without them, our world as we know it would come to a sudden halt. Computers have become necessary tools in almost every type of activity and in almost every type of business. They are capable of performing many different tasks. Think of the many ways computers affect *you* every day. Any time you go to the movies, shop in a grocery store, watch the instant replay of a tackle in a football game, or take a trip on an airplane, you are benefiting from the capabilities of computers. See Figure 1-4.

> **Hot Tip**
>
> Original music can be created using computers. People do not need a lot of musical talent or even specific instruments to make music. They just need to press a button or key on a MIDI keyboard.

FIGURE 1-4
Computers are everywhere in our lives today

How Does a Video Store Use Computers?

If you are employed at a video store as a sales clerk, you will see the computer used a lot. You thought it was just being used as a cash register and to enter customers' information when they rented a video. If you were to ask your supervisor how the computer is used in the operation of the store, you would probably be surprised at the answer. You would learn that the computer is used to:

- maintain inventory of all the videos.
- maintain records of all the members.
- maintain personnel records.
- maintain the store's budget.
- record sales figures.
- interact with the computers at headquarters.
- order inventory and other items.
- advertise on the Internet.
- communicate with other stores, suppliers, customers, and so on.

See Figure 1-5.

FIGURE 1-5
An employee at a video store uses the computer

Types of Computers

1-1.1.2-1 The personal computer is only one type of computer. There are other types more suited for various tasks and organizations. Computers are classified by their size, speed, and application.

1-1.1.2-2 1-1.4.1 The ***microcomputer,*** also called a personal computer or desktop computer, is the type of computer used at home or at the office by one person. Its size and shape allow it to fit on top or under a desk. The PC is typically used for writing papers or letters, tracking personal finances, playing games, and surfing the Internet. See Figure 1-6.

FIGURE 1-6
Microcomputer

1-1.1.1-2 1-1.4.2 1-1.4.4 1-1.4.8 The ***notebook computer*** has the same capabilities as the desktop computer. However, it is much smaller and more expensive. Because of its small size, it is portable and can run on power from an electrical outlet or batteries. Businesspeople find the notebook computer very convenient to use when they are away from the office. See Figure 1-7.

FIGURE 1-7
Notebook computer

The ***personal digital assistant (PDA)***, also known as a palm-top computer, is even smaller
than the notebook computer. It has limited capabilities and may lack traditional components
1-1.4.3 such as the keyboard. On such a PDA, a touch-sensitive screen accepts characters drawn with
1-1.4.5 your finger. PDAs can connect to desktop computers to exchange and update information. The
cost of a PDA is not necessarily lower than a microcomputer. See Figure 1-8.

FIGURE 1-8
A personal digital assistant, or palm-top computer

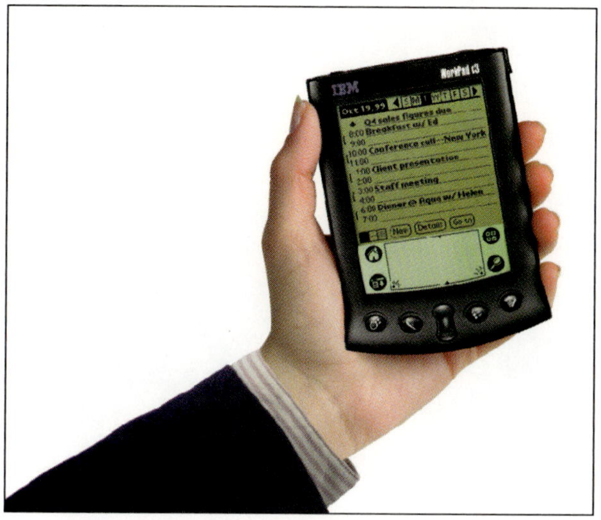

Minicomputers are larger than microcomputers and basically have the same capabilities. The
cost, however, is much higher. A company would choose to use minicomputers rather than
1-1.1.10 microcomputers if there are many users and large amounts of data.

Mainframe computers are much larger and more powerful than minicomputers. They also per-
form processing tasks for many users. They are used for centralized storage, processing, and man-
1-1.1.11 agement of very large amounts of data. Mainframe computers cost hundreds of thousands of
1-1.4.7 dollars and are used by large institutions and government installations. See Figure 1-9.

FIGURE 1-9
Mainframe computers are capable of performing several billion operations per second

Supercomputers are the largest and fastest computers. These computers are used by large corporations with tremendous volumes of data to be processed. The processing speed is much faster than any other type of computer. A supercomputer can cost several million dollars! See Figure 1-10.

Hot Tip

Supercomputers are often used as testers for medical experiments.

FIGURE 1-10
The supercomputer was first developed for high-volume computing tasks such as predicting the weather

IC³ 1-1.1.6-1

What Is a Computer System?

What makes it possible for the computer to perform the work it does? It uses a combination of several parts working together called a ***computer system.*** It consists of four parts:

- ***Hardware*** is the tangible, physical equipment that can be seen and touched. Examples include the keyboard, processor, monitor, and printer.
- ***Software*** is the intangible set of instructions that tells the computer what to do. These sets of instructions are called programs or software programs. There are two types of software programs: system software programs and application software programs.
- ***Data*** is the new facts entered into the computer to be processed. Data consists of the following:
  - text
  - numbers
  - sounds and images

> **Did You Know?**
>
> A computer won a World Chess Championship game against a human.

It is entered into the computer as raw data and the computer manipulates (processes) it into the final form that the user needs. This data can be entered into the computer in several ways including:

- the keyboard
- voice activation
- diskettes
- scanning

Likewise there are various sources from which data can come including:

- handwritten notes
- diskettes
- voice input
- typed reports
- bar codes

- ***People*** are the users of the computers who enter the data and use the output. See Figure 1-11.

FIGURE 1-11
The components of a microcomputer system

Data Communications

In the early years (1950s) of computers, they did not "talk" to each other. There were many reasons for this. One was that they didn't talk the same language. It was as if Computer "A" spoke French and Computer "B" spoke Swedish. As technology expanded, standards were developed that enabled computers to communicate.

Data communications, the technology that enables computers to communicate, is defined as the transmission of text, numeric, voice, or video data from one machine to another. Popular examples are the Internet, electronic messages (e-mail), faxes, and electronic or online banking. Data communications has changed the way the world does business and the way we live our lives. This technology has made it possible to communicate around the globe!

These are the four components of data communications:

- ***Sender:*** the computer that is sending the message.
- ***Receiver:*** the computer receiving the message.
- ***Channel:*** the media that carries or transports the message. This could be telephone wire, coaxial cable, microwave signal, or fiber optic.

- ***Protocol:*** the rules that govern the orderly transfer of the data sent. See Figure 1-12.

FIGURE 1-12
Data communications use modems to send and receive messages

Networks

One of the most utilized types of data communications in the business world is a ***network*** connection. A network connects one computer to other computers and peripheral devices. This connection enables the computers to share data and resources. If the computers are located in a relatively close location such as in the same building or department, they are part of a local area network. The data and software for these computers are stored on a central computer called the file server. See Figure 1-13.

These local area networks can be expanded to include several local area networks within a city, state, region, territory, country, continent, or the world. These are called ***wide-area networks.***

FIGURE 1-13
A network system consists of workstations, servers, and printers

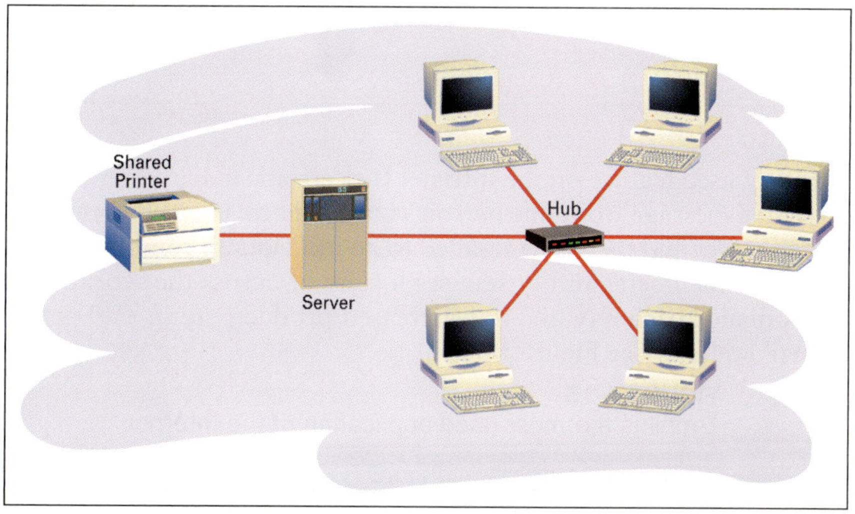

The Internet

1-2.2.9-1

The ***Internet*** was originally developed for the government to enable researchers around the world to be able to share information. Today, it is the largest network (computers connected together) in the world. It is used every day by millions of users. It has become an invaluable communication tool for businesses, individuals, and governments. See Figure 1-14.

> **Internet**
>
> Visit NASA's site, *www.nasa.gov*, to learn how computers and computer-related technologies are used in space exploration.

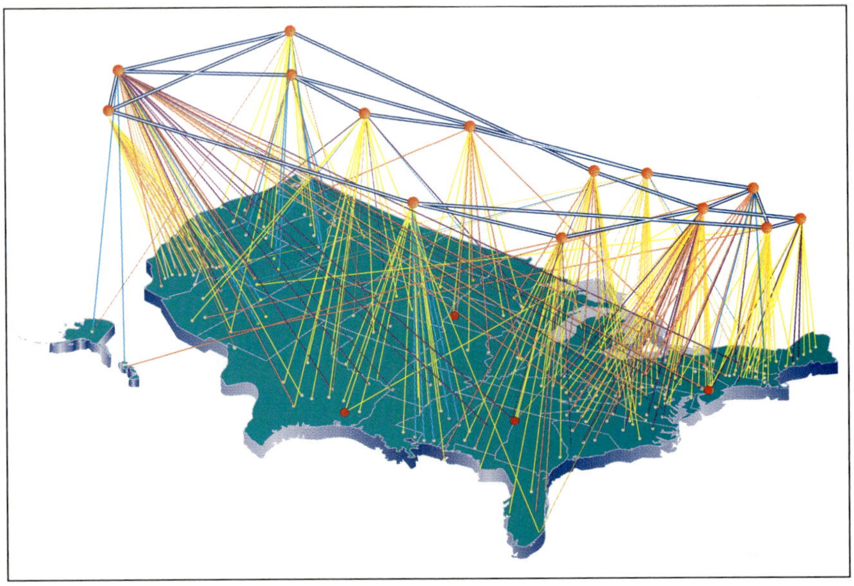

FIGURE 1-14
A graphical representation of the Internet in the United States

E-Mail

The most commonly used feature on the Internet is electronic mail, better known as ***e-mail.*** This is the capability to send a message from one person's computer to another person's computer. E-mail is stored on someone's server and then downloaded to an individual's computer. E-mail messages can be sent to friends, family members, and businesses locally or across the world. E-mail has reduced the number of letters mailed each day and has increased productivity in the workplace. Just about everyone has an e-mail address! See Figure 1-15.

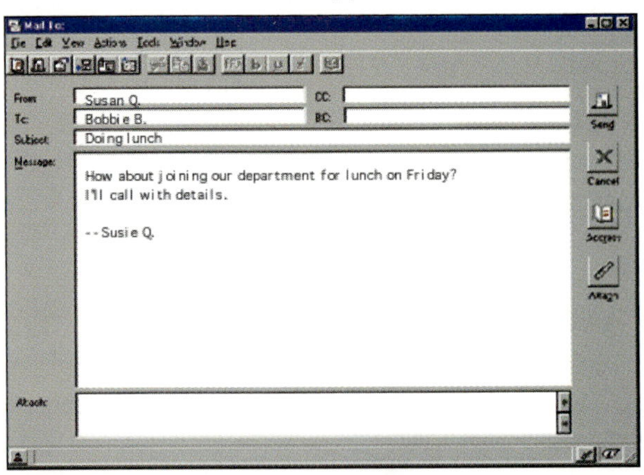

FIGURE 1-15
E-mail is the most used application of the Internet

Intranets

Many companies have implemented intranets within their own organizations. An ***intranet*** is for the exclusive use of users within the organization and contains only company information. Company manuals, handbooks, and newsletters are just a few of the types of documents distributed via an intranet. Online forms are also made available on an intranet. The major advantage of using an intranet is reliability and security—possible because the organization can control access.

Extranets

Extranets are applications that allow outside organizations to access internal information systems. Access is controlled very tightly. These are usually reserved for suppliers or customers.

Computers in Our Future

It is a fair assumption that computers of the future will be much more powerful and less expensive. It is also a fair assumption that almost every job will somehow involve a computer.

One of the major areas of change in the computer evolution will be connectivity, the ability to connect with other computers. We will be able to do the things we are now doing with computers but on an even bigger scale. This bigger and better computer age will affect how and where we work, how we communicate with other people, how we shop, as well as how we communicate and share information.

SUMMARY

In this lesson, you learned:

- A computer is an electronic device that receives data, processes data, and stores data to produce a result.
- The first computers were used by the military and government installations.
- The first personal computer was sold in 1977.
- Computers can be found in almost every aspect of our lives.
- There are different types of computers including microcomputers, notebook computers, personal digital assistants, minicomputers, mainframe computers, and supercomputers.
- Computers are classified by size, speed, and application.
- A computer system consists of the following components:
    - Hardware: tangible, physical equipment that can be seen and touched.
    - Software: the intangible set of instructions that tell the computer what to do. This set of instructions is called a software program.
    - Data: the information entered into a computer to be processed.
    - People: the users who enter the data and use the output.

- Data communication is the transmission of text, numeric, voice, or video data from one machine to another. The four components of data communication are as follows:
  - Sender: the computer that is sending the message.
  - Receiver: the computer receiving the message.
  - Channel: the media that carries or transports the message. This could be telephone wire, coaxial cable, microwave signal, or fiber optic.
  - Protocol: the rules that govern the orderly transfer of the data sent.
- A local area network connects multiple computers within a building. It allows the sharing of data and resources.
- The Internet was originally developed so information could be shared by government researchers around the world.
- E-mail is the most common experience most people have with the Internet. It lets us send messages from one computer to another locally and around the world.
- The World Wide Web is a huge database of information that allows public access.

VOCABULARY *Review*

Define the following terms:

Channel	Internet	Personal Digital Assistant (PDA)
Computer	Intranet	Protocol
Computer system	Mainframe computers	Receiver
Data	Microcomputer	Sender
Data communications	Minicomputers	Software
E-mail	Network	Supercomputers
Extranet	Notebook computer	Wide-area networks
Hardware	People	

REVIEW *Questions*

MULTIPLE CHOICE

Select the best response for the following statements.

1. The first personal computer was sold in ________.
   A. 1967
   B. 1977
   C. 1987
   D. 1999

2. The Internet's most popular feature is _________.
   A. e-mail
   B. buying on the Web
   C. viewing videos
   D. creating Web pages

3. A _________ consists of hardware, software, data, and users.
   A. computer
   B. computer system
   C. telecommunications
   D. Web pages

4. The _________ was developed for government researchers.
   A. Internet
   B. mainframe computer
   C. electronic mail
   D. World Wide Web

5. _________ computers share files, data, and software.
   A. Apple
   B. IBM
   C. Networked
   D. Protocol

TRUE/FALSE

Circle the T if the statement is true or F if the statement is false.

T F 1. Computers have been a part of society for over 100 years.

T F 2. The Internet was first developed for government use.

T F 3. Computers are classified by size, cost, and Internet abilities.

T F 4. Because notebook computers are much smaller than microcomputers, they are less expensive than microcomputers.

T F 5. Software is a set of instructions that tells the computer how to perform certain tasks.

WRITTEN QUESTIONS

Write a brief answer to the following questions.

1. What are the basic functions of a computer?

2. What are four types of computers?

3. What are the components of a computer system?

4. What is e-mail?

5. What is a network?

PROJECTS

PROJECT 1-1

Select a career in the field of mathematics such as teachers or statisticians. Use the Internet or other resources to research information explaining how computers are being used in a specific mathematics career. Write a two-page report. Use the keyword *mathematics careers* with one or two search engines (Excite, Mamma, askjeeves, etc.).

PROJECT 1-2

Use the Internet and other resources to locate information regarding computers in our future. We know that computers are getting more and more powerful every day and are making our lives easier. One example is robotics. These computerized helpers perform many activities that may be dangerous or unpleasant for humans to perform. What are some other capabilities we can anticipate? Write a one- to two-page report describing these capabilities. Use *www.AskJeeves.com* to ask for information for this report.

PROJECT 1-3

Using the Internet or other resources, see what information you can find on computers that were developed in the early 1950s and 1960s. Write a one- to two-page report on the capabilities of these computers. Also include specific uses of these early computers. Visit *www.looksmart.com* to locate information regarding earlier computers. The Obsolete Computer Museum will also be helpful.

WEB PROJECT

E-mail is a tool that allows you to communicate with friends and family members using the Internet. E-mail has other capabilities such as replying to messages. If you have access to e-mail, study the e-mail screen and identify and describe the various options available. Also use the Internet to find the names of at least three providers of e-mail services, such as America On-Line. Prepare a two-page report on your findings.

TEAMWORK PROJECT

Your supervisor is considering putting a computer in her office as well as one in the office used by the part-time supervisor and other employees. She wants to look into the possibilities of having these two computers networked with the main computer in the store. She knows this is possible, but she is not really sure about what is involved.

She needs to know if there is a minimum number of computers needed to be networked. What kind of information and resources can be shared? What special hardware is required? Working with the other part-time sales clerk, research information on local area networks and find answers to your supervisor's questions. You may also include any other information about networks you think will be beneficial. Prepare a written report of your findings. You may find useful information at *www.officelans.com/Office_lan.htm* and at *www.AskJeeves.com*.

CRITICAL *Thinking*

ACTIVITY 1-1

The computer has greatly influenced the way we communicate. Use the Internet and other resources to locate information on some of these ways. Write a two-page report on your findings.

LESSON 2

How Does a Computer Process Data?

OBJECTIVES

Upon completion of this lesson, you should be able to:

- Identify computer system components.
- Explain how the CPU works.
- Differentiate between RAM and ROM.
- Describe how data is represented.

Estimated Time: 1.5 hours

VOCABULARY

American Standard Code for Information Interchange (ASCII)
Arithmetic/logic unit (ALU)
Bit
Byte
Cache memory
Central processing unit (CPU)
Control unit
Controller
Execution cycle (E-cycle)
Extended Binary Coded Decimal Interchange Code (EBCDIC)
Input
Instruction cycle (I-cycle)
Main memory
Memory
Modem
Motherboard
Random access memory (RAM)
Read-only memory (ROM)
Universal Serial Bus (USB)

With today's technology a little knowledge about what's inside a computer can make you a more effective user and help you select the right computer for the job you need it to do. In this lesson you will learn how the CPU processes data and turns it into information. And you will learn about some of the basic components contained on the computer's motherboard.

Computer System Components

We use computers for all kinds of tasks—to predict weather, to fly airplanes, to control traffic lights, to play games, to access the Internet, to send e-mail, and so on. You might wonder how a machine can do so many things.

To understand what a computer really does takes a degree in computer engineering. But most of us don't need that level of understanding. Instead, we need an overview for a basic understanding.

IC³ -1.1.6-1

Just about all computers, regardless of size, take raw data and change it into information you can use. The process involves input, process, output, and storage (IPOS). For example,

- You input data with some type of input device.
- The computer processes it to turn it into information.
- You output the information to some type of output device.
- You store it for later retrieval.

Input, output, and processing devices grouped together represent a computer system. In this lesson, we look at the components that the computer uses to process data. These components are contained within the system case. See Figure 2-1.

> **Hot Tip**
>
> Research companies and universities are designing wearable computer systems.

FIGURE 2-1
Computer system components

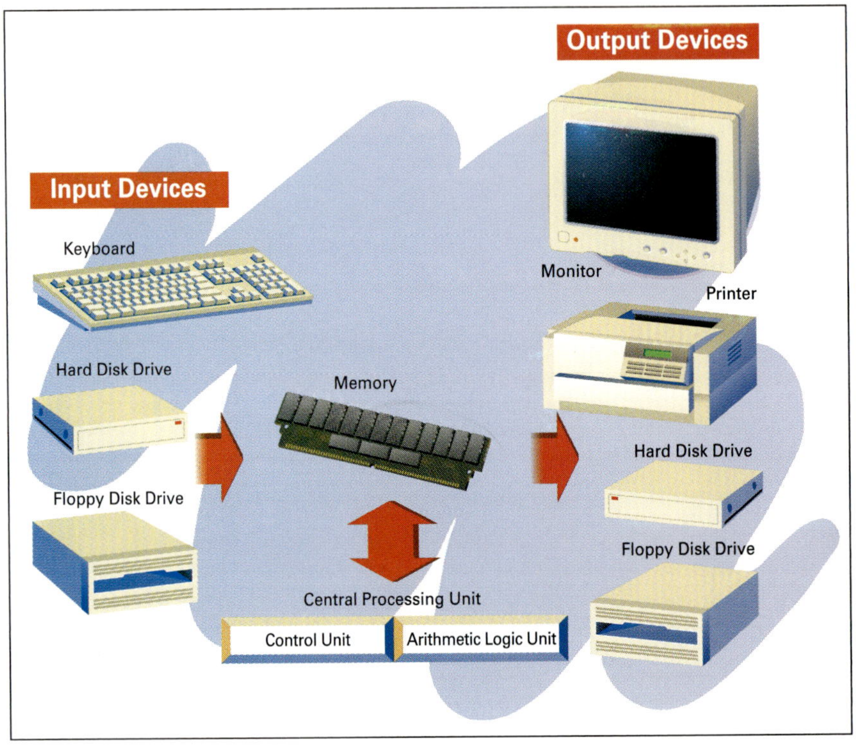

System Components

1-1.1.3-3 The PC system case is the metal and plastic case that houses the main system components of the computer. Central to all of this is the ***motherboard*** or system board that mounts into the case. The motherboard is a circuit board that contains many integral components. A circuit board is simply a thin plate or board that contains electronic components. See Figure 2-2. Some of the most important of these components are as follows:

- The central processing unit
- Memory
- Basic controllers
- Expansion ports and expansion slots

FIGURE 2-2
Simplified motherboard

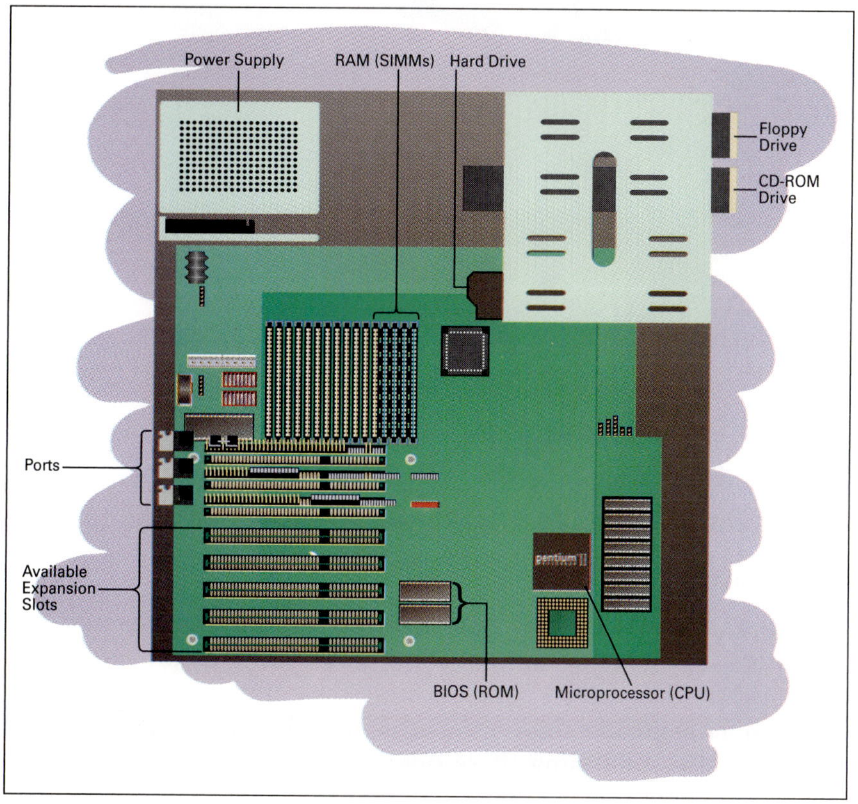

The Central Processing Unit

The ***central processing unit*** (CPU), also called the microprocessor, the processor, or central
1-1.1.3-4 1-1.1.3-1 processor, is the brains of the computer. The CPU is housed on a tiny silicon chip. See Figure 2-3.
1-1.2.2 This chip contains millions of switches and pathways that help your computer make important decisions. The switches control the flow of the electricity as it travels across the miles of pathways. The CPU knows which switches to turn on and which to turn off because it receives its instructions from computer programs. Programs are a set of special instructions written by programmers that control the activities of the computer. Programs are also known as software.

FIGURE 2-3
The brains of the computer

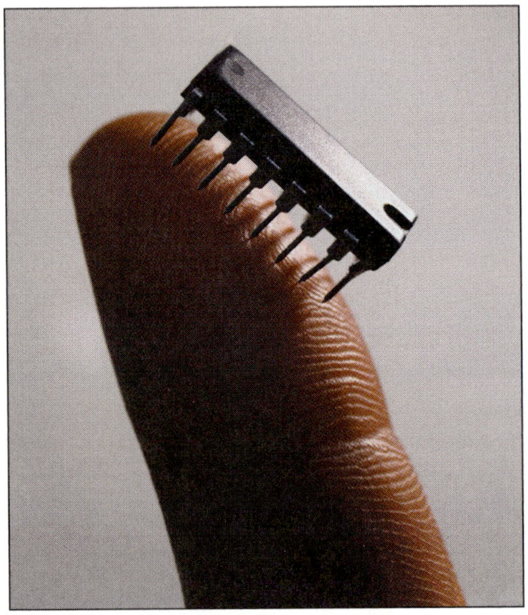

The CPU has two primary sections: the arithmetic/logic unit and the control unit.

The Arithmetic/Logic Unit

The ***arithmetic/logic unit*** (ALU) performs arithmetic computations and logical operations. The arithmetic operations include addition, subtraction, multiplication, and division. The logical
1-1.3.1 operations involve comparisons. This is simply asking the computer to determine if two numbers are equal or if one number is greater than or less than another number. These may seem like simple operations. However, by combining these operations, the ALU can execute complex tasks. For example, your video game uses arithmetic operations and comparisons to determine what displays on your screen.

The Control Unit

The ***control unit*** is the boss, so to speak, and coordinates all of the CPU's activities. Using
1-1.1.3-2 programming instructions, it controls the flow of information through the processor by control-
1-1.2.7 ling what happens inside the processor.

We communicate with the computer through programming languages. You may have heard of programming languages called BASIC, COBOL, C++, or Visual Basic. These are just a few of the many languages we can use to give the computer instructions. For example, we may have a programming statement such as Let X = 2 + 8. With this statement, we are using a programming language to ask the computer to add 2 + 8. However, when we input this instruction, something else has to happen. The computer does not understand our language. It only understands machine language, or binary, which is ones and zeros. This is where the control unit takes over.

The control unit reads and interprets the program instruction and changes the instruction into machine language. Recall that earlier we discussed the CPU and pathways and switches. It is through these pathways and the turning on and off of switches that the CPU represents the ones and zeros. When electricity is present, it represents a one. The absence of electricity represents a zero. After changing the instructions into machine language, the control unit then sends out the necessary messages to execute the instructions.

Internet

Jones Telecommunications and Multimedia Encyclopedia Web site has a wealth of information on computer history and development. You can find this Web site at *www.digitalcentury.com/encyclo/update/comp_hd.html*.

Memory

Memory is also found on the motherboard. Sometimes understanding memory can be confusing because it can mean different things to different people. The easiest way to understand memory is to think of it as "short term" or "long term." When you want to store a file or information permanently, you use secondary storage devices such as the computer's hard disk drive or a floppy disk. You might think of this as long term.

Random Access Memory

IC3 1-1.1.6-1 1-1.1.5-2

You can think about the memory on the motherboard as short term. This type of memory is called ***random access memory***, or ***RAM***. You may have heard someone ask, "How much memory is in your computer?" Most likely they are asking how much RAM is in your computer. Data, information, and program instructions are stored temporarily on a RAM chip or a set of RAM chips. See Figure 2-4.

FIGURE 2-4
RAM Chip: memory

1-1.3.2

When the computer is turned off or if there is a loss of power, whatever is stored in the RAM memory chips disappears. Therefore, it is considered volatile. The computer can read from and write to this type of memory. RAM is also referred to as ***main memory*** and primary memory.

> **Hot Tip**
>
> Can't afford that new computer, but need more speed? Try adding more RAM or purchase one of the optimizer software programs.

To better understand how RAM works and how the computer processes data, think about how you would use a word-processing program to create an address list of your family and friends. First, you start your word-processing program. The computer then loads your word-processing program instructions into RAM. You would input the names, addresses, and telephone numbers (your data). Your data is also stored in RAM. Next you would give your word-processing program a command to process your data by arranging it in a special format. This command and your processed data, or information, is also now stored in RAM. You would then click the Print button. Instructions to print are transmitted to RAM and your document is sent to your printer. Then, you click the Save button. Instructions to provide you with an opportunity to name and save your file are loaded into RAM. Once you save your file, you exit your word-processing program and turn off the computer. All instructions, data, and information are erased from RAM.

1-1.1.7-3
1-1.1.7-4

This step-by-step process is known as the **Instruction cycle** or I-cycle and the **Execution cycle** or E-cycle. When the CPU receives an instruction to perform a specified task, the instruction cycle is the amount of time it takes to retrieve the instruction and complete the command. The execution cycle refers to the amount of time it takes the CPU to execute the instruction and store the results in RAM. See Figure 2-5.

FIGURE 2-5
Processing cycle

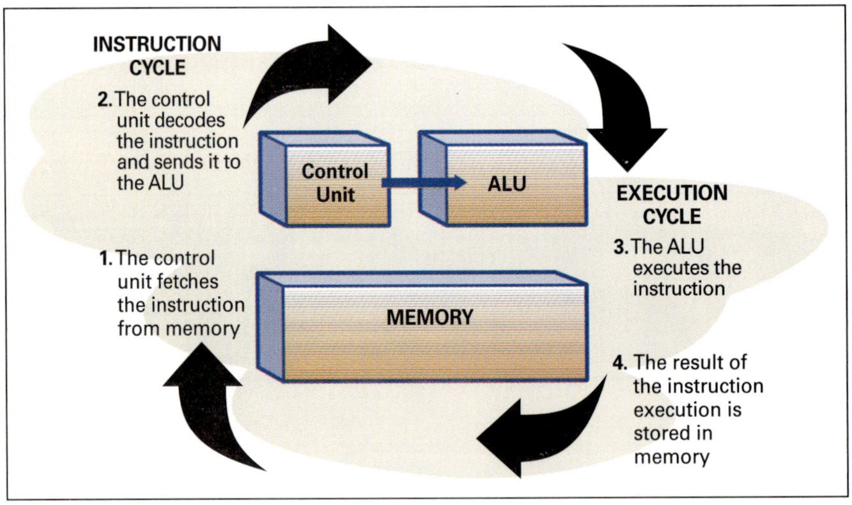

1-1.3.4

Together, the instruction cycle and one or more execution cycles create a machine cycle. Machine cycles are measured in microseconds (millionths of a second), nanoseconds (billionths of a second), and even pico seconds (trillionths of a second) in some of the larger computers. The faster the machine cycle, the faster your computer processes data. The speed of the processor has a lot to do with the speed of the machine cycle. However, the amount of RAM in your computer can also help increase how fast the computer processes data. The more RAM you have, the faster the computer processes data. See Figure 2-6.

FIGURE 2-6
Machine cycle

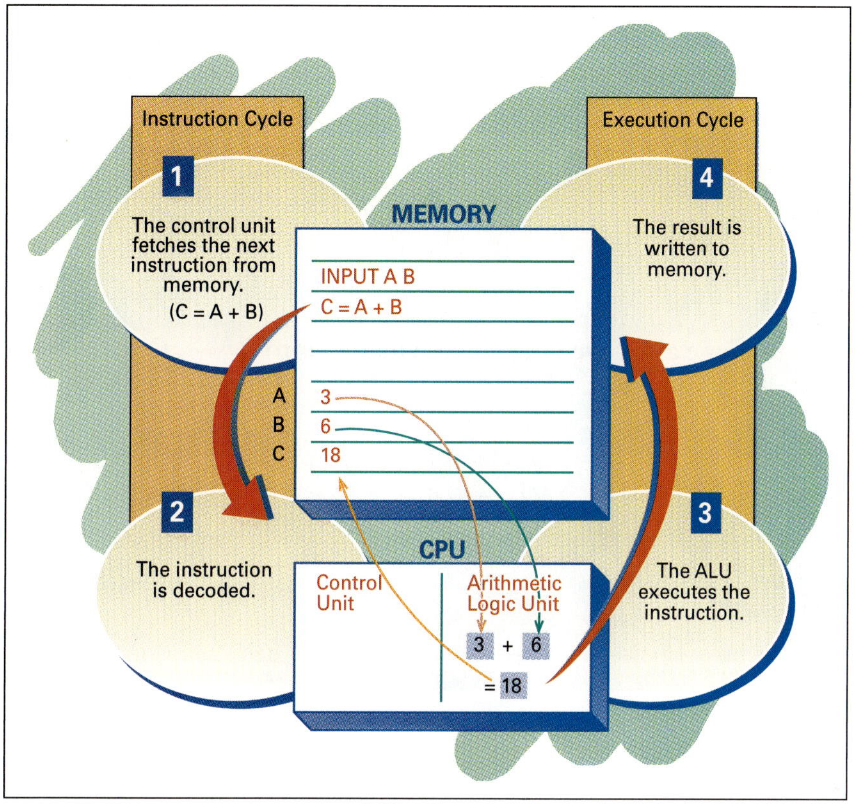

IC3 1-1.1.5-3

Read-Only Memory

Another type of memory you will find on the motherboard is ***ROM***, or ***read-only memory.*** ROM chips are found throughout a computer system. The computer manufacturer uses this type of chip to store specific instructions that are needed for the computer operations. This type of memory is nonvolatile. These instructions remain on the chip regardless if the power is turned on or off. The most common of these is the BIOS ROM. The computer uses instructions contained on this chip to boot or start the system when you turn on your computer. A computer can read from a ROM chip, but cannot write or store data on the chip.

> **Did You Know?**
>
> Another type of memory is called ***cache memory***. This very high-speed RAM is used to increase the speed of the processing cycle.

Basic Controllers

The motherboard also contains several controllers. A ***controller*** is a device that controls the transfer of data from the computer to a peripheral device and vice versa. Examples of common peripheral devices are keyboards, mouse, monitors, and printers. Controllers are generally stored on a single chip. When you purchase a computer, all the necessary controllers for the standard devices are contained on the motherboard. See Figure 2-7.

FIGURE 2-7
A close-up of a motherboard

Serial and Parallel Ports and Expansion Slots

We use serial and parallel ports to connect our peripheral devices to the computer. Serial devices transmit data one ***bit*** at a time. Parallel devices transfer several bits at a time. A bit is a zero or one. Most computers have at least one parallel port and one serial port. You will most likely find a printer connected to your parallel ports and perhaps a modem connected to your serial port. A ***modem*** is a device that allows one computer to talk to another.

The ***Universal Serial Bus (USB)*** is a new standard that supports data transfer rates of up to 12 million bits per second. You can use a single USB port to connect up to 127 peripheral devices. USB is expected to replace serial and parallel ports.

Expansion slots are openings on the motherboard where a circuit board or expansion board can be inserted. Let's suppose that you want to add pictures to your list of names and addresses. You need a scanner to scan the pictures and you need some way to connect the scanner to the computer. You could accomplish this by adding an expansion board and then connecting the scanner to the board.

Perhaps you would like to add more memory. Motherboards contain special expansion slots for additional memory. Expansion boards are also called expansion cards, add-ins, and add-ons. See Figure 2-8.

FIGURE 2-8
Expansion card

Data Representation

Earlier in this lesson, you read about binary and that a bit is either a zero or a one. You may wonder, though, just exactly how the computer determines what combination of zeros and ones represent the letter A or the number 1. It's really very simple. This is accomplished through standardized coding systems. The most popular system is called ***ASCII*** (pronounced as-kie) and stands for ***American Standard Code for Information Interchange***. There are other standard codes, but ASCII is the most widely used. It is used by nearly every type and brand of microcomputer and by many large computers as well.

Eight bits or combinations of ones and zeros represent a letter such as A. Eight bits are called a ***byte*** or character. Each capital letter, lowercase letter, number, punctuation mark, and various symbols has its own unique combination of ones and zeros.

Another type of standard code is called ***Extended Binary Coded Decimal Interchange Code***, or ***EBCDIC*** (pronounced EB-si-dik). This code is mostly used in very large computers.

Internet

Find out more about the ASCII standard by visiting the Webopedia Web site located at *webopedia.internet.com/TERM/A/ASCII.html*. Type the URL exactly as shown here.

SUMMARY

In this lesson, you learned:

- Just about all computers perform the same general options: input, process, output, and storage.
- Input, output, and processing devices grouped together represent a computer system.
- The motherboard is the center of all processing.
- The motherboard contains the CPU, memory, and basic controllers for the system.
- The motherboard also contains ports and expansion slots.
- The central processing unit is the brains of the computer.
- The computer is given instructions through computer programs.
- The CPU has two main sections—the arithmetic logic unit and the control unit.
- All calculations and comparisons take place in the ALU.
- The control unit coordinates the CPU activities.
- The motherboard contains different types of memory.
- Random access memory is volatile and is used to store instructions, data, and information temporarily.
- The machine cycle is made up of the instruction cycle and the execution cycle.
- Read-only memory is nonvolatile and is used to store permanent instructions needed for computer operations.
- A controller is used to control the transfer of data between the computer and peripheral devices.
- Peripheral devices are connected to the computer through serial and parallel ports.
- The Universal Serial Bus is a new standard expected to replace serial and parallel ports.
- Expansion boards are used to connect specialized peripheral devices or to add more memory to the computer.
- The ASCII code is a standard code used to represent the alphabet, numbers, symbols, and punctuation marks.

VOCABULARY *Review*

Define the following terms:

American Standard Code for Information Interchange (ASCII)
Arithmetic/logic unit (ALU)
Bit
Byte
Cache memory
Central processing unit (CPU)
Control unit
Controller
Execution cycle (E-cycle)
Extended Binary Coded Decimal Interchange Code (EBCDIC)
Input
Instruction cycle (I-cycle)
Main memory
Memory
Modem
Motherboard
Random access memory (RAM)
Read-only memory (ROM)
Universal Serial Bus (USB)

REVIEW *Questions*

MULTIPLE CHOICE

Select the best response for the following statements.

1. Eight __________ make one character.
   A. characters
   B. bits
   C. bytes
   D. codes

2. The __________ contains the CPU, memory, and basic controllers.
   A. memory
   B. motherboard
   C. processor
   D. expansion slot

3. The __________ is considered the brains of the computer.
   A. program
   B. ALU
   C. CPU
   D. control unit

4. Random access memory is __________.
   A. permanent
   B. volatile
   C. nonvolatile
   D. the same as ROM

5. A printer would be considered a(n) __________.
   A. controller
   B. peripheral device
   C. input device
   D. USB

TRUE/FALSE

Circle the T if the statement is true or F if the statement is false.

T F 1. You would most likely use a serial port to connect a modem to your computer.

T F 2. The ASCII code is the most widely used standardized coding system.

T F 3. A bit has eight bytes.

T F 4. The two primary sections of the CPU are the ALU and the control unit.

T F 5. The computer only understands machine language.

FILL IN THE BLANK

Complete the following sentences by writing the correct word or words in the blanks provided.

1. You can think of RAM as ________-term memory.
2. The instruction cycle and the execution cycle create a(n) ________ cycle.
3. The ________ the machine cycle, the faster your computer.
4. A(n) ________ is a board that contains electronic components.
5. You would add memory to a computer by inserting it into a(n) ________ slot.

PROJECTS

PROJECT 2-1

Collect three or four computer ads from your local Sunday paper. Using either a spreadsheet program or paper and pencil, complete a comparison table. Include the following elements in your table: processor speed, amount of memory, number of expansion slots, and price. Based on your comparisons, write a short paragraph explaining which computer you would purchase and why.

PROJECT 2-2

If possible, find a computer system with the case removed. Examine the motherboard and the components connected to the motherboard. Locate and count the number of available expansion slots. Locate the RAM chips. See if you can find the CPU. Can you see the chip itself? Create a drawing of the system and label as many of the components as you can.

PROJECT 2-3

Using the Internet or other resources, see what you can find about the history of computers. See if you can find the answers to the following questions: (1) What is the name of the first commercially available electronic digital computer? (2) In what year was the IBM PC first introduced? (3) What software sent Bill Gates on his way to becoming the richest man in the world? (4) In what year did Apple introduce the Macintosh computer? Use your word processing program to answer each of these questions and/or to provide some additional historical facts.

WEB PROJECT

Launch your Web browser and key the following URL: *www.AskJeeves.com*.

When the Web site is displayed, ask Jeeves "Who invented the microprocessor?" and click **ASK**. Jeeves will provide several answers for you. Choose the one most appropriate and click **ASK**. This takes you to the Web site where you can find the answer to your question. Use your presentation systems program to create a presentation on what you found at this Web site. Include the name of and an overview of the person who developed the first transistor. Add two or three more slides to your presentation with information you find at this Web site. Share your presentation with your friends or coworkers.

CRITICAL *Thinking*

ACTIVITY 2-1

Many people compare the computer to our brain. We input data into the computer, process the data, and then output it in the form of information. Consider how we function as a human—that we input through our five senses, process what we input by thinking about it, and then talk or perform some action as output. If we as humans can function like a computer, then what's so great about this technology and why do we need it? Do you think there will ever be a computer that can rival the human brain?

LESSON 3

How Do I Input Data and Output and Store Information?

OBJECTIVES

Upon completion of this lesson, you should be able to:

- Identify and describe the most common input devices.
- Identify and describe the most common output devices.
- Identify and describe how input and output devices are connected to the computer.
- Identify and describe storage devices.

Estimated Time: 1.5 hours

VOCABULARY

CD-ROM
Dot pitch
DVD
File allocation table (FAT)
Function keys
Graphic tablet
Input devices
Jaz drives
Magnetic tape drives
Management Information Systems (MIS)
Modifier keys
Non-impact printers
Optical storage devices
Output devices
Parallel ports
PhotoCD
Printhead
Resolution
Serial ports
Special-purpose keys
Touch display screen
Trackball
Tracks
Virus
Voice recognition
WORM disks
Zip drives

We all can agree it is the computer that does all of the work of processing data! However, it needs help. Data must be entered into the computer. Once the data has been entered and processed, it has to be "presented" to the user. Special devices are used for these tasks. Such devices are called input and output devices.

When customers come into the video store to rent videos, they leave with the rented videos and a receipt. In order for the receipt to be printed, you enter the customer's information into the computer and the printer produces a receipt.

You used the keyboard or a scanner to enter the information or to input the data. The printer produced a copy of the transaction, or the output of the information.

Input devices enable you to input data and commands into the computer and ***output devices*** enable the computer to give you the results of the processed data.

Some devices perform both input and output functions. The modem is an example. When it is used for transmitting an e-mail message, it is an input device when the sender inputs the message to be sent to the receiver. The message received is the output.

1-2.1.1-1

Input Devices

The type of input device used is determined by the task to be completed. An input device can be as simple as the keyboard or as sophisticated as those used for specialized applications such as voice or retinal recognition devices.

1-2.1.1-2

Keyboard

The ***keyboard*** is the most common input device for entering numeric and alphabetic data. Therefore, if you are going to use the computer efficiently, it is very important that you learn to keyboard. ***Keyboarding*** means being able to key without having to look at the keys.

When you enter information into the computer at the video store, it is important to be able to enter the information in a reasonable amount of time. You would not want to have the customer standing around waiting too long.

The keyboard comes in many different sizes and shapes. The standard keyboard, similar to the typewriter keyboard, is divided into four sections: the typewriter keyboard, the function keys, the directional keys, and the numeric keypad. See Figure 3-1.

FIGURE 3-1
A typical computer keyboard divided into four sections: function keys, typewriter keyboard, numeric pad, and directional keys

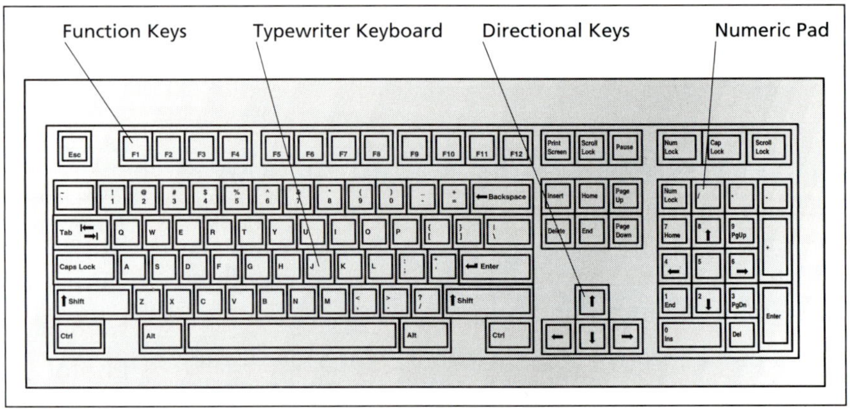

- The computer keyboard is much like the keyboard of a typewriter. They both have alphabetic and numeric keys; however, the computer keyboard has some additional keys called ***modifier keys***. They are used in conjunction with other keys. These are the Shift, Ctrl (control), and Alt (alternate) keys. A letter or number must be depressed while the modifier key is held.
- The numeric keypad is located on the right side of the keyboard and looks like an adding machine. However, when you are using it as a calculator, be sure to depress the Num Lock key so the light above Num Lock is lit.
- The ***function keys*** (F1, F2, and so forth) are usually located at the top of the keyboard. These keys are used to give the computer commands. The function of each key varies with each software program. For example, F2 in Corel WordPerfect performs a different function than F2 in Microsoft Excel.

- The ***arrow keys*** allow you to move the position of the cursor on the screen.
- ***Special-purpose keys*** perform a specialized function. The Esc key's function depends on the program being used. Usually it will back you out of a command. The PRINT SCRN sends a copy of whatever is on the screen to the printer. The Scroll Lock key, which does not operate in all programs, usually controls the strolling of the cursor keys. The Num Lock key controls the use of the number keypad. Remember: In order for the keypad to operate as a calculator, the light on Num Lock must be lit. The Caps Lock key controls typing text in all capital letters.
- Some keyboards may have additional keys. Many keyboards are now ergonomic, which means they have been designed to fit the natural placement of your hands and should reduce your risk of repetitive motion injuries such a carpal tunnel syndrome. See Figure 3-2.

Internet

Many companies specialize in developing ergonomic keyboards that minimize the stress caused by keying data for long periods of time. Use a search engine such as *AskJeeves.com* or *Dogpile.com* to locate several of these companies and see the types of products they produce.

FIGURE 3-2
An example of a keyboard

Mouse

The ***mouse*** is a pointing device that rolls around on a flat surface and controls the pointer on the screen. The ***pointer*** is an on-screen arrow-shaped object used to select text and access menus. As you move the mouse, the "arrow" on the screen also moves.

IC3 1-2.1.3-2

The mouse fits conveniently in the palm of your hand. It has a ball located on the bottom that rolls around on a flat surface as the mouse is moved. Most of these devices have two buttons; however, some have three buttons. You usually use the left button for most mouse operations. Once you place the on-screen pointer where you want it, depress a button on the mouse. This will cause some type of action to take place in the computer; the type of action depends on the program being used.

Everything that you do with the mouse will be done by these techniques:

- ***Pointing:*** placing the on-screen pointer at a designated location.
- ***Clicking:*** pressing and releasing the mouse button.
- ***Dragging:*** pressing down the mouse button and dragging the mouse while continuing to hold down the button.
- ***Double-clicking:*** pressing and releasing the mouse button twice in rapid succession.
- ***Right-clicking:*** pressing the right mouse button. See Figure 3-3.

FIGURE 3-3
The mouse is used as a pointing device to select an option

Technology Careers

PC SUPPORT SPECIALIST

The PC support specialist provides support for application software and related hardware via telephone and/or site visits to all workstation users.

As a PC support specialist you need to be knowledgeable about current software and have good oral communication and organizational skills. You will be required to interface with all departments within the company and users with various skill levels ranging from novice to expert. You must be willing to learn other areas of ***Management Information Systems (MIS)*** such as networking, printer maintenance, and e-mail.

A bachelor's degree is preferred for most of these jobs; however, impressive experience is also accepted. Experience performing actual hands-on hardware and software upgrades is important.

Joystick

1-1.2.3-1 1-1.2.3-2

The *joystick* is also a pointing device. It consists of a plastic or metal rod mounted on a base. It can be moved in any direction. Some joysticks have switches or buttons that can input data in an on/off response. Joysticks are most often used for games. See Figure 3-4.

FIGURE 3-4
Joystick

Trackball

1-1.2.3-3

The *trackball* is a pointing device that works like a mouse turned upside down; the ball is on top of the device. You use your thumb and fingers to operate the ball, thus controlling the arrow on the screen. See Figure 3-5.

FIGURE 3-5
Trackball

Graphics Tablet

A ***graphic tablet*** is a flat drawing surface on which the user can draw figures or write something freehand. The tablet is connected to the computer. Once the drawing has been inputted to the computer, it can be manipulated like a regular graphic.

Touch Display Screen

The ***touch display screen*** has pictures or shapes. You use your fingers to "point" to the desired object to make a selection. These screens can be found in many public establishments such as banks, libraries, delivery services, and fast-food restaurants. These are very user-friendly input devices. See Figure 3-6.

FIGURE 3-6
Touch screens are often used in retail stores where keyboards are impractical

Voice Recognition Devices

IC³ 1-2.1.3-1

Voice recognition devices are used to "speak" commands into the computer and to enter text. These devices are usually microphones. The computers must have some type of voice recognition software installed on the computer. Directory assistance is also a type of voice recognition technology. Voice recognition technology has also enabled disabled persons to command wheelchairs and other objects that will make them more mobile. See Figure 3-7.

Did You Know?

Microsoft has a text-only version of Internet Explorer, and Netscape has a version of its Navigator browser that incorporates speech recognition capabilities in an effort to assist visually impaired persons.

FIGURE 3-7
Speech recognition devices can be used by handicapped persons to command wheelchairs

Scanners

Scanners are devices that can change images into codes for input to the computer. There are various sizes and types of scanners:

- *Image scanners* convert images into electronic form that can be stored into a computer's memory. The image can then be manipulated.
- *Bar code scanners* read bar lines that are printed on products (for example, in a grocery store or department store).
- *Magnetic scanners* read encoded information on the back of credit cards. The magnetic strip on the back of the cards contains the encoded user's account number. See Figure 3-8.

FIGURE 3-8
Optical character-reading equipment is frequently used in grocery stores to read the price on an item

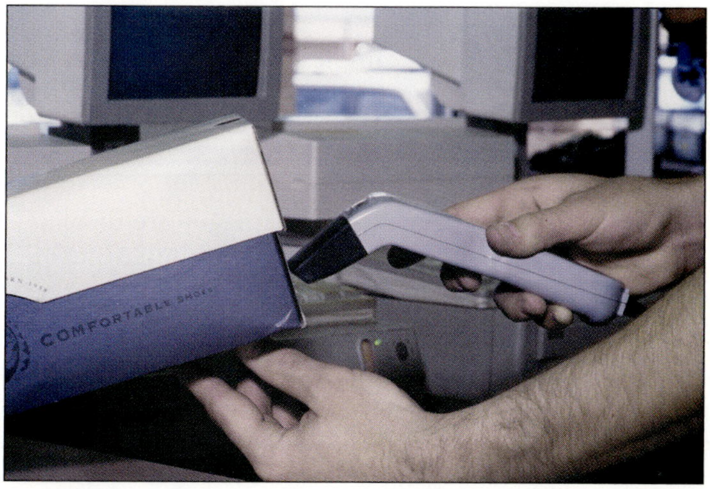

Video Input

Video input allows images generated with camcorders and VCRs to be transferred to the computer. Once input into the computer, the images can be viewed on the screen and even edited.

Digital Cameras

IC3 1-2.1.2-2 1-2.1.2-1

The pictures taken with a digital camera are stored in the camera's memory and can be transferred to the computer's memory. These pictures can be viewed quickly and any imperfections can be edited. See Figure 3-9.

Did You Know?

You don't need a digital camera to have digital pictures. Your photo lab can deliver your photos to you via the Internet or on a disk in digital format.

FIGURE 3-9
Digital cameras store photographs that can later be transferred to a computer system and viewed on a monitor

Output Devices

IC3 1-1.2.1-1 1-1.2.4-1

Output devices display information. Examples of output are printed text, spoken words, music, pictures, or graphics. The most common output devices are monitors and printers.

Monitors

Monitors are called video display screens because images are displayed on the screen. They can be either monochromatic or color. A monochromatic (monochrome) monitor screen is a one-color display. It could be white, green, or amber. Color monitors display thousands of colors. Most computers today are color.

Factors that influence the quality of a monitor are screen size, resolution, and dot pitch. ***Screen size*** is the diagonal measurement in inches from one corner of the screen to the other. Common measurements for monitors are 15, 17, 19, and 21 inches. With large monitors you can make the objects on the screen appear larger, or you can fit more information on the screen. The larger screens are more expensive. Most computers are sold with 15–17-inch monitors. ***Resolution*** is the number of pixels or dots that a monitor can display. Most 15-inch monitors have pixel grid settings of 640 × 480, 800 × 600, and 1024 × 768. ***Dot pitch*** measures the distance between pixels. See Figure 3-10.

FIGURE 3-10
Monitors come in various sizes, while notebook computers use flat-panel displays that are built into the lid

Printers

IC3 1-1.2.4-2

Printers are used to produce a paper or hard copy of the processing results. There are several types of printers with tremendous differences in speed, print quality, price, and special features.

When selecting a printer, consider the following features:

- *Speed:* Printer speed is measured in ppm, pages per minute. The number of pages a printer can print per minute varies for text and for graphics. Graphics print slower than regular text.
- *Print quality:* Print quality is measured in dots per inch, dpi. This refers to the resolution.
- *Price:* The price includes the original cost of the printer as well as what it costs to maintain the printer. A good-quality printer can be purchased very inexpensively; a high-output system can cost thousands of dollars. The ink cartridges and toners need to be replaced periodically.

Hot Tip

Downloading graphic and text files from the Internet is another form of computer input. Once you download a file from the Internet, you can save it on your computer's hard drive or to a floppy disk if there is enough space to hold it.

IC3 1-1.2.4-3

The three most popular types of printers are laser, ink jet, and dot matrix. Printers are classified as either impact or nonimpact. ***Impact printers*** use a mechanism that actually strikes the paper to form images. Dot matrix printers are impact printers. ***Non-impact printers*** form characters without striking the paper. Laser printers and ink-jet printers are examples of nonimpact printers.

Laser Printers

Laser printers produce images using the same technology as copier machines. The image is made with a powder substance called toner. A laser printer produces high-quality output. The cost of a laser printer has come down substantially. Color laser printers are much more expensive, costing thousands of dollars. See Figure 3-11.

FIGURE 3-11
How a laser printer works

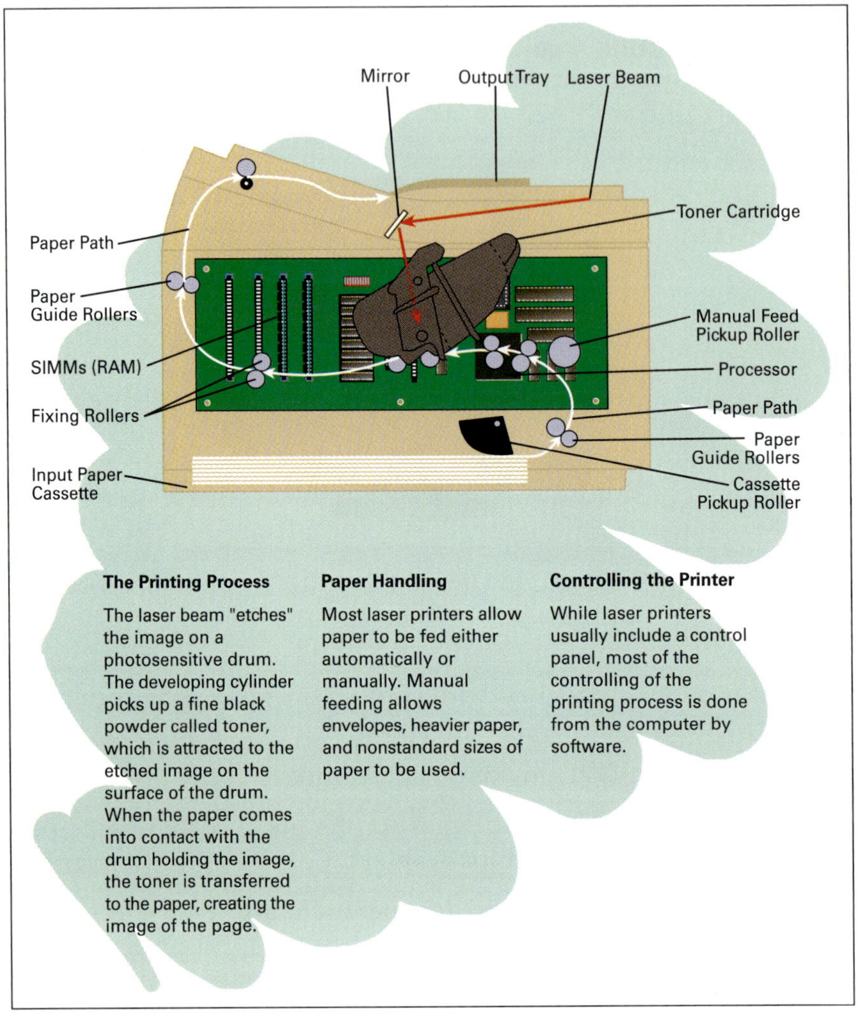

Ink-Jet Printers

The use of ***ink-jet printers*** is a less expensive way to have color printing available. The color is sprayed onto the paper. The same process used in laser printers is used in ink-jet printers; it just works slower. Unlike earlier versions of the ink-jet printers, the new versions can use regular photocopy paper. Ink-jet printers are also combined with other technologies to create complete "three-in-one" office machines. These machines combine printer, copier, and fax capabilities into one. See Figure 3-12.

FIGURE 3-12
How an ink-jet printer works

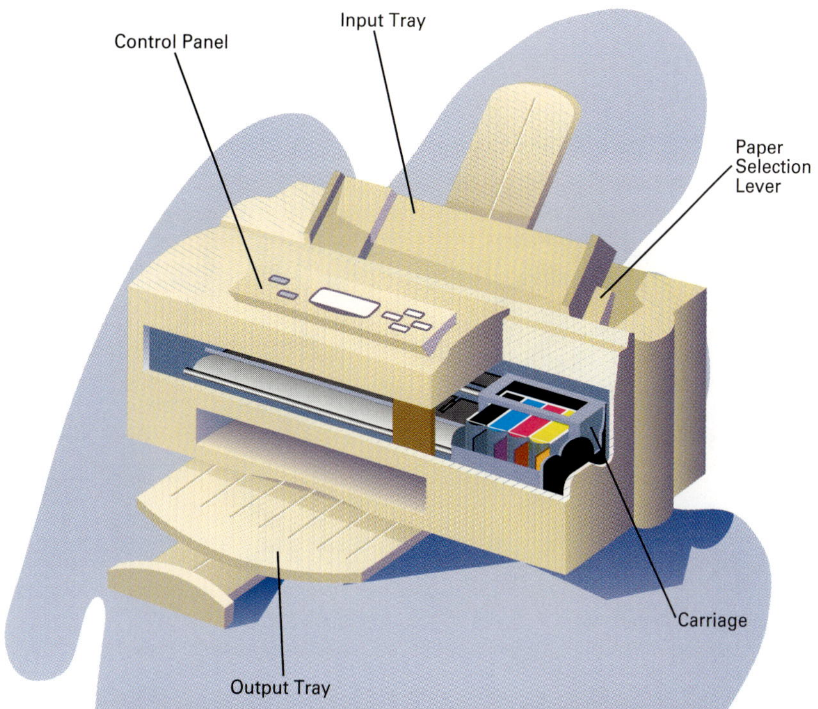

The Printing Process

During printing, the paper passes below the carriage, which holds the ink cartridges and print head. As the carriage moves back and forth over the paper, ink is sprayed in minute droplets onto the page.

Paper and Ink

Ink-jet printers use single sheets of paper. Since plain paper can be too absorbent for ink-jets, manufacturers recommend special ink-jet paper, which has a harder surface.

Controlling the Printer

The control panel includes the on/off switch, an online button, and an LCD panel that displays messages and menus.

Dot Matrix Printers

Impact printers have been around for a long time. They print by transferring ink to the paper by striking a ribbon with pins. The higher the number of pins (DPI), the better the resolution or output. The mechanism that actually does the printing is called a ***printhead.*** The speed of the dot matrix printer is measured in characters per second (cps). See Figure 3-13.

FIGURE 3-13
Dot matrix printer

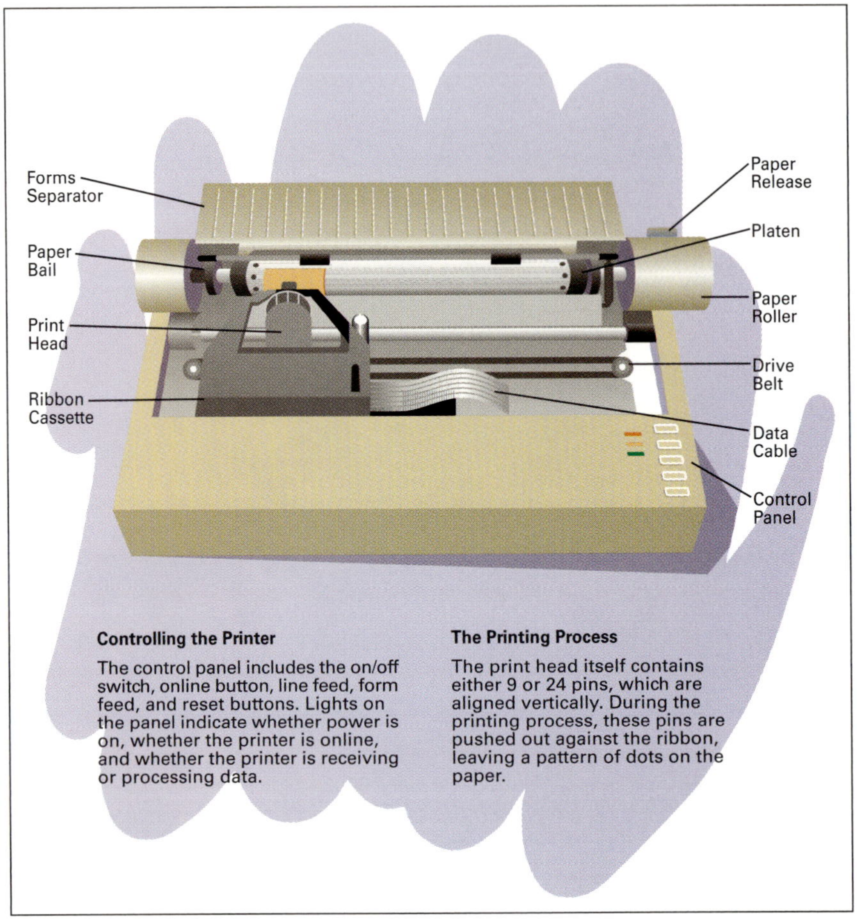

Connecting Input/Output Devices to the Computer

Input and output (I/O devices) must be physically connected to the computer. There are two ways to connect these devices to a computer. You can plug the device into an existing socket or port located on the back of the computer, or you can install a circuit board with the port you need already included.

Serial and Parallel Ports

IC3 1-1.2.6-1

Computers can have several types of ports, including the following:

- ***Parallel ports*** transmit data eight bits at a time.
- ***Serial ports*** transmit one bit at a time. It is like a narrow one-lane road. A mouse, keyboard, and modem are connected in serial ports.

Special Ports

- *SCSI* (pronounced “scuzzy”) stands for small computer system interface. One SCSI port can provide connection for one or more peripheral devices; they allow many devices to use the same port.

- *MIDI* (pronounced "middy") ports are used to connect computers to electronic instruments and recording devices.
- *PC cards* are used to add memory and to connect peripheral devices to notebook computers. They act as the interface between the motherboard and the peripheral device. The use of expansion cards in notebook computers is impractical because of the size of the notebook computer. These slots allow for the attachment of printers, modems, hard disks, and CD-ROM drives.
- *USB* ports can replace other types of ports such as serial and parallel ports, and they can plug up to 127 devices.

IC³ 1-1.1.5-4 1-1.2.5-1

Storage Devices

As data is entered into the computer and processed, it is stored in RAM. If you want to keep a permanent copy of the data, you must store it on some type of storage medium such as the following:

- Floppy diskettes
- Hard disks
- CDs
- Magnetic tape cartridges
- WORM disks (Write once, read many)
- Zip and Jaz diskettes
- Super floppy

Storage devices are categorized by the method they use to store data. Magnetic storage devices use oxide-coated plastic storage media called mylar. As the disk rotates in the computer, an electromagnetic read/write head stores or retrieves data in circles called ***tracks***. The number of tracks on a disk varies with the type of diskette. The tracks are numbered from the outside to the inside. As data is stored on the disk, it is stored on a numbered track. Each track is labeled and the location is kept in a special log on the disk called a ***file allocation table*** (FAT).

The most common types of magnetic storage media are floppy diskettes, hard drives, and magnetic tape.

IC³ 1-1.2.5-2

Floppy Diskettes

Floppy diskettes, usually just called diskettes, are flat circles of iron oxide-coated plastic enclosed in a hard plastic case. Most floppy diskettes are 3½ inches, although you may see other sizes. They have a capacity to hold 1.44 MB or more of data. To protect unwanted data from being added to or removed from a diskette, write protection is provided. To write-protect a diskette, open the write-protect window on the diskette. See Figure 3-14.

FIGURE 3-14
The parts of a diskette

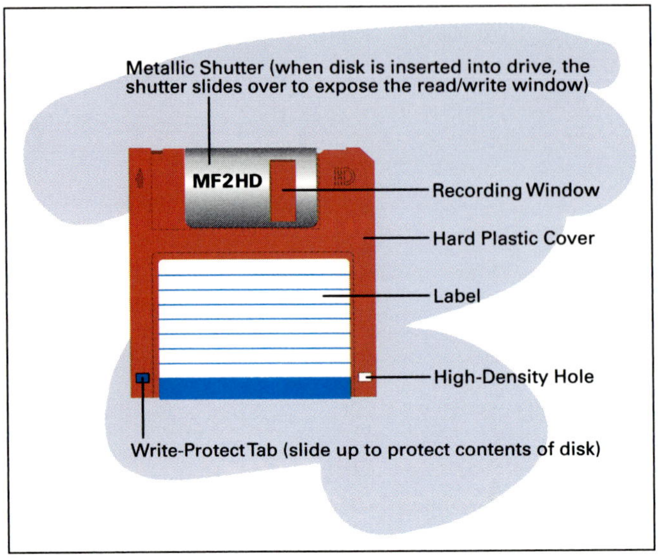

Hard Disk Drives

1-1.3.3-1

Hard disk drives are used to store data inside of the computer. They provide two advantages: speed and capacity. Accessing data is faster and the amount of data that can be stored is much larger than what can be stored on a floppy diskette. The size of the hard drive is measured in megabytes or gigabytes. See Figure 3-15.

FIGURE 3-15
How a hard drive works

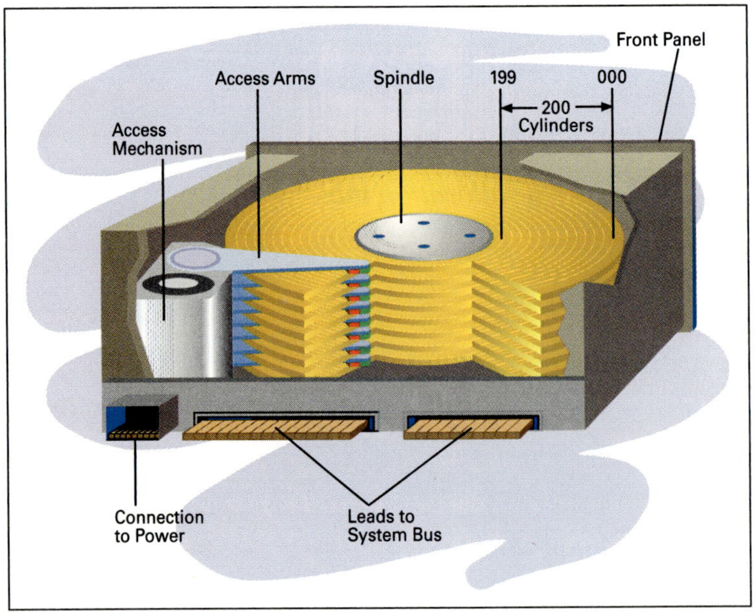

1-1.2.5-3

Zip Drives and Jaz Drives

Zip drives and *Jaz drives* house disks that are capable of storing tremendous amounts of storage. Even though they are only the size of a 3-inch diskette, they can hold as much as 1 GB of data. The Zip drives are slower than the Jaz drives; they can hold as much as 70 floppy diskettes but are less expensive than the Jaz drive. The Jaz drive is much faster and can store up to 1 GB of data. See Figure 3-16.

FIGURE 3-16
Types of removable storage

Magnetic Tape Drives

Magnetic tape drives are used for making backup copies of large volumes of data. This is a very slow process and therefore not used for regularly saving data. The tape can be used to replace data that may have been lost on the hard drive.

Optical Storage Devices

Optical storage devices use laser technology to read and write data on silver platters.

CD-ROM

The *CD-ROM* (Compact Disk Read-Only Memory) can store up to 680 MB. This is the equivalent of about 450 floppy diskettes! You can only read data from the CD; you cannot store data on a CD unless you are using the new writable CDs.

WORM Disks

WORM (Write Once Read Many) *disks* are optical disk storage devices that use laser beams and optical technology. They are usually used for permanently storing large volumes of data. The data is stored by making imprints into the surface of the disk that cannot be removed.

CD-R Drives

CD-R (Recordable) *drives* make it possible for you to create your own CD-ROM disks that can actually be read by any CD-ROM drive. Once information has been written to this type of disk, it cannot be changed.

PhotoCD

The ***PhotoCD*** is used to store digitized photographic images on a CD. The photos stored on these disks can be uploaded into the computer and used in other documents.

DVD Media

Full-length movies can be stored on the ***DVD*** (Digital Versatile Disk). It is the size of a regular CD and can be played in a regular CD. However, the DVD movie player can connect to your TV and play movies like a VCR.

Caring for Removable Storage Media

Removable storage media require special care if the data stored is to remain undamaged. Here are some safeguards that should be taken:

- Keep away from magnetic fields such as those contained in televisions and computer monitors.
- Avoid extreme temperatures.
- Never open the data shutter or attempt to disassemble a removable disk cartridge. Never touch the surface of the media itself.
- Remove media from drives and store them properly when not in use.
- Write-protect important data to prevent accidental erasure.
- When handling CD-ROMs and other optical disks, hold them at the edges.
- Never try to remove the media from a drive when the drive indicator light is on.
- Keep disks in a sturdy case when transporting.

Ethics in Technology

COMPUTER VIRUSES

The word "viruses" can put fear into anyone who uses the Internet or exchanges diskettes. How can such a small word cause such fear? It is because a virus can cause tremendous damage to your computer files!

A ***virus*** is simply a computer program that is intentionally written to attach itself to other programs or disk boot sectors and duplicates itself whenever those programs are executed or the infected disks are accessed. A virus can wipe out all of the files that are on your computer.

Viruses can exist on your computer for weeks or months and not cause any damage until a predetermined date or time code is activated. Not all viruses cause damage. Some are just pranks; maybe your desktop will display some silly message. Viruses are created by persons who are impressed with the power they possess because of their expertise in the area of computers, and sometimes they create them just for fun.

To protect your computer from virus damage, install an anti-virus software program on your computer and keep it running at all times so that it can continuously scan for viruses.

SUMMARY

In this lesson, you learned:

- Input devices enable you to input data and commands into the computer.
- The most common input devices are the keyboard and mouse.
- The keyboard is divided into four sections: alphabetical keys, function keys, cursor keys, and the numeric keypad.
- Additional special-purpose keys perform specialized functions.
- The mouse is a pointing device used to input data.
- Other types of input devices include joysticks, trackballs, graphic tablets, touch display screens, voice recognition devices, scanners, and electronic pens.
- Printers are used to produce a paper or hard copy of the processed result.
- Criteria for selecting a printer include speed, print quality, and cost.
- Printers are classified as either impact or non-impact.
- The most popular types of printers are laser, ink-jet, and dot matrix.
- Input and output devices must be physically connected to the computer.
- There are two ways to connect I/O devices to a computer: Plug the device into a port in the back of the computer or install a circuit board with the needed port included.
- There are several types of ports: USB, SCSI, MIDI, parallel, and serial.
- To maintain a permanent copy of data, you must store it on some type of storage medium. These may include floppy diskettes, hard drives, CDs, magnetic tape cartridges, and WORM disks.

VOCABULARY *Review*

Define the following terms:

CD-ROM
Dot pitch
DVD
File allocation table (FAT)
Function keys
Graphic tablet
Input devices
Jaz drives
Magnetic tape drives
Management Information Systems (MIS)
Modifier keys
Non-impact printers
Optical storage devices
Output devices
Parallel ports
PhotoCD
Printhead
Resolution
Screen size
Serial ports
Special-purpose keys
Touch display screen
Trackball
Tracks
Virus
Voice recognition
WORM disks
Zip drives

REVIEW *Questions*

MULTIPLE CHOICE

Select the best response for the following statements.

1. Laser, ink-jet, and dot matrix are types of ________.
   - **A.** monitors
   - **B.** printers
   - **C.** storage devices
   - **D.** input devices

2. Monitors and printers are types of ________.
   - **A.** input devices
   - **B.** output devices
   - **C.** storage devices
   - **D.** ports

3. All of the following are types of ports *except* ________.
   - **A.** MSO
   - **B.** USB
   - **C.** SCSI
   - **D.** MIDI

4. Floppy diskettes are also called ________.
   - **A.** diskettes
   - **B.** hard drives
   - **C.** CDs
   - **D.** magnetic disks

5. All of the following are sections of the keyboard *except* ________.
   - **A.** alphabetic keys
   - **B.** function keys
   - **C.** Esc key
   - **D.** numeric keypad

TRUE/FALSE

Circle T if the statement is true or F if the statement is false.

T F 1. Modifier keys are used in conjunction with other keys.

T F 2. Input and output devices perform the same function.

T F 3. The mouse is a pointing device that rolls around on a flat surface and controls the pointer.

T F 4. Factors that influence the quality of a monitor are screen size, resolution, and dot pitch.

T F 5. PPM refers to the number of pages that a printer prints per minute.

FILL IN THE BLANK

Complete the following sentences by writing the correct word or words in the blanks provided.

1. A(n) __________ is used to enter data into the computer.
2. __________ and __________ are the most popular output devices.
3. Input and output devices are connected to computers through __________.
4. The two types of ports are __________ and __________.
5. Hard disks and floppy diskettes are types of __________ media.

PROJECTS

PROJECT 3-1

Contact computer vendors, read computer magazines, research the Internet, and use any other resources to collect data concerning the prices of at least five storage devices. Find sales information for the same product from three vendors. Determine the average cost of each device. Prepare a chart like the one here to show your findings.

Storage Device	Capabilities	Vendor	Cost	Vendor	Cost	Vendor	Cost	Avg. Cost

PROJECT 3-2

There are many styles of keyboards for computers. Many of the designs were developed to address various health issues related to keyboard use. Use appropriate research sources to locate information on various keyboard designs and report on the theory on which they are designed. You may also visit retail stores that sell computers to obtain information and sales documents. Prepare a written report of the information you locate.

PROJECT 3-3

Prepare a written report in table format of early storage media. Your table should have the columns shown here. Include at least five types of early storage media.

Type	Media	Capacity	Advantages	Disadvantages

WEB PROJECT

Christopher Sholes is given credit for inventing the first typewriter (keyboard). How did he design his keyboard? Why did he design it the way that he did? Who invented the one before his? Why was this person not given credit for inventing the first typewriter? Use a search engine on the Internet to answer these questions and to find other information concerning the early typewriter. Prepare a written report of your findings. The following keywords may be helpful in your search: *Christopher Sholes*, *typewriter*, and *keyboard*.

TEAMWORK PROJECT

Your supervisor at the video store is interested in setting up a teleconference with several of the stores throughout the state. However, she would like to get more information on this capability. She has asked you and the assistant manager to research this technology for her and let her know the steps needed to set up such a conference. Research the Internet and any other materials to prepare a step-by-step guide for setting up a teleconference. Include an introduction that gives basic information about teleconferencing.

CRITICAL *Thinking*

ACTIVITY 3-1

Prepare a report describing several applications in which a user would need to use the Jaz or Zip drive to store data. Describe the application and explain why it would be necessary to use the Zip or Jaz drive. Also explore the alternatives to using these drives. You may find useful information at *www.iomega.com*.

LESSON 4

WHAT IS SOFTWARE?

OBJECTIVES

Upon completion of this lesson, you should be able to:

- Distinguish between software and hardware.
- Describe the difference between applications software and systems software.
- Describe the three categories of system programs.
- Describe operating systems for microcomputers.
- Describe network operating systems.

Estimated Time: 1.5 hours

VOCABULARY

Applications software
Graphical user interfaces (GUIs)
Hardware
MS-DOS
Multitasking
Network operating system
Operating systems
Software
Systems software
Unix
User interface

Over the last 50 years or so, computer technology has changed the world. Not so long ago, workers would not have used computers. Customers would not have ID cards that could be scanned. Accounting was done using ledgers.

When most of us think about computers, we think of hardware and how the hardware has changed—that computers have become smaller and faster. If we look at the history of computers, however, we find that the early computers were used for little more than high-speed calculators. This alone would not have had such a major influence on our culture and economy. The reason that computers have had such an impact is through the vision and desire of software developers. These software creators came up with hundreds of ideas and ways in which to use computers. They created programs that affect us in every aspect of our lives.

Hardware vs. Software

You have probably heard the words software and hardware many times. Sometimes it is difficult to distinguish between these two terms. ***Hardware*** refers to anything you can touch. This includes objects such as the keyboard, mouse, monitor, printer, chips, disks, disk drives, and CD recorders. You cannot touch software because it has no substance. ***Software*** is instructions issued to the computer so that specific tasks may be performed. Another word for software is program.

IC3 1-2.1.4

For example, a computer programmer may write a program that lets the user download music from the Internet. Or suppose a bookkeeper has a problem with his computer. You might hear him say, "The problem lies in the software." This means there is a problem with the program or data, and not with the computer or hardware itself. He may also say, "It's a software problem." A good analogy here is a book. The book, including the pages and the ink, is the hardware. The words and ideas on the pages are the software. One has little value without the other. The same is true of computer software and hardware.

Types of Software

1-2.2.14 There are two basic types of computer software: ***applications software*** and ***systems software.*** Applications software helps you perform a specific task. Systems software refers to the operating system and all utility programs that manage computer resources at a low level. Figuratively speaking, applications software sits on top of systems software. Without the operating system and system utilities, the computer cannot run any applications program.

Applications Software

1-2.2.4 1-3.3.8 1-2.2.11 1-2.2.6 1-2.2.7 Applications software is widely referred to as productivity software. Applications software is comprised of programs designed for an end user. Some of the more commonly used application programs are word processors, database systems, presentation systems, spreadsheet programs, and desktop publishing programs. Some other applications categories are as follows:

- Education, home, and personal software—reference, entertainment, personal finance, calendars, e-mail, browsers
- Multimedia software—authoring, animation, music, video and sound capturing and editing, virtual reality, Web site development
- Workgroup computing software—calendars and scheduling, e-mail, browsers, electronic conferencing, project management

Systems Software

1-2.2.13-1 1-3.3.7 Systems software is a group of programs that coordinate and control the resources and operations of a computer system. Systems software enables the many components of the computer system to communicate. There are three categories of systems software: operating systems, utilities, and language translators.

Did You Know?

Some operating systems software programs are DOS, Windows 2000, Windows NT, Macintosh OS, and Unix. Some software applications include word processing, spreadsheets, database, and desktop publishing. These software applications are frequently sold as suites, such as Microsoft Office.

Operating Systems

1-2.2.1-1 1-3.1.4-1 1-3.1.6-1 ***Operating systems*** provide an interface between the user or application program and the computer hardware. See Figure 4-1. There are many brands and versions of operating systems software. Each of these is designed to work with one or more particular processors. For example, an operating system like Windows is designed to work with a processor made by Intel. Many IBM PC-compatible computers contain this brand of processor. Most Macintosh computers contain a processor manufactured by Motorola. The Windows operating system does not work with this Motorola processor.

FIGURE 4-1
Operating systems: an interface between users and computers

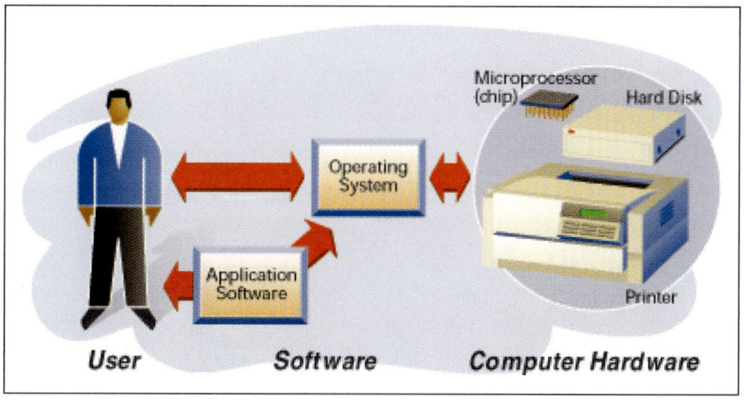

Utilities

Utility programs help you perform housekeeping chores. You use these programs to complete
1-2.2.10-1 specialized tasks related to managing the computer's resources, file management, and so forth.
1-3.1.1-1 Some utility programs are part of the operating system, and others are self-contained programs.
1-2.1.5 See Figure 4-2. Some examples of utility program functions are as follows:

- You format a disk—a disk formatting utility provides the instructions to the computer on how to do this.
- You copy a file from the hard drive to a floppy disk—the file management utility provides the instructions to the computer.
- To do a backup of the hard drive, you use the backup utility.

FIGURE 4-2
File conversion utility

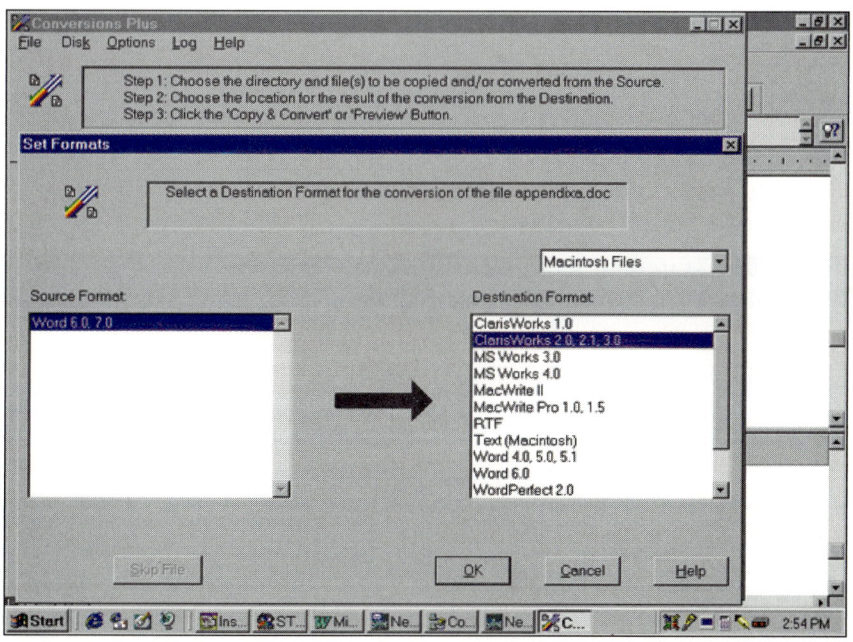

See Table 4-1 for a list and purpose of the most commonly used utilities.

1-2.2.10-2
1-2.1.6

TABLE 4-1
Utlility Programs

TYPE OF UTILITY	PURPOSE
Disk formatting	Prepares a disk to have files stored on it
File management	Allows the user to perform tasks such as copying, moving, and deleting files
File recovery	Attempts to recover a file that has been erased
Disk defragmentation	Attempts to place the segments of each file on the hard disk as close to one another as possible
Uninstall	Removes an application that is no longer needed
Diagnostic	Provides detailed information about the computer system and attempts to locate problems
File conversion	Converts a file from one format to another
Disk compression	Frees up storage space on a disk by compressing the existing files
Backup	Makes a duplicate copy of the contents of a secondary storage device
Anti-virus	Protects the computer system from viruses

Language Translators

Language translators convert English-like software programs into machine language that the computer can understand. A company will hire a programmer to write a software program to inventory all of the items in the store. The programmer writes the program statements using a programming language called Visual Basic. A program statement directs the computer to perform a specified action.

The computer, however, cannot read the Visual Basic programming statements because they are written in a language that we understand. This is where the language translator takes over. The translator changes each of the Visual Basic programming statements into machine language. A single statement in a high-level language can represent several machine-language instructions. Now the statements can be executed and the company's inventory can be processed.

Hot Tip

If you have a computer, you should have an emergency boot disk. Sooner or later, your computer may not boot from the hard drive. You can use your emergency boot disk to get your computer started. Each operating system has its own unique way of creating a boot disk. Check your operating system help files for information on how to create this disk. Then be sure to store it in an easy-to-find and safe place.

Microcomputer Operating Systems Interfaces

All computers, big and small, have operating systems. For most of us, however, the computer we most often use is a microcomputer. So our focus in this module is on microcomputer operating systems.

The ***user interface*** is the part of the operating system with which we are most familiar. This is the part of the operating system we interact with when using our computer. The two most common types of user interfaces are command-line interfaces and graphical interfaces.

Command-line Interfaces

All early computers used command-line interfaces. With this type of interface, you must type the exact command you wish to execute. One of the most widely used command-line interfaces for microcomputers is ***MS-DOS***. Using DOS, you want to look at a list of files on your computer's hard drive. You key the DOS command dir and press the Enter key. See Figure 4-3. This type of interface is not considered very user friendly. You must memorize the commands and key them without any spelling errors. Otherwise, they do not work.

FIGURE 4-3
Command line interface

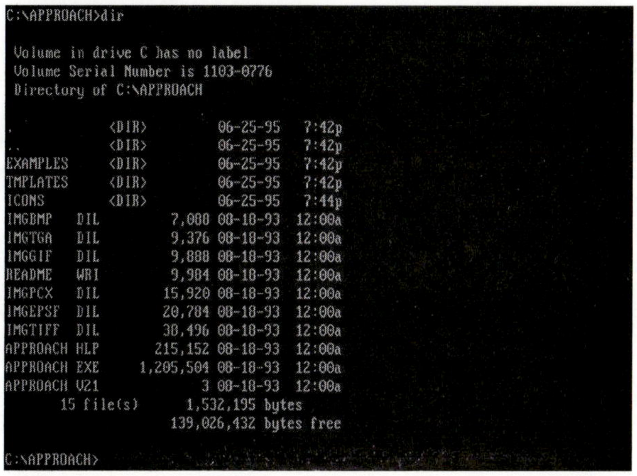

Graphical User Interfaces

As microcomputer technology developed, so did the operating system interface. The next step in this progression was menus. The user could choose commands from a list.

The big breakthrough in ease of use came with the development of ***graphical user interfaces (GUIs).*** When the user turns on the computer and starts the operating system, a symbolic desktop is displayed. On this desktop are various objects, or icons. These graphical symbols represent files, disks, programs, and other objects. GUIs permit the user to manipulate these on-screen icons. Most people use a pointing device such as a mouse to click on the icons and execute the commands. See Figure 4-4.

FIGURE 4-4
Graphical user interface

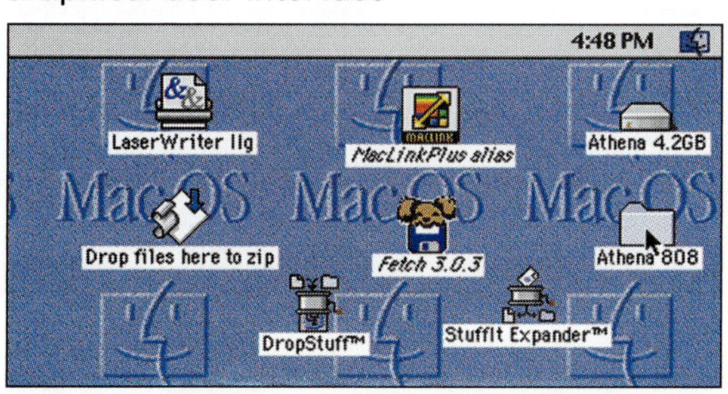

Microcomputer Operating Systems

There are several popular operating systems for microcomputers. If you are using a Macintosh or a Macintosh clone, you will most likely be using a version of the Mac OS.

1-2.2.1-2 If your computer is what is commonly referred to as a PC or an IBM PC compatible, you most likely are using one of these three operating systems:

- DOS
- A combination of DOS and Windows
- A stand-alone version of Windows

> **Internet**
>
> The history of Apple Computer and Steve Jobs and Steve Wozniak is a fascinating story. For an overview of this story and some interesting facts about the Macintosh operating system, check out the Web site at *www.hypermall.com/History/ah01.html*.

Mac OS

1-2.2.1-4 The Mac OS is used with Apple's Power Macintosh computers and Power Macintosh clones. The Macintosh was introduced in 1984. One of the main features of this new computer was a GUI. The GUI was called the Finder and contained icons or symbols that represented documents, software, disks, and so forth. To activate the icon, the user clicked on it with a mouse. See Figure 4-5. This operating system was also the first OS to provide on-screen help or instructions. In 2002, Macintosh released OS v.X.

> **Did You Know?**
>
> Macintosh popularized the first graphical user interface; however, Apple did not invent the interface. Xerox Corporation developed the idea for a graphical user interface.

FIGURE 4-5
Macintosh operating system

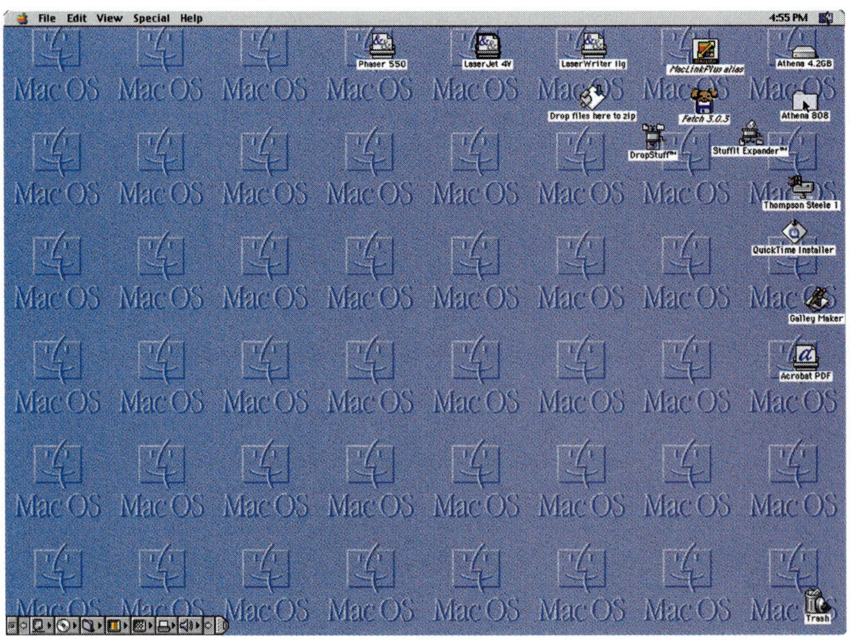

DOS

1-3.1.2-2 IBM introduced its first IBM PC in 1981. With the introduction of this new microcomputer came a new operating system (OS). This system was called DOS (Disk Operating System). IBM referred to this operating system as PC DOS. They licensed this software from a small start-up company called Microsoft. But as agreements go, Microsoft retained the rights to market its own version of the OS. Microsoft called their version MS-DOS. This OS was the catalyst that launched Microsoft into the multibillion dollar company it is today.

1-2.2.1-3 1-3.1.2-1 DOS is a character-based operating system. The user interacts with the system by typing in commands. DOS is a single-user or single-tasking operating system because the user can run only one program at a time.

Windows

In response to the competition from the Macintosh, Microsoft introduced its own GUI in 1987. This OS was called Windows.

- The first versions of Windows contain a graphical shell and were called operating environments because they work in combination with DOS.
- The different applications installed on a computer appear as icons.
- The user activates the icons by clicking on them with a mouse.
- These early versions of Windows are consecutively numbered beginning with Windows 3.0, Windows 3.1, and so forth.

1-3.1.4-3

Technology Careers

SOFTWARE DEVELOPER

A software developer maintains and helps develop new application and operating systems programs. When you see a job listing for software developer, it could include many requirements.

A company may be looking for someone to develop software using a particular programming language such as Visual Basic, C, or C++. Or a company may be looking for someone to develop add-ons to operating systems programs. This could include enhancements to utility programs, updates to language translators, or new additions to the operating system itself. Many companies seek employees with skills in operating systems programs such as Unix and Windows NT.

If you go online and look for software developer jobs, you will find that many of them refer to Oracle, a large information technology software company. Oracle products support database technology, data design and modeling, Web applications, and much more.

There is a great variation in salaries and educational requirements. Salaries can range from $25,000 to $100,000 plus. Educational requirements range from some college to a bachelor's or master's degree or maybe even a Ph.D. Generally, but not always, the more education you have, the higher your starting salary. Most companies require some experience, but a few have entry-level positions.

1-1.1.4-2 1-3.3.6 Windows 95 was Microsoft's first true multitasking operating system. ***Multitasking*** allows a single user to work on two or more applications that reside in memory at the same time. Some advantages of Windows 95 include the following:

- An improved graphical interface.
- Programs run faster than with earlier Windows versions.
- Includes support for networking, which allows a group of two more computers to be linked.
- Uses Plug and Play technology, the goal of which is to just plug in a new device and immediately be able to use it, without complicated setup maneuvers.

> **Internet**
>
> Want to learn more about Windows CE, Microsoft's operating system for small handheld devices? Access the Web site *www.whatis.com*; in the Quick Search text box, key **Windows CE** and click **Go**. You can also find additional information at *www.microsoft.com/windowsce/*.

Windows 98 is easier to use than Windows 95 and has additional features. Some of these new features include the following:

1-3.1.4-4 1-3.1.4-5 1-3.1.6-1 1-3.1.6-2

- Internet integration.
- Windows Explorer has a Web browser look option.
- Faster system startup and shutdown.
- Support for the Universal Serial Bus that is used to easily add and remove devices on the computer.

Windows 2000 is an update to the Windows 98 and Windows NT operating systems. See Figure 4-6. Some new features include the following:

- Tools for Web site creation.
- Wizards that guide the user through various operations.
- Monitoring programs.

FIGURE 4-6
Windows 2000 operating system

The most recent update is Windows XP, which provides increased stability and improved device recognition. Even though the Windows versions have changed, some features remain consistent, such as the Start Menu, Task Bar, and Desktop.

1-3.1.4-2
1-3.1.4-6

Windows CE is a scaled-down Windows operating system. It is used on small handheld computers and wireless communication devices.

Still another operating system is ***Unix***. Unix is frequently used by scientists and programmers. This operating system, developed by AT&T, is considered a portable operating system. This means it can run on just about any hardware platform. There are several variants of the language, such as Linux and IBM's AIX. See Figure 4-7.

1-3.1.5-1
1-3.1.5-2

FIGURE 4-7
Unix operating system

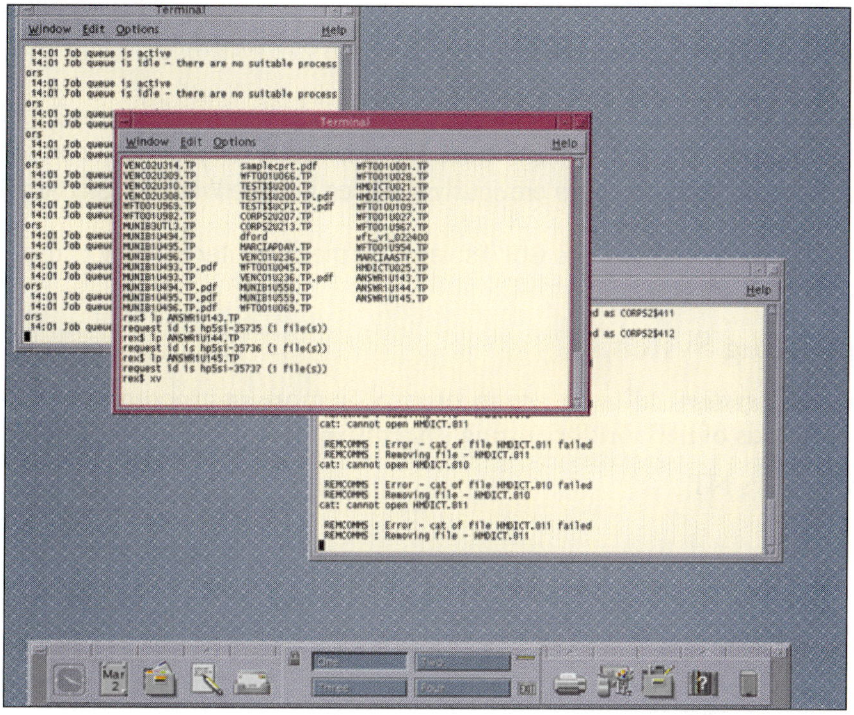

STEP-BY-STEP 4.1

-1.1.7-1
-1.1.7-2
1-3.3.5
1-3.3.9
1-3.3.7

When you start your computer, operating system commands are loaded into memory. Each operating system boots or starts the computer in its own individual way. Understanding the boot process is the key to diagnosing many computer start-up problems.

The Step-by-Step given in this example is based on the Windows OS system. Keep in mind, however, that the boot process is similar for all operating systems.

1. When you turn on the computer, the first thing that happens is POST, an acronym for Power-on Self Test. This is a series of diagnostic tests to check RAM and to verify that the keyboard and disk drives you may have are physically connected to the computer.

STEP-BY-STEP 4.1 Continued

2. The BIOS (Basic Input Output System) searches for the boot record—first on drive A and then on drive C. The BIOS is built-in software that is normally placed on a ROM chip. It contains all of the code that controls the most common devices connected to your computer. This includes the monitor, keyboard, disk drives, and other components. This chip comes with your computer when you purchase it.

3. The boot record is loaded into RAM. The boot record contains several files. These files contain programming configuration instructions for hardware devices and software applications that you may have installed on your computer.

4. Next, the software drivers are loaded. Drivers are what enable you to use your printer, modem, scanner, or other devices. Generally, when you add a new device to your system, you install drivers for that device.

5. Next to be loaded is the GUI or graphical user interface. In this instance, the GUI is Windows. When loading the GUI, the operating system reads the commands for your desktop configuration. It also loads whatever programs you have previously specified into the Windows Start-up Folder.

6. If everything goes as it should, the GUI displays and the computer is ready to use.

Network Operating Systems

Network operating systems allow a group of two or more microcomputers to be connected. There are several brands of network operating systems. Three of the most popular are as follows:

- Microsoft Windows NT
- Novell's Netware
- IBM's Warp Server

Ethics in Technology

WHAT IS COMPUTER ETHICS?

Webster's Online Dictionary[1] offers the following definition of ethics:

(1)the discipline dealing with what is good and bad and with moral duty and obligation

(2)a: a set of moral principles or values, b: a theory or system of moral values <the present-day materialistic ethic>, c: plural but singular or plural in construction: the principles of conduct governing an individual or a group <professional ethics>, d: a guiding philosophy.

Ethical judgments are no different in the area of computing than they are in any other. The use of computers can raise many issues of privacy, copyright, theft, and power, to name just a few. In 1990 the Institute of Electrical and Electronics Engineers created the following code of ethics. Many businesses and organizations have adopted this code as their code. Remember that this is just a code—not a law. People choose to follow it voluntarily.

CODE OF ETHICS

We, the members of the IEEE, in recognition of the importance of our technologies affecting the quality of life throughout the world, and in accepting a personal obligation to our profession, its members, and the communities we serve, do hereby commit ourselves to the highest ethical and professional conduct and agree:

1. to accept responsibility in making engineering decisions consistent with the safety, health, and welfare of the public, and to disclose promptly factors that might endanger the public or the environment;
2. to avoid real or perceived conflicts of interest whenever possible, and to disclose them to affected parties when they do exist;
3. to be honest and realistic in stating claims or estimates based on available data;
4. to reject bribery in all its forms;
5. to improve the understanding of technology, its appropriate application, and potential consequences;
6. to maintain and improve our technical competence and to undertake technological tasks for others only if qualified by training or experience, or after full disclosure of pertinent limitations;
7. to seek, accept, and offer honest criticism of technical work, to acknowledge and correct errors, and to credit properly the contributions of others;
8. to treat fairly all persons regardless of such factors as race, religion, gender, disability, age, or national origin;
9. to avoid injuring others, their property, reputation, or employment by false or malicious action;
10. to assist colleagues and co-workers in their professional development and to support them in following this code of ethics.

[1] Webster's Online Dictionary: courses.ncsu.edu:8020/classes-a/computer_ethics/basics/principles/

SUMMARY

In this lesson, you learned:

- Hardware refers to anything you can touch.
- Software is instructions that tell the computer what to do.
- Software is also called a program.
- The two basic types of computer software are applications software and systems software.
- Applications software is also known as productivity software.
- Systems software coordinates and controls the resources and operations of a computer system.
- Three major categories of systems software are operating systems, utilities, and language translators.
- Operating systems provide an interface between the user and application program and the computer hardware.
- Utility programs help users complete specialized tasks such as file management.
- Language translators convert English-like software programs into machine language.
- A programmer uses a programming language to write program statements.
- All computers have operating systems.
- The user interface is the part of the operating system with which we are most familiar.
- The two most common user interfaces are command-line interfaces and graphical user interfaces.
- The Mac operating system is used with Apple's Power Macintosh computers and Power Macintosh clones.
- Icons are symbols that represent documents, software programs, disks, and so forth.
- DOS was introduced with the IBM PC in 1981 and is a character-based operating system.
- Microsoft introduced the first version of Windows in 1987; this was an operating environment.
- Windows 95 was Microsoft's first true multitasking operating system.
- Windows CE is a scaled-down Windows operating system used for small handheld computers.
- Unix is a portable operating system.
- Network operating systems allow a group of two or more microcomputers to be connected.

VOCABULARY *Review*

Define the following terms:

Applications software	MS-DOS	Software
Graphical user interfaces (GUIs)	Multitasking	Systems software
	Network operating system	Unix
Hardware	Operating systems	User interface

REVIEW *Questions*

MULTIPLE CHOICE

Select the best response for the following statements.

1. Another word for software is ________.
   A. hardware
   B. program
   C. programming statement
   D. interface

2. The two basic types of computer software are ________ and ________.
   A. program, applications
   B. productivity, applications
   C. applications, systems
   D. systems, networking systems

3. A group of programs that coordinate and control the resources of a computer system is called ________.
   A. systems software
   B. applications software
   C. language translator
   D. utility program

4. The ________ is the part of the operating system with which we are most familiar.
   A. formatting utility
   B. programming statement
   C. language translator
   D. user interface

5. DOS was first introduced with the ________.
   A. Apple Macintosh
   B. IBM PC
   C. Unix operating system
   D. Windows

TRUE/FALSE

Circle T if the statement is true or F if the statement is false.

T F 1. The first version of Windows was a true operating environment.

T F 2. DOS is a multitasking operating system.

T F 3. Apple Computer Company developed the GUI.

T F 4. Computer hardware is anything you can touch.

T F 5. There are five categories of systems software.

FILL IN THE BLANK

Complete the following sentences by writing the correct word or words in the blanks provided.

1. The second step in the progression of the operating system interface was __________.
2. Word processing is an example of __________ software.
3. Novell NetWare is an example of __________ system.
4. One of the main features of Apple's Power Macintosh was the __________ interface.
5. DOS is a(n) __________-user operating system.

PROJECTS

PROJECT 4-1

To use a floppy disk, you must first format it. Use the Internet or other written resources and write step-by-step instructions on how to format a floppy disk. If you have a computer available, give your instructions to one of your friends or coworkers. Ask them to use your instructions and format a floppy disk. Were they able to follow the instructions easily? At the end of the formatting process, a summary displays telling you the number of available bytes on the disk. Include the name in your report. If there are any bad bytes in bad sections, include that information as well.

PROJECT 4-2

Operating systems have come a long way over the last few years. They are much easier to user and support many more features. If you were going to design an operating system for computers for the year 2010, what features would you include? How would your operating system be different from those that are currently available? Use your word processing program to write a report or give an oral report to the class.

PROJECT 4-3

You have been hired to create an icon to represent a new software program that has just been developed. This is an interactive encyclopedia. It also contains games to help reinforce the topics presented in the encyclopedia. Think about the icons on your computer's desktop or that you see in the figures throughout this chapter. Using graph paper or a computer drawing program, create an icon for this new interactive encyclopedia.

WEB PROJECT

Office 2000 is a popular applications suite of programs. For an online tutorial of some of the ways you can use Office 2000, go to *www.actden.com/o2k/HTML/index_h.htm.*

When you complete the tutorial, use your word processing program to write an overview of what you learned. Your report should be at least one page.

TEAMWORK PROJECT

IC³ 1-2.2.13-1

You and two team members have been given the responsibility for purchasing new computers for a company. One team member wants to purchase an Apple Macintosh with the Mac OS v.X with the latest software suite, another wants to purchase a PC with the latest version of the Windows OS, and the third wants to purchase a PC with the Unix operating system. The manager has requested that your team do some research and present her with a report so that she can make the best choice. Your report should include the positives and negatives for each of these operating systems.

CRITICAL *Thinking*

ACTIVITY 4-1

The more recent versions of operating systems include accessibility options for people with visual or hearing disabilities. Research the operating system on your computer and complete a report on the accessibility options.

LESSON 5

WHAT BASIC SKILLS DO I NEED TO USE THE COMPUTER?

OBJECTIVES

Upon completion of this lesson, you should be able to:

- Describe a graphical user interface.
- Start and shut down a graphical user interface.
- Open and close a window.
- Format a disk.
- Create files and folders.
- Start a program.
- Manage Windows.
- Manage files.
- Access Help.

Estimated Time: 1.5 hours

VOCABULARY

Desktop
Details
Finder
Folder
Formatting
Icons
Maximize
Menus
Minimize
Pointer
Pointing device
Restore
Scroll bar
Size box
Window
Windows
Zoom box

Graphical User Interface

IC3 1-3.1.3-1

As introduced in Lesson 4, you learned that most of today's computers come with some type of GUI. This type of interface lets you interact with your computer using pictures and symbols as opposed to text. A well-designed graphical user interface makes a computer easier to use by freeing you from memorizing complicated text commands. Instead, you point and click with a mouse, or some other type of input device, to activate programs or commands.

IC3 1-3.1.3-2

A true graphical interface includes standard text and graphic formats. This makes it possible for the user to share data among different programs. For instance, you can create a chart in Excel and copy it into a PowerPoint document.

To work with a GUI, it is important to understand the associated terminology. Some of the more popular components are as follows:

- ***Desktop:*** The desktop is the first screen you see when the operating system is up and fully running. It is called the desktop because the icons symbolize real objects on a real desktop.
- ***Icons:*** A small picture that represents a file, command, or some other computer function. You execute the associated command by clicking or double-clicking the icon.

- ***Pointer:*** An on-screen symbol that shows the current position of the mouse. It usually appears as an arrow or an I-beam pointer.
- ***Pointing device:*** A device, such as a mouse or trackball, that allows the user to select objects, such as icons or text.
- ***Menus:*** A text interface that includes drop-down options; the user clicks on one of the choices to execute a command.
- ***Scroll bar:*** A horizontal or vertical bar that allows the user to control which part of a list or document is currently in the window's frame. The scroll bar makes it easy to move to any part of a file.
- ***Window:*** Rectangular area of the screen; used to display a program, data, or other information. Windows can be resized and moved around the screen.

Important note: ***Windows*** is the operating system for the PC. A ***window*** is an object within both the Macintosh and Windows operating systems. Both Macintosh and Windows operating commands are covered in this lesson.

Despite the convenience of these GUI features, it is still necessary to use a keyboard for many programs. For instance, trying to enter a document in a word processor with a mouse would be impossible.

IC3 1-3.1.3-3

Starting and Shutting Down the GUI

To start a graphical user interface is as simple as turning on your computer. When you turn on the computer, it first performs a self-test. Next, it loads the system software. Once the computer is up and running, you're looking at the desktop. The two most popular GUIs are the Macintosh OS and Windows. The program that displays the Macintosh desktop is called ***Finder***. There is no comparable name in Windows; it is simply called the desktop.

Desktop

The desktop contains windows and icons. Refer to Figures 4-5 and 4-6 in Lesson 4 for what the Macintosh and Windows' desktops look like. It is a representation of how people work at a desk. Think about how you work at your desk. You look at and read documents or files, you move the documents around, put them in folders, and store and retrieve them from a file drawer. The computer desktop works in a similar way. You have documents that you can read. You can store those documents in folders and retrieve those documents from folders. These documents and folders are represented by icons. These activities may seem very basic, but they are an essential part of any job. They help you stay organized.

Did You Know?

The first graphical user interface was designed by Xerox Corporation's Palo Alto Research Center in the 1970s. It was not, however, until the 1980s and the development of the Apple Macintosh that graphical user interfaces became popular.

IC3 1-3.2.3-2

Shutting Down the System

If you are using Windows, point to Start and select Shut Down. When the Shut Down Windows dialog box displays, select Shut down and click OK. If you are using a Macintosh, point to the Special menu option to display the drop-down menu. Select Shut Down.

Opening a Window

To open a window means to double-click an icon. This executes a command and opens a window on the desktop. It is easy to open and close windows and to move windows from one place to another on the screen. One of the windows you may want to view often is the Trash (Macintosh) or Recycle Bin (Windows).

To view the Trash or Recycle Bin, you point to the Trash or Recycle Bin icon and double-click the mouse. This executes the program and opens a new window. If there is anything in the trash, it is either represented by icons or by text. You will notice that the window contains a title bar. This title bar contains lines (Macintosh) or is highlighted (Windows), indicating that the window is the active window. See Figures 5-1 and 5-2.

FIGURE 5-1
Windows Recycle Bin window

FIGURE 5-2
Macintosh Trash window

-3.2.2-4

Closing a Window

To close a window within Windows, on the File menu, you click Close or click the Close button [X] in the upper right corner. To close a window within the Macintosh environment, you click Close Window on the File menu or make the window active and press Command + W.

-1.1.8-1
-1.1.8-2

Formatting a Disk

If you want to save your work on a floppy disk, you must first format the disk. A floppy disk is a portable storage medium. This means you can store data on the disk and take it with you from computer to computer. A floppy disk is a type of magnetic media. It uses magnetic patterns to store data on the disk's surface.

When you purchase a new floppy disk, chances are it is not formatted, although you can purchase preformatted disks. ***Formatting*** is the process of preparing the disk so that you can write data to and read data from the disk. When a disk is formatted, it is organized into tracks and sectors. A sector is pie shaped and can hold 512 bytes of data. A track is a narrow band that forms a full circle on the surface of the disk.

Sometimes when you format a disk, you may receive a message that the disk has a bad sector. This doesn't necessarily mean the entire surface of the disk is bad—just a small portion. However, it is generally best to discard the disk if you have one with a bad sector. There may be occasions when you store data on a disk and find a sector becomes damaged. If so, you may be able to recover the data with special utility programs.

If you have a floppy disk with a lot of data you would like to discard, you can just reformat the disk. Keep in mind that when you format a disk, any data contained on that disk is erased. See Figure 5-3.

Did You Know?

Formatting a disk does not erase the data on the disk. It only erases the address tables. Unless you write something else to the disk, you can probably recover your files. There are special operating commands that can help you recover your data. If this doesn't work, there are utility programs available for purchase. Most of the time, You can retrieve your data with one of these programs.

FIGURE 5-3
Formatting a disk

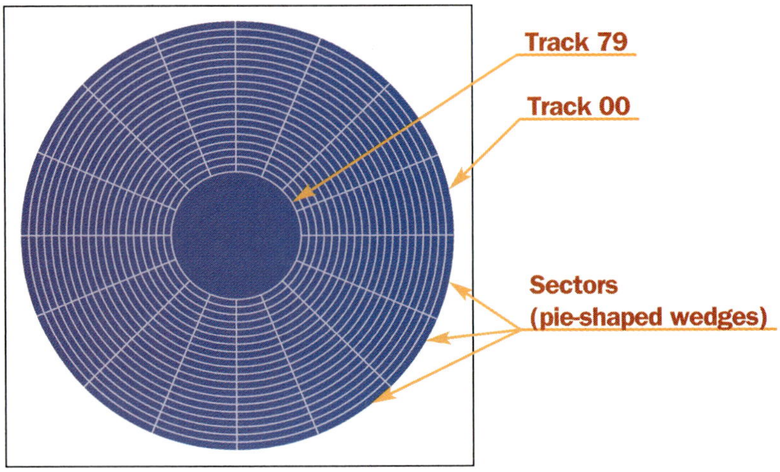

STEP-BY-STEP 5.1

To format a new floppy disk with Windows:

1. Insert the floppy disk into the drive.
2. On the desktop, double-click the **My Computer** icon to open the window.
3. Click the **Floppy disk (A:)** icon to select it.
4. Move the mouse pointer over the selected icon and right-click to display the Shortcut menu.
5. Select **Format** to display the Format dialog box.
6. Under File Type, select **Full**.

STEP-BY-STEP 5.1 Continued

7. Click **Start** to begin formatting your disk. The line at the bottom of the dialog box indicates the format progress. See Figure 5-4.

8. When your disk is formatted, check to make sure there are no bad sectors.

1-3.2.2 9. Click **Close** to close the Format Results dialog box. See Figure 5-5.

FIGURE 5-4
Format Dialog Box

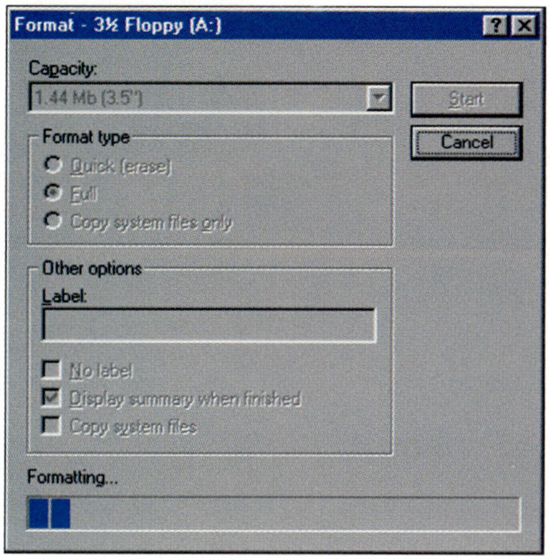

FIGURE 5-5
Format Results Dialog Box

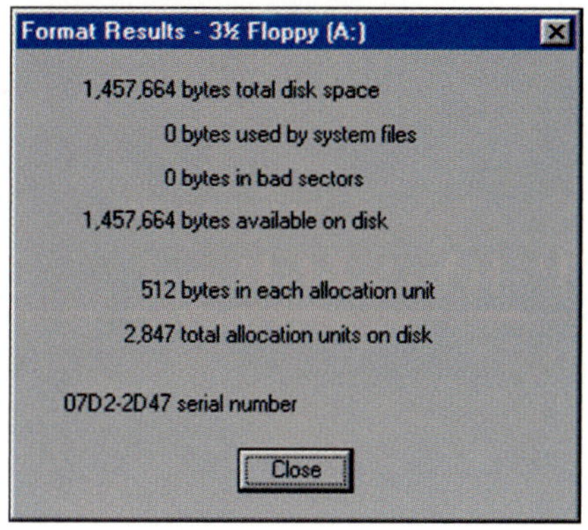

To eject a disk from a Windows computer, press the eject button on the floppy disk drive.

STEP-BY-STEP 5.2

To format a new floppy disk with the Macintosh:

1. Insert the disk into the drive. A prompt is displayed asking if you want to initialize the disk.

2. In the Format drop-down list, choose **Format**.

3. Click **Initialize** and then click **Continue**.

To eject the disk, drag the floppy disk icon to the Trash icon. The disk icon is removed from the desktop and the floppy disk is automatically ejected. The disk content is not erased.

Here are some floppy disk precautions:

- Do not expose disks to magnetic fields such as monitors, calculators, telephones, and so forth.
- Do not drink, eat, or smoke near a disk.
- Do not expose disks to extreme temperatures.

Internet

If you're looking for links to Macintosh tutorials, including Hypercard, try the MacInstruct site at *www.macinstruct.com/tutorials/index.html*.

- Do not place heavy objects on the disk.
- Do not touch the flexible plastic part of the disk.

Files and Folders

1-3.2.8-1 1-3.2.8-2 When you start using a computer you will quickly accumulate a large number of files. These files can easily become unmanageable. One of the best ways to organize your files is to do what you would do with paper files—create folders. ***Folders*** are represented by icons that look like a traditional manila folder. You can even create and move a folder inside another folder on the Windows desktop.

The following Step-by-Step instructions involve creating a folder on a floppy disk. You would typically not create many folders on a floppy disk. However, for illustration purposes, we use the floppy disk.

STEP-BY-STEP 5.3

Create a folder—Windows:

1. Insert a formatted floppy disk into drive A.
2. On the desktop, double-click the **My Computer** icon to open the window.
3. Double-click the **Floppy disk (A:)** icon to open the window.
4. 1-3.2.13-6 On the file menu, point to New and select **Folder**. The new folder appears, displaying a temporary name, New Folder.
5. 1-3.2.8-6 Type a name for the new folder, such as Assignments.
6. Press **Enter**.

To delete a folder in Windows, select the folder, move the mouse pointer over the selected folder, and right-click. Select Delete from the Shortcut menu. In response to the Confirm Folder
1-3.2.8-3 Delete dialog box, click Yes. Or click the folder, hold down the mouse button, and drag the folder to the Recycle Bin.

STEP-BY-STEP 5.4

Create a folder—Macintosh:

1. Insert the formatted floppy disk into the drive. The floppy disk icon appears on the disk.
2. Double-click the floppy disk icon.

STEP-BY-STEP 5.4 Continued

3. On the File menu, select **New Folder**. A folder icon is displayed and the name "untitled folder" is selected.

4. Type a new name, such as Assignments.

To delete a folder from a Macintosh desktop, select the folder, hold down the mouse button, and drag the folder to the Trash icon. The folder and its contents are deleted.

> **Hot Tip**
>
> You can even create folders within folders. These are called subfolders. For example, you may have a folder called Science, and within your Science folder, have two subfolders—one called Project 1 and another called Project 2.

Starting a Program

Almost everything you do within a GUI environment requires working with windows and icons. Windows contain the programs you run and the data with which you are working. To get a better overview of how to manage windows, we will start a program. For Windows, we use an application called WordPad.

STEP-BY-STEP 5.5

1. Click the **Start** button.

2. Point to Programs, then Accessories, and then click **WordPad**. See Figure 5-6.

FIGURE 5-6
Starting WordPad

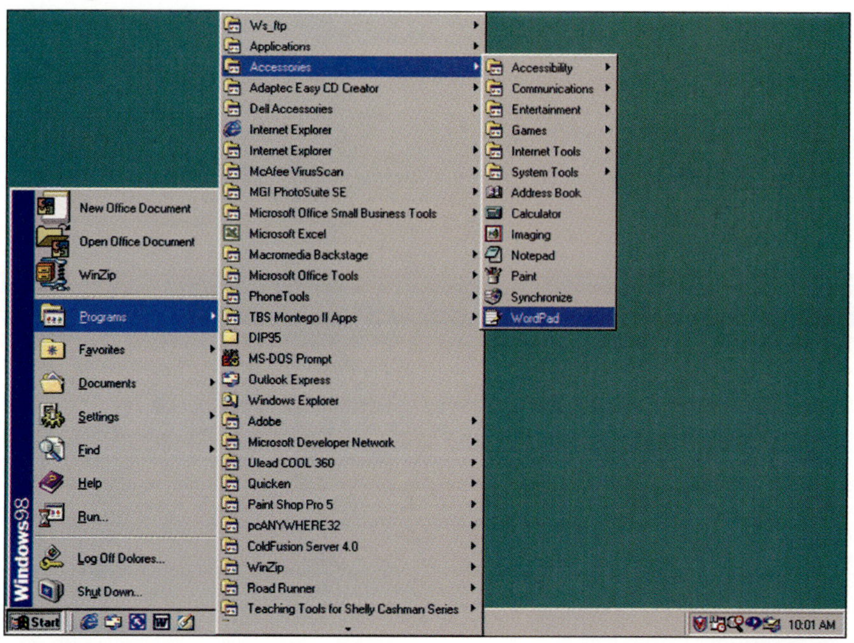

STEP-BY-STEP 5.5 Continued

3. Key a sentence or two about your favorite school subject.

4. On the File menu, click **Save**.

5. When the Save As dialog box displays, click the **Save in** drop-down arrow and select floppy disk drive A. The contents of your disk in drive A displays.

6. Double-click the **Assignments** folder; this opens the folder so you can store your data within the folder.

7. In the File name text box, key **Science**.

8. In the Save as type text box, click the drop-down arrow and select **Text Document**. See Figure 5-7.

FIGURE 5-7
Wordpad Save as dialog box

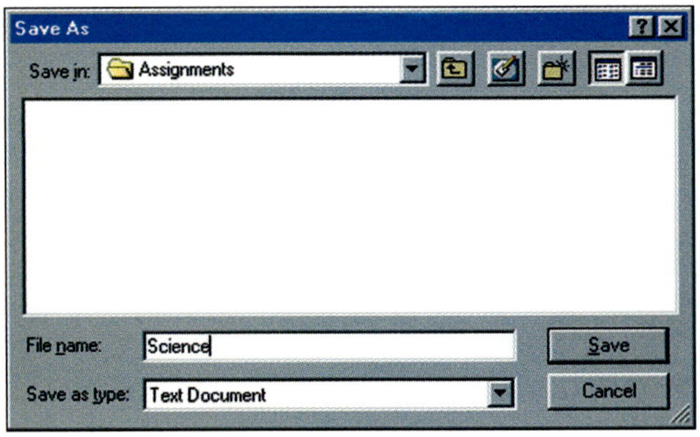

9. Click **OK** to save your file.

Exploring a Window

A window contains many parts. In our illustration, we point out the various parts of a window. See Figures 5-8 and 5-9. To help you manage the desktop effectively, you have the following options you can use to manipulate windows:

FIGURE 5-8
WordPad Window showing parts of the window

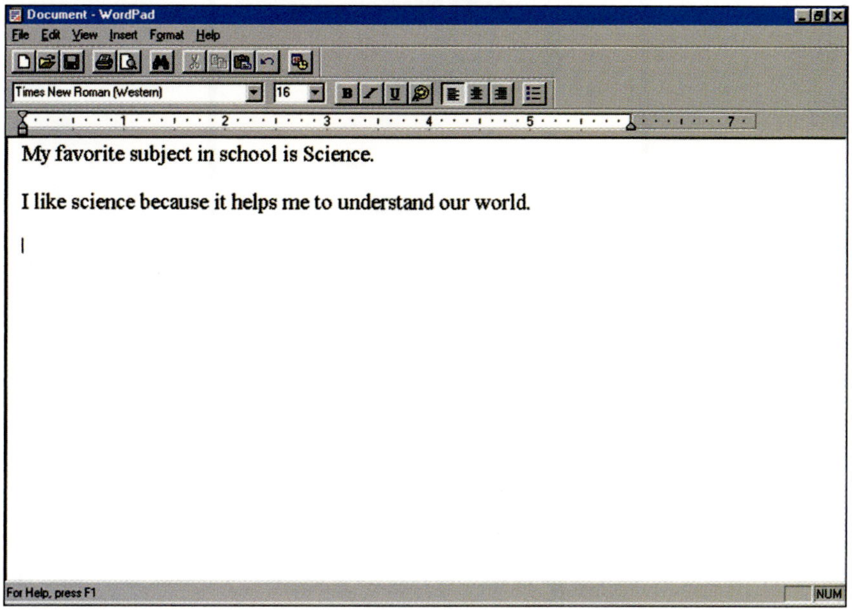

FIGURE 5-9
Macintosh window showing parts of the window

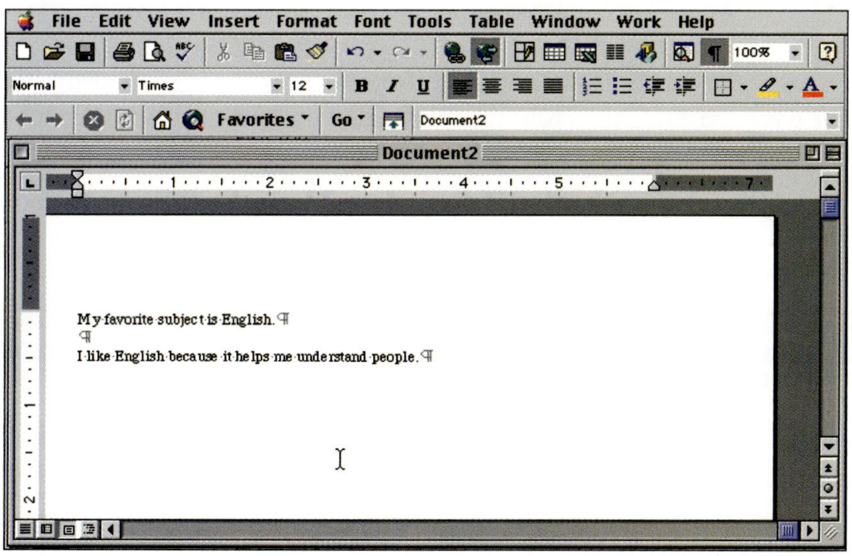

1-3.2.2-1

- ***Maximize:*** Move the mouse pointer over the Maximize button and click the button. The window fills the full screen. Notice that the shape of the Maximize button changes and now becomes the Restore button. See Figure 5-10.

FIGURE 5-10
Maximize button/Restore button

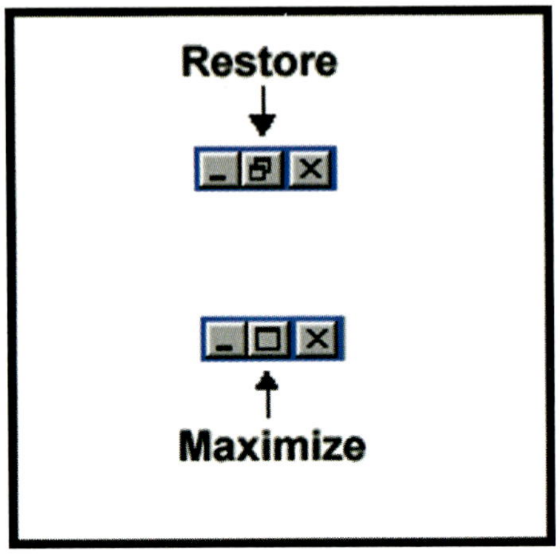

- ***Restore:*** Move the mouse pointer over the Restore button and click the button. The window returns to its previous size.

1-3.2.2-2

- ***Minimize:*** Move the mouse pointer over the Minimize button and click the button. The window disappears from the screen and is displayed as a button on the task bar. See Figure 5-11.

FIGURE 5-11
WordPad displayed as button on Taskbar

1-3.2.2-3

- ***Move:*** If you don't like where the window is located on the screen, just move it. Move the mouse pointer over the title bar. Hold down the button and drag the window to its new location.
- ***Resize:*** You can easily change the size of a window. Move the mouse pointer over an edge of the window; hold down the button and drag to make the window smaller or larger. You can change both the width and height of a window at the same time by dragging a corner.

Within the Macintosh environment, you have two different options to resize windows. The first is the ***Size box***. This box is located in the lower right corner of the window. See Figure 5-12. Just drag the box to make the window larger or smaller. When you drag the box, an outline follows the mouse pointer. When you release the mouse button, the window becomes the new size.

FIGURE 5-12
Macintosh Size and Zoom boxes

The second option is the ***Zoom box***. This feature functions like a switch. When you click it, the window reduces or enlarges. When you click it again, the window returns to its previous size.

Switching Between Windows

Another advantage of working with a GUI is that you can have many windows open at one time. For instance, suppose you want to open a paint program and a word-processing program and switch back and forth between the two. This is very easy to do.

Hot Tip

If you have used the Minimize button to reduce an application to a button on the toolbar and you want to close the application window, you have two choices. First, you can click the button to open the window and then click **Close**, or you can move the mouse pointer over the button and right-click. Choose **Close** from the Shortcut menu.

Internet

For a history of the graphical user interface, visit the Apple Museum Web site at *www.applemuseum,seastar.net/ sections/gui.html.*

STEP-BY-STEP 5.6

1. Click the **Start** button.

2. Point to Programs, then Accessories, and then click **Paint**. You now have two programs open on the desktop—WordPad and Paint.

3. To move the window you want to work with to the front, move the mouse pointer over its taskbar button and click the button. See Figure 5-13.

FIGURE 5-13
Two open windows

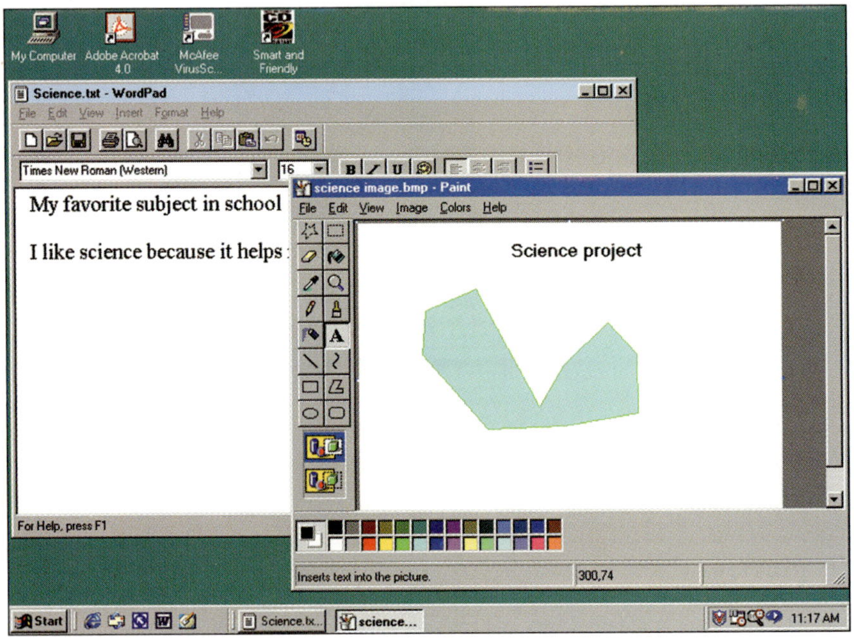

This example illustrates only two open programs. However, you can have as many open programs as the memory in your computer will support. You can also have more than one instance of the same program open; that is, you can have two or more WordPad windows open, and so forth.

Managing Files

1-3.2.13-2
1-3.2.13-3

You can move a file or copy a file from one folder to another or from one disk to another. You cannot, however, have more than one file in a folder with the same name. You can also move, copy, and delete entire folders.

Moving a File

1-3.2.8-4

When you move a file, it is copied to a new location. Then the version in the original location is erased. You will find this feature very useful if you want to organize or reorganize files by moving them into folders.

STEP-BY-STEP 5.7

1. Click the **Start** button.

2. Point to Programs, then Windows Explorer.

1-3.2.14-1 3. Locate, point to, and select the file you want to move.

4. Move the mouse pointer over the selected filename and right-click to display the shortcut menu. Click **Cut**. See Figure 5-14.

FIGURE 5-14
Moving a file

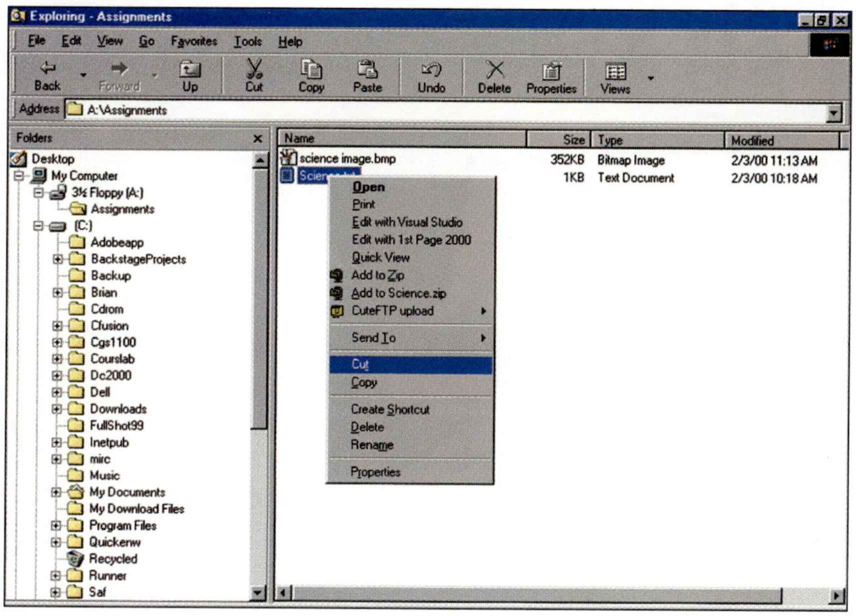

5. Locate and select the destination folder.

6. Move the mouse pointer over the selected folder and right-click to display the shortcut menu. Click **Paste** to move your file into the destination folder.

To move a file within the Macintosh environment, drag the file from one location to another on the same disk.

Copying a File

When you copy a file, you create an exact duplicate of your original file. For example, you may want to transfer a copy from your hard drive at home to a floppy so you can transport it to a different computer. Or you may want to share a copy of a file with a friend. With one exception, you use the same basic procedure to copy a file as you do to move a file.

STEP-BY-STEP 5.8

1. Click the **Start** button.
2. Point to Programs, then Windows Explorer.
3. Locate, point to, and select the file you want to copy.
4. Move the mouse pointer over the selected filename and right-click to display the shortcut menu. Click **Copy**. See Figure 5-15.

FIGURE 5-15
Copying a file

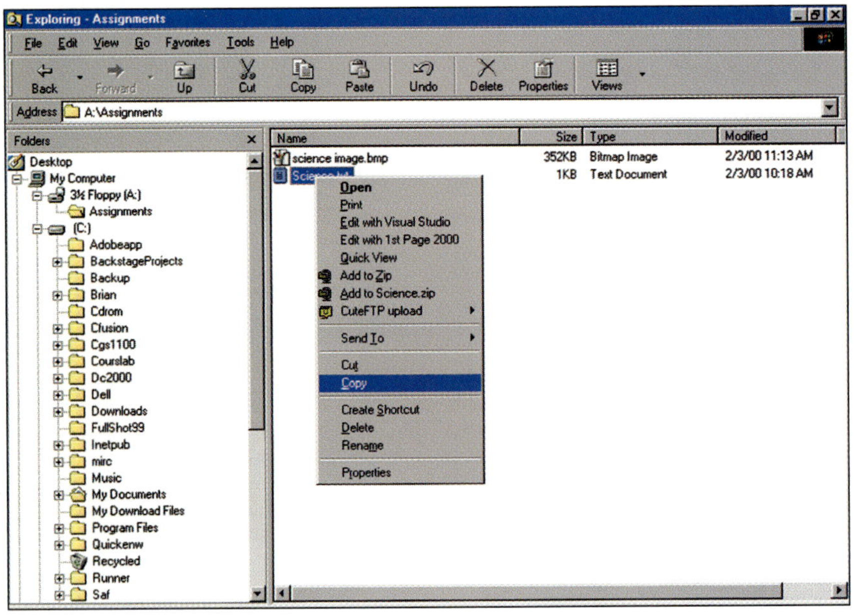

5. Locate and select the destination folder.
6. Move the mouse pointer over the selected folder and right-click to display the shortcut menu.
7. Click **Paste** to copy your file into the destination folder.

To copy a file within the Macintosh environment, drag a file from one disk to another. If you want to make a copy of the file on the same disk, but in a different folder, hold down the Option key as you drag the file.

Deleting a File

To delete a file within Windows, select the file, right-click to display the shortcut menu, and select Delete. To delete a file within the Macintosh environment, drag the file icon to Trash.

When you delete a file, it is removed from the list of available files. It is sent to the Recycle Bin (Windows) or Trash (Macintosh). What if you discover you have deleted the wrong file or need to retrieve a deleted file? This is easy as long as you have not "emptied" the trash. Simply open the Recycle Bin or Trash, locate and click the filename, right-click, and select Restore.

Views

Windows offers several options that control how file folders and filenames are displayed in a window. Depending on the task and your goal, you can choose the option to best meet your objectives.

- ***Large icons:*** A large icon and title for each file displays and provides a visual clue to the type of file and the file contents.
- ***Small icons:*** Small icons provide basically the same information as large icons—they're just smaller. Small icons are generally arranged horizontally across the screen.
- ***List:*** Provides a list of all files and folders. Displays small icons and the name; generally in a vertical arrangement.
- ***Details:*** With details, you get much more information than you do with the other view types. Details shows the file icon, the filename, the file size, the associated application, and the date and time the file was created or last modified.

STEP-BY-STEP 5.9

1. Click the **Start** button.
2. Point to Programs and click **Windows Explorer**. Most likely when this window opens, the view will be large icons. See Figure 5-16.

FIGURE 5-16
Windows Explorer – large icon view

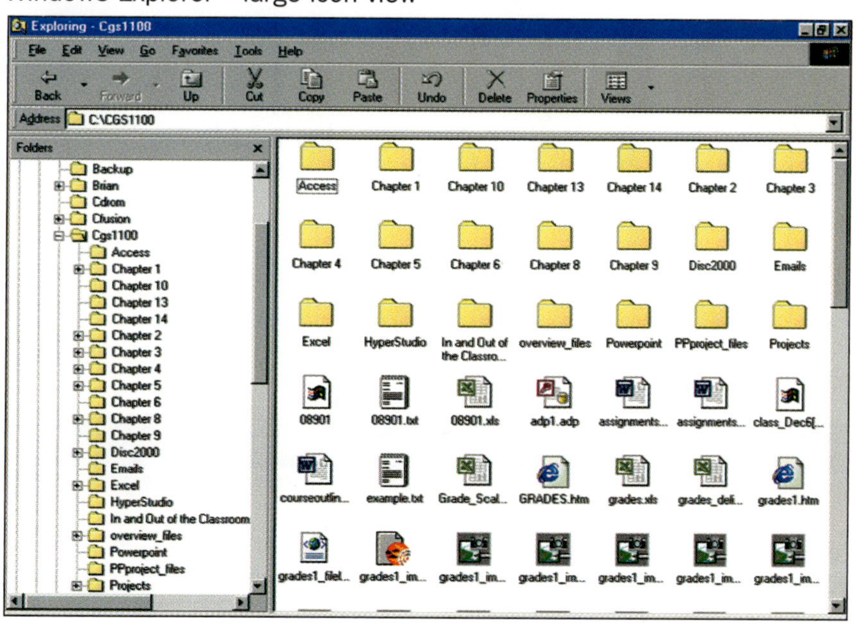

3. On the View menu, click **Small Icons**. The display now shows a horizontal arrangement of folders and files represented by icons and titles.
4. On the View menu, click **List**. The display now shows a vertical arrangement of folders and files represented by icons and titles.

STEP-BY-STEP 5.9 Continued

5. On the View menu, click **Details**. The display now shows a detailed list of each folder, including name, size, type, and date and time created or last modified. See Figure 5-17.

FIGURE 5-17
Windows Explorer – details view

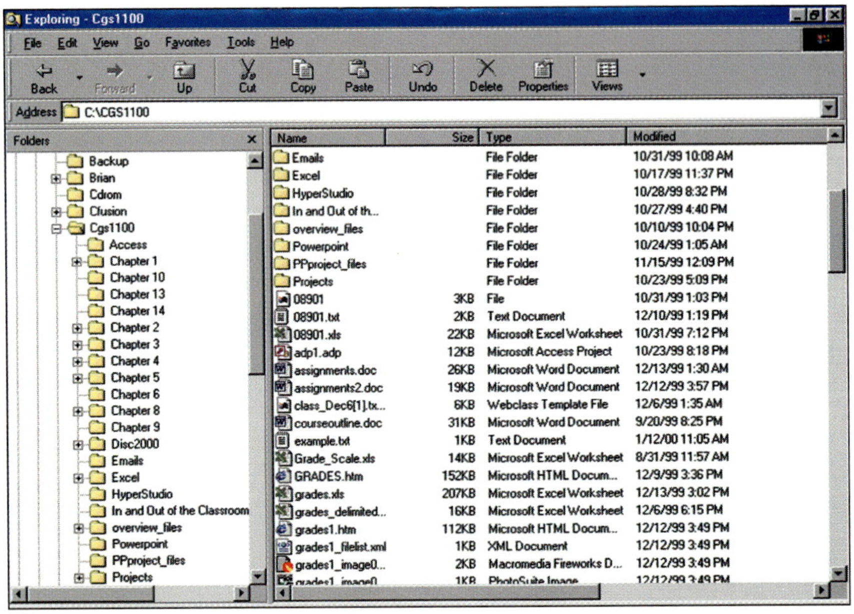

If you're working with a Macintosh computer, you can use the Finder View menu to view the list of files. On the View menu, select By_Icon to view the full-size icon or select By_Small Icon to see many files at one time. You can select By_Name to obtain additional information, such as the time and date the file was created or last updated.

Sorting

To help you more easily locate files and folders, you can also sort the items displayed in a window. For example, you're looking for a file, but you can't remember the name. However, you know you created the file within the last few days. Your best option is to sort by date. You can also sort by name, size, and type. To sort by any of these four options, just click the column name. See Figure 5-18.

FIGURE 5-18
Windows Explorer – files sorted by type

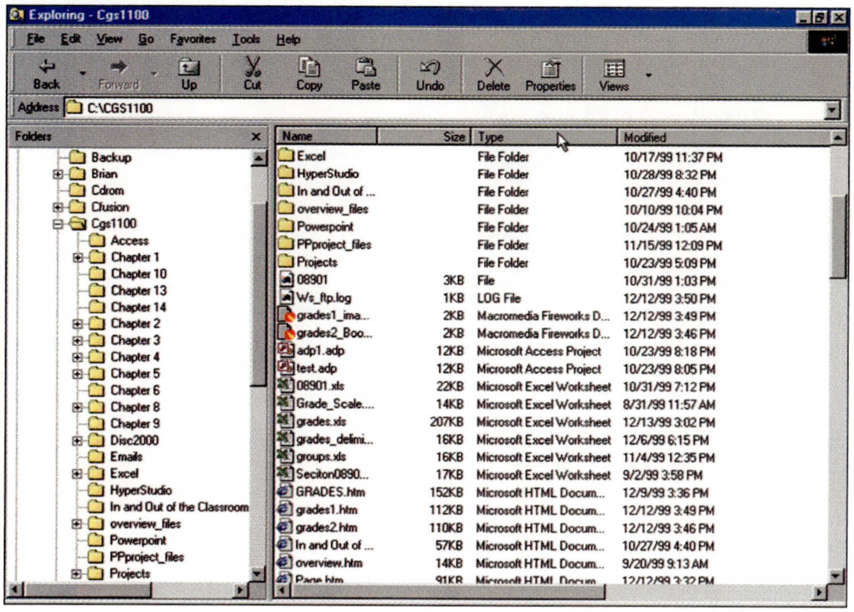

You can also sort files within the Macintosh environment. You can sort on the name or you can sort on the date and time the file was created.

Selecting Files

You've already learned how to copy and/or delete a single file. But what if you have a group of files you would like to delete? It could be a time-consuming chore if you had to do these one by one. You can, however, easily select a group of files. The files can be next to each other or they can be separate.

1-3.2.14-2

Within the Windows desktop, to select a group of adjacent files, click the first file to select it. Then hold down the Shift key and select the last file in the list. See Figure 5-19.

FIGURE 5-19
Adjacent selected files

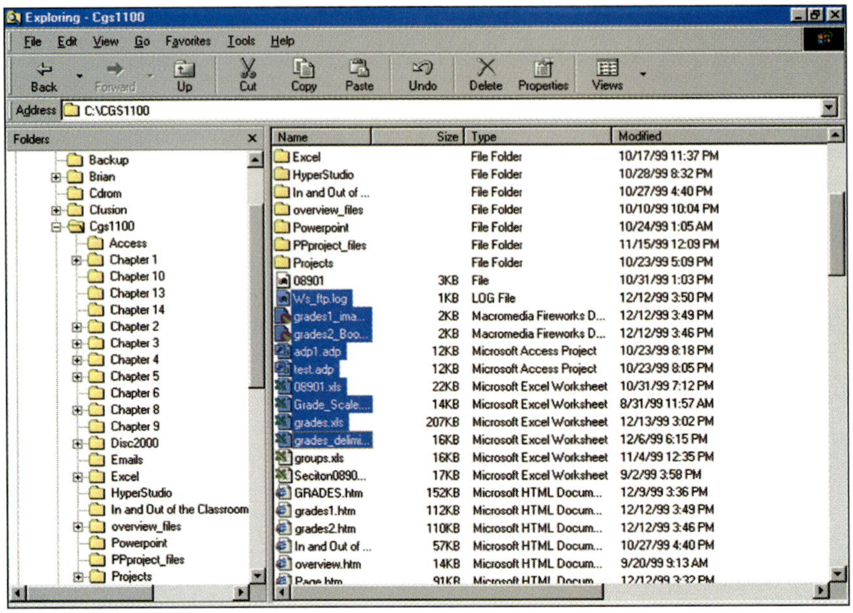

Technology Careers

PROJECT MANAGEMENT

Project Management is one of the components that a System Analyst might find in a job description. However, because the job of a system analyst can sometimes be so detailed, many companies are hiring a project manager to work with the analyst and other team members.

This could cover a wide array of projects—from Web site development to implementing an entire new computer system. The responsibilities of the project manager would be to manage, guide, keep everyone on task, and coach the team.

People who work in this profession need strong leadership abilities and good organizational skills. Many people use a software program called Project Management to help them with this job.

Educational requirements vary depending on the company and job requirements—some employers may require a two-year degree, whereas others require a master's degree. Likewise, salary levels also vary—anywhere from $22,000 to $35,000 for entry level.

To select a group of nonadjacent files, select the first file, hold down the Control [CTRL] key, and click on the remaining filenames you want to select. See Figure 5-20.

FIGURE 5-20
Nonadjacent selected files

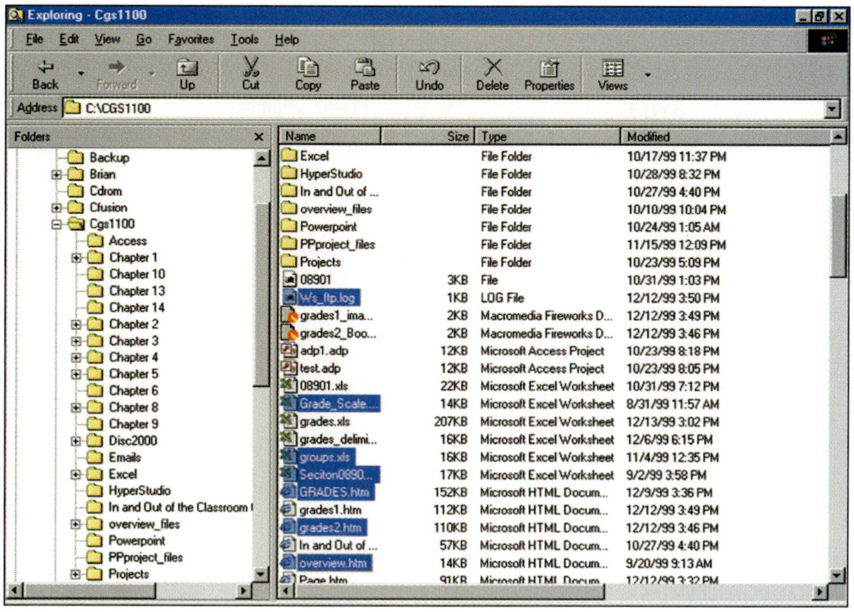

After you select the files, move the mouse pointer over any of the selected filenames, right-click to display the context menu, and then choose Delete or Copy.

If you're using a Macintosh, hold down the Shift key as you select the files. Then drag the entire group of files to a new folder in one single step.

Getting Help

1-3.2.7-1
1-3.2.7-2
1-3.2.7-4

Both the Macintosh and Windows programs offer a help program. If you are using Windows, on the File menu, click Help. If you are using a Macintosh computer, use the Apple Guide Help Balloons feature.

> **Hot Tip**
>
> For the Macintosh computer, Apple Guide provides a reference system that you can use to learn more about the computer and applications. This guide can lead you step by step through tasks such as formatting a disk, creating a folder, and so forth.

Ethics in Technology

SPAM

If you use the Internet often and have an e-mail account, you have most likely encountered SPAM. Some people define SPAM as junk mail or junk newsgroup postings. However, real SPAM is unsolicited e-mail advertising or advertising posted to a newsgroup.

The first thing that you must be aware of is that if you sign Web site guest books, post to newsgroups, or request information from a Web site, you are leaving information about yourself. This information can be collected by various software programs and your e-mail address added to a list that can be sold over and over again.

You will not be able to avoid all SPAM, but there are some ways that you can eliminate some of this unwanted advertising.

- If you post to newsgroups, go through the Web site *www.dejanews.com*; this site provides you with a special e-mail account so that your "real" e-mail address is not recorded.
- If you sign a guest book, don't use your real e-mail address. Instead, use another one that you can check at your leisure. There are many places on the Internet that provide free e-mail.
- Most sites post their privacy policy regarding selling of e-mail addresses. Read this policy before you fill out all of those online forms.

SUMMARY

In this lesson, you learned:

- Most of today's computers come with some type of graphical user interface.
- A graphic interface includes standard text and graphics.
- Some of the components of a GUI are the desktop, icons, pointer, pointing device, menus, scroll bar, and window.
- A window is an object within both the Macintosh and Windows operating systems.
- The desktop is a representation of how people work at a desk and contains windows and icons.
- Double-click an icon to open a window.
- Close a window in Windows by clicking the Close button and by selecting Close Window from the File menu in the Macintosh environment.
- Formatting is the process of preparing a disk so you can write data to and read data from the disk.
- If you have a disk with a bad sector, it is better not to use the disk.
- Use folders to organize your files.
- Delete folders and files in both Windows and Macintosh by dragging to the Trash or Recycle Bin.

- With a window, you can move it, resize it, maximize it, minimize it, or restore it to its original size.
- You can have several windows and/or programs open at one time.
- You can move a file or copy a file from one folder to another.
- When you move a file, it is moved to a new location.
- When you copy a file, you create a duplicate of your original file in another location.
- When viewing files and file folders, you can view these as large icons, small icons, a list, or details.
- You can sort files and folders by date, name, size, and type.
- You can select and copy a group of adjacent or nonadjacent files and folders.
- You can select and move a group of adjacent or nonadjacent files and folders.
- To get help within Windows, select Help from the File menu.
- Use the Apple Guide Help Balloons feature to get help on the Macintosh.

VOCABULARY *Review*

Define the following terms:

Desktop	Maximize	Scroll bar
Details	Menus	Size box
Finder	Minimize	Window
Folder	Pointer	Windows
Formatting	Pointing device	Zoom box
Icons	Restore	

REVIEW *Questions*

MULTIPLE CHOICE

Select the best response for the following statements.

1. The __________ is the first screen you see after the operating system is loaded.
   A. WordPad
   B. menu options
   C. desktop
   D. format

2. To keep your files organized, you create ________.
   A. menus
   B. icons
   C. folders
   D. desktops

3. Graphical representations of files and programs are called ________.
   A. icons
   B. menus
   C. pictures
   D. scroll bars

4. To move a window, move the pointer over the ________, press down the button, and drag.
   A. scroll bar
   B. icon
   C. desktop
   D. title bar

5. When you create a duplicate of a file, you are ________ the file.
   A. moving
   B. copying
   C. deleting
   D. executing

TRUE/FALSE

Circle T if the statement is true or F if the statement is false.

T F 1. Within both the Macintosh and Windows environments, you can only copy files, not move them.

T F 2. You can only open one window at a time.

T F 3. When viewing files as large icons, you can see the date and time the file was created and/or modified.

T F 4. To more easily locate a particular file, you can use the Sort option.

T F 5. To select a group of adjacent files, select the first file, then hold down the Shift key and select the last file in the group.

FILL IN THE BLANK

Complete the following sentences by writing the correct word or words in the blanks provided.

1. A small picture that represents a file or program is called a(n) ________.
2. ________ provide drop-down options from which to choose commands.
3. The program that displays the Macintosh desktop is called ________.
4. A disk must be ________ before you can use it.
5. When you change the size of a window, you are ________ it.

PROJECTS

PROJECT 5-1

When you format a floppy disk, it is formatted with sectors and tracks. Do some research, either on the Internet or from reference books, and determine the total number of bytes or characters you can store on the floppy disk you are using. Then convert that into bits.

PROJECT 5-2

Examine the desktop of the computer you are using and write a report on the various elements on the desktop. Describe the system you are using and then describe what you think is the best operating system—a visual system with icons or a text-based system.

PROJECT 5-3

Your rich grandmother has told you she will buy you any type of computer you want. Describe for your grandmother what type of computer you would like to have and why. Explain to her about the desktop and why you would choose this type of desktop.

WEB PROJECT

At *www.microsoft.com/education/tutorial/classroom/win98/default.asp*, you can find a Windows tutorial. Complete this tutorial and submit the results to your teacher.

TEAMWORK

You now have some information and knowledge about using a computer. Team up with a friend or coworker and create an outline for a training program. Include all the main elements that you think are necessary for someone to be an effective computer user.

CRITICAL *Thinking*

ACITIVITY 5-1

In social studies, you often learn about working as together as a group. Now think about putting groups of files into folders. Are there any similarities between this and people working together as groups? Any differences?

LESSON 6

How Can I Use Technology to Solve a Problem?

OBJECTIVES

Upon completion of this lesson, you should be able to:

- Define problem solving.
- Identify technology tools for solving problems.
- Identify problem-solving steps.
- Explain how other forms of technology are used to solve problems.

Estimated Time: 1.5 hours

VOCABULARY

Database

Database software

Distance learning

Personal information management software (PIMS)

Problem solving

Search engines

Spreadsheet software

Technology

Telecommunications

Teleconferencing

Word-processing software

World Wide Web (WWW)

How Does Technology Solve Problems for You?

Did your Spanish instructor give you an assignment to write a report in Spanish? Did your math instructor assign you to find the average temperatures for a month in your town? Did your adviser for Future Business Leaders of America ask for a printout of all members who have still not paid their dues or to determine how much candy you would need to sell to make a $250 profit? Do you have a classmate who has a disability that prevents him or her from being able to key information into the computer? If you can answer "yes" to even one of these scenarios, technology is your solution!

IC³ -2.2.12-1

Technology is the application of scientific discoveries to the production of goods and services that improve the human environment. The computer is a major element of technology and has aided in improvements in medical research, space travel, and exploration, just to name a few.

Technology provides tools for dealing with the many situations that could affect business operations as well as our individual lives. Technology is responsible for transporting us to a make-believe universe when we play arcade games at the mall, making getting cash from our banks any time of the day or night as easy as locating an ATM machine, and making it possible for employees to send messages over networks. The Internet's capabilities are endless.

IC³ -2.2.12-2

The computer plays a major role in the technology boom. It addresses and solves many of the technical types of issues and concerns in our society. A basic function of a computer is to solve problems, that is, to answer questions and to provide an easier and better way to perform certain tasks. Computer software controls the versatility of the computer. In other words, with the appropriate software, you can solve just about any problem or simplify any task.

The amount and kinds of technology available are astounding. You can find technology for almost every situation, from finding and purchasing stock over the Internet to finding personnel for a space shuttle! See Figure 6.1.

FIGURE 6-1
Clockwise from top left: A technician uses a computer to evaluate data; students use a variety of computers for researching and writing papers; a businessperson is using a general-purpose computer to keep track of inventory; a scientist is using a computer containing a special math processor to conduct an experiment

Selecting the correct technology to address a specific task or problem requires careful investigation. A logical guideline needs to be followed in order to identify the situation that could use technology to alleviate problems or to enhance a specific task and to identify the exact technology that would address the situation.

What Is Problem Solving?

Problem solving is a systematic approach of going from an initial situation to a desired situation that is subject to some resource constraints.

Problem-Solving Steps

To solve a problem successfully, a logical plan should be used that will act as a guide or road map. It will assist in defining the problem, gathering information concerning the problem, identifying possible solutions, and selecting and implementing the best solution. A guide is listed here.

- Define the problem.
- Investigate and analyze the problem.
- Identify possible solutions.
- Select and implement a solution.
- Evaluate solutions.

Each of the listed steps is very important in the problem-solving process. Each step should be fully completed before going to the next step. Let's explore each step closely.

Identify the Problem

In this stage, you ensure that there really is a problem and identify what it is. Sometimes the problem may not be as transparent as you might think. You need to investigate the situation to determine what is the real issue. Ask questions, use what-if statements, eliminate some facts, include others, clarify the current situation, and identify what the situation should be or perhaps what you would like it to be. If necessary, make notes or sketches; identify the known and unknown facts. Once you have identified the problem, you can now begin to determine why the problem exists, possible causes, and so forth.

Investigate and Analyze the Problem

Before you can begin to solve the problem, you need all the facts. Collect all available data and facts regarding the situation. This step will provide information needed to make an accurate decision. Sometimes during this step, it may be decided that a problem really does not exist at all or that what you thought was the problem is actually being caused by something else. However, if there is a legitimate problem or need, your detective work at this stage should provide you with this information.

Identify Possible Solutions

Once the problem has been pinpointed, possible solutions need to be identified. What can be done to alleviate the problem? What needs to be done differently? What needs to be deleted or added? These are the types of questions that would need to be answered in looking for a solution. In exploring possible answers, several solutions may be identified.

Choose and Implement the Chosen Solution

If more than one possible solution is identified, critique and test each solution to determine what would be the outcome of the situation. Based on this information, you would choose the solution that provides the best outcome. Once the solution is selected, implement it.

Evaluate Solutions

After putting the chosen solution into place, you will need to evaluate its performance on the situation. Did it eliminate the problem? Did it accomplish what you needed to have done? If your answer is yes, you now have a solution to a situation that caused you concern.

Problem Solving with Computers in Action

Now that we have discussed the guideline for solving problems using technology, let's use it to solve a company's scheduling problem. Employees have been missing meetings, so let's explore how technology can help this issue.

Identifying the Problem

What needs to be accomplished? What information is needed and how is it to be presented?

- Selecting appropriate software to be used
- Eliminating scheduling conflicts
- Knowing employees' schedules

Investigating and Analyzing Problem

- How can a manager know all employees' schedules?
- How can a manager notify all employees of a meeting in a timely fashion?
- What type of software is available for these needs?

Ethics in Technology

DIGITAL WATERMARKS

A watermark is a faded-looking image in the background of a document. A digital watermark is an image embedded within graphics and audio files that is used to identify the owner's rights to these files. In other words, a digital image can be added to music files, pictures, and so forth, that identifies the creator's work in a way that is invisible to the human eye.

These watermarks also serve the purposes of identifying quality and assuring that the work is the original. Watermarking technology makes it possible for copyright owners to find illegal copies of the work and take appropriate legal action.

Digital watermarks are also an excellent tool for Webmasters. It ensures that only lawful image and audio files are used so that they are not guilty of copyright infringement.

Identify Possible Solutions

- Use word-processing software to key a memo to send to all employees announcing a meeting.
- Manually check everyone's schedule to see when they are at work and available for a meeting.
- Identify a software program that can be used to enter and maintain employees' schedules, has the capability to notify employees of meetings, and will let a manager know that they have received the message.

Choose a Solution and Implement the Chosen Solution

After studying the possible solutions, it was decided that the company would purchase a software program to solve the problem of missed meetings.

Using Technology Tools to Solve Problems

Computers and the Internet have made it much easier to find solutions to many of the tasks that individuals and businesses need to address on a daily basis. Typical software programs used are word processing, database, spreadsheet, utility programs, scheduling, collaboration, telecommunications, and multimedia (graphics, animation, digital video, sound, authoring, presentation).

Once you have learned to use the mechanics of computer software, you can determine how to use this software to perform various types of tasks. Here are some examples:

IC3 1-2.2.2-1

- *Word-processing software* is used to key data, but it has many applications that it can perform other than just keying. What are these applications and how can you use them to, say, prepare envelopes for a group of customers?
- Web pages can be designed using HTML codes or word-processing software. You have just started a new small business and want to advertise on the Internet. How can you go about having a Web page prepared?
- You know that grades can be averaged in a spreadsheet, but how can you determine what grade you would need to make on the final exam to receive an "A" in your math class?

All of these situations pose problems that need to be solved or at least pose situations that could use some type of technology. Each software application mentioned can solve one of the problems. However, you will need to determine which software program to use and how to use its capabilities to solve the problem at hand.

IC3 1-2.2.9-3

The Internet offers electronic communication, distance learning and teleconferencing, networking, and electronic research tools. These tools are used to collect and analyze data for use in problem-solving activities. As a user, this means you must be adequately familiar with the mechanics or the "know-how" of the software plus how to use search engines and other features available for Internet research.

You can see technology in use almost everywhere! It assists in the development of new treatments in the medical field, guides you through tourist attractions such as museums, simulates space travels, assists law enforcement activities, and makes those special effects in movies seem so real! In what ways can you see technology in your life?

Using Software to Solve Problems

There are many different types of software programs available to address various types of applications. There are basic software programs as well as software programs for specialized areas such as banking, medicine, real estate, insurance, law, and so forth.

> **Did You Know?**
>
> Many word-processing programs have advanced features that allow you to perform spreadsheet and database-like functions. You can create files using mathematical functions similar to those found in spreadsheet programs. Data files can be created that can sorted, selected, and even merged into other documents.

Word-Processing Software

1-2.2.2-2 There are several word-processing programs. Microsoft Word, WordPerfect, and Lotus WordPro are just a few. Word-processing software allows you to create and modify documents. It greatly reduces the need for keying documents. Most word-processing programs have features that make creating various types of documents such as newsletters, reports, and tables an easy task. The merge feature saves hours in preparing multiple documents. Do you need an alphabetical listing of members of an organization? This is a simple task for word-processing software. Footnotes and endnotes can be entered effortlessly. This software addresses many of the document needs of an organization or individual. See Figure 6-2.

FIGURE 6-2
Word-processing document

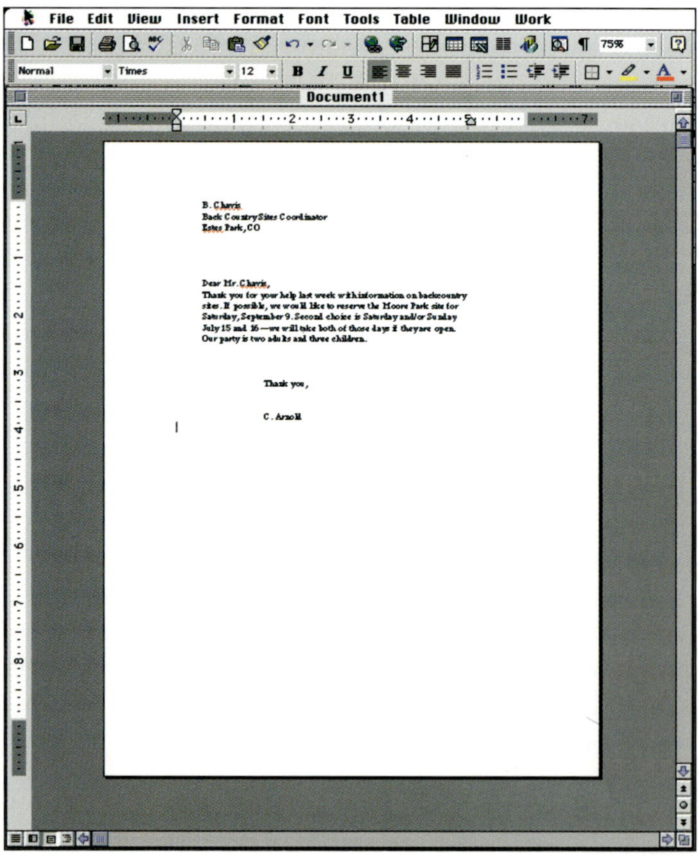

Spreadsheet Software

1-2.2.3-2 1-2.2.3-1 Spreadsheet programs, such as Microsoft Excel or Lotus 1-2-3, are designed to store and manipulate numeric data. They are used extensively in business to produce financial analyses such as budgets, financial statements, and forecasts. Formulas are entered into a spreadsheet to calculate various conditions. The beauty of the spreadsheet is its ability to recalculate itself when different information is entered.

Spreadsheet software has become a vital tool to businesses because it helps in predicting the outcome of various situations and factors. There are times when businesses need to know what an outcome will be under certain circumstances. Spreadsheet software allows this type for forecasting with "what-if" statements. It is quite evident how this type of software solves problems for businesses. See Figure 6-3.

FIGURE 6-3

Spreadsheets are used for documents such as budgets, inventories, etc.

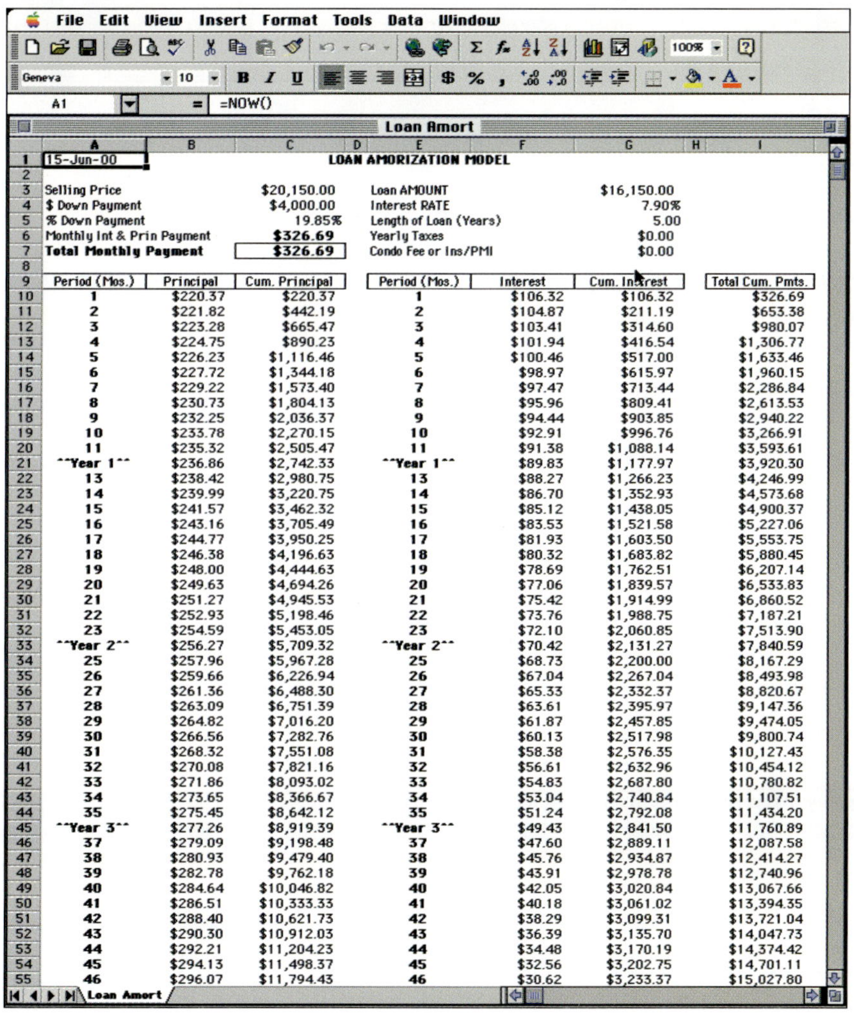

	A	B	C	E	F	G	I
1	15-Jun-00		LOAN AMORIZATION MODEL				
2							
3	Selling Price		$20,150.00	Loan AMOUNT		$16,150.00	
4	$ Down Payment		$4,000.00	Interest RATE		7.90%	
5	% Down Payment		19.85%	Length of Loan (Years)		5.00	
6	Monthly Int & Prin Payment		**$326.69**	Yearly Taxes		$0.00	
7	**Total Monthly Payment**		**$326.69**	Condo Fee or Ins/PMI		$0.00	
8							
9	Period (Mos.)	Principal	Cum. Principal	Period (Mos.)	Interest	Cum. Interest	Total Cum. Pmts.
10	1	$220.37	$220.37	1	$106.32	$106.32	$326.69
11	2	$221.82	$442.19	2	$104.87	$211.19	$653.38
12	3	$223.28	$665.47	3	$103.41	$314.60	$980.07
13	4	$224.75	$890.23	4	$101.94	$416.54	$1,306.77
14	5	$226.23	$1,116.46	5	$100.46	$517.00	$1,633.46
15	6	$227.72	$1,344.18	6	$98.97	$615.97	$1,960.15
16	7	$229.22	$1,573.40	7	$97.47	$713.44	$2,286.84
17	8	$230.73	$1,804.13	8	$95.96	$809.41	$2,613.53
18	9	$232.25	$2,036.37	9	$94.44	$903.85	$2,940.22
19	10	$233.78	$2,270.15	10	$92.91	$996.76	$3,266.91
20	11	$235.32	$2,505.47	11	$91.38	$1,088.14	$3,593.61
21	^^Year 1^^	$236.86	$2,742.33	^^Year 1^^	$89.83	$1,177.97	$3,920.30
22	13	$238.42	$2,980.75	13	$88.27	$1,266.23	$4,246.99
23	14	$239.99	$3,220.75	14	$86.70	$1,352.93	$4,573.68
24	15	$241.57	$3,462.32	15	$85.12	$1,438.05	$4,900.37
25	16	$243.16	$3,705.49	16	$83.53	$1,521.58	$5,227.06
26	17	$244.77	$3,950.25	17	$81.93	$1,603.50	$5,553.75
27	18	$246.38	$4,196.63	18	$80.32	$1,683.82	$5,880.45
28	19	$248.00	$4,444.63	19	$78.69	$1,762.51	$6,207.14
29	20	$249.63	$4,694.26	20	$77.06	$1,839.57	$6,533.83
30	21	$251.27	$4,945.53	21	$75.42	$1,914.99	$6,860.52
31	22	$252.93	$5,198.46	22	$73.76	$1,988.75	$7,187.21
32	23	$254.59	$5,453.05	23	$72.10	$2,060.85	$7,513.90
33	^^Year 2^^	$256.27	$5,709.32	^^Year 2^^	$70.42	$2,131.27	$7,840.59
34	25	$257.96	$5,967.28	25	$68.73	$2,200.00	$8,167.29
35	26	$259.66	$6,226.94	26	$67.04	$2,267.04	$8,493.98
36	27	$261.36	$6,488.30	27	$65.33	$2,332.37	$8,820.67
37	28	$263.09	$6,751.39	28	$63.61	$2,395.97	$9,147.36
38	29	$264.82	$7,016.20	29	$61.87	$2,457.85	$9,474.05
39	30	$266.56	$7,282.76	30	$60.13	$2,517.98	$9,800.74
40	31	$268.32	$7,551.08	31	$58.38	$2,576.35	$10,127.43
41	32	$270.08	$7,821.16	32	$56.61	$2,632.96	$10,454.12
42	33	$271.86	$8,093.02	33	$54.83	$2,687.80	$10,780.82
43	34	$273.65	$8,366.67	34	$53.04	$2,740.84	$11,107.51
44	35	$275.45	$8,642.12	35	$51.24	$2,792.08	$11,434.20
45	^^Year 3^^	$277.26	$8,919.39	^^Year 3^^	$49.43	$2,841.50	$11,760.89
46	37	$279.09	$9,198.48	37	$47.60	$2,889.11	$12,087.58
47	38	$280.93	$9,479.40	38	$45.76	$2,934.87	$12,414.27
48	39	$282.78	$9,762.18	39	$43.91	$2,978.78	$12,740.96
49	40	$284.64	$10,046.82	40	$42.05	$3,020.84	$13,067.66
50	41	$286.51	$10,333.33	41	$40.18	$3,061.02	$13,394.35
51	42	$288.40	$10,621.73	42	$38.29	$3,099.31	$13,721.04
52	43	$290.30	$10,912.03	43	$36.39	$3,135.70	$14,047.73
53	44	$292.21	$11,204.23	44	$34.48	$3,170.19	$14,374.42
54	45	$294.13	$11,498.37	45	$32.56	$3,202.75	$14,701.11
55	46	$296.07	$11,794.43	46	$30.62	$3,233.37	$15,027.80

Database Software

1-2.2.5-1 1-2.2.5-2 ***Database software*** makes it possible to create and maintain large collections of data. This type of software is critical to the success of many businesses. A few database products are Microsoft Access, dBASE, and SOL. A ***database*** is a collection of files. Customer lists and inventory lists are just two examples of how database software is used in business. The data stored in a database can easily be accessed in a variety of ways. Do you need to know how many of your customers live within a certain zip code area? Your database software can render this information. See Figure 6-4.

FIGURE 6-4
Database documents

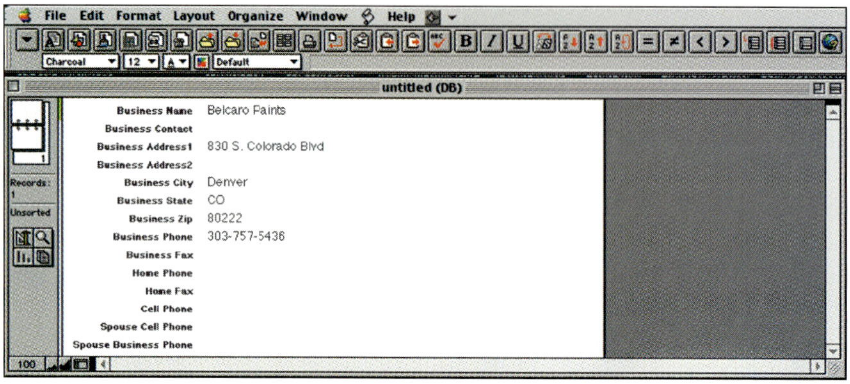

Telecommunications

1-1.4.6-2 ***Telecommunications*** is electronically transferring data. Two of the most popular features of telecommunication are ***distance learning*** and ***teleconferencing***. Distance learning addresses the problem of not being able to actually attend classes, and teleconferencing reduces the cost of travel, schedule conflicts, and accommodations for busy executives by providing conferencing capabilities without having to leave their offices.

> **Hot Tip**
>
> The Information Superhighway is the result of cable-television companies and telephone companies, which used to be separate types of companies, beginning to provide the same services.

Personal Information Management Software

Personal information management software (PIMS) is used to organize appointments, telephone messages, projects, and tasks to be completed. Some examples of PIMs are Microsoft Scheduler+, Microsoft Outlook, and Lotus Organizer.

Other Software Programs

Many other types of software programs on the market provide specific capabilities for specific applications. For example, there is software for real estate agents, builders, doctors, musicians, cooks, and so forth. The list goes on and on.

Using the Internet to Solve Problems

The capabilities of the Internet are numerous! Users can exchange messages, participate in discussion groups, and transfer files from one location to another. Researchers can access information from remote sources, information can be shared around the world, businesses can sell services and products, and so forth. A brief discussion of some Internet services follows.

IC3 1-2.2.8-1 1-2.2.8-2

E-mail

Electronic mail is the most popular service of the Internet. It allows users to communicate with each other at any time day or night. Businesses find that e-mail makes communication more efficient by eliminating interruptions from telephone calls and playing phone tag. E-mail definitely addresses a need. Examples of electronic mail products include Microsoft Outlook, Eudora, and Lotus cc Mail.

IC3 1-2.2.9-2

World Wide Web

The ***World Wide Web***, or **WWW**, as it is sometimes referred to, is a collection of interlinked multimedia documents stored on tens of thousands of independent servers around the world. In simpler terms, it consists of pages and pages of businesses, individuals, and organizations. Many businesses advertise on the Internet. Do you need to purchase a new car? Linking to the car dealer's Web page will give you all the information you need including cost, options, local dealerships, and so forth. If you want to know what kinds of business are in your area, go to *www.bigbook.com*. Two popular Web-browsing products are Microsoft Internet Explorer and Netscape Navigator.

Internet

Establish a link to the manufacturer of a car that you may be interested in purchasing or just want information on. Determine the cost and the availability of pre-owned cars in your locality.

Technology Careers

ADMINISTRATIVE ASSISTANT

The administrative assistant oversees the overall functioning of an office. The position requires the person to work with considerable initiative in the absence of the supervisor and to exercise independent judgment within the framework of established policies and objectives.

The computer is the main tool that the administrative assistant uses to complete many of the required tasks. Word processing, database management, spreadsheet, and desktop-publishing software programs are used daily. The administrative assistant also uses other types of computer capabilities depending on the type of office in which he or she works.

The qualifications required include excellent communication skills, both verbal and written; knowledge of modern office practices, systems, and equipment; the ability to handle multiple projects simultaneously; strong math, interpersonal, and organizational skills; and a professional, friendly, and outgoing personality. A sense of humor is also an asset.

A college degree is usually preferred. Evidence of some training and impressive experience, however, is sometimes acceptable. The average salary for an administrative assistant ranges between $25,000 and $35,000 a year depending on experience and location of the company.

Search Engines

Not sure of the name of an organization or business, but know the subject or topic on which you need information? Use a search engine. ***Search engines*** allow you to enter a keyword to find sites that contain information that you need. Some popular search engines include Excite, Hotboot, Mamma, AskJeeves, and Dogpile. See Figure 6-5.

> **Hot Tip**
>
> You can ask a complete question to locate information on the Internet. Go to *AskJeeves.com.*

FIGURE 6-5
Search engines are helpful in locating needed information on the Web

Other Technologies

The use of technology has affected our daily lives in so many different ways. This section briefly looks at some of these situations and their benefits to us as individuals and as businesses.

- *Entertainment:* Computer games can be found in many places including homes, arcades, and schools. These games range from action games to simulations.

> **Hot Tip**
>
> Voice mail is the most popular example of the combination of telephone technology and computer technology. It has proven to be a very important asset to businesses because it helps to alleviate the many problems caused in trying to make contact with customers, suppliers, etc.

- *Electronic banking:* Nearly every bank offers electronic banking. This service permits customers to bank whenever they want. They can take money out of their accounts at any place there is an ATM machine. They can also do on-line banking, which allows them to pay bills, check balances, and even reconcile their statements.
- *Medical and health care:* For quite some time, computers have been used in hospitals for record keeping. They now have a greater role in the care of patients. Sensors can be attached to patients to indicate when changes occur within their bodies. Tests that used to take a long time to complete can now be done quickly with computers. See Figure 6-6.

FIGURE 6-6
Computers help medical personnel provide more effective treatment

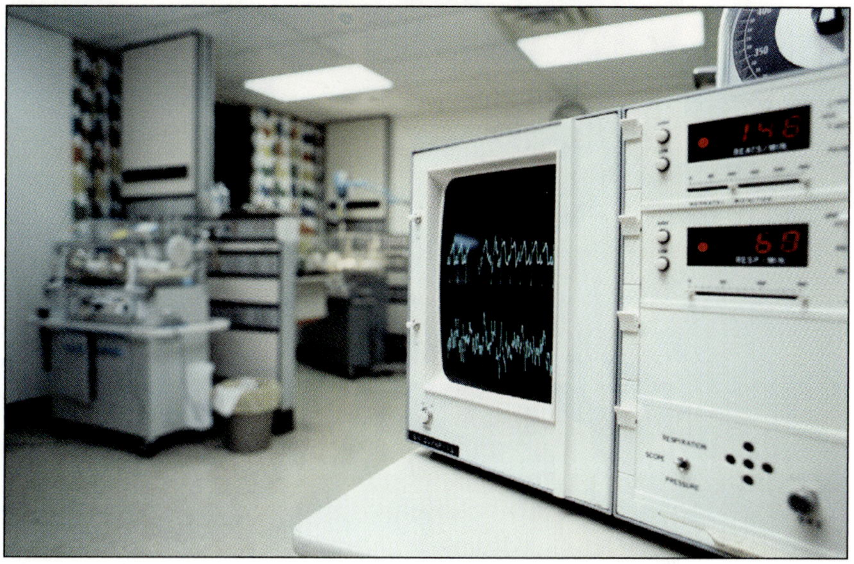

- *Dangerous tasks:* Some jobs are too dangerous for humans to perform. Computers can perform these jobs as well or even better than humans. See Figure 6-7.

FIGURE 6-7
Computers can perform tasks in environments too dangerous for humans

Repetitious tasks are performed by computers. An example is the manufacture of the microprocessor chip. Each one must be made exactly alike. This is done by using computers to control the processing equipment down to the exact timing and chemical mixtures.

SUMMARY

In this lesson, you learned:

- Technology has made a great impact on our lives.
- The computer plays a major role in the technology boom.
- Computer software controls the versatility of the computer.
- Problem solving involves defining a problem and finding a solution.
- Typical software programs such as word processing, spreadsheet, database management, and telecommunications are used to solve problems.
- The Internet offers electronic communication, distance learning, teleconferencing, networking, and electronic research tools to solve problems.

- Other technologies that have affected our lives in solving problems include the areas of entertainment, medicine, transportation, banking, and the performance of dangerous tasks.
- The sequence of problem solving includes defining the problem, investigating and analyzing the problem, identifying possible solutions, selecting and implementing the best solution, and evaluating the chosen solution.

VOCABULARY *Review*

Define the following terms:

Database
Database software
Distance learning
Personal information management software (PIMS)
Problem solving
Search engines
Spreadsheet software
Technology
Telecommunications
Teleconferencing
Word-processing software
World Wide Web (www)

REVIEW *Questions*

MULTIPLE CHOICE

Select the best response for the following statements.

1. Word processing, database, spreadsheets, and telecommunications are types of ________ used to solve problems.
   A. search engines
   B. software
   C. URLs
   D. technology

2. Being able to withdraw cash from your checking account any time you want is made possible through the use of ________.
   A. ATMs
   B. online banking
   C. debit cards
   D. postdated checks

3. Electronic communication, distance learning, and teleconferencing are examples of ________ tools for solving problems.
   A. software
   B. Internet
   C. e-mail
   D. hardware

4. ________ software provides the ability to make what-if statements in order to perform forecasts.
   A. Database
   B. Spreadsheet
   C. Word-processing
   D. Web page design

5. A ________ is a collection of files.
   A. database
   B. spreadsheet
   C. search engine
   D. list

TRUE/FALSE

Circle T if the statement is true or F if the statement is false.

T F 1. Technology can solve every imaginable problem a person could have.

T F 2. The first step in the problem-solving process is to select a solution.

T F 3. Telecommunications is electronically transferring data.

T F 4. Electronic mail is the most popular service on the Internet.

T F 5. Many businesses advertise on the World Wide Web.

FILL IN THE BLANK

Complete the following sentences by writing the correct word or words in the blanks provided.

1. Use ________ when using search engines to locate information.
2. The first step in the problem-solving process is to ________ the problem.
3. The ________ plays a major role in the technology boom.
4. The name of one search engine is ________.
5. The last step in the problem-solving process is to ________ the chosen solution.

PROJECTS

PROJECT 6-1

Computer games have become a booming business. There are usually two or three that are very popular every year. Locate sales data for the top five computer games over the past two years. Prepare a report indicating the total sales for the two-year period as well as indicating the share of the market each one held. You may find useful information at *www.pcdata.com*. You may also find information at individual computer games companies.

PROJECT 6-2

You heard one of your instructors say that he needed to take a course next semester, but the course was being offered at an inconvenient time for him. He had been told the course was also being offered as a distance learning class, which is sometimes called online learning. Write a report that explains just what this means. How are the computer and other technology involved in making this type of class possible? You may find useful information at *www.hoyle.com/distance*. Also try using the keyword *distance learning* with several search engines.

WEB PROJECT

Using search engines to locate information on the Internet was discussed in this lesson. As with anything, there are rules and guidelines to follow in order to use search engines effectively. If you can narrow your search by using precise keywords, you have a better chance of finding just the information you want. Use the Internet to locate information on using search engines effectively. Prepare a handout you can share with your friends or coworkers. You may find useful information at *www.webreference.com*, *www.monash.com*, and *http://daphne.palomar.edu/TGSEARCH*.

CRITICAL *Thinking*

ACTIVITY 6-1

Did you ever wonder how the design of stamps is selected? What criteria does the post office use in selecting images for stamps? You can find information at *www.usps.com* and *www.AskJeeves.com*

LESSON 7

How Is Technology Changing the Workplace and Society?

OBJECTIVES

Upon completion of this lesson, you should be able to:

- Describe the impact of technology on education.
- Describe the impact of technology on science and medicine.
- Describe the impact of technology on work and play.

Estimated Time: 1.5 hours

VOCABULARY

Artificial intelligence
Bot
Computer-based learning
Digital cash
Electronic commerce
Simulations
SPAM
Virtual reality
Voice recognition
WebQuest

As the age of innovation blazes its way into the world of technology, dramatic changes are taking place in every aspect of life—from home to school to the workplace. And the changes are swift and dramatic. Just as soon as we settle in and become comfortable with a new technological change, along comes something more innovative and different. As things look now, the world is in for a lot more of this type of change.

Education

There are many similarities between today's schools and those of 40 or 50 years ago. In many classrooms, the students still sit in rows and the teacher stands at the front of the class, lecturing and using a chalkboard. However, in other classrooms, a technological revolution is taking place.

Many people predict that technology will change the entire structure of education. Others believe the way in which most students receive education today—students and teacher in a traditional classroom—will remain for many years. Regardless of who is right, one thing is certain: Technology is having a tremendous impact on education in general and in more and more classrooms around the world.

Internet

The Internet and the World Wide Web are the biggest factors affecting education today. For instance, not so long ago, if a science teacher gave the class a project to find out how a television works, the students would go to the library and do the research. In many of today's classrooms, the students most likely go to the Internet, and maybe to the How Stuff Works Web site, to find this information. See Figure 7-1. Using the Internet, it is fast and easy to find the information you need.

FIGURE 7-1
How Stuff Works Web site

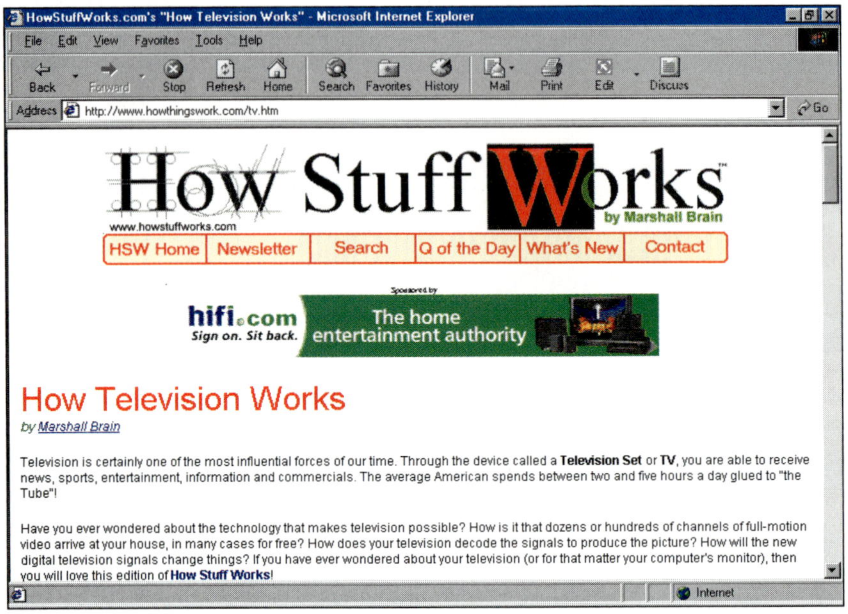

Perhaps you're taking a trip next week, and you would like to pretest your geography knowledge. You can again use the Internet as your resource. One site you might visit is the CIA Geography Quiz Page. See Figure 7-2.

FIGURE 7-2
CIA Geography Quiz Page

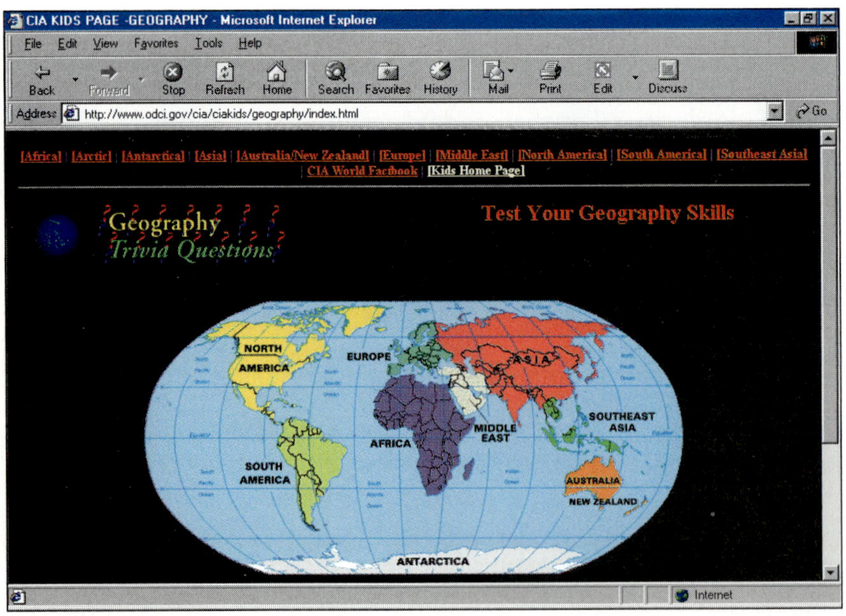

You may have had an opportunity to participate in or work with a ***WebQuest***. Bernie Dodge and Tom developed the WebQuest Model March at San Diego State University. This type of activity uses the Internet for investigation and problem solving. Dozens of WebQuests have been developed by schools all over the country. Example WebQuests include countries around the world, politics, learning about money, and so forth. You can find a list and a link to some of these at *www.macomb.k12.mi.us/wq/webqindx.htm*. One of the more popular of these is Ancient Egypt. See Figure 7-3.

FIGURE 7-3
Ancient Egypt WebQuest

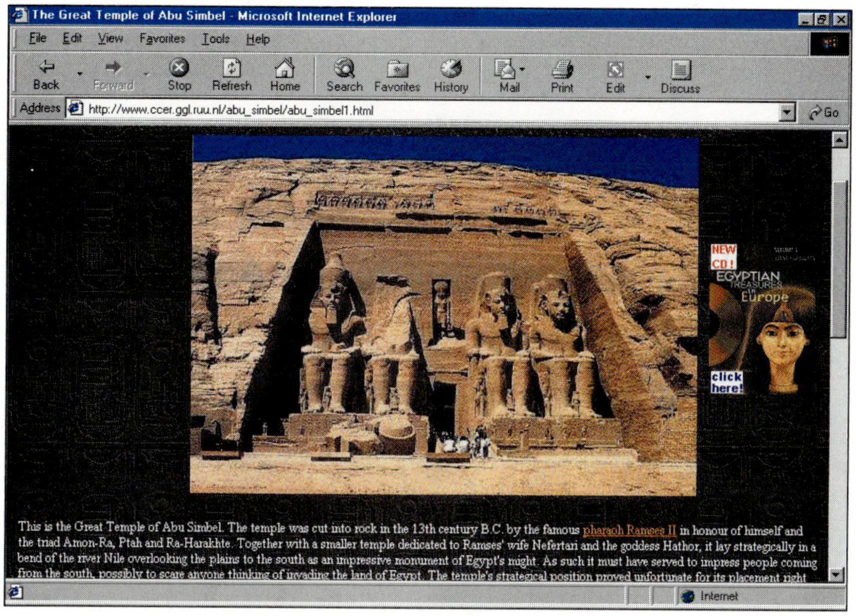

Distance Learning

For years many people have been receiving their education via distance-learning methods. These methods include television and correspondence courses that are completed through the mail. In the last few years, however, the Internet has become a way to deliver distance learning. At the elementary and secondary school levels, the Department of Education supports an initiative called the Star Schools Program. This program provides distance education learning to more than millions of learners annually. Imagine being able to complete high school from home. This is possible in some states.

Did You Know?

According to the National Center for Education Statistics, 93% of public schools are connected to the Internet.

New types of programs are on the market that help teachers develop online courses. These programs are an integrated set of Web-based teaching tools that provide guidance and testing for the student. Two of the most popular of these are Blackboard and WebCT.

Computer-Based Learning

Everyone learns in different ways and at different rates. Likewise, information can be presented in many formats and at different levels. This could be presented through lecture, homework, group projects, movies, and so forth. The more ways in which information can be presented, the more opportunities everyone has to use their own learning style so they can master the particular topic.

You may have heard the terms ***computer-based learning*** or computer-assisted instruction (CAI). These are examples of ways your instructor can use the computer for instruction. It is basically using a computer as a tutor. For many students, this is one of the most effective ways for them to learn. For example, you may have difficulty understanding a specific mathematics concept, such as how to calculate percentages. Your instructor may suggest a special computer program to help reinforce that difficult concept. Using such a program provides you with the opportunity to master the idea by reviewing the concept as many times as necessary. See Figure 7-4.

FIGURE 7-4
Students at work in a computer lab

Simulations

Learning doesn't have to be dull, boring work. Learning can actually be fun especially if it is done through computer simulation. ***Simulations*** are models of real-world activities.

They are designed to allow you to experiment and explore environments that may be dangerous or unavailable. Using simulations, you can explore other worlds and settings without leaving your classroom. With this type of model, you learn by doing.

You can find simulations on the Internet or on a CD-ROM disk that you would run from a local computer.

Some example simulations are as follows:

- Many of you have probably heard about fortunes being made and lost in the stock market. If you would like to see how good your investing skills are, you might want to try The Stock Market game located at *www.smgww.org/*. This simulation is for students of all ages—from middle school to adults. By playing this game, you learn about finance and the American economic system. To participate in this game, you invest a hypothetical $100,000 in the stock market and follow your investments over a 10-week time period. See Figure 7-5.

FIGURE 7-5
Stock Market simulation game

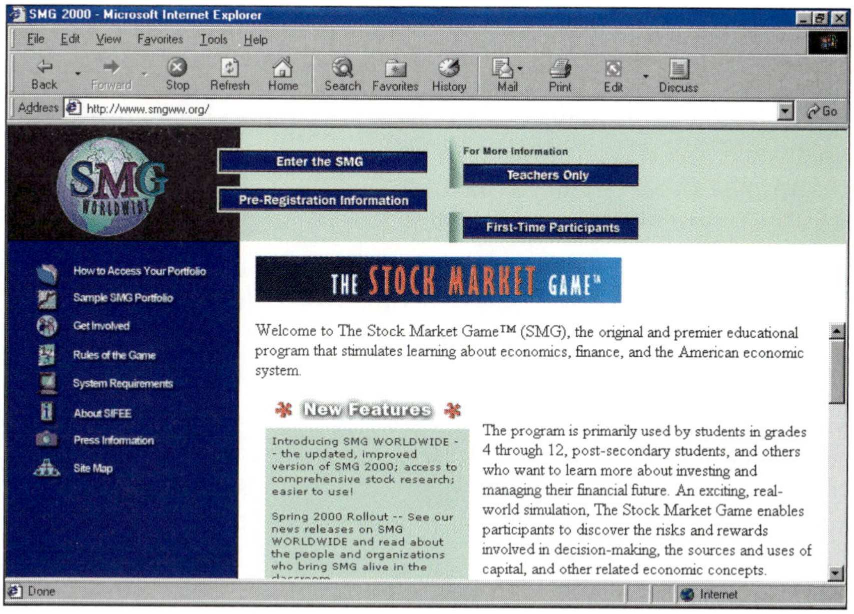

- Maybe you are interested in outer space and would like to explore Mars. You can do this through simulation.
- One of the earliest and still most popular simulations is SimCity. Go to *www.simcity.com* to visit this exciting site. Several versions of this program have been released. It is used extensively in schools throughout the world. This problem-solving software program allows the user to create a city, including highways, buildings, homes, and so forth. See Figure 7-6.

FIGURE 7-6
SimCity simulation

Scientific Discovery and Technological Innovations

Our world is changing at an ever-increasing pace. Currently, people around the world are able to communicate with each other almost instantaneously. The amount of available information is increasing each and every day. In fact, it is continuing to increase faster than we can process it. On the positive side, the information and discoveries are contributing to a better lifestyle for many people. Predictions are that we will learn to cure illnesses and to continue to increase our life span.

But there's another aspect to all of this. Within all of this change, other predictions are that an anti-technology backlash is possible. Many people feel technology is creating a world out of control. Moral and cultural dilemmas are becoming more and more common, and many people want to return to a simpler, slower way of life.

Whether society could and would return to something simpler is highly debatable. Even today, there are very few places in the world one can live that are not being affected by technology. And many scientists say we're "only at the Model-T stage" of what's to come. Let's take a brief look at some of the predicted and possible scientific changes on the horizon.

Artificial Intelligence

Some of you who enjoy science fiction may have read the book or seen the movie *2001: A Space Odyssey*. In this movie, originally released in the late 1960s and re-released in 2000, controlling the spaceship on its way to Mars is a computer referred to as HAL. This computer has a type of artificial intelligence so it never makes a mistake. No computer such as HAL yet exists, but the concept of artificial intelligence is still a branch of computer science. Computer scientists have made many advancements in this area.

Ethics in Technology

WHO IS RESPONSIBLE?

Increasingly, computers participate in decisions that affect human lives. Consider medical safety, for instance, and consider that just about everything in a hospital is tied to a computer. So what happens if these machines don't produce the expected results? What happens if they have been incorrectly programmed?

When programmers write a program, they check for as many conditions as possible. But there is always the chance they might miss one. So what happens if a computer malfunctions and applies a high dosage of radiation? Or what happens if two medications are prescribed to an individual and the computer doesn't indicate the medications are incompatible? Or what happens when someone calls for an ambulance and the system doesn't work and there is no backup?

Then the question becomes who is responsible for these mishaps. Is it the programmer? Is it the company? Is it the person who administered the radiation treatment?

The incidents described here actually happened. These are ethical issues that are being decided in court.

The concept of ***artificial intelligence*** (AI) has been around for many years. In fact, it was coined in1956 by John McCarthy at the Massachusetts Institute of Technology. The goal for this software is to process information on its own without human intervention. There are many ways in which artificial intelligent applications are being developed and used today. Some examples are as follows:

- *Game playing:* An area where the most advances have been made.
- *Natural language:* Offers the greatest potential rewards by allowing people to interact easily with computers by talking to them.
- *Expert systems:* Computer programs that help us make decisions. For instance, an expert system may help your parents determine the best type of insurance for their particular needs.
- *Robotics:* When we think of robotics, we may think of humanoid robots like those in Star Wars. In real life, however, we do not see this type of robot in our society. Robots, mostly used in assembly plants, are only capable of limited tasks. One of the newest types of robots is called a ***bot***, commonly used by search engines.

Genetic Engineering

The human life span has almost tripled in the last 200 years. We can now expect to live 80+ years. Implications are that the average life span in the 21st century will continue to increase, possibly dramatically. One of the major factors contributing to this increase is genetic engineering, which refers to changing the DNA in a living organism. There are groups of people who argue against this technology. The supporters, however, point out the many benefits. Here are some examples:

- Increasing resistance to disease
- Enabling a plant or animal to do something it would not typically do
- Enabling a fruit to ripen without getting too soft

Virtual Reality

The term ***virtual reality*** (VR) means different things to different people. A general definition is an artificial environment that feels like a real environment. This environment is created with computer hardware and software. Virtual reality and simulation share some common characteristics. Simulation is sometimes referred to as desktop VR. However, with virtual reality, there is more of a feeling of being in the actual environment—of using all or almost all of the five senses. The user is completely immersed inside the virtual world, generally through some head-mounted display. This helmet contains the virtual and auditory displays.

Virtual reality is used in many different ways and areas. Some examples are as follows:

- *Education:* The creation of virtual environments so students may have a better understanding of history, for instance. Imagine experiencing World War II as though you were really there. Or maybe you would like to experience what it would be like to live during the age of dinosaurs. With a virtual world, you feel as though you are really there.
- *Training:* You may have had an opportunity to play Doom or Torok: Dinosaur Hunter or some of the other virtual games. If so, you may have felt you were part of the action. You could control much of the environment and make choices as to what your next move would

be. A variation of this type of virtual reality is being used to train pilots, navigators, and even astronauts. These individuals are put into virtual life-and-death situations where they must make decisions. This helps prepare them in the event that a similar situation occurs in real life.

- *Medicine:* One example of a medical VR application is the "Anatomic VisualizeR," being developed at the University of California, San Diego. This project is a virtual reality–based learning environment that will enable medical students to actively learn human anatomy. Or, at a university in Germany, a VR system allows student surgeons to practice operations.
- *Miniaturized chips:* Researchers at Texas Instruments have developed an advanced semiconductor manufacturing technology. The transistors are so small that more than 400 million of them will fit onto a single chip the size of a fingernail. And we can expect that this type of technological advance will continue.

These are just a few examples of activities taking place today. As in the past, it is fairly certain that scientific discovery and technological innovation will greatly affect our economic and military developments in the future. Predictions are that science and technology will continue to advance and become more widely available and utilized around the world. Some people forecast, however, that the benefits derived from these advancements would not be evenly distributed.

Technology Careers

SIMULATION ANALYSTS

Simulation analysts work with large and small companies. Their primary job is to investigate different options to determine which would be the best for a particular situation. For instance, health care company administrators might want to implement a new system for filing and processing insurance claims. Before spending a huge amount of money, they may hire a simulation analyst to determine which system would best meet their needs. Perhaps a bank is going to bring in a new system to process checks. It hires an analyst to do simulation modeling of what the system might and might not do.

Simulation analysts work with all types of companies and industries. Some necessary skills include the ability to see detail in a system and to be a good technical writer. The person should be a logical thinker and have good analytical skills. A good memory is an additional asset.

Opportunities and the need for simulation analysts are increasing. One of the reasons for the increase is that simulation is being applied to a larger variety of problems by more and more companies.

As a consultant, you would probably do some traveling. Consulting fees are generally quite generous, with some simulation analysts making as much as $75,000 or more. You may find some analysts with only a two-year degree, but generally you need at least a bachelor's degree in computer information systems or computer engineering.

Work and Play

How will technology affect us as individuals in our work and social life? Although no one knows what the future will bring, predictions are many. Many people predict that, with high-skilled work more in demand, semi-skilled work will start to disappear. We've already discussed some of the changes taking place in education and how genetic engineering is helping increase life expectancy. As a result of these advances, what types of changes can we expect in the economy and in our personal lives?

Global Economy

One thing for certain about the new economy: knowledge is the greatest asset. However, knowledge will be limited by time—it can be incredibly valuable one moment and worthless the next. The spread and sharing of knowledge, the development of new technologies, and an increased recognition of common world problems present unlimited opportunities for economic growth.

Consider banking, finance, and commerce. Electronic technology is having a dramatic effect on these industries. Think about money. Will it become obsolete? Most likely so. Already, huge amounts of money zip around the globe at the speed of light. Technology is affecting the way information and money is transmitted. See Figure 7-7.

FIGURE 7-7
Transmitting data

Electronic Commerce

You have probably read about the Industrial Revolution and how it affected our world. The Internet economy is being compared to the Industrial Revolution. ***Electronic commerce***, or E-commerce, which means having an online business, is changing the way our world does business.

Within this electronic business, one can buy and sell products through the Internet. We find e-commerce in every corner of the modern business world. Predictions are that over a billion people will be connected to the Internet by the year 2005. Internet speed will increase as more people add cable modems or digital subscriber lines (dsl). All of this activity and high-speed connections indicate more online businesses. Some analysts predict that, within the next 10 years, the value of Internet-based business will account for up to 10% of the world's consumer sales. The Center for Research in Electronic Commerce at the University of Texas indicates that, out of the thousands of online companies, over two thirds of them are not the big Fortune 500 companies—they are smaller companies.

Hot Tip

The economy created by the Internet is generating enormous environmental benefits by reducing the amount of energy and materials consumed by businesses. It is predicted that the Internet will revolutionize the relationship between economic growth and the environment.

When it comes to buying online, many people hesitate because they fear someone will steal their credit card number. However, ***digital cash*** is a new technology that may ease some of those fears. The digital cash system allows someone to pay by transmitting a number from one computer to another. The digital cash numbers are issued by a bank and represent a specified sum of real money; each number is unique. When one uses digital cash, there is no way to obtain information about the user.

As you read about electronic commerce, you may wonder about what effects it will have on you personally. You or someone in your family may have already made a purchase online. Buying online will become much more common in the future, and you may find it becomes a way of life.

Rarely a day goes by that you or someone in your family doesn't receive junk mail. In the future, much of the postal junk mail will be replaced by ***SPAM***, junk mail sent to your e-mail address. Several states are already looking at ways to legislate this new junk mail.

Other aspects you might consider are the number of and new categories of jobs being generated due to electronic commerce. These might be something you want to consider as you look toward a future career. Some examples include Webmasters, programmers, network managers, graphic designers, Web developers, and so forth. You may also think about going into an online business for yourself. Individuals with imagination and ambition will discover that the greatest source of wealth is their ideas.

Hot Tip

Want to find out more about the Internet and electronic commerce? The Internet Economy Indicators Web site located at *www.internetindicators.com/* provides lots of statistics and links to other sites on how to start your own online business.

Personal Lives

Will our personal life become almost like Star Trek? Many people predict it will. Just as technology is affecting our work environment, it is also affecting our personal lives.

In the 20th century, society witnessed all types of changes in the places people lived. They moved from the farms to the cities and then to the suburbs. The 21st century will also witness changes as the home becomes the center for work, entertainment, learning, and possibly even health care. More and more people will telecommute or run a business from their home. As a result, they will have to manage their lives in a world of uncertainty. This will be a great change for many people. They will have to make decisions about how to separate their business and personal lives.

Some examples of potential technological advances that can affect our personal lives are as follows:

- *Clothes that fight odor and bacteria:* Some clothing companies are manufacturing clothes that keep you comfortable and smelling good. For example, when the temperature drops, jackets grow warmer and sweat socks resist bacteria and odors. Or how about clothing that kills mosquitoes on contact?
- *The flying car:* This has long been a fantasy of the American public, but the question is how long will it be before we all have flying cars? It will probably be a few more years before we're flying around like the Jetsons, but there are possibilities on the horizon. Moller International has developed a personal vertical takeoff and landing vehicle (VTOL). The Skycar is able to operate in a much less restrictive area than a helicopter or airplane and is less expensive and safer. These factors allow this type of future transportation to be addressed and investigated for the first time. See Figure 7-8.

FIGURE 7-8
Moller Web site – Skycar

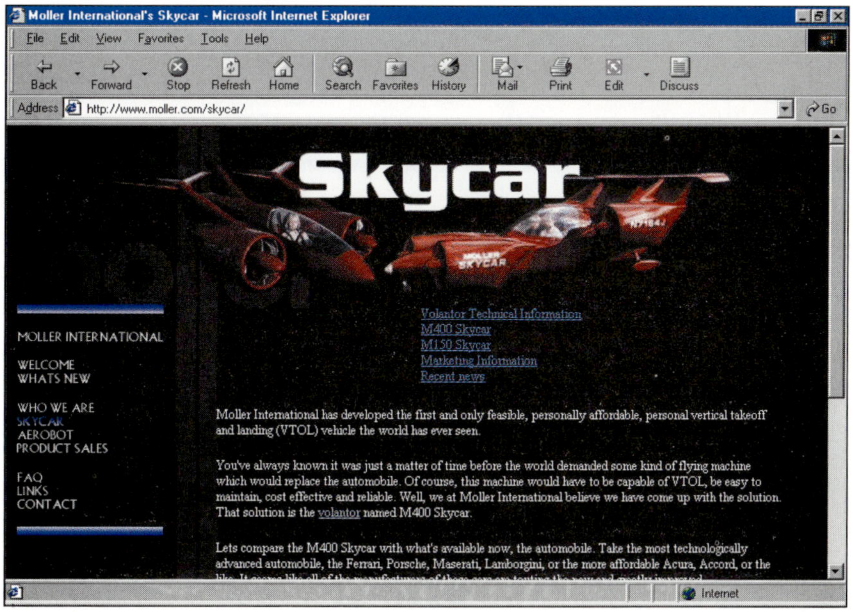

- *Voice recognition:* Some people forecast that, within the next few years, written language will be dead and writing may become an ancient art form. Instead, we will talk to computers or computerlike devices, and they will reply. We will curl up in the bed with our electronic book, and it will read us to sleep.
- *Nonlethal weapons:* A company in San Diego is working on a nonlethal weapon that uses two ultraviolet laser beams. These two beams of UV radiation ionize paths in the air to create "wires" in the atmosphere. This device is harmless, but it can immobilize people and animals at a distance.

- *Space travel:* Would you like to take a trip around the world—that is, by low-earth orbit? You may be able to do so in the near future. The Roton Rocket Company is developing a fleet of commercial vehicles to provide the public the opportunity to access space.
- *Smart shoes and smart seats:* When we think of technology, not too many of us consider our shoes. No matter how expensive our shoes are, they can still become uncomfortable after wearing them for long hours. A technology called expansive polymer gel uses a micro voltage to expand or contract the gel. Weight can be evenly distributed and heat dissipated. This technology is also being applied to car seats.
- *Smart houses:* The smart house uses computers to help the family live a healthy, happy, and safe life. A smart house, among other things, keeps the temperature at a comfortable level while monitoring the amount of electricity being used, helps the family plan and prepare healthy meals, monitors devices within the home and schedules maintenance, and provides accommodations for individuals with disabilities.

> **Internet**
>
> Electronic ink will have a far-reaching impact on our society. The ink itself is a liquid that can be printed onto nearly any surface. You can learn about electronic ink at *www.eink.com*.

- *Electronic shopping:* No longer do we have to fight the crowds and search for parking spaces. We can do all of our shopping online. Regardless of what you are shopping for—electronics, jewelry, flowers, clothes, food, or even a snack from Pizza Hut—you can have it delivered to your door. See Figure 7-9.

FIGURE 7-9
Pizza Hut Web site

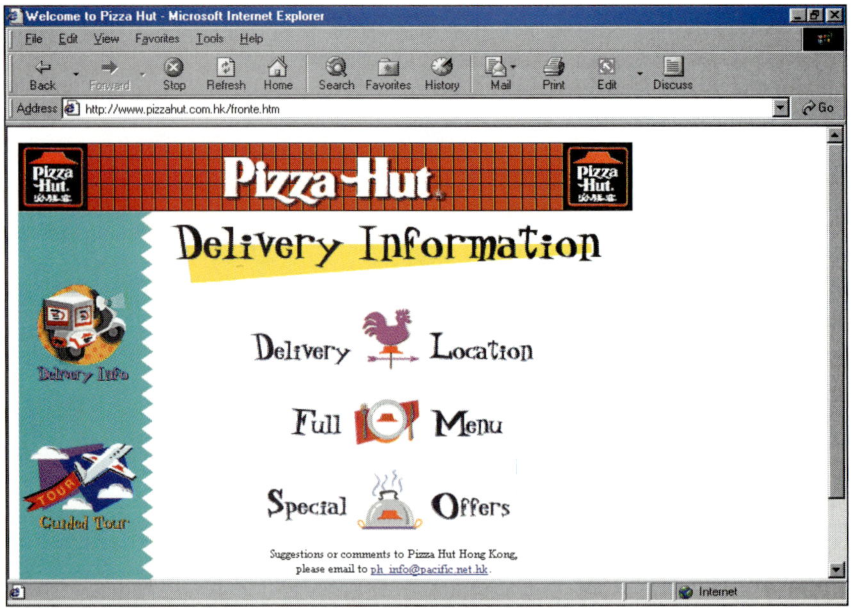

So what does the future hold? No one really knows. You can be assured, however, that it will be exciting and ever changing.

SUMMARY

In this lesson, you learned:

- Many people predict that technology will change the entire structure of education.
- Technology is having a tremendous impact on education.
- The Internet and the World Wide Web are the biggest factors affecting education today.
- Online courses through the Internet are becoming very popular.
- Many schools use computer-based learning to reinforce concepts.
- Simulations are models of real-world activities.
- Information is continuing to increase faster than we can process it.
- Some people predict an anti-technology backlash.
- Artificial intelligence is software that can process information on its own without human intervention.
- Genetic engineering refers to changing the DNA in a living organism.
- Virtual reality is an artificial environment that feels like a real environment and is used in education, training, medicine, research, and other areas.
- In the new global economy, knowledge is the greatest asset.
- Electronic commerce is the buying and selling of goods and services using the Internet and is predicted to grow at an ever-increasing rate.
- Digital cash allows someone to pay online by transmitting a number from one computer to another.
- New jobs and new job categories are being developed because of the Internet and electronic commerce.
- In the 21st century, many people will work from their homes.
- Some technological advances are clothes that fight odors, flying cars, voice recognition, nonlethal weapons, space travel, smart shoes and smart seats, smart houses, and electronic shopping.

VOCABULARY *Review*

Define the following terms:

Artificial intelligence	Electronic commerce	Virtual reality
Bot	Simulations	Voice recognition
Computer-based learning	SPAM	WebQuest
Digital cash		

REVIEW *Questions*

MULTIPLE CHOICE

Select the best response for the following statements.

1. New technology is causing ________ changes in our society
   A. some
   B. none
   C. major
   D. a few

2. One of the biggest factors affecting education is the ________.
   A. government
   B. school board
   C. Internet
   D. other students

3. ________ is the delivery of education over the Internet.
   A. Simulation
   B. Distance learning
   C. Virtual reality
   D. None of the above

4. If you were participating in a ________ application, you would wear a helmet.
   A. simulated
   B. cloning
   C. virtual reality
   D. computer-based training

5. The buying and selling of goods on the Internet is called ________.
   A. economic commerce
   B. electronic commerce
   C. on-hand business
   D. local commerce

TRUE/FALSE

Circle T if the statement is true or F if the statement false.

T F 1. With digital cash, you can pay someone by transmitting a number from one computer to another.

T F 2. Life in the 21st century will probably be very similar to that of the 20th century.

T F 3. It is a real possibility that, within the next 25 years or so, individuals will be able to purchase a ticket to orbit the earth.

T F 4. There are only a few applications for virtual reality.

T F 5. Simulations are models of real-world activities.

FILL IN THE BLANK

Complete the following sentences by writing the correct word or words in the blanks provided.

1. A(n) __________ uses the Internet for investigation and problem solving.
2. Using __________ you learn by doing.
3. SimCity is a popular __________ activity.
4. __________ is the changing of the DNA in a living organism.
5. __________ is software that works without human intervention.

PROJECTS

PROJECT 7-1

See what information you can find on flying cars. Prepare a report and a chart showing the possibilities for these cars. Include price, speed, size, and any other relevant numbers you can locate.

PROJECT 7-2

Robots, and particularly bots, have become a very important element in searching and finding information online. Do some research, using whatever resources are available, and write a report on what the bots are and how they work. If you have an Internet connection, check out *info.webcrawler.com/mak/projects/robots/faq.html.*

PROJECT 7-3

The year is 2070. You were born in 2055. Use your word-processing program to write a letter to someone who lived 50 years ago and tell him or her about your life and your community.

WEB PROJECT

Visit the U.S. Geological Survey's Water Science for Schools Web site located at *ga.water.usgs.gov/edu/*. Review the Web site and then go to the Activity Center. Complete the Surveys and Challenge Questions.

CRITICAL *Thinking*

ACTIVITY 7-1

It is predicted that, in the next few years, the home and business will merge for many people; more and more people will work from home. Would you consider working from home? Why or why not? What advantages and disadvantages do you see?

LESSON 8

INTRODUCTION TO WINDOWS XP PROFESSIONAL

OBJECTIVES

Upon completion of this lesson, you should be able to:

- Describe the general features of Windows XP.
- Start Windows.
- Examine the elements of the Windows opening screen.
- Use a mouse to move around the desktop.
- Shut down Windows.

Estimated Time: 1.5 hours

VOCABULARY

Clicking
Double-click
Dragging
Graphical User Interface (GUI)
Icons
Linking
Log off
Log on
Mouse
Mouse buttons
Mouse pointer
Multitasking
Primary button
Right-clicking
Select (highlight)
Shortcut menu button
Standard desktop
Start button
Windows

Introduction

Windows . . . a simple, familiar word. Not a high-tech word. Yet Windows is, as you will see, an accurate name for a rich, powerful, high-tech software program. Reason: The word ***windows*** represents a visual or picture-oriented environment, the type of environment that Windows uses. This environment provides an easy way for users to communicate or interact with the computer by way of pictures, often called a ***Graphical User Interface*** or ***GUI***. Indeed, Windows' visual environment is the key to understanding and to using this impressive program.

But a graphical user interface does more than make Windows easy to use. One key benefit of a GUI is that it provides a consistent way to work within each program, a consistent way to work with other programs, and a simple and consistent way to switch between programs.

The Windows World

Imagine an electronic (not a physical) version of your desktop, complete with electronic tools and supplies, all accessible at your fingertips. That's the Windows desktop. Its parallels with the physical desktop are not accidental; Windows is designed to be your workplace.

Here you will work with your mouse by moving and clicking. Here you can set up a clock, use your calculator, grab your files and folders, dial your phone, surf the Net, and open your briefcase. You can instantly see a complete listing of all your tools and supplies, a complete log of all your files and folders—a complete inventory of everything on your computer. And don't forget that wastebasket, which Windows calls a Recycle Bin. You can even decorate your Windows desktop, as you will see later.

Windows Empowers You

You can't appreciate the full potential of Windows until you understand its powerful capabilities, such as file linking and automatic file updating. This powerful yet friendly software is an operating system; that means it manages everything—both the hardware and the software that operate your entire computer system. With Windows, you shift to each new task and open or close programs as effortlessly and quickly as when you use your remote control to switch between TV channels. While one window remains open and active on the desktop, others remain open but inactive—either on the desktop or as buttons on the taskbar. Just click a taskbar button to reactivate it, and place it in an open window.

1-3.2.6-1 1-3.2.6-2 This capability of running several tasks, or programs, at the same time is called ***multitasking***. Multitasking allows you to process data in one program while you are working in another. For instance, while you are working on a spreadsheet in one window, you might be printing a word-processing document in another window.

And with Windows' ***linking*** features, you can easily transfer data among programs and update the data automatically.

Windows XP—An Easy Transition

1-3.1.4-2 1-3.1.4-5 Whether you are new to Windows software or not, adapting to new software—even a new version of familiar software—can be taxing. Learning new tools and unfamiliar features can be time-consuming and may require training. But Windows simplifies the process considerably. Consequently, if you've used an older version of Windows, you'll make the transition easily to Windows XP Professional. As you make the transition, you'll see that Windows XP provides

- Easier, faster, and more powerful ways to work with application programs, as well as special hardware settings and increased speed for your network connections.
- Greater reliability and built-in support for hardware and software improvements, such as being able to use up to four monitors at a time.
- Enhanced versions of desktop tools, the taskbar, and the Start menu.
- Upgraded support for multimedia that allows you to receive high-quality movies and audio directly on your desktop.
- A single, easy way to have automated access to and delivery of information—whether it is located on your machine, the local area network, or the Internet.
- A mechanism that schedules delivery of information from the World Wide Web that you want to monitor, without requiring that you physically visit the site or even connect to the Web.
- Advanced capabilities for Internet Explorer and support for all Internet standards.

Starting Windows

Windows XP automatically starts when you turn on your computer. If you are the only person using your computer, Windows XP displays your desktop, ready for you to begin your work. However, Windows may ask you to click a user name before it will give you access to the computer. This is because Windows XP lets many different users create their own accounts. Each account contains all the settings the user likes, such as screen colors, placement of items on the desktop, and other program options. In order to do this, Windows XP needs to know who is going to use the computer. If your computer uses this feature, each time you start the computer, a Welcome screen appears, as shown in Figure 8-1, with each user's account name and an associated icon. You must ***log on***, or tell the computer who you are, by clicking one of the user names and, if prompted, entering a password. Windows loads all your preferred settings and opens to the Windows ***standard desktop,*** as shown in Figure 8-1.

FIGURE 8-1
Windows XP may ask users to log on

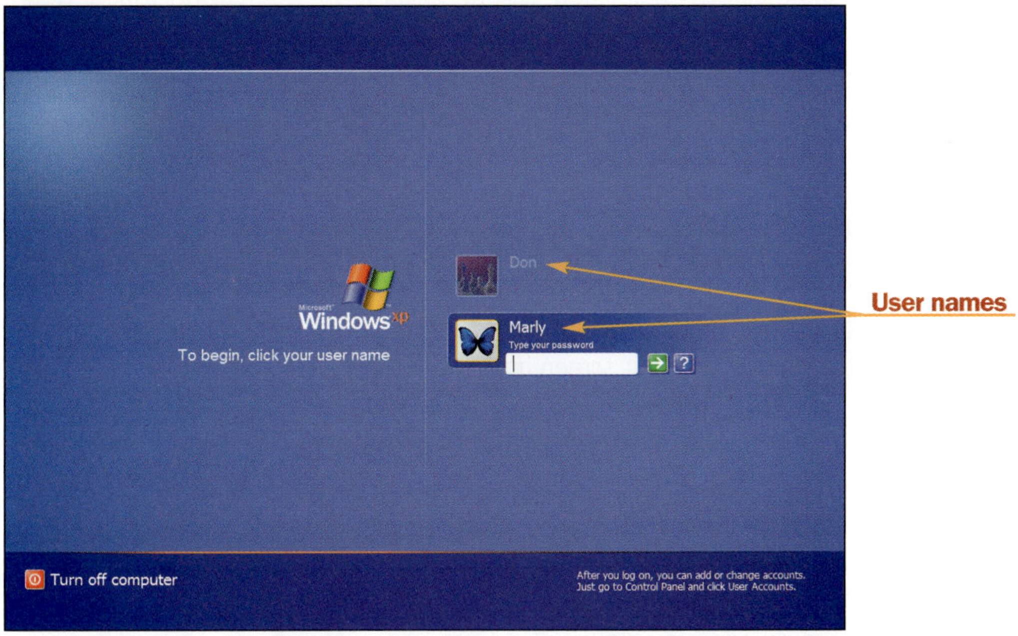

STEP-BY-STEP 8.1

1. Turn on your computer system.
2. Windows will start automatically.
   a. If prompted, click one of the user names or enter the user name you have been assigned. (You may need to ask your system administrator for assistance with which user name and password to use.)
   b. If prompted, key your password. As you key your password, the password box will fill with black circles—one for each character in your password. Your password won't display for security reasons, so key your password carefully. If you can't remember your password and you had a password clue entered to help you remember, click the blue box with the question mark to the right of the password box to display a memory clue to your password.
   c. If your system is set up for multiple users, click the green arrow to the right of the password box or press **Enter** on the keyboard or click the **OK** button. Windows should then start.

> **Extra for Experts**
>
> If you are a user of an earlier version of Windows, you can set up the Windows desktop to look like the classic desktop. To switch from the standard desktop to the classic desktop, right-click anywhere on a clear area on the desktop. A shortcut menu displays. Click **Properties** on the submenu. Click the **Appearance** tab, select the **Windows Classic style** option on the Windows and buttons drop down list, and then click the OK button. You can also change the Start menu to the Classic style: Right-click on **Start**, click **Properties** and then choose the **Classic Start menu** option on the Start menu tab in the taskbar and Start Menu Properties dialog box.

3. Compare your screen with that illustrated in Figure 8-2. Your screen may differ slightly, but the basic elements should be the same. Spend a few minutes looking at the layout of your screen and the position of the elements. If your screen does not display elements similar to those shown in Figure 8-2, ask for assistance. Remain on the Windows desktop for the next Step-by-Step.

IC3 1-3.1.4-6

FIGURE 8-2
Windows XP standard desktop

Examining the Windows Opening Screen

Now that you have started Windows, you are ready to explore its many features. As you explore Windows, remember what you have already learned about its graphical environment. As you work through each lesson in this course, you will be using the same consistent way of performing common tasks for different programs within Windows.

The Desktop

The standard *desktop* (see Figure 8-2) provides the overall work area on the screen and is the Windows equivalent of the top surface of your desk. Most Windows activity takes place on the desktop. You put things on your desk, take things off your desk, and move things around on your desk. In the same way, you can place items on, remove items from, and rearrange items on your Windows desktop.

Like any new desk, the Windows desktop is relatively neat when Windows is first installed on your computer. A new Windows desktop may have a number of elements, depending on your system's configuration. As you work, placing elements on and removing elements from your desktop, these system elements will generally stay on your desktop.

Look again at Figure 8-2, which identifies the main components of the opening Windows screen: the desktop, the taskbar, the Quick Launch toolbar, the Start button, and one or more small pictures, or ***icons***, you can use to work with Windows programs and features.

The opening Windows XP desktop typically only displays the Recycle Bin icon. The Recycle Bin contains files you delete from your hard disk. You can retrieve files from the Recycle Bin if you deleted them by mistake. This "undo" feature can be a lifesaver. Your desktop may show other icons if your system has been set up differently from the initial installation.

The Taskbar

IC3 1-3.2.4-2

Locate the taskbar in Figure 8-2. There you will see the taskbar in its usual default location at the bottom of the screen, but you can move it to the top, left, or right side of the desktop to suit your needs. Wherever you choose to position it, you will find the taskbar to be a very convenient helper.

You use the taskbar for two important tasks: to display the Start menu and to switch among currently running programs that you want to keep open. Every program you keep open is represented by a button on the taskbar that offers easy access to all your running programs—just click the button. For example, if you open Excel, the taskbar displays a button for that program. If you then decide to run Paint, the taskbar adds a button for that program. One glance at the icons on the taskbar buttons tells you which programs are running (active). Want to switch to another active program? Just click the appropriate button on the taskbar.

The Start Menu

1-3.2.5-1
1-3.2.4-1

You click the ***Start button*** on the taskbar to display the Start menu, as shown in Figure 8-3. The Start menu contains a list of options you will use throughout this book that enables you to complete frequently performed tasks quickly and easily. For example, you can launch programs from the Start menu, open recently used files, change your system's settings, find files or folders, access Help topics, and close or shut down Windows.

FIGURE 8-3
Start menu

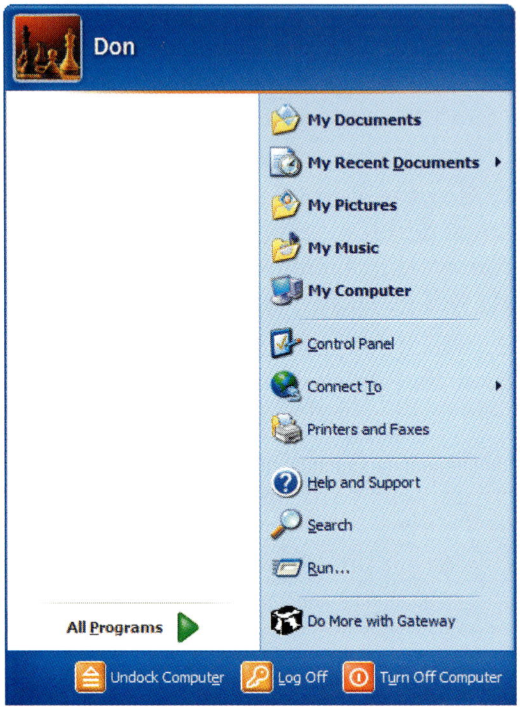

Look closely at the Start menu shown in Figure 8-3. Notice that the items on the menu are placed in one of four sections. These sections are at the top, bottom, left, and right of the menu. The login user name is displayed in large letters in the section across the top of the menu, and options for logging off or shutting down Windows are displayed along the bottom of the menu. A list of folders and programs is displayed on the left and right side of the separator line in the middle portion of the start menu.

The items on the right side of the separator line are known as the pinned items list. These items remain there and are always available for you to click to start them. You can add items to the pinned items list. The list of programs on the left of the separator line is known as the most-often-used-programs list. The programs displayed on the most-often-used-programs list appear there when you use them. Clicking the All Programs item opens a list of programs currently installed on your computer. When you click one of these programs, the program is placed in the often-used-programs list. Windows has a default number of programs that are displayed on this list. When that number of programs is reached, a program you have not opened recently is replaced in the list. You can change the default number of programs displayed on the most-often-used list, if you wish.

Following is an explanation of the options commonly found on the Start menu:

- 1-3.2.1-1 *All Programs* contains a complete list of the programs installed on your computer and allows you to launch any program quickly from the desktop.
- *My Documents* contains a list of the documents saved in this folder for quick access.
- *My Recent Documents* contains a list of the documents that were recently opened or created.
- *My Pictures* contains a list of the digital photos, images, and graphic files saved in this folder.
- *My Music* contains a list of music and other audio files saved in this folder.
- *My Computer* displays the contents of your computer. You can see the hardware devices, resources, programs, and files that are stored on your computer. My Computer also provides information about different system resources, such as the size of the hard disk and how much space is available on it. You can also use My Computer to format disks and to run programs.
- *Control Panel* provides options for customizing the "look and feel" of your desktop. For instance, the Control Panel option lets you change settings, such as the computer's date/time, desktop background, display colors, keyboard language, and mouse controls. The Taskbar & Start Menu option lets you make changes to what appears on your taskbar and Start menu.
- *Printers and Faxes* lists all of the printers and any fax machines that can be accessed from your computer.
- The *Help and Support* option opens the Windows Help facility, an easy-to-use program that provides you with information about Windows and its programs.
- The *Search* option is one of the most important capabilities in the Windows program. It helps you find files and folders. This option also lets you search for Web sites you visit frequently, plus it provides a quick way to find people whose names are stored in a variety of electronic address books.
- The *Run* command allows you to begin a program quickly from the Start menu. You can also use this command to find a file or program.
- The *Log Off* option permits you to exit the account you are using and keep the computer on for you or another user to log on at a later time.
- The *Turn Off Computer* (or *Shut Down*) option provides options for safely shutting down and/or restarting Windows and your computer.

The Mouse Pointer

The arrow you see on the desktop is the ***mouse pointer***, a graphical element you move around the screen to select items (such as icons and menu options), issue commands, and move or manipulate screen elements (such as text or windows). The arrow is one of several shapes the pointer may assume. Other shapes and their meanings will be explained later in this lesson.

Moving Around the Desktop

Question: "How do I move around the Windows desktop?" Answer: "With a mouse." The mouse lets you race all over the screen—and, if you want, carry materials with you as you move.

Introducing the Mouse

The ***mouse*** is an input device that allows you to find files, access tools, grab folders you need to move, or place items on the Windows desktop. Of course, you can also use the mouse to put those tools, files, or folders away. But that's not all. The mouse serves a number of other convenient uses. Your desktop is a visual work area, and the mouse is the key to that work area.

IC3 1-1.2.3-1

Most computers include a mouse as standard equipment. However, some systems, especially portable laptop and notebook models, may have an integrated trackball, touchpad, or Trackpoint on or next to the keyboard. These input devices work like a mouse, but they take less space and don't require a desk to move around on. Think of a trackball as an upside-down mouse. You use your thumb to rotate the ball and move the pointer. If you have a touch-sensitive pad, you move the mouse pointer on the display screen by moving a finger or other object along the pad. And you click by tapping the pad or an adjacent button. The Trackpoint is a small knob found in the middle of the keyboard. It works like a very short joystick. You move the pointer on the screen by pressing the Trackpoint toward or away from you or from side to side.

Many other alternatives to the conventional roller-ball mouse exist. A tailless mouse, or hamster, transmits its information with infrared impulses. An optical mouse uses a light-emitting diode and photocells instead of a rolling ball to track its position. Some optical designs may require a special mouse pad marked with a grid; others work on nearly any surface.

Basics

If you're using a conventional mouse, clear an area (at least 1 square foot) next to the keyboard on your computer desktop for moving the mouse. This area must be clean and smooth because the mouse uses a rotating ball to sense movement: Any grease or dust on the desk surface can clog the ball and cause difficulty in operating the mouse. For best performance, use a mouse pad. It's specially designed to sit under your mouse and facilitate its movement.

Hold the mouse so the cable extends outward (away from your hand) and the body of the mouse rests under the palm of your hand. Rest your index finger lightly on one of the buttons.

The Mouse Pointer and Its Shapes

The mouse controls the on-screen mouse pointer, which was explained earlier in this lesson. To move the pointer up or down or to the left or right, slide the mouse in that direction. When you get "cornered" (that is, when you run out of room on your real desk or mouse pad), just lift the mouse off your desk (or mouse pad), move the mouse, and set it back down—all without moving the on-screen pointer.

The on-screen pointer changes its appearance depending on the task in which Windows is engaged. Most of the time, the pointer looks like an arrow, but it may assume a number of other shapes. For example:

- When you are working with text, the pointer changes to an I-beam.
- When Windows is working on an instruction and isn't ready to accept further input from you, the pointer changes to an hourglass. The hourglass means "Wait. Windows is busy finishing a task."
- When an arrow is attached to the hourglass, it indicates that Windows is working on a task but you can still select and move objects.
- When the pointer turns into a circle with a slash through it—the international "no" symbol—the message is: "This action is not allowed."

When you move the pointer over parts of a window, the different pointer shapes give you visual clues about how you can move the mouse.

Mouse Buttons

So, the mouse lets you move around the screen quickly, but what do you do when you "get there?" Besides moving the pointer around the screen, the mouse allows you to move windows and to choose various programs. How? By using ***mouse buttons***.

> **Extra for Experts**
>
> You can change your desktop settings so different shapes appear to indicate the different tasks. If you choose a desktop theme, the shapes will be changed automatically to match the theme.

Every mouse has one, two, or three buttons, depending on the manufacturer. By default, the button on the left is the ***primary button*** (the one you will use most often). It is also referred to as the select/drag button because it is the one you use to select and move elements around the screen. The secondary button, usually the button on the right, is called the ***shortcut menu button*** (shortcut menus are discussed later in this lesson), and using it is called ***right-clicking***. You'll learn when to right-click as you practice using Windows.

Your mouse may also have a "Fast Wheel" located between the primary and secondary buttons. Basically the wheel lets you move through documents quickly by allowing you to roll to scroll. If you click this wheel once, your pointer changes to a large arrow and you can scroll extremely rapidly just by moving the mouse pointer up or down on the screen.

Are you left-handed? Windows allows you to reverse the primary and secondary mouse buttons so you can use your left hand. You'll learn how to do this in a later lesson. For the purpose of this book, however, we will always consider the left button to be the primary button and the right button to be the secondary button.

Operating the Mouse

In addition to moving the pointer, the mouse is used to select objects and to move objects or icons around the screen. You ***select***, or ***highlight***, an item by pointing to it and pressing and then releasing the left (primary) mouse button. Pressing and then releasing the left mouse button is referred to as ***clicking***; some commands require you to ***double-click*** (that is, click twice quickly). If you don't double-click the button fast enough, Windows interprets your action as two single clicks rather than one double-click. (With a little experience, you'll double-click expertly.)

Moving objects with the mouse is known as ***dragging***. You drag an object by placing the mouse pointer on the item to be moved, then pressing and holding down the primary mouse button while moving the object. When the pointer is at the right location, release the mouse button.

Table 8-1 lists and explains five common techniques for using a standard two-button mouse device.

TABLE 8-1
Operating the mouse

TO	DO THIS
Drag	Press and hold the mouse button and move the mouse in the desired direction, then release.
Click	Press and release the left (primary) mouse button.
Double-click	Click the left mouse button twice in rapid succession.
Right-click	Press and release the right (secondary) mouse button.
Select	Point to an item and click the mouse button.

Using the mouse proficiently requires a little practice—and a little patience. In a very short time, you'll use the mouse comfortably and smoothly.

STEP-BY-STEP 8.2

1. Move the mouse (or other pointing device) on your desk (or mouse pad). As you move the mouse, watch the screen to see how the pointer moves:
   - **a.** Move the pointer to the far left of your screen by sliding the mouse to the left on the desk or mouse pad. Do not lift the mouse.
   - **b.** Move the pointer to the far right of your screen by sliding the mouse to the right.
   - **c.** Move the pointer to the top of your screen by moving the mouse toward the top of your desk or mouse pad.
   - **d.** Move the pointer to the bottom of your screen by moving the mouse toward the bottom of your desk or mouse pad.

2. Display and then close the Start menu:
   - **a.** Point to the Start button in the corner of the taskbar.
   - **b.** Click the left mouse button.
   - **c.** Point to a clear area of the desk, and click the left mouse button. The Start menu closes.

3. Select and rearrange an icon on the desktop:
   - **a.** Point to the Recycle Bin icon, and hold (do not click) the pointer on the icon for a few seconds. Notice that a small window opens displaying a description of the icon. Click the mouse button. Notice that when you click an icon, it changes color. The change in color means the icon is selected.
   - **b.** Click anywhere on the desktop. As you do so, notice that Recycle Bin is deselected (that is, it returns to its original color).
   - **c.** Again point to the Recycle Bin icon.
   - **d.** While holding down the mouse button, drag the icon about one inch to the right and release the mouse button. As you drag the icon, note how a "ghost image" of the icon follows the mouse pointer to indicate where the icon will be placed when you release the mouse button.
   - **e.** Drag the **Recycle Bin** icon back to its original position.

STEP-BY-STEP 8.2 Continued

4. Double-click the **Recycle Bin**. The Recycle Bin window opens similar to that shown in Figure 8-4.

FIGURE 8-4
Results of double-clicking an icon

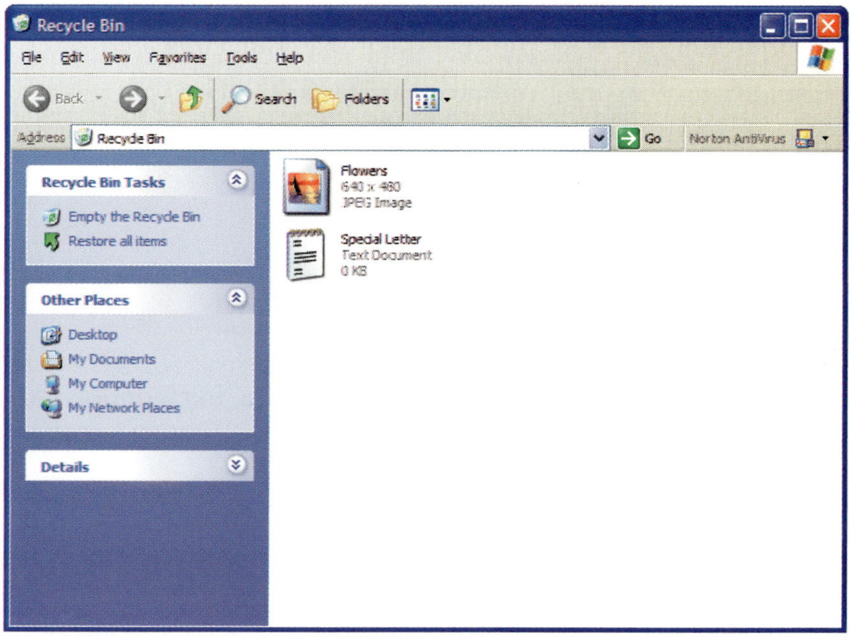

5. Close the Recycle Bin window by clicking the **X** in the upper right corner of the window.

1-3.2.4-1 6. Open an application from the Start menu:
   a. Point to the Start button in the corner of the taskbar.
   b. Click the left mouse button.
   c. Point to Programs on the pop-up menu.
   d. Point to and click the Word application from the submenu.
   1-3.2.4-2 e. Notice that the Word application is now open and listed on the taskbar.
   f. Close the Word application.

1-3.2.6-3 7. Open an application from the taskbar.
   a. Point to and click the Word icon on the taskbar.
   b. Notice that the Word application opens.
   c. Close the Word application.

Shutting Down Windows

1-3.2.3-1
1-3.2.3-2
1-3.2.3-3
1-3.2.3-4

You shut down Windows by using the Start button. You have two choices along the bottom of the Start menu: Log Off or Turn Off Computer (or Shut Down). Each of these choices has options, as explained below.

- *Log off*—Selecting this choice keeps your computer running while you log off the computer so someone else can use it. If you select this option (and your system is set up for multiple users), Windows will open a message box asking if you want to Switch User or Log Off, as shown in Figure 8-5. (If your system is not set up for multiple users, the message box gives you the choice between logging off or canceling this action.)

FIGURE 8-5
Log Off Windows message box

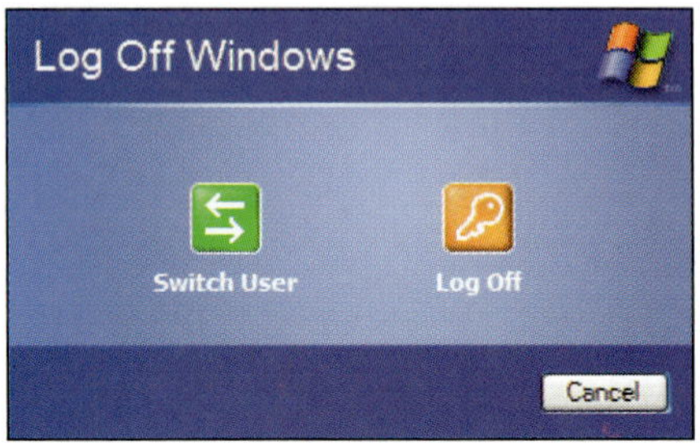

  - If you choose Switch User, the Welcome screen appears, but Windows keeps your open programs waiting for you. When the new user logs off, Windows switches back to you as the user and everything is just as you left it.
  - If you choose Log Off, Windows saves your work and your settings and returns to the Welcome screen for the next user. Windows does not turn the computer off when this option is selected.

- *Turn Off Computer* (or *Shut Down*)—Selecting this choice instructs Windows to prepare to shut down. Each time you select Turn Off Computer, a message box displays, giving you options similar to those shown in Figure 8-6. These options are discussed below.

FIGURE 8-6
Turn off computer message box

  - *Stand By*—Select this option if you want to save electrical energy but keep your current programs open so you can resume where you left off.
  - *Turn Off*—This option closes all programs (if you didn't close them first) and shuts down Windows. Depending on how your computer system is set up, your computer's and monitor's power may also turn off. If it is not set up to do this, a message box will appear informing you that it is safe to turn off the power to your computer.
  - *Restart*—This option quits Windows and restarts your computer – opening Windows back up.

IC³

STEP-BY-STEP 8.3

1-3.2.3-2
1-3.2.3-1

1. Click the **Start** button, and select the **Turn Off Computer** option (or **Shut Down** option if applicable) from the Start menu. Shutting down the computer is good to do each time you are finished working for the day.

1-3.2.3-4
1-3.2.3-3

2. Select the **Restart** option. Windows will shut down and then automatically start running again. This is helpful if you decide you need to continue working or if your computer locks up.

3. Log on to Windows if necessary to start Windows.

4. Shut down Windows again. This time select the **Turn Off** option (or **Shut Down** option if applicable).

5. If instructed, turn off your computer when the message window informs you that it is safe to do so.

Note

If your Start menu choice is Shut Down as opposed to Turn Off Computer, your message box will be named Shut Down Windows and it will contain a drop-down list of options. These options are Log off [User Name], Shut down, and Restart. Log off works the same as clicking Log Off from the Start menu. Shut Down is comparable to Turn Off. And Restart functions in the same manner as Restart from the Turn off computer message box.

SUMMARY

In this lesson, you learned:

- Windows XP Professional allows multitasking—that is, processing information in more than one program at the same time—and linking of data.
- The opening screen on the standard desktop is mostly empty except for the Recycle Bin icon and any others that may be added by users.
- Most Windows activity takes place on the desktop.
- The Windows opening screen has the following basic components: the desktop, the taskbar, the Quick Launch toolbar, the Start button, the mouse pointer, and one or more desktop icons.
- You use the taskbar to open programs and documents and to switch back and forth between running programs.
- The Start menu options let you launch programs, open recently used files, change your system's settings, find files or folders, access Help topics, and close and shut down Windows.
- The mouse controls an on-screen pointer. The shape of the pointer will change depending on where you are on-screen and what you are doing.
- Mouse buttons let you make selections by clicking, right-clicking, and double-clicking. The primary button is used most frequently. The secondary button is used for shortcuts.
- The mouse lets you move (drag) objects.
- When you want to shut down Windows, you select either the Log Off or the Turn Off Computer option (or the Shut Down option) from the Start menu.

VOCABULARY *Review*

Define the following terms:

Clicking
Double-click
Dragging
Graphical User Interface (GUI)
Icons
Linking
Log off
Log on
Mouse
Mouse buttons
Mouse pointer
Multitasking
Primary button
Right-clicking
Select (highlight)
Shortcut menu button
Standard desktop
Start button
Windows

REVIEW *Questions*

MATCHING

Match the correct term in Column 2 to its description in Column 1.

	Column 1		Column 2
___ 1.	Desktop component that contains buttons for open programs	A.	dragging
___ 2.	Item on the Start menu that provides options for customizing the look and feel of your desktop	B.	Control Panel
___ 3.	Graphical element you move around the screen to select, move, and manipulate screen elements	C.	Recycle Bin
___ 4.	Act of moving an object with the mouse	D.	taskbar
___ 5.	Icon on the desktop that contains deleted files	E.	mouse pointer

TRUE / FALSE

Circle T if the statement is true or F if the statement is false.

T F 1. The standard desktop is the name of the Windows XP operating system.

T F 2. The Recycle Bin stores newly created documents.

T F 3. A trackball is similar to an upside-down mouse.

T F 4. By default, the taskbar is usually located at the bottom of the screen.

T F 5. Multitasking means running two or more programs simultaneously.

CRITICAL *Thinking*

SCANS ACTIVITY 8-1

In two weeks, your computer will be upgraded to Windows XP Professional. This will be your first exposure to this operating system. You would like to be somewhat prepared for the transition.

Develop a list of off-line research resources where you can explore the vocabulary and basic procedures of running a Windows PC as well as develop an understanding of some of the pros and cons of desktop automation. These resources can include people, bookstores, and broadcast media. Access at least one of these resources, and write a summary of your findings.

LESSON 9

MANIPULATING WINDOWS

OBJECTIVES

Upon completion of this lesson, you should be able to:

- Identify parts of the window.
- Open, move, resize, minimize, maximize, and restore windows.
- Work with menus and menu elements.
- Work with dialog boxes.
- Manipulate multiple windows.

Estimated Time: 1.5 hours

VOCABULARY

Active window
Address Bar
Commands
Command buttons
Default
Dialog box
Menu
Menu bar
Option buttons
Radio buttons
Shortcut keys
Shortcut menu
Standard toolbar
Status bar
Submenu
Title bar
Window

In Lesson 8, you became familiar with the Windows desktop. In this lesson, the various parts of a window are identified. You will learn how to work with a window and how to manage multiple windows. This lesson also describes the use of menus and dialog boxes to issue commands.

Identifying the Parts of a Window

A ***window*** is an on-screen area in which you view program folders, files, and icons. At first sight, a window, such as the one in Figure 9-1, may look rather complicated because you aren't familiar with its symbols and labels. Let's examine the features of the window shown in Figure 9-1. The elements labeled are common to most windows you'll work with in Windows.

FIGURE 9-1
Parts of the window

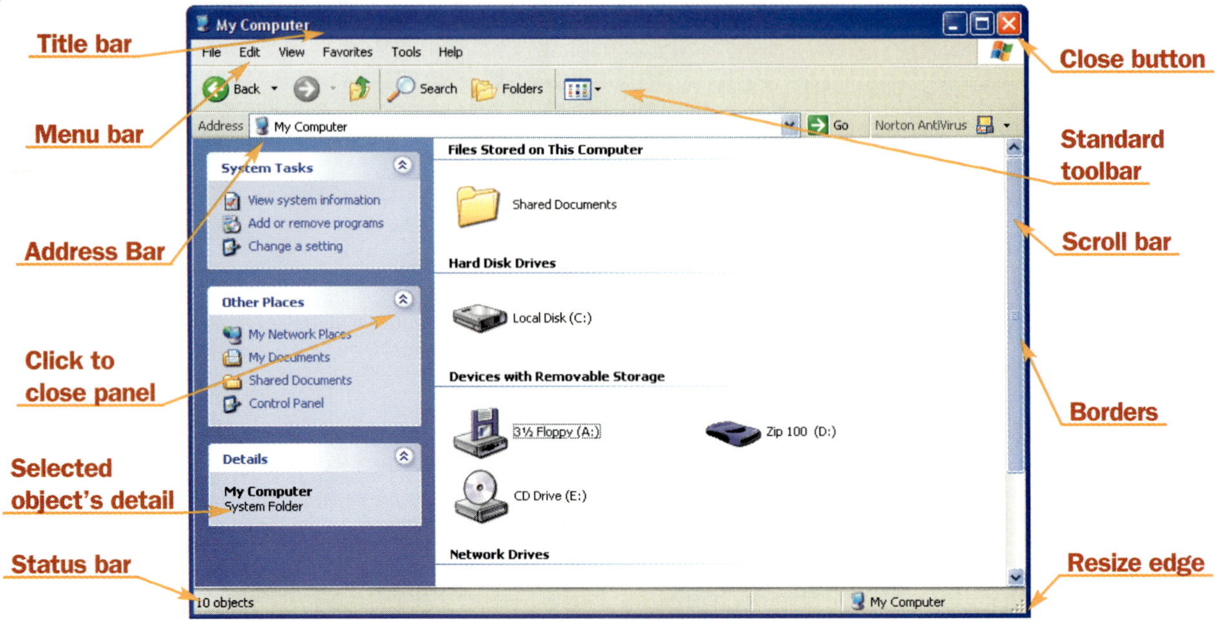

- In Figure 9-1, find the title bar at the top of the window. The ***title bar*** displays the name of the program running in a window—in this case, "My Computer."
- Directly below the title bar is a ***menu bar***, which lists available menus (the specific choices depend on the program you are running). The menu bar in Figure 9-1 lists six choices: File, Edit, View, Favorites, Tools, and Help.
- The ***Standard toolbar*** contains buttons that permit you to access various functions and to issue commands. The toolbar in the My Computer window has buttons for navigating your computer's resources and for changing the display of the objects in the window. If the toolbar is not displayed, open the View menu, select Toolbars, and select Standard Buttons.

> **Did You Know?**
>
> When you load Windows, default settings are in place that may cause your screen to look slightly different from the screens shown in this text's figures.

- The ***Address Bar*** displays the name of the open folder or object. It also permits you to key the address of a Web page quickly without opening your browser. If it is not displayed, open the View menu, select Toolbars, and select Address Bar.
- In the rectangular window are icons, which you learned about in Lesson 8. In this window, the icons represent the parts of your computer system and programs to control the system. The icons in your window may be different from those shown in Figure 9-1. When you select an icon, a description of it displays on the left side of the window.
- The Minimize, Maximize/Restore Down, and Close buttons appear at the upper-right corner of the window on the same line as the title bar. The Minimize button reduces the window to a button on the taskbar, and the Maximize button enlarges the window to fill the screen. Once the window is full-screen size, the Maximize button changes to a Restore Down button, which enables you to restore the window to its previous (smaller) size. The Close button quickly closes the window. (These are shown more clearly in Figure 9-2.)

- The borders are the four lines that define the limits of the window.
- The ***status bar*** provides information on the currently selected object or the task you are performing. As you choose menu items, select window objects, or issue commands, the actions are described on the status bar.
- The resize edge provides a large spot to grab when you want to resize a window without moving the upper-left corner.
- When the window is not large enough to display everything, scroll bars are displayed. Clicking the scroll bar moves (scrolls) the contents of a window so you can view objects that are hidden.

Manipulating Windows

When you open a window, the software determines the window size and location on the desktop. A predetermined software choice or setting is called the ***default***. If you wish, you can change many defaults; for example, you can control the position and size of your windows by changing the default settings.

Moving a Window

At times, you may need to move a window to uncover another window or an object on the desktop. The quickest way is to drag the window by its title bar. If the window is maximized, you must first restore it to its previous size before you move it.

Resizing a Window

If you want greater control over the position of the resized window, resize the window by dragging one of the three types of window borders (horizontal, vertical, or corner), as shown in Figure 9-1.

- If you drag on a horizontal border, you make the window taller or shorter. The pointer changes to a vertical double-headed arrow, indicating that you can drag the border up or down.
- If you drag on a vertical border, you make the window wider or narrower. The pointer changes to a horizontal double-headed arrow, indicating that you can drag the border right or left.
- If you drag from one of the corners, you can change two window dimensions with one movement. The pointer changes to a diagonal double-headed arrow, indicating that you can drag in either a vertical or a horizontal direction.

Minimizing, Maximizing, and Restoring a Window

IC3
-3.2.2-1
-3.2.2-2
-3.2.2-3

Although it is easy to resize a window by dragging its borders, Windows XP also gives you three additional ways to resize a window. The Maximize, Restore Down, and Minimize buttons allow you to change the window's size with one click of the mouse.

Study the resizing buttons shown in Figure 9-2. To use one of these buttons, you simply click it.

- The Minimize button reduces the active window to a button that appears on the taskbar. The window is still available but it is hidden, allowing more room on your desktop.
- The Maximize button enlarges the active window to its maximum size so it fills the entire window—helpful if you need a larger view of one window. Once you select the Maximize button, it is replaced by the Restore Down button.
- When a window has been maximized, clicking the Restore Down button returns the window to its former size.

FIGURE 9-2
Minimize, Maximize, and Restore Down buttons

STEP-BY-STEP 9.1

1. If necessary, start your computer and log on to Windows. Click **Start**, and then click **My Computer** in the pinned list.
2. To set up your views of windows to look like those shown in this text, open the **Tools** menu and select **Folder Options**.
3. In the Tasks section on the General tab, make sure the **Show common tasks in folders** option is selected. In the Browse folders section, make sure the **Open each folder in the same window** option is selected and click **OK**.
4. If the Standard toolbar and Address Bar are not displayed, open the **View** menu, select **Toolbars**, and then select **Standard Buttons**. Display the Toolbars submenu again, and select **Address Bar**.
5. Move the My Computer window until its upper-left corner is 1 inch from the top and 1 inch from the left side of the desktop:
   a. Position the pointer over the title bar, and then press and hold down the mouse button.
   b. Drag the window to the desired position.
6. Resize the window by using the resize edge:
   a. Position the pointer over the lower-right corner border (see Figure 9-1). The pointer should change to a diagonal double-headed arrow.
   b. Drag the border up and to the right to enlarge the window.
7. Click the **Minimize** button. The window minimizes to a button on the taskbar. Did you notice the visual effect of the window minimizing to a button on the taskbar?
8. Click the **My Computer** button on the taskbar to restore the window to its former position on the desktop.

STEP-BY-STEP 9.1 Continued

9. Click the **Maximize** button. The window expands to fill the display, and the Maximize button changes to a Restore Down button.

10. Click the **Restore Down** button to restore the My Computer window to its former size.

11. Resize the My Computer window by dragging a vertical border:
    a. Position the pointer over the left border of the My Computer window. When the pointer is in the correct position, it will change to a horizontal double-headed arrow.
    b. Drag the border to the left until it is at the left edge of the desktop.

12. Leave the My Computer window open for the next Step-by-Step.

Working with Menus

A ***menu*** is a list of options or choices. Every window you open in Windows XP contains a menu bar offering menus. The My Computer window currently on your screen has a menu bar with six menus: File, Edit, View, Favorites, Tools, and Help. Each of these menus, in turn, offers a number of ***commands*** you can issue to perform a task or function.

If all these menu choices appeared on the desktop at the same time, your work area would be too cluttered to be useful. Windows' menus organize the choices so they are out of sight but within reach.

To find out what choices are available on a particular menu, you display the menu by clicking it. When you click the menu name, the menu drops down, as shown in Figure 9-3.

FIGURE 9-3
Menu in the My Computer window

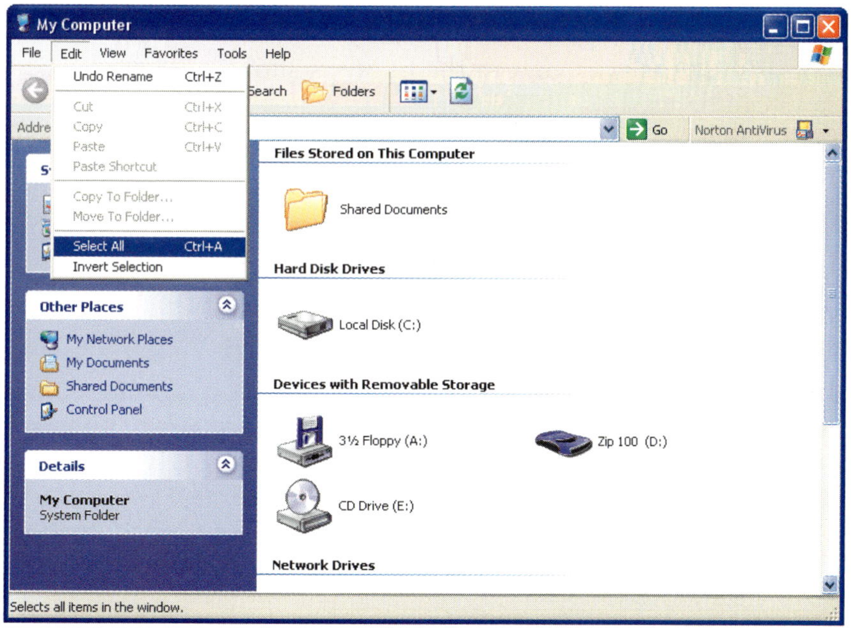

Before you learn how to choose an item from a menu, read the following section to understand more about menus.

Identifying Menu Elements

Look again at Figure 9-3, and notice the differences among the listed options. One is highlighted, some are in black letters, some are in a light color, and some are followed by three periods. All menu choices have one letter underlined. Each visual element has a special meaning, as explained below.

Highlighting

In Figure 9-3, the Select All menu option is highlighted; that is, the words appear in white letters within a dark box. Highlighting indicates that an option is currently selected.

Colors

Not all menu options are available to you all the time. The dark or black letters indicate options that are currently available. Light or grayed letters indicate options that are not available. Look closely at the Edit menu in Figure 9-3. Which options are currently available?

Ellipses

An ellipsis is a series of three periods (...) following some commands. See the Copy To Folder and Move To Folder commands in Figure 9-3, for example. An ellipsis tells you that if you choose this option, a second window or dialog box will be displayed, requesting more information from you. (You'll learn more about dialog boxes later.)

Selection Letters

Each menu option has one underscored letter or number, indicating a keyboard command you can use as an alternative to the mouse. On the keyboard, press the underscored letter or number to choose that command. You can press the selection letters only while the menu is displayed.

Shortcut Keys

Some menu options list ***shortcut keys*** to the right, as shown in Figure 9-3. Unlike selection letters, shortcut keys can be used even when the menu is not displayed. Shortcut keys also offer the advantage of not having to remove your hands from the keyboard while you are keying.

Shortcut keys generally combine the Alt, Ctrl, or Shift key with a letter key. In this text, such combinations are expressed as follows: Alt+X or Ctrl+O. Look again at Figure 9-3. The shortcut keys for the Select All command are Ctrl+A. To execute this command using the shortcut keys, press the Ctrl key and hold it down while pressing the A key. Then release both keys at the same time.

Right-Pointing Arrow

A right-pointing arrow next to a menu option indicates that if you point to that option, another menu will appear with more options. This second menu is a ***submenu***. Windows automatically opens submenus after the pointer has been resting on an option for a short period of time. You can click the option to display the submenu immediately.

Selecting an Option from a Menu

To select an option from a menu, first open the menu. You'll find that as you move the pointer down the menu, the highlight also moves. Stop the pointer on the option you want to choose, and then click. The command you have chosen will execute.

You can also execute a command using the command's shortcut keys, if available. After you have become familiar with commands, you may find it easier to use shortcut keys for the commands you use most often.

> **Hot Tip**
>
> You can use either uppercase or lowercase letters for shortcut keys.

STEP-BY-STEP 9.2

1. Display a topic from the Help menu in the My Computer window:
   a. Click the **Help** menu name in the menu bar.
   b. Select **About Windows** by pressing the **A** key.
   c. Close the Help window by clicking the **Close** button on that window.
2. Select all the icons in the My Computer window:
   a. Click the title bar on the My Computer window to verify that it is selected.
   b. Key the shortcut **Ctrl+A**. All the icons are now selected.
   c. Click somewhere in the blank (white) space in the My Computer window to deselect the icons.
3. Close the My Computer window by clicking its **Close** button.
4. Open the Start menu by clicking the **Start** button.
5. Point to All Programs. Notice how another menu opens overlaying the Start menu.
6. Deselect the submenu (and return to the Start menu) by pointing to the part of the Start menu that is visible to the left of the submenu.
7. Move the pointer to the **Run...** command on the Start menu and click. The Run dialog box appears, as shown in Figure 9-4.

FIGURE 9-4
Run dialog box

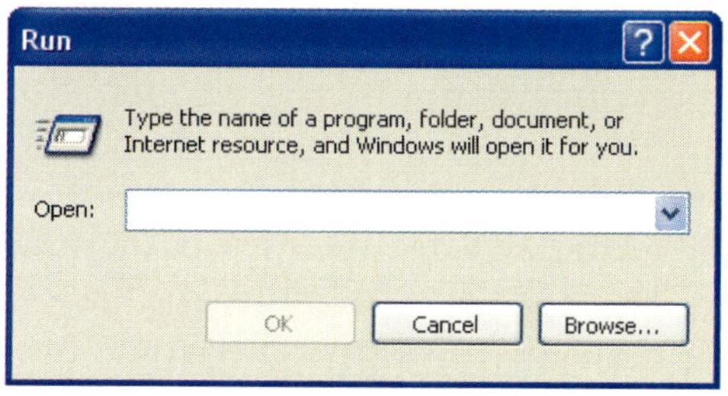

8. Leave the Run dialog box open for the next Step-by-Step.

Working with Dialog Boxes

Some menu options, such as the Run... command you selected in the last Step-by-Step, need more information before they can be executed. For example, before Windows can run (start) a program, it needs to know the program name. The ellipsis (...) that follows such a command signals that need for additional information. You provide the needed information by responding to a ***dialog box***, such as the one shown in Figure 9-4.

A dialog box is itself a window and has some of the same features as a window, such as an identifying title bar and a Close button. But dialog boxes contain a number of other elements that help you give information to your computer.

Let's take a look at the elements you will find most often in dialog boxes.

Buttons

There are two types of buttons: command buttons and option buttons.

- ***Command buttons*** carry out your instructions using the information selected in the dialog box. Command buttons are always rectangular. When you press a command button, the program accepts your instructions. If there is an ellipsis on the button (for example, Browse...), choosing it will open another dialog box. Typical command buttons are Open, Help, Cancel, and OK (see Figure 9-5). The Run dialog box currently on your screen contains three command buttons: OK, Cancel, and Browse....
- ***Option buttons*** (sometimes called ***radio buttons***) allow you to choose one option from a group of options (see Figure 9-5). To change a selection, simply choose a different button.

FIGURE 9-5
Command buttons, option buttons, and text boxes

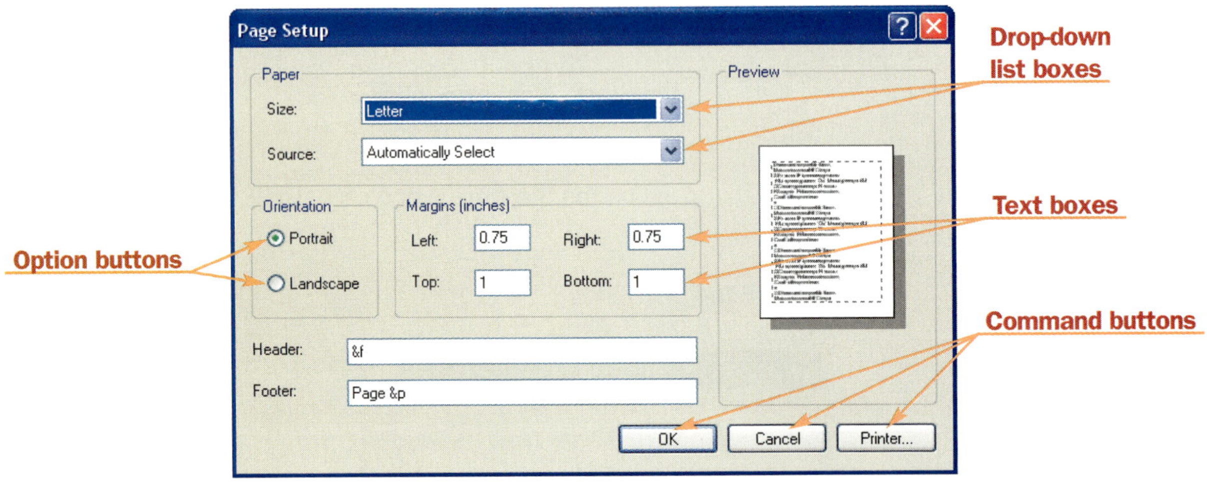

Boxes

There are four types of boxes: text boxes, check boxes, list boxes, and drop-down list boxes. A combo box combines two types of boxes.

Text Boxes

Text boxes allow you to key information in the dialog box. A text box may contain a blinking insertion point to show you where to begin keying, or it may already contain text that you can change as necessary. To change existing text, highlight it by double-clicking it and then key the new text. Figure 9-5 shows several text boxes.

Check Boxes

Check boxes allow you to make choices from a group. However, unlike option buttons, you can check several boxes; that is, you can select a variety of options. Clicking with the mouse selects (✓) or deselects a check box. Figure 9-6 shows two check boxes.

FIGURE 9-6
A dialog box containing several kinds of boxes

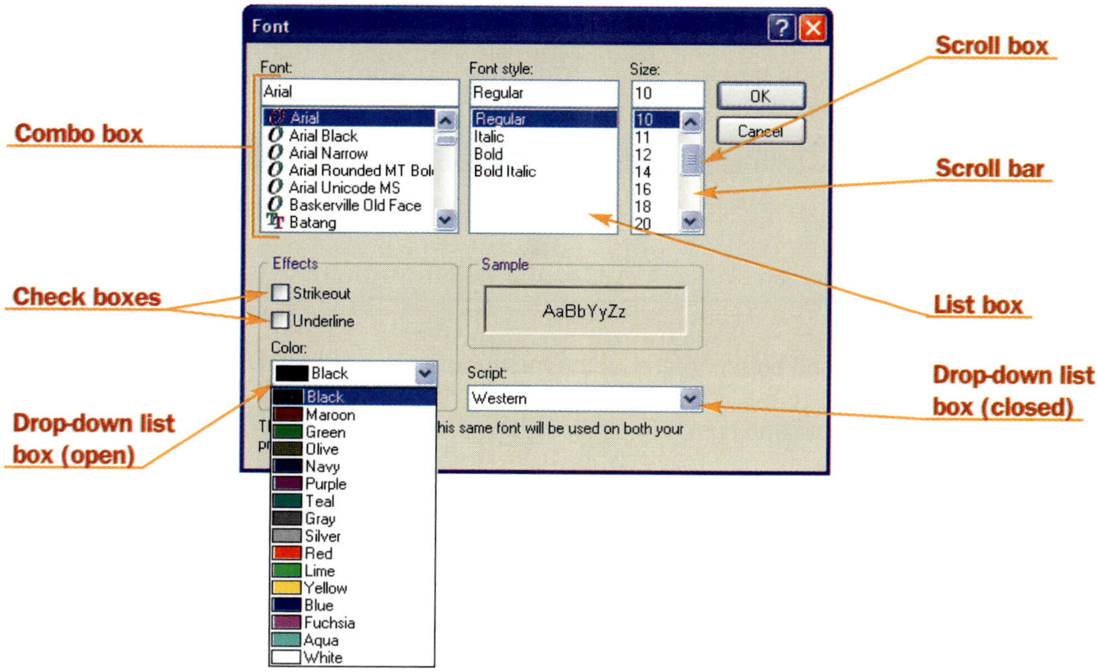

List Boxes

List boxes present a set of options in list format. List boxes are found in both windows and dialog boxes. When the list of options is too lengthy to fit in the box, scroll bars are available to allow you to scroll through the items. Drag the scroll box to move up or down the list. Figure 9-6 shows scroll bars on the Font list box.

Drop-Down List Boxes

Drop-down list boxes display only one option and a special arrow symbol. Click the arrow symbol to reveal the entire list box. Figure 9-6 shows two drop-down list boxes, with one of the lists displayed.

Combo Box

A combo box is a combination of a text box and a list box. You can select from the list or enter your own choice by keying it in the text box part of the combo box. Figure 9-6 shows a combo box.

STEP-BY-STEP 9.3

1. If the Run dialog box on your screen contains text, make sure the text is highlighted.
2. Key your first name in the text box—do not press Enter.
3. Click the **OK** command button. You now see a message box (another form of dialog box) similar to the one illustrated in Figure 9-7. Windows is telling you that it cannot locate the file you asked to run.

FIGURE 9-7
Message box

4. Click the **OK** command button to cancel the message display.
5. Click the **Cancel** command button to close the Run... dialog box.

Managing Multiple Windows

Windows' multitasking ability allows you to perform more than one task at a time. As a result, you may have a lot of windows open on the desktop at one time, and this can be confusing. How can you manage those windows and switch between them? By rearranging the windows on your desktop.

Arranging Windows on the Desktop

Earlier you learned to drag a window to a different location on the desktop. Dragging can be very time-consuming when you have a number of open windows. A shortcut menu hidden on the taskbar makes it easy to arrange open windows. The ***shortcut menu*** contains the options that are most commonly performed from the current window display. While the shortcut menu is handy, not all options are included on it. To access the shortcut menu, point to any portion of the taskbar that does not contain a button and right-click. The shortcut menu shown in Figure 9-8 displays, allowing you to instruct Windows to organize the open windows on your desktop. You can choose one of three different arrangements: Cascade, Tile Horizontally, or Tile Vertically.

FIGURE 9-8
Shortcut menu

- The Cascade Windows option cascades the open windows into a stack with title bars showing; the active window is always in front of the stack, on the top layer.
- The Tile Windows Horizontally option tiles the open windows across the desktop from top to bottom, without overlapping any portion of any window.
- The Tile Windows Vertically option divides the desktop evenly among the open windows and aligns the windows across the screen, left to right, without overlapping any window.

The shortcut menu also contains a Show the Desktop command, which reduces all windows to buttons on the taskbar. You can cancel whichever option you select by using the Undo command. For example, the shortcut menu would list an Undo Cascade option once you selected the Cascade Windows option. Selecting this option restores the display to its previous arrangement.

Switching Between Windows

1-3.2.6-3

When multiple windows are open on your desktop, the one you are working with is called the ***active window***. The active window is easy to recognize because its title bar is a different color or intensity. You can make any open window the active window in one of two ways:

- If any portion of the window you want to work with is visible, click it. It will come to the front and become the active window.
- At any time, press and hold down the Alt key; then press Tab. A small window appears in the center of the display. The window contains icons for all items currently open. This display includes those items open on the desktop as well as those items minimized on the taskbar. If you hold down the Alt key and then press and release Tab, you can cycle through all the icons. A box surrounds the item's icon and a description appears at the bottom of the window as each item is selected. When the one you want is selected, release the Alt key. That item comes to the front and becomes the active window. This is called the fast Alt+Tab method for switching to a different window.

STEP-BY-STEP 9.4

1. Double-click the **Recycle Bin** icon on the desktop to open the Recycle Bin window.
2. Click the **Start** button, then click the **My Computer** option on the pinned list to open the My Computer window.

STEP-BY-STEP 9.4 Continued

3. Click the **Start** button, then click the **Search** option on the pinned list to open the Search Results window.
4. Tile the open windows using the shortcut menu:
   a. Point to a blank area in the taskbar and right-click to display the shortcut menu.
   b. Select the **Tile Windows Vertically** option. The windows are now arranged differently – they are arranged in a tiled format.
5. Right-click on the taskbar and select the **Tile Windows Horizontally** option from the shortcut menu. The windows are rearranged into this tiled format.
6. Right-click on the taskbar and select the **Cascade Windows** option from the shortcut menu. The windows are rearranged into a cascade format.
7. Change the active window:
   a. Click the **My Computer** window. If it wasn't in front, it comes to the foreground and becomes the active window.
   b. Click the **Recycle Bin** window to make it the active window. The Recycle Bin comes to the front as the active window.
   c. Click the **Search Results** window to make it the active window. This window comes to the front as the active window.
8. Undo the cascade format and return the windows to the Tile Windows Horizontally format:
   a. Point to a blank area in the taskbar and right-click to display the shortcut menu.
   b. Select the **Undo Cascade** option. The windows are again arranged in a horizontal tiled format.
9. Right-click on the taskbar and select the **Show the Desktop** option on the shortcut menu to minimize all windows to buttons on the taskbar.
10. Open the Recycle Bin window using the Alt+Tab feature:
    a. Press and hold down the **Alt** key.
    b. Press and release the **Tab** key until the Recycle Bin icon is outlined, then release the **Alt** key.
11. Notice that this window is still in tile format. Display the Recycle Bin window in the cascade format by right-clicking on the taskbar and selecting the **Cascade Windows** option on the shortcut menu.
12. Open the My Computer window and the Search Results window using the **Alt+Tab** feature. Display all the open windows in cascade format.

1-3.3.2-4

13. Close all open windows by clicking their **Close** buttons. If instructed to do so, shut down Windows and your computer.

SUMMARY

In this lesson, you learned:

- Any window with Minimize and Maximize/Restore Down buttons can be resized. A window can also be resized by dragging one of its borders or corners. The resize tab provides a large spot to grab when you want to resize a window.
- A menu is a list of options or choices. You make selections from a menu by pointing at and clicking an option or using the up or down arrow keys.
- On a menu, a highlighted option (white letters within a dark box) indicates that this option is currently selected, and light or grayed letters (as opposed to black or dark) mean that an option is not available.
- A series of three periods (...), called an ellipsis, following a command tells you that if you choose this option, a dialog box will open to request more information.
- A dialog box is a window. In it you will find command buttons and option buttons. Command buttons are rectangular and, as their name clearly indicates, clicking a command button executes a command. Option buttons (also known as radio buttons) let you choose one option from a group of options.
- A dialog box may also have check boxes, list boxes, text boxes, and drop-down list boxes, each of which allows you to make selections or key information.
- Windows is able to multitask (do more than one task at a time). This means more than one window can be open at a time. The windows can be arranged on the desktop in a cascade, horizontally tiled, or vertically tiled format. Click any window or use Alt+Tab to bring a desired window to the front and make it the active window.

VOCABULARY *Review*

Define the following terms:

Active window	Menu	Standard toolbar
Address Bar	Menu bar	Status bar
Commands	Option buttons	Submenu
Command buttons	Radio buttons	Title bar
Default	Shortcut keys	Window
Dialog box	Shortcut menu	

REVIEW *Questions*

MATCHING

Match the correct term in Column 2 to its description in Column 1.

	Column 1		Column 2
___	**1.** A list of options or choices	**A.**	option buttons
___	**2.** A predetermined choice made by the software	**B.**	default
___	**3.** The window in which you are presently working	**C.**	menu
___	**4.** In a dialog box, the buttons that carry out your instructions using the information selected	**D.**	command buttons
___	**5.** In a dialog box, the buttons that represent a group of choices from which you can select one	**E.**	active window

MULTIPLE CHOICE

Select the best response for each of the following statements and write the answers in the lines provided.

1. The list of choices on a Windows menu bar _________.
   A. is the same for all programs
   B. will vary according to the program
   C. displays as icons
   D. None of the above

2. Shortcut keys _________.
   A. can be used even when the menu is not displayed
   B. are keystrokes that must be used in place of the mouse
   C. always use the Alt key
   D. cannot be used unless the menu is displayed

3. When a window is not large enough to display everything, _________.
   A. you can click the Restore button to enlarge it
   B. the status bar will indicate there is more to be displayed
   C. you should drag its title bar to resize it
   D. scroll bars will be displayed

4. The visual element that indicates whether a menu option is available is _________.
   A. an ellipsis
   B. the color of the option
   C. an underscored letter
   D. highlighting

5. If additional information is needed before a command can be executed, Windows displays a __________.
   A. message box
   B. dialog box
   C. control-menu box
   D. prompt box

CRITICAL *Thinking*

SCANS ACTIVITY 9-1

The local library has computers available with Windows XP Professional installed. You will be using one of these computers but can only spend one hour on it. Develop a strategy to maximize your time. Using the information from Lessons 1 and 2 of this unit, create a priority list, ranking the most important features to explore and skills to practice.

LESSON 10

GETTING HELP

OBJECTIVES

Upon completion of this lesson, you should be able to:

- Start the Windows Help and Support system.
- Locate help topics using the Help and Support Center, the Index, and the Search box.
- Add topics to and delete topics from a Favorites list.
- Print a Help topic.
- Use the "What's This?" feature.
- Use Window's Help System.
- Access help inside a Windows XP application program.

Estimated Time: 1.5 hours

VOCABULARY

Help Viewer
Link
Newsgroup
Pop-up
Scroll
Search qualifiers
Shortcut button
What's This?

Windows Help and Support System

IC³ 1-3.2.7-4

If you need assistance while working in Windows XP, use Windows' built-in Help and Support system. The Help and Support system includes both local help that relies on files on your computer for answers to many of your questions and Web help that utilizes Microsoft's online help resource. In this lesson, you will learn to use Windows Help and Support system.

There are many ways you can get help while working in Windows XP and XP applications. This lesson focuses on the three most common ways:

1. Select the Help and Support option from the Start menu.
2. Press F1 whenever you see Help on a menu bar (almost every menu bar has this item).
3. Select Help whenever you see a Help command button or Help as an item on a menu.

Using the Help and Support Center

One of the easiest ways to get Windows XP help is from the Start menu. The Start menu is available to you no matter what you are doing in Windows XP. If the Start button is not visible on-screen, the Start menu will display as soon as you press the Windows key on your keyboard (see Figure 10-1).

FIGURE 10-1
Start menu

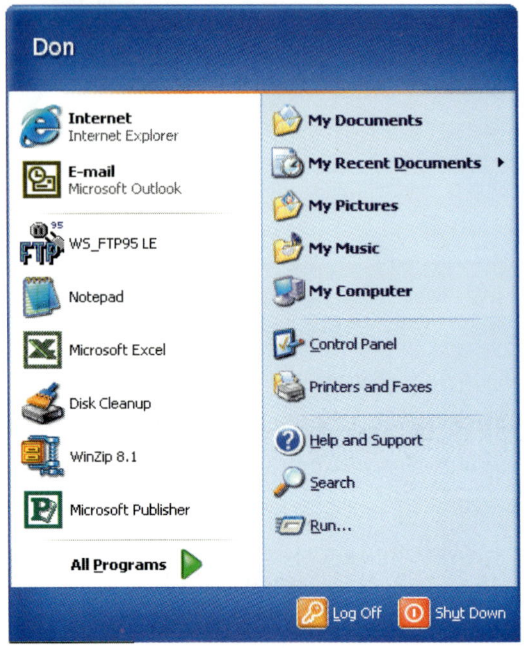

Selecting the Help and Support option from the Start menu opens the Help and Support Center window. The Help and Support Center offers support in four categories, as shown in Figure 10-2.

FIGURE 10-2
Help and Support Center window

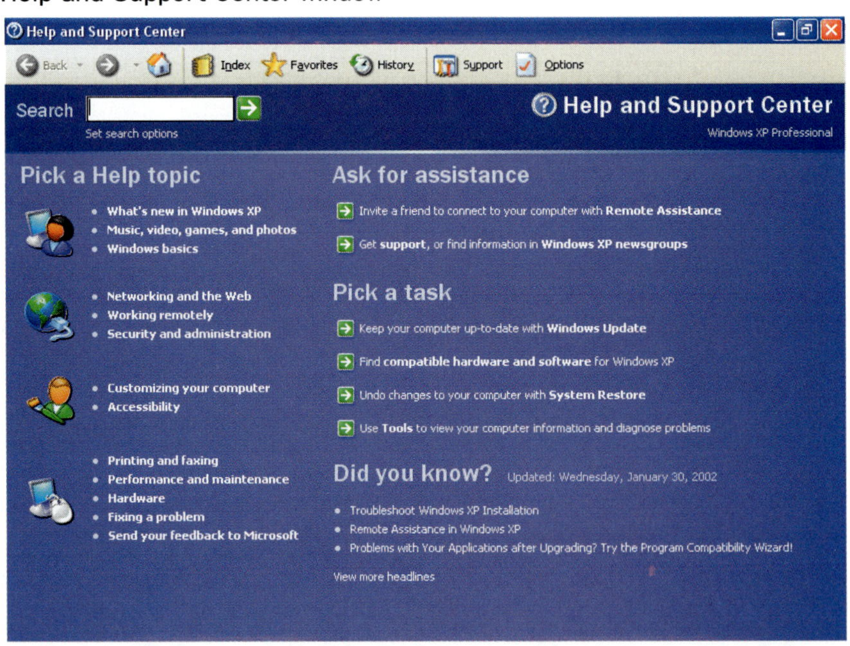

1-3.2.7-3
1-3.2.7-5

- *Pick a Help topic* contains general information about a topic. For example, clicking What's new in Windows XP displays a list of resources that you can use to learn about Windows XP features.

- *Ask for assistance* provides two ways for getting outside help. The Remote Assistance option allows you to invite someone to help you. Using an Internet connection, anyone running Windows XP can view your screen and, with your permission, work on your computer. The Support option enables you to get help from Microsoft, from product experts, or to discuss your questions with other Windows XP users online.
- *Pick a task* provides access to the latest updates for your computer's operating system, hardware, and software. You can also use this category to find Windows XP–compatible hardware and software, restore your computer to a previous working state, or access helpful tools to keep your computer running smoothly.
- *Did You Know?* displays a tip on using Windows XP. Each time the Help and Support Center is opened, the tip that is displayed is selected at random from a group of tips, so be sure to read the tip each time you access the Help and Support Center.

The Help and Support Center is designed to look and work much like a Web page. When you point to an underlined topic, the pointer changes to a hand with the index finger pointing to the topic or word. This indicates that the topic is actually a ***link***. When you click a link, the Help and Support entry is displayed in the right pane. For example, if you click the *Fixing a Problem* link in the Pick a Help topic menu (see Figure 10-2), the Help and Support entry shown in Figure 10-3 will be displayed in the right pane. Notice the various links for this topic in the left pane.

FIGURE 10-3
Displaying a Help topic

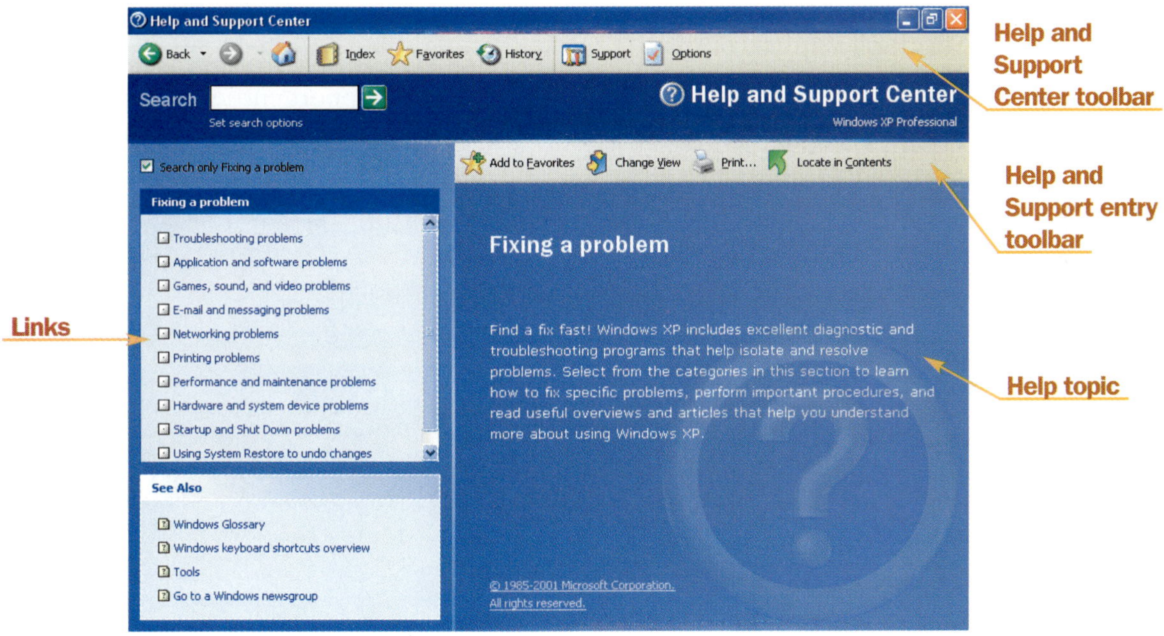

STEP-BY-STEP 10.1

1-3.2.7-1
1-3.2.7-2

1. Start Windows, if necessary. Select the **Help and Support** option on the Start menu.

2. Maximize the Help and Support Center window, if necessary.

3. Click the **Fixing a problem** link under the Pick a Help topic menu to display the Help and Support entry, as shown in Figure 10-3.

1-3.2.7-3
1-3.2.7-4

4. Read the choices in the listing in the left pane, and then click the **Application and software problems** link to display the Help and Support entry for this topic in the right pane. Notice that as you point on the topic, it becomes underlined, indicating that it is a link. Also notice that after you click, the topic is highlighted, indicating that the Help and Support entry for this link is displayed in the right pane.

5. Read the choices for this Help and Support entry in the right pane, and then click **Print Troubleshooter** to display its Help and Support entry. Leave this window open for the next Step-by-Step.

Using the Help and Support Toolbar

Look closely at the Help and Support Center window shown in Figure 10-3. Notice the two toolbars: one at the top of the Help and Support Center window and one above the Help and Support entry displayed in the right pane. The toolbar buttons let you navigate the Help and Support Center and print Help and Support entries. Each button's function is explained below:

The Help and Support Center Toolbar

- Clicking the Back button returns you to previous Help and Support entries. Clicking this button once takes you to the most recent entry; clicking again takes you to the next most recent entry.
- Clicking the Forward button (the button to the right of the Back button) takes you to the next Help topic in the previously displayed sequence of topics.
- Clicking the Home button (the house icon) takes you to the Help and Support Center home page.
- Clicking the Index button displays the Help and Support Center index. When you know exactly what you're looking for, the index provides you with a fast, easy way to locate topics and resources. You will learn more about the Help and Support Center index later in this lesson.
- Clicking the Favorites button displays a list of topics that you've "bookmarked" because you refer to them often. Once a topic is bookmarked, you can quickly and easily access it.
- Clicking the History button displays a list of topics you've displayed in the Help and Support entry pane during the current help session.
- Clicking the Support button displays the online support and information page. This page contains several links that will take you to various areas on Microsoft's Web site.
- Clicking the Options button displays different options you can use to customize the Help and Support Center, set search options to find help and information, install Windows help, and share Windows help with others.

The Help and Support Entry Toolbar

- Clicking the Add to Favorites button bookmarks the currently displayed topic. The topic is placed on the Favorites list that is displayed when you click the Favorites button on the Help and Support Center's toolbar.
- Clicking the Change View button changes the number of panes displayed in the Help and support window. Clicking the Change View button when the Help and Support window is fully open hides the left pane. Clicking the Change View button when the left pane is hidden displays the left pane.
- Clicking the Print button prints a copy of the currently displayed topic.
- Clicking the Locate in Contents button (which is only available within Search and Index) displays in the left pane all of the table of contents' topics in which the selected topic is discussed.

STEP-BY-STEP 10.2

1. Click the **Back** button on the Help and Support Center toolbar twice to return to the Fixing a problem help topic.
2. Click the **Back** button again to return to the Help and Support Center home page.
3. Click the **Forward** button once. Notice that you are back to the Fixing a problem topic.
4. Click the **Home** button to return to the Help and Support Center home page.
5. Click the **Fixing a problem** link, and then click the **Printing problems** link in the left pane.
6. Click the **Install new or updated printer drivers** link in the right pane. Leave this window open for the next Step-by-Step.

Printing a Help Topic

When you are working with a new Windows program or feature, you may find it handy to have a hard copy (printout) of selected Help topics so you don't have to keep the Help and Support Center open while you are learning.

You can print a chosen topic by clicking the Print button on the Help and Support entry toolbar. A Print dialog box, similar to that shown in Figure 10-4, opens. (Your screen will appear different based upon the printer(s) that is hooked up to your system.) You will learn more about the options in the Print dialog box in later lessons. For now, you only need to know how to verify that your computer is connected to the appropriate printer (as indicated in the Select Printer section of the dialog box). If you want to print the topic, you click the Print button.

FIGURE 10-4
Print dialog box

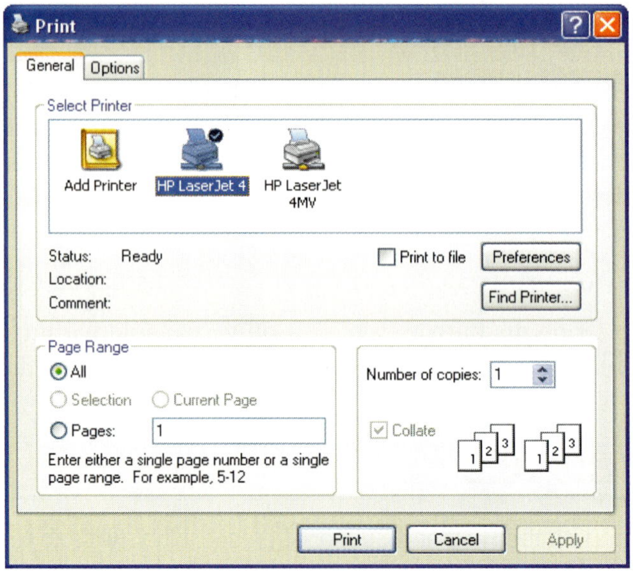

You can also print the topic displayed in the right pane of the Help and Support window by right-clicking the entry and then selecting Print on the shortcut menu.

STEP-BY-STEP 10.3

In order to complete this Step-by-Step, you must have a printer connected to your computer system. If you are sharing a printer, be sure you have access to the printer and be sure it is online. If you do not know how to access your printer, ask for assistance before you begin.

1. Verify that the Install new or updated printer drivers entry is displayed in the Help and Support Center right pane.
2. Click the **Print** button.
3. Make sure you are connected to the appropriate printer, and click **Print** in the Print dialog box. Leave this window open for the next Step-by-Step.

Help and Support Entry Objects

Look carefully at the Help and Support entry shown in Figure 10-5. Notice the format of the Printer and Faxes item in instruction 1 in the Help and Support entry pane. As you have learned, the underlining indicates that it is a link. The color of the link indicates its status: A link that has not been opened is one color (often blue), and a link that has been jumped to in the past is another color (often red). The color of the links is controlled by the settings in your system.

FIGURE 10-5
Links, shortcuts, and subtopics

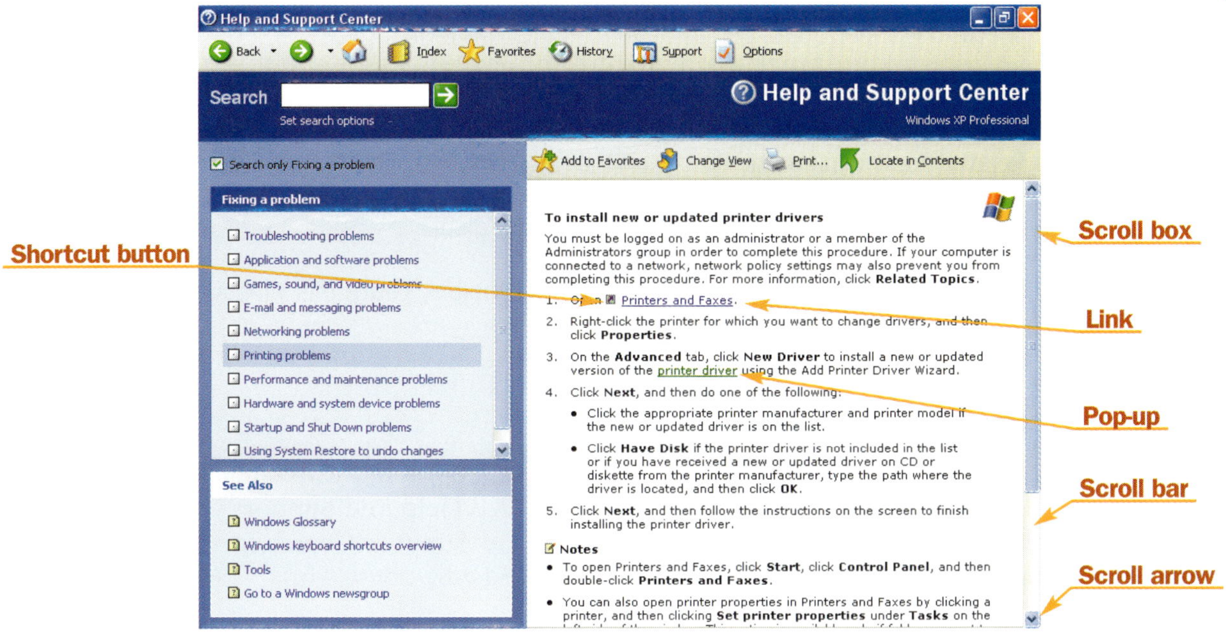

Look again at Figure 10-5. Do you see the small button with an arrow pointing upward in front of the Printers and Faxes link? This identifies the link as a ***shortcut button***. In addition to text, many Help and Support entries contain one or more such buttons, each of which is a shortcut for performing an action associated with the topic you are viewing. For example, clicking the shortcut button in front of the Printers and Faxes link opens the Printers and Faxes window in which you can install new printers, set the default printer, and so on.

A Help and Support entry might contain a word or term that is formatted as a link but in a different color, such as green. This is known as a ***pop-up***. The words printer driver in Figure 10-5 are an example of this type of link.

Notice the Related Topics link at the bottom of the window (you may need to scroll down to see it). Clicking this link will display a menu of related topics. You can jump to any one of the topics on the menu by clicking on it.

When a window is too small to show all the text of an entry, scroll bars are displayed so you can ***scroll*** the text into view. Scroll bars are especially important for dialog boxes and other windows that cannot be resized by dragging on the borders or clicking the Maximize button.

To scroll text, click the up or the down scroll arrow. Clicking the up arrow moves the text downward; clicking the down arrow moves text upward. Each time you click, the text scrolls one line in the direction you've chosen. If you hold down the mouse button instead of clicking, the text continues to scroll.

The scroll bar also has a scroll box. You can move through the text quickly by dragging the scroll box to a position that corresponds to the approximate location you want to view. For example, to view the middle of the text, move the scroll box to the middle of the scroll bar.

STEP-BY-STEP 10.4

1. Click the **printer driver** pop-up to display a definition for the term.

1-3.2.7-5 2. Read the definition, and then click anywhere to close the box.

3. Click the **Related Topics** link at the bottom of the page (you may have to scroll to bring it into view).

4. Click the **Printer drivers overview** item on the menu that displays.

5. Click the **Home** button on the Help and Support Center toolbar. Leave this window open for the next Step-by-Step.

Using the Help Index

You use the Help Index to search for information. Like a book index, the Help Index provides an alphabetical listing of topics covered in the Windows XP Help and Support system. To access the index, simply click the Index button on the Help and Support Center toolbar to bring an alphabetical listing of topics into view, as shown in Figure 10-6.

FIGURE 10-6
Help Index

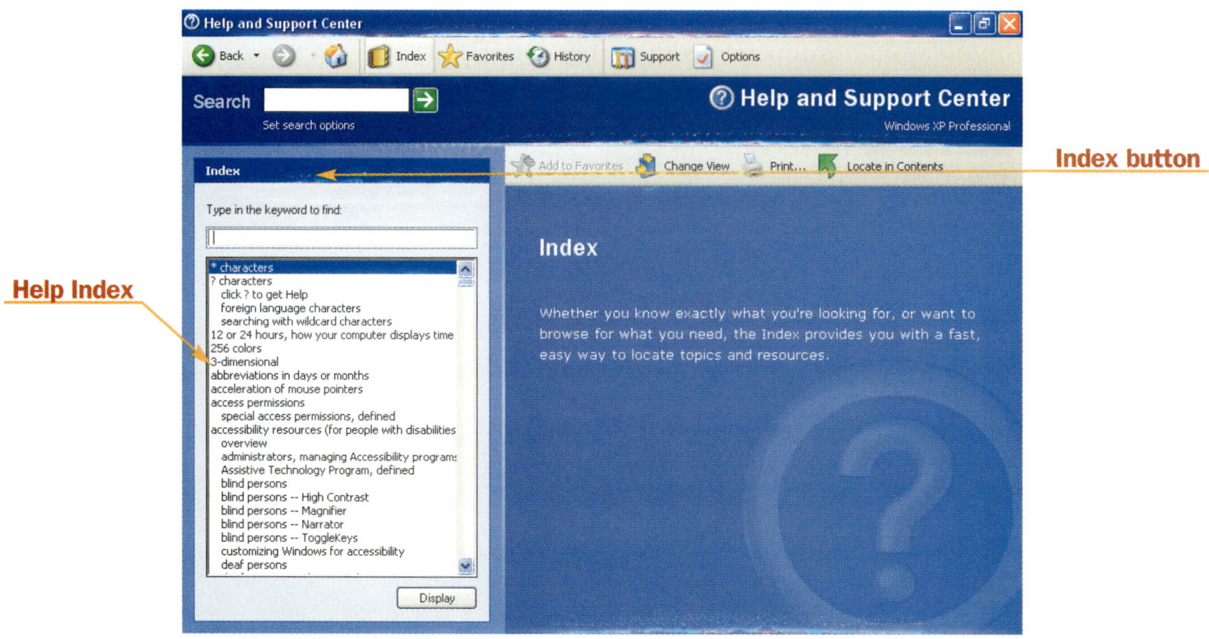

If you're the first user of the Help Index, a message box will display telling you that the Help Wizard is preparing the Help system's alphabetical index. To find a topic using the Index, key a word or a phrase in the text box (or select one from the list) and then click the Display button at the bottom of the pane. When you start keying a word in the text box, the list automatically scrolls to any matching or closely matching words in the index. You can also use the scroll bars to locate a word or feature.

STEP-BY-STEP 10.5

1. Click the **Index** button on the Help and Support Center toolbar.

2. Key the word **creating** in the Type in the keyword to find text box, but do not press Enter. The highlight moves to the first entry that matches the word you keyed.

3. Click the **Display** button. The Help and Support entry for the topic displays in the right pane. Read through the entry.

4. Highlight the word **creating** in the Index text box, and then key **printing**.

5. Double-click the **banner pages** item under the key word *printing*.

6. Click **Separator pages** in the Topics Found window, and then click the **Display** button.

7. Read through the entry; then click the **Home** button on the Help and Support Center toolbar. Leave this window open for the next Step-by-Step.

Using the Search Feature

Have you ever tried to locate a specific topic in an index when you weren't quite sure of the precise wording? If so, you probably tried a number of different words or phrases until you guessed the correct one. In the Windows XP Help and Support system, the Search box enables you to search for specific words and phrases within a Help topic, select among listings, and display the topics.

The Search box looks like that shown in Figure 10-7. In the search box, you key the word or phrase for which you want to find more information. The Search feature is case-sensitive. Click the Start searching arrow (the green arrow to the right of the Search box) to display all the Help and Support entries that contain the word or phrase. Click a topic to display the Help and Support entry in the right pane.

FIGURE 10-7
Search box

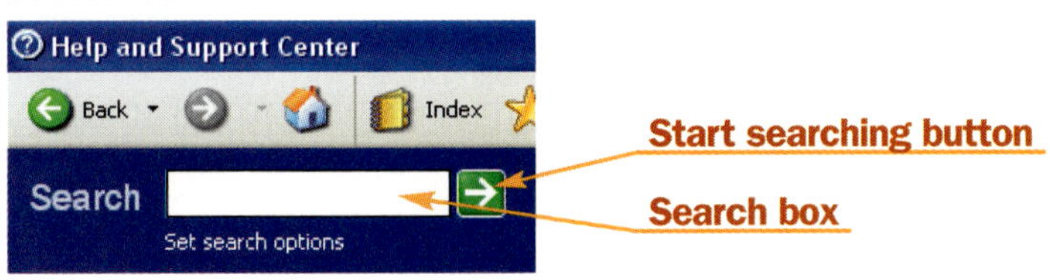

STEP-BY-STEP 10.6

1. Click in the **Search** box, key the word **schedule**, and then click the **Start searching** button. 

2. The Help system finds a number of entries that contain the word *schedule* or that have the word *schedule* in the entry text. Click **Schedule a new task** to display the entry in the right pane.

3. Read through the entry. Notice how the occurrences of the word *schedule* in the right pane are highlighted to show you where the term is used. Leave this window open for the next Step-by-Step.

Using Search Qualifiers

You can also use ***search qualifiers*** to refine or narrow your search. Following are the qualifiers you can use:

- AND to search for more than one word. This will find Help and Support entries that contain all the terms specified.
- NEAR to search for a string of text in which one term is within a certain number of words from another term.
- OR to search for Help and Support entries that contain one term or another.
- NOT to exclude any topic containing a specified term.

You key the qualifiers as part of the text you enter in the Search box. For example, if you want to display all the Help and Support topics containing the word *schedule* except for those topics that also contain the word *backup*, you would key *schedule NOT backup* in the Search box.

STEP-BY-STEP 10.7

1. The search results for the word *schedule* should still be displayed. Count the number of topics that are displayed under the Pick a task heading in the list box.
2. Click in the **Search** box after the word *schedule*, press the spacebar, and key **NOT backup**.
3. Click the **Start searching** button. Notice that fewer topics are now listed under the Pick a task heading.
4. Click in the **Search** box after the word *backup*, press the spacebar, and key **AND new**.
5. Click the **Start searching** button. Notice that even fewer topics are now listed.
6. Click the **Home** button. Leave this window open for the next Step-by-Step.

Bookmarking Favorite Topics

Just as you use bookmarks to mark places in printed matter, you can place electronic bookmarks in the Windows Help and Support system to locate frequently used topics quickly and easily. For example, if you often look up the same procedures in a particular application, you could create a bookmark for that topic instead of using the Index or Search functions to locate it.

Creating a bookmark is simple. First, display the Help topic you wish to bookmark in the right pane and click the Add to Favorites button on the Help and Support entry toolbar. A message window similar to the one shown in Figure 10-8 will display, informing you that the page has been added to your Favorites list.

FIGURE 10-8
Message window informing you that a page has been added to your Favorites list

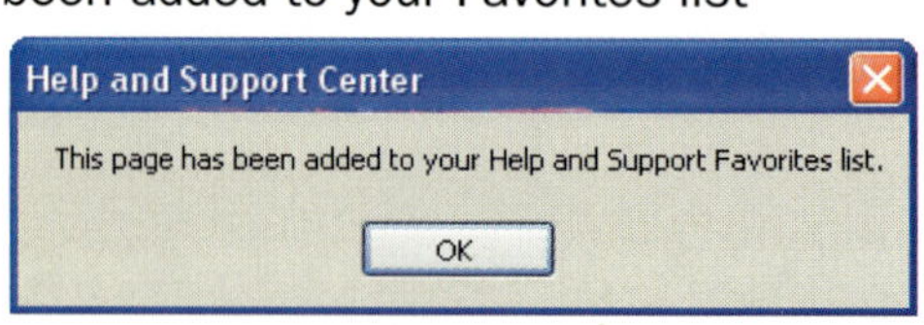

When you wish to display one of your bookmarked pages, click the Favorites button on the Help and Support Center toolbar to display the Favorites list, as shown in Figure 10-9; then double-click the desired topic in the list to display the page. If you want to remove a bookmark, click once on the entry, then click the Remove button at the bottom of the Favorites list window.

FIGURE 10-9
Favorites list

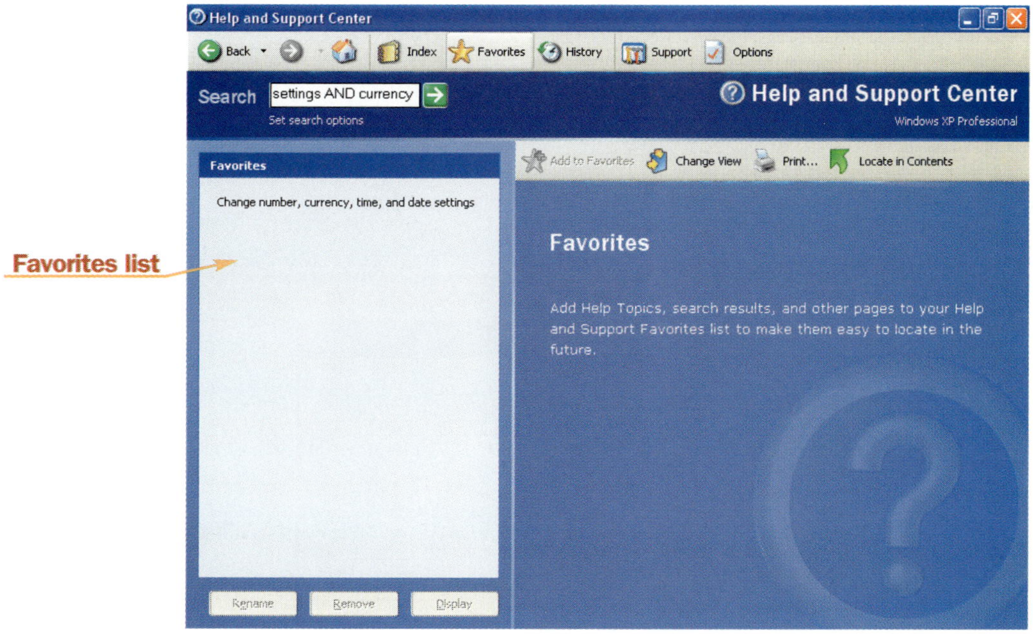

STEP-BY-STEP 10.8

1. Click three times rapidly in the Search box to select all the text.
2. Key **settings AND currency** in the Search box, and click the **Start searching** button.
3. Click the **Change number, currency, time, and date settings** item.
4. Click the **Add to Favorites** button on the Help and Support entry toolbar, then click **OK** on the message window.
5. Click the **Favorites** button on the Help and Support Center toolbar to display the Favorites list.
6. Double-click the **Change number, currency, time, and date settings** item in the Favorites listing to display the topic.
7. Verify that the Change number, currency, time, and date settings bookmark is highlighted, and then click the **Remove** button. Leave this window open for the next Step-by-Step.

Getting Help on a Specific Item

All dialog boxes and some windows have their own special Help feature called ***What's This?*** This feature employs a special pointer with which you select any option in a dialog box. Thus, "What's This?" means "What's this option?"

Here's how it works: Look at Figure 10-10. Do you see the ? icon in the upper-right corner of the dialog box? When you select the ? icon, a large question mark attaches to the mouse pointer. With this question mark pointer, you can click any option in the dialog box or window. When you click an option, a box displays with a short description of the item you selected. The mouse pointer returns to its normal arrow shape after displaying a description.

You can also right-click any option in a dialog box to display a small box labeled What's This? Click this box to display a description of the option that you right-clicked.

FIGURE 10-10
The What's This? feature

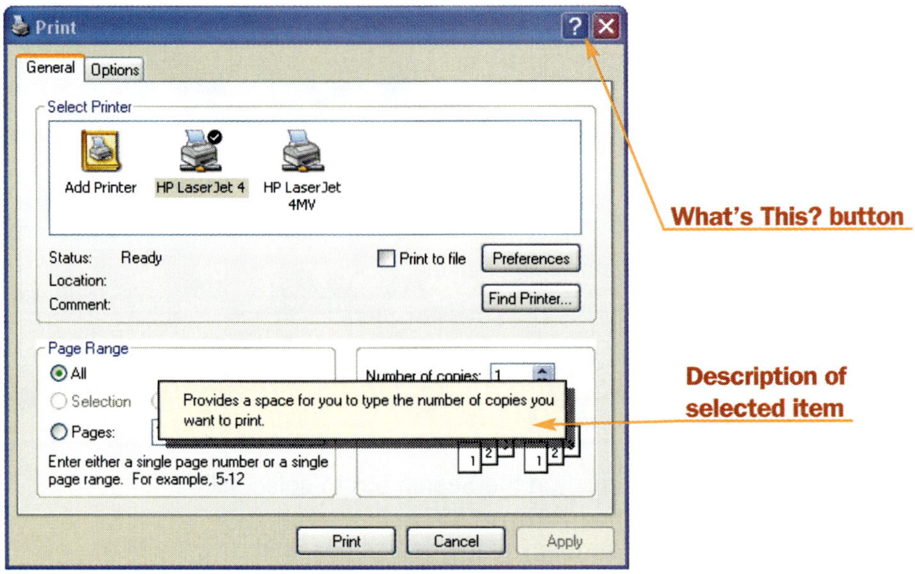

STEP-BY-STEP 10.9

1. Click the **Print** button on the Help and Support entry toolbar. The Print dialog box opens.
2. Click the **?** icon in the upper-right corner of the dialog box. The mouse pointer becomes an arrow with a large question mark beside it.
3. Click the **Number of copies** option to display a description of this option.
4. Click anywhere to close the description box. Click **Cancel** to close the Print dialog box.
5. Close the Windows Help system by clicking the **Close** button on the Help and Support Center title bar.

Using Windows XP Application Help System

Selecting the Help option and then the Help Topics menu item from any Windows XP application menu displays the ***Help Viewer*** for that program. For example, when you click Help in the Windows Paint program, you see the Help Viewer window shown in Figure 10-11. Like the Help and Support Center, an application's Help Viewer contains two panes when fully opened, as shown in Figure 10-11.

FIGURE 10-11
Windows Paint program's Help Viewer

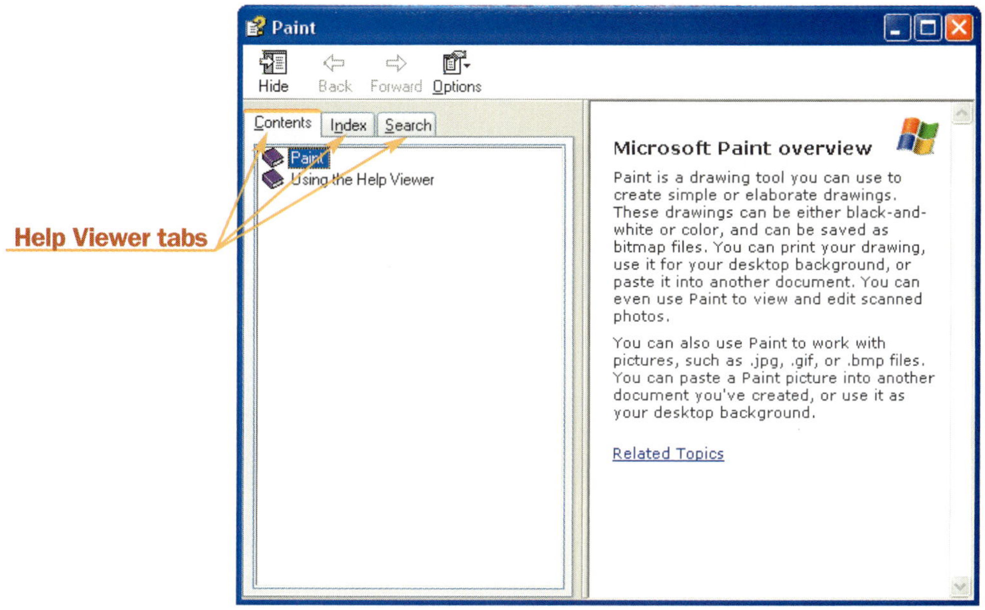

The three tabs in the left pane of the Help Viewer let you locate and navigate Help topics in different ways.

- The Contents tab groups topics into general categories. The Contents tab permits you to browse an application's Help system's table of contents to locate a topic. Each main topic has a book icon next to it. When you click a book icon, a list of topics within that main topic displays. Each of these topics represents a link to relevant information.
- The Index tab provides an alphabetical listing of key words and terms. This tab functions in a manner similar to the Index button on the Help and Support Center toolbar, except the available topics are specific to the application you are using.
- The Search tab lets you search the Help topics for a term or feature. This tab functions in a manner similar to the way the Search box functions in the Help and Support Center. Again, the available help topics are specific to the application you are using.

The Application Help Toolbar

Notice the toolbar buttons in the Window's Paint Help window shown in Figure 10-11. You are already familiar with the Forward and Backward buttons. The function of two new buttons, Hide and Options, is explained next.

- Clicking the Hide button hides the left pane of the Applications Help Viewer. When the left pane is hidden, the Hide button turns into a Show button. Clicking the Show button displays the left pane again.
- Clicking the Options button displays a menu with options to hide or display the left pane of the application's Help Viewer, to navigate displayed topics, and to print help entries.

STEP-BY-STEP 10.10

1. Click the **Start** button, select **All Programs**, select **Accessories**, and then select **Notepad** from the menu. The Windows Notepad program opens, as shown in Figure 10-12.

FIGURE 10-12
Windows Notepad program window

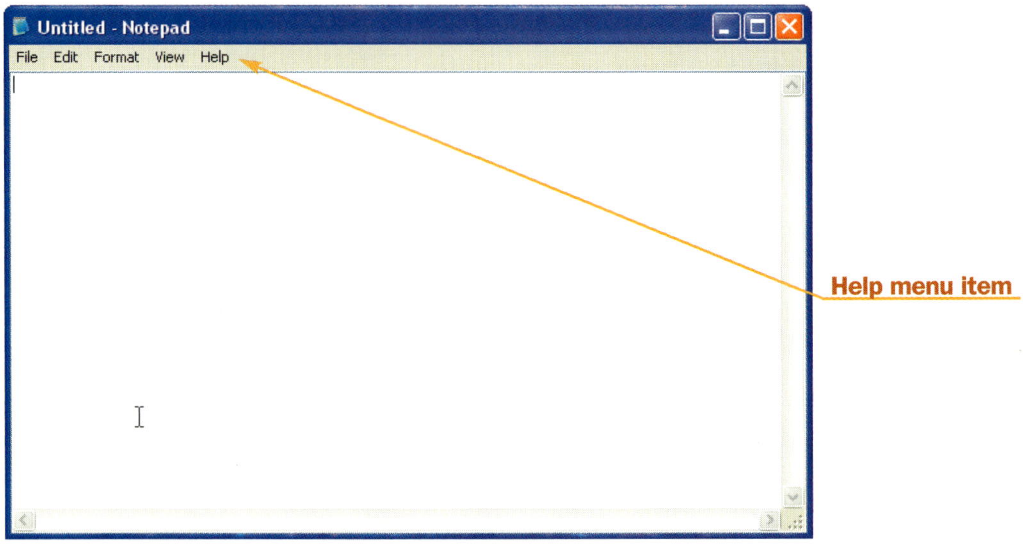

2. Click **Help** on the Menu bar, then select the **Help Topics** option to open Notepad's Help Viewer.
3. Click the **Show** button, if necessary, to display the navigation pane.
4. Click the **Contents** tab, if necessary, to bring it to the front.
5. Click the **Notepad** book icon to display its subtopics.
6. Click the **Find specific characters or words** topic. The topic entry is displayed in the Help Viewer's right pane.
7. Click the **Wrap text to the window size** topic in the navigation page. The new topic replaces the old topic in the Help Viewer's right pane.
8. Click the **Notepad** book icon in the navigation pane to close the book.

STEP-BY-STEP 10.10 Continued

9. Close the Notepad program Help system by clicking the **Close** button on Notepad's Help Viewer's title bar.

10. Close Notepad by clicking the **Close** button on the title bar. If instructed, shut down Windows and your computer.

Using Windows XP Remote Assistance

Windows XP, through the Support page (shown in Figure 10-13) offers several ways for getting remote assistance if your computer has a connection to the Internet. The Support page can be accessed in several ways.

- Click the Support button on the Help and Support Center toolbar. This button is always available no matter where you are in the Help and Support Center.
- Click the *Get support*, or *find information in Windows XP newsgroups* link in the Ask for assistance section on the Help and Support Center's home page.
- Click the *Invite a friend to connect to your computer with Remote Assistance* link in the Ask for assistance section on the Help and Support Center's home page. The page that opens as a result of choosing this option varies slightly from that shown in Figure 10-13 in that you are taken directly to the Remote Assistance options—which are shown in the right pane instead of Welcome to Support.

FIGURE 10-13
Support options page

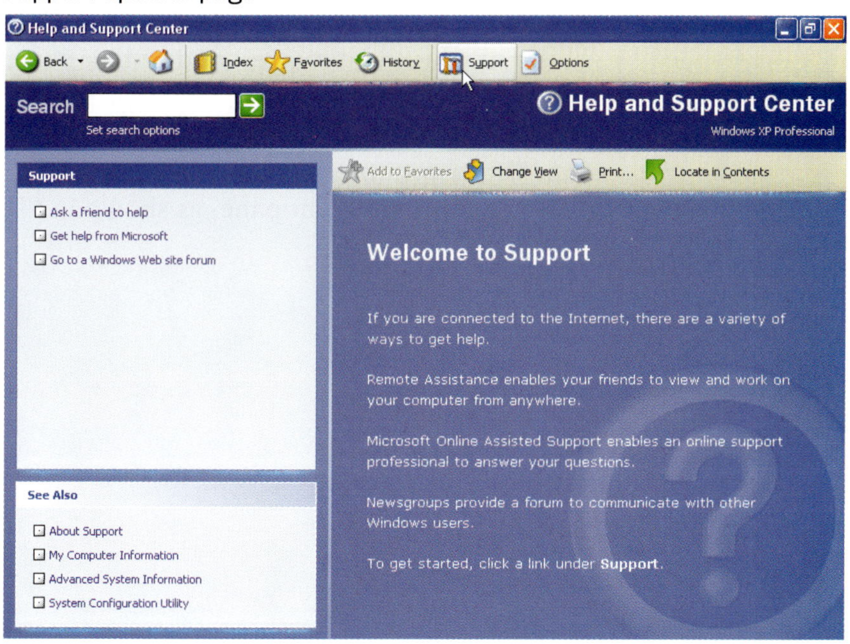

Getting Assistance Online

Some individuals better understand the answer to a question by watching a live demonstration. Remote Assistance is a convenient way for someone you know to connect to your computer from another computer running Windows XP, chat with you, and observe your computer screen as you work. With your permission, you can receive the remote user's keystrokes as if he or she were keying on your keyboard. In this way, you are able to watch the remote user demonstrate the solution to your problem.

The Remote Assistance option can also be used to let a technician diagnose a problem you are experiencing with your computer and correct the problem without coming to your home or office. Of course, you would not use Remote Assistance in this way without knowing the other person.

Following are the general steps you would go through when using the Remote Assistance:

- Send the remote user an e-mail invitation to connect to your system.
- Open the Help and Support Center.
- Click the *Invite a friend to connect to your computer with Remote Assistance* link in the Ask for assistance group.
- Click the link labeled *Invite someone to help you.*
- After your remote user responds to your invitation and clicks the appropriate link on the remote computer, Windows XP will connect your computer to your remote user's computer and give control of your computer to the remote user. You will be able to control your computer as well as communicate with the remote user during the session using the pop-up chat window.

Getting Help from Windows XP Newsgroups

Microsoft provides a number of newsgroups that give you access to a community of users and experts who may be able to answer your questions. A ***newsgroup*** is an online discussion group in which participants with common interests exchange messages. A typical newsgroup consists of hundreds of messages arranged by subject to which you can respond or that you can read.

The *Get support, or find information in Windows XP newsgroup* link on the Help and Support Center home page takes you to the Windows XP Support page (shown in Figure 10-13). You then click *Go to a Windows Web site forum* in the Support topics section (left pane). The Windows Newsgroups information will appear in the right pane, as shown in Figure 10-14.

FIGURE 10-14
Windows XP Newsgroup page

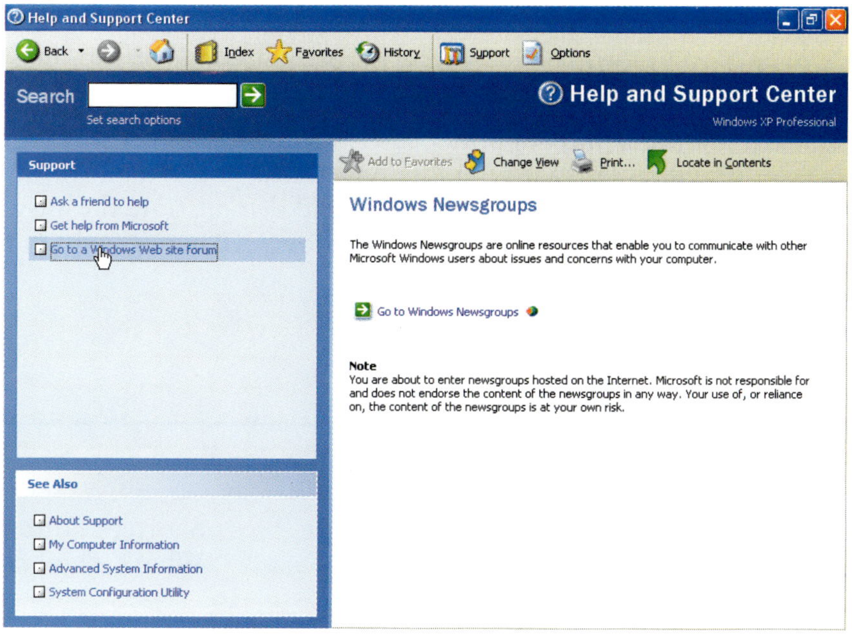

Because there are so many variations of equipment and types of communication connections, it is impossible to include a step-by-step exercise for Windows Remote Assistance. You will, however, learn to communicate with other computers in a later lesson.

SUMMARY

In this lesson, you learned:

- To access Windows Help, press F1 whenever you see Help on the menu bar, select the Help option from the Start menu, or select Help whenever you see a Help command button. Different applications provide different kinds of help.
- Windows' Help system is like an electronic reference book with a table of contents and an index. Files can be searched by word or phrase. An entry displayed in the Help and Support Center's right pane can be printed for easy reference.
- The Help and Support entry toolbar provides buttons for navigating through the Help files and for printing Help and Support entries.
- Help and Support entries may contain different objects. Shortcut buttons perform an action associated with the selected topic. Pop-ups display a definition or short description of the pop-up word or term. The Related Topics option is used to review topics related to the selected topic.
- You use the search qualifiers AND, NEAR, OR, and NOT to combine several words or phrases to refine or narrow a Help topic search.

- Every Windows XP application has the word Help on its menu bar that opens the application's Help Viewer. The left pane of the Help Viewer contains three tabs that provide different options for searching the Help system. When you select an entry on one of the three tabs, the right pane displays detailed help information that may contain links to additional information.
- The Support page in the Help and Support Center offers a variety of ways for you to get help, including over the Internet. With Remote Assistance, you can allow someone you know to connect to your computer, chat with you, and demonstrate the answer to a question. The Support page also gives you access to Windows XP newsgroups where you may be able to find an answer to your questions.

VOCABULARY *Review*

Define the following terms:

Help Viewer	Pop-up	Shortcut button
Link	Scroll	What's This?
Newsgroup	Search qualifiers	

REVIEW *Questions*

TRUE/FALSE

Circle T if the statement is true or F if the statement is false.

T F 1. When using the Help Search feature, keying in the text box with uppercase or lowercase letters will produce the same results.

T F 2. Most dialog boxes contain the "What's This?" icon.

T F 3. The Help and Support Center is designed to function like a Web page.

T F 4. You use search qualifiers to refine a Help topic search.

T F 5. Color is used in Help and Support entry objects as a design element but serves no other useful purpose.

MULTIPLE CHOICE

Select the best response for each of the following statements and write the answers in the lines provided.

1. Terms in a Help and Support entry that are underlined are called __________.
   - **A.** pop-ups
   - **B.** annotations
   - **C.** "What's This?" terms
   - **D.** None of the above

2. An alphabetical listing of topics covered in the Help system is found in the ________.
   A. Options button drop-down menu
   B. Help Index
   C. Search box
   D. toolbar

3. Windows Help and Support system ________.
   A. is accessed from the Start menu
   B. is a menu option on all menu bars
   C. is an optional feature that must be purchased separately
   D. None of the above

4. To display a previously selected topic quickly in the Help and Support Center, use the ________.
   A. Back button
   B. Home button
   C. Related Topics button
   D. Support button

5. When you want to find Help and Support entries that contain a certain word or phrase, you key the words or phrase you want to find in the ________.
   A. "What's This?" box
   B. Search box
   C. Print dialog box
   D. All of the above

PROJECTS

PROJECT 10-1

Be sure you have access to a printer before beginning the activity.

1. Start Windows XP if it is not already active.

2. Select the **Help and Support** option on the Start menu.

3. Click the **What's new in Windows XP** link, and then click the **What's new topics** link.

4. Display the entry for the following links, then print each entry by right-clicking on the entry and selecting **Print** on the shortcut menu. Remember to click the **Back** button to return to the What's new topics listing after you print each entry.
   A. What's new on your desktop
   B. What's new for home networking
   C. What's new for browsing the Internet

5. Click the check box next to **Search only What's new in Windows XP** to deselect this option.

6. Using the **Search** feature, locate the topics for *printing*.

7. Click the **Suggested Topics** header to verify that the Suggested Topics results list is displayed.

8. Click the **Print a picture** link in the Pick a task list.

9. Click the **Print** option on the Help and Support entry toolbar to print a copy.

10. Using the **Search** feature, locate the topics for *printers AND sharing*.

11. Click the **Full-text Search Matches** header to display the full-text search matches for this search session.

12. Click the **What's new in home networking** link to display the topic in the Help and Support window.

13. Click the **Home networking made easy** topic to expand the topic in the Help and Support window.

14. Click the **Print** button on the Help and Support entry toolbar to print a copy.

15. Click the **Home networking made easy** heading to collapse (close) the entry.

16. Quit the Help system.

17. Assemble your printed pages for submission to your instructor as follows:
    - A. Arrange the printouts in the order in which they were produced.
    - B. Write your name and class information in the upper right corner of each printout.

PROJECT 10-2

1. Start Windows XP, if necessary, then open the **Notepad** application program.
    - A. Click the **Start** button, then click **All programs, Accessories,** and **Notepad.**
    - B. Maximize the Notepad window.

2. Select the **Help Topics** option on the Help menu.

3. Using the **Search** tab, locate the topics for searching.
    - A. Key **searching.**
    - B. Click **List Topics.**

> **Hot Tip**
>
> Notepad may be one of the options in the left column of your Start menu if it was a program you used recently.

4. Click the **Getting Help** topic entry, then click the **Display** button at the bottom of the window.

5. Click the **Find a Help topic** entry, then click the **Related Topics** link at the bottom of the window.

6. Select **Help viewer overview** on the pop-up menu, and print a copy of the entry by right-clicking it and selecting **Print** on the shortcut menu.

7. Using the **Help** Index, locate the topics for *margins*, then double-click it in the listing. The topic entry will appear in the Help Viewer window.

8. Print a copy of the entry by right-clicking it and selecting **Print** on the shortcut menu.

9. Click the **Contents** tab, then click the **Notepad** icon to open it.

10. Click the **Find specific characters or words** topic.

11. Print a copy of the entry by right-clicking it and selecting **Print** on the shortcut menu.

12. Quit the Help Viewer, then quit Notepad.

13. Assemble your printed pages for submission to your instructor as follows:
    A. Arrange the printouts in the order in which they were produced.
    B. Write your name and class information in the upper right corner of each printout.

PROJECT 10-3

1. Start Windows, if necessary, then access Windows Help and Support system.

2. Click the **Index** button, then key **color** in the Type in the keyword to find text box.

3. Double-click several items in the list (your choice).

4. Pick two topics (your choice) and print them.

5. Highlight the words in the Index text box and key **menu.**

6. Locate the topic **adding programs to QuickLaunch bar**, and then double-click the topic.

7. Locate the term **taskbar**, then click the term to display its definition.

8. With the definition displayed, right-click it and print a copy of the topic.

9. Click the **Home** button to display the Help and Support home page.

10. Using the **Search** feature, display the topics using the search phrase **color NOT printing.**

11. Click the **Full-text Search Matches** header to display the results list.

12. Scroll to locate the topic **Using rendering intents**, then click on it.

13. Print a copy of the topic by clicking the **Print** button on the Help and Support entry toolbar.

14. Assemble your printed pages for submission to your instructor as follows:
    A. Arrange the printouts in the order in which they were produced.
    B. Write your name and class information in the upper-right corner of each printout.

15. Close the Help and Support Center window. If instructed, shut down Windows and your computer.

CRITICAL *Thinking*

SCANS ACTIVITY 10-1

On Monday morning, you arrive at your office and find that Windows XP Professional has been loaded on your computer. You notice that the Start menu looks a little different.

Using the Windows Help system, look up information on the items that now appear on your Start menu and print copies of the Help and Support entries. Write a brief report on why you selected these topics to print. Then assemble the topics in a fashion that would make it easy for a new user of Windows to get acquainted quickly with the changes in the desktop.

LESSON 11

CUSTOMIZING THE DESKTOP

OBJECTIVES

Upon completion of this lesson, you should be able to:

- Apply a predefined theme to the desktop.
- Change the Windows desktop background.
- Use a graphic file as a desktop background.
- Customize the icons on the desktop.
- Clean up your desktop.

Estimated Time: 1 hour

VOCABULARY

Active desktop
Background
Control Panel
Desktop shortcuts
Desktop theme
Internet Explorer
My Computer
My Documents
My Network Places
Wizard

Windows programs run on the desktop, and objects are placed on the desktop. When you install Windows XP, the original desktop you see may not be the kind of desktop you want, but you can customize it to suit your personal tastes. In this lesson, you will learn how to change the look of your desktop's ***background*** (the color or image that covers your on-screen desktop).

Changing Display Properties

IC3 -3.3.4-2

You customize the desktop using the ***Control Panel***, which is found on the Start menu. Specifically, you select the Control Panel's Display icon, and the Display Properties dialog box appears, as shown in Figure 11-1.

FIGURE 11-1
Display Properties dialog box

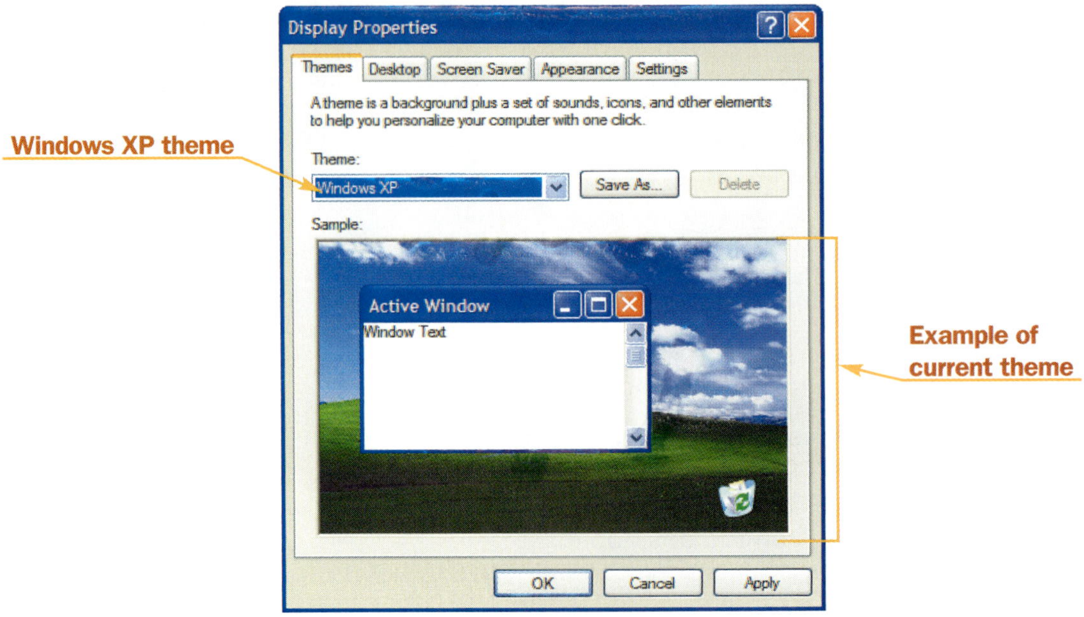

As you see in Figure 11-1, the Display Properties dialog box has several tabs you can use to change the appearance and the behavior of your desktop.

IC3 1-3.3.2-1

- The Themes tab permits you to assign a predefined set of icons, fonts, colors, sounds, and other window elements to your desktop. Collectively these elements are called a ***desktop theme*** and give the desktop a unified and distinctive look.
- The Desktop tab offers you a wide selection of pictures and graphics that you can place as a background on your desktop. You can use one of the backgrounds that come with Windows or create one of your own.
- The Screen Saver tab permits you to display static or moving graphics or a blank screen when your system is idle.
- The Appearance tab permits you to control the colors, fonts, and sizes of various screen elements. You can change the appearance of these elements by selecting from a set of predefined schemes or by creating your own scheme.
- The Settings tab permits you to change the resolution and the number of colors used by the display, change the display type, and change other display characteristics.

Hot Tip

Right-clicking an empty area on your desktop (a place where there is no folder or icon) and clicking **Properties** will also open the Display Properties dialog box.

Customizing the Background

When Windows is first installed, the ***background*** that covers your desktop is a picture of a green hill beneath a blue sky with white clouds. (The name of this background is Bliss.) However, the Display Properties dialog box allows you to change the background by selecting a different desktop theme or by modifying the existing background.

Selecting a Desktop Theme

Using the Themes tab, you can quickly modify your desktop background by selecting from a set of predefined themes. If your computer has other users with their own user accounts, each person can have a different theme.

To apply a new desktop theme, simply use the drop-down menu (beneath the word Theme) to select one of the preconfigured themes (see Figure 11-2). When you click a theme, the new background will appear in the sample window in the center of the Display Properties dialog box. Click the Apply button; after a short wait, the new theme will be set on the desktop.

FIGURE 11-2
Theme drop-down list

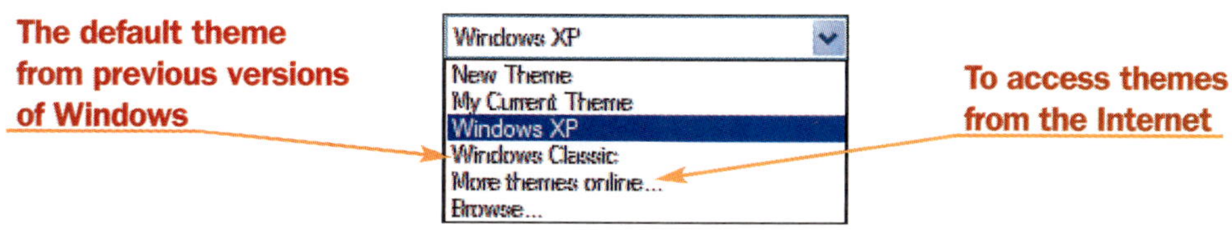

If your computer has an Internet connection, you can access a number of themes from the Microsoft Web site by clicking the More themes online option on the drop-down list.

STEP-BY-STEP 11.1

-3.3.1-1
-3.3.1-2

1. Open the **Control Panel**, then double-click the **Display** icon.

2. On a sheet of paper, write the name of the desktop theme that is currently displayed in the Theme list box.

1-3.3.4

3. Click the **Theme** drop-down list arrow, and then select **Windows Classic** if it is not already selected. If it is already selected, select one of the other backgrounds.

4. Click the **Apply** button. Your theme will take effect after a short wait. The new desktop background will appear in the Sample window in the Display Properties dialog box.

5. Click the **Theme** drop-down arrow, select the desktop theme that you wrote on your paper in Step 2, and then click **Apply**. After a short wait, your desktop background will return to its former appearance. Leave the Display Properties dialog box open for the next Step-by-Step.

1-3.3.4-1

Setting a Background Design

You can change a theme's settings by making modifications to the other tabs available on the Display Properties dialog box. For example, if you wish to change the background design, click the Desktop tab and select one of the backgrounds. You can select from Windows' preexisting backgrounds, which are listed on the Background list box (see Figure 11-3), or you can use other graphic files (for instance, from a digital camera) as your background. By default, the background is set up to stretch across your screen so it takes up the entire desktop area. You can center the background on the desktop or tile it to fill the entire desktop. These options are shown in Figure 11-4. You select the option from the Position drop-down list box.

FIGURE 11-3
Display Properties Desktop tab

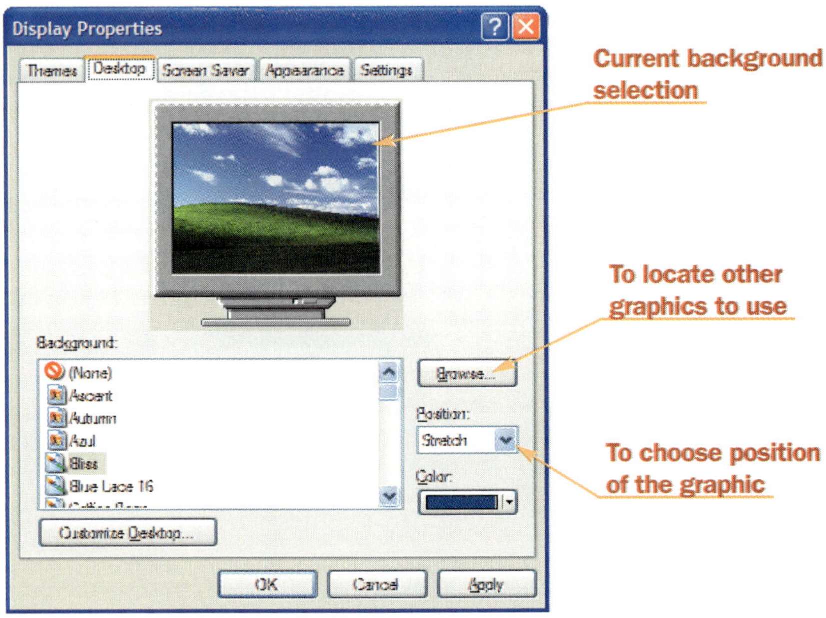

FIGURE 11-4
Background that is stretched, centered, and tiled

STEP-BY-STEP 11.2

1. Click the **Desktop** tab.
2. Select the Windows XP background:
   a. Click the scroll down arrow in the **Background** list box until the **Windows XP** option appears, and then select it.

STEP-BY-STEP 11.2 Continued

- **b.** Notice that a preview of your selection is displayed in the monitor graphic in the upper portion of the Desktop tab.
- **c.** Verify that the **Stretch** option is displayed in the Position drop-down list box. The Windows XP background is a picture file, and by default, all picture files are stretched to cover the entire desktop.

3. Center the background on the desktop:
   - **a.** Click the **Center** option from the Position drop-down list. Notice that the preview of your selection in the monitor graphic changes according to your selection.
   - **b.** Click the **Apply** button to set the background. Do not click the OK button.
   - **c.** Notice that the background is centered on your desktop and a background color fills the area of the desktop not covered by the background graphic.

4. Tile the background on the desktop:
   - **a.** Click the **Tile** option from the Position drop-down list.
   - **b.** Click the **Apply** button to reset the background. Notice that the background now fills the desktop by repeating the graphic.

5. Click the **Stretch** option from the Position drop-down list, and then click the **Apply** button to reset the background. Do not click the OK button. Leave the Display Properties dialog box open for the next Step-by-Step.

Windows XP can display any picture or graphic file (usually files with a GIF, JPEG, or BMP extension) as a background. If you have picture files already stored on your computer, you can simply browse and select the desired picture. You can also create your own graphic in the Windows Paint program or some other graphics program and use it as a background.

STEP-BY-STEP 11.3

1. Use the **Flowers** file in the Lesson 11 folder of the data files as a background:
   - **a.** Click the **Browse** button on the Desktop tab to open the Browse dialog box.
   - **b.** Select the drive and folder that contain your data files.
   - **c.** Double-click the **Lesson 11** folder, and then double-click the **Flowers.jpg** file. The Browse dialog box closes, and the Display Properties dialog box reappears.
   - **d.** Verify that the **Stretch** option is selected from the Position drop-down list.
   - **e.** Click the **Apply** button to set the background.

2. Reset the background to (None):
   - **a.** Scroll the background list box, locate the **(None)** option, and click it.
   - **b.** Click the **Apply** button to set the background to (None). Leave the Display Properties dialog box (Desktop tab) open for the next Step-by-Step.

Hot Tip

You can download a picture or an image from the Web and use it as a background. Simply right-click the picture or image you want to use as a background and click **Set As Wallpaper**.

Customizing the Icons on Your Desktop

The Customize Desktop button toward the bottom of the Desktop tab provides a convenient way for you to select which Windows program icons are to appear on your desktop and to determine which icons are used to represent those programs. Click this button, and the Desktop Items dialog box opens (see Figure 11-5). This dialog box contains a General and a Web tab.

FIGURE 11-5
The Desktop Items dialog box

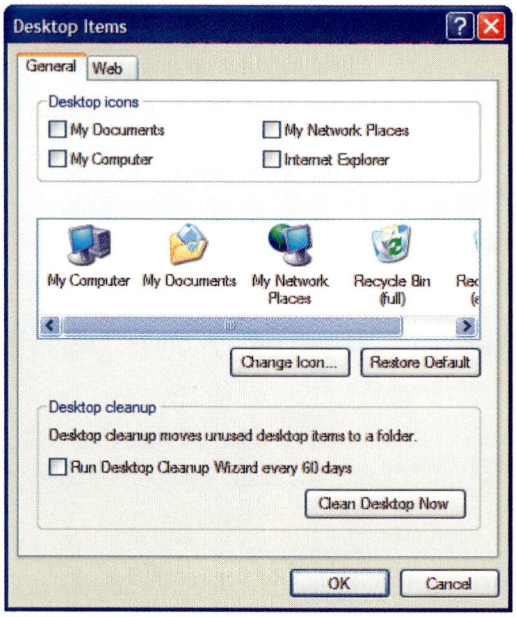

On the General tab (see Figure 11-5), you can select the desktop icons you wish to appear by checking one or more of the check boxes: My Documents, My Computer, My Network Places, and Internet Explorer. These icons are discussed in detail below.

- ***My Documents*** is your personal folder where you can save the files you create and use. By default, the My Documents folder contains two additional personal folders: My Pictures and My Music. As the names imply, the My Picture folder is provided as a place for you to save your picture files and the My Music folder is provided as a place for you to save your music files.
- ***My Computer*** displays the contents of your computer. You can see the hardware devices, resources, programs, and files that are stored on your computer. My Computer also provides information about different system resources, such as the size of the hard disk and how much space is available on it. You can also use My Computer to format disks and to run applications. (You may recall that My Computer is also accessible from the Start menu.)
- ***My Network Places*** lists all of the computers on your network, if you are connected to a network. It permits you to browse through files on a networked computer.
- With ***Internet Explorer***, you get a fast, personalized Web browser. It provides you with far-reaching communication capabilities, including sending and receiving e-mail, surfing the Internet, designing your own Web site, and building a videoconference.

Just below the Desktop icons, you will see a window showing the default icons that are used for each of these items, as well as the Recycle Bin icon that is placed on your desktop by default. If you want to use a different icon for any of these items, click the item you wish to change, click the Change Icon button, and select a different icon from the choices provided. If you change your mind or don't like your choice, just click the Restore Default button to return to the Windows XP default icon settings.

STEP-BY-STEP 11.4

1. Click the **Customize Desktop** button. The Desktop Items dialog box (Figure 11-5) is displayed.

2. Click the **General** tab to verify that it is in the foreground.

3. Display the My Documents and My Computer icons on your desktop:
   a. Click the **My Documents** check box in the Desktop icons area. (This will place a check mark in the check box.)
   b. Click the **My Computer** check box.
   c. Click the **OK** button. The Desktop Icons dialog box will close.

4. Click the **Apply** button on the Display Properties dialog box to place the selected icons on your desktop. Do not click the OK button on the Display Properties dialog box.

5. Change the My Documents desktop icon:
   a. Click the **Customize Desktop** button to display the Desktop Items dialog box.
   b. Click the **My Documents** icon in the display window, and then click the **Change Icon** button.
   c. Click the folder icon shown in Figure 11-6, and then click the **OK** button. Notice that the icon changes in the display window.

FIGURE 11-6
Folder icon

   d. Click the **OK** button on the Desktop Items dialog box, and then click the **Apply** button on the Display Properties dialog box. Notice that the icon on your desktop has changed to your selection.

6. Remove the My Computer icon from your desktop:
   a. Click the **Customize Desktop** button to display the Desktop Items dialog box.
   b. Click the **My Computer** check box to deselect (uncheck) it, leave the My Documents check box checked, and then click the **OK** button.
   c. Click the **Apply** button on the Display Properties dialog box. Notice that the My Computer icon is no longer displayed on the desktop. Leave the Display Properties dialog box open for the next Step-by-Step.

Cleaning Up Your Desktop

Windows XP provides a number of utility programs that help you perform a task quickly and easily. Each of these programs is called a *Wizard* and performs a special function. For example, as you use windows, you will place icons on your desktop. Because these icons function as shortcuts to an application or a document, they are often referred to as ***desktop shortcuts***. Windows XP contains a Desktop Cleanup Wizard that can check your desktop to see which desktop shortcuts you have not used during the previous 60 days; it then lets you decide if you want to remove them. The desktop shortcuts you remove are moved to an Unused Desktop Shortcuts folder from which you can recover them at any time.

Look again at the General tab on the Desktop Items dialog box shown in Figure 11-5. Notice the Desktop cleanup area at the bottom of the sheet. In this area, you can set the Desktop Cleanup Wizard to run automatically every 60 days, or you can run it any time by clicking the Clean Desktop Now button.

STEP-BY-STEP 11.5

1. Create a desktop shortcut:
   a. Right-click the **My Documents** icon on the desktop, and then click the **Create Shortcut** option on the pop-up menu.
   b. A desktop shortcut for the My Documents icon appears on the desktop, as shown in Figure 11-7.

FIGURE 11-7
My Documents desktop shortcut

2. Click the **Customize Desktop** button on the Display Properties dialog box.

3. Click the **Clean Desktop Now** button near the bottom on the Desktop Items dialog box.

4. When the Desktop Cleanup Wizard welcome screen appears (see Figure 11-8), click the **Next** button to continue.

FIGURE 11-8
Desktop Cleanup Wizard welcome window

STEP-BY-STEP 11.5 Continued

5. The Shortcuts window appears (Figure 11-9) listing all the shortcut icons on your desktop.

FIGURE 11-9
Desktop Cleanup Wizard shortcuts window

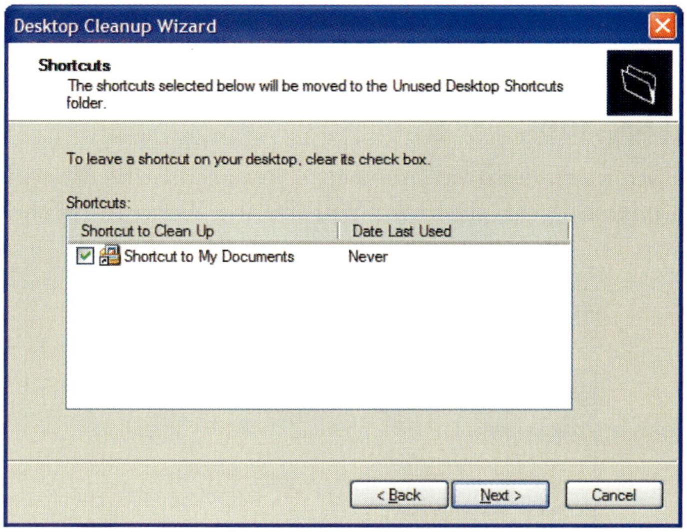

6. Review the list of shortcut icons in the Shortcuts window. Notice the shortcut has a date next to it, noting the last time it was used.

7. Verify that the **Shortcut to My Documents** icon is checked. If you have more than one shortcut on your desktop, the wizard may have selected some of them for you. Make certain that only the Shortcut to My Documents is checked or the others, too, will be removed.

8. Click the **Next** button. Verify that only the **Shortcut to My Documents** is listed in the Shortcuts window, and then click the **Finish** button.

9. Look at your desktop. Notice that the Shortcut to My Documents icon has been replaced with a yellow folder called Unused Desktop Shortcuts (see Figure 11-10). As its name implies, this is the folder where all the unused desktop shortcuts are saved.

FIGURE 11-10
Unused Desktop Shortcuts folder icon

10. Drag the **Unused Desktop Shortcuts** folder to the Recycle Bin.

STEP-BY-STEP 11.5 Continued

11. Remove the My Documents icon from your desktop:
    a. Verify that the General tab on the Desktop Items dialog box is still displayed.
    b. Click the **My Documents** check box to deselect (uncheck) it, and then click the **OK** button.

12. Click the **OK** button to close the Display Properties dialog box.

Setting an Active Desktop

If your computer is connected to the Internet, you can use the Windows XP ***active desktop*** feature to place a Web page on your desktop. You use the Web tab on the Desktop Items dialog box (see Figure 11-11) to do this.

FIGURE 11-11
The Web tab is used to display a Web page on your desktop

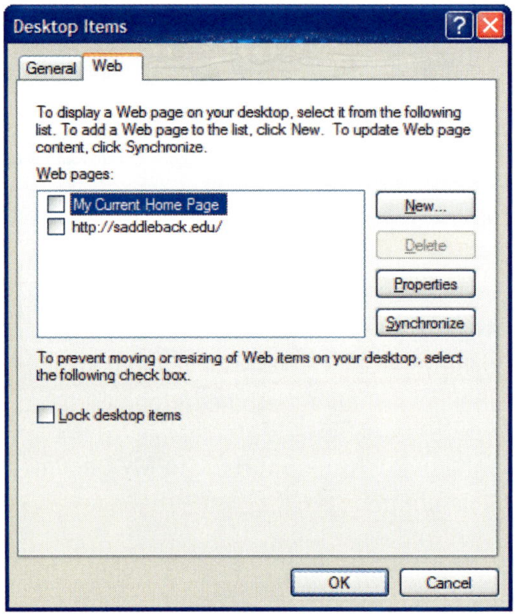

To place a Web page on your desktop, click the New button and key the URL of the desired Web page. The entire Web page is downloaded and stored on your computer. Once you have the Web page displayed on your Desktop, you can lock the items in place so no items can be moved or resized by accident.

The advantage of placing a Web page on your desktop is that, unlike regular backgrounds, the Web page contents can frequently change. However, Windows XP stores the page in an off-line format, meaning that the Web page will not change on its own. Whenever you want the Web page to be updated, you must tell Windows XP to synchronize the page or go to the Internet and update the page at specified time intervals. The Synchronize button on the Web tab (see Figure 11-11) is used for this purpose.

SUMMARY

In this lesson, you learned:

- Double-clicking the Display icon in the Control Panel opens the Display dialog box, where you can modify your desktop's background.
- You can select from Windows' existing themes. You can also choose a different background on the Background tab.
- Windows comes with a number of preexisting desktop themes that give your desktop a unified and distinctive look. A picture can be tiled to fill the whole screen, centered on the screen, or stretched across the screen.
- You can use most any picture or graphic file as a background. For example, you might take a photograph on a digital camera or download a graphic from the Web and then use it as a desktop background.
- The Desktop Cleanup Wizard is used to remove any unwanted or unused desktop shortcuts from the desktop.

VOCABULARY *Review*

Define the following terms:

Active desktop	Desktop theme	My Documents
Background	Internet Explorer	My Network Places
Control Panel	My Computer	Wizard
Desktop shortcuts		

REVIEW *Questions*

TRUE/FALSE

Circle T if the statement is true or F if the statement is false.

T F 1. The Background tab in the Display Properties dialog box lets you change the colors, fonts, and sizes of various screen elements.

T F 2. By default, your desktop's background is a solid color.

T F 3. Even though other users share your computer, you must all have the same theme for your desktops.

T F 4. Windows XP can display any picture or graphic file with a GIF, JPEG, or BMP extension.

T F 5. My Computer does not allow you to see programs stored on your computer.

MATCHING

Write the letter of the term in Column 2 that matches the definition in Column 1.

Column 1	Column 2
___ 1. Tab in the Display Properties dialog box that lets you create a static or moving graphic that displays when your system is idle	A. Settings
___ 2. Tab in the Display Properties dialog box that offers you a wide selection of pictures and graphics that you can place as a background on your desktop	B. Themes
___ 3. Tab in the Display Properties dialog box that lets you assign a predefined set of icons, fonts, colors, sounds, and other window elements to your desktop	C. Appearance
___ 4. Tab in the Display Properties dialog box that lets you control the colors, fonts, and sizes of various screen elements	D. Desktop
___ 5. Tab in the Display Properties dialog box that lets you change the resolution and the number of colors used by the display, change the display type, and change other display characteristics	E. Screen saver

PROJECTS

PROJECT 11-1

Before you begin, ask if your instructor wants to see the background you create in this project.

1. Open the **Control Panel**, and then double-click the **Display** icon.
2. Click the **Themes** tab if necessary, and write down the name of the desktop theme that is currently displayed in the Theme list box.

3. Modify the theme:
   A. Click the **Desktop** tab, select the **Ascent Background**, and then click the **Apply** button.
   B. Click the **Themes** tab, click **Save As**, Key **Project 11-1 Theme** in the File name textbox, and then click **Save**.
4. Click the arrow in the **Themes** list box and verify that the Project 11-1 Theme is displayed in the list.
5. Delete the Project 11-1 Theme:
   A. Select **Project 11-1 Theme** from the Theme list box.
   B. Click the **Delete** button.

PROJECT 11-2

1. Open the **Control Panel** if necessary, and then double-click the **Display** icon.
2. Use the Browse button on the Desktop tab to apply the **Boats**.jpg file from your data files as a background:
   A. Click **Browse**.
   B. Select the drive and/or folder containing your data files.
   C. Double-click the **Boats.jpg** file.
   D. Click the **OK** button to set the background.
3. Reopen the **Display Properties** dialog box, and reset the background to **None**.
4. Click **OK** to close the dialog box, and then close the Control Panel.

PROJECT 11-3

1. Open the **Control Panel** if necessary, and then double-click the **Display** icon.
2. On the Themes tab, select **Windows XP** from the Theme drop-down list.
3. On the Desktop tab, click the **Browse** button, locate the **Boats.jpg** file in your data files, and double-click it. Change the background position to **Center**.
4. Click the **Color** button, and select the **light gray** color from the color palette. Click the **Apply** button. The boat picture should appear in a large box in the center of the display, with a light gray background surrounding the picture.
5. Display the My Documents and My Computer icons on your desktop:
   A. Click the **Customize Desktop** button to display the Desktop Items dialog box.
   B. Click the **My Computer** and **My Documents** check boxes in the Desktop icons section of the sheet, then click **OK**.
   C. Click the **Apply** button to display the icons.
6. Right-click the **My Documents** icon from the desktop, and then click the **Create Shortcut** option on the pop-up menu to create a desktop shortcut.

7. Remove the My Documents icon (not the My Documents Shortcut icon) from your desktop:
   A. Click the **Customize Desktop** button, and then uncheck the **My Documents** check box on the General tab of the Desktop Items dialog box.
   B. Click the **OK** button, and then click the **Apply** button.

8. Clean up your desktop:
   A. Click the **Customize Desktop** button, and verify that the **General** tab is selected.
   B. Click the **Clean Desktop Now** button.
   C. When the Desktop Cleanup Wizard welcome screen appears, click the **Next** button to continue.
   D. Review the list of shortcut icons in the Shortcuts window, and verify that **Shortcut to My Documents** is checked.
   E. Click the **Next** button.
   F. Verify that Shortcut to My Documents is listed in the Shortcuts window, and then click the **Finish** button.

9. Drag the **Unused Desktop Shortcuts** folder to the Recycle Bin.

10. Restore your desktop to its original Theme:
    A. Open the **Desktop Properties** dialog box.
    B. On the Themes tab, click the theme name that you wrote down on a sheet of paper in Project 11-1. Click **OK** to close the Display Properties dialog box.

CRITICAL *Thinking*

ACTIVITY 11-1

Beyond aesthetics, is there a practical use for applying a desktop background? Include a brief explanation in your answer. If your answer is yes, include an example of a practical application. If your answer is no, cite an example of how a desktop background might impair productivity.

LESSON 12

INTRODUCING MY COMPUTER

OBJECTIVES

Upon completion of this lesson, you should be able to:

- Start and exit My Computer.
- Set My Computer options.
- Customize the Standard toolbar.
- Access disk drives and view their contents.
- Identify object icons.

Estimated Time: 1.5 hours

VOCABULARY

Disk
Disk drive
Disk drive icons
File
Floppy disk
Folder
Hard disk
Subfolders

Files, folders, and disks—these are your key system resources. Windows offers two tools for browsing, accessing, and managing these resources: My Computer and Explorer. Both are easy to access. You can access My Computer from the Start menu, and you access Explorer from the All Programs option on the Start menu. This lesson will introduce you to My Computer; later lessons will work with Explorer.

Understanding File Management Concepts

Before you can appreciate and use either of Windows' file management tools, you must understand the foundation on which they are built: Files, folders, and disks.

Files

Imagine large file drawers for paper files. If papers were simply stacked in the drawer, not separated or grouped in any way, finding what you wanted would be a nightmare. But if one folder contained all reports, another all letters, and another all memos, then you'd be able to find what you wanted much faster with less searching. The same principle applies to storing computer data.

In terms of paper documents, a file may describe a wide range of documents—short or long, formal or informal, handwritten or keyed, and so forth. In computer terms, file describes a wide range of objects. A ***file*** may be the instructions the computer needs to operate (called program files or executable files), or a file may contain a text document you can read (often referred to as a document file).

Folders

Files are stored on a disk. Disks are discussed in greater detail below, but for now, note that some common disks can store the equivalent of many thousands of pages of information. But as with paper files, finding what you want may be time-consuming. In both cases, folders are helpful.

For example, a disk can be organized to have a ***folder*** that contains only files relating to application programs, another folder only for correspondence files, another only for reports, another only for forms, and so forth. Like paper folders, disk folders organize files into manageable groups, and ***subfolders*** further separate groups of files within a folder. As you start working with disks later in this lesson, you will see more clearly how files are grouped into subfolders and how subfolders are grouped within folders.

Disks

Files, folders, and subfolders are stored on disks. Think of a computer disk as an electronic file cabinet. Instead of storing paper files, however, computers store electronic files—program instructions or data documents.

A ***disk*** is the magnetic medium on which data is stored. A ***disk drive*** is the hardware that finds, reads, and writes information to and from a disk. To clarify the distinction, just pick up a portable floppy disk (or diskette) and insert it into a built-in disk drive.

While a ***floppy disk*** is small and portable, a second kind of disk, a ***hard disk***, is not. A hard disk and a hard drive are one integrated unit; further, the unit cannot easily be removed from the computer. In fact, because it is permanently installed, a hard disk is also called a fixed disk. Because a hard disk drive is one unit, people sometimes use the terms disk and drive interchangeably.

The My Computer Window

As you learned earlier, you start My Computer from the Start menu. The My Computer window that appears contains the familiar title bar, menu bar, display area, and several other parts, as seen in Figure 12-1. The objects displayed in the window reflect your computer's setup and differ from computer to computer. When you select My Computer from the Start Menu, the window that appears will have My Computer showing in the title bar and the majority of the window should be split into two panes. The left pane is called the Explorer Bar, and it contains three drop-down bars: System Tasks, Other Places, and Details, which are described later in this lesson. What you will notice as you select different tasks from the Explorer Bar is that the name on the title bar and the features available in both panes will continue to change to reflect what you have most recently selected.

> **Note**
>
> When My Computer opens, what you see in the right window pane will depend on the number and type of drives your system has installed on it.

FIGURE 12-1
My Computer window

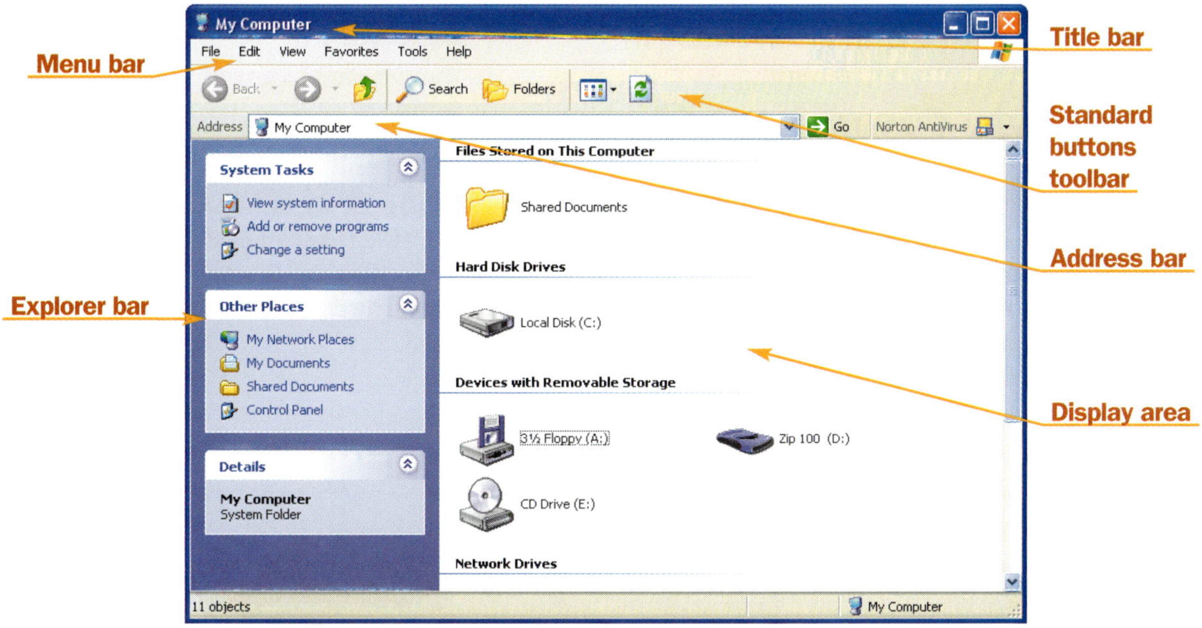

STEP-BY-STEP 12.1

1. Click the **Start** button, then click once on **My Computer** in the second column. The My Computer window opens.

2. In its display window, examine the icons that represent your system's computer resources. Leave the My Computer window open for the next Step-by-Step.

Identifying the Icons in the Display Window

As indicated on Figure 12-1, the My Computer window contains two types of icons: disk drive icons and folder icons.

Disk drive icons identify (by letter and type) the disk drives you can access on your system. Thus, the icons will vary depending on the computer system. The appearance of each disk drive icon varies according to the type of drive—hard disk drive, floppy disk drive, or CD-ROM drive.

A disk drive is named by letter. For most computers:

- Drives A and B are generally floppy disk drives, although drive B is not often used.
- Drive C typically designates the hard disk. Some computers have more than one hard disk, and some computers have partitioned hard disks—disks divided into separate sections, or logical drives. Additional hard drives and partitions, such as a CD-ROM or a DVD/CD-RW, are usually labeled D, E, F, and so forth.

Figure 12-1 shows a computer system with one Hard Disk Drive, called Local Disk (C), and three Devices with Removable Storage: a floppy drive, called 3½ Floppy (A), a CD-ROM, called CD Drive (E), and a Zip 100 (D). The My Computer window shown in Figure 12-1 also contains a folder icon for Shared Documents displayed under Files Stored on This Computer (as well as in the Other Places section).

Setting My Computer Options

You learned about the key options of the View menu (Figure 12-2) of My Computer earlier when preparing to use the Control Panel Accessibility Options. (Please see Lesson 11 if you need to refresh your memory.) The following section explains how to add toolbar buttons to further control the way the My Computer window looks and functions. To reach the Customize Toolbar dialog box, select View, Toolbars, and then Customize.

FIGURE 12-2
My Computer's View menu and expanded Toolbars submenu

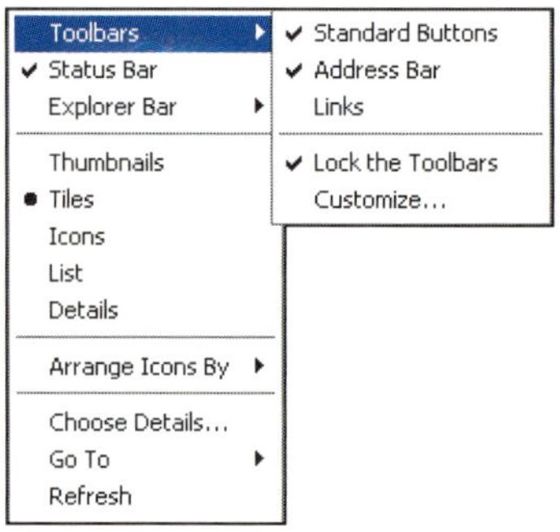

Customizing the Standard Toolbar

When you select the Customize option on the Toolbars submenu, the Customize Toolbar dialog box appears. As shown in Figure 12-3, the Customize Toolbar dialog box has two list boxes. The Current toolbar buttons list box on the right lists the buttons currently shown on the Standard toolbar. The names and icons shown in the list box on the left identify those toolbar buttons that are available, but not currently shown on the Standard toolbar. The Add and Remove buttons are the keys to customizing the Standard toolbar buttons.

FIGURE 12-3
Customize Toolbar dialog box

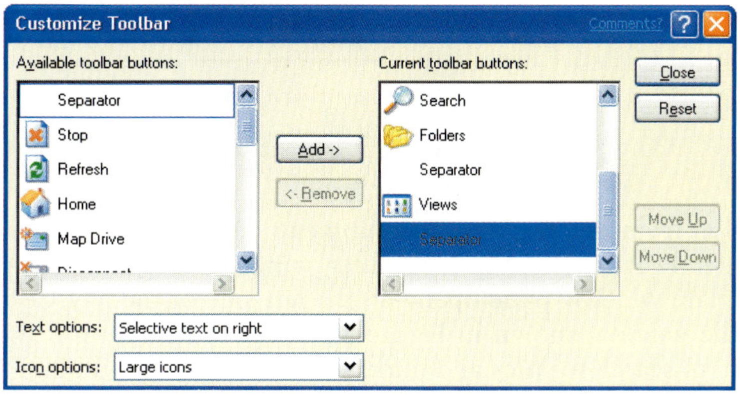

To add a toolbar button, simply click the button name in the Available toolbar buttons list box, then click the Add button. As the arrow indicates, the button name will move to the Current toolbar buttons list box on the right, and the button will appear on the Standard toolbar. You remove a button from the Standard toolbar in a similar manner. You select the button name in the Current toolbar buttons list box, then click the Remove button. The button name will move to the Available toolbar buttons list box on the left. The button will no longer appear on the Standard toolbar.

You can display small icons or large icons on the Standard toolbar using the Icon options drop-down list at the bottom of the dialog box.

You can choose to display the toolbar with or without identifying text by selecting one of the options from the Text options drop-down list. If you choose to identify the icons, you have the option of displaying the text on the right of the icon or beneath the icon.

Explorer Bar

Windows Explorer, also called Explorer, was created to help you do just that—explore the contents of your computer. It is probably one feature of the Windows XP operating system you will use more than any other. There are a few ways to start Explorer. One way is in My Computer: Click View, then Explorer Bar. Another option is if your display is not showing the Explorer Bar: Click Tools, click Folder Options, select Show common tasks in folders, and then click OK.

When you select Explorer Bar on the View menu, a submenu like that shown in Figure 12-4 appears.

FIGURE 12-4
Explorer Bar submenu displaying the Search pane

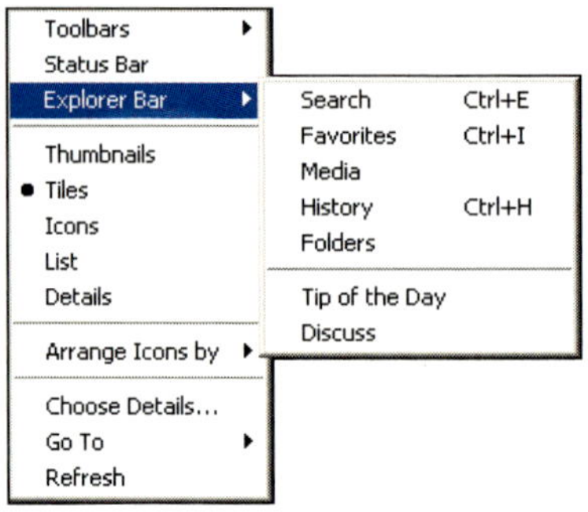

Selecting an option from the Explorer Bar submenu permits you to explore, or search, your computer system directly from the My Computer window. Depending on the submenu item selected, the appropriate window pane opens on the left side of the My Computer window. For example, to get to the window shown in Figure 12-5, the Search button was selected from the toolbar, allowing you to search for files and folders stored on your computer system from the My Computer window.

FIGURE 12-5
The Search Companion

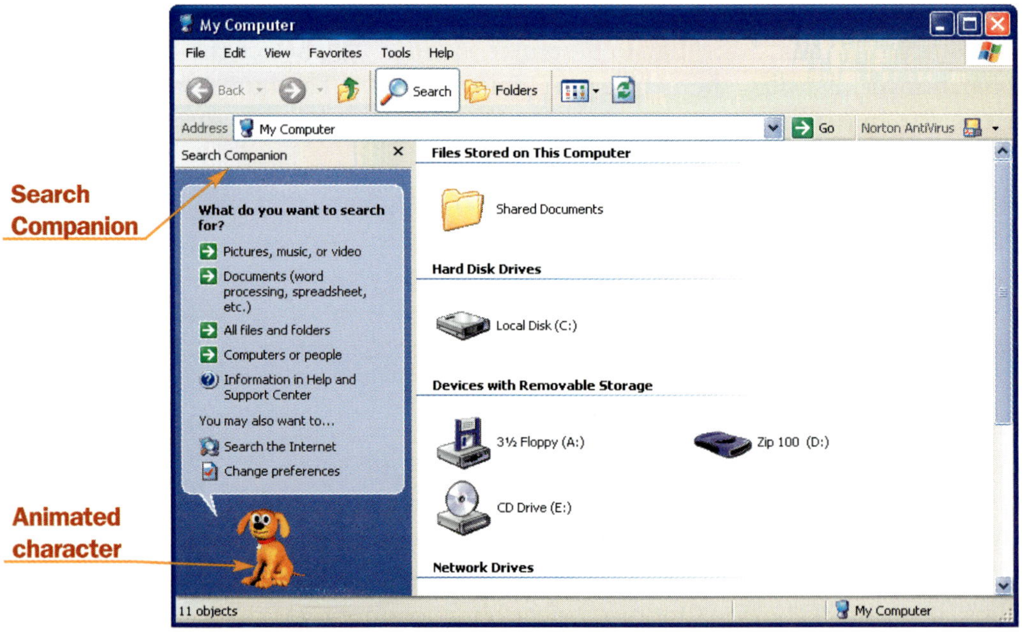

Look once again at the options on the Explorer Bar submenu shown in Figure 12-4. Notice that some of these options may also be available as buttons on the Standard toolbar.

When you select the Tip of the Day option from the Explorer Bar submenu, a pane containing a timesaving tip or shortcut opens in the My Computer window, as shown at the bottom of Figure 12-6. The tip window will be displayed until you close it by clicking the Close button (the X in the upper left corner of the tip window) or until you close the My Computer window.

FIGURE 12-6
Tip of the Day

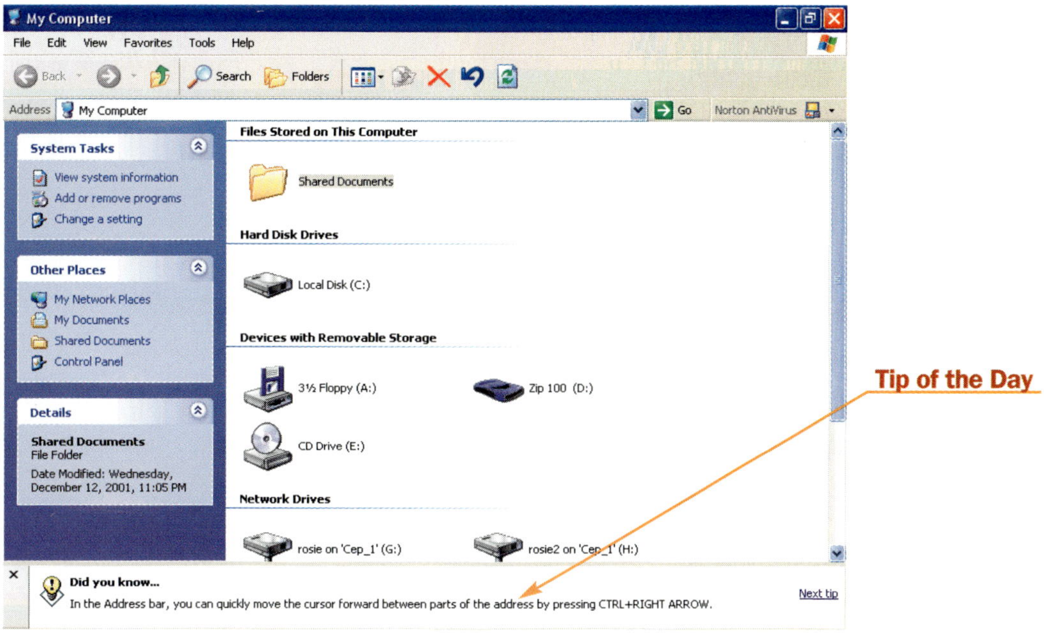

STEP-BY-STEP 12.2

1. Select the **Toolbars** option on the View menu, and verify that **Standard Buttons** is selected (checked); then select the **Customize** option from the submenu.

2. Click the first item in the **Current toolbar buttons** list box, then click the **Remove** button. The name of this button will be moved from the Current toolbar buttons list box to the Available toolbar buttons list box. At the same time, this button will be removed from the Standard toolbar in the My Computer window.

STEP-BY-STEP 12.2 Continued

3. Continue clicking the **Remove** button until all the button names in the Current toolbar buttons list box are moved to the Available toolbar buttons list box on the left side. A grayed separator button that cannot be removed will be highlighted in the Current toolbar buttons list box.

4. Click the **Back** button in the Available toolbar buttons list box, then click the **Add** button. The Back button name will appear in the Current toolbar buttons list box and will reappear on the Standard toolbar.

5. Click the **Reset** button to redisplay the default buttons on the Standard toolbar.

6. Click the **Close** button.

7. Open the **View** menu, and verify that the **Status Bar** option is selected. If it is not, select it. Leave the My Computer window open for the next Step-by-Step.

Accessing Disk Drives

When My Computer is displayed in the Address Bar, each disk drive available is represented by an icon in the display window. To select a drive, click the appropriate drive icon; the drive is then highlighted, as shown in Figure 12-7. Information on the selected object appears in the Details section on the bottom left side of the window. You access a drive by selecting its name in the Address Bar drop-down list or by double-clicking its icon in the window.

FIGURE 12-7
Selected disk drive is highlighted

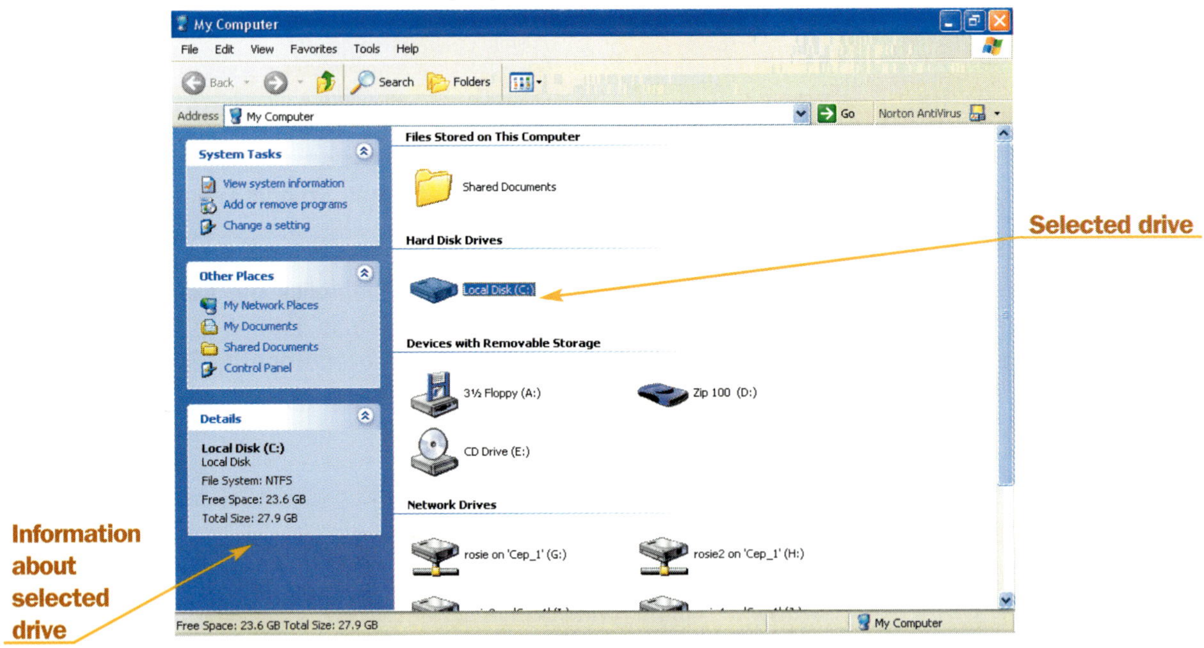

Viewing the Contents of a Drive or Folder

You can display the contents of a selected drive or folder by double-clicking the object in the My Computer window. Once displayed, the objects can be viewed as large icons, small icons, a simple list, or a detailed list.

You can select the Folder Options command on the Tools menu to further customize the display of the My Computer window. The Folder Options dialog box opens, as shown in Figure 12-8.

FIGURE 12-8
Folder Options dialog box

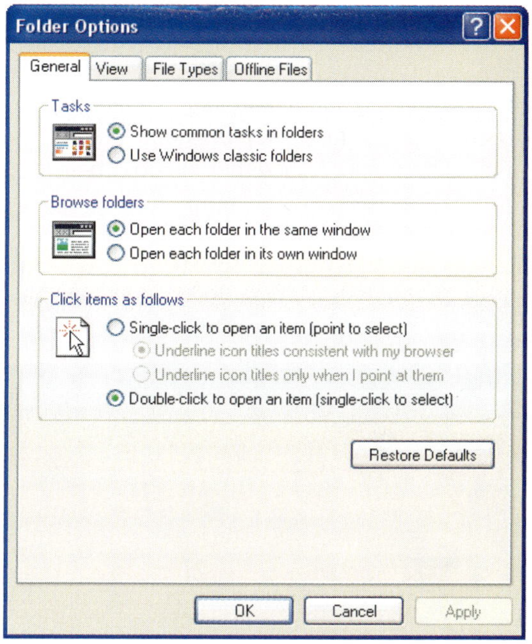

The General tab contains options for the style of your desktop and for customizing the way you organize and manage objects and files on your computer. You can use the Help (?) feature to learn more about the various options in the dialog box.

Browse Folders Options

Open Each Folder in the Same Window

Select this option to display the contents of each folder you open in the same window. In other words, only one window is open on-screen at a time—a handy feature when you have to open several folders before you get to the one you really want.

Open Each Folder in Its Own Window

This option opens a new window every time you open a folder or resource in My Computer. The previous folder is still displayed in another window, so you can switch between them.

STEP-BY-STEP 12.3

1. Select **Folder Options** on the Tools menu. Select the **Open each folder in the same window** Browse folders option, and then click **OK**.
2. From the View menu, select **Toolbars**, then select **Address Bar** on the submenu if it is not already selected.
3. Click on the arrow on the far right of the Address Bar, scroll to the top if necessary, and click on **Desktop**.
4. Select the **Tiles** option on the View menu. Notice that the objects listed are the same objects that appear on your desktop, although they may differ somewhat from those shown in Figure 12-9 based upon what you have placed on your desktop.

FIGURE 12-9
Selecting Desktop shows all objects on the desktop

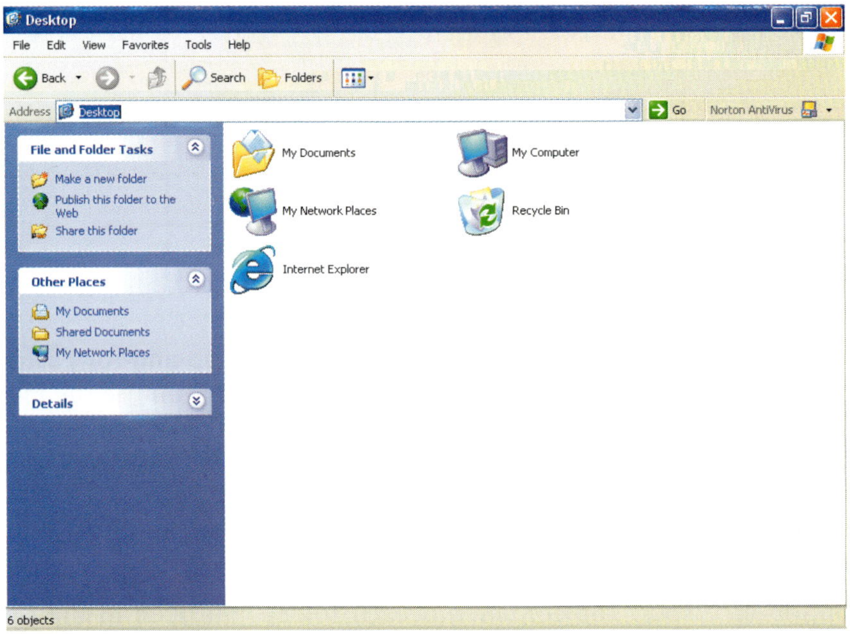

5. Select **View** and **Toolbars**. Make certain you have selected the **Standard Buttons** from the expanded Toolbars submenu so the Back button is displayed.
6. Click the **Back** button to redisplay the My Computer window.
7. Choose **Details** on the View menu, then change back to the **Tiles** view.
8. Click the **Forward** button to return to the Desktop window. Make sure the view selected is Tiles.

STEP-BY-STEP 12.3 Continued

9. Click the **Back** button to return to the My Computer window.

10. Select the WINDOWS folder from your hard drive:

a. Double-click the drive containing the **WINDOWS** folder (usually drive C).

b. Locate the WINDOWS folder on your hard drive, then double-click the **WINDOWS** folder. Notice that the window's title bar now consists of an open file folder icon and the word WINDOWS, indicating you have selected the WINDOWS folder. Notice also that the WINDOWS folder and drive information is displayed in the Address Bar. Look at the status bar. How many objects are within the WINDOWS folder? How much disk space do these objects use?

11. Make sure the **Tiles** view is selected. Scroll in this window until your screen resembles Figure 12-10 (with the system folder at the top). Leave this window open for the next Step-by-Step.

> **Note**
>
> If the WINDOWS folder has not previously been opened on your system, instead of the folders appearing, a message may appear that says *These files are hidden* which advises you not to modify the contents of this folder. If you see this message, you can click on the last line of the message that says *Show the contents of this folder*. You can also click the **Show the contents of this folder** link under System Tasks (in the Common Tasks panel) to display the objects in the WINDOWS folder.

FIGURE 12-10
Contents of the Windows folder

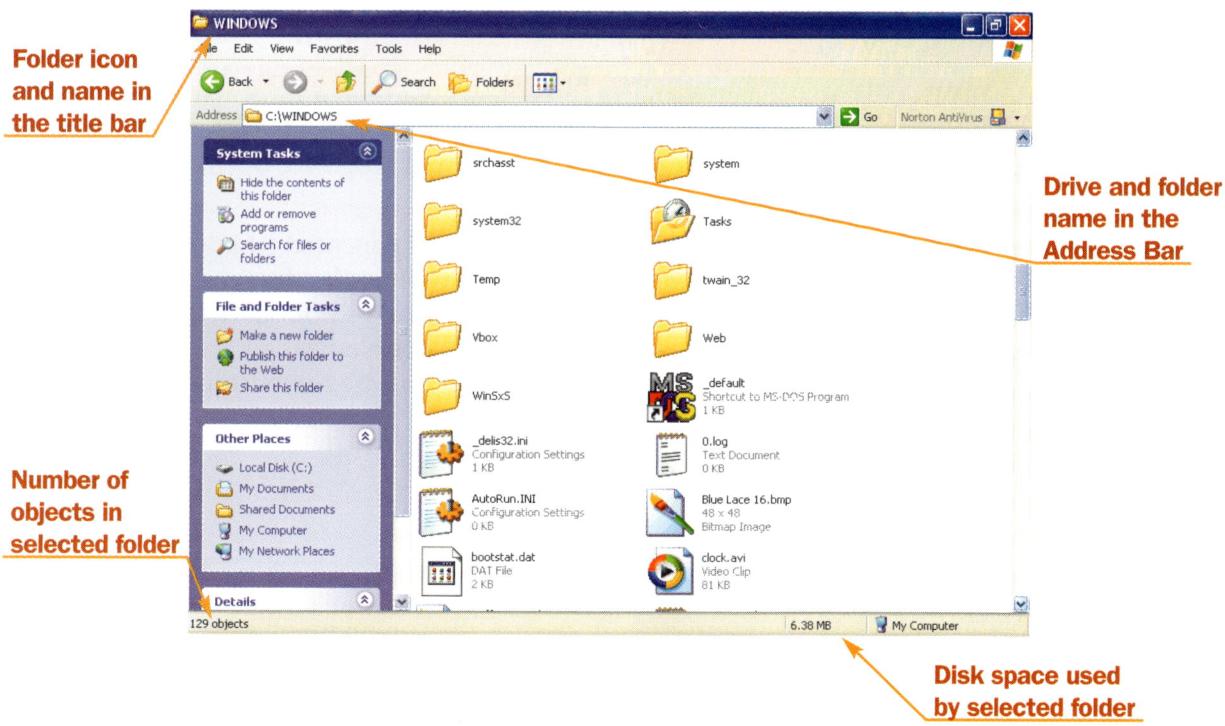

Identifying Object Icons and Using the Details View

With practice, you'll easily identify many icons. But what about those icons you don't know? A simple solution is to display the window in the Details view (Figure 12-11). To do so, select the Details option from the View menu.

FIGURE 12-11
The Type column identifies the file type for each object in the Details view

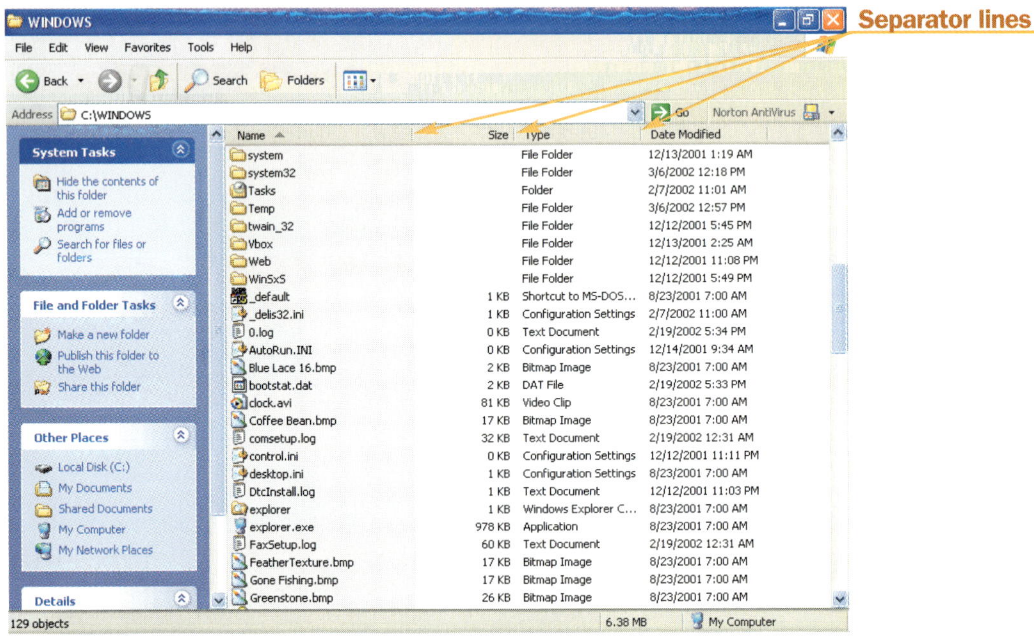

When you choose Details, the screen displays three new columns of information: Size, Type, and Date Modified. You can customize the columns that appear in Details view by selecting the Choose Details option on the View menu. A Column Settings dialog box opens where you can choose to display or hide different types of information.

As you can see in Figure 12-11, listings under Type may be truncated (that is, cut off) if the Type column is narrow. You can easily change the width of a column by dragging one of the vertical separator lines (labeled in Figure 12-11) that mark the column's boundaries. To drag a separator line, place the mouse pointer on the line. It becomes a double-headed arrow. Hold down the main mouse button and drag in the desired direction, then release the button.

STEP-BY-STEP 12.4

1. Click the **View** button drop-down list arrow, and select **Details** to expand the display.
2. Expand the Type column to see all entries:
   - **a.** Place the mouse pointer over the separator line between the Type and Date Modified columns. The pointer becomes a double-headed arrow.
   - **b.** Drag the separator line to the right until you can read all the entries in the column.
3. Click the **Up** button on the toolbar to close the WINDOWS folder.
4. Click the **Up** button again to return to My Computer and display your system's resources.
5. Click the **Close** button on the My Computer window.
6. If instructed to do so, shut down Windows XP and your computer.

SUMMARY

In this lesson, you learned:

- Computer disks store electronic files, which they organize into folders and subfolders. Using My Computer to create folders and subfolders lets you group and organize electronic files, just as cabinets and folders allow you to organize paper documents—systematically.
- When you start My Computer, you see a window with the familiar title bar, menu bar, display window, and status bar. The My Computer window may also contain a toolbar and an Address Bar.
- The My Computer window contains two types of icons: disk drive icons, which identify the disk drives you can access on your system; and folder icons, which represent the folders containing files on your system.
- A floppy disk drive is generally labeled A; the initial hard drive is usually labeled C; and additional drives, such as CD-ROM or DVD/CD-RW, are labeled D, E, and so forth. To access a drive, double-click the drive icon in the My Computer display window.
- Buttons on the My Computer Standard toolbar let you navigate among your system's resources and control the display of objects. You can customize the Standard toolbar by adding and removing a number of editing, navigating, and functional buttons.
- You can display the contents of a selected drive or folder by double-clicking the icon in the display window.
- You can display the contents of a selected drive or folder in five views: Thumbnails, Tiles, Icons, List, and Details. The specific details shown and the icon arrangement will vary depending on the view you choose.
- Various types of icons represent objects within folders.

VOCABULARY *Review*

Define the following terms:

Disk	File	Hard disk
Disk drive	Floppy disk	Subfolder
Disk drive icons	Folder	

REVIEW *Questions*

MULTIPLE CHOICE

Circle the best response for each of the following statements.

1. Double-clicking an object in the My Computer window opens the item and displays its name in the
   A. menu bar.
   B. Standard toolbar.
   C. Address Bar.
   D. status bar.

2. A hard disk is different from a floppy disk. Specifically, a hard disk
   A. is portable and easy to remove.
   B. is normally inserted into a built-in disk drive.
   C. cannot be easily removed from the computer.
   D. is sometimes called a diskette.

3. To customize the Standard toolbar, you select Customize on the
   A. View menu.
   B. Toolbars submenu on the View menu.
   C. View submenu on the Edit menu.
   D. Tools menu.

4. In My Computer, the Details display does not, by default, include a file's
   A. size.
   B. type.
   C. filename.
   D. author.

MATCHING

Write the letter of the term in Column 2 that matches the definition in Column 1.

Column 1	Column 2
___ 1. Magnetic medium on which data is stored	A. floppy disk
___ 2. Hardware that finds, reads, and writes information to and from a disk	B. disk
___ 3. Small, portable storage device	C. folder
___ 4. Fixed unit within the computer	D. hard disk
___ 5. Used to organize files and subfolders on a disk	E. disk drive

PROJECTS

PROJECT 12-1

1. Start Windows if it is not already running.
2. Open **My Computer**, and perform the following steps:
   A. Change the view to **Details**.
   B. Change the view to **List**.
   C. Change the view to **Icons**.
3. Click the **Address Bar** drop-down list arrow, and select **Recycle Bin**.
4. Click the **Back** button to return to My Computer.
5. Double-click the icon that represents your computer's hard disk.
6. Double-click a folder on your computer's hard disk to view its contents.
7. Change the view to **Tiles**.
8. Click the **Up** button until My Computer appears in the Address Bar.
9. If necessary, change the view to **Tiles**.
10. Click the **Close** button to close My Computer.

PROJECT 12-2

1. Open **My Computer**.
2. Click the icon that represents your computer's hard disk.
3. Select **Folder Options** on the Tools menu bar.
4. Select **Show common tasks in folders** on the Tasks section of the General tab, and then click **OK**.
5. Double-click your computer's hard disk icon, and then double-click any folder on your hard disk.
6. Change the view to **Details**.
7. Point to the separator line between the Name and Size columns. When the mouse pointer becomes a double-headed arrow, drag the separator line to the left until the Name column is approximately the same width as the Size column.
8. Adjust the widths of the Type and Date Modified columns to approximately the same width as the Name and Size columns.
9. Readjust all column widths so the full contents of each are displayed.
10. In the Other Places section of the Explorer Bar, click **Local Disk (C:)** to return to the hard disk.
11. Change the view to **Tiles** if necessary.
12. Close the My Computer window.

PROJECT 12-3

1. Open the **My Computer** window.
2. Select **Folder Options** from the Tools menu. Click the **Use Windows classic folders** option in the General tab under Tasks, and then click **OK**. Note the change in the window appearance.
3. Scroll up and down if necessary to review the full contents of the window.
4. Change the view to **List**.
5. Change the view to **Details**.
6. Open the **Folder Options** dialog box again, and click the **Show common tasks in folders** option on the General tab. Click **OK**.
7. Close My Computer. If instructed to do so, shut down Windows XP and your computer.

CRITICAL *Thinking*

ACTIVITY 12-1

One of your coworkers is collecting informal inventories of all employees' PC systems and desktop setups. She has requested a list of desktop contents and system resources on your computer. Use My Computer to compile the list. Write a short explanation of how you found this information.

LESSON 13

WORKING WITH DISKS, FOLDERS, AND FILES

OBJECTIVES

Upon completion of this lesson, you should be able to:

- Format a floppy disk.
- Magnetically label a floppy disk.
- Use Disk Cleanup to clear your disk of unnecessary files.
- Run the Disk Defragmenter.
- Create folders and subfolders.
- Name and rename folders.
- Delete folders and restore (undelete) a deleted folder from the Recycle Bin.
- Manage the display and organization of files.
- Copy and move files from one folder to another.
- Recognize and distinguish between different file icons.
- Run applications from My Computer.

Estimated Time: 4.5 hours

VOCABULARY

8.3 alias
Application file icons
Copy
Destination
Disk Cleanup
Disk Defragmenter
Document file icons
Extension
Filename
Formatting
Fragmented files
Move
Parent folder
Source
Subfolder

My Computer gives you a number of options for working with disks, folders, and files. In this lesson, you will learn how to use My Computer to manage and format floppy disks; create new folders on a disk and then name, rename, delete, and restore folders; and how to identify, manage, and open files.

Formatting and Labeling Disks

Floppy disks are commonly used to save and transfer files from one computer to another. It is important that you know how to prepare a disk properly to store your files safely. Formatting and labeling are two procedures you should be familiar with when working with floppy disks.

Formatting a Floppy Disk

Formatting prepares a disk for use on a specific type of drive—that is, it imprints a disk with the information it needs to work in that particular kind of drive. But beware: The formatting process removes all the information from a disk. Of course, Windows provides a safety net in the form of a message box that appears before you start the formatting process.

The Format dialog box shown in Figure 13-1 offers you a number of options for formatting a disk. These options are discussed below.

FIGURE 13-1
Format dialog box

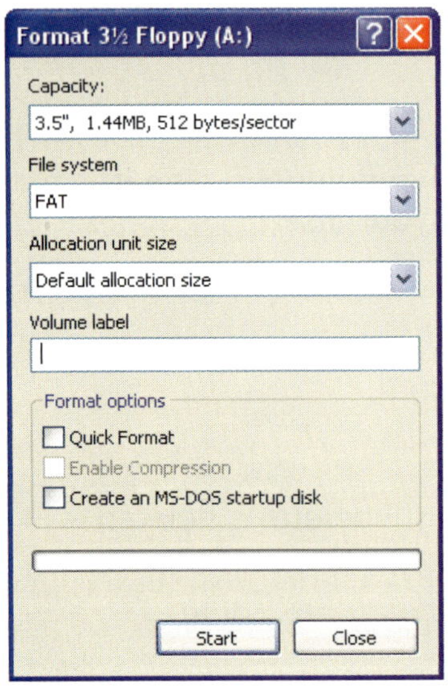

Capacity

First, the dialog box asks you to identify the disk by its capacity—such as 1.44MB for 3½-inch disks, 100MB, or 250MB. The dialog box will indicate whatever your system has the capacity to use.

Computer Concepts

Many manufacturers of floppy disks sell their products preformatted, so there is no need to format these disks. Just use them straight from the box.

File System

Windows XP supports one of the file allocation table file systems (FAT or FAT32) or the NTFS file system. While you must use the default system when formatting a floppy disk, you can select from among the options when formatting a hard disk. The options appear on the File system drop-down list.

Note

Most floppy disks manufactured today are high density.

Allocation Size

All file systems used by Windows XP organize your hard disk in clusters, which represent the smallest amount of disk space that can be allocated to hold a file. If you are formatting a floppy disk, Windows will select the appropriate allocation unit size indicated by the setting Default allocation size. You can select from among several options if you are formatting a hard disk, but the default settings are strongly recommended for general use.

Volume Label

Electronic volume labels are not essential, but they can be very helpful. For example, you may label one disk *Invoices* and another *Reports*. Unlike paper labels, electronic volume labels are visible only when you access the media. If you want to add an electronic volume label, enter the label text in the Volume label text box. If you prefer not to label, leave the text box blank. The file system determines the maximum number of characters that can be used in the volume label name: The volume label for FAT and FAT32 systems disks can contain up to 11 characters; the labels for NTFS system disks can contain up to 32 characters.

Format Options

You have a choice of formatting your disks using the full format option (the default) or the Quick Format option. Click the Quick Format option in the Format dialog box to select it, or leave it blank to use the full formatting option. The full format option checks a disk for problem areas (bad sectors); the Quick Format option does not. Use the Quick Format option only if the disk has been previously formatted and you are sure it is not damaged. You can also choose to compress folders and files by selecting the Enable Compression option.

Create an MS-DOS Startup Disk

Creating an MS-DOS startup disk will allow you to boot *only* into MS-DOS by giving you an MS-DOS prompt. The MS-DOS startup disk will contain no additional tools, so you need to be familiar with MS-DOS commands to go any further. To create the startup disk, insert a floppy disk into your computer's floppy drive, open My Computer, and then click the floppy drive to select it. On the File menu, click Format. In the Format dialog box, click Create an MS-DOS startup disk, then click Start. Click OK in the warning message dialog box.

The Formatting Process

To format a disk, insert it into the appropriate disk drive, select the drive, and choose Format from the File menu in My Computer. Select the desired options from the Format dialog box, and click Start. Click OK in the warning message dialog box. A formatting scale displays a progress report at the bottom of the dialog box as the task is completed. When the format is completed, a Format Complete message box appears.

Click the OK button to close the message box. When you return to the Format dialog box, you may choose to format additional disks. If you do, make the appropriate selections for each disk, and when you are ready, click the Start button to format. If you don't want to format additional disks, click the Close button to close the Format dialog box.

IC3

STEP-BY-STEP 13.1

1. Using a pen, write **Windows Practice** on an external disk label. Then place the label on your disk.

2. Insert the Windows Practice disk in the correct drive.

3. Start **My Computer** by clicking its icon on the Start menu. Select the **List** option from the View menu if necessary.

4. Click the icon of the drive where you inserted the disk.

-3.2.18-2

5. Select **Format** from the File menu. The Format dialog box appears.

STEP-BY-STEP 13.1 Continued

1-3.2.18-1

6. Verify that the appropriate capacity is indicated: This could be a high-density of 1.44MB on a floppy disk, or 238 MB on a zip disk.

7. Leave the volume label text box blank.

8. Make sure the Quick Format option is not selected.

9. Click the **Start** command button. Click **OK** in the warning box. The bar at the bottom of the dialog box shows the progress of the format.

10. When the format is complete, click **OK** in the message box.

11. Click the **Close** button to close the Format dialog box.

Electronically Labeling Disks

Just as a paper label identifies a disk on the outside, a volume label identifies a disk on the inside—that is, electronically—with a magnetic label. You can label a disk when you format the disk as discussed above, or you can add the label after the disk is formatted. You can also change the label whenever you wish. To label a disk or change the label of a disk that has already been formatted, select the Properties option on the File menu. The Properties dialog box for your floppy disk drive opens, as shown in Figure 13-2. On the General tab, key the name of the disk in the text box at the top of this page. Note that many symbols and characters (such as *, ?, /, \, |, ;, :, +, =, [,], <, >, and ") are considered invalid characters and cannot be used in FAT volume labels.

FIGURE 13-2
Label a disk in the Properties dialog box

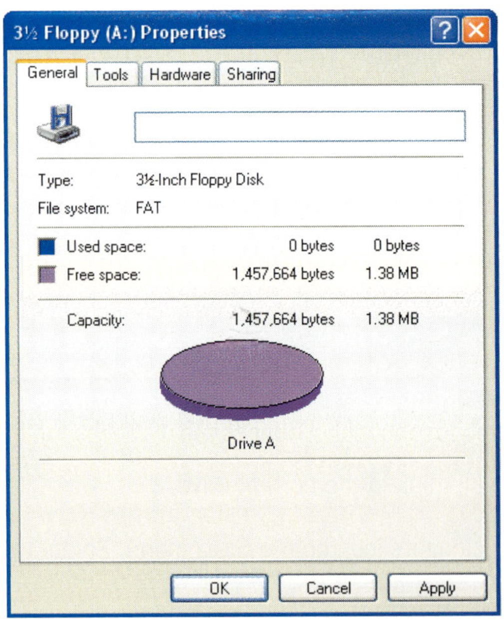

The disk label will not appear in the My Computer window. The label can be viewed only by displaying the Properties dialog box.

STEP-BY-STEP 13.2

1. Verify that your Windows Practice disk is in one of the floppy drives. Then select that drive.
2. Select the **Properties** option on the File menu.
3. Verify that the **General** tab is selected.
4. An insertion point is blinking in the text box at the top of this page. Key your last name (or a shortened version if it is longer than 11 characters or 32 characters if you are using NTFS). If the disk already has a label, the text box will display it. Keying a new label replaces the former name.
5. Click the **OK** button to record the label, or click **Cancel** if you do not want to record the label. The Properties dialog box closes.
6. Close My Computer.

Managing Disks

A trouble-free hard disk is extremely important to the Windows program. Windows uses your hard disk for temporary storage, and many Windows application programs create temporary files on the hard disk as you use the application. If your hard disk is not in good working order, you may find your system slow in responding or you may have problems running programs and opening documents.

Windows comes with a number of tools to keep your system in good working order. You can review all of these by looking up system tools in the Windows Help facility. For the remainder of this lesson, we'll discuss two important disk maintenance tools: Disk Cleanup and Disk Defragmenter.

Disk Cleanup is a program that enables you to clear your disk of unnecessary files. ***Disk Defragmenter*** rearranges the files on your disk, repositioning the files in one place so the disk performs optimally. An error-checking tool that reads a disk's vital signs and either warns you about problems or fixes them is also available in the My Computer Properties dialog box; it is called the Check Disk tool.

Locating and Deleting Unnecessary Files

You can use Disk Cleanup to help free up space on your hard drive. Disk Cleanup will not work on floppy drives or CD-ROM disks. The Disk Cleanup program searches your drive and then shows you temporary files and unnecessary program files you can safely delete. You can direct Disk Cleanup to delete some or all of those files.

Note

If you have more than one hard drive on your system, you will see a Select Drive dialog box before the Disk Cleanup dialog box. Select the drive to be cleaned and click **OK**.

STEP-BY-STEP 13.3

1. Open the **Start** menu.
2. Select the **All Programs** option, select the **Accessories** option, choose the **System Tools** option, and then select the **Disk Cleanup** option. The Disk Cleanup message box appears showing the progress of the scan of your hard drive.

STEP-BY-STEP 13.3 Continued

3. When the scan of the hard drive is complete, the Disk Cleanup for (C:) (or the drive selected) dialog box indicates how much disk space you can gain by cleaning up the disk (see Figure 13-3).

4. Only certain file types are selected for deletion by default. Scroll through the list of files to see what other files could be deleted and how much space could be gained on the hard drive by their deletion.

FIGURE 13-3
Disk Cleanup dialog box

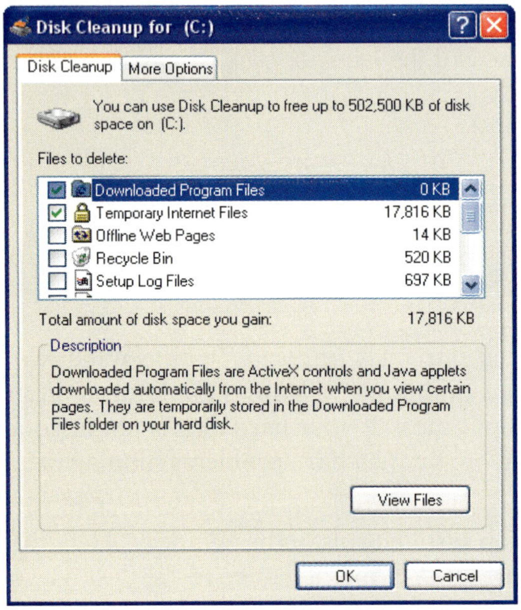

5. Click the **More Options** tab in the Disk Cleanup dialog box. You will see you have three additional options for cleaning up your disk (see Figure 11-4). The Windows components option permits you to remove optional Windows program components you do not use. The Installed programs option permits you to remove programs you may no longer need or use. The System Restore option tracks changes to your computer and creates a restore point when it detects the beginning of a change. It permits you to remove all but the most recently saved system restoration point or to restore your computer to an earlier state in which your computer was functioning the way you liked.

STEP-BY-STEP 13.3 Continued

FIGURE 13-4
Additional disk cleanup options

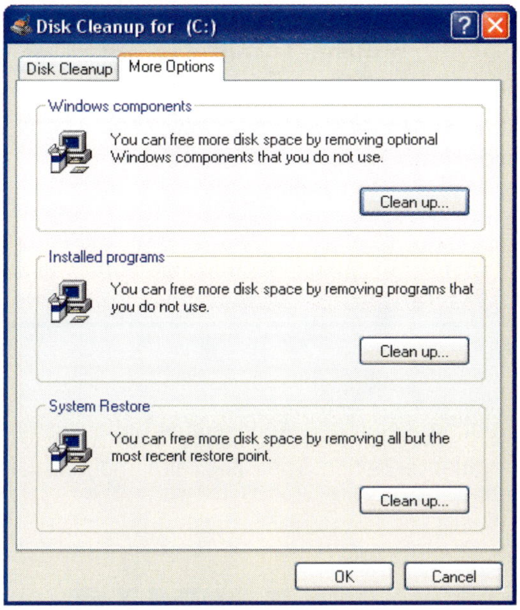

6. Click the **Cancel** button to close Disk Cleanup without performing any actions.

Each option on the More Options tab launches a separate program to perform the actions described. You would need to select each of these options independently. If you wanted to actually clean up the hard drive on your system (deleting the files listed on the Disk Cleanup tab), you would click OK in the Disk Cleanup dialog box. A message box would ask you to verify that you wanted to perform this action—in which you would click OK. Then the disk cleanup would proceed. Depending upon the number of files involved, the speed of your system, and so on, a disk cleanup can take anywhere from just a couple of minutes up to a half an hour or more.

Defragmenting a Disk

Disks—both hard and floppy—store data in clusters, also referred to as allocation units. A cluster is the smallest amount of disk space the operating system can handle when it writes or reads a file and is usually equal to 512 bytes or the default size of the disk. When you store files on a newly formatted disk, Windows writes each file's data in adjacent clusters. For example, the data for the first file saved might be stored in clusters 3 through 15, the next file's data might use clusters 16 through 30, and a third file's data might use clusters 31 and 32. In this way, Windows stores data in contiguous clusters; that is, in clusters that are adjacent on the disk.

What happens when you delete files? Each time you delete a file, you empty clusters and make them available for new data. To optimize your disk space, Windows uses these now-empty clusters as you save new files. First, Windows saves as much data as possible in the first available cluster, then the next available cluster, and the next, and so on, until it has stored all the remaining file data. In this way, Windows splits file data among clusters that are not contiguous. In other words, in its efforts to optimize disk space, Windows creates ***fragmented files***, files that are not stored in contiguous clusters. In the normal process of saving new files and deleting old files, your disk becomes quite fragmented.

Fragmentation does not harm a disk, but heavy fragmentation can slow down the disk's read and write times, thus reducing disk efficiency. To enhance disk performance, use Windows' Disk Defragmenter or a similar program. Disk Defragmenter rearranges disk files, storing each file in contiguous blocks.

First, Defragmenter looks at your disk and tells you what percentage of the disk is fragmented. If the disk is not heavily fragmented, you may not want to proceed; in that case, the Defragmenter gives you an option: continue or quit. If you continue, Disk Defragmenter begins to reposition the files. While Defragmenter is working, you can click the Show Details button to see a graphic display of the program's progress. Note that you cannot use Disk Defragmenter on floppy disks.

STEP-BY-STEP 13.4

1. Open the **Start** menu.

2. Select the **All Programs** option, select the **Accessories** option, choose the **System Tools** option, and then select the **Disk Defragmenter** option. The Disk Defragmenter dialog box appears (see Figure 13-5).

FIGURE 13-5
Disk Defragmenter dialog box

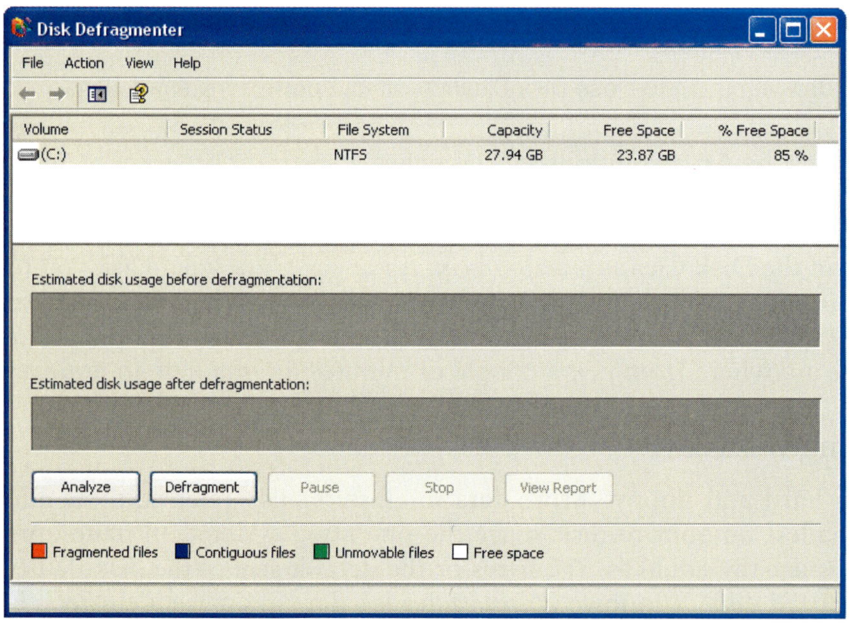

3. Select your hard disk, and then click the **Analyze** button. Be patient; it may take Windows a minute or two to analyze the disk.

4. A message box like that shown in Figure 13-6 appears, indicating that the analysis is complete.

STEP-BY-STEP 13.4 Continued

FIGURE 13-6
Defragmenter message box

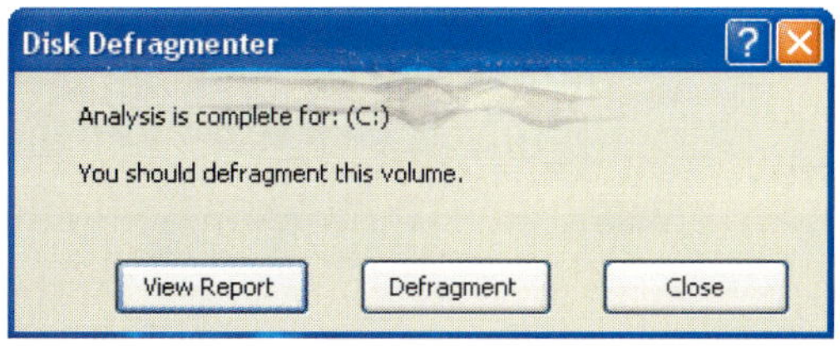

5. Click **View Report**. The Analysis Report dialog box opens, as shown in Figure 13-7.

FIGURE 13-7
Analysis Report dialog box

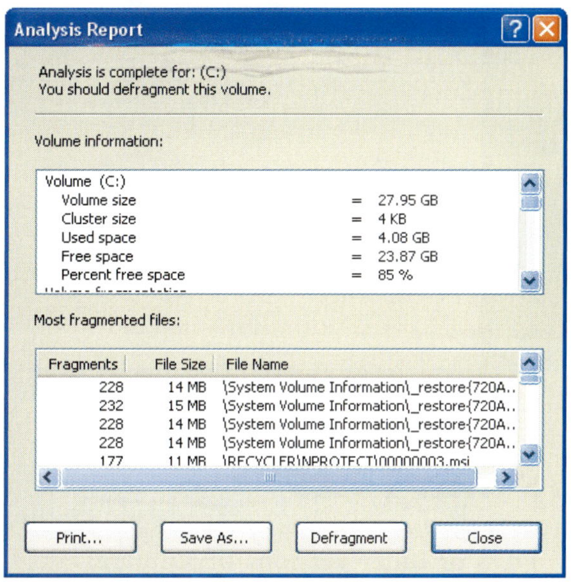

6. Click **Close** to close the report window.
7. If you have permission from your instructor to run Disk Defragmenter, click the **Defragment** button. Otherwise, proceed to Step 8.
8. Click the **Close** button to close the Disk Defragmenter. Remove your Windows Practice disk from the floppy disk drive. If instructed, shut down Windows and your computer.

Creating Folders

As you have learned, folders are used to organize files on a disk. When you want to create a folder to store files, your first decision is "On which disk will I place the new folder?" To create a ***subfolder***, your decision is "Under which ***parent folder*** will I place the new subfolder?" Remember, this is a creation process, a building process. You decide where to create or where to build.

Computer Concepts

There are a couple of other ways to make a new folder. You can choose **New** from the File menu and then select **Folder** from the submenu. Or you can right-click in the contents pane of the drive or folder in which you want to place the new folder and then choose **New** from the shortcut menu and **Folder** from the submenu.

With My Computer, you create folders and subfolders using a similar process. To create a folder, open the disk where you want the new folder to appear, then click the Make a new folder option in the Tasks panel on the left. A New Folder icon (see Figure 13-8) appears in the display window. To create a subfolder, double-click the folder where you want the subfolder to appear, then follow the instructions for creating a folder.

FIGURE 13-8
New Folder icon

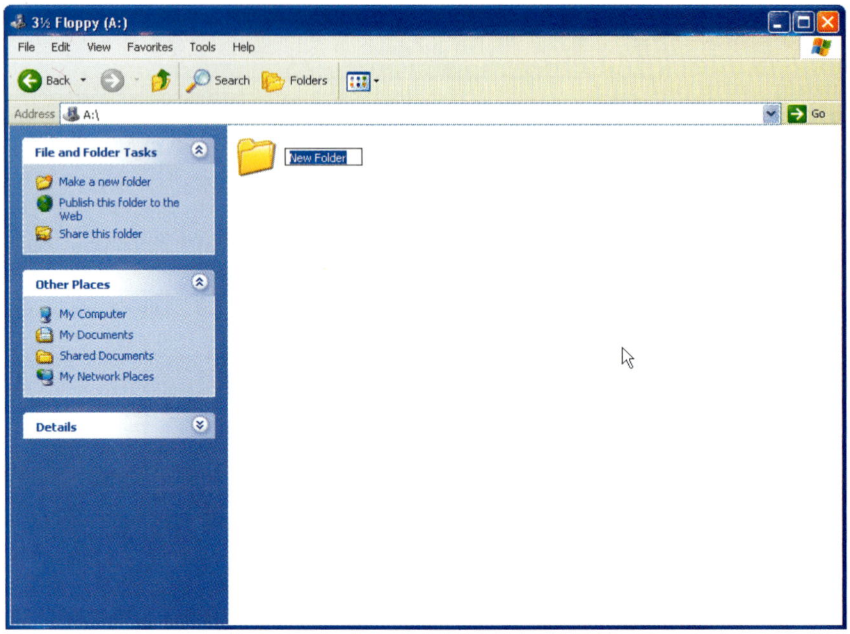

Naming Folders and Files

Are you familiar with DOS or older versions of Windows? If so, perhaps you know that both use a file-naming convention called *8.3* (pronounced "eight dot three"). The "eight" part means that a file's name may be up to eight characters long. The "three" part is an ***extension*** (no longer than three characters) to the name. And the "dot" is the period that separates the 8 from the 3. Neither spaces nor special characters can be used in the DOS naming system. For example, in the ***filename*** *letter.doc*, the name is *letter*, the separator is the standard period, and the extension is *doc*. There you have it: 8.3.

Newer versions of Windows, including Windows XP, allow long names (up to 255 characters) for folders and files, and they allow spaces, punctuation marks, and most characters in the names. They allow you to name a folder *JL Smith & Company Contract* instead of a code name such as *jlscocon.doc*.

But only application programs designed specifically for Windows 95 and later versions will permit long filenames. To compensate, Windows (and Windows application programs) assigns a short filename, called an ***8.3 alias***. Programs that don't support long filenames see this 8.3 alias as the file's name.

Be extra careful working with programs that don't recognize long filenames:

- If you copy a folder or file with a long filename to a system that doesn't support long filenames, the system will use an 8.3 alias.

- When you open a file that has a long filename in a program that doesn't recognize long filenames, the long filename could get lost.
- Backup and restore programs that don't support long filenames will destroy the long filenames.

After you create a new folder (and before you click anywhere else or press Enter), simply key the folder name. As you key, your folder name replaces the words *New Folder*. Press Enter to display the new folder name.

STEP-BY-STEP 13.5

1. Start Windows if necessary, and then start **My Computer** from the Start Menu.
2. If necessary, change the view in the My Computer window to **Icons**.
3. Verify that your Windows Practice disk (or another disk you can work with) is in the appropriate floppy drive, then double-click the disk's icon in the display window (most likely labeled A: or 3 ½ floppy). Notice that the drive is now displayed in the Address Bar. Notice also that there are no icons in the display window. Why? Because your Windows Practice disk is a newly formatted disk—a clean disk.
4. Create a new folder called Reports:
   - **a.** Click **Make a new folder** in the File and Folder Tasks panel.
   - **b.** The New Folder icon—with the name *New Folder* highlighted—appears in the display window. Key the folder name **Reports**. Be sure to key upper- and lowercase as shown.
   - **c.** Press **Enter**. Do you see the new Reports folder in the display window?
5. Create three subfolders in the Reports folder:
   - **a.** Double-click the **Reports** folder icon to open it. The Reports folder icon and name are now displayed in the Address Bar (and the path may be included as well).
   - **b.** Click **Make a new folder**. The new folder appears.
   - **c.** Key the folder name **Monthly**, then press **Enter**.
   - **d.** Click anywhere in the display window, except on the newly created folder, to deselect it.
6. Following the instructions in Steps 5b–5d, create two additional subfolders in the Reports folder; name them **Quarterly** and **Final**. Your screen should resemble Figure 13-9. Remain in this screen for the next Step-by-Step.

STEP-BY-STEP 13.5 Continued

FIGURE 13-9
Three subfolders in the Reports folder

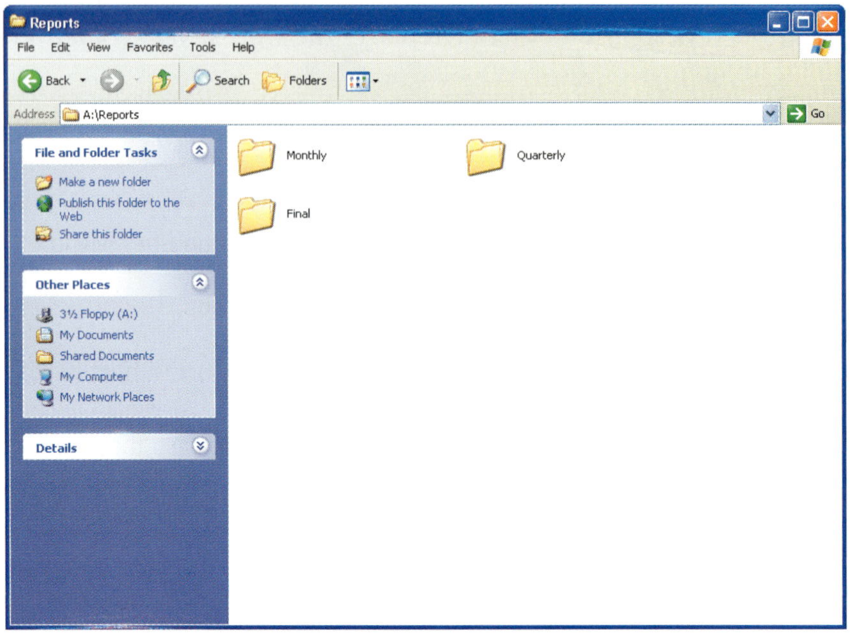

Renaming a Folder

It often happens that after you have used a folder for a time, you find you need to rename it. This is a simple process in My Computer. There are four ways to rename a folder:

- Click the folder to select it; click Rename this folder in the File and Folder Tasks panel; then key the new name in the text box.
- Click the folder to select it; press the F2 key; then key in the new name in the text box.
- Click the folder to select it; choose Rename from the File menu; then key the new name in the text box.
- Right-click the folder name; choose Rename on the shortcut menu; then key the new name in the text box.

Notice that folder maintenance tasks appear in the File and Folder Tasks panel displayed to the left of the folder contents. If no subfolder is selected, the File and Folder Tasks panel includes only Make a New Folder and Publish this folder to the Web. (If you are on a network, you may also see Share this folder.) If a subfolder is selected, the task list includes folder tasks such as Rename this folder, Move this folder, and Copy this folder.

Hot Tip

Make sure the parent folder in which you want to create a subfolder is displayed in the Address Bar before you create a new folder.

STEP-BY-STEP 13.6

1. Click the **Up** button to close the Reports folder, and return to the floppy disk display window.

STEP-BY-STEP 13.6 Continued

2. Click the **Reports** folder icon in the display window to select it.

3. Click **Rename this folder** in the File and Folder Tasks panel.

4. Key the new name **Status Reports**, and then press **Enter**. Leave this window open for the next Step-by-Step.

Deleting a Folder

You can delete a folder in four ways:

- Click the folder to select it; then select Delete from the File menu.
- Click the folder to select it; then select Delete this folder from the File and Folder Tasks panel.
- Click the folder to select it; then press the Delete key.
- Right-click the folder; then select Delete on the shortcut menu.

> **Computer Concepts**
>
> Rename folders with care. Application programs will not work if they cannot locate the folder names for which they are searching.

When you delete a folder or subfolder, you also delete all the files in it. Use extreme caution, therefore, before you attempt to delete a folder. To make sure this is what you really want to do, Windows displays a Confirm Folder Delete message box (see Figure 13-10). Windows provides one additional safety net when you are deleting a folder from a hard disk. Folders deleted from a hard disk are transferred by default to the Recycle Bin, from which they can be recovered. But a folder or a file deleted from a floppy disk is gone—period. No Recycle Bin is available.

FIGURE 13-10
Confirm Folder Delete message box

STEP-BY-STEP 13.7

1. Double-click the **Status Reports** folder to open the folder and display its subfolders.

2. Delete the Monthly subfolder:
   a. Click the **Monthly** subfolder to select it.
   b. Click **Delete this folder** on the File and Folder Tasks panel. The Confirm Folder Delete message box appears.
   c. Verify that the correct folder name (Monthly) is shown before you click the **Yes** button. Watch as Windows graphically illustrates the folder being deleted from the Status Reports folder.

STEP-BY-STEP 13.7 Continued

3. Click the **Up** button until you return to My Computer in the Address Bar.

4. Click the **Close** button to close My Computer.

5. Remove your Windows Practice disk from the floppy disk drive. If instructed to do so, shut down Windows and your computer.

> **Computer Concepts**
>
> My Computer allows you to turn off this Confirm Folder Delete message by checking the appropriate box in the Recycle Bin Properties dialog box. To prevent accidents, keep this option checked.

Restoring a Deleted Folder

As discussed above, a folder deleted from a hard disk goes to the Recycle Bin. The Recycle Bin acts as a temporary storage folder for files you delete and keeps track of where deleted files and folders were originally stored. Then if you need to recover a deleted folder, you can use the Recycle Bin to restore the folder to its original location on the hard disk.

To restore a deleted folder from the Recycle Bin you must restore them before you empty the Recycle Bin because emptying the Recycle Bin permanently deletes all the files currently in the Recycle Bin. Double-click the Recycle Bin icon on the desktop to open the Recycle Bin window (see Figure 13-11), which displays files deleted from the hard disk. To restore a file or folder, right-click it and choose Restore from the shortcut menu. To restore multiple items, select the items you want to restore; right-click any selected item; then select Restore this item from the Recycle Bin Tasks panel or the File menu. The selected file will be returned to its original location and it will no longer appear within the Recycle Bin.

> **Computer Concepts**
>
> The Recycle Bin stores only hard disk deletions, not floppy disk deletions.

FIGURE 13-11
Recycle Bin window

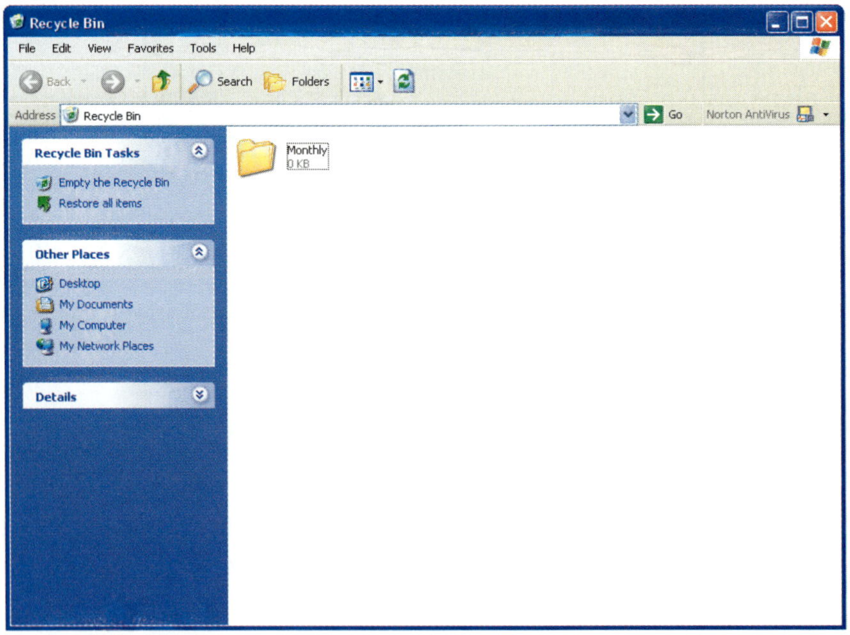

You can also choose to restore all items in the Recycle Bin by choosing Restore all items from the Recycle Bin Tasks panel.

Note

If you choose to Empty the Recycle Bin, the files are permanently deleted and cannot be restored.

Selecting Files

My Computer permits you to control how your files are organized by allowing you to *move* and *copy* files between disks and folders and to delete files. The first step in performing any of these functions is to select the files.

To select a single file, click it. To select two or more files that are adjacent to one another, click the first file in the series, press and hold down the Shift key, and then click the last file in the series (see Figure 13-12).

FIGURE 13-12
Selecting adjacent files

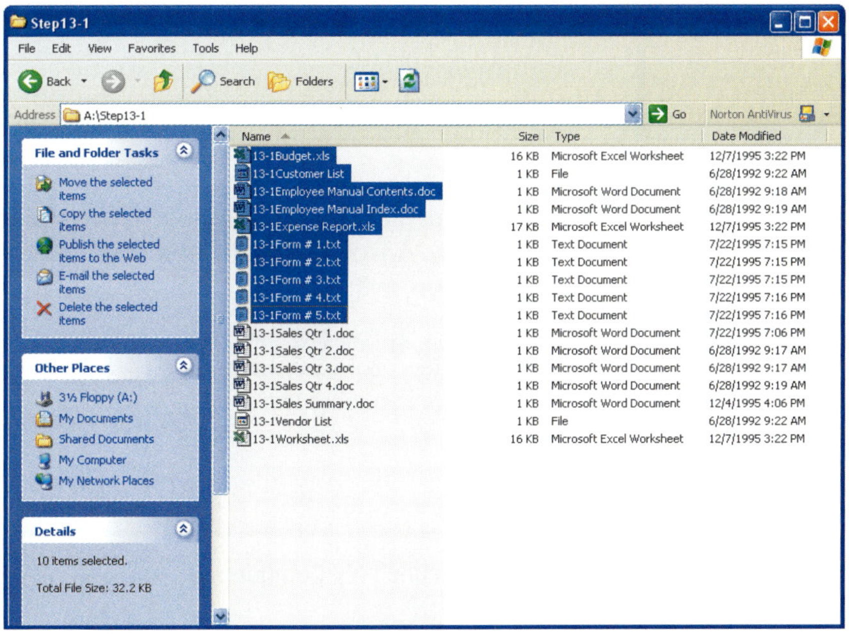

To select files that are not adjacent, press and hold down the Ctrl key and then click each of the files. In Figure 13-13, for example, nine nonadjacent objects are selected. Notice the information that appears about your selection in the Details section in the Common Tasks panel.

FIGURE 13-13
Selecting nonadjacent files

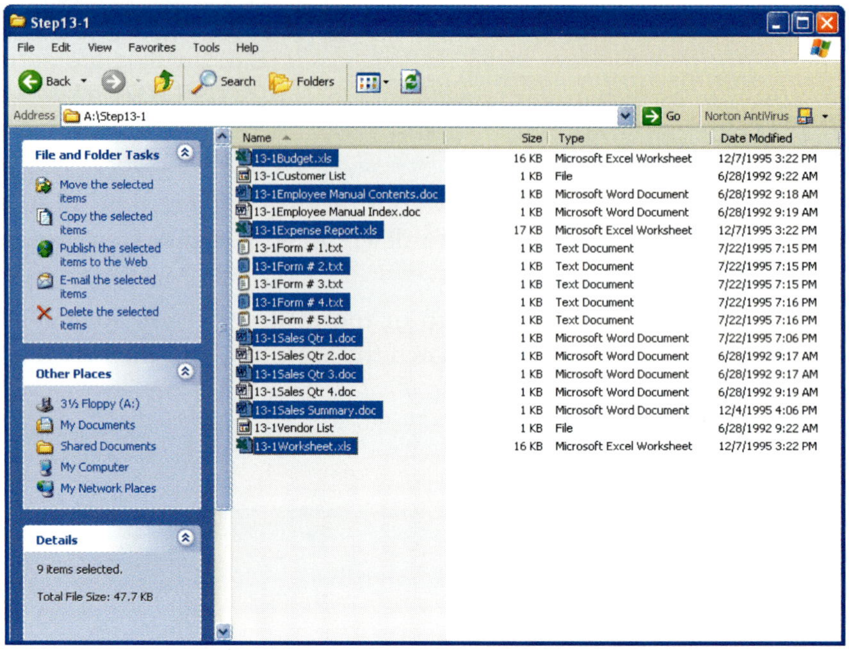

You can use the scroll bars to move around the display window when selecting files. Don't worry if the selected object moves out of view. An object will remain selected until you select another object or cancel the selection. When you want to cancel all the selections in a window, click a blank area in the window.

In the next Step-by-Step exercise, you will need to access the Step13-8 folder from your data files. Ask your instructor for further instructions if necessary.

STEP-BY-STEP 13.8

1. Start your computer if necessary, and then launch My Computer.
2. In the display window, double-click the drive that contains your data files for this lesson.
3. If necessary, scroll the window until the **Step13-8** folder is in view, then double-click it to open it. (You might have to click the **Show the Contents of This Folder** link in the Common Tasks panel to display the files and folders.)
4. Maximize the window.
5. Select the **Details** view if necessary.
6. Select the first file in the display window by clicking it once. (Be careful not to double-click, or you may open the file.)
7. Select nonadjacent files:
   a. Press and hold down **Ctrl**.
   b. Click every other filename you currently see in the window.

STEP-BY-STEP 13.8 Continued

8. Deselect the first selected file by pressing **Ctrl** and clicking the file's icon in the display window.

9. Deselect all the selected files by clicking once on a clear area in the display window.

10. Select adjacent files:
   a. Click the first file in the list.
   b. Press and hold down **Shift**. Then click the tenth file in the listing. All the intervening files will be selected.

11. Deselect all the selected files by clicking once on a clear area in the display window.

12. Click the **Up** button until My Computer is displayed in the Address Bar. Keep the window open for the next Step-by-Step.

Changing the Order of Files Listed in the Display Window

So far you have used My Computer's defaults to display the order of folders and files in the display window. But at times, you may want to change the display order—for example, you may want to see all files of one type grouped together. The Arrange Icons by options on the View menu (see Figure 13-14) allow you to control the order in which objects are arranged in the display window.

FIGURE 13-14
Arrange Icons by options on My Computer's View menu

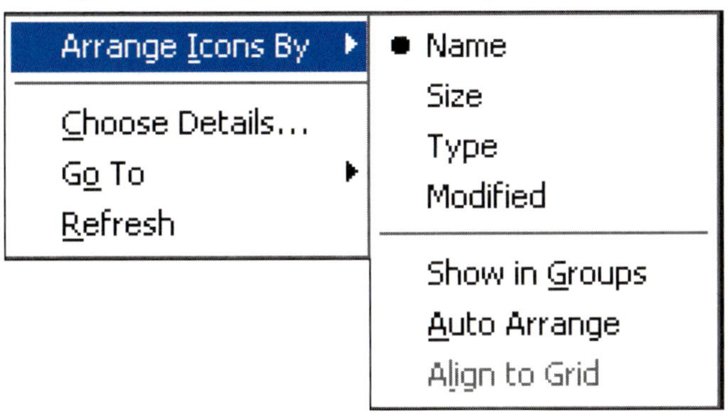

The Arrange Icons by submenu includes the following options:

- Name. This option sorts and displays folders and files in normal alphabetical order by folder or filename (with symbols first, then numbers, and finally letters). Names are case-sensitive: *Windows* is not the same as *windows* or *WINDOWS*. Folders are always placed before files when using this option.
- Size or Total Size. This option lists folders and files in order by size. By default, folders are listed first. Files are listed in ascending order.

- Type. This option displays folders and files grouped according to type (application, bitmapped image, folder, and so on). By default, folders are shown first.
- Modified. The Modified option lists folders and files in order by date from most recent to oldest.
- Show in Groups. This option displays items in groups (folders, files, and so on) under classifications based on the item by which the list is sorted.
- Auto Arrange. This option allows icons to be automatically repositioned to fill any gaps in the arrangements.
- Align to Grid. This option snaps the icons to an invisible grid so that they line up with each other even though the alignment might leave gaps in the arrangement.

You can use the above options in combination. For example, you can arrange the folders and files first by size and second by name. This gives you a list of files arranged by size, with objects of the same size arranged in alphabetical order by name. You may also click on the column heading bars (i.e, Name) to sort files and folders by that column. Click again on the column heading bar to toggle between ascending and descending order.

STEP-BY-STEP 13.9

1-3.3.3

1. Verify that the **My Computer** window is displayed on your screen. Locate your data files for this lesson.
2. Open the **Step13-9** folder from the data files and, if necessary, change the view to **Details**.
3. List the files by type in the display window:
   a. Select **Arrange Icons by** from the View menu.
   b. Click **Type**. Notice that a gray arrow has been placed to the right of the column heading *Type*.
4. List the files by size in the display window:
   a. Select **Arrange Icons by** from the View menu.
   b. Click **Size**. Notice that the files are now arranged by size.
5. List the files by the date modified in the display window:
   a. Select **Arrange Icons by** from the View menu.
   b. Click **Modified**.
6. Scroll the list, and notice that the files are now arranged by the date modified.
7. Change the listing back to **by Name**.
8. Click the **Up** button until My Computer is displayed in the Address Bar. Remain in this screen for the next Step-by-Step.

Displaying File Properties

1-3.2.16-1
1-3.3.3-1
1-3.3.3-2

The Properties dialog box for a file or folder in Windows displays information about the file or folder, including the type of file, the name of the program that opens the file, the file size, the file location, and the date the file was created and last modified. To display the properties for a file or folder in Windows, right-click the filename or folder in Windows Explorer, and then click Properties. Figure 13-15 shows the properties for a Microsoft Word file named Letter.doc.

FIGURE 13-15
Properties dialog box in Windows

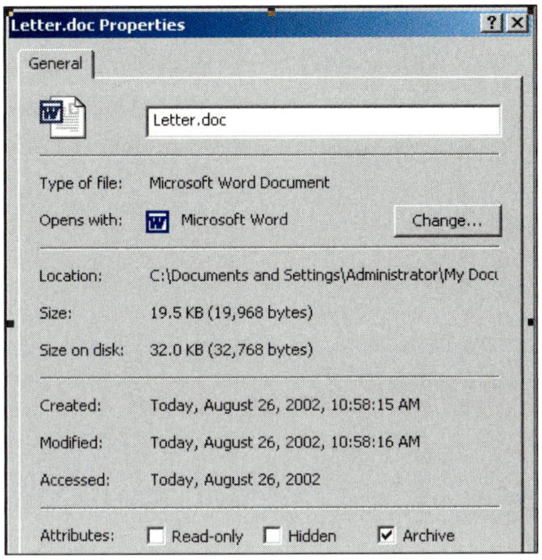

1-3.2.16-3 Files created in different programs can have additional properties that are displayed in the Properties dialog box within that program. For example, in addition to General properties, a Microsoft Word document can have Summary, Statistic, Contents, and Custom properties, which might include the document's author, the number of words and paragraphs in the document, and the name of the client for whom the document was created. Figure 13-16 shows the Summary tab of the Properties dialog box in Word for the file Letter.doc.

FIGURE 13-16
Properties dialog box in Microsoft Word

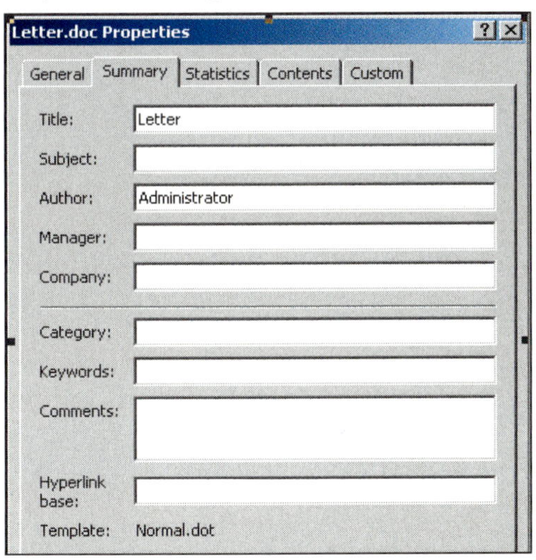

STEP-BY-STEP 13.10

1-3.2.16-1

1. Open Windows Explorer. To do this, right-click the **Start** button, and then click **Explore**.

STEP-BY-STEP 13.10 Continued

1-3.2.16-3
2. Search for two different file types—a word processing file (.doc) and a spreadsheet file (.xls).
3. Right-click on the file/folder.

1-3.2.16-2
4. Click **Properties**. Notice which properties are displayed.
5. Click **Print Screen**.
6. Open a graphics-capable program such as Microsoft Word.
7. Click **Edit** on the menu bar, and click **Paste** to paste the screen into Word.
8. Click **Ctrl + P** to print the screen.
9. Compare properties between the two types of files. Mark the differences/similarities directly onto the print-outs.
10. Close Windows Explorer.

Finding Files and Folders Using Windows

The Windows Search feature allows you to find files and folders by specifying a variety of search criteria. For example, you can search for files and folders by name, by date, by type, by size, or by a string of text that they contain.

To find a file, click the Start button on the taskbar, point to Search, and then click For Files and Folders. Figure 13-17 shows the Search Results window that opens.

FIGURE 13-17
Search Results window

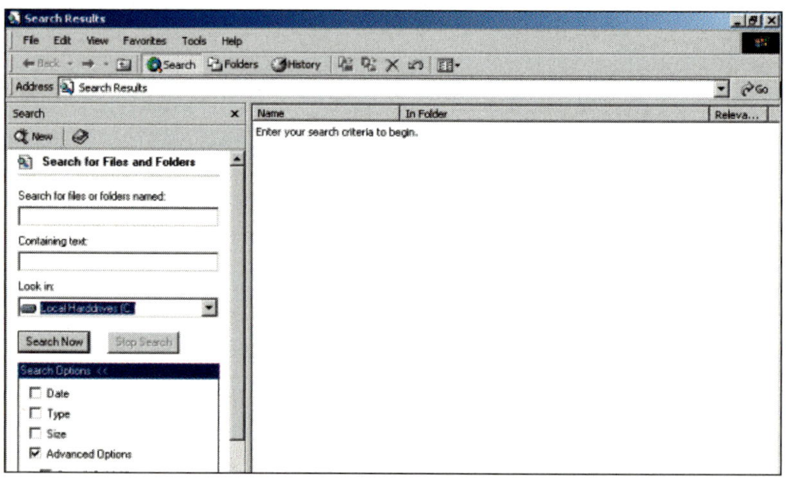

1-3.2.17-2
In the Search for files or folders named text box, type all or part of the name of the file you want to find. You can also type the wildcards * or ? to substitute for characters in a filename. Use * to substitute for zero or more characters; use ? to substitute for only one character.

To search for files containing specific text, type the text you want to find in the Containing text dialog box. Use the Look in list arrow to select the drive or folder you want to search. To specify additional search criteria, click Search Options, and then select one or more of the options to narrow your search. Table 13-1 describes the search options available in the Search Results window. When you are finished selecting search options, click Search Now.

TABLE 13-1
Search options

SEARCH OPTION	USE TO
Date	Find files that were created or modified on or between specific dates
Type	Find files of a specific type, such as a Microsoft Word document
Size	Find files of a specific size
Search subfolders	Search all the subfolders in a drive or folder
Case sensitive	Find files with upper- and lowercase letters that match the filename search criteria
Search slow files	Find files stored on removable storage devices, such as a tape backup device

IC3

STEP-BY-STEP 13.11

1-3.2.17-1

1. Click the **Start** button on the taskbar, point to Search, and then click **For Files and Folders**.
2. Key the name of a file from My Documents for which you would like to search in the Search for files or folders named field.
3. Choose **My Documents** from the drop-down menu of the Look In field.

1-3.2.17-2

4. Go to the Search Options box and check **Advanced Options**. Make sure that **Search Subfolders** is also checked.
5. Click on **Search Now**.
6. Select the file you searched for from the list of Search Results on the right side of the screen. Double-click on the file to open it.
7. Close the file.

Copying and Moving Files

IC3

1-3.2.19-1

One of the key advantages of using Windows is the ease with which you can copy or move files from one location to another. You move or copy files from a source to a destination. The ***source*** is the file to be copied, and the ***destination*** is the location (folder or disk) where the copied file will then reside. Whenever you need to move or copy files, make both the source and destination visible. In this way, you can see what you are moving or copying and where it is going. In

My Computer, you make the source and destination windows visible at the same time by changing the browsing option in the Folder Options dialog box to Open each folder in its own window. Folder options are available from the Tools menu.

When you **copy** a file, you place a duplicate of the file in a different location and the original file remains in place. To copy a file to a new location on a different disk, select it. You can select more than one file to copy using the techniques you learned earlier. You can also select a folder to copy. Then drag the object from its current location and drop it onto its destination; that is, to where you want to copy it.

The moving process is similar to the copying process. When you ***move*** a file, however, you remove it from its original location and place it in the destination window. To move an object to a new location on a different disk, select it, hold down the Shift key, and drag it to the destination window.

Rather than try to remember when to hold down the Shift key, an alternate method of moving and copying files is to drag the file using the right mouse button. When the file is dropped in the destination, a menu appears; you can then click on your preference: move, copy, or create shortcut.

If you attempt to copy or move a file to a destination where an identically named file exists, Windows displays the Confirm File Replace message box, shown in Figure 13-18. Click the Yes button to replace the existing file; click No to cancel the copy or move.

FIGURE 13-18
Confirm File Replace message box

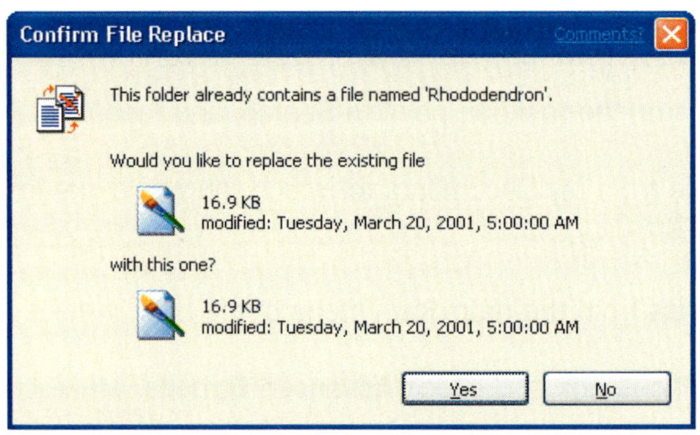

1-3.2.20 Take special care when moving, copying, or renaming files so that a file is not lost. You may inadvertently move a file to a location or rename a file and then forget the name or location. Another common error is that, when you rename a file using a different application than the original, the file is no longer associated with that original file and you won't be able to locate it.

Common problems associated with manipulating and working with files include lost files and file or disk corruption. You can avoid these problems by naming and storing files systematically, backing up data files regularly, checking for corrupted floppy diskettes before you start moving files to a disk, and checking for compatibility.

STEP-BY-STEP 13.12

1. Locate the data files for this lesson.

STEP-BY-STEP 13.12 Continued

2. Change the browsing option so each folder is opened in its own window:
   a. Select **Folder Options** from the Tools menu.
   b. Click **Open each folder in its own window** in the Browse folders section. Click the **OK** button.

3. In the My Computer window, click the **Up** button twice to open the Desktop in a new window. Notice that the taskbar button indicates that multiple windows are open.

4. Switch back to the My Computer window.

5. Double-click the icon representing the drive that contains your data files.

6. In the data files window, double-click the **Step13-12** folder to open it in a new window.

> **Note**
>
> If you open two or more My Computer windows, only one button will appear on the taskbar showing the total number of open windows in front of the name *Windows Explorer*. To access a specific window, click the button and choose the window you want from the pop-up menu. This grouping feature can be turned off in the Taskbar Properties dialog box by deselecting the Group similar taskbar buttons option. You can also close the whole group of open windows by right-clicking and choosing **Close Group**.

7. Double-click the **Status Reports** folder icon.

8. Double-click the **Final** folder.

9. Close all open windows except the Final folder window and the Desktop window (see Figure 13-19).

FIGURE 13-19
Copying and moving files in My Computer

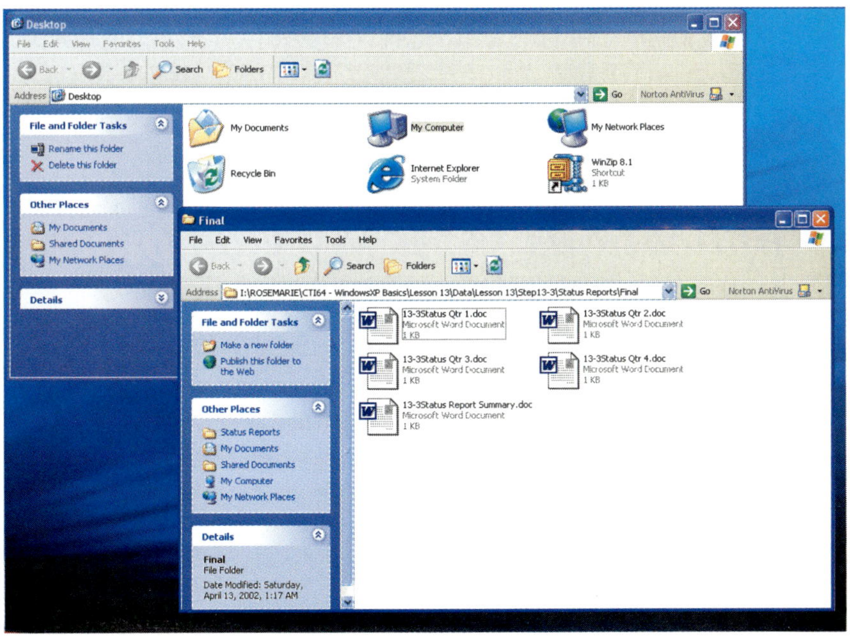

10. Right-click a blank area of the taskbar, then select the **Tile Windows Vertically** option from the shortcut menu.

STEP-BY-STEP 13.12 Continued

11. In the Final folder window, bring the **13-12Status Report Summary** file into view.

1-3.2.15-2 **12.** Point to the 13-12Status Report Summary file. Then drag the icon from the Final folder window to the Desktop window. Notice that, as you move the icon onto the Desktop window, there is a small plus sign (+) next to the pointer. This plus sign is a visual clue that you are copying the file. You will see the copied file in the Desktop window.

13. Select the **13-12Status Qtr 1** file from the Final folder window. Hold down the **Shift** key, and drag the file to the Desktop window. Release the Shift key. The 13-12Status Qtr 1 file now appears only in your Desktop window.

1-3.2.15-1 **14.** Move the **13-12Status Qtr 1** file back to the Final folder window using the shortcut menu. Hold down the right mouse button, and drag the file from the Desktop window to the Final folder. A shortcut menu will appear when you drop the file in its destination window. Use either the right or left mouse button to click on **Move Here** on the shortcut menu. The file will reappear at the end of the Final folder file list.

15. Move the **13-12Status Report Summary** from the Desktop back to the Final folder using the shortcut menu. Right-drag the file in the Desktop window to the Final folder window. Click **Move Here** when the menu appears. Because a copy of this file already exists in this window, you will see the dialog box to confirm that the existing file is to be overwritten. Click **Yes** to proceed. The file will no longer appear in the Desktop window.

16. Change the browsing option back to display each folder in the same window.

17. Close both open windows, but leave Windows XP running for the next Step-by-Step.

Hot Tip

To copy an object to a new location on the same disk, you must hold down the **Ctrl** key as you drag the object. Otherwise, Windows moves the file rather than copies it. Again, by using the right mouse button to drag the item to the new location, you will avoid having to remember which keystroke to use to move or copy.

Running Applications from My Computer

There are several ways to run an application, and one is by using My Computer. To start an application program with My Computer, you can double-click an icon or select the icon and then choose the Open option on the File menu. However, you cannot click just any icon to start an application. Only certain icons will start applications. Windows typically contains several types of icons, so you need to learn how to recognize the different types.

Recognizing File Icons

Running applications from My Computer is easy when you can distinguish among the different types of icons. My Computer's display window shows two basic file icons—***application file icons*** and ***document file icons***. Each has distinguishable characteristics.

Application File Icons

An application file icon starts an application. The icon may look like a miniature version of the program icon, or it may look like a miniature window (see Figure 13-20). In both cases, double-clicking an application file icon will start the application program.

FIGURE 13-20
Application file icons

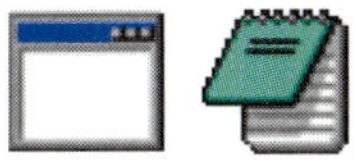

Document File Icons

Document file icons share the same distinctive feature: a piece of paper with a superimposed graphic (see Figure 13-21). When you create a document file, you can associate that file with an application. For Windows, this means you can create a link between a document and an application. In practical terms, this means you can open a document file directly—you do not need to open the application first.

FIGURE 13-21
Document file icons

Starting an Application Using the Open Command

One of the easiest ways to start an application from My Computer is to use the Open command on the File menu. As you will see in the next Step-by-Step, this is a simple process: Click the application icon, then choose Open from the File menu.

STEP-BY-STEP 13.13

1. Open **My Computer**.
2. Double-click the drive containing the data files.
3. Double-click the **Step13-13&14** folder. If necessary, change the view to **Icons**.
4. Click to select the NOTEPAD application icon (a small notepad with a blue cover and the caption *NOTEPAD*).
5. Select **Open** from the File menu. The Notepad application program opens in a window on top of the Step13-13&14 window, as shown in Figure 13-22.

STEP-BY-STEP 13.13 Continued

FIGURE 13-22
Starting an application using the Open command on the File menu

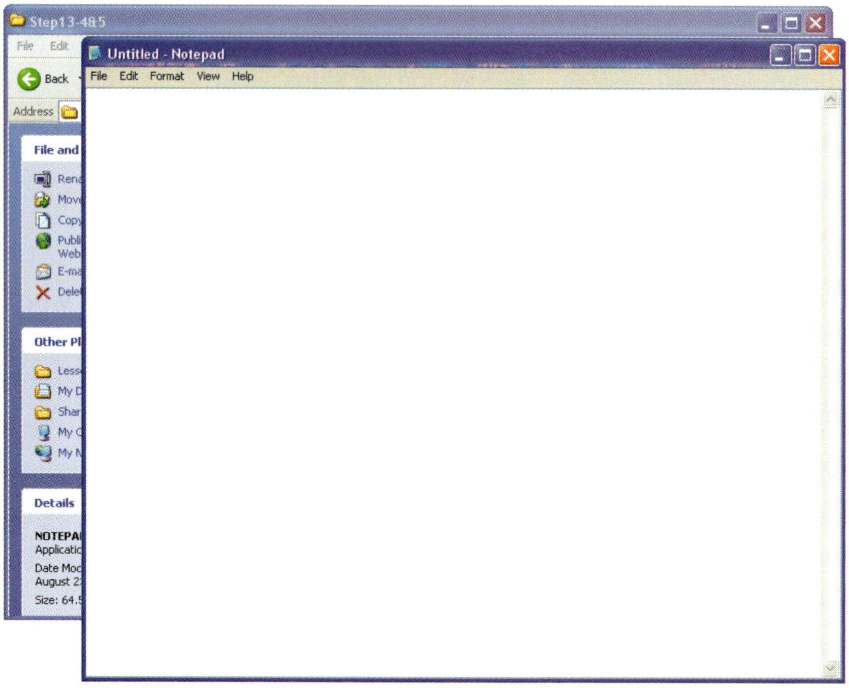

6. Click the **Close** button on the Notepad window to close the Notepad application program. Remain in this screen for the next Step-by-Step.

Starting an Application Using an Application File Icon

Rather than using the Open option, you can double-click an application file icon in My Computer's display window to start the application.

STEP-BY-STEP 13.14

1. The contents of the Step13-13&14 folder should still be displayed in the My Computer window.
2. Locate the CALC application icon (looks like a calculator), then double-click it to open it. The Calculator application program opens in the Step13-13&14 window, as shown in Figure 13-23.

STEP-BY-STEP 13.14 Continued

FIGURE 13-23
Starting an application by double-clicking its icon

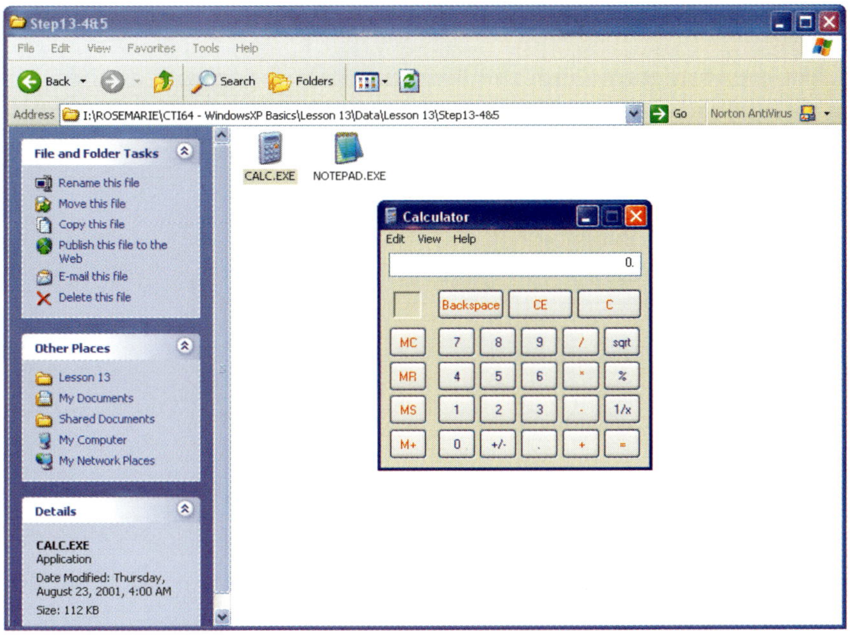

3. Click the **Close** button on the Calculator application window to close the application. Remain in this screen for the next Step-by-Step.

Starting an Application Using a Document File Icon

To open an application from a document file icon, double-click any document that is associated with an application. A document file icon is easy to spot because it shows the application icon on top of a sheet of paper (often with the upper right corner of the paper turned down).

STEP-BY-STEP 13.15

1. Click the **Up** button to return to the window that displays disk drive icons. Double click the icon for the drive that contains your data files. Open the **Step13-15** folder.

2. Locate the 13-15FL # 3 document file icon. Look closely at the icon. Does it look familiar? This icon resembles the Notepad application because the document file is associated with the Notepad application program.

3. Double-click the **13-15FL # 3** icon. The Notepad application opens with the title bar 13-15FL # 3 – Notepad displayed.

4. Click the **Close** button on the Notepad application window to close the document and the application.

5. Close My Computer. Leave Windows open for the next Step-by-Step.

Using the Run Command

You have learned how to open and run applications and their associated documents using several methods. Windows offers yet another way to start applications and open files and folders: the Run command on the Start menu.

When you select the Run command, the Run dialog box appears, as shown in Figure 13-24. The Open line in the dialog box contains the highlighted last document or program opened using the command.

FIGURE 13-24
Run dialog box

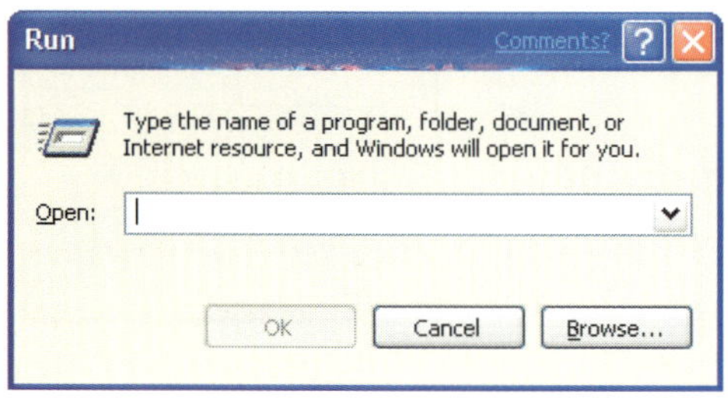

If you know the name of the document or program you want to open, you can key it in the Open text box and then click the OK button to carry out the command. Your keying automatically replaces the highlighted text. If you're not sure of the name or location of the file or program, you can browse for it by clicking the Browse button. Windows then displays a Browse dialog box that closely resembles the My Computer window. In this dialog box, you can open folders and scroll among files until you find the one you want. Double-clicking the found object returns you to the Run dialog box, where you'll find that Windows has filled in the name and path of the object. You then click the OK button to run the file or program.

STEP-BY-STEP 13.16

1. Select **Run** from the Start menu.
2. If the Open line contains text, make sure it is highlighted.
3. Key **Notepad**, and click the **OK** button. The Notepad application appears in a window.
4. Close the Notepad window.
5. Select **Run** again from the Start menu. This time use the Browse button to find the Notepad file named 13-15FL # 3:
   - **a.** Make sure any entry in the Open line is highlighted.
   - **b.** Click the **Browse** button. In the Browse window, make sure **My Computer** is displayed in the Look in text box, then double-click the drive where your data files are located.
   - **c.** Open the **Step13-15** folder. Click the down arrow on the **Files of type** drop-down list, and select **All Files**.
   - **d.** Scroll to locate the **13-15FL # 3** document file, then double-click it.
6. Notice that the filename and its path now appear in the Open text box. Click the **OK** button. The 13-15FL # 3 document appears in a Notepad window.

STEP-BY-STEP 13.16 Continued

7. Close the 13-15FL # 3 document.

8. Close all folders. Remain in this screen for the next Step-by-Step.

The commands you key on the Open line in the Run dialog box are stored on the Open drop-down list. Clicking the drop-down list arrow displays a list of up to 20 of your most recently used Run commands. Simply click any "stored" Run command on the Open drop-down list, click the OK button, and Windows does the rest.

The drop-down list also appears as you key text. This is called AutoComplete. You can continue keying a filename, or if you see the filename you intend to key in the listing, you can select the filename from the list.

Opening a Folder Using the Run... Command

You can also use the Run command to open folder windows without actually running any program. To open a window for the folder C:/Windows, for example, simply key that string of characters in the Open text box and click the OK button.

STEP-BY-STEP 13.17

1. Select **Run** from the Start menu.

2. Click the **Open** drop-down list arrow to display the list of previously used commands.

3. Click **Notepad**, and click the **OK** button. The Notepad window appears.

4. Close the Notepad window.

5. Select **Run** again from the Start menu.

6. In the Open text box, key **c:**. Notice that the drop-down list appears as you key the text.

7. Finish keying **c:\Windows**, and then press **Enter**.

8. Close the folder window. If instructed to do so, shut down Windows XP and your computer.

Computer Concepts

If you have AutoComplete turned off, the drop-down list will not appear as stated in Step 6 of Step-by-Step 13.17. With AutoComplete turned off, you always need to key in the entire path and filename.

SUMMARY

In this lesson, you learned:

- Formatting prepares a disk for use on a specific type of drive. In this context, formatting means imprinting a disk with the information it needs to work in that kind of drive. At the same time, formatting erases any information previously stored on the disk.

- You can give a disk an electronic (or magnetic) volume label. You can relabel a disk by keying a new name in the text box in the disk's Properties dialog box.
- You can use Disk Cleanup to clear your disk of unnecessary files.
- Disk Defragmenter rearranges the files on a hard disk so the disk performs optimally.
- You can assign descriptive names up to 255 characters long to folders and files; however, only Windows 95 and higher can accommodate long names. Windows will assign a short filename, called an alias, to each of these files so they can be used with programs that don't support long filenames.
- You can easily rename folders.
- Deleting a folder or subfolder deletes all the files within the folder as well. Folders deleted from a hard disk are transferred to the Recycle Bin. Folders deleted from a floppy disk are deleted permanently.
- You can restore a deleted folder from the Recycle Bin by double-clicking the Recycle Bin icon on the desktop, selecting the folder to be restored, and then selecting Restore this item from the Recycle Bin Tasks panel or the File menu.
- Files are moved or copied from a source to a destination. The source is the file to be copied, and the destination is the location (folder or disk) where the moved or copied file will be placed.
- When you copy a file, you duplicate the original. When you move a file, it is removed from its original location and placed in a new location.
- An application file icon may look like a miniature version of the program icon, or it may look like a miniature window.
- A document file icon looks like a piece of paper with a graphic on it. You can open an associated document file without opening the application first.
- To run an application, select the application's icon and then choose the Open command on the File menu. If you prefer, double-click the application's icon in the My Computer display window. If a document is associated with an application program, you can double-click the document's icon.
- Use the Run command to open a file or window. You can key the path of the file or window, choose it from the Open drop-down list, or use the Browse button to locate it.
- The AutoComplete feature displays a list of suggestions immediately below the text box as you key a filename. You can continue keying the filename, or you can pick a matching filename from the list of suggestions.

VOCABULARY *Review*

Define the following terms:

8.3 alias	Disk Defragmenter	Fragmented files
Application file icons	Document file icons	Move
Copy	Extension	Parent folder
Destination	Filename	Source
Disk Cleanup	Formatting	Subfolder

REVIEW *Questions*

TRUE/FALSE

Circle T if the statement is true or F if the statement is false.

T F 1. A single cluster is the smallest amount of space on a disk that the operating system can handle when storing data.

T F 2. If you format a previously used floppy disk, you can retain all the information on the disk.

T F 3. All application programs can recognize long filenames.

T F 4. Folders deleted from the hard disk can be retrieved from the Recycle Bin.

T F 5. A destination file is the file you are copying.

FILL IN THE BLANK

Complete the following sentences by writing the correct word or words in the blanks provided.

1. A(n) __________ label identifies a disk electronically.
2. The __________ format option checks a floppy disk for problem areas.
3. A long filename cannot exceed __________ characters.
4. The Windows program that enables you to clear your disk of unnecessary files is called __________.
5. Removing a file from its original location and placing it in a new location is called __________ the file.

PROJECTS

PROJECT 13-1

1. Start Windows, if necessary, and insert a blank floppy disk in the appropriate drive.
2. Start My Computer and click the icon of the drive where you inserted the disk.
3. Format the disk:
   - A. Select **Format** from the File menu.
   - B. Verify that the Quick Format button is unchecked and that there is nothing displayed in the Volume label text box.
   - C. Click the **Start** command button.
   - D. When the warning window appears, click the **OK** button.
   - E. When the format is complete, click **OK** in the message box, then click the **Close** button to quit the Format dialog box.
4. Apply a label to the disk:
   - A. Select **Properties** on the File menu.
   - B. Verify that the **General** tab is selected.

   C. Key your last name (or a shortened version if it is longer than 11 characters) in the text box.
   D. Click the **OK** button to record the label.

5. Close My Computer.

6. Remove the disk from the floppy disk drive. If instructed to do so, shut down Windows XP and your computer.

PROJECT 13-2

1. Start Windows if it is not already running, and open **My Computer**.

2. Set the Browse folders option in the Folder Options dialog box to **Open each folder in its own window**.

3. Copy the Project 13-2 folder from the data files to the desktop:
   A. Double-click the disk drive and/or folder containing the data files.
   B. Switch to the My Computer window, and click the **Up** button to display Desktop in the Address Bar.
   C. Drag the Project 13-2 folder in the My Computer folder in data files to the Desktop window.

4. Move the Project 13-2 folder to your Windows practice disk:
   A. Insert your Windows practice disk.
   B. Hold down the **Shift** key and drag the Project 13-2 folder from the Desktop window to the floppy disk drive window.

5. Open the Project 13-2 folder on your Windows Practice disk, and do the following:
   A. Add a new subfolder called **Special Report #1**.
   B. Copy all the files with the words *Sales Manual* in their filenames to the Special Report #1 subfolder.
   C. In the Special Report #1 subfolder, rename the files that contain the word *Chapter* in their filenames by changing the word *Chapter* to **Part**.
   D. Add a new subfolder to the Project 13-2 folder called **Quarterly Reports**.
   E. Move the Progress Reports (Q 1, Q 2, Q 3, and Q 4)files from the Progress Reports subfolder to the Quarterly Reports subfolder.
   F. Delete the Progress Reports subfolder.

6. Change the browsing option to **Open each folder in the same window**.

7. Close all folder and subfolder windows. Close My Computer.

CRITICAL *Thinking*

ACTIVITY 13-1

Why would you want to use Disk Defragmenter? Survey at least three PC users whose usage could be described as heavy and ask whether they use Disk Defragmenter on their computers. Summarize your findings and conclusions.

ACTIVITY 13-2

Design a folder structure to organize files you might create for one of the following: your home organization, your job environment, your volunteer work. Create a parent folder and at least two more levels, with at least two folders in each level under one parent. Outline the structure on your Windows practice disk.

LESSON 14

USING SHORTCUTS AND WINDOWS EXPLORER

OBJECTIVES

Upon completion of this lesson, you should be able to:

- Explain what a shortcut is and how it is used.
- Create a shortcut using drag and drop and using the File menu.
- Assign a shortcut key to a shortcut.
- Delete a shortcut.
- Add a program to the Quick Launch bar.
- Define uses for Windows Explorer.
- Start Windows Explorer.
- Identify the parts of the Explorer window.
- Identify the icons in the Explorer display window.
- Use Explorer to view the contents of a drive or folder.
- Expand and collapse the folder list.
- Select Explorer Toolbar options.

Estimated Time: 2.5 hour

VOCABULARY

Contents pane
Folders bar
Shortcut
Shortcut key
Tree pane
Windows Explorer

If you use particular programs or documents frequently, you might want to create shortcuts for them so you can access them quickly and easily. Like My Computer, ***Windows Explorer*** is designed to help you find, view, and manage files and to use files easily and effectively. In this lesson, you will learn how to create and use shortcuts and how to start Explorer and set options to control the display of files and folders.

What Is a Shortcut?

A ***shortcut*** functions as a pointer to an application or a document file, wherever the file is located. When you double-click the shortcut icon, you're opening the actual item to which the shortcut is pointing.

The shortcut is represented by an icon on your desktop. A shortcut icon is identified by a small arrow in its lower-left corner (see Figure 14-1). Here's how a shortcut works. Suppose you create a shortcut to the OEWABLog file you opened in the last lesson. When you double-click the OEWABLog shortcut icon to open it, you are actually opening the WINDOWS folder, running the Notepad application program, and opening the OEWABLog file. So you can see why it is called a shortcut. Shortcuts save time because you don't have to open and browse through several folders to find the file you need.

FIGURE 14-1
Shortcut icon

Creating Shortcuts

You can create a shortcut by dragging a file to the desktop or by using the Create Shortcut command on the File menu. Shortcut menus also appear when you right-click a file or folder on your desktop, in the right pane of a folder window, or when you right-click an empty space on the taskbar or desktop.

Creating a Shortcut Using Drag and Drop

If you can display an item in the My Computer window, you can create a shortcut for it by dragging and dropping an item to the desktop with the right mouse button:

- Using the right mouse button, right-drag the item (file, program, folder, printer, computer) from its current location to wherever you want the shortcut to appear.
- Drop the item where you wish to place it by releasing the mouse button.
- A shortcut menu appears, giving you several options. Click Create Shortcuts Here.
- The icon appears with the shortcut arrow and a default name.

You may want to change the shortcut's default name to something different. To rename the shortcut, right-click the shortcut icon to display the Shortcut menu, shown in Figure 14-2. Choose Rename, and key the new name in the shortcut icon's text box. You can use this shortcut menu for a number of tasks, such as deleting a shortcut or changing its properties.

FIGURE 14-2
Shortcut menu

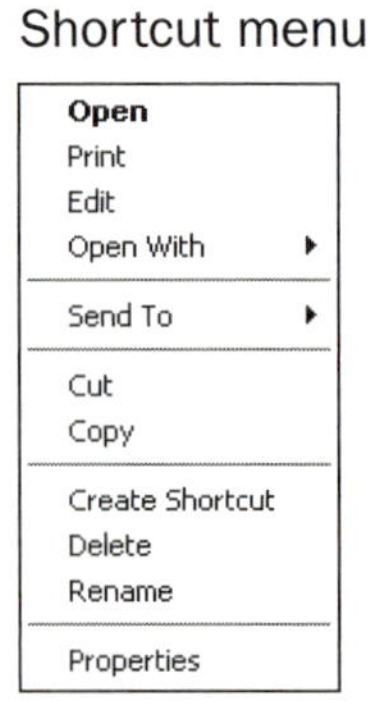

Computer Concepts

Your shortcut menu may have additional options besides those shown in Figure 14-2. For instance, if you have certain virus protection programs, you may see the Scan for viruses option on your shortcut menu.

STEP-BY-STEP 14.1

1. Start your computer, and open **My Computer** from the Start menu. If necessary, double-click on the icon for your hard disk drive, open the **WINDOWS** folder, and click the **Show the contents of this folder** link.

2. Locate the setuplog document file icon in the WINDOWS folder. The My Computer Window should NOT be maximized.

1-3.2.9-4 3. Make sure that part of your desktop is visible, and using the right mouse button, drag the setuplog document file icon to the desktop. Release the mouse button.

1-3.2.5-1 4. Select **Create Shortcuts Here** from the shortcut menu. The setuplog document shortcut appears on your desktop.

5. Rename the shortcut:
   - **a.** Right-click the **Shortcut to setuplog** icon.
   - **b.** Select **Rename** from the shortcut menu. Notice that the icon's name is now highlighted and has a blinking insertion point.

1-3.2.9-6 **c.** Key **My Shortcut** and press **Enter** to rename the icon. Remain in this screen for the next Step-by-Step.

> **Computer Concepts**
>
> If you use the left mouse button to drag a file from a folder on the C drive to the desktop, you will move the file and its icon to the desktop.

Creating a Shortcut Using the File Menu

You can also create a shortcut by selecting the item for which you want (a file, program, folder, printer, or computer) to create the shortcut in My Computer. Then from the File menu select Create Shortcut. Resize the window so you can see the desktop. A shortcut icon for the item appears as the last item in the My Computer window (see Figure 14-3). Drag the new shortcut icon to the desktop. Then you can rename it—as you have already learned.

> **Note**
>
> The icons shown with your .txt files may differ from those shown in Figure 14-3 depending upon what application is associated with text files on your system.

FIGURE 14-3
Using the Create Shortcut command on the File menu

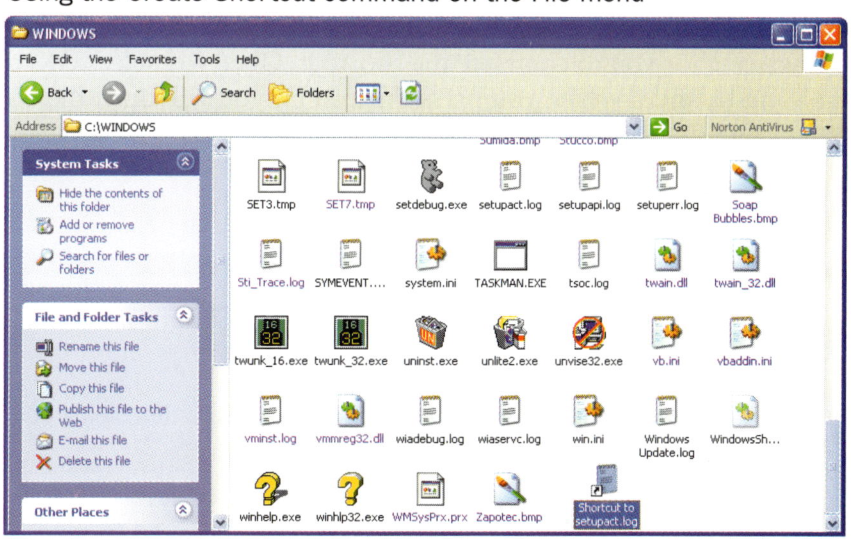

STEP-BY-STEP 14.2

1. Open the **system32** folder within the WINDOWS folder. If necessary, click the **Show the contents of this folder** link. *Note*: The capitalization of your system32 folder may vary. Yours may be System32 or SYSTEM32.

2. Locate and select the **calc** program icon.

3. Select **Create Shortcut** from the File menu. A *Shortcut to calc* icon will be placed at the end of the file listing.

1-3.2.9-5 4. Drag the shortcut (using the left mouse button) from the system32 folder in the My Computer window to the desktop.

1-3.2.9-2 5. Click the **Up** button in the system32 window, and locate and select the **NOTEPAD** program icon in the WINDOWS folder.

6. Select **Create Shortcut** from the File menu.

7. Drag the **Shortcut to NOTEPAD** icon from the WINDOWS window to the desktop.

8. Close the WINDOWS window. Leave Windows open for the next Step-by-Step.

Assigning a Shortcut Key to a Shortcut

A ***shortcut key*** is a keystroke combination that runs a program or opens the dialog box to which it is linked. For example, if you assign the shortcut key *Ctrl+Alt+N* to your My Shortcut, your new shortcut key will then open the setuplog document. You assign a shortcut key in the shortcut's Properties dialog box, which is accessible from the shortcut menu. You make the assignment by pressing and holding the Ctrl key and then pressing the key you want to complete the shortcut keystroke combination. When you press the Ctrl key, the combination Ctrl+Alt+ appears in the Properties dialog box. It ends with + because it is waiting for you to complete the shortcut. Once you select OK, the shortcut keystroke assignment is made, and anytime you press those keys, you will open the document.

Computer Concepts

If Windows is already using your selected keystroke combination for another shortcut, it will still allow you to make the assignment. When you enter the keystroke combination, however, Windows will run the other shortcut. In this case, just open the shortcut's Properties dialog box and select a different keystroke combination.

You can activate a shortcut in two ways: Double-click the shortcut icon, or issue the shortcut key combination.

STEP-BY-STEP 14.3

1. Right-click the **My Shortcut** icon.

2. Select **Properties** from the shortcut menu. The My Shortcut Properties dialog box appears.

STEP-BY-STEP 14.3 Continued

3. Make sure the Shortcut tab is displayed as shown in Figure 14-4.

FIGURE 14-4
Shortcut tab in the My Shortcut Properties dialog box

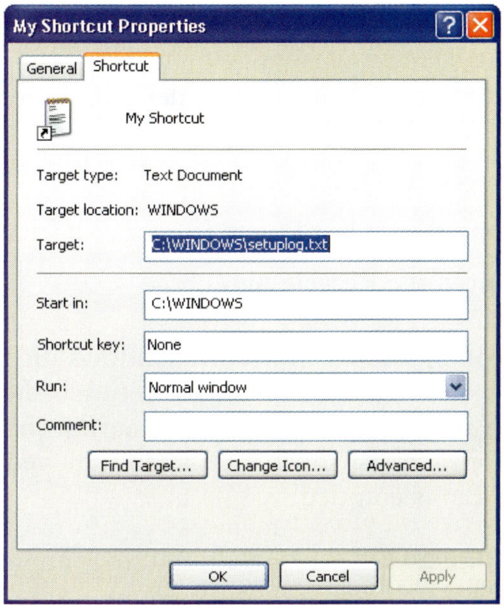

4. Click in the **Shortcut key** text box.

5. Press and hold down **Ctrl**, press **n**, and then release Ctrl. The shortcut key Ctrl+Alt+N is displayed in the Shortcut key text box.

6. Click the **OK** button to save the shortcut keystroke combination, and close the My Shortcut Properties dialog box. Remain in this screen for the next Step-by-Step.

> **Note**
>
> The letter name of your hard disk may appear different from that shown in the Target and Start in text boxes shown in Figure 14-4.

STEP-BY-STEP 14.4

1. Double-click the **My Shortcut** icon. Did the setuplog document open?

2. Close the setuplog document window.

3. Issue the shortcut keystroke combination Ctrl+Alt+N:
   - **a.** Press and hold down **Ctrl**.
   - **b.** Press and hold down **Alt**.
   - **c.** Press **n**, and release all keys.

4. The setuplog document once again opens. Close the document. Remain in this screen for the next Step-by-Step.

Which method do you prefer—double-clicking the icon or issuing the shortcut key? You probably found the first method simpler, but as you become more familiar with creating shortcuts, you will see that shortcut keys are very useful when the shortcut is not in view or if you prefer to keep your hands on the keyboard.

Deleting a Shortcut

Like most Windows elements, shortcuts can be deleted. There are several ways to delete a shortcut:

- Select the shortcut, then press the Delete key.
- Right-click the shortcut, and then select Delete from the shortcut menu.
- Drag and drop the shortcut in the Recycle Bin.

If you double-click the icon or issue a shortcut, Windows displays the message box shown in Figure 14-5, asking you to confirm the deletion. Deleting a shortcut deletes only the shortcut, not the file to which the shortcut points. If you drag the shortcut to the Recycle Bin, no confirmation message box appears; the shortcut is simply moved to the Recycle Bin where it will remain until the Recycle Bin is emptied.

FIGURE 14-5
Confirm File Delete message box

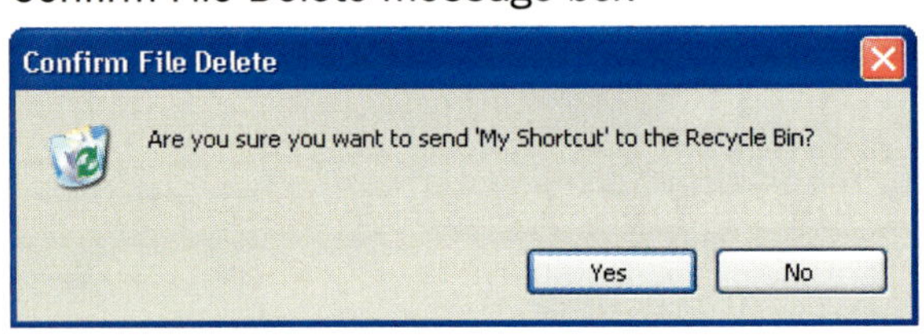

1-3.2.9-3

STEP-BY-STEP 14.5

1. Right-click the **My Shortcut** icon on the desktop, and then select **Delete** from the shortcut menu.
2. Confirm that you do intend to delete the shortcut by clicking the **Yes** button on the message box.
3. Click the **Shortcut to calc** icon on the desktop, and then press the **Delete** key.
4. Click **Yes** in the message box to confirm the deletion. Remain in this screen for the next Step-by-Step.

Adding a Shortcut to the Quick Launch Bar

With Windows, you have another choice for shortcuts: The Quick Launch bar on the taskbar (see Figure 14-6). Always visible, the Quick Launch bar is great for those items you need to reach fast. If you don't see the Quick Launch bar, right-click the taskbar, point to Toolbars, and then click Quick Launch.

FIGURE 14-6
Quick Launch bar

To add a button to the Quick Launch bar, drag a program, document, or desktop shortcut icon to the Quick Launch bar.

To remove a button from the Quick Launch bar, right-click the shortcut and then select Delete from the shortcut menu.

STEP-BY-STEP 14.6

1. Verify that the Quick Launch bar is displayed. If not:
   a. Right-click a clear area on the taskbar, then select **Toolbars** from the shortcut menu.
   b. Select the **Quick Launch** option.

2. Move the **Shortcut to Notepad** icon to the beginning of the Quick Launch bar:
   a. Right-drag the **Shortcut to Notepad** icon from the desktop to the Quick Launch bar.
   b. Select the **Move Here** option from the menu.

3. Test the shortcut:
   a. Click the **Notepad** icon on the Quick Launch bar to run the program.
   b. Close the Notepad window.

4. Delete the shortcut from the Quick Launch bar:
   a. Right-click the **Notepad** icon on the Quick Launch bar, and then click **Delete** on the shortcut menu.
   b. Click **Yes** in the message box to confirm the deletion.

5. Leave Windows XP and your computer on for the next Step-by-Step.

Introducing Windows Explorer

3.2.10-1

Explorer is a handy Windows XP program that gives you control over the organization and management of your files and folders. Like My Computer, which you learned about earlier, Explorer makes it easy to view the contents of selected disks and folders. In earlier versions of Windows, My Computer and Windows Explorer were separate programs. In Windows XP, My Computer and Windows Explorer are actually the same program. This is because My Computer takes on Windows Explorer features whenever the Folders button is pressed on the Standard buttons toolbar. All the disk and folder maintenance operations you use with My Computer are available in Windows Explorer. Explorer simply provides additional features to make the tasks easier and faster. Windows Explorer gives you the capability to search for certain files and folders. That's why the Explorer icon is a magnifying glass superimposed over a file folder (see Figure 14-7).

FIGURE 14-7
Explorer icon

The right pane of the Explorer window looks similar to and functions like the My Computer window. The major difference between the My Computer window and the Windows Explorer window is how the left pane is used.

1-3.2.11-1 As you can see in Figure 14-8, My Computer's left pane contains a resource bar that provides links to system tasks and your computer's resources.

FIGURE 14-8
My Computer window

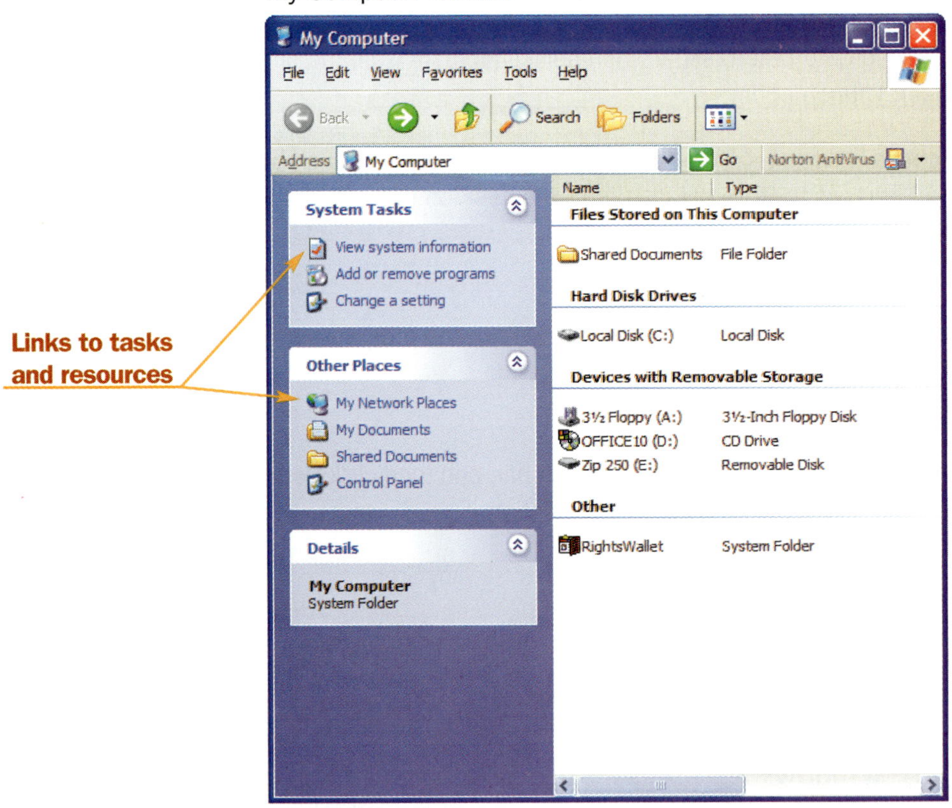

-3.2.11-2 Explorer's left pane (see Figure 14-9) contains a folders bar that lets you see the structure of your folders at a glance and allows you to move and copy files by dragging them from the right pane to the left. If you've worked in previous versions of Windows, this pane should look familiar to you.

FIGURE 14-9
Windows Explorer window

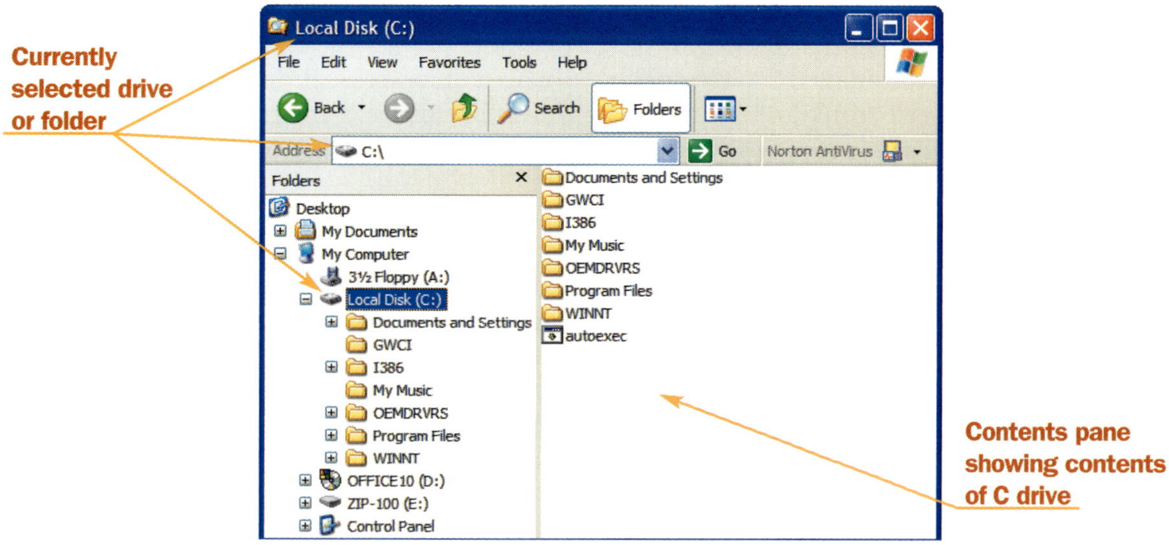

Note that with either of these windows, because they are really working from the same program, you can alter your view to appear like the other. For example, if you are in the My Computer window and you click the Folders button on the toolbar, the links will disappear and be replaced with the folders bar. If you are in the Windows Explorer window and you click on the Close button at the top right of the Folders panel, the folders bar will disappear and be replaced by the links to System Tasks and Other Places.

There are three ways to start Explorer:

- Click Start, point to All Programs, point to Accessories, and then click Windows Explorer.
- Right-click over the Start menu, and then select Explore from the pop-up menu.
- Click Start, click My Computer, and then click the Folders button on the Toolbar.

STEP-BY-STEP 14.7

1. Start your computer, and launch Windows XP if necessary.

-3.2.10-2

2. Click **Start**, point to All Programs, point to Accessories, and then click **Windows Explorer**. If Windows Explorer does not appear on the Accessories menu, click the down arrow at the bottom of the menu.

3. Click **View** on the menu bar, and select the **List** option. Leave this window open for the next Step-by-Step.

Hot Tip

Windows XP continually monitors the programs you use. The programs and files that have not been accessed in some time will not be displayed on a menu until you click the down arrows at the bottom of the menu. The menu listing will expand to show all the options on the menu.

Identifying the Parts of the Explorer Window

By now, you should recognize the window features common to many Windows XP screens. If you are new to Windows XP, however, you may not know the function of the two panes in the Explorer window. The ***Folders bar*** (left pane) is commonly referred to as the ***tree pane***. The right pane is called the ***contents pane***. These panes are discussed below.

Folders Bar (Tree Pane)

The Folders bar is also called the tree pane because its hierarchical display of all objects on the desktop is like a tree's trunk and branch system. But in this case, the tree is upside down: Its main root (Desktop) is at the top, with folders and subfolders branching off below it.

Contents Pane

The display shown in the right pane (the contents pane) changes depending on the folder, disk,
1-3.2.11-3 or other object selected in the left pane. In other words, the two panes—tree and contents—work together. For example, note in Figure 15-3 that Local Disk (C:) is selected. Also note that the Address Bar says C:\, thus matching the object selected in the left pane. If the WINNT folder is selected in the tree pane, the listing in the contents pane changes to show what's in the WINNT folder and the Address Bar reads C:\WINNT. Explorer's title bar also displays the name of the disk or folder you're currently exploring in the contents pane.

Identifying the Icons in the Explorer Window

1-3.3.5 At the top of the tree pane is the Desktop icon. You may have to scroll to bring it into view. This icon represents the Windows desktop, and all icons are shown in the tree pane as stemming from the Desktop icon. Look at Figure 14-10. Note how the My Documents, My Computer, and My Network Places icons appear below and to the right of the Desktop icon. The placement of these icons makes it clear that these folders are subordinate to—or down one level from—the Desktop.

FIGURE 14-10
Icons in the Explorer window

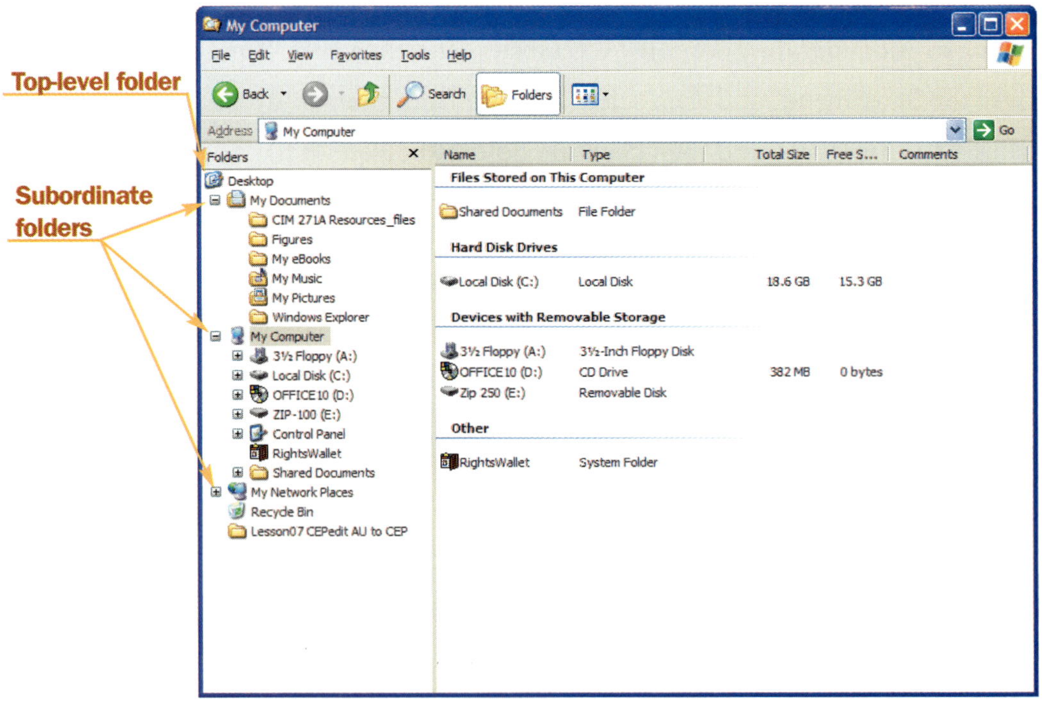

Each of these icons, in turn, has icons below and to the right of them. Under the My Computer icon, for example, there is at least one floppy drive and the hard drive. The hard drive icon has a number of folders displayed below and to the right of it. These are the applications and other folders stored on the drive.

Finally, Explorer shows you whether each of these folders has subfolders within it. Notice in Figure 14-10 the small boxes to the left of some icons. Boxes containing a plus sign (+) indicate folders that have subfolders not currently displayed. If a box contains a minus sign (–), the subfolders are displayed below the folder. In Figure 14-10, for example, the minus sign next to the My Computer icon indicates that all folders on that drive are displayed below. The plus sign next to the Shared Documents folder indicates that this folder contains subfolders that are not displayed. (See the Expanding and Collapsing the Tree section, which follows.)

> **Hot Tip**
>
> If you're displaying the contents of a folder for the first time, you may have to click the **Show Files** link in the contents pane first.

As you can see from a careful look at the tree pane, Explorer uses one view to show the same information that would require several views in My Computer. You'll find this view makes it very easy to handle file-management tasks.

The contents pane also shows several types of icons, depending on the object selected in the tree pane. Look at Figure 14-11. This figure shows that the WINNT Folder has been selected. The label *WINNT* is highlighted in the tree pane, and the folder icon appears to be open. The contents pane shows the contents of this folder, which include both subfolders (identified by the yellow folder icons) and files (identified by icons other than that of a folder).

FIGURE 14-11
Displaying the contents of a folder

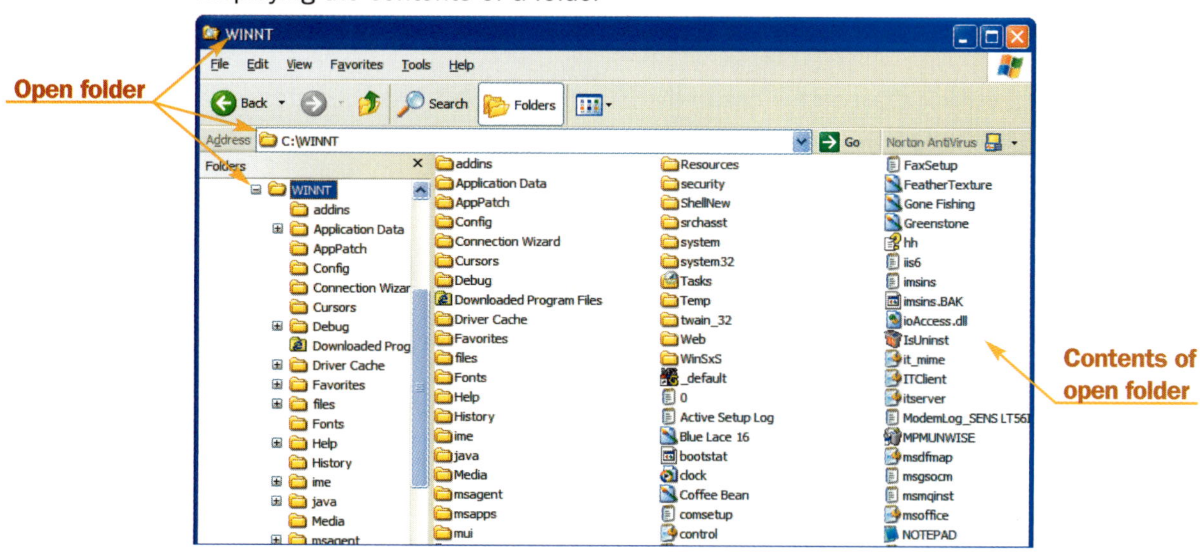

You can see the subfolders in the contents pane even when they are not displayed in the tree pane. Being able to control each pane independently of the other gives you great flexibility when you are copying, moving, viewing, or otherwise manipulating files.

Expanding and Collapsing the Tree

When you open Explorer, it does not display subfolders. If you want to display subfolders for any folder, you must expand the folder list (increase the subfolder display level). To expand the folder list, just click the plus sign in the box to the left of the folder. As the subfolders appear below the folder, the plus sign changes to a minus sign. When you click the minus sign, you collapse the folder list (decrease the subfolder display level).

Collapsing a folder makes it possible to view more objects in the tree. This is useful if you are trying to copy or move files between different folders. Collapsing folders also makes the folder list less cluttered, so it is easier to locate files and folders.

STEP-BY-STEP 14.8

1. Click the **My Computer** icon in the tree pane.
2. Find the drive on which the WINNT folder is stored (generally drive C). If the box to the left of the drive has a plus sign, click the **plus sign**.
3. Locate the WINNT folder, and note whether there is a plus or a minus sign in the box to the left of the icon.

1-3.2.12-1
1-3.2.12-2

4. Click the box to the left of the **WINNT** folder icon. If the box has a plus sign, the tree will expand, showing the subfolders below the WINNT folder; if the file icon displays a minus sign, the tree will collapse.

Note

On your system, the folder may have a different name than WINNT. It may, for instance, be WINDOWS or Windows. If you are uncertain, ask your instructor for assistance. In this and subsequent Step-by-Step instructions, substitute the appropriate name of your folder wherever you see the name WINNT.

5. If necessary, click again on the box to the left of the **WINNT** folder icon to display the WINNT subfolders in the tree pane.
6. Notice that a number of the WINNT subfolders have additional subfolders, as indicated by a plus sign in the box to the left of the subfolder.

1-3.2.12-4

7. Expand the system32 folder (you may have to use the tree pane's scroll bar to find it), and display all of its subfolders and their subfolders:
   a. Click the **plus sign** in front of the system32 folder.
   b. Click the **plus sign** in front of the drivers folder.
8. Click the **minus sign** in front of the drivers folder. Notice that the drivers folder list collapses.
9. Click the **minus sign** in front of the system32 folder and the **minus sign** in front of the WINNT folder. Remain in this screen for the next Step-by-Step.

Setting Explorer Options

Explorer's View menu is similar to all View menus. You can choose to display the Standard buttons and the Status Bar, for example, and you can change the view of the contents pane to Icons, List, or Details. You also have a view option called Thumbnails. This option shows a miniature picture of each object. Additionally, if a folder contains all graphic files, the Filmstrip view becomes an option as well. With the Filmstrip view, you see a larger image than you do with the Thumbnail view and you can scroll through all the files in the folder.

Explorer's toolbar is also similar to the My Computer toolbar. You will see the familiar Back, Forward, and Up navigation buttons that help you navigate in the tree pane. The Views button at the far right of the toolbar lets you change the way objects are displayed in the contents pane only. The options from the Views button are the same as those listed above: Icons, List, Details, Thumbnails, and Filmstrip.

STEP-BY-STEP 14.9

1. Click the **Views** drop-down list arrow on the toolbar, and select **Details** if this view is not already selected. Note that the display is the same as the Details view in My Computer.
2. Select each of the other views on the Views drop-down list to see how the display in the contents pane changes.
3. Select **List** to display the contents pane in List view. Leave this window open for the next Step-by-Step.

Viewing the Contents of a Drive or Folder

Most folder and file operations require you first to identify the drive you want to use. In Explorer, icons in the tree pane represent the available disk drives. To select a drive, click the appropriate drive icon. The drive is highlighted in the tree pane, and its contents appear in the contents pane (see Figure 14-12).

FIGURE 14-12
Highlighting shows which disk drive is selected

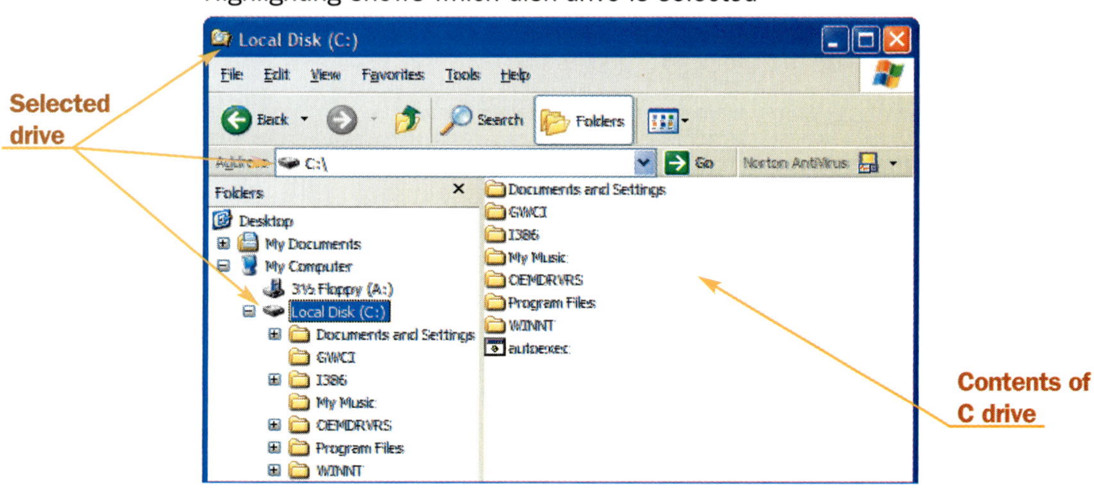

You can also select a drive or another desktop object (such as the Recycle Bin) by clicking the object in the Address Bar drop-down list. This action moves you directly to the object in the tree pane. If you have a very large tree displayed, it may be easier to select an object this way than to scroll in search of it.

To view the contents of a folder, click the folder in the tree pane. The folder opens and its contents appear in the contents pane. If the folder has subfolders, you can double-click a subfolder in the contents pane. When you do so, the subfolder's contents are displayed in the contents pane and the tree pane expands to show any subfolders.

STEP-BY-STEP 14.10

1. Insert your Windows Practice disk in the appropriate disk drive.
2. Click the icon of the drive where your Windows Practice disk is located. The contents pane shows the contents of the disk.
3. Double-click the **Project Reports** folder in the contents pane. Notice that the folder's contents now appear in the contents pane and that the tree pane shows the open folder under the drive icon.

1-3.2.13-1
4. Click the **WINNT** folder in the tree pane to display the contents of the WINNT folder on your hard drive.

1-3.2.15-3
5. In the contents pane, double-click the **system** folder. (If necessary, click **Show Files** in the contents pane.) Make sure **List view** is selected. Your display should resemble Figure 14-13.

FIGURE 14-13
Contents of the system folder

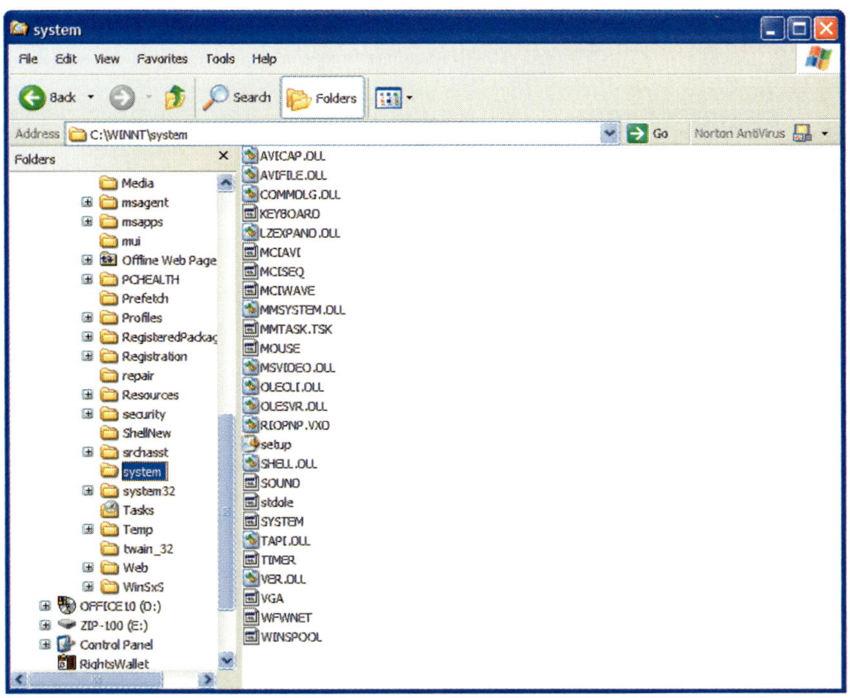

STEP-BY-STEP 14.10 Continued

6. Click the **Up** button on the toolbar to select the WINNT folder again.
7. From the Address Bar drop-down list, select the drive that contains your Windows Practice disk.
8. Click the **Close** button to close Windows Explorer. Then if instructed to do so, shut down Windows XP and your computer.

SUMMARY

In this lesson, you learned:

- A shortcut functions as a pointer to a file—wherever it is located. Double-click the shortcut icon to open the actual item to which the shortcut is pointing.
- You create a shortcut by dragging and dropping or by using the Create Shortcut option on the File menu. When you no longer need a shortcut, it can be deleted without impacting the original instance.
- You can add a shortcut key to a Windows shortcut. A shortcut key is a keystroke combination that runs a program—or in this case, runs the Windows shortcut to which it is linked. Shortcut keys to Windows shortcuts always use Ctrl+Alt+ and one additional character.
- You can place a program, document, or desktop shortcut icon that you plan to use often on the Quick Launch bar.
- Windows Explorer and My Computer are actually the same program. This is because My Computer takes on Windows Explorer features whenever the Folders button is pressed on the Standard buttons toolbar.
- When you start Explorer, you see a window with the familiar title bar, menu bar, display window, and status bar. The display window is divided vertically into two panes—a left pane, which displays the Folders bar, and a right pane, which displays the contents.
- The Folders bar, also referred to as the tree pane, displays all the objects on the desktop in a hierarchical structure, and it displays the folder structure for the currently selected disk. The contents pane displays the contents of the folder selected in the tree pane.
- In the tree pane, the open folder is the active folder. In the contents pane, a folder icon represents a subfolder of the open folder.
- Explorer's View menu options and Views button allow you to control how files are displayed in the contents pane. You can select Icons, List, Details, Thumbnails, and sometimes Filmstrip.
- In the tree pane, you can collapse (decrease the levels shown in) the tree so the folders and subfolders do not appear. You can also expand (increase the levels shown in) the tree so it shows folders of all levels.

VOCABULARY *Review*

Define the following terms:

Contents pane	Shortcut	Tree pane
Folders bar	Shortcut key	Windows Explorer

REVIEW *Questions*

TRUE/FALSE

Circle T if the statement is true or F if the statement is false.

T F 1. When you double-click a shortcut icon, you're opening a copy of the item to which the shortcut is pointing.

T F 2. To start Windows Explorer, you select All Programs on the Start menu and then select Windows Explorer.

T F 3. In Windows Explorer, the Folders bar is also called the contents pane.

T F 4. Right-clicking a shortcut icon displays the shortcut menu.

T F 5. A plus sign next to a folder in Explorer's tree pane indicates folders that have subfolders not currently displayed.

FILL IN THE BLANK

Complete the following sentences by writing the correct word or words in the blanks provided.

1. You can create a shortcut by using the Create Shortcut command on the __________ menu.
2. A(n) __________ is a keystroke combination that runs a program or opens the dialog box to which it is linked.
3. The left pane of Explorer contains a(n) __________ __________ that lets you see the structure of your folders.
4. The __________ icon is at the very top of the tree pane.
5. A(n) __________ is represented by a small arrow in the lower-left corner of its icon.

PROJECTS

PROJECT 14-1

1. Start Windows if it is not already running.
2. Open **My Computer**, and display the **Lesson 14** data files.
3. Create a shortcut to the Project14-1 folder in the data files:
   A. Right-drag the **Project14-1** folder to the desktop.
   B. Choose **Create Shortcuts Here** from the shortcut menu.
   C. Rename the shortcut **Project14-1 Folder**.
4. Using the **Project14-1 Folder** shortcut, access and print a copy of the Project14-1 Report Form in the Project Reports folder:
   A. Double-click the shortcut to open the **Project14-1** folder.
   B. Double-click the **Project Reports** subfolder.
   C. Verify that your printer is accessible and ready.
   D. Select the **Project14-1 Report Form** file, then select **Print** from the File menu.
5. Using the Project14-1 Report Form you printed in step 4, do the following:
   A. Fill in the heading with the appropriate information.
   B. Answer all questions on the Report Form using My Computer to display the subfolders and files in the Project14-1 folder.
   C. Turn the report in to your instructor if requested.
6. Close all windows, then close My Computer.
7. Delete the **Project14-1 Folder** shortcut from the desktop.
8. If instructed to do so, shut down Windows XP and your computer.

PROJECT 14-2

1. Start your computer and Windows XP if it is not already running.
2. Open **Windows Explorer**, and select the **Details** view. Display the Folders bar in the left pane of the window if necessary. Maximize the Explorer window if necessary.
3. Select the **Status Bar** option on the View menu to display the status bar at the bottom of the window.
4. In the tree pane, select the disk drive and/or folder in which the data files for this lesson are stored.
5. In the tree pane, highlight and expand the Project14-2 folder.
6. Double-click the **Project Reports** folder in the contents pane.
7. In the contents pane, select the **Project14-2 Report Form**, and then select **Print** from the File menu.

8. Using the Project14-2 Report Form, do the following:
   - **A.** Fill in the heading with the appropriate information.
   - **B.** Answer all questions on the Report Form using Windows Explorer to display the subfolders and files in the Project14-2 folder.
9. Collapse all open folders in the tree pane.
10. Close Windows Explorer.

CRITICAL *Thinking*

ACTIVITY 14-1

Shortcuts are handy tools, but too many shortcuts on the desktop can make it look cluttered and confusing (which is the primary reason why Windows XP removed all the shortcuts except the Recycle Bin from its default desktop). List other advantages and disadvantages of using shortcuts, including the pros and cons of assigning shortcut keys.

ACTIVITY 14-2

During lunch, a coworker asked when, if ever, there would be an advantage to working with Windows Explorer rather than My Computer. You told him you would have to think about it and would give him an answer later in the day. You now have a few minutes to think about your response. Consider features that might be available in Explorer but not in My Computer; determine what, if any, operations are easier to perform in Explorer than in My Computer; and prepare a response for your coworker.

COMPUTING FUNDAMENTALS

REVIEW *Questions*

TRUE/FALSE

Circle T if the statement is true or F if the statement is false.

T F 1. Computers have been around since the 1920s.

T F 2. The GUI is the brains of the computer.

T F 3. Downloading graphic and text files from the Internet is a form of computer input.

T F 4. DOS is a character-based operating system.

T F 5. The WWW is a collection of interlinked multimedia documents stored on one independent server.

T F 6. The taskbar is used to display the Start menu and to switch among currently running programs that you want to keep open.

T F 7. The menu bar contains buttons that permit you to access various functions.

T F 8. The Help Index provides an alphabetical listing of topics covered in the Windows XP Help and Support system.

T F 9. Even if your computer is not connected to the Internet, you can use the Windows XP active desktop feature to place a Web page on your desktop.

T F 10. The Windows Search feature allows you to find files and folders by specifying a variety of search criteria.

MATCHING

Match the description in Column 2 to the correct term in Column 1.

Column 1	Column 2
___ 1. Mainframe computers	A. Online business
___ 2. RAM	B. Used to organize appointments, telephone messages, projects, and other tasks to be completed
___ 3. Scanners	C. Short term memory found on the motherboard
___ 4. Software	D. An easy way for users to communicate or interact with the computer by way of pictures
___ 5. PIMS	E. Used by large institutions and government installations to process very large amounts of data
___ 6. Electronic commerce	F. A utility program that helps you perform a task quickly and easily
___ 7. GUI	G. Used to refine or narrow a search
___ 8. Search qualifiers	H. Also called the Folders bar, it is the left pane of the Explorer window
___ 9. Wizard	I. Devices that can change images into codes for input to the computer
___ 10. Tree pane	J. Instructions issued to the computer so that specific tasks may be performed

PROJECTS

PROJECT 1

1. Click the **Start** button.
2. Point to Programs, then Accessories, and then click **Word**.
3. Key a few paragraphs about your favorite charity organization.
4. On the File menu, click **Save**.
5. Name your file **Favorite Charity**.
6. On the File menu, click **Save As**.
7. Name your file **Favorite Charity2** and save it in the folder designated by your instructor.
8. Click **Ok** and close the file.

PROJECT 2

1. Start your Web browser. Create a Favorites folder and give the folder a name of your choice, such as Project 2 Sites.
2. Use a Search engine such as Excite, AskJeeves, or Dogpile to find information on the following topics:
   A. Electronic banking
   B. Medical and health care
   C. Dangerous tasks that computers can perform better than humans
   D. How technology has made a great impact on our daily lives
3. Save the information you find and the Web sites to your Favorites folder.
4. Create a word-processing document that summarizes each of the topics in step 2.
5. Save the document with a filename of your choice and then print the document. Close all open files.

PROJECT 3

1. Go to the My Computer window and click on the **Help** menu.
2. Key **How to use My Computer** in the Search text box.
3. Choose one of the topics that you'd like to learn more about from the list that comes up.
4. Create a report that summarizes your findings.
5. Close all open files and windows.

SIMULATION

JOB 1

You are in the technical support division of a medical facility. The head of the department has asked you to research and make suggestions on why the current computer system needs to be updated. Use the Internet for your research, and prepare two reports. One report should list the pros of upgrading the system, and the second report should summarize the cons of not upgrading the system.

JOB 2

A new employee of your company is having a hard time understanding the differences between Windows Explorer and My Computer. Your boss has asked for your help and wants you to create a document for the new employee that lists the similarities and differences of the two programs, as well as the advantages and disadvantages of each.

KEY APPLICATIONS

Unit

Part 1 Microsoft Office XP

Lesson 1 **Introduction to Office XP Applications and Internet Explorer**	**1.5 hrs.**
Lesson 2 **Introduction to Word**	**1 hr.**
Lesson 3 **Editing Documents**	**1 hr.**
Lesson 4 **Formatting Documents**	**1.5 hrs.**
Lesson 5 **Working with Tables**	**1.5 hrs.**
Lesson 6 **Desktop Publishing**	**1 hr.**
Lesson 7 **Working with PowerPoint Presentations**	**1 hr.**
Lesson 8 **Enhancing PowerPoint Presentations**	**1 hr.**
Lesson 9 **Working with Visual Elements**	**1 hr.**
Lesson 10 **Creating and Formatting an Excel Worksheet**	**1 hr.**
Lesson 11 **Organizing the Worksheet**	**1 hr.**
Lesson 12 **Creating Worksheet Formulas**	**1 hr.**
Lesson 13 **Using Function Formulas**	**1 hr.**
Lesson 14 **Using the Worksheet to Communicate Information**	**1 hr.**
Lesson 15 **Working with Access Databases**	**1 hr.**
Lesson 16 **Editing Records and Using Forms**	**1 hr.**
Lesson 17 **Ordering and Finding Data and Creating Reports and Mailing Labels**	**1 hr.**
Lesson 18 **Working with Outlook**	**1 hr.**
Unit Review	**1 hr.**

Estimated Time for Unit: 20.5 hours

Key Applications

Part 1 Microsoft Office XP

Lesson 1
Introduction to Office XP Applications and Internet Explorer

2-1.1.1, 2-1.1.2, 2-1.1.3, 2-1.1.4, 2-1.1.5, 2-1.1.6, 2-1.2.1, 2-1.2.8, 2-1.2.9, 2-1.2.10, 2-1.2.11, 2-1.4.4, 2-1.4.5

Lesson 2
Introduction to Word

2-1.1.5, 2-1.2.1, 2-1.2.2, 2-1.2.3, 2-1.2.4, 2-1.2.6, 2-1.2.9, 2-1.3.1

Lesson 3
Editing Documents

2-1.3.2, 2-1.3.3, 2-1.3.4, 2-1.3.5, 2-1.3.6, 2-1.3.7, 2-1.3.8, 2-1.3.9

Lesson 4
Formatting Documents

2-1.2.5, 2-1.3.10, 2-1.3.11, 2-1.3.12, 2-1.3.13, 2-1.3.14, 2-1.3.15, 2-1.4.1, 2-1.4.2, 2-1.4.3, 2-1.4.6, 2-2.1.1, 2-2.1.2, 2-2.1.3, 2-2.1.5, 2-2.1.6, 2-2.1.7, 2-2.1.8, 2-2.1.12

Lesson 5
Working with Tables

2-2.2.1, 2-2.2.2, 2-2.2.3, 2-2.2.4, 2-2.2.5, 2-2.2.6, 2-2.2.7, 2-2.2.8, 2-2.2.9, 2-2.2.10

Lesson 6
Desktop Publishing

2-1.1.4, 2-1.2.7, 2-2.1.9, 2-2.1.10, 2-2.1.11, 2-2.1.13, 2-2.2.11, 2-2.2.12, 2-2.2.13, 2-2.2.14

Lesson 7
Working with PowerPoint Presentations

2-1.2.1

Lesson 10
Creating and Formatting an Excel Worksheet

2-1.2.1, 2-1.3.1, 2-1.3.2, 2-1.3.7, 2-3.1.1, 2-3.1.2, 2-3.1.7, 2-3.1.8, 2-3.3.1, 2-3.3.5, 2-3.3.6

Lesson 11
Organizing the Worksheet

2-1.3.3, 2-1.3.4, 2-1.3.5, 2-1.3.6, 2-3.1.2, 2-3.1.3, 2-3.1.4, 2-3.1.5, 2-3.1.6, 2-3.1.9, 2-3.2.1, 2-3.2.2, 2-3.3.2, 2-3.3.3, 2-3.3.4, 2-3.3.7, 2-3.3.8, 2-3.3.9, 2-3.3.10, 2-3.3.11, 2-3.3.12

Lesson 12
Creating Worksheet Formulas

2-3.2.3, 2-3.2.6, 2-3.2.7, 2-3.2.8, 2-3.2.10

Lesson 13
Using Function Formulas

2-3.2.4, 2-3.2.5

Lesson 14
Using the Worksheet to Communicate Information

2-3.2.9, 2-3.4.1, 2-3.4.2, 2-3.4.3, 2-3.4.4, 2-3.4.5, 2-3.4.6

Lesson 15
Working with Access Databases

2-1.2.1

Lesson 18
Working with Outlook

2-1.2.1

LESSON 1

INTRODUCTION TO OFFICE XP APPLICATIONS AND INTERNET EXPLORER

OBJECTIVES

Upon completion of this lesson, you should be able to:

- Start Office XP applications.
- Open, save, and print documents.
- Close documents and applications.
- Use onscreen help.
- Use speech and handwriting recognition.
- Launch Microsoft Internet Explorer.
- Access and browse the Internet.

Estimated Time: 1.5 hours

VOCABULARY

Client

Hypertext transfer protocol (HTTP)

Internet

Internet Service Provider (ISP)

Links

Path

Server

Uniform Resource Locator (URL)

Web browser

World Wide Web (WWW)

Microsoft Office XP is an integrated software package that enables you to share information between several applications. The applications available to you are dependent upon the Office XP suite that is installed and the selections made during the installation. Microsoft offers several different Office XP suites, each with a different combination of applications. Among the Office XP applications are Word, Publisher, FrontPage, PowerPoint, Excel, Access, Outlook, and Designer. Each application performs specific tasks. Table 1-1 provides a brief description of the uses for the Office applications you will learn about in this unit.

TABLE 1-1
Office applications you will learn about in this text

APPLICATION	DESCRIPTION
Word	A word-processing application that enables you to create documents such as letters, memos, and reports.
Publisher	A desktop publishing application that enables you to design professional-looking documents such as brochures, calendars, signs, and posters.
FrontPage	A Web page application that enables you to create and maintain your own Web site.
PowerPoint	A presentation application that enables you to create multimedia slide shows, transparencies, outlines, and organizational charts.
Excel	A spreadsheet application that enables you to work with text and numbers to create tables, worksheets, and financial documents involving calculations.
Access	A database application that enables you to organize and manipulate information such as addresses and inventory data.
Outlook	A schedule/organization application that enables you to efficiently keep track of e-mail, appointments, tasks, contacts, and events.

Start an Office XP Application

2-1.1.1-2

Depending on your computer setup, you can start Office XP applications by double-clicking the application icon on the desktop or by using the Start menu. When you launch most Office applications, a new Office document (word processing document, spreadsheet, database, etc.) is displayed. You can have multiple applications open at the same time. Each open application will display in the taskbar at the bottom of the screen. To switch from one application to another, click on the application button in the taskbar. The taskbar, with three open applications, is illustrated in Figure 1-1.

2-1.2.1-1

FIGURE 1-1
The taskbar

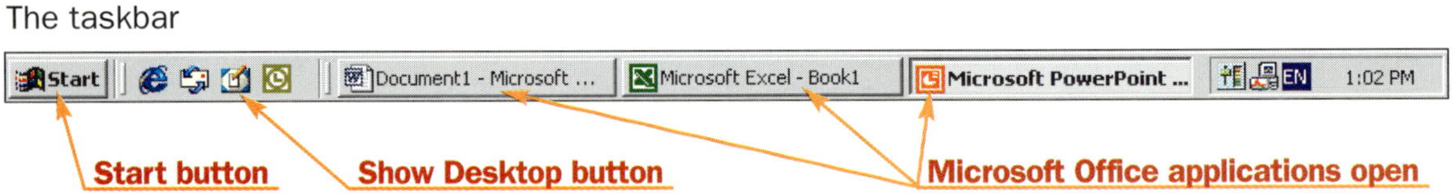

2-1.1.1-1

STEP-BY-STEP 1.1

1. Do one of the following:

a. Click the **Start** button on the taskbar and point to the Programs folder. When the submenu appears, click **Microsoft Word**.

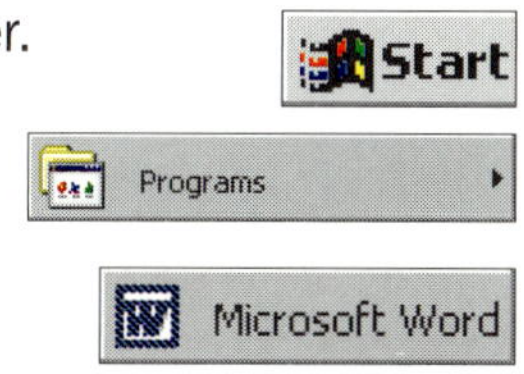

OR

b. Double-click the **Microsoft Word** icon on the desktop.

2. Do one of the following:

a. Click the **Start** button, point to Programs, and click **Microsoft Excel**.

OR

b. Click the **Show Desktop** button on the taskbar to display the desktop, and then double-click the **Microsoft Excel** icon on the desktop.

3. Microsoft Excel is now the active application, although Microsoft Word is still open and running. Do one of the following:

a. Click the **Start** button, point to Programs, and click **Microsoft PowerPoint**. The PowerPoint application opens with a dialog box presenting options for opening a presentation or creating a new presentation.

OR

b. Click the **Show Desktop** button on the taskbar, and then double-click the **Microsoft PowerPoint** icon on the desktop.

4. Microsoft PowerPoint is now the active application, although Microsoft Word and Microsoft Excel are both still open and running. The taskbar should show buttons for Word, Excel, and PowerPoint. Click the **Document1 - Microsoft Word** button in the taskbar to switch to that application. See Figure 1-1.

5. Leave the Word, Excel, and PowerPoint applications open for the next Step-by-Step.

Did You Know?

If the Microsoft Office Shortcut Bar is installed, you can use it to open an Office application. The Shortcut Bar floats on the screen and often appears in the top right corner of the screen.

Open, Save, and Print Documents

You use the same procedures to open and save documents in all Office applications. Opening a document means to load a file from a disk into the open application. A file is a collection of information saved on a disk. The terms "document" and "file" are used interchangeably. Each file is identified by a filename.

To save a document means to store it on a disk. A file extension is automatically added to the filename when the document is saved. A period separates the filename and the extension. The extension is three characters and varies depending on the application used to create the document. For example, Word automatically assigns the extension *doc*, PowerPoint assigns *ppt*, Excel assigns *xls*, and Access assigns *mdb*.

2-1.2.10-1 Folders can be used to organize the documents within a disk. The ***path*** is the route the operating system uses to locate a document. The path identifies the disk and any folders relative to the location of the document. Figure 1-2 illustrates a typical path and identifies the items in the path.

FIGURE 1-2
A typical path

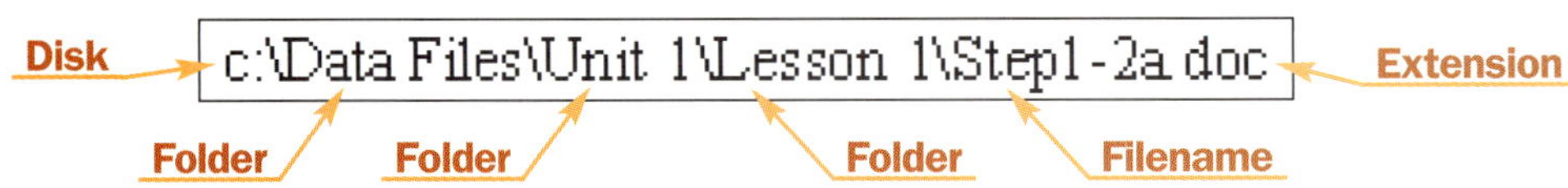

Figure 1-2 illustrates that the Word document called Step1-2a.doc is saved in a folder called Lesson 1. The Lesson 1 folder is, in turn, stored in a folder called Unit 1 which can be found in the Data Files folder on the local (this computer's) hard drive—drive C.

Open a Document

2-1.2.8-1 You have several choices for the way in which you open a file. You can choose Open Office Document on the Start menu; you can choose Open in the File menu of the Office application; or you can simply click the Open button on the Office application's toolbar. All of these procedures display the Open dialog box which enables you to open a file from any available disk and folder. By using the Open dialog box, you can work with multiple files at the same time—in either the same Office program or different programs.

To locate a specific drive or folder, you select from the options available in the *Look in* box. You can use the *Up one level* button to return to the next highest level in the path. Clicking the *Back* button will return you to the previous drive, folder, or Internet location.

Computer Concepts

To display file extensions in Windows 2000, click the **Start** button, choose **Programs**, choose **Accessories**, and then choose **Windows Explorer**. Open the **Tools** menu and choose **Folder Options**. Select the **View** tab and turn off the option *Hide file extensions for known file types*. The option is turned off when the checkmark is removed.

2-1.2.8-1

STEP-BY-STEP 1.2

1. Word should be displayed in the active window. Click **File** in the Menu bar, then click **Open** in the drop-down menu. (To see the Open command in the menu, you may need to click on the double arrow at the bottom of the menu for the full menu to display.) An Open dialog box similar to the one shown in Figure 1-3 will display. Use the Places Bar on the left side of the Open dialog box to go to the folders and locations you use the most.

FIGURE 1-3
The Open dialog box

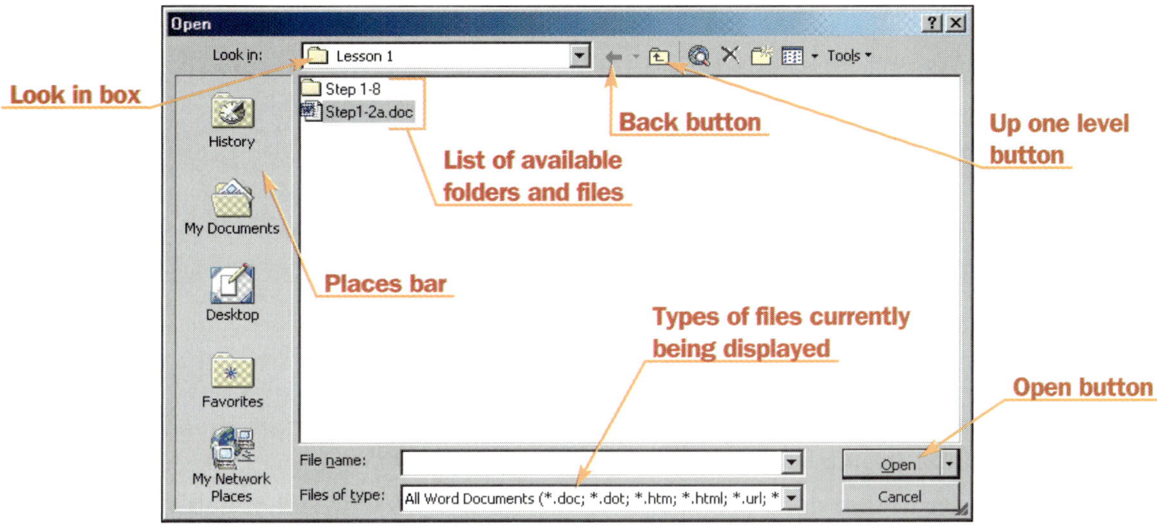

2. Click the down arrow to the right of the **Look in** box to see the available disk drives. Select the drive that contains your data files.

3. Double-click the **Data Files** folder. Double-click the **Unit 2 – Key Applications** folder. Double-click the **Lesson 1** folder. There is one folder (*Step 1-8*) and one Word file (*Step1-2a*) in the Lesson 1 folder.

4. Click the down arrow at the right of the *Files of type* box at the bottom of the dialog box and select **All Files (*.*)**. The names of all files in the **Lesson 1** folder are displayed, including those created in applications other than Word.

> **Hot Tip**
>
> Word remembers the last file you opened and automatically takes you to the drive and folder where the last file came from, so your Open dialog box may look very different from the one shown.

5. Click the filename **Step1-2a** once to select it, then click **Open** in the dialog box.

6. Click the **Microsoft Excel** button in the taskbar to switch to that application.

7. Click the **Open** button on the Standard toolbar.

STEP-BY-STEP 1.2 Continued

8. Find the data files again and open the **Unit 2 – Key Applications** folder. Select the **Lesson 1** folder, and click **Open**.

9. Click the **Up One Level** button in the Open dialog box toolbar to return to the list of folders/files in the Unit 2 folder. Click the **Up One Level** button again to return to the list of Unit folders.

10. Click the **Back** button in the Open dialog box toolbar to return to the list of folders/files in the Unit 2 folder. Click the **Back** button again to see the contents of the Lesson 1 folder.

11. Double-click the filename **Step1-2b** to open it.

12. Leave the applications and files open for the next Step-by-Step.

Computer Concepts

When you click the **History** button in the Places Bar, you will see the last 20 to 50 documents and folders that you have accessed.

Save a Document

2-1.2.9-1
2-1.2.9-2

The quickest and easiest way to save a document is to click the Save button on the Standard toolbar. The document is saved with the same filename and in the same location. To save a file with a new filename or a new location, open the File menu and choose the Save As command. If the file does not already have a name, the application prompts you to name the file upon saving.

To make it easier to find documents, choose filenames with words that help describe the document. The complete path to the file can include up to 255 characters. Filenames cannot include any of the following characters: /, \, >, <, *, ?, “, |, :, ;.

2-1.2.9-3 You should make a habit of saving frequently and after any major changes to your document. If you do this you will avoid the possibility of losing work should there be a power outage or should your computer stop running for some other reason.

2-1.2.10-6 It is also important to note that each application offers you a number of choices for formats in which to save your files. The default is always the format for the application in which you are working. Click the down arrow next to the Save as type text box and you will see the list of other file formats in which the current document can be saved.

STEP-BY-STEP 1.3

1. Click the Word **Step1-2a** button in the taskbar to switch to that document.

STEP-BY-STEP 1.3 Continued

IC3 2-1.2.9-2

2. Open the **File** menu and choose **Save As**. The Save As dialog box shown in Figure 1-4 is displayed.

FIGURE 1-4
The Save As dialog box

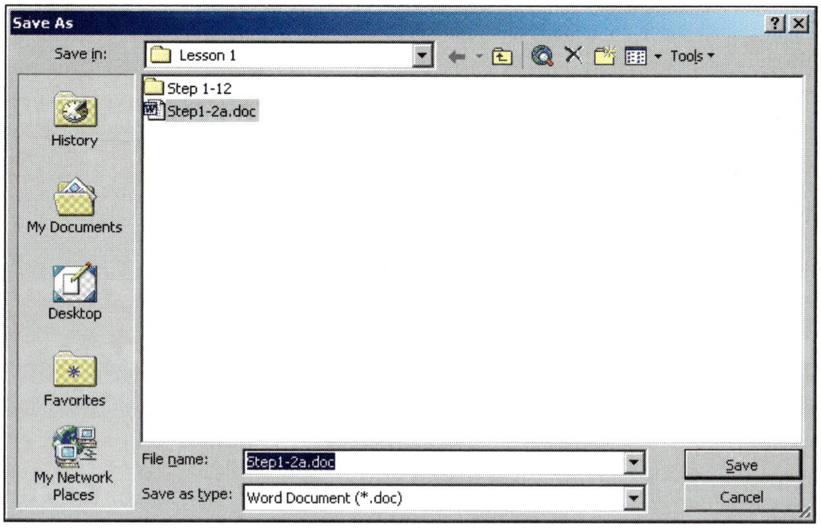

3. In the File name box, with Step1-2a.doc already selected, key **Vehicle Recycling**. (If the text in the File name box is not highlighted, click in the box and select or delete that text and then key the new filename.)

4. Click the **Save** button in the dialog box. The document is saved to the same folder where you opened it, but with a different name. (The original document, with the original name, remains also.)

5. Click the Excel **Step1-2b** button in the taskbar to switch to that document.

-1.2.10-2
-1.2.10-3
-1.2.10-4
-1.2.10-5
-1.2.10-7

6. Open the **File** menu and choose **Save As**. Name this document **Travel Expenses** and change its type to **Text (Tab Delimited)** (.txt).

7. Place a floppy diskette into the floppy drive and then use the **Up one level button** to locate and select the floppy drive. Click **Save**.

8. Keep the documents and applications open for the next Step-by-Step.

Print a Document

2-1.4.4-1
2-1.4.5-1
The quickest and easiest way to print a document is to click the Print button on the Standard toolbar when the document is active. The document is sent to the printer using all the default print settings (such as paper size, paper orientation, number of copies, etc.). If your computer accesses more than one printer, however, you will probably want to print from the File menu. This option displays the Print dialog box. Here you can view the selected printer and change it, or the printer settings, if necessary. Depending upon which application you are using, your options within the Print dialog box will vary.

Check with your instructor about the policy for printing documents in this course.

STEP-BY-STEP 1.4

1. Click the Word **Vehicle Recycling** button in the taskbar to switch to that document.

2-1.4.4-1
2. Open the **File** menu and choose **Print**. The Print dialog box shown in Figure 1-5 is displayed. The Print dialog box looks different for each Office application, but most of the print options are similar for all applications.

3. Click the down arrow in the **Name** box. If your computer is connected to more than one printer, the other printers will be listed in this drop-down box. Click to select the printer from which you would like to print this file.

2-1.4.5-2
4. Click to select **Current Page** under *Page Range*. When this option is selected, only the page where you last left the insertion point will print.

5. Click the option for **Pages**. When this option is selected, you can enter a specific page number in the text box (for example, 2). Use hyphens for a page range (for example, 1-3), and use commas to separate pages or page ranges (for example, 1, 3-5).

6. Click **Cancel** to close the dialog box without printing. (To print, you would click **OK**.)

FIGURE 1-5
The Print dialog box

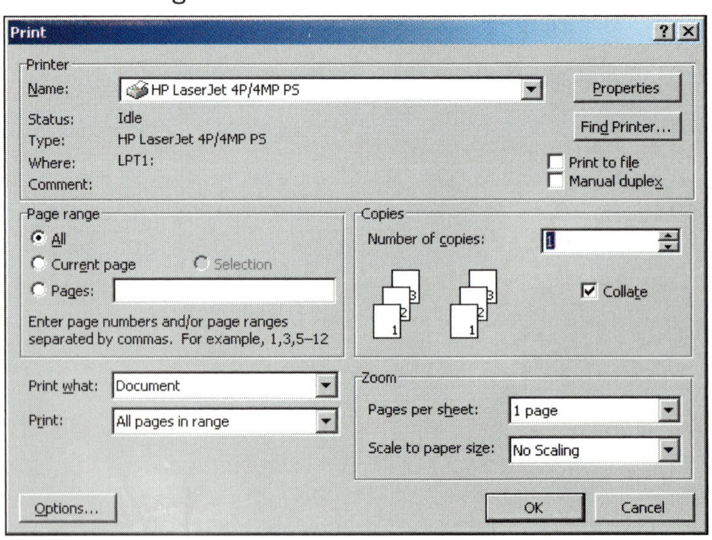

Close Documents and Applications

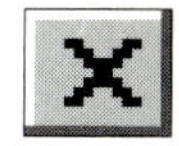

2-1.1.2-1 You use the same procedures to close documents and applications in all Office applications. To close a document, you can open the File menu and choose the Close command or you can use the Close button on the document window. To close an application, you can open the File menu and choose the Exit command or you can use the Close button on the application window. When you close a document, the application remains open and so do any other files you have open. If you have no other files open, the application shows a blank screen and is ready for you to open or create another document. When you close an application, you will also close any open files.

STEP-BY-STEP 1.5

1. Click the Excel **Travel Expenses** button in the taskbar to switch to that document.

2-1.1.2-1
2. Click the **Close** button on the right side of the Travel Expenses document window. Be sure to click the document window **Close** button. See Figure 1-6.

FIGURE 1-6
The Close buttons for the document window and the application window

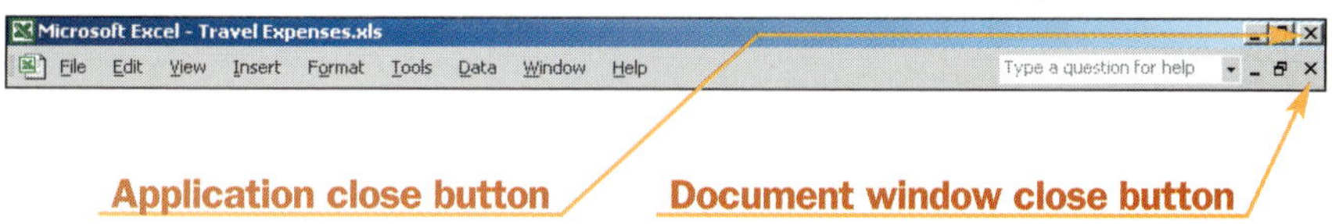

3. Open the **File** menu and choose **Exit** to close the Excel application.
4. Click the **PowerPoint** button in the taskbar to switch to that application. Click the **Close** button on the right side of the application window. Be sure to click the application window **Close** button.
5. Keep the Word document Vehicle Recycling open for the next Step-by-Step.

Problems with Files

-1.2.11-1 Each of the applications within the Microsoft Office Suite creates, by default, specific types of files — files in a specific format. Word, for example, creates *doc* files while Excel creates *xls* files. There are a number of ways that documents can be shared between the applications within the Office XP suite. Primarily you can export files from one application to another application's file type or you can import files from one application into another. An Access file can be exported as an Excel file. An Excel file can be saved as a text file and then opened in Word. This kind of data sharing gives you a great deal flexibility in how you want to view, manage, and use your data.

Within the Office XP suite you can usually move files back and forth between applications with relative ease as long as you save them in formats that each application can read. Occasionally, however, you may encounter some problems with opening files.

Finding Files

2-1.2.11-2

You may use the Open command from the File menu but not see the file for which you are looking. This could be caused by a number of things. First you need to verify that you are looking in the right drive and the right folder. It could be that the file for which you are looking is stored in a different location. If you are unsure of the location of the file, you may want to use the Find command (available from within the Open dialog box) to locate the file.

2-1.2.11-4

Another reason that you cannot see a file could be that the file is in a format that cannot be read by the application you are using. For example, if you want to open an Access file but you are in Word, you will not see the file listed. You could switch the file type within the Open dialog box to show All Files, so that you could see the file, but that does not necessarily mean that the application you are using will be able to open the file. In general, it is better to open a file in its native application and then save as or export to the appropriate file format for the application in which you want to open the file.

File Corruption

2-1.2.11-4

Occasionally you may encounter a corrupted file or a file that will not open. The application may give you an error message when you try to open the file, it may cause the application to shut down, or it may just not open. In these cases you can try to open the file on a different computer to verify that the file is indeed corrupt and that there isn't something wrong with your computer. You may also want to try to open the file from within Windows Explorer or using another file management tool. It may be that the file is associated with an application different than the one in which you are trying to open it.

File Compatibility

2-1.2.11-3

Yet another problem you may encounter is with file compatibility. In most cases, files that were created with older applications can be opened in the newer applications. But sometimes, files created in newer applications are not backwards compatible—meaning that they cannot be opened in older versions of the software. In most cases, you can resolve this issue by opening the file in the newer software and then choosing to save the file in the older application format.

You may also encounter problems if you are working in a different operating system than the one in which the file was created. For example, if a file was created in PowerPoint on a Macintosh, it may not be able to be opened in PowerPoint on a PC. This problem generally occurs if you are working with different versions of the software across the different platforms.

Work Arounds

2-1.2.11-4

In almost all cases—the file actually being corrupted being the exception—there is some way to get to or open the file you are seeking to use. It may involve going back to the application in which the file was originally created and saving it again with a different format. Or it may mean trying to open it in different applications or on different machines. Usually, with a little effort, you can find a way to open and use almost any Office file.

Help with Applications

IC3 2-1.1.3-1

The Microsoft Office XP applications have some very powerful Help features that will assist you as you work. You have access to online help and documentation as well as Internet help. You should also not overlook a vital source of help — assistance from others. There may be classmates or co-workers that are familiar with the application you are using. Or perhaps your workplace has a help desk. Additionally, many software manufacturers offer a support line.

IC3 2-1.1.3-2

The key to using these various sources of help is determining what sort of help you need and the quickest or most efficient way to access that help. The idea is to find the assistance you need without interrupting or delaying your work. Whenever you encounter a problem, your first source of help should be the online help. This is always readily available and is just a few mouse clicks away. Online help includes the ToolTips, ScreenTips, and the Office Assistant discussed below.

If the online help does not have the information you need and you have access to the Internet, you should look there for your answer. If you can't find the answers you need there and you have technical support available or a classmate or co-worker is available to assist you, this should be your next avenue to find the answers you need. Be cautious, however, about asking co-workers or classmates for assistance. You should not interrupt the work they need to complete in order to get your work completed.

Use ToolTips and ScreenTips

If you do not know the function of a toolbar button, rest the mouse pointer on the button, but do not click it. After a few seconds, the name of the function appears in a ToolTip. If you want more information about an option in a dialog box, click the Help button in the title bar of the dialog box, then click the option for which you want to display a ScreenTip. You can also right-click the option in the dialog box. A pop-up dialog box will appear displaying *What's This?*. Click *What's This?*, and the ScreenTip will appear.

STEP-BY-STEP 1.6

1. Position the pointer over the **Print** button on the Standard toolbar. (If the name doesn't display at first, you may need to move the pointer slightly so that it rests fully on the button.) The name of the button (Print), as well as the name of the printer currently selected, will appear in the ToolTip.
2. Point to other buttons on the toolbar to see the name of each button.
3. Open the **File** menu and choose **Print**.
4. Click the Question Mark icon (the **Help** button) at the top right-hand corner of the dialog box. The question mark will display with the pointer until you click an area to display a Screen Tip.

5. Click the **Properties** button in the dialog box. You should see a ScreenTip that explains the option in the dialog box.

6. Click anywhere and the ScreenTip and dialog box will disappear.
7. Click the **Cancel** button in the Print dialog box.

2-1.1.4-1

Use the Office Assistant

As you worked through the first three Step-by-Steps in this lesson, you may have seen the Office Assistant displayed on your screen. The Office Assistant is an animated Help character that offers tips and messages to help you work more efficiently. For example, if you close a document without saving it, the Office Assistant will ask you if you want to save the changes before closing. If you have a specific question, the Office Assistant will help you search for the answer. To access the Office Assistant, you must have an application open. You can then ask the Office Assistant for help with information about the active Office application.

Hot Tip

Office displays ScreenTips for all toolbar buttons. However, ScreenTips do not display for all options or items in a dialog box.

2-1.1.4-1

STEP-BY-STEP 1.7

1. If the Office Assistant is not displayed on the screen, open the **Help** menu and choose **Show the Office Assistant**.

2. Click the **Office Assistant**. An Office Assistant dialog box similar to Figure 1-7 appears. Your dialog box will look different depending on what application you are using and what information was last requested of the Office Assistant.

3. The existing search text is already selected. Key the following request to replace the existing search text: **How do I use the Office Assistant?**

Did You Know?

You can change the way the Office Assistant provides help by right-clicking the Office Assistant, selecting **Choose Assistant**, and then making selections. You can also use this shortcut menu to hide the Office Assistant if it gets in the way!

FIGURE 1-7
The Office Assistant dialog box

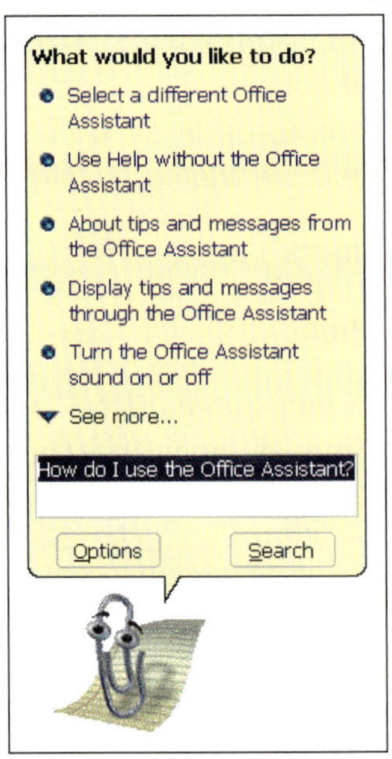

IC3

STEP-BY-STEP 1.7 Continued

4. Click **Search** (or press **Enter**). A list of topics that may provide an answer is displayed.

2-1.1.5-2

5. Click the topic **Display tips and messages through the Office Assistant**.

6. Click the topic **View a tip** and read the information about the light bulb that appears next to the Office Assistant.

7. Click the **Close** button to close the Help dialog box. Leave Word open for the next Step-by-step.

Hot Tip

Sometimes the Office Assistant gets in the way. To move the Office Assistant, simply point to it, hold down the left mouse button, and drag it to a new location on the screen.

Online and Internet Help

The Ask a Question box is another alternative to using the Office Assistant. The Ask a Question box appears at the right side of the menu bar in all Office applications. Simply click in the box, key your question, and press Enter. To repeat a question, click the down arrow in the box and select the question.

IC3 2-1.1.6-1

Although not as convenient as using the Ask a Question box and the Office Assistant, you will find more options in the Help window. To open the Help window, the Office Assistant must be turned off. To turn off the Office Assistant, open the Help window and choose Hide the Office Assistant. You can then display the Help window by opening the Help menu and choosing Help (i.e., Microsoft Word Help) or by pressing the F1 key. You can also access the Help window from the New Document task pane.

Additionally, you can find answers for frequently asked questions for all Office products at the Microsoft Office Assistance Center Web site. You'll also find other information such as important product updates, online services, and clip art. To go to the Microsoft Web sites, open the Help menu and choose Office on the Web.

IC3 2-1.1.6-1

STEP-BY-STEP 1.8

1. If necessary, establish a modem (dial-up) connection to the Internet.

2. Select **Office on the Web** from the Help menu.

3. If this is the first time this site has been visited from this system, you may see the Tools on the Web welcome page. Click on the area that represents the part of the world in which you live.

4. In the Office Assistance Center Web site, select **Word** in the Assistance By Product area.

5. Select the **Printing** topic.

6. Select and read the information concerning keeping cover letters with your resume.

7. Close your browser. If necessary, disconnect your modem (dial-up) connection.

8. Close the Word document window and the Word application window. (This can be done in one step using the Close button for the application window.)

Use Speech and Handwriting Recognition

You've probably seen people talk to computers in movies or television programs. Have you ever wished that you could talk to your computer? Imagine what it would be like to sit back and dictate your reports instead of keyboarding pages of text. Or, imagine writing your name and phone number on a graphics tablet and having your computer automatically recognize and store the data for future use. Well, you no longer have to imagine. You have access to the technology in Office XP applications. Office XP offers two new and exciting methods of input: handwriting and speech recognition.

> **Computer Concepts**
>
> Over time, as you become proficient in using the features, the speech and handwriting features can save you considerable time entering text and controlling menus. However, neither feature is intended to replace the need for using the keyboard for input. Instead, the features are designed to help you become more productive and to make your experience with Office applications more enjoyable.

The handwriting feature allows you to input information, either by controlling a mouse or an input device such as a graphics tablet, computer aided drafting (CAD) software, or a tablet-PC. You can choose to leave the text in handwritten form, or you can convert the handwriting to typed characters and insert the characters in a line with existing text. The handwriting feature is easy to learn, but it requires a custom installation. Check with your instructor to see if handwriting features are installed on your computer.

The speech feature enables you to speak to your computer via a microphone. You can dictate commands (such as to save or print a document), and you can dictate text (such as the paragraphs of a report). The speech recognition feature also requires some special installation, and you will need to spend some time learning how to use the feature successfully. In each lesson throughout this unit you will see speech recognition tips describing how you can use the speech recognition technology to complete tasks. Moreover, the tips will illustrate how the technology is integrated into each of the applications.

Use Internet Explorer to Access the Internet

The ***Internet*** is a network of computers that makes the exchange of information possible. To connect to the Internet, you need special hardware and software, and you also need an ***Internet Service Provider (ISP)***. It is the ISP that directs the flow of information.

Although the term "Web" is often used interchangeably with the term "Internet," they are actually two different things. The ***World Wide Web (WWW)*** is a system of interlinked documents that work together using ***HTTP***. HTTP stands for "***hypertext transfer protocol.***" It is a set of rules that enables computers to "talk" with each other. All of these documents reside at different locations (i.e., different computers). The Web uses a ***Uniform Resource Locator (URL)*** to locate documents on the Internet. The following are examples of URLs:

http://www.nps.gov
http://www.microsoft.com

To access the Web, you need a particular type of software known as a ***Web browser***. Microsoft Internet Explorer is an example of a Web browser. The browser is known as a ***client***, and it accesses data from a remote computer called a ***server***. The server can be located across town or it may be located on another continent. The amount of time it takes for a browser to access data depends on the size of the files, the modem speed, the ISP's modem speed, how busy the server is, and the "traffic" (flow of data) on the Internet.

> **Did You Know?**
>
> The World Wide Web was originally developed in 1990 at CERN, the European Laboratory for Particle Physics. The WWW is managed by The World Wide Web Consortium, also known as the World Wide Web Initiative.

Navigate Web Pages

When you first open Internet Explorer, your home page will appear. Your home page is the page that is displayed every time you open Internet Explorer. When the Internet Explorer image in the top right corner of your screen is animated, it means that Internet Explorer is accessing data from a remote computer.

> **Computer Concepts**
>
> There are two basic types of Internet connections: dial-up access and direct access. Dial-up access uses a modem and a telephone line. Direct access uses a special high-speed connection that is faster.

The buttons on the Internet Explorer Standard Buttons toolbar will help you browse the Web faster and easier. ***Links*** are connections to specific locations on the Web. They make it easy to navigate Web sites because they enable you to quickly jump from one site to another.

You can open Web pages using the Open command if you know where they are located on your system or the Internet.

Sometimes you may get a message that a Web page cannot be displayed; sometimes when a file transfer is interrupted, not all of the elements of a Web page are loaded. In either case, click the Refresh button.

STEP-BY-STEP 1.9

1. If necessary, connect to your ISP and then launch the Internet Explorer application by double-clicking the **Internet Explorer** button on your desktop. Your screen should look similar to Figure 1-8. However, your home page will likely be a different site. Even if your default setting is the Microsoft Web site, your screen will look different because the site is updated daily.

2. Click any link in your home page. You will know that an item is a link when you point to the item and the mouse pointer changes to a hand.

3. Click in the Address bar on the Standard Buttons toolbar to select the current URL. With the text selected, key **www.msn.com** and then click **Go** (or press **Enter**). The MSN home page is displayed.

STEP-BY-STEP 1.9 Continued

FIGURE 1-8
The Microsoft home page

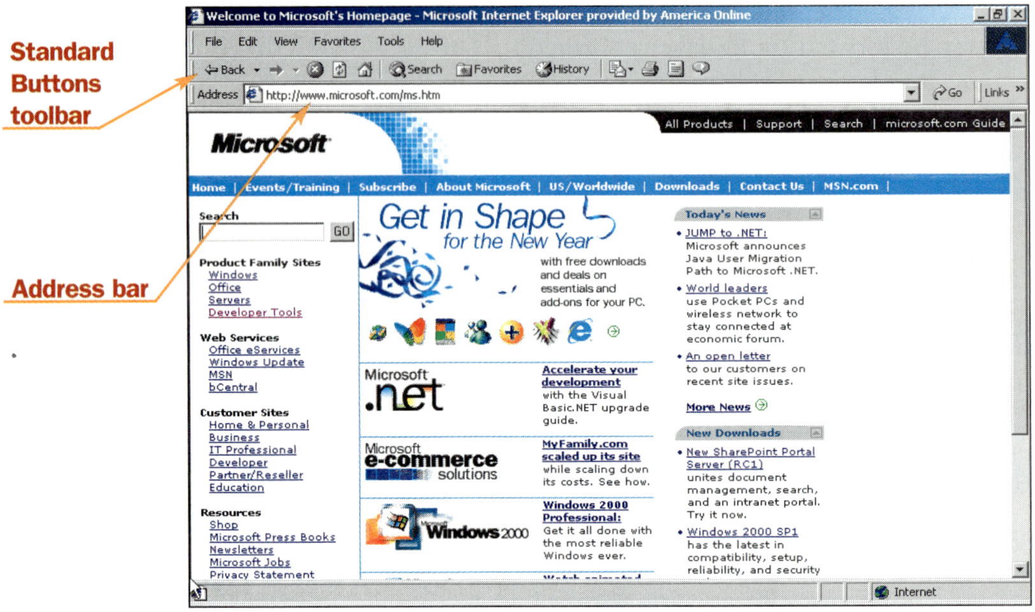

4. Open the **File** menu and choose **Open**. The Open dialog box appears.

5. Click **Browse** to open the Microsoft Internet Explorer dialog box. Locate your **Data Files** folder, open the **Unit 2 – Key Applications** folder, open the **Lesson 1** folder, and then open the **Step 1-8** folder.

> **Hot Tip**
>
> If a page you are trying to view takes too long to open, you can stop the process by clicking the **Stop** button on the Standard Buttons toolbar.

6. Select the **index.htm** document and then click **Open**. Click **OK** in the Open dialog box. Internet Explorer displays the home page of a Web site created in Microsoft FrontPage. Notice the three links to other pages in the last paragraph of the home page.

7. Click the **Flowering Trees** link to open a new page. You will see the series of links below the heading that can take you to other pages or back to the home page.

8. Click the **Deciduous Trees** link, and then click the **Evergreen Trees** link.

9. Click the **Back** button to return to the previous link, Deciduous Trees.

STEP-BY-STEP 1.9 Continued

10. Click the list arrow next to the **Back** button on the Standard Buttons toolbar to see a list of the pages you have viewed. Select **Flowering Trees** in the list to return to the Flowering Trees page.

11. Click the **Forward** button to go to the next page, Deciduous Trees. On the Deciduous Trees page, click the **Home** link to return to the Greenwood Arboretum home page.

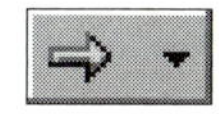

12. Click **History** on the Standard buttons toolbar to display the History bar. Click the link that will take you back to the MSN home page (the link might read *Welcome to MSN.com.*) Click the **Close** button at the top right of the History bar.

13. Leave Internet Explorer open for the next Step-by-Step.

Search the Web

You can search for Web sites, e-mail addresses, businesses, previous searches, and maps. With hundreds of millions of Web pages online, finding specific information can be very time consuming. You can narrow down the search results by using several search words. After you go to a Web page, you can search for specific text within that Web site.

Another way to search the Web using Internet Explorer is to key the search words directly into Internet Explorer's Address bar. Internet Explorer performs an AutoSearch to try to locate your key words in Web page URLs.

Computer Concepts

When you locate Web pages that you like, you can save them in a list—often called Favorites or Bookmarks—so you can return to the pages quickly. The bookmarks are saved in a folder for quick reference. The process for creating the bookmark depends on your Internet browser. For example, in Internet Explorer, you simply open the **Favorites** menu, choose **Add to Favorites**, and then identify the folder where you want the bookmark to be saved.

STEP-BY-STEP 1.10

1. In the Search the Web text box on the MSN home page, key **flowering trees** and click **Go**.
2. The search results in a number of links. The first fifteen matches are displayed.
3. In the Address bar on the Standard Buttons toolbar, key **Microsoft** and then click **Go**. Even though you did not enter the URL for the Microsoft Web site, the Microsoft home page opens.
4. The search box provided on this home page enables you to search for words within the Microsoft site. In the Search box for this page, key **Office XP** and click **Go**. The search results display links related to the search text.
5. Explore the site and click on any of the links that interest you.
6. Close the Internet Explorer application window and, if necessary, disconnect from your ISP.

Hot Tip

Most search engines provide tips for refining searches. Read these tips so you know how to make your searches more effective and productive.

Historically Speaking

In the 1840s, George Boole, a self-educated mathematician from England, developed ways of expressing logical processes using algebraic symbols. The Boolean logic uses words called operators to determine whether a statement is true or false. This Boolean logic has become the basis for computer database searches. The most common operators used are AND, OR, and NOT. These three simple words can be extremely helpful when searching for data online. For example, if you search for "railroad AND models," the results will include documents with both words. If you search for "railroad OR models," the results will include the greatest amount of matches listing documents with either word. A good way to limit the search is to search for "railroad NOT models." The results will then include all documents about railroads but not documents about models.

SUMMARY

In this lesson, you learned:

- You can start Office applications by clicking the Start button on the taskbar and selecting the application from the Programs folder, or you can double-click the application icon on the Desktop.
- The Open dialog box enables you to open a file from any available disk and folder.
- To save a document using a new filename, open the File menu and choose the Save As command.
- To print a document, you can use either the Print button on the application's toolbar or you can open the File menu and choose Print.
- To close document windows and application windows, you click the Close button or open the File menu and choose Close or Exit.
- ToolTips and ScreenTips provide immediate Help without interrupting your work. The Office Assistant offers tips and will help you search for answers to specific questions.
- You can input information using your own handwriting. The handwriting feature enables the computer to recognize your handwriting. You can also convert your handwriting to typed characters and insert them in a line of existing text.
- If your computer has speech recognition capability, you can use the speech feature to dictate commands and text.
- To access the Web, you need browser software such as Microsoft Internet Explorer.
- Internet Explorer provides many tools to help you navigate Web pages and search for information.

VOCABULARY *Review*

Define the following terms:

Client	Internet Service Provider (ISP)	Uniform Resource Locator (URL)
Hypertext Transfer Protocol (HTTP)	Links	Web browser
Internet	Path	World Wide Web (WWW)
	Server	

REVIEW *Questions*

TRUE/FALSE

Circle T if the statement is true or F if the statement is false.

T F 1. You use the same procedures to open and save documents in all Office applications.

T F 2. To save a file with a new filename or to a new location, open the File menu and choose the Save command.

T F 3. The Office Partner is an animated Help character that offers tips and messages to help you work more efficiently.

T F 4. To access the World Wide Web, you need a Web browser.

T F 5. One way to find information on the Internet is to perform a search using several search words.

FILL IN THE BLANK

Complete the following sentences by writing the correct word or words in the blanks provided.

1. The Office application you would use to organize and manipulate information such as addresses and inventory data is __________.
2. __________ are used to organize the documents within a disk.
3. Rest the mouse pointer on a toolbar button to see the name of the button appear in a(n) __________.
4. When viewing a Web page, you can click a(n) __________ to jump quickly to another page or location on the Web.
5. Click the __________ button on the Standard Buttons toolbar to return to a page you have already visited.

PROJECTS

In the following projects, you will become familiar with other Office applications.

PROJECT 1-1

If you do not have Microsoft Publisher installed, go to Project 1-2.

1. Using a desktop shortcut or the **Start** menu, launch Microsoft Publisher. The Microsoft Publisher Quick Publications dialog box appears on your screen. You can use the Catalog to choose the type of publication you want to create.

2. At the left of the Quick Publications is a list of new publications in the pane on the left. Click the **Flyers** option in the New Publications pane. Notice that a list of types of different flyers appears below the Flyers heading and sample flyers display in the window at the right.
3. Click **Event** in the list of flyers at the left to see the different event flyers available.
4. Select other publication types in the New Publications list to see what kinds of publications you can create using Publisher.
5. Close Publisher by clicking the application **Close** button.

PROJECT 1-2

1. Using a desktop shortcut or the **Start** menu, launch Microsoft Outlook.
2. Using a desktop shortcut or the **Start** menu, launch Microsoft PowerPoint.
3. Click **More presentations** in the task pane (or just **Presentations**) to display the Open dialog box.
4. Open **Project1-2** from the data files. The PowerPoint window displays a slide, an outline of the current presentation, and an area where you can make notes.
5. Move the mouse pointer over some of the toolbar buttons to display a ToolTip for each button.
6. To learn more about the different views you can use in PowerPoint, click the Office Assistant, key **PowerPoint views**, and then click **Search**. In the list of topics that displays, choose **About PowerPoint views**.
7. Read about the different views available in PowerPoint, then close the Help window.
8. Save the PowerPoint presentation as **Three Rs**.
9. Click the **Outlook** button on the taskbar to return to Outlook. Notice the vertical bar at the left of the Outlook window named *Outlook Shortcuts*.
10. Click the **Calendar** shortcut. The calendar for the current date opens in the Outlook window. If you wanted to schedule a time to present your Three Rs slide show, you could do so using this Outlook tool.
11. Close Outlook by clicking its application **Close** button.
12. Close PowerPoint by clicking its application **Close** button.

PROJECT 1-3

1. If necessary, connect to your ISP and then launch Internet Explorer.
2. If the MSN home page does not appear when you launch Internet Explorer, click in the Address bar to select the current URL and key **www.msn.com**.
3. Explore the site and click on some of the links that interest you.
4. Click the **Search** button on the Standard Buttons toolbar. The default search engine for your connection will appear.

5. In the *Search* box, key **nasa** and then click **Search**. How many matches were found for your search word?

6. Click any of the links that look interesting to you to display the page.

7. If you are going to complete the Web project next, keep Internet Explorer open and do not disconnect. Otherwise, close the Search bar and then close Internet Explorer. If necessary, disconnect from your ISP.

WEB PROJECT

1. If necessary, connect to your ISP and open Internet Explorer. In Internet Explorer, click in the Address bar to select the current URL and then key **national park service** and click **Go**.

2. Internet Explorer should correctly locate the home page for the National Park Service. Explore this site briefly by clicking on any links that interest you.

3. Use the **Back** button to return to the National Park Service home page.

4. Select the current URL in the Address bar and key **smithsonian** and click **Go**. Internet Explorer should locate the Smithsonian Institution home page. (Notice the URL in the Address bar does not contain the word "smithsonian," but Internet Explorer was able to find the home page anyway.)

5. Follow links to find out how much it costs to visit the Smithsonian museums and what days during the year they are closed.

6. Close Internet Explorer and, if necessary, disconnect from your ISP.

TEAMWORK PROJECT

Using Internet Explorer to search the Web can help you find a lot of information. To make your searches more specific, however, you should use a search engine. A search engine is software that creates indexes of Internet sites. You enter text describing what you're looking for, and the search engine presents results of the Internet sites that match your search. There are many search engines available on the Web, with new ones appearing all the time. Team up with a partner to learn about and test some of the most popular search engines.

1. Frequently used search engines include AltaVista, Excite, Lycos, Hotbot, MSN, Google, Ixquick, and Yahoo. Evenly divide this list of search engines with your teammate so that each of you has a list to check.

2. Locate each search engine on the Web by keying its name in the Internet Explorer Address bar.

3. Search engines usually display a Help link that gives you specific information on how to perform a search. Read the tips and suggestions on searching using each search engine.

4. With your teammate, select a search topic that can be used to compare search results for all the search engines on your lists. This search topic can either be a single keyword (such as "grapefruit"), a phrase (such as "ruby red grapefruit"), or a proper name. If you decide to search for a phrase, follow any special instructions given by the search engine so that you find only instances of the entire phrase, not each word in the phrase. For example, some search engines suggest enclosing the phrase in quotation marks.

5. Run your search in each of the search engines on your list. Write down the links to the first three matches and then compare them with those your teammate received.
6. If time allows, try to refine your search using more keywords as well as AND, OR, or NOT.
7. Compare notes with your teammate on speed, ease of use, and useful results provided by each search engine.

CRITICAL *Thinking*

ACTIVITY 1-1

In exchange for riding privileges, you have agreed to help the owner of a local riding stable with a number of computer-related tasks. The owner has created the following list of jobs she needs to have done:

- Write letters to people who board their horses at the stable to tell them feed bills will go up at the beginning of the year.
- Store information on owners, frequent riders, equipment, and employees.
- Schedule regular visits by the vet, keep track of regular chores, and plan activities in coming months.
- Create flyers to place at local clubs with information about riding clinics and other special activities.
- Create a Web site to provide information on classes, boarding fees, and facilities at the stable.
- Calculate expenses for running the stable as well as income from riders and boarders.
- Come up with a presentation that can be used to train new employees and new riders.

What Office applications can you use to complete each of these jobs? Make a table that lists each job and the Office application you would use to complete the task. Are there other jobs you could do for the stable owner using Office applications?

ACTIVITY 1-2

As you have visited various Web pages in this lesson, you might have wondered what all those letters in the pages' URLs really mean. You might be able to guess that www stands for World Wide Web. But what are the letters after www for? And if an URL ends with the suffix .edu and not .com, what does that mean?

Use Internet Explorer's Help files to locate information on Internet addresses. Read the explanation of each part of an Internet address and how it directs the browser to a specific location on the Web. Then explain each part of the following URL:

http://www.msn.com

LESSON 2

INTRODUCTION TO WORD

OBJECTIVES

Upon completion of this lesson, you should be able to:

- Create a new document.
- Switch between document windows.
- Enter text in a document.
- Navigate through a document.
- Use Click and Type.

Estimated Time: 1 hour

VOCABULARY

Default

I-beam

Normal view

Print Layout view

Scroll

Word wrap

Word is a powerful, full-featured word processor. You can use Word to create reports, tables, letters, memos, Web pages, and much more. The Word lessons in this course will introduce you to features that enable you to prepare documents efficiently. You will also learn how to edit documents and enhance their appearance.

IC3 2-1.2.6-1

Create a New Document

When you first open the Word application, a new blank document is displayed. The document is currently titled Document1. This filename will remain until you open the File menu and choose Save As and assign the document a new filename.

The New Document task pane is also displayed. This task pane enables you to quickly open documents that you have recently accessed or to create a new document. You can open additional documents on top of the blank Document1. Thus, you can have multiple Word documents open at the same time.

When you open a new document using the *Blank Document* option in the task pane, the document contains ***default*** settings to create a traditional printed document. Default settings are preset options or variables. You can change the default settings as you work with the document.

After you open an existing document or create a new document, the task pane will disappear. You can open additional documents by using the New Blank Document button or the Open button on the Standard toolbar.

STEP-BY-STEP 2.1

1. Launch the Word application. Your screen will look similar to Figure 2-1. Do not be concerned if your screen does not match the figure exactly.

2-1.2.4-2
2. If necessary, click the **Normal View** button in the lower left corner of the screen, just above the status bar, to switch to Normal view.

3. Take some time to review Figure 2-1 to become familiar with the various parts of the Word application window. As you work through these Word lessons, refer to the figure if you need help remembering the names of parts of the Word window.

2-1.2.2-1
2-1.2.2-2
4. If your screen does not show the Standard toolbar or Formatting toolbar, open the **View** menu and select the appropriate toolbar. If your screen is displaying other toolbars not shown in Figure 2-1, such as the Drawing toolbar or the Reviewing toolbar, open the **View** menu and deselect the toolbar.

Hot Tip

If the New Document task pane is not displayed, open the **View** menu and choose **Task Pane**. If a task pane other than New Document displays, click the down arrow on the task pane title bar and select **New Document**.

Hot Tip

To display or hide toolbars, open the **View** menu and select the desired toolbar to turn the option on or off. A checkmark in front of the toolbar name indicates that the toolbar is displayed.

2-1.2.1-1

FIGURE 2-1
Document in Normal view

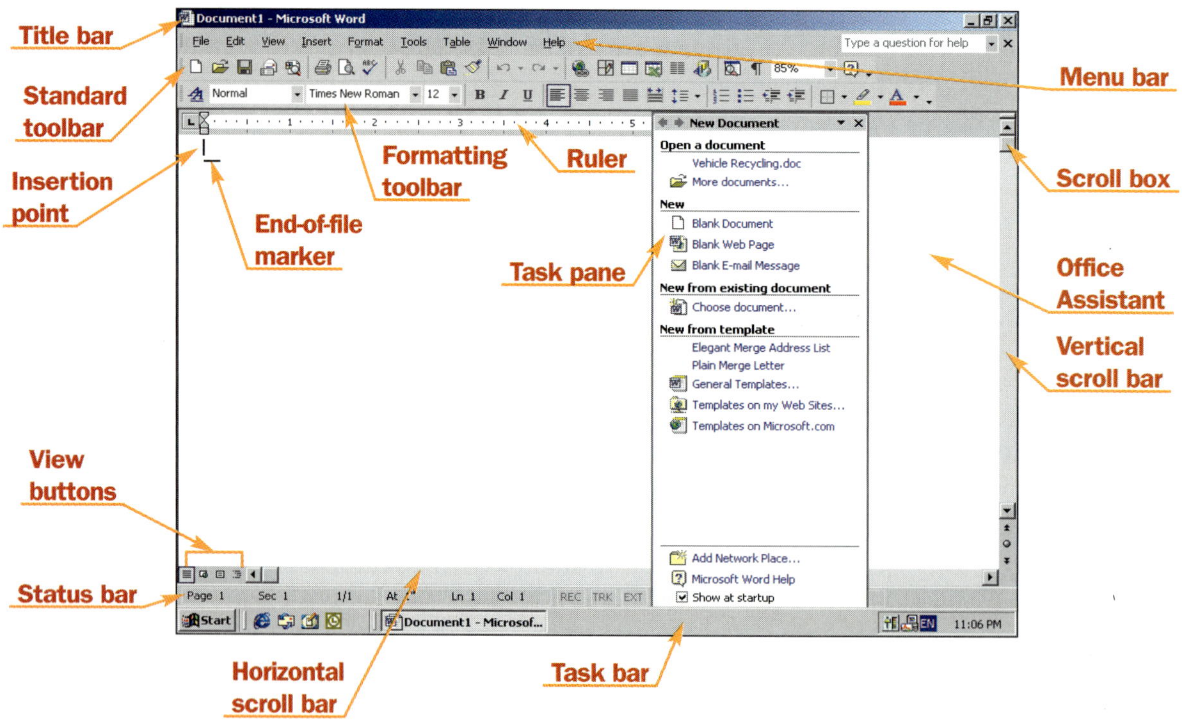

2-1.2.6-1

STEP-BY-STEP 2.1 Continued

5. In the New Document task pane, under New, click the **Blank Document** option to open a second blank document. Notice that the document title bar displays Document 2.

6. Click the **New Blank Document** button on the Standard toolbar to open a third document.

7. Leave all three documents open for the next Step-by-Step.

Did You Know?

Although Figure 2-1 is an illustration of an open Word document, many of the elements shown are common to all Office applications.

Computer Concepts

Word offers different options for viewing a document. Normal view provides a simple layout so you can enter and edit text quickly.

2-1.2.3-1
2-1.2.3-3

Switch between Document Windows

You can have several Word documents open at the same time. However, regardless of how many documents you have open, you can only work in one document at a time. The document you are working in is called the active document. To switch between documents and make a different document the active document, click the document name in the taskbar. Having multiple documents or applications open at the same time can be extremely useful, especially when you want to use information from one document in another or when you want to compare the information in multiple documents.

2-1.2.3-2

STEP-BY-STEP 2.2

1. Click the **Document1** button in the taskbar to switch to that document.

2. Click the **Close** button for that document window to close the document.

3. Click the **Document2** button in the taskbar to switch to that document.

4. Click the **Close** button for that document window to close the document.

5. The Document3 window should still be open. Leave the document open for the next Step-by-Step.

Hot Tip

Pressing **Ctrl + F4** is an alternative to clicking the **Close** button to close the active document window.

Enter Text in a Document

As you enter text in a Word document, the insertion point will move to the right and the status bar will change to reflect the position of the insertion point. As you key, you may see a red or green wavy line under some of the words. Word automatically checks the spelling and grammar in a document as you enter the text. The red wavy line identifies a word that may be misspelled. The green wavy line identifies a possible grammatical error. If you make any errors while keying, press Backspace to remove the errors, then rekey your text correctly.

If the text you are keying extends beyond the right margin, Word will automatically wrap the text to the next line. This feature is called ***word wrap***. Press Enter only to start a new paragraph. To insert a blank line between paragraphs, press Enter twice.

Computer Concepts

Before word processors, typewriters were used to create formal documents. It was common practice to create two blank spaces between sentences. The extra blank space created more white space between sentences and made it easier to read the text. However, today's word processing applications are more sophisticated and the extra spaces are not necessary because the fonts generally allow for proportional spacing which eliminates excess white space between characters, and therefore, the white space between sentences is more obvious. Consequently, you need only key one blank space between sentences.

IC3

STEP-BY-STEP 2.3

1. Key the sentences illustrated in Figure 2-2 into **Document3**. Notice as you enter the text that the insertion point moves and the status bar reflects the position of the insertion point. Remember: do not press **Enter** until you reach the end of the paragraph, then press **Enter** twice to create a blank line between paragraphs.
2. Open the **File** menu and choose **Save As** to display the Save As dialog box.
3. Click the down arrow in the Save in box and locate the folder where you are to save your work.
2-1.2.9-1
4. In the File name box, key **Greenways** followed by your initials, then click **Save** in the dialog box.
5. Leave the document open for the next Step-by-Step.

Speech Recognition

If your computer has speech recognition capability, enable the Dictation mode and dictate the two paragraphs.

Hot Tip

F12 is a shortcut to open the Save As dialog box.

Speech Recognition

If your computer has speech recognition capability, enable the Command mode and say the commands to open the Save As dialog box, locate the folder, name the file, and save the document.

FIGURE 2-2
Text for Step-by-Step 2.3

> Today the majority of the American population lives in cities and suburbs. The people who live in metropolitan areas depend on parks and recreational paths close to their homes for both recreation and contact with nature.
>
> To preserve acres of green open space, greenways are interconnected open spaces surrounding and running through metropolitan areas. Sometimes these greenways even link cities together.

2-1.3.1-1

Navigate through a Document

To insert new text or change existing text, you must know how to ***scroll*** and how to reposition the insertion point. Scrolling enables you to move through the document on the screen without repositioning the insertion point. You can use either the mouse or the keyboard to move the insertion point and scroll.

> **Computer Concepts**
>
> By default, the AutoRecover feature automatically saves a temporary copy of your document every 10 minutes. The temporary copy will open automatically when you start Word after a power failure or similar problem.

Use the Mouse

When you use the mouse to scroll, you use the horizontal or vertical scroll bars. When you use the mouse to reposition the insertion point, you simply move the mouse pointer to the desired location within the document. The pointer changes to an ***I-beam***, indicating you can now key text. Position the I-beam where you want the insertion point to be, and then click the mouse button. Figure 2-3 shows an I-beam and some quick ways to scroll using the mouse.

FIGURE 2-3
Ways to scroll with the mouse

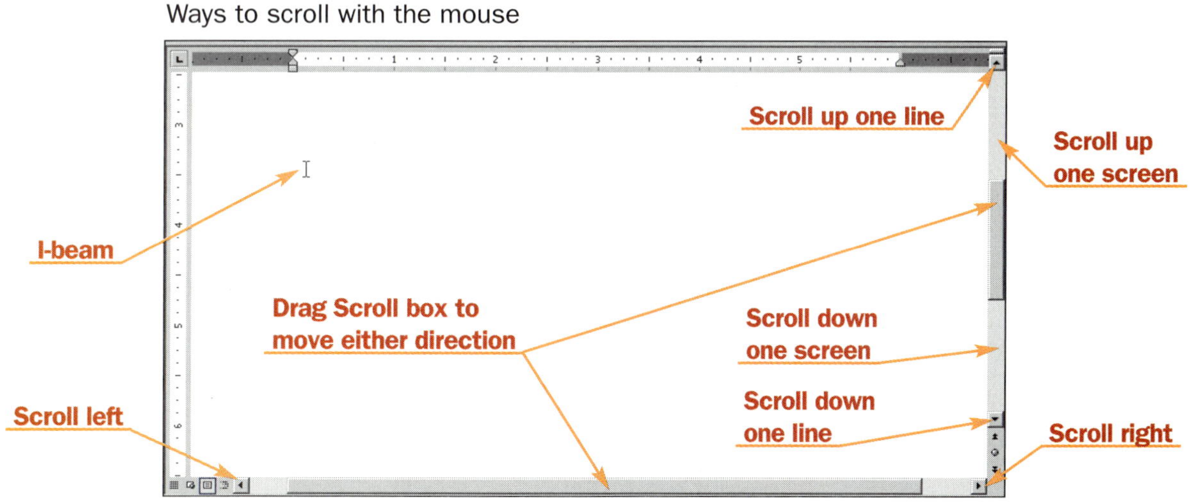

IC3 2-1.3.1-1

STEP-BY-STEP 2.4

1. Move the I-beam to the end of the first paragraph and click once. The insertion point is positioned at the end of the paragraph.

2. Click below the scroll box in the vertical scroll bar. The view of the document moves down one screen and the text disappears.

3. Click the scroll up arrow until you can see the first line of text in the document.

4. Drag the scroll box to the bottom of the vertical scroll bar to view the end of the document.

5. Drag the scroll box to the top of the vertical scroll bar to view the beginning of the document.

6. Click the right scroll arrow twice to display the right edge of the document.

7. Drag the scroll box to the left side of the horizontal scroll bar to display the left edge of the document.

8. Find the insertion point. Notice that even though you scrolled to several different parts of the document, the insertion point never moved.

9. Leave the document open for the next Step-by-Step.

Use the Keyboard

You can use the arrow keys on the keyboard to move the insertion point one character at a time or one line at a time. If you need to move across several characters or lines, however, the keyboard shortcuts shown in Table 2-1 will make the task easier and quicker.

TABLE 2-1
Keyboard shortcuts for moving the Insertion point

TO MOVE THE INSERTION POINT	PRESS
Right one character	right arrow
Left one character	left arrow
To the next line	down arrow
To the previous line	up arrow
To the end of a line	End
To the beginning of a line	Home
To the next screen	Page Down
To the previous screen	Page Up
To the next word	Ctrl+right arrow
To the previous word	Ctrl+left arrow
To the end of the document	Ctrl+End
To the beginning of the document	Ctrl+Home

STEP-BY-STEP 2.5

1. Press **Home** to move the insertion point to the beginning of the line.
2. Press the **down arrow** twice to move the insertion point down two lines.
3. Press the **right arrow** three times to move the insertion point three characters to the right.
4. Hold down **Ctrl** and then press the **left arrow** to move the insertion point to the previous word.
5. Press **End** to move the insertion point to the end of the line.
6. Hold down **Ctrl** and then press **End** to move the insertion point to the end of the document.
7. Hold down **Ctrl** and then press **Home** to move the insertion point to the beginning of the document.
8. Hold down **Ctrl** and then press the **right arrow** to move the insertion point to the next word.
9. Leave the document open for the next Step-by-Step.

Did You Know?

If you have good keyboarding skills, learning keyboard shortcuts to move the insertion point can speed your work. Using the keyboard shortcuts eliminates the need to take your hands from the keyboard to navigate through the document. Table 2-1 provides a list of shortcuts for common commands to move the insertion point. You can find a comprehensive list of keyboard shortcuts in online Help by searching for the keywords *keyboard shortcuts*.

Speech Recognition

If your computer has speech recognition capability, enable the Command mode and say the commands to move the insertion point.

IC3 2-1.1.5-1

Use Help to Find More Ways to Scroll and Move the Insertion Point

Figure 2-3 and Table 2-1 described some of the ways to scroll and position the insertion point. In the following Step-by-Step you will use the Help feature to find a more comprehensive list of ways to scroll through a document and move the insertion point.

Word proposes a list of topics that will link you to information related to the key words. A link is represented by colored, underlined text. When you click the link, you will "jump" to a different Help screen. There you may see even more links. Using these links will help you locate information that explains the features of Word. Once you have clicked a link, the text color of the link will change to show that you have used that link.

IC3 2-1.1.5-3

STEP-BY-STEP 2.6

1. Click the **Office Assistant**, or open the **Help** menu and choose **Microsoft Word Help**.
2. In the What would you like to do? text box, key **viewing and navigating documents** and then click **Search**.

STEP-BY-STEP 2.6 Continued

3. The Assistant displays a list of topics. Point to the topic *Move around in a document*. Your mouse pointer changes to a hand, indicating a link to information about the topic. Click the link **Move around in a document**.

4. The Microsoft Word Help dialog box opens and the topic *Move around in a document* is displayed at the right. Click the link **Scroll through a document** to display information about using the scroll bar features.

5. Use the vertical scroll bar to view the information above and below the current topic.

6. If necessary, drag the scroll box in the vertical scroll bar until you see the link *Tips*. Click the link **Tips** to display more information about scrolling more slowly and using built-in scrolling and zooming capabilities.

7. Click the **Close** box on the Help window to close the Help screens.

8. Leave the document open for the next Step-by-Step.

Use Click and Type

2-1.2.4-1 Click and Type is a feature that enables you to quickly position the insertion point within a blank area of a document. Different applications allow you to view your files in different ways. Most likely the documents you have been working with have been displayed in ***Normal view*** or in ***Print Layout view***. Normal view shows a simplified layout of the page. Print Layout view shows how a document will look when it is printed. To use the Click and Type feature, the document must be displayed in Print Layout view. To switch between these views, open the View menu or click one of the buttons at the bottom left of the document window.

STEP-BY-STEP 2.7

1. Make sure that the Click and Type feature is turned on. Open the **Tools** menu and choose **Options**. Click the **Edit** tab to display the dialog box shown in Figure 2-4.

2. If necessary, select the Enable click and type check box to toggle the option on. The option is turned on when there is a checkmark in the box as shown in Figure 2-4.

3. Click **OK** to apply the option and close the dialog box.

2-1.2.4-2

4. Click the **Print Layout View** button at the bottom left corner of the screen to switch to Print Layout view.

5. Point to the middle of the screen just above the status bar and double-click. The insertion point is now positioned in the center of the document at the bottom of the screen.

STEP-BY-STEP 2.7 Continued

6. Key your name.

7. Click the **Save** button on the Standard toolbar to save the changes. Click the **Close** box on the title bar to close the Greenways document window and the Word application simultaneously.

FIGURE 2-4
Edit tab in the Options dialog box

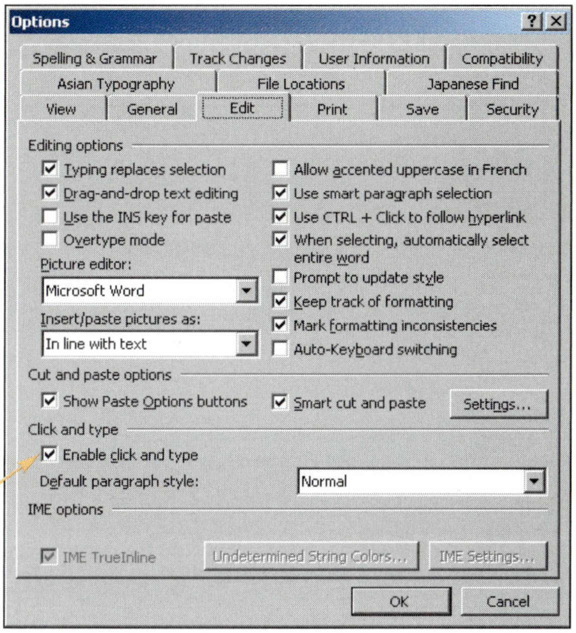

Make sure this box has a checkmark

SUMMARY

In this lesson, you learned:

- You can open multiple Word documents, but you can only work in one document at a time. The document you are working in is called the active document.
- If you have multiple documents open, you can quickly switch to a different document by clicking the document button in the status bar.
- Word automatically wraps text to the next line when the line of text extends beyond the right margin.
- When you scroll through the document, the insertion point does not move. To reposition the insertion point, you can use either the mouse or the keyboard.
- The Click and Type feature enables you to quickly position the insertion point in a blank area of the document.

VOCABULARY *Review*

Define the following terms:

Default	Normal view	Scroll
I-beam	Print Layout view	Word wrap

REVIEW *Questions*

TRUE/FALSE

Circle T if the statement is true or F if the statement is false.

T F 1. The task pane provides an easy and quick way to open a recently accessed document or create a new document.

T F 2. To switch from one document to another, click the document name in the status bar.

T F 3. As you key a paragraph of text, you should press Enter to stop each line at the right margin.

T F 4. Clicking the mouse pointer below the scroll box on the vertical scroll bar lets you scroll down one screen.

T F 5. To move quickly to the beginning of a document, click the Home key.

FILL IN THE BLANK

Complete the following sentences by writing the correct word or words in the blanks provided.

1. Preset options already in place in a new document are called __________ settings.
2. The __________ feature automatically moves text to the next line when you reach the end of the current line.
3. To relocate the insertion point in a document, point the __________ at the proper location and then click the left mouse button.
4. To move to the next word in a document, press __________ and then the right arrow key.
5. To use Click and Type, you must be in __________ view.

PROJECTS

PROJECT 2-1

1. Open a new Word document.
2. Open **Project2-1** from the data files. Save the document as **Tiger**, followed by your initials.
3. Click the document button in the taskbar to return to the new blank document you created when you started Word.
4. Key the following text:

   ```
   Someone Else's Fault

   Almost everyone knows about the San Andreas Fault in California.
   Shifting along this fault line resulted in numerous damaging earthquakes
   throughout the twentieth century.

   Relatively unknown by comparison, the New Madrid Fault in the central
   United States caused three of the most powerful earthquakes in U.S. his-
   tory in the nineteenth century. One earthquake along this fault line was
   so powerful it caused the Mississippi River to run backward for a brief
   stretch. Damage from the earthquake was reported as far away as
   Charleston, South Carolina, and Washington, DC.
   ```

5. Save the document as **New Madrid**. Print the document and then close it.
6. Leave the **Tiger** document open for the next Project.

PROJECT 2-2

1. The document **Tiger** should still be open. Position the insertion point following the period after the number *1,000* in the second paragraph of the document.
2. Press the spacebar once and key the following sentences:

   ```
   The South China tiger is dangerously close to extinction. Only 20 to 30
   tigers are thought to be alive in a few isolated areas. Because there
   have been no recent sightings of this tiger, some people believe it
   might already be extinct.
   ```

3. Use **Ctrl + End** to move to the end of the document. Key the following sentence:

   ```
   They state that only an immediate, widespread effort by concerned indi-
   viduals and support from governments of countries where tigers still
   exist will keep tigers alive in the wild.
   ```

4. Navigate to the top of the document. If you are not already in Print Layout view, change to this view.

5. Position the I-beam pointer so that it is in the white space immediately above the first paragraph and in the center of the document. Double-click to insert the insertion point, and then key **Tiger, Tiger** to create a title for the document. After you key the title, press **Enter** to insert a blank line between the title and the first paragraph of text.

6. Save your changes and close the document.

WEB PROJECT

In Project 2-1, you keyed information about the New Madrid Fault. Using Web resources such as an encyclopedia or a search engine, find out where the New Madrid Fault is located. Use Word to write a brief report describing the location. Print a page from the Web site that shows a map of the area. Try to find out what area of the United States would be affected by a major earthquake along this fault. Would your home, school, or workplace be affected?

TEAMWORK PROJECT

As you worked through this lesson, you may have noticed that Word offers a total of four views to help you work with specific types of documents. Learn more about the different Word views in this project.

1. Divide into four groups. Each group should be assigned a different Word view: Normal, Web Layout, Print Layout, or Outline.

2. Each group should use observation and the Word Help system to learn as much as possible about its assigned view. Be sure to answer these questions as you gather information:
   A. How can you tell where the top and bottom of the page are in this view?
   B. This view is designed for working with what kinds of documents?
   C. What happens to the document window when you change to this view?
   D. Are there any objects that will not display in this view?
   E. How many ways can you find to switch to this view?

3. Each group should write a short report on the information it has gathered on its view. One member of the group should summarize the group's findings in a brief presentation.

CRITICAL *Thinking*

ACTIVITY 2-1

Use the Word Help system to find information on Word's personalized menus and toolbars. Write a brief summary of this feature and state whether you feel this feature will be useful to you in this course.

LESSON 3

EDITING DOCUMENTS

OBJECTIVES

Upon completion of this lesson, you should be able to:

- Display nonprinting characters.
- Use the Backspace and Delete keys.
- Use the Overtype mode.
- Use the undo, redo, and repeat features.
- Select text.
- Use drag-and-drop editing.
- Use cut, copy, and paste commands.
- Highlight text.
- Insert a file.
- Find and replace text and formats.

Estimated Time: 1 hour

VOCABULARY

Clipboard
Drag-and-drop
Insert mode
Overtype mode
Select
Toggle

Editing involves adding, deleting, changing, or moving text in a document. Editing enables you to correct errors and refine the appearance of the document.

Display Nonprinting Characters

Word considers characters to be letters, numbers, and graphics. All of these elements are visible on your screen just as they will look when printed. To simplify editing, you can also display some special characters. These characters are known as nonprinting characters because, although you can display these symbols on the screen, they do not print.

The Show/Hide ¶ button on the Standard toolbar enables you to ***toggle*** the display of these nonprinting characters. Toggling is the process of turning an option on or off using the same procedure, such as clicking a button.

Nonprinting characters include hard returns, blank spaces, and tabs. Initially, you may not like displaying nonprinting characters while you work with a document, but give it a try. Once you get used to seeing the nonprinting characters on the screen, you will find them very useful as you create and edit the document.

STEP-BY-STEP 3.1

1. Open **Step3-1** from the data files for this lesson.

2. Save the document as **Carbohydrates** followed by your initials.

> **Computer Concepts**
> Descriptive filenames help you locate files on your computer.

3. Compare your document to Figure 3-1. The nonprinting symbols are identified in the figure. If you do not see the nonprinting characters on your screen, click the **Show/Hide ¶** button on the Standard toolbar. ¶

4. Leave the document open for the next Step-by-Step.

FIGURE 3-1
Document with nonprinting characters displayed

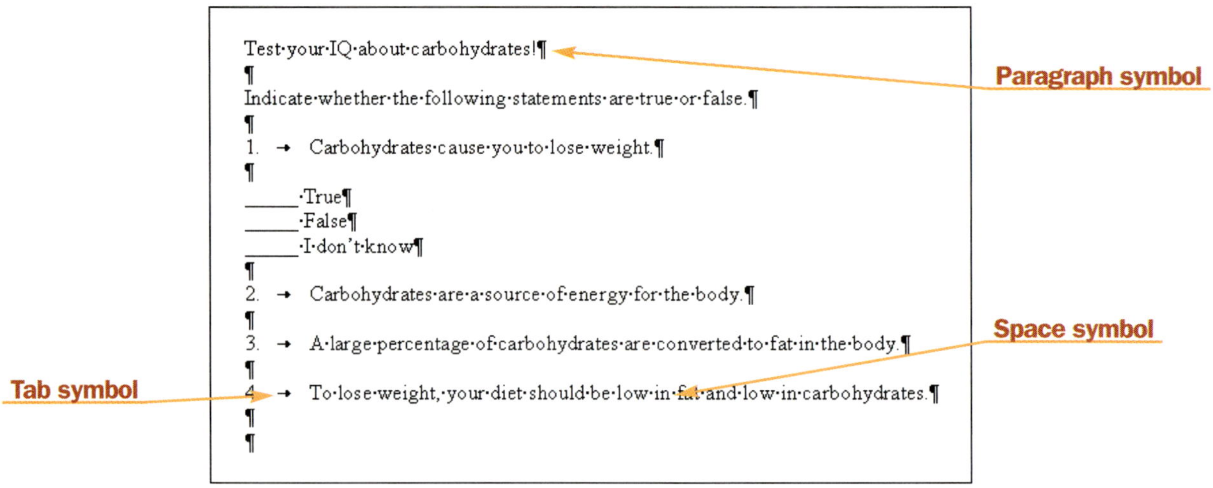
Test·your·IQ·about·carbohydrates!¶
¶
Indicate·whether·the·following·statements·are·true·or·false.¶
¶
1. → Carbohydrates·cause·you·to·lose·weight.¶
¶
_____·True¶
_____·False¶
_____·I·don't·know¶
¶
2. → Carbohydrates·are·a·source·of·energy·for·the·body.¶
¶
3. → A·large·percentage·of·carbohydrates·are·converted·to·fat·in·the·body.¶
¶
4. → To·lose·weight,·your·diet·should·be·low·in·fat·and·low·in·carbohydrates.¶
¶
¶

Delete and Replace Characters

When you edit documents, you often need to delete and replace existing text. This is very easy to do in Word.

Use the Backspace and Delete Keys to Delete Characters

2-1.3.3-1

You can quickly delete characters one at a time by using either the Backspace or the Delete keys. The Backspace key deletes the character to the left of the insertion point. The Delete key removes the character to the right of the insertion point. If you hold down either of these keys, the characters will continue to delete until you release the key.

STEP-BY-STEP 3.2

1. Position the insertion point at the end of the first sentence in your document.

2-1.3.3-1

2. Press **Backspace** several times to erase the last two words in the sentence (*about carbohydrates!*).

STEP-BY-STEP 3.2 Continued

3. Move the insertion point to the beginning of the first sentence.

4. Press **Delete** several times to erase the remaining words in the sentence. Leave at least one paragraph symbol above the line that begins, *Indicate whether...*

5. Save the changes and leave the document open for the next Step-by-Step.

Use Overtype Mode to Replace Characters

By default, Word enters text in a document using the ***Insert mode***. In this mode, when you type new text in front of existing text, the existing text shifts to the right to make room for the new text. When the Insert mode is turned off, the ***Overtype mode*** is activated. In the Overtype mode, new text you key replaces the existing text. You can toggle between the Insert mode and the Overtype mode by double-clicking OVR in the status bar or by pressing the Insert key (on the keyboard). Regardless of how you toggle, when OVR is dimmed, Insert mode is on; when OVR is dark or bold, Overtype mode is on.

STEP-BY-STEP 3.3

1. Make sure *OVR* in the status bar is dimmed. If the option is bold in the status bar, double-click it to toggle off the Overtype mode.

2. Position the insertion point to the right of the letter "C" in the word *Carbohydrates* in Question 1. See Figure 3-2.

FIGURE 3-2
Position the insertion point in the word Carbohydrates

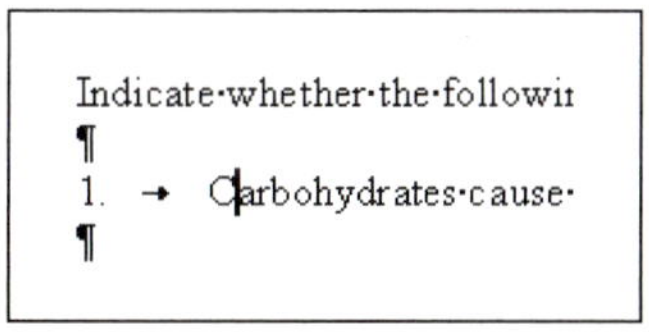

3. Key **omplex c**. In Insert mode, Word inserts the text between the existing characters.

4. Position the insertion point in front of the word *source* in Question 2. Key **primary** and press the **Spacebar**.

5. Double-click **OVR** in the status bar to toggle on the Overtype mode.

6. Position the insertion point in front of the word *lose* in Question 1.

7. Key **gain**. Word replaces the word *lose* with the new text.

8. Double-click **OVR** in the status bar to switch back to the Insert mode.

9. Save the changes and leave the document open for the next Step-by-Step.

Use Undo, Redo, and Repeat

2-1.3.7-1
2-1.3.7-2

Sometimes you may delete or replace text unintentionally. Whenever you perform an edit that you want to change back, you can use the Undo command. If you undo an edit and then change your mind, you can reverse the undo action by using the Redo command. You can undo and redo multiple actions at one time by choosing from the Undo or Redo drop-down list on the Standard toolbar. When you undo or redo an action from the drop-down list, Word will also undo or redo all the actions listed above it on the list.

There may be times when you want to repeat your last action. For example, you may enter your name in a document and then want to add your name in other locations in the document. You can use the Repeat command to repeat your last action. You can access the Repeat command in the Edit menu, or you can use the shortcut key combination Ctrl + Y to execute the command. If you can't repeat the last action, the Repeat command in the Edit menu will change to *Can't Repeat*.

STEP-BY-STEP 3.4

1. Position the insertion point at the end of the document and press **Enter** three times.

2. Key your name.

3. Position the insertion point at the beginning of the document.

4. Open the **Edit** menu and choose **Repeat Typing**. The three blank lines and your name are inserted in the document.

2-1.3.7-1 5. You change your mind. Click the **Undo** button on the Standard toolbar. The blank lines and your name disappear from the top of the document.

6. Click the down arrow next to the **Undo** button and select *Typing "primary"*. (You may have to scroll down.) All the previous actions will remain highlighted. See Figure 3-3. The last six actions are reversed.

FIGURE 3-3
Select multiple actions in the Undo list box

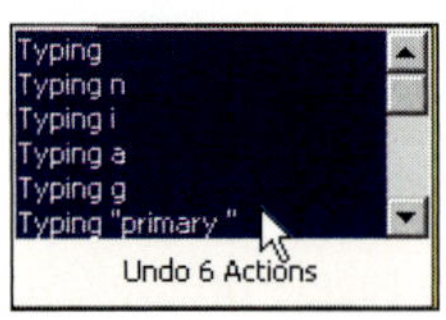

2-1.3.7-2 7. Click the **Redo** button on the Standard toolbar to undo only the last undo. The word *primary* is reinserted in Question 2.

Hot Tip

The shortcut key combination for the Undo command is **Ctrl + Z**.

Speech Recognition

If your computer has speech recognition capability, enable the Command mode and say the commands to undo and redo edits.

STEP-BY-STEP 3.4 Continued

8. Click the down arrow next to the **Redo** button and select *Typing n*. The word *lose* is replaced with the word *gain*.

9. Save the changes and keep the document open for the next Step-by-Step.

Hot Tip

If the Redo button is not visible on the Standard toolbar, you can display it by clicking **More Buttons** on the toolbar and then choosing it from the list of buttons.

IC³

2-1.3.2-1

Select Text

When you ***select*** text, you identify blocks of text you want to edit. The text can be a single character, several characters, a word, a phrase, a sentence, one or more paragraphs, or even the entire document. Once you select text, you can edit it by deleting it, replacing it, changing its appearance, moving it, copying it, and so on.

Computer Concepts

To make many editing changes, you must first select text. Become familiar with the different ways to select text.

Computer Concepts

Be cautious when working with selected text. If you press keys on the keyboard when text is selected, the new keystrokes will replace the selected text. Pages of text could accidentally be replaced with a single character.

You can use the mouse or the keyboard to select text. The quickest way to select text using the mouse is to drag the mouse pointer over the desired text. Sometimes it is difficult to select precisely when you are dragging the mouse. The click-Shift-click method makes it easy to select the right text on the first try. Click where you want the selection to begin, hold down Shift, then click where you want the selection to end. Table 3-1 lists several options for selecting text using the mouse and the keyboard. To deselect the text (remove the selection), click an insertion point anywhere in the document or press an arrow key. If you accidentally delete or replace selected text, or if you just change your mind, click the Undo button.

TABLE 3-1
Ways to select text

TO SELECT TEXT USING THE MOUSE	DO THIS
Any amount of text	Drag over the text.
A word	Double-click the word.
A sentence	Hold down the Ctrl key, then click anywhere in the sentence.
A paragraph	Triple-click anywhere in the paragraph, or double-click in the left margin.
An entire document	Move the pointer to the left of any text. When the pointer changes to a right-pointing arrow, triple-click, or open the Edit menu and choose Select All.
A line	Click in the left margin.

TABLE 3-1 Continued
Ways to select text

TO SELECT TEXT USING THE MOUSE	DO THIS
Multiple lines	Drag in the left margin.
One character to the right	Hold down Shift and press the right arrow.
One character to the left	Hold down Shift and press the left arrow.
To the beginning of a word	Hold down Ctrl + Shift and press the left arrow.
To the end of a word	Hold down Ctrl + Shift and press the right arrow.

2-1.3.2-1

STEP-BY-STEP 3.5

1. Move the I-beam mouse pointer until it is at the beginning of the first line of text.

2. Hold down the mouse button and drag through the entire line of text including the paragraph mark. When all the text is selected, release the mouse button. The sentence is now selected as shown in Figure 3-4.

FIGURE 3-4
Selected text

¶
Indicate·whether·the·following·statements·are·true·or·false.¶
¶
1. → Complex·carbohydrates·cause·you·to·gain·weight.¶

3. Double-click on the second occurrence of the word low in Question 4.

4. Key **high**. The selected text is replaced with the new text.

5. Press **Ctrl + A** to select the entire document.

6. Click at the beginning of Question 1 to position the insertion point there. Hold down **Shift**, then click at the end of Question 4. All the questions are selected.

7. Click at the end of Question 3 to position the insertion point there. Hold down **Ctrl + Shift** and then press **Home**. All the text from the insertion point to the beginning of the document is selected.

8. Practice other methods of selecting text following the instructions in Table 3-1.

9. Click anywhere in the document window to deselect the text. Then save the changes and leave the document open for the next Step-by-Step.

Copy and Move Text

Selected text can be copied or moved from one location in a Word document to a new location in the same document, to a different Word document, or even to a different document in another application program. There are several ways to copy and move text. You can use the mouse to drag selected text from the existing location and then drop the selected text in its new location. This is called ***drag-and-drop*** editing. You can also use the Cut and Paste commands to relocate selected text.

> **Hot Tip**
>
> If the selected text is not replaced with the new text, click **Undo**, then open the **Tools** menu and choose **Options**. Make sure *Typing replaces selection* is turned on in the Edit sheet.

Use Drag-and-Drop Editing

Drag-and-drop editing makes moving text quick and easy, especially when you are moving the text short distances. You simply drag selected text to the next location and then release the mouse button.

You can also copy text using drag-and-drop editing. Hold down Ctrl as you drag, and the selected text will be copied instead of moved.

STEP-BY-STEP 3.6

1. Select all of the text in Question 3 including the number 3 at the beginning of the line and the blank paragraph after the question.

2. Point to the selection and hold down the left mouse button. An arrowhead, a small dotted box, and a dotted insertion point will be displayed. See Figure 3-5.

FIGURE 3-5
Selected paragraph before dragging to a new location

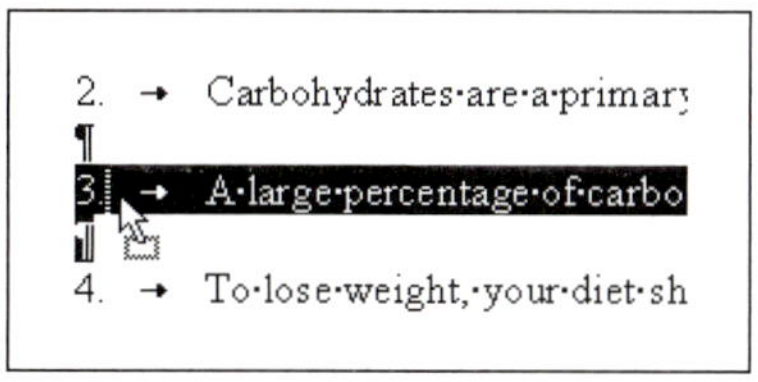

3. Drag the dotted insertion point in front of the number 2 at the beginning of Question 2, then release. See Figure 3-6.

FIGURE 3-6
Position of pointer after dragging selected paragraph to a new location

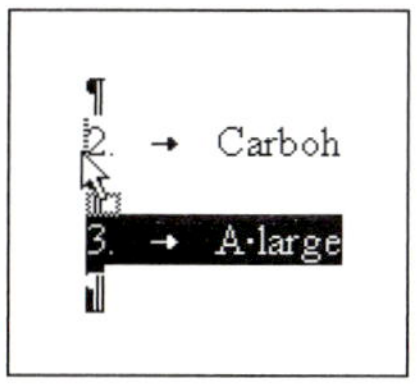

STEP-BY-STEP 3.6 Continued

4. With Question 3 still selected, hold down **Ctrl** and use the left mouse button to drag the text to the end of the document. The text is copied to the new location.

5. Click **Undo**.

6. Click to deselect the text, then renumber the questions in the new order.

7. Save the changes and leave the document open for the next Step-by-Step.

Did You Know?

To drag text beyond the current screen of text, drag the pointer toward the top or bottom of the screen. As you hold the pointer at the edge, the document will automatically scroll in that direction.

Use the Cut, Copy, and Paste Commands

IC3 2-1.3.4-1 2-1.3.5-1 2-1.3.6-1

You can access the Cut, Copy, and Paste commands by clicking the appropriate buttons on the Standard toolbar. You can also access the commands by right-clicking the selected text. Then choose the desired command from the shortcut menu that is displayed.

When you use the Cut, Copy, and Paste commands, Word stores the selected text in the ***Clipboard***. The Clipboard is a temporary storage place in your computer's memory. The Clipboard is a shared item between all the Office applications. It can store data of all Office types and that data can be pasted from the Clipboard to other office programs. You send selected contents of your document to the Clipboard by using the Cut or Copy commands. Then you can retrieve those contents by using the Paste command.

Hot Tip

The shortcut keys for Cut are **Ctrl + X**; for Copy, **Ctrl + C**; and for Paste, **Ctrl + V**. Cut, Copy, and Paste can also be found on the **Edit** menu.

The Clipboard will store up to 24 items. If you display the Clipboard task pane, you can see the items that are stored in the Clipboard. To display the Clipboard task pane manually, open the View menu and choose Task Pane. If necessary, click the down arrow in the title bar of the task pane and select Clipboard. A shortcut to open the Clipboard task pane is to press Ctrl + C twice. See Figure 3-7. Make sure that nothing is selected when you press Ctrl + C. If text is selected, the shortcut will copy the selected text to the Clipboard instead of opening the Clipboard task pane.

Computer Concepts

It is not necessary to display the Clipboard task pane when you are cutting or copying text. The Clipboard still functions even if the task pane is not displayed.

FIGURE 3-7
Clipboard task pane

You can select any one of the items in the task pane and paste it, or you can choose the Paste All button to paste all the Clipboard items at once. If you choose the Clear All button, all the contents are removed from the Clipboard. The items are inserted at the location of the insertion point. Pasting the contents of the Clipboard does not delete the contents from the Clipboard. Therefore, you can paste Clipboard items as many times as you want. When you turn off the computer, the Clipboard contents are lost.

Did You Know?

If you cut or copy text and fail to leave a blank space between sentences, Word will automatically adjust the spacing by adding a blank space.

STEP-BY-STEP 3.7

1. Press **Ctrl + C** twice to display the Clipboard task pane. If any items are displayed in the task pane, click the **Clear All** button in the task pane.

2. Select the blank paragraph and the three lines of text under Question 1. Be sure to include the paragraph mark at the end of the third line of text. See Figure 3-8.

FIGURE 3-8
Selected lines of text

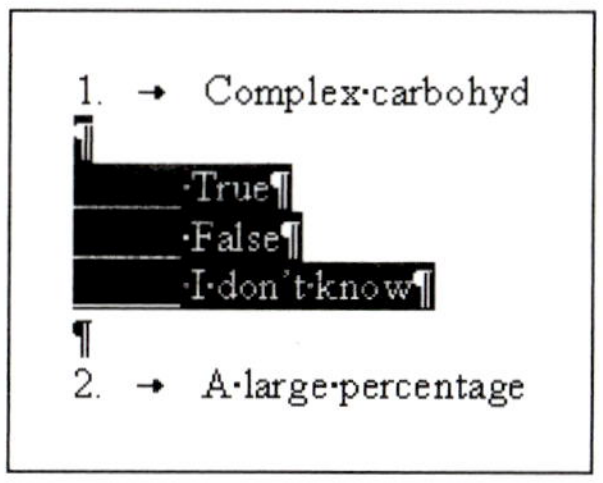

STEP-BY-STEP 3.7 Continued

2-1.3.5-1

3. Click the **Copy** button on the Standard toolbar. Word copies the selected text to the Clipboard and displays the item in the task pane. See Figure 3-7 on page 47.

4. Position the insertion point in the blank paragraph below Question 2.

2-1.3.6-1

5. Click the **Paste** button on the Standard toolbar. Word pastes the contents of the Clipboard at the location of the insertion point. Notice that the item is still displayed in the Clipboard task pane.

6. Position the insertion point in the blank paragraph below Question 3, then click the item in the task pane.

7. Select the entire line of text for Question 4, then click the **Copy** button.

8. Select the entire line of text for Question 3, then click the **Copy** button again.

9. You should see three items in the Clipboard task pane. Position the insertion point in the blank paragraph below Question 4. Click on the last item in the Clipboard task pane with the____*True*____*False* contents.

10. Click the **Clear All** button to remove the items from the Clipboard.

11. Save the changes and leave the document open for the next Step-by-Step.

Did You Know?

If the Office Clipboard icon is displayed on the right side of the taskbar, the Clipboard is already displayed in at least one active Office application. Double-click the Office Clipboard icon to open the Clipboard task pane in the active application.

Speech Recognition

If your computer has speech recognition capability, enable the Command mode. Then select the text and say the commands to copy and paste the text.

Hot Tip

To cut text, select the text and click the **Cut** button on the Standard toolbar.

Computer Concepts

Cutting removes text from the document and stores it in the Clipboard. Copying also stores the text on the Clipboard, but it leaves the text in the document.

Use Help to Learn More about Clipboard Options

Word offers many options for using the Office Clipboard. Word's Online Help is a good resource for reviewing the features and determining which option will best meet your needs. One way to access Help is to enter keywords and begin a search for that text. Often times when you access Help, you will see words in the topics that are formatted as hyperlinks. These hyperlinks will either link you to demonstrations on how to do something or the links may define words and provide additional details. When you see *Show All* above the topic information, details regarding the topic have been collapsed. You can click on each of the hyperlinks to toggle the display of the details on and off. Or, you can click on *Show All* to display all the details at once.

STEP-BY-STEP 3.8

1. If the Office Assistant is not displayed, open the **Help** menu and choose **Show the Office Assistant**. Click the **Office Assistant**, enter the keywords **Clipboard options** in the text box, and then click the **Search** button.

2. When the Office Assistant suggests some topics, select *Turn Office Clipboard command options on or off.*

3. When the topic is displayed, click the first link **task pane**. The definition of *task pane* is displayed. Click the **task pane** link again to hide the definition.

4. Click the link **How?** to display the linked information. Click the link again to hide the information.

5. Click the **Show All** link at the top of the Help screen. All the information for each of the links related to the current topic is displayed.

6. Scroll down through the list and read the descriptions of the four options available for the Clipboard.

7. Click the **Hide All** link at the top of the Help screen. Click the **Close** box in the Help window to exit Help.

8. If necessary, display the Clipboard task pane. Then, click the **Options** button at the bottom of the task pane and turn on the option for *Show Office Clipboard Automatically.* The option is turned on when there is a checkmark next to it.

9. Click outside the options list to close it and leave the document open for the next Step-by-Step.

Highlight Text

To emphasize important text within a document, you can use Word's highlight feature. Color highlights are most effective when the recipient of the document is going to be viewing the document online or on a color printout. If the document is to be printed in black and white, light highlight colors work best.

To remove the highlight from text, select None for the highlight color.

STEP-BY-STEP 3.9

1. If necessary, scroll to display the first line of text.

2. If necessary, click the down arrow to the right of the **Highlight** button on the Formatting toolbar and select **Yellow**. The I-beam pointer changes to a highlighter.

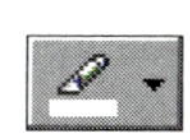

3. Highlight the first line of text. You can drag the highlighter pointer across the text and release at the end, or click in the left margin alongside the line of text. The selected text is highlighted in yellow.

STEP-BY-STEP 3.9 Continued

4. Click the down arrow to the right of **Highlight**, select a new color, and highlight Question 1.
5. Highlight Questions 2, 3, and 4 in different colors.
6. Select **None** for the highlight color.
7. Drag across the highlighted text for the first line of text.
8. Click the **Highlight** button to turn off the highlight option.
9. Save the changes and leave the document open for the next Step-by-Step.

Speech Recognition

If your computer has speech recognition capability, enable the Command mode and then say the commands to open the Insert menu and choose the File command.

Hot Tip

When you position the pointer on one of the highlight colors, a ScreenTip will display with the color name.

Insert a File

You can quickly insert all of the contents of one file into an open document without even opening the file. Simply position the insertion point where the file contents should be inserted, and then open the Insert menu and choose the File command.

Hot Tip

Before you insert files, be sure the insertion point is positioned correctly. Files are inserted at the insertion point.

STEP-BY-STEP 3.10

1. Position the insertion point at the end of the document.
2. Open the **Insert** menu and choose **File**.
3. Select **Step3-10** from the data files and click **Insert** in the dialog box. The entire file is inserted at the insertion point.
4. Save the changes and close the document.

Find and Replace Text and Formats

Scrolling through a long document to locate a specific section of text is time-consuming and not very efficient. The Find feature in Word makes searching for text and/or formats much easier. When you need to replace or reformat multiple occurrences of the same text, you can use the Replace feature to replace each occurrence automatically.

Find Text

2-1.3.8-1 You use the Find command to search a document for every time a specific word or phrase occurs. The search will begin at the location of the insertion point. If you want to search only a specific portion of a document, you can select the desired text before beginning the search.

STEP-BY-STEP 3.11

1. Open **Step3-11** from the data files. Save the document as **Treadwall** followed by your initials.

2. If necessary, move the insertion point to the top of the document.

2-1.3.8-1

3. Open the **Edit** menu and choose **Find**. The Find sheet in the Find and Replace dialog box is displayed. See Figure 3-9.

FIGURE 3-9
The Find sheet in the Find and Replace dialog box

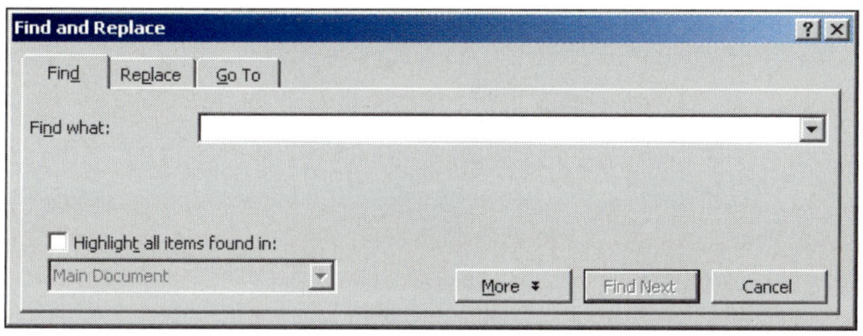

4. In the *Find what* box, key **workout**, then click **Find Next**. Word locates the first occurrence of the word, and the word is selected in the document window. The dialog box remains open.

5. Click **Find Next** again. Word finds the next occurrence of the word in the open document.

6. Click **Cancel** to close the dialog box.

7. Leave the document open for the next Step-by-Step.

> **Hot Tip**
>
> The shortcut keys to execute the Find command are **Ctrl + F**.

Find and Replace Text

-1.3.9-1 If you want to replace the search text with new words, you choose the Replace command. The replacements can be made individually, or all occurrences can be replaced at once.

STEP-BY-STEP 3.12

1. Move the insertion point to the beginning of the document. (*Hint*: Hold down **Ctrl** and press **Home**.)

STEP-BY-STEP 3.12 Continued

2-1.3.9-1

2. Open the **Edit** menu and choose **Replace**. The Replace sheet in the Find and Replace dialog box is displayed. See Figure 3-10. Notice the word *workout* from your last search is still displayed in the *Find what* box.

FIGURE 3-10
The Replace sheet in the Find and Replace dialog box

3. Key **tread wall** in the *Find what* box.
4. Click in the *Replace with* box and key **Treadwall**.
5. Click **Find Next**. Word locates and selects the first occurrence of the words *tread wall*. (Notice that the Find function ignores case.)
6. Click **Replace**. Word changes the selected text to *Treadwall* and then locates the next occurrence of the search text. The dialog box remains open.
7. Click **Replace All**. Word replaces all occurrences of the search text with the replace text. The Assistant balloon (or a message box) is displayed indicating that three replacements were made. Click **OK**.
8. Click **Close** in the Find and Replace dialog box.
9. Save the changes and leave the document open for the next Step-by-Step.

> **Hot Tip**
> The shortcut keys to execute the Replace command are **Ctrl + H**.

Find and Replace Formats

You can also use the Find command to search for character and paragraph formats. You can search for combined formats such as bold and italic. When you need to replace multiple occurrences of the same format, you can use the Replace command to reformat each occurrence automatically.

STEP-BY-STEP 3.13

1. Position the insertion point at the beginning of the document. Then open the **Edit** menu and choose **Replace**.
2. Delete the text in the *Find what* and *Replace with* boxes.

STEP-BY-STEP 3.13 Continued

3. Click **More** in the Find and Replace dialog box. The expanded dialog box shown in Figure 3-11 is displayed.

FIGURE 3-11
The Replace sheet with More

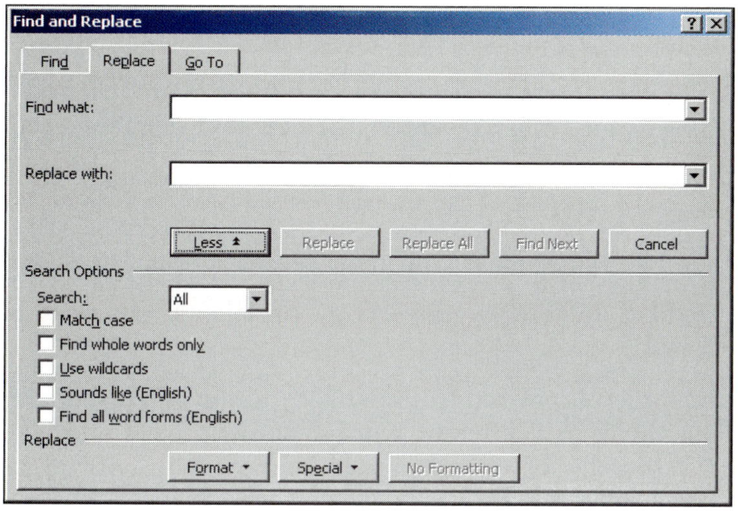

4. Position the insertion point in the *Find what* box.

5. Click **Format**. A shortcut menu is displayed.

6. Click **Font** to display the Find Font dialog box. Under *Font style*, select **Bold** and then click **OK**. Notice that the words *Font: Bold* are displayed below the *Find what* box.

7. Click in the *Replace with* box. Click on **Format**, then select **Font** in the shortcut menu.

8. Under *Font style*, select **Italic** and click **OK**.

9. Click **Replace All**. A balloon (or message box) is displayed indicating that four occurrences of bold text are changed to bold and italic. Click outside the balloon to close it (or click **OK**).

10. Click in the *Find what* box and then click **No Formatting**. This removes the format from the search box. Click in the *Replace with* box and then click **No Formatting** to remove the format.

11. Click **Less** to return the dialog box to the condensed view, then click **Close** in the Find and Replace dialog box.

12. Save the changes and close the document.

SUMMARY

In this lesson, you learned:

- The Show/Hide ¶ button on the Standard toolbar toggles the display of nonprinting characters such as tab symbols, blank spaces, and paragraph marks.
- The Delete key and the Backspace key can be used to delete characters.
- When you add new text in Insert mode, the new characters are inserted between existing text. When text is entered in Overtype mode, the new text replaces existing text.
- The Undo and Redo commands make editing easy when you make mistakes or change your mind.
- The Repeat command lets you repeat your most recent action.
- Text must be selected before you can move, copy, or delete it. Text can be selected using the mouse or the keyboard.
- Selected text can be copied or moved from one location in a Word document to a new location in the same document, to a different Word document, or to another application. Drag-and-drop editing is especially helpful when you are moving or copying text short distances.
- When you use the Cut, Copy, and Paste commands, Word stores the selected text in the Clipboard. The Clipboard stores up to 24 items.
- The highlight feature emphasizes important text and is most effective when the recipient views the document online or from a color printer.
- The File command on the Insert menu quickly inserts all of the contents of one file into an open document.
- The Find command makes searching for text and/or formats easy. The Replace command replaces multiple occurrences of text automatically.

VOCABULARY*Review*

Define the following terms:

Clipboard	Insert mode	Select
Drag-and-drop	Overtype mode	Toggle

REVIEW *Questions*

TRUE/FALSE

Circle T if the statement is true or F if the statement is false.

T F 1. Characters can be letters, numbers, or graphics.

T F 2. In Overtype mode, new text is inserted between existing text.

T F 3. To repeat your last action, you can use the Redo command.

T F 4. To copy text using drag-and-drop, hold down the Ctrl key as you drag.

T F 5. The Clipboard stores up to 10 items.

FILL IN THE BLANK

Complete the following sentences by writing the correct word or words in the blanks provided.

1. Use the ________ key to remove characters to the left of the insertion point.
2. Before you can copy or move text, you must first ________ it.
3. You can find the Cut, Copy, and Paste buttons on the ________ toolbar.
4. Use the ________ feature to emphasize text in a document that will be viewed online or printed in color.
5. Use the ________ command on the ________ menu to add the entire contents of one document to another.

PROJECTS

PROJECT 3-1

1. Open **Project3-1a** from the data files.
2. Save the document as **Walking Weather**, followed by your initials. If nonprinting characters are displayed, turn them off.
3. Turn on Overtype mode and replace the word *dangerous* in the first sentence with **hazardous**. Turn Overtype mode off.
4. Position the insertion point at the end of the second sentence in the second paragraph of the document. Backspace to remove the words *or lightheaded*. If necessary, replace the period at the end of the sentence.
5. Turn on the display of nonprinting characters. Select the heading *Walking in Hot Weather* (including the paragraph symbol at the end of the heading) and copy it.

6. Position the insertion point to the left of the tab symbol at the beginning of the first paragraph on walking in cold weather.

7. Paste the heading at the location of the insertion point. Delete the word *Hot* in the pasted heading and key **Cold** in its place.

8. Position the insertion point to the left of the tab symbol at the beginning of the last paragraph that begins *On a cold*,.... Insert the **Project3-1b** file at the location of the insertion point.

9. Highlight the second sentence under the *Walking in Hot Weather* heading using the **Yellow** color. Highlight the second sentence under the *Walking in Cold Weather* heading using the **Turquoise** color.

10. Save your changes. Print and close the document.

PROJECT 3-2

You've been helping out at your local community center. Today, the director of programs gave you a file containing a description of some of the courses offered at the center. She admitted she created the document in a hurry and asked you to edit the document for her using her file and her notes.

1. Open **Project3-2** from the data files. Save the document as **Languages**, followed by your initials.

2. Display the Clipboard task pane, and clear all items from the Clipboard.

3. Scroll down the page and notice that there is a course title separated from its description. Cut the *Japanese for Beginners* title from its current location and paste it above the course description that begins *Build a solid foundation for communicating in Japanese...*

4. Remove the blank line below the *Japanese for Beginners* heading. (Display nonprinting characters, if necessary, to see the paragraph symbol for the blank line.)

5. According to the director's notes, Spanish for Beginners and Japanese for Beginners are offered on the same day and time and for the same number of weeks. You need to add information to both class descriptions.
   A. First, copy the class dates (*September 25–November 13*) that appear below the Japanese instructor's name. Do not include the paragraph symbol at the end of the dates in the selection.
   B. Then, position the insertion point below the Spanish instructor's name and paste the dates. Press **Enter** to insert a blank line below the dates.
   C. Next, position the insertion point after the Spanish instructor's name (*Ken Grazzi*) and press **Enter** to insert a new line. Key **Tuesday, 6–8 p.m.**
   D. Position the insertion point after the Japanese instructor's name (*Hiroki Sasaki*) and use the Repeat command. Word should move to a new line and insert the same day and time you keyed for the Spanish class.

6. Clear all the items from the Clipboard. Copy to the clipboard the name of the German for Beginners instructor and the fee for the German for Beginners class.

7. Paste the German instructor's name after the course number for *Continuing German for Beginners*.

8. All classes have the same fee, so you can paste the class fee after the dates for each class.

9. The director's notes indicate that Ken Grazzi may not be able to teach the Spanish class. Delete his name.

10. After checking with the director, you learn that Mr. Grazzi will be able to teach the class after all. Use Undo to restore his name.

11. Using cut and paste and/or drag-and-drop, reorganize all information for the classes to be in alphabetical order by the class title.

12. Save your changes. Print and close the document.

WEB PROJECT

In this lesson, you learned some facts about carbohydrates and weight control. Proper weight control is important for good health. One way to measure the fitness of a person is to find out their body mass using the body mass index. Use a Web search tool to find information on the body mass index. How is it calculated? Find a Web site that contains a table of values or a body mass index calculator and check the body mass for a 5' 2", 20-year-old female weighing 122 pounds. Then check the body mass for a 5' 11", 20-year-old male weighing 160 pounds. Using Word, write a brief report that states what you have learned about the body mass index.

TEAMWORK PROJECT

If you completed Project 3-1, you learned a bit about exercising in both hot and cold weather. Many people have preferences for warm or cool weather for a variety of reasons. Team up with a partner to explore these reasons.

1. With your partner, decide who will take the warm weather topic and who will take the cool weather topic. If both of you prefer the same season, flip a coin to decide who will take which season.

2. Using Word, create lists of advantages and disadvantages of your "temperature." If you live in a climate that is more or less warm all year round, use your imagination to list the advantages and disadvantages of cold weather.

3. Use the editing skills you have learned in this lesson to organize your advantages and disadvantages in order of importance. Use your own personal opinion to determine the importance.

4. Compare your lists with your partner and discuss whose arguments are more persuasive.

5. Take a poll of family members or friends to determine how many prefer warm weather and how many prefer cool weather.

CRITICAL *Thinking*

ACTIVITY 3-1

You have been copying multiple items to the Clipboard. You learned in this lesson that the Clipboard will hold up to 24 items. What do you think will happen when you copy the 25th item? Use the Help feature to see if your answer was correct.

LESSON 4

FORMATTING DOCUMENTS

OBJECTIVES

Upon completion of this lesson, you should be able to:

- Change fonts and point sizes.
- Change line spacing and align text.
- Change margins and page orientation.
- Use Print Preview and zoom in or out of a document.
- Check and correct spelling and grammar.
- Format tabs.
- Format indents.
- Format bullets and numbering.
- Insert page numbers and create a header and footer.

Estimated Time: 1.5 hours

VOCABULARY

First line indent
Font
Footer
Hanging indent
Hard page break
Header
Landscape orientation
Points
Portrait orientation
Soft page break

Format features enable you to change the appearance of a document so you can make it more attractive and easier to read. Word offers a number of formats. Character formats and paragraph formats can be applied to specific portions of text. Character formats can be applied to as much text as desired, from a single character to the entire document. Text color and underline are examples of character formats. You can apply more than one character format at a time. For example, you can format characters in both bold and italic formats.

A paragraph format is applied to an entire paragraph and cannot be applied to only a portion of a paragraph. For example, you cannot single-space part of a paragraph and double-space the rest. Word defines a paragraph as any amount of text that ends with a paragraph mark—which is caused by a *hard return* (pressing the Enter key).

Computer Concepts

If you change the format *before* you enter text, all the text you enter will be formatted with the new format until you change the format again. If you have already entered the text, you can change the paragraph formats by clicking in the paragraph and then applying the new format. To change a paragraph format in more than one paragraph or for more than one character, select all the text before applying the format.

Another format Word offers is document formats. Document formats apply to an entire document. For example, margins and paper size are document formats. You can position the insertion point anywhere in a document to change the entire document format. Document formats can be applied either before or after you key text in your document.

Format Fonts and Point Sizes

A *font* is the design of the typeface in your document. Fonts are available in a variety of styles and sizes, and you can use multiple fonts in one document. The size of the font is measured in ***points***. The higher the points, the larger the font size.

You can quickly change font style and point size by using the Formatting toolbar. However, when you open the Font dialog box from the Format menu to change the font, you can also
2-1.3.14-1 apply other font options such as color, outline, superscript, and shadow. The Font dialog box can
2-1.3.13-1 be very useful when you want to make several font changes at one time or if you want to explore
2-1.3.11-1
2-1.3.12-1 what options are available and what they would make the text look like.

STEP-BY-STEP 4.1

1. Open **Step4-1** from the data files and save the document as **Wild Things** followed by your initials.

2. Select the first line of text, then open the **Format** menu and choose **Font**. If necessary, click the **Font** tab to display the Font sheet. See Figure 4-1. Do not be concerned if your dialog box does not exactly match the dialog box illustrated in the figure.

2-1.3.11-1
2-1.3.12-1
3. In the *Font* list box (or in the *Latin text font* box), scroll up and select **Arial**. In the *Font style* list box, scroll down if necessary and select **Bold Italic**. Notice the text in the *Preview* box changes as you select different character formats.

2-1.3.14-1
4. In the *Size* list box, scroll down and select **48**. Click **OK**.

FIGURE 4-1
The Font tab in the Font dialog box

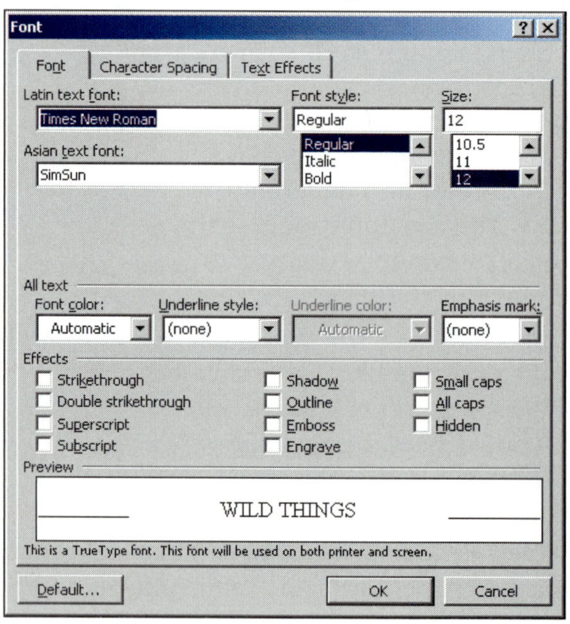

STEP-BY-STEP 4.1 Continued

5. Select the second line of text, then click the down arrow at the right of the *Font* box in the Formatting toolbar. A list of fonts appears. The fonts you used most recently are shown at the top of the list, and separated by a double line from the rest of the font list.

2-1.3.13-1

6. Select any font style and any font color. The text in the document changes, and the name of the selected font displays in the *Font* box.

7. Click in the *Font Size* box and key **32**, then press **Enter**. The text in the document is enlarged, and the size of the font displays in the *Font Size* box. Do not be concerned if the text wraps to the next line.

8. With the text still selected, click the **Bold**, **Italic**, and **Underline** buttons on the Formatting toolbar.

9. Click anywhere in the document to deselect the text so you can see all the font changes. Click **Undo** once to remove the underline format.

2-1.3.14-1

10. Select each of the remaining paragraphs, and format each paragraph with a different font and point size. Also practice applying bold, italic, underline, superscript, and subscript formats.

11. Save the changes and leave the document open for the next Step-by-Step.

Hot Tip

2-2.1.12-1

When you apply multiple character formats to text, you can use the **Format Painter** button to quickly copy the formatting to other text. Select the text with the formatting you want to copy. Double-click the **Format Painter** button on the Standard toolbar. When the pointer changes to a paintbrush, click on the word to which you want to apply the formatting. If you want to apply the formatting to a group of words, drag the pointer across the words to select them. To turn off the feature, click the **Format Painter** button again or press **ESC**.

Change Line Spacing and Align Paragraphs

2-2.1.1-1

The default line spacing in Word is single spacing. When text is double-spaced, there is a blank line between each line of text. The blank line between each line of text is half the space for 1½-line spacing. You can choose from several line spacing options by using the Line Spacing button on the Formatting toolbar or by opening the Format menu, choosing Paragraph, and selecting from the line spacing options in the Paragraph dialog box. You can also adjust the spacing both before and after the paragraph itself in the spacing section of the Paragraph dialog box.

Hot Tip

The shortcut key combination for single spacing is **Ctrl + 1**. For 1½ spacing, the shortcut key combination is **Ctrl + 5**; and for double spacing it is **Ctrl + 2**.

2-1.3.15-1

Alignment refers to how text is positioned between the left and right margins. Text can be aligned in four different ways: left, center, right, or justified. The default setting is left alignment. Center alignment is often used for titles, headings, and invitations. Right alignment is often used for page numbers and dates. You can quickly apply any of these alignments using the buttons on the Formatting toolbar. See Figure 4-2.

FIGURE 4-2
Alignment options on the Formatting toolbar

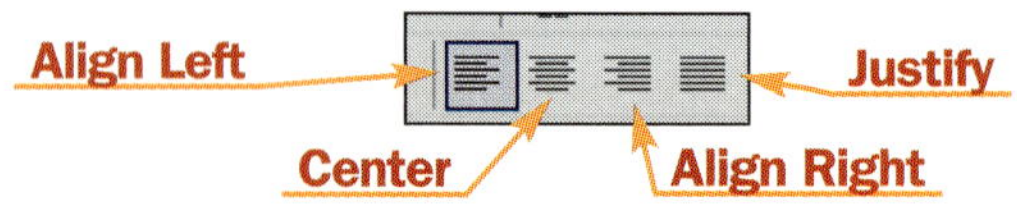

STEP-BY-STEP 4.2

2-2.1.1-2 1. Select the entire document, then click the down arrow on the **Line Spacing** button on the Formatting toolbar. Select **2.0**. The lines are now double-spaced.

2. With the entire document still selected, click the down arrow on the **Line Spacing** button and select **1.5**. The spacing between lines is reduced to 1 ½ line spacing.

3. With the entire document still selected, click **Format** on the menu bar and then click **Paragraph**.

2-2.1.1-3 4. Select the **Indents and Spacing** tab if necessary and then set both the Before and After spacing to **6pt**. Click **OK**.

5. Click **Undo** on the Standard toolbar.

2-1.3.15-1 6. Click in the first line of the document, then click the **Center** button on the Formatting toolbar.

7. Select all the remaining lines in the document, then click **Center**. All the lines are centered on the page.

8. Position the insertion point in the paragraph of the document that begins, *Join us in...* Click **Justify**.

9. Position the insertion point in the last line of text in the document and click the **Align Right** button to align the text at the right margin.

10. Save the changes and leave the document open for the next Step-by-Step.

Speech Recognition

If your computer has speech recognition capability, enable the Command mode. Position the insertion point (or select the designated paragraphs) and say the toolbar button name to align the current or selected paragraph.

Hot Tip

Click the **Align Left** button on the Formatting toolbar to align all the lines in a paragraph at the left.

Change Page Orientation and Margins

2-1.4.2-1 ***Portrait orientation*** formats the content of the document with the short edge of the page at the top. This is the default setting, and most printed documents are formatted this way. You can change to landscape orientation in the Page Setup dialog box. ***Landscape orientation*** formats the content of the document sideways with the long edge of the page at the top. Figure 4-3 illustrates the two options for page orientation. Your onscreen document will accurately reflect the page orientation you choose.

FIGURE 4-3
Portrait and landscape orientations

2-1.4.1-1 Margins are the blank space around the edges of the page. In general, text only appears in the printable area inside the margins. The default settings are 1 inch for top and bottom margins, and 1.25 inches for left and right margins.

> **Computer Concepts**
>
> You can also change margins by dragging the margin markers on the Ruler.

2-1.4.1-1

STEP-BY-STEP 4.3

1. Open the **File** menu and choose **Page Setup**. If necessary, click the **Margins** tab to display the Page Setup dialog box illustrated in Figure 4-4.
2. Notice that the top and bottom margins are 1" and the left and right margins are 1.25".
3. 2-1.4.2-1 Select the **Landscape** option under Orientation. When you select landscape orientation, Word automatically reverses the default margins settings. The top and bottom margins are now 1.25".

> **Speech Recognition**
>
> If your computer has speech recognition capability, in Command mode you can say the commands to open the Margins tab in the Page Setup dialog box. Then continue to dictate the commands to change the selected options in the dialog box.

4. Select the text in the *Top* box, then key or select **1**. It is not necessary to key the inch symbol. Then, change the value in the *Bottom* text box to **1** and click **OK**.
5. Save the changes and leave the document open for the next Step-by-Step.

FIGURE 4-4
Margins sheet in the Page Setup dialog box

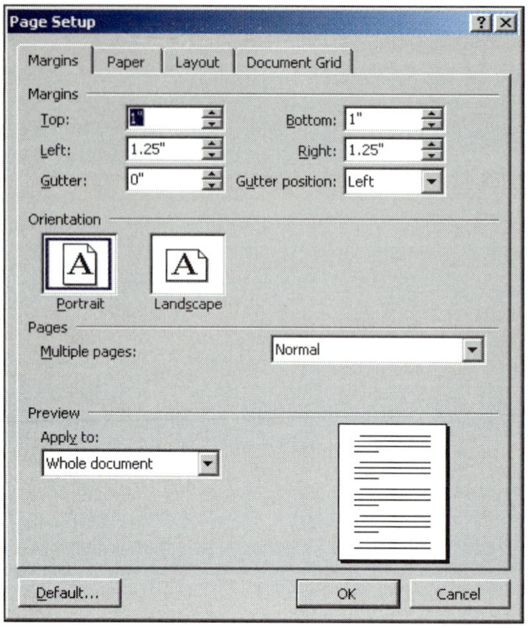

View a Document before Printing

To avoid wasteful printing, it is a good idea to preview your document and make adjustments before you print it.

Use Print Preview to Display a Document

Print Preview is an on-screen, reduced view of the layout of a completed page or pages. In Print Preview, you can see such things as page orientation, margins, and page breaks. If you find
2-1.4.3-1 errors or necessary changes, you can edit the document in print preview or you can change back to Normal view.

STEP-BY-STEP 4.4

2-1.4.3-1

1. Click the **Print Preview** button on the Standard toolbar. The Print Preview toolbar similar to the one shown in Figure 4-5 is displayed.

2. If necessary, click the **One Page** button on the Print Preview toolbar to display the entire page in Normal view.

3. Click the **Close** button on the Print Preview toolbar to return to the document window.

4. Leave the document open for the next Step-by-Step.

Speech Recognition

If your computer has speech recognition capability, enable the Command mode. Say the toolbar button name to display the document in Print Preview. Then say the commands to view one page and to close Print Preview.

FIGURE 4-5
Print Preview toolbar

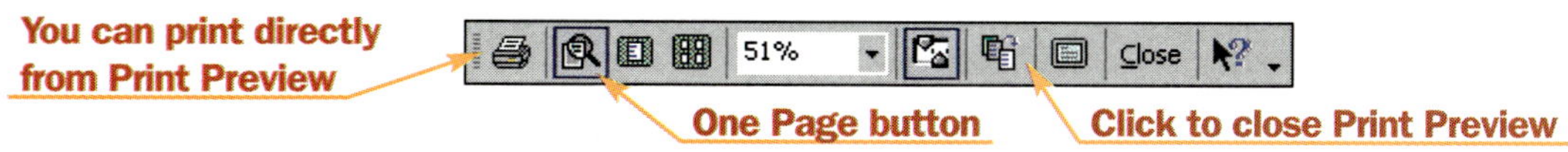

Use Help to Learn How to Edit a Document in Print Preview

In Lesson 3, you learned that the Office Assistant can help you with many Word features and problems you may have. Some people prefer not to have the Office Assistant displayed. If you choose not to use the Office Assistant, you can still access the Help screens using the Microsoft Word Help command. To get help without the Office Assistant, the Assistant must be turned off. With the Assistant turned off, you can access the Help screens using the Contents tab, the Answer Wizard, or the Index tab.

STEP-BY-STEP 4.5

1. If the Office Assistant is not displayed, open the **Help** menu and choose **Show the Office Assistant**. Then point to the Office Assistant and right-click. Then, choose **Options** in the shortcut menu. Uncheck the box for *Use the Office Assistant* and click **OK**.

2. Open the **Help** menu and choose **Microsoft Word Help**. If necessary, click the **Show** button on the toolbar to display the *Contents*, *Answer Wizard*, and *Index* tabs.

3. If necessary, click on the **Index** tab to display the dialog box shown in Figure 4-6.

FIGURE 4-6
Index sheet in Microsoft Word Help window

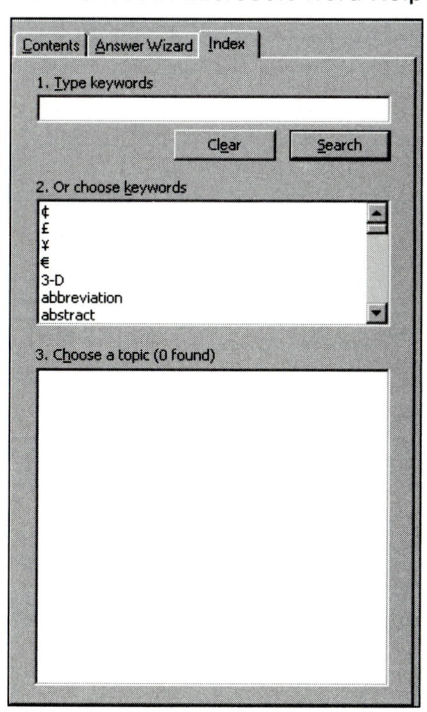

STEP-BY-STEP 4.5 Continued

4. Click in the text box below *1. Type keywords*, and key **print**. As you enter the text, the list in the section below (*2. Or choose keywords*) will scroll to display the keywords beginning with those characters.

5. Double-click **print preview** (in the *2. Or choose keywords* section) to open a list of applicable topics. Under *3. Choose a topic*, click the topic **Edit text in print preview**. Information related to that topic will display in a separate popup box at the right. Read this information.

6. Under *3. Choose a topic*, click on the topic **Change page margins**. Read the topic, then close the Help window.

7. To turn the Office Assistant back on, open the **Help** menu and choose **Show the Office Assistant**.

8. If you noticed when you viewed the document in Print Preview (in the previous Step-by-Step) that your document was more than one page long, change the point sizes so that the entire document fits on one page.

9. If you made any changes, save your work and leave the document open for the next Step-by-Step.

Use Zoom to View How a Document Will Print

2-1.2.5-3
2-1.2.5-1

An alternative to viewing a document in Print Preview is to zoom in or out of a document. You can "zoom in" to get a close-up view of your document or "zoom out" to see more of the page at a reduced size. This allows you to get an overall view of your document or to closely inspect one part of your document.

STEP-BY-STEP 4.6

2-1.2.5-2

1. Click the down arrow in the **Zoom** box on the Standard toolbar to display the zoom options.

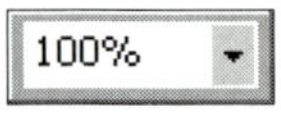

2. Select **50%**. Word provides a reduced view of the document.

3. Experiment with different view percentages, then return the zoom to **100%**.

4. Close the document.

Did You Know?

Instead of selecting the zoom percentage in the *Zoom* drop-down box, you can select the current zoom percentage and key the new percentage.

Did You Know?

If you're using the Microsoft IntelliMouse, you can use it to zoom in or out. Hold down **Ctrl** as you rotate the wheel forward or backward.

Common Printing Problems

IC³ 2-1.4.6-1 2-1.4.6-2

Even when using the Print Preview, there are times when what you think will print out and what you actually get on the printed page are different. This could be due to a variety of different things.

Sometimes the text that prints appears different from the text on the screen or the font you have chosen isn't showing up in the printed document. Microsoft Word might be using draft fonts to display text. To change this, click Options on the Tools menu, and then click the View tab. Under Outline and Normal options, clear the Draft font check box. Word also might be printing a draft of your text. To change this, click Options on the Tools menu, and then click the Print tab. Clear the Draft output check box.

Alternately, the font in your document might not be available on the printer you are using. Change the font in your document to a TrueType font, which looks the same on the printed page as it does on the screen. Or change the font to one that is available on your printer. Another possibility is that the font in your document might be one that is available on your printer but doesn't have a matching screen font. Microsoft Windows substitutes a TrueType font to display the text on the screen. Try changing the font in your document to a TrueType font. You can change the font that Microsoft Word substitutes for the unavailable font from the Compatibility tab in the Options dialog box (accessible from the Tools menu). Here you can set what font is substituted if the one used in the document is missing.

You should also keep in mind that animated text effects are not printed. If text in your document is animated, it will print with the underlying text formatting—such as bold or italic—but the animated effects will not be printed.

If the layout of your page looks wrong when you print it, you may be printing a document that was created with a different language version of Microsoft Word and formatted for a different paper size. To have Word format the document to your printer's paper size for this printing session only, click Print on the File menu. Under Zoom, select the paper size you want to use in the Scale to paper size box. Word will scale the page to fit the paper size you choose, similar to the reduce/enlarge feature on a photocopy machine.

If your document contains graphics but they are not printed with the document, you might be printing in draft mode. To print the borders and graphics in the document, click Options on the Tools menu, click the Print tab, and then clear the Draft output check box.

You may try to print a document and it appears that nothing happens. You should be aware that printing from your computer is primarily controlled by settings in Microsoft Windows. Therefore you need to determine whether your printer setup in Windows is correct by using the Windows Print Troubleshooter. To access the Troubleshooter, click Help on the Windows Start menu. Click the Index tab, and then key *print troubleshooter*. Click Display, and then follow the instructions in the Print Troubleshooter. If the Microsoft Windows printer setup looks correct, check the Word printer settings to make sure that the selected printer matches the printer you're using. Lastly, make sure that the page range you've selected in the Print dialog box corresponds to the pages you want to print.

If, when you try to print, you not only do not get a printed document, but Microsoft Word itself stops responding, it is likely that you do not have the correct or an updated printer driver. Try obtaining and installing an updated printer driver from the printer's manufacturer to resolve this problem.

Check Spelling and Grammar

2-1.3.10-1

Spell checking a document can significantly reduce the amount of time you spend proofreading and editing. Word can help you with both spell checking and proofreading. Word has a standard dictionary that you can use to check your spelling. You can check the spelling of one word, a selected group of words, or the entire document. To spell check the entire document, use the Spelling and Grammar dialog box.

Good proofreading skills also include checking grammar. When you check for the grammar in a document, you read for content and make sure each sentence makes sense. Word can also help you find grammatical errors such as incomplete sentences, the wrong use of words, and capitalization and punctuation errors.

As you enter text in a document, Word automatically checks the spelling of each word against its standard dictionary. If Word cannot find the word in its dictionary, it will underline the word with a wavy red line. This does not always mean the word is misspelled. It simply means the word is not listed in Word's dictionary. To view suggestions for alternative spellings of the word, you can right-click the underlined word to display a shortcut menu. You can select an alternative spelling from the shortcut menu, or you can choose to ignore the misspelling. In any case, once you have indicated your preference, the red wavy line disappears until you close and reopen the document.

Word also automatically checks for grammar errors as you enter text. When it finds a possible error, Word underlines the word, phrase, or sentence with a wavy green line. You can then access a shortcut menu to view suggestions for changes.

Computer Concepts

Although the spell checker is very helpful for identifying spelling errors, you still need to proofread. The spell checker simply verifies that the word is spelled correctly. It does not, however, confirm that you have used the correct word. For example, if you use the word *their* instead of *there*, the spell checker will not identify the error.

Computer Concepts

Although the grammar checker is a helpful tool, you still need to have a good working knowledge of English grammar. The grammar checker can identify a possible problem, but it's up to you to decide if the change should be made depending on the context of the sentence.

Computer Concepts

The red or green underlines are only visible when you display your document. They will not appear when you print the document.

2-1.3.10-1

STEP-BY-STEP 4.7

1. Open a new document. Open the **Tools** menu, choose **Options**, and click the **Spelling & Grammar** tab. Make sure the selected options match those shown in Figure 4-7 and then click **OK**.

2. Key the following text: **In the erly 1800s,**. Notice that as you press the spacebar after *erly*, Word underlines the word with a red wavy line.

STEP-BY-STEP 4.7 Continued

FIGURE 4-7
Spelling & Grammar Options dialog box

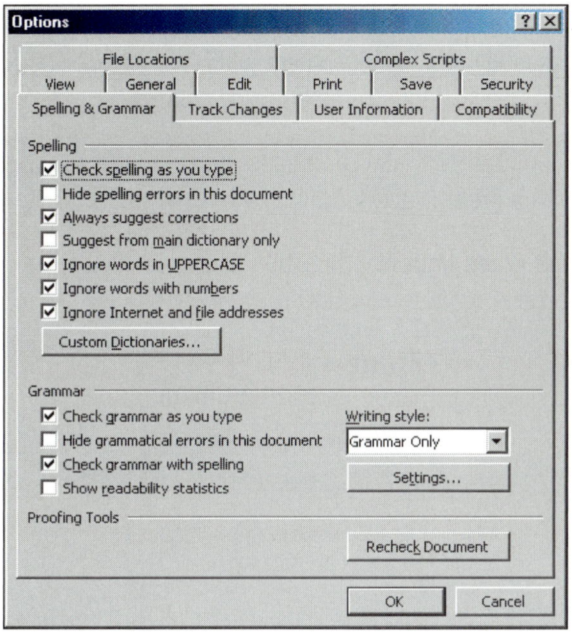

3. Point to the word *erly* and right-click. A shortcut menu is displayed as shown in Figure 4-8 and several word choices are displayed at the top of the menu.

FIGURE 4-8
Spelling shortcut menu

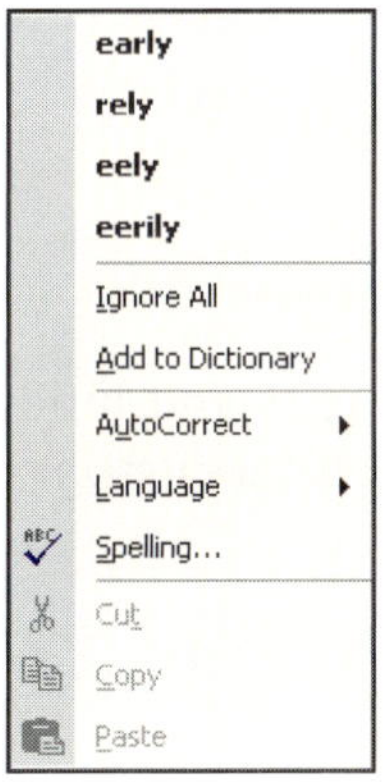

4. Select **early** in the shortcut menu. The correct spelling replaces the original spelling in the document.

5. Position the insertion point after the comma you keyed and press **Spacebar**. Then key **Potawatomi Indians**. Notice that as you press the spacebar after *Potawatomi*, Word underlines the word with a red wavy line.

STEP-BY-STEP 4.7 Continued

6. Right-click on the word *Potawatomi*. The proposed spelling *Pottawatomie* in the shortcut menu is an alternative way to spell the name of the Indian tribe. However, the spelling you entered is also correct. Click **Ignore All** in the shortcut menu. The red wavy line is removed, and the word *Potawatomi* will not be flagged as misspelled again in this document until you check the Recheck Document (or Check Document) button in the Spelling and Grammar dialog box.

7. Position the insertion point after the word *Indians*. Key a period and then press **Enter**. The entire sentence is underlined with a green wavy line.

8. Point to any part of the green underlined portion of the sentence and right-click. A shortcut menu is displayed, and the words *Fragment (consider revising)* appear at the top of the menu. See Figure 4-9.

FIGURE 4-9
Grammar shortcut menu

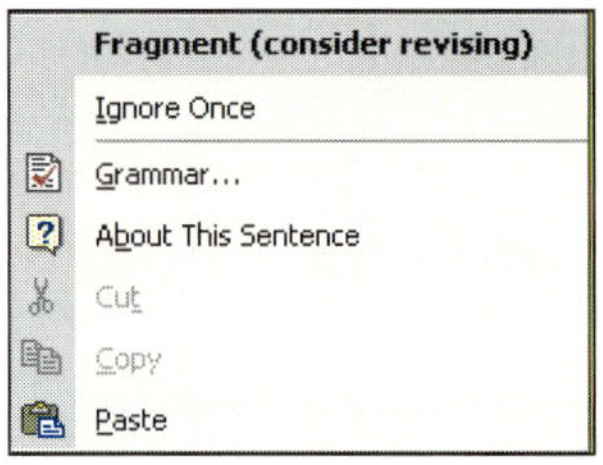

9. Click outside the shortcut menu to close it. Then edit the sentence to read *In the early 1800s,* ***the*** *Potawatomi Indians* ***made the path***.

10. Close the document without saving the changes.

> **Speech Recognition**
>
> If your computer has speech recognition capability, make sure you are in Command mode and say the appropriate command to position the insertion point at the end of the document.

Format Tabs

Tabs are useful for indenting paragraphs and lining up columns of text. Word's default tabs are set at every half inch. You can, however, set custom tabs at other locations. When you set new tabs, the default tab(s) to the left of the new tab stop are automatically removed. The default tab style is left-aligned. When you begin to enter text at the tab, the text lines up at the left and extends to the right. With a center-aligned tab, the text is aligned evenly on either side of the tab position. With a right-aligned tab, the text lines up at the right and extends to the left. A decimal tab can be used to align numbers or text. Numbers with decimals are all aligned at the decimal point; text aligns on either side of the tab.

2-2.1.5-1 To set custom tabs, position the insertion point in the paragraph where you want to set a tab stop. Then choose the alignment by clicking the tab alignment symbol at the left edge of the Ruler. Next, click the Ruler where you want to set the tab. A tab marker appears on the Ruler to show the tab setting. Figure 4-10 shows the Ruler with some tab markers and what each of the tab markers looks like for different alignment settings. Dragging any tab marker to a new position on the Ruler changes the location of the tab. To remove the tab setting, drag and drop the marker off the Ruler. If you want to set precise measurements for tabs, open the Format menu and choose Tabs.

FIGURE 4-10
Tab symbols on the Ruler

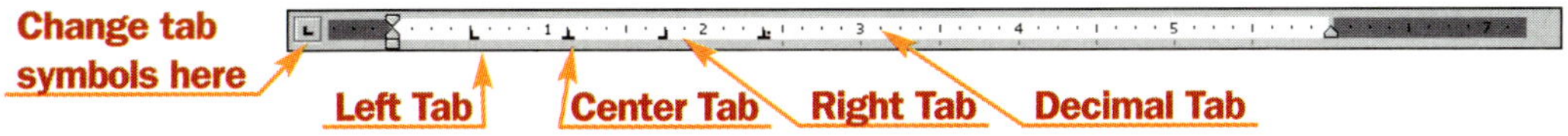

STEP-BY-STEP 4.8

1. Open **Step4-8** from the data files and save the document as **Parks** followed by your initials. If necessary, open the **View** menu and choose **Ruler** to display the Ruler.

2. Position the insertion point anywhere in the line that begins *Mount Rushmore....*

3. Click the tab symbols at the left end of the Ruler until the **Right Tab** symbol is displayed.

2-2.1.5-2 2-2.1.5-3

4. Click near the 5-inch mark on the Ruler (just to the left of the Right Margin marker). Then, drag the **Right Tab** marker on the Ruler and position it exactly at the right indent marker.

5. Position the insertion point in front of *April 11* and press the **Tab** key. The date is now aligned at the right margin.

6. Position the insertion point in the paragraph beginning *Yellowstone....* Notice that there are no tab markers displayed on the Ruler. The tab you set in the *Mount Rushmore* paragraph was applied to that paragraph only.

7. Format a right tab at the right margin, then insert a tab character in front of the date in the *Yellowstone...* paragraph to align the date at the right margin.

8. Format a right tab at the right margin for the paragraph beginning *Glacier....* Then insert a tab character in front of the date in that paragraph.

9. Save the changes and leave the document open for the next Step-by-Step.

Format Indents

2-2.1.2-1

An indent is a space insert between the margin and where the line of text appears. You can indent text from the left margin, from the right margin, or from both the left and right margins. For example, to draw attention to specific paragraphs in a document, you can indent all the lines of the paragraph from the left and right margins. If you are creating a long document and you want the first line of all the paragraphs to be indented, you can format a ***first line indent***. A first line indent can make a document easy to read, because a person can easily tell where a new paragraph begins. If you are creating a bibliography for a report, you can format a ***hanging indent***. A hanging indent is when the first line of text begins at the left margin, and all other lines of the paragraph "hang," or are indented, to the right of the first line. To quickly format an indent, position the insertion point in the paragraph to be formatted and then drag the indent markers on the Ruler. See Figure 4-11.

FIGURE 4-11
Indent markers on the Ruler

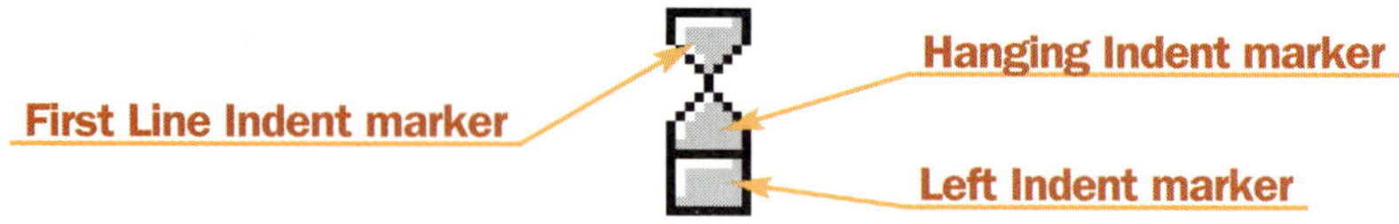

2-2.1.2-2

STEP-BY-STEP 4.9

1. Position the insertion point in the paragraph that begins *This national memorial....*
2. Drag the **Left Indent** marker to the ½" mark on the Ruler. (Notice that the First Line Indent and Hanging Indent markers move also.)
3. Drag the **Right Indent** marker to the 5" mark on the Ruler.
4. Click in the paragraph that begins *The park was established....* Notice that the Left Indent marker is positioned at the 0" mark on the Ruler. When you moved the Left Indent marker in Step 2, the indent format was applied only to that paragraph.
5. Drag the **Left Indent** marker to the ½" mark on the Ruler. Then, drag the **Right Indent** marker to the 5" mark on the Ruler.
6. Format similar left and right indents for the paragraph beginning *This national park....*
7. Position the insertion point in the paragraph that begins *Each documentary....* Drag the **First Line Indent** marker to the ½" mark on the Ruler. Notice that just the first line of the paragraph is indented from the left ½".
8. Position the insertion point in the last paragraph in the document. Point to the **Hanging Indent** marker and drag the marker to the ½" mark on the Ruler. All lines but the first line are indented from the left ½".
9. Save the changes and close the document.

Computer Concepts

If you drag the bottom half of the **Hanging Indent** marker, the **First Line Indent** marker will also move. If you point to the middle of these markers, a two-headed arrow will display and you can drag to change the left margin.

Format Bullets and Numbering

2-2.1.3-1

Bullets and numbers are easy to add using the Bullets and Numbering buttons on the Formatting toolbar. In general, you should use a numbered list for steps that must be completed in a specific order. This is sometimes referred to as an ordered list. Bullets are used to list items whose order does not matter – an unordered list.

Computer Concepts

If you apply the bullet or number format before you enter text, each new paragraph will be formatted with the bullet or number. To end the format, press **Enter** a second time and backspace over the unwanted bullet or number, or click the button on the toolbar to toggle the option off.

Bulleted and numbered lists are automatically formatted with a hanging indent. Word automatically calculates the best distance for the hanging indent. You can change the bullet symbol, the number style, or the distance for the hanging indent in the Bullets and Numbering dialog box.

STEP-BY-STEP 4.10

1. Open **Step4-10** from the data files and save the document as **Expo** followed by your initials.

2. Select all the lines (paragraphs) in the list below the first heading that begins *Displays and Demonstrations....*

2-2.1.3-2 3. Click the **Bullets** button on the Formatting toolbar. Each paragraph in the selection is formatted with a bullet symbol. The symbol will vary depending on the symbol last used for bullets.

4. Select the list below the second heading that begins *A Look at....* Open the **Format** menu and choose **Bullets and Numbering**. If necessary, click the **Bulleted** tab to display the bullet options.

5. Select one of the bullet symbols, then click **OK**.

2-2.1.3-3 6. Select the list below the third heading *Seminars and Films*. Click the **Numbering** button on the Formatting toolbar.

7. Save the changes and leave the document open for the next Step-by-Step.

Format Page Numbers and Headers and Footers

Word begins new pages when needed by inserting ***soft page breaks***. A soft page break is automatically inserted for you when you fill a page with text or graphics. You can also break pages manually by inserting ***hard page breaks***. A hard page break forces a page break at a specific location, regardless of how full the page of text is. The location of a soft page break will change if you add or delete text so that each page remains completely filled with text. A hard page break will remain where you insert it until it is deleted.

In addition to hard page breaks, you can also insert section breaks in your documents. Whereas a page break just forces the start of a new page, a section break allows you to vary the
2-2.1.6-1 layout of a document within a page or between pages. For example, you may want part of your document to appear as a single column and then have a portion of it appear in two columns. Or you may want different portions of your document to have different headers or footers.

When your document has multiple pages, you may want to insert page numbers. The Page Numbers command on the Insert menu is a quick way to add page numbers that do not need accom-
2-2.1.7-1 panying text. (What this actually does is create a ***header*** or ***footer*** with a page number as the only text.)

Headers and footers are information and/or graphics that print in the top and bottom margins of each page. Your document can have a header, a footer, or both. Headers and footers can
2-2.1.8-1 be a single paragraph or multiple paragraphs. Creating a header or footer is another way to add page numbers to a document. The advantages of formatting a header or footer rather than just using the Insert Page Numbers command is that you can include text with the page number. (Note that you can always edit the header or footer—and hence the page number—if you change your mind about how you want them to appear.)

STEP-BY-STEP 4.11

1. Select the entire document and change to double-spacing.

2-2.1.6-3 2. Position the insertion point in front of the second heading that begins *A Look at....* Open the **Insert** menu and choose **Break**. Select **Next page**.

3. Use the Page Setup dialog box (from the File menu) to set all the margins for this section to 1.5". Click **OK**. (Make sure the **Apply to this section** option in selected.)

4. Note that margin changes did not affect the first page of the document. Click **Undo** two times to reverse the margin change and section break.

2-2.1.6-2 5. With the insertion point still positioned in front of the second heading, open the **Insert** menu and choose **Break**. **Page break** should already be selected. Click **OK**.

Hot Tip

The shortcut for inserting a hard page break is **Ctrl + Enter**.

2-2.1.7-2 6. Open the **Insert** menu and choose **Page Numbers**. The dialog box shown in Figure 4-12 is displayed.

FIGURE 4-12
Page Numbers dialog box

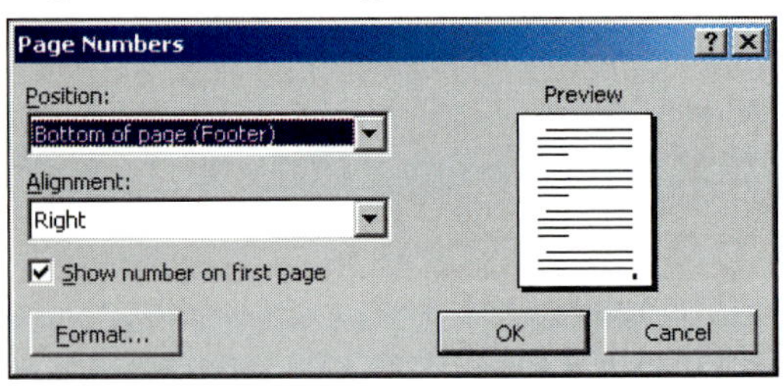

2-2.1.7-3 7. In the *Position* box, verify that **Bottom of page (Footer)** is selected. In the *Alignment* box, select **Center**. Click **OK**. If your document is displayed in Print Layout View, you can scroll to the bottom of the first or second page to see the page number. These are dimmed because they are part of the footer and you must open the header or footer pane to edit them.

2-2.1.8-2 8. Open the **View** menu and choose **Header and Footer**. The Header and Footer toolbar and a blank header pane appear. The document pane is dimmed as shown in Figure 4-13. This indicates that you can now edit the header (and footer) but not the document.

FIGURE 4-13
Header and Footer toolbar and header pane

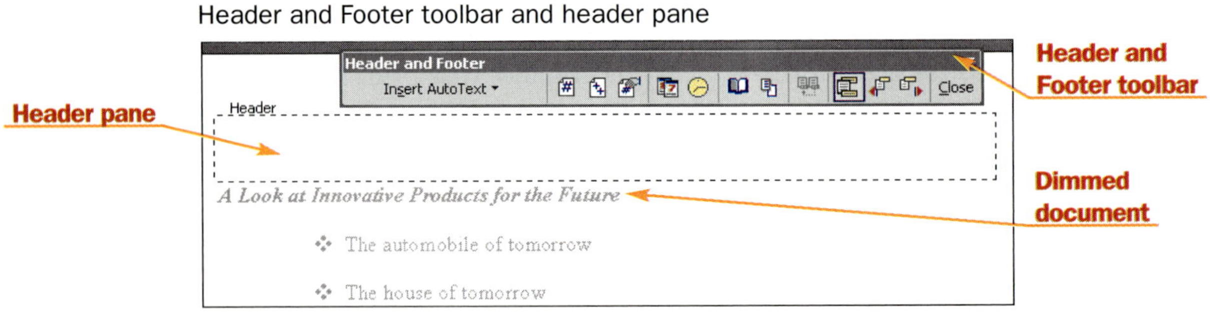

STEP-BY-STEP 4.11 Continued

2-2.1.8-3

9. Key **Environmental Expo** and then press **Tab** twice. (Notice that, by default, the headers and footers have a left-align tab, a center tab, and a right-align tab.) The insertion point is now positioned at the right margin in the header pane.

10. Click the **Insert Date** button on the Header and Footer toolbar. The current date is inserted in the header pane. This will automatically be updated each time the document is opened.

11. Click the **Switch Between Header and Footer** button. The footer pane is displayed and you can see the page number that you inserted in the last Step-by-Step.

12. Click **Close** in the Header and Footer toolbar to close it and to return to working in the document.

13. View the document in Print Preview or change the zoom to view the document in a reduced image.

14. Save the changes and close the document.

SUMMARY

In this lesson, you learned:

- Fonts are available in a variety of styles and point sizes.
- You can adjust the line spacing in a paragraph to create more or less white space between the lines of text. Formatting the paragraph alignment for left, center, right, or justified positions the text appropriately between the left and right margins.
- The page orientation determines how the document will print on the page. Adjusting the margins affects the white space around the edges of the page.
- Print Preview shows a reduced view of the layout of a document. You can also reduce the view of a document by changing the zoom. Print Preview can help eliminate wasteful printing.
- Word checks spelling and grammar as you key text. Misspelled words are marked with red wavy lines and possible grammar errors are marked with green wavy lines. Spelling and grammar errors can be corrected as you enter text by using a shortcut menu. To check all spelling and grammar at once, use the Spelling and Grammar dialog box.
- Custom tabs can be set by clicking on the Ruler.
- Options for indenting text include left indents, right indents, first line indents, and hanging indents.
- The Bullets and Numbering feature automatically adds and formats bullets and numbers in lists.
- The Insert Page Number command automatically numbers all the pages in a document. You can include text with the page number by formatting a header or footer.

VOCABULARY *Review*

Define the following terms:

First line indent	Hard page break	Points
Font	Header	Portrait orientation
Footer	Landscape orientation	Soft page break
Hanging indent		

REVIEW *Questions*

TRUE/FALSE

Circle T if the statement is true or F if the statement is false.

T F 1. It is best to use only one font in a document.

T F 2. Landscape orientation prints sideways with the long edge of the page at the top.

T F 3. You can edit a document while in print preview.

T F 4. When you set a tab, you position the tab marker on the Formatting toolbar.

T F 5. Bulleted and numbered lists are automatically formatted using a first line indent.

MATCHING

Match the correct term in Column 1 to its description in Column 2.

Column 1	Column 2
___ 1. font	A. Space you insert between the margin and the line of text
___ 2. indent	B. How text is positioned between the left and right margins
___ 3. margin	C. Break you insert manually to end a page
___ 4. alignment	D. Break Word automatically inserts when a page is full
___ 5. hard page break	E. Design of a typeface
	F. Blank space around the edges of a page

PROJECTS

PROJECT 4-1

Your good work at the community center has convinced the director to give you another assignment. Help her create the title and contents pages for the Recreation Commission's fall program guide.

1. Open **Project4-1** from the data files. Save the document as **Contents** followed by your initials.
2. Change the page orientation to landscape. Change the top and bottom margins to 1 inch, and change the left and right margins to 2 inches.
3. Center the first eight lines of text, beginning with *Oak Creek Recreation Commission* and ending with *Mt. Washington Recreation Center*.
4. Format the centered text as follows:
   A. Change the font style of the first line (*Oak Creek Recreation Center*) to bold and the font size to 28 point.
   B. Change the size of the next two lines (*Community Center* and *Program Guide*) to 20 point.
   C. Change the size of the next line (*Fall*) to 20 point and apply bold style.
   D. Change the size of the last four centered lines to 20 point.
5. Position the insertion point in front of the word *Contents* and insert a page break. On the new page, format the word *Contents* as 20 point bold.
6. Select all the text below the *Contents* heading and then set a right tab at the 6.5-inch mark on the ruler. Format the program listings as follows:
   A. Apply bold and italic formatting to the first three lines below the *Contents* heading (*Registration*, *Memberships*, and *Hours*) and the last two lines (*Special Events* and *Community Meetings*). Change the size of these lines to 12 point and the font to Arial.
   B. Apply bold and underline formatting to the headings (including the page number) for each age group (*ELEMENTARY PROGRAMS*, *TEEN PROGRAMS*, and *ADULT PROGRAMS*). Change the size of these headings to 11 point and the font to Arial.
   C. Apply a 0.25-inch left indent to the lists of programs under each age group heading and change their point size to 12.
7. View the document in Print Preview. You decide that the first page could be "spread out" a little to fill up more of the page. Close Print Preview and display the first page. Add blank lines as desired to improve the look of the first page. Check your adjustments using Print Preview.
8. Save your changes and close the document.

PROJECT 4-2

IC3 -2.1.12-2

1. Open **Project4-2** from the data files. Save the document as **Hummingbirds** followed by your initials.
2. Format the document as described in Figure 4-14. Use the Format Painter wherever possible to repeat formatting that is the same.

FIGURE 4-14
Document with formatting notes

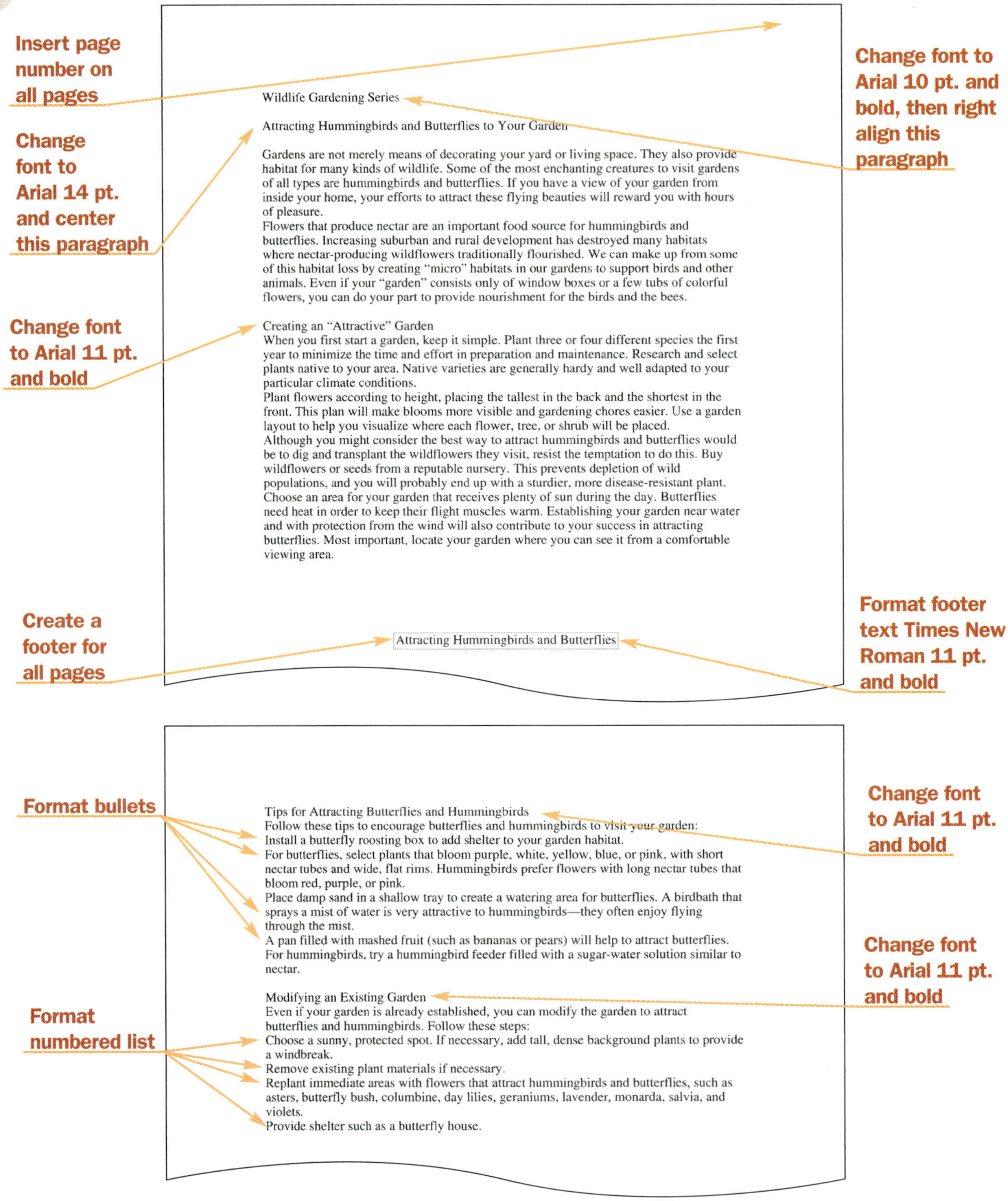
Wildlife Gardening Series

Attracting Hummingbirds and Butterflies to Your Garden

Gardens are not merely means of decorating your yard or living space. They also provide habitat for many kinds of wildlife. Some of the most enchanting creatures to visit gardens of all types are hummingbirds and butterflies. If you have a view of your garden from inside your home, your efforts to attract these flying beauties will reward you with hours of pleasure.
Flowers that produce nectar are an important food source for hummingbirds and butterflies. Increasing suburban and rural development has destroyed many habitats where nectar-producing wildflowers traditionally flourished. We can make up from some of this habitat loss by creating "micro" habitats in our gardens to support birds and other animals. Even if your "garden" consists only of window boxes or a few tubs of colorful flowers, you can do your part to provide nourishment for the birds and the bees.

Creating an "Attractive" Garden
When you first start a garden, keep it simple. Plant three or four different species the first year to minimize the time and effort in preparation and maintenance. Research and select plants native to your area. Native varieties are generally hardy and well adapted to your particular climate conditions.
Plant flowers according to height, placing the tallest in the back and the shortest in the front. This plan will make blooms more visible and gardening chores easier. Use a garden layout to help you visualize where each flower, tree, or shrub will be placed.
Although you might consider the best way to attract hummingbirds and butterflies would be to dig and transplant the wildflowers they visit, resist the temptation to do this. Buy wildflowers or seeds from a reputable nursery. This prevents depletion of wild populations, and you will probably end up with a sturdier, more disease-resistant plant.
Choose an area for your garden that receives plenty of sun during the day. Butterflies need heat in order to keep their flight muscles warm. Establishing your garden near water and with protection from the wind will also contribute to your success in attracting butterflies. Most important, locate your garden where you can see it from a comfortable viewing area.

Attracting Hummingbirds and Butterflies

Tips for Attracting Butterflies and Hummingbirds
Follow these tips to encourage butterflies and hummingbirds to visit your garden:
Install a butterfly roosting box to add shelter to your garden habitat.
For butterflies, select plants that bloom purple, white, yellow, blue, or pink, with short nectar tubes and wide, flat rims. Hummingbirds prefer flowers with long nectar tubes that bloom red, purple, or pink.
Place damp sand in a shallow tray to create a watering area for butterflies. A birdbath that sprays a mist of water is very attractive to hummingbirds—they often enjoy flying through the mist.
A pan filled with mashed fruit (such as bananas or pears) will help to attract butterflies. For hummingbirds, try a hummingbird feeder filled with a sugar-water solution similar to nectar.

Modifying an Existing Garden
Even if your garden is already established, you can modify the garden to attract butterflies and hummingbirds. Follow these steps:
Choose a sunny, protected spot. If necessary, add tall, dense background plants to provide a windbreak.
Remove existing plant materials if necessary.
Replant immediate areas with flowers that attract hummingbirds and butterflies, such as asters, butterfly bush, columbine, day lilies, geraniums, lavender, monarda, salvia, and violets.
Provide shelter such as a butterfly house.

3. For every paragraph except the bulleted paragraphs and the numbered list, change the line spacing to 1 ½ lines.

4. For every paragraph except the headings, the bulleted paragraphs, and the numbered list, create a first line indent of 0.5 inches.
5. Use the Zoom feature to view your document at the Two Pages setting.
6. Save your changes and close the document.

WEB PROJECT

If you have ever seen a hummingbird up close, you are aware of how rapidly they beat their wings to stay in flight. Use a Web search tool to locate sites relating to hummingbirds on the Web. Find out some basic facts about hummingbirds, such as how fast they flap their wings and how often and how much they eat. Use Word to write a brief report on what you have learned. Be sure to cite your Web sources!

TEAMWORK PROJECT

The fonts you use to format a document can be divided into two types: serif and sans serif. Serif faces are often used for the main body of a document, while sans serif faces are used for headings and other display items. Learn more about the differences between these two types of typefaces with a partner.

1. With your partner, decide who will research serif typefaces and who will research sans serif typefaces.
2. Use the Web, an online encyclopedia, or other reference to read about typography, the art of designing typefaces. Concentrate on your chosen type, either serif or sans serif.
3. You and your partner should be able to answer these questions after your research:
   A. What is a serif?
   B. What is the main difference between a serif typeface and a sans serif typeface?
4. Select a paragraph of text and a heading from any source and key the material using the type of typeface you have been studying (you key in serif, for example, and your partner keys in sans serif). Copy the text several times and apply different fonts of either serif or sans serif to each copy.
5. With your partner, decide which of the fonts is most readable and appropriate for each type of text.

CRITICAL *Thinking*

ACTIVITY 4-1

If you completed Project 4-1, you had to add blank lines to center the text vertically on the first page of the document. There is another way to center text vertically. Use Word's Help feature to find out how to do this. Using Word, write a brief explanation of the steps you need to take. What would happen to the second page of the Contents document if you follow these steps? Describe at least two other documents in which you could use this feature.

LESSON 5

Working with Tables

OBJECTIVES

Upon completion of this lesson, you should be able to:

- Create a table.
- Insert and delete rows and columns.
- Adjust column width and center a table.
- Edit table text.
- Use the Draw Table and Eraser tools to create a table grid.
- Format text alignment and direction within a table cell.
- Format borders and shading.
- Convert text to a table and AutoFormat the table.

Estimated Time: 1.5 hours

VOCABULARY

Cell
Gridlines
Merging cells
Splitting cells

Suppose you need to arrange several lines of information in two or three columns. How could you create the columns? If your answer is "Set tab stops," you're correct. However, there's also an easier and faster way. The table features in Word make the task of arranging text and numbers in columns both quick and easy.

Create a Table

A table consists of cells (boxes) to which you add text or graphics. A ***cell*** represents one intersection of a row and a column in a table. In a table, rows go across and columns go down.

By default, Word formats a border around all the cells in a table. If you don't want this border to print, you can remove the border. However, the boundary lines for each of the cells still remain. These boundary lines in a table are called ***gridlines***. Gridlines are used for layout purposes; they do not print.

Insert a Table

To create a table, you must first decide how many columns and rows you want in the table. Then you create a table grid and enter the data.

> **Computer Concepts**
>
> The Insert Table button appears on the Standard toolbar and on the Tables and Borders toolbar. However, the button on the Tables and Borders toolbar will not display a grid. Instead, it will open the Insert Table dialog box. Or, if you click the down arrow next to the button, it will display the options available in the Insert Table command.

STEP-BY-STEP 5.1

1. Launch Word and open a blank document. Click the **Insert Table** button on the Standard toolbar. A grid of table cells appears.
2. Click in the first cell in the grid and drag down the grid until seven rows of cells are displayed; then drag across until the bottom of the grid reads *7 × 3 Table*. See Figure 5-1. The table appears in the document.
3. Leave the document open for the next Step-by-Step.

FIGURE 5-1
Table grid

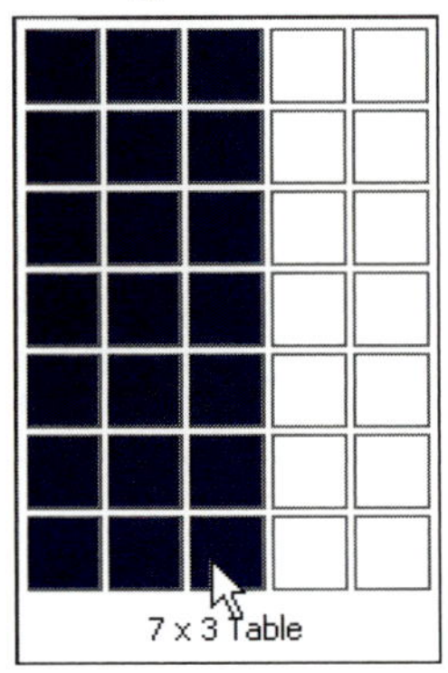

Enter Text in the Table

To move the insertion point from one cell to another, you can press the arrow keys or Tab. If the text that you enter is wider than the column, Word automatically wraps the text to a new line within the cell. When you reach the end of a row and press Tab, the insertion point moves to the first cell in the next row.

> **Did You Know?**
>
> IC³ 2-2.2.1-1
>
> You can also manually enter the table size (number of columns and rows) through the Insert Table dialog box. To open the dialog box, click the **Insert Table** button on the Tables and Borders toolbar or open the **Table** menu, choose **Insert**, and then select **Table** in the submenu.

STEP-BY-STEP 5.2

1. The insertion point should be positioned in the first cell. Key **Activity**.

2. Press **Tab** to move the insertion point to the next cell to the right in the same row. Key **20 Minutes**. Press **Tab** and then key **40 Minutes**.

> **Hot Tip**
>
> To move the insertion point to the cell that is to the left of the current cell, press **Shift + Tab**.

3. Press **Tab** to move the insertion point to the first cell in the next row.

4. Press the down arrow to move the insertion point down to the third row.

5. Key the rest of the table as illustrated in Figure 5-2. Use **Tab** or the arrow keys to move from one cell to another.

6. Save the document as **Calories** followed by your initials. Leave the document open for the next Step-by-Step.

FIGURE 5-2
Completed table for Step-by-Step 5.2

Activity	20 Minutes	40 Minutes
Cross-country skiing	192	384
Downhill skiing	144	288
Golf: carrying clubs	132	264
Mountain biking	204	408
Running: 9 min/mile	264	528

Use Help to Learn about Table Gridlines and Borders

As you worked with the table you created, you probably thought you were looking at the gridlines for your table. But the lines you saw on the screen are actually borders. You can go to the Help screen to find out more about borders.

You can use the Answer Wizard in Help to ask a question or key search words. A list of topics related to your question is displayed, and when you click on one of the proposed topics, details about the topic are provided in the same dialog box at the right.

> **Did You Know?**
>
> If you have access to the Internet, you can click the **Search on Web** button and access technical resources from the Microsoft Office as well as other Microsoft Web sites. If a topic begins with "Web:," the Office Web article is available when you are connected to the Internet.

STEP-BY-STEP 5.3

1. If necessary, display the Office Assistant by opening the **Help** menu and choosing **Show the Office Assistant**.

2. Click the **Office Assistant**, key **table gridlines**, and press **Enter**. In the list of topics, click on **Display or hide gridlines in a table**. Read the information about the gridlines.

STEP-BY-STEP 5.3 Continued

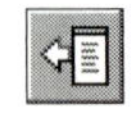

3. You decide you want to remove the default border, but you don't know how. If necessary, click the **Show** button on the Help toolbar to display the Contents, Answer Wizard, and Index tabs. (If you do see the Contents, Answer Wizard, and Index tabs, the Hide button will be displayed in the toolbar.)

4. If necessary, click the **Answer Wizard** tab to display the dialog box shown in Figure 5-3.

FIGURE 5-3
Answer Wizard sheet of the Help dialog box

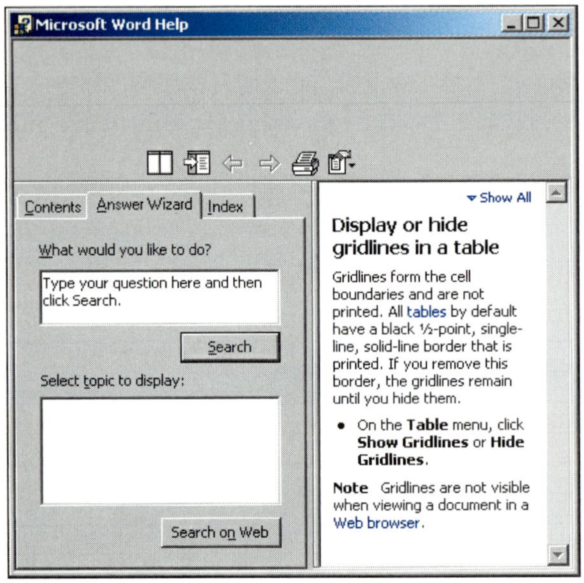

5. Click in the **What would you like to do?** text box, key **remove a border**, then click **Search**. Notice the list of topics that display in the Answer Wizard folder under Select topic to display.

6. At the right, click on the link **Remove a border from a picture, a table, or text**.

7. Study the directions in Steps 1–3. Click the hyperlinks for **table** and **cells**. The first time you click on the hyperlink, a definition will display. When you click on the hyperlink again, the definition will be hidden.

8. Change the text in the What would you like to do? box to **select cells** and click **Search**. Then click the link **Select items in a table with the mouse**. Study the examples. Be sure to read the section *Multiple cells, rows, or columns.*

9. Leave the Help screen open. Click the **Calories** document button in the taskbar.

STEP-BY-STEP 5.3 Continued

2-2.2.2-1

10. Experiment with selecting cells, rows, and columns. If you need to refresh your memory, refer back to the Microsoft Help screen to reread the directions.

11. Switch back to Help, then close the Help screen. Leave the document open for the next Step-by-Step.

> **Hot Tip**
>
> You can click on the **Help** button in the task bar to display the Help window on top of the Calories document. You can click the **Hide** button in the Help window to reduce its size, and you can also resize the window so it doesn't take up as much space on the screen. Drag the title bar of the Help window to move it out of the way.

Remove Table Borders

Now that you have read about how to remove borders from a table, give it a try. In the following Step-by-Step, you will practice one of the Tips provided in the Help screen. However, you can explore the other methods of removing table borders on your own.

STEP-BY-STEP 5.4

1. Position the insertion point anywhere inside the table.

2. Open the **Format** menu and choose **Borders and Shading**. If necessary, select the **Borders** tab to display the dialog box shown in Figure 5-4.

FIGURE 5-4
Borders and Shading dialog box

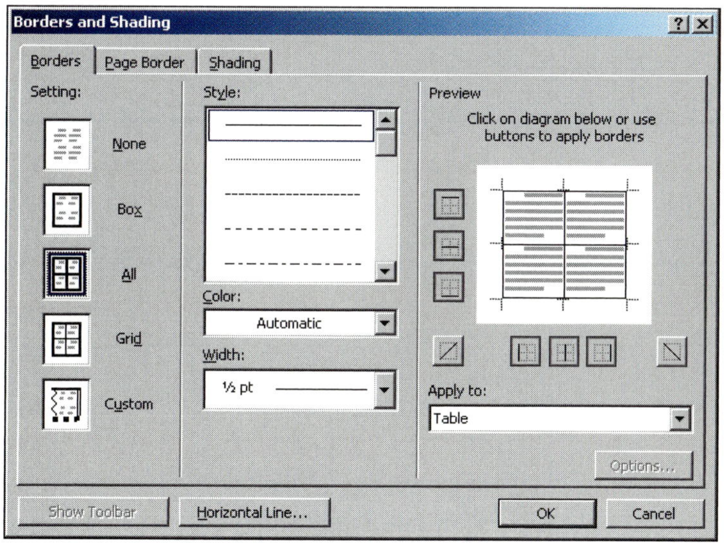

STEP-BY-STEP 5.4 Continued

3. Under Setting, select **None** and then click **OK**.

4. Your document should now display lines that indicate the cell boundaries. If you don't see any lines in your document, open the **Table** menu and choose **Show Gridlines**. The gridlines are similar to the borders you removed, but they are much lighter in color. (If you do see gridlines, the menu item on the Table menu would read **Hide Gridlines**.) Leave the document open for the next Step-by-Step.

Speech Recognition

If your computer has speech recognition capability, enable the Command mode and say the commands to open the Borders and Shading dialog box and select the options.

Insert and Delete Rows and Columns

After you create a table, you may decide to change it. For example, you may need to add more rows or delete a column. Word has many features that make these changes easy.

Change the Number of Rows and Columns

2-2.2.3-1 If you want to insert a new row at the end of the table, you can position the insertion point in the last table cell and press Tab. To insert a new row anywhere else in the table, use the Insert command in the Table menu.

2-2.2.4-1 If you select the content in a cell or group of cells and press Delete, the text is deleted but the cells are still there. To remove rows or columns, you must choose the Delete command in the Table menu. When you delete a row or column, the text is also deleted.

STEP-BY-STEP 5.5

1. Position the insertion point in the last cell in the table (the cell contains the text *528*). Press **Tab** to create a new row.

2. Key the following information in the new row:
   Walking: 15 min/mile 108 216

3. Press **Tab** and key the following information in the new row:
   Weight lifting 72 140

2-2.2.3-1

4. Move the insertion point to the cell containing the text *Golf: carrying clubs*. Open the **Table** menu and choose **Insert**, then select **Rows Below** in the submenu.

5. Key the following information in the new row:
   Golf: using a cart 84 168

2-2.2.4-1

6. Position the insertion point in the blank row (the second row). Open the **Table** menu and choose **Delete**, then select **Rows** in the submenu.

STEP-BY-STEP 5.5 Continued

7. Position the insertion point in any cell in the *40 Minutes* column. Open the **Table** menu and choose **Delete**, then select **Columns** in the submenu.

8. Click **Undo** to restore the column you deleted.

9. Move the insertion point to the second cell in the third column (the cell contains the text *384*). Open the **Table** menu and choose **Insert**, then select **Columns to the Left** in the submenu.

10. Click in the first cell of the new column and key **30 Minutes**. Press the down arrow to move down one cell below the current cell and key **288**. Key the following numbers to complete the column:
    216
    198
    126
    306
    396
    162
    108

11. Save the changes and leave the document open for the next Step-by-Step.

Hot Tip

To insert or delete multiple rows and columns at one time, first select the desired number of rows or columns. For example, if you want to insert or delete three rows, select three rows in the table. Then choose the **Table Insert** or **Table Delete** command.

Speech Recognition

If your computer has speech recognition capability, enable the Dictation mode and dictate the cell contents. (*Hint:* Say "Tab" to move to the next cell.)

Did You Know?

You can use the number pad on your keyboard to enter numbers. Make sure that NUMLOCK is turned on.

Merge and Split Table Cells

IC3 2-2.2.6-1

When you remove the boundary between two cells, it is called ***merging cells***. You can merge cells horizontally or vertically. You can merge cells when you want to create a heading to span across two or more columns. To merge cells, the cells must be selected.

IC3 2-2.2.5-1

When you convert a cell into multiple cells, it is called ***splitting cells***. You can split a cell into two or more rows and/or two or more columns. To split a cell, the insertion point must be positioned in the cell.

IC3 2-2.2.8-1

You can also split a table into two separate tables by selecting Split Table from the Table menu. A new table will begin with the row in which you have placed your insertion point. You will practice this in Step-by-Step 5.7

STEP-BY-STEP 5.6

IC3 2-2.2.5-1 2-2.2.6-1

1. Position the insertion point in the first cell in the table (*Activity*).

2. Open the **Table** menu and choose **Insert**, then select **Rows Above**. A new row is added and the four cells in the new row are selected.

STEP-BY-STEP 5.6 Continued

3. With the new row still selected, open the **Table** menu and choose **Merge Cells**. (*Hint:* You may need to expand the menu to see the Merge Cells command.)

4. Click anywhere in the window to deselect the row. The four cells have been converted into a single long cell.

5. Position the insertion point in the new blank row, then open the **Table** menu and choose **Split Cells**. (*Hint:* You may need to expand the menu to see the Split Cells command.) The dialog box shown in Figure 5-5 is displayed.

FIGURE 5-5
Split Cells dialog box

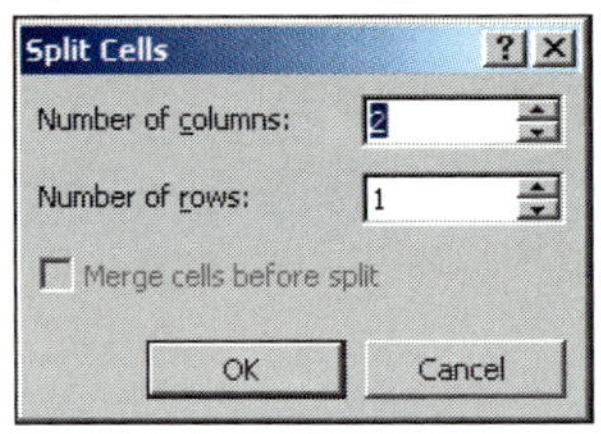

6. Change the number in the Number of columns box to **1**. Change the number in the Number of rows box to **2**. Click **OK**. Click anywhere in the window to deselect the row. You will see that the row is split into two rows.

7. Position the insertion point in the top blank row and key the following title for the table: **NUMBER OF CALORIES BURNED**. Press **Enter**, and then key **Body weight: 150 lbs.** The height of the cell is automatically adjusted to accommodate the two lines of text.

8. Save the changes and leave the document open for the next Step-by-Step.

Adjust Column Width and Height and Center the Table

2-2.2.7-1
2-2.2.7-2
2-2.2.7-3
2-2.2.7-4

When you create a table grid, Word makes all the columns the same width. Sometimes, you'll want to adjust the column widths or the row heights in a table to make the text easier to read or to fit a certain style or content. If you want to specify an exact column width or row height, you should use the Table Properties command on the Table menu. However, it's usually easiest to drag a border to a new position. You can also adjust the width of each column automatically using the AutoFit feature. Word offers five AutoFit options. In this lesson, you will learn and practice AutoFit to Contents. With AutoFit to Contents, Word automatically adjusts all column widths and heights as needed to accommodate the contents within the cells.

> **Computer Concepts**
>
> If a table cell is formatted for AutoFit, Word will automatically adjust the cell width each time the cell contents change.

To align a table on the page horizontally, you must first select the entire table. Then you format the alignment in the same way you align text paragraphs.

IC³

STEP-BY-STEP 5.7

2-2.2.7-1

1. Position the insertion point on the second column. Open the **Table** menu and choose **Table Properties**. Select the **Column** tab, click in the **Preferred width** text box, and set the width to **1** inch. Click **OK**.

2-2.2.7-3

2. Position the insertion point in the third row. Open the **Table** menu and choose **Table Properties**. Select the **Row** tab, click in the **Specify height** text box, and set the height to **0.25.** inches. Click **OK**.

2-2.2.7-2
2-2.2.7-4

3. Position the insertion point anywhere within the table. Open the **Table** menu and choose **AutoFit**. In the submenu, choose **AutoFit to Contents**. The text in the first column no longer wraps within the cell, and the extra white space in the other three columns is eliminated.
4. With the insertion point still positioned in the table, open the **Table** menu and choose **Select**. Then select **Table** in the submenu. All the cells in the table are selected.
5. Click the **Center** button on the Formatting toolbar. The table is now positioned in the middle between the left and right margins.

2-2.2.8-1

6. Click anywhere in the third row. Open the **Table** menu and select **Split Table**. The heading rows are now a separate table that is centered between the left and right margins.
7. Click **Undo** to return the two tables to one table.
8. Save the changes and leave the document open for the next Step-by-Step.

Hot Tip

If you want rows or columns to be spaced evenly throughout the table, select the particular rows or columns and then click the **Distribute Rows Evenly** or **Distribute Columns Evenly** button on the Tables and Borders toolbar.

Edit Text in a Table

Editing table text is similar to editing other document text. You can insert, delete, copy, or move text within the table cells. You can apply several formats to change the font and alignment of the text within a cell.

Computer Concepts

If you have the **Show/Hide ¶** button on the Standard toolbar toggled on, small squares will display in the left corner of each table cell. These squares are called end-of-cell markers. They will move to the right as you enter text in the cell. End-of-cell markers do not print.

STEP-BY-STEP 5.8

1. Click in the last cell in the table (*140*). Change the number to **144**.
2. Click in the first cell to the right of *Cross-country skiing* (*192*).
3. Click the **Align Right** button on the Formatting toolbar. The number shifts to the right edge of the cell.
4. With the insertion point still in the *192* cell, hold down **Shift** and then click in the last cell of the table (*144*). All of the cells containing numbers are selected.
5. Click the **Align Right** button.

STEP-BY-STEP 5.8 Continued

6. Position the pointer to the left of the first row. When the pointer changes to a right-pointing arrow, click to select the entire row.

7. Click the **Center** and **Bold** buttons on the Formatting toolbar.

8. Select the row beginning with *Activity* and apply the center and bold formats.

9. Save the changes and close the document.

Use the Draw Table and Eraser Tools

2-2.2.1-2

There may be occasions when you need to create and customize a more complex table. For example, the table may require cells of different heights or a varying number of columns per row. The Draw Table tool is very useful for creating complex tables. You use the Draw Table tool much the same way you use a pen to draw a table on a sheet of paper. When you use the Draw Table tool, you draw the table using the mouse. The document must be displayed in Print Layout view when you use the Draw Table tool.

The Eraser tool enables you to remove cell boundaries. Click on the Eraser button, and the pointer changes to an eraser. When you point and click on a cell gridline, the line will be selected. When you release, the gridline is deleted. The Eraser tool is especially useful if you want to delete a gridline or if you want to change the layout by moving a gridline.

STEP-BY-STEP 5.9

1. Open a new blank document. If necessary, open the **View** menu and choose **Ruler** to display the Ruler at the top of the document. The Ruler is displayed when there is a checkmark to the left of the command in the menu.

2. If necessary, display the Tables and Borders toolbar. Open the **View** menu, choose **Toolbars**, and turn on the **Tables and Borders** toolbar shown in Figure 5-6.

FIGURE 5-6
Tables and Borders toolbar

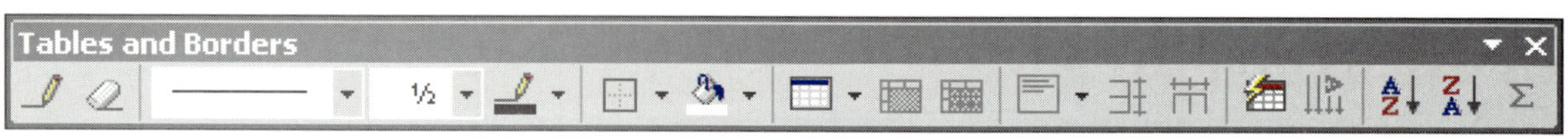

2-2.2.1-2

3. Click the **Draw Table** button on the Tables and Borders toolbar. The pointer changes to a pencil and Word automatically changes to Print Layout View. 

4. To draw the outside boundary of the table grid, position the pointer at the left margin. Then click and drag down and to the right to create a table boundary. Release when the table (box) is approximately 6 inches wide by 2 ½ inches high.

STEP-BY-STEP 5.9 Continued

5. Create the vertical and horizontal lines inside the table. Position the point of the pencil where you want the line to begin. Then click and drag to the point where you want the line to end. A broken line will display as you drag the mouse. Repeat to draw all of the lines illustrated in Figure 5-7. Note that there are four horizontal lines at ½ inch apart, and three vertical lines at 1 inch, 4 ½ inches, and 5 ½ inches on the ruler.

Computer Concepts

Sometimes when you display a toolbar, it is floating on the screen. You can move a floating toolbar anywhere on the screen by dragging the title bar. If you drag the toolbar to the edge of the program window or to a location beside another docked toolbar, it becomes a docked toolbar. To move a docked toolbar, drag the move handle at the left side of the toolbar.

FIGURE 5-7
Table grid for Step-by-Step 5.9

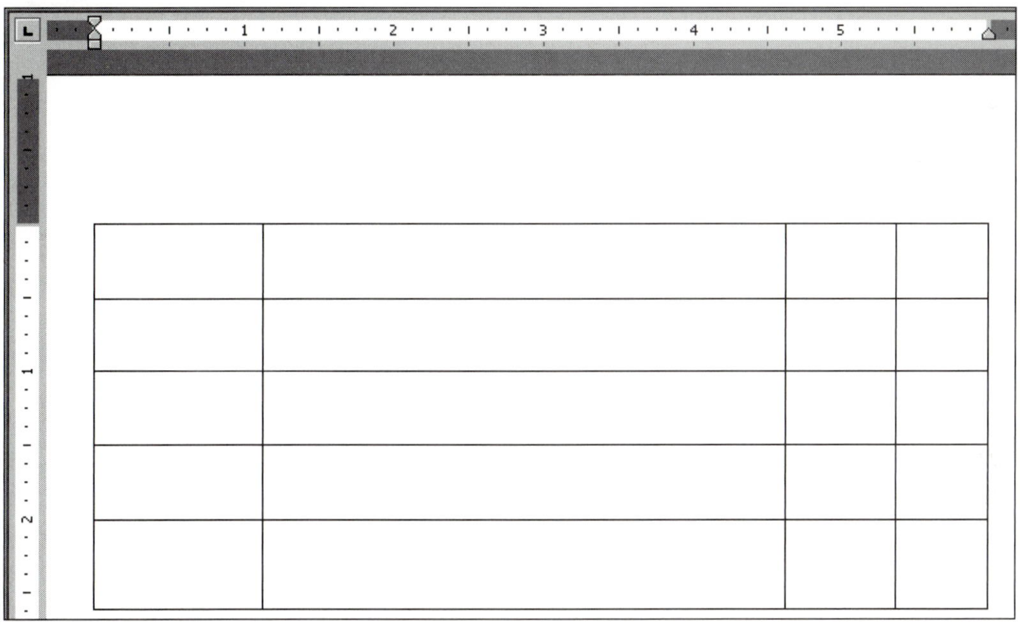

6. Click the **Draw Table** button to deselect it.

7. Click the **Eraser** button. The pointer changes to an eraser. 

8. Point the eraser on the first vertical line in the first row.
When the bottom corner of the eraser is positioned over the line, click to select the line and delete it. If you click and the line is not selected, reposition the eraser and try again. The line will only be deleted if it is selected when you click. See Figure 5-8.

FIGURE 5-8
Eraser tool with selected line

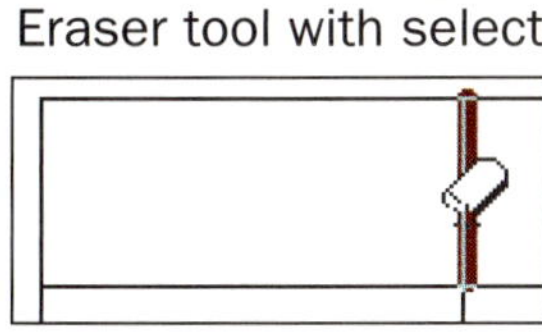

STEP-BY-STEP 5.9 Continued

9. Erase two more lines in the first column so your table grid matches the grid illustrated in Figure 5-9.

FIGURE 5-9
Layout grid for Step-by-Step 5.9

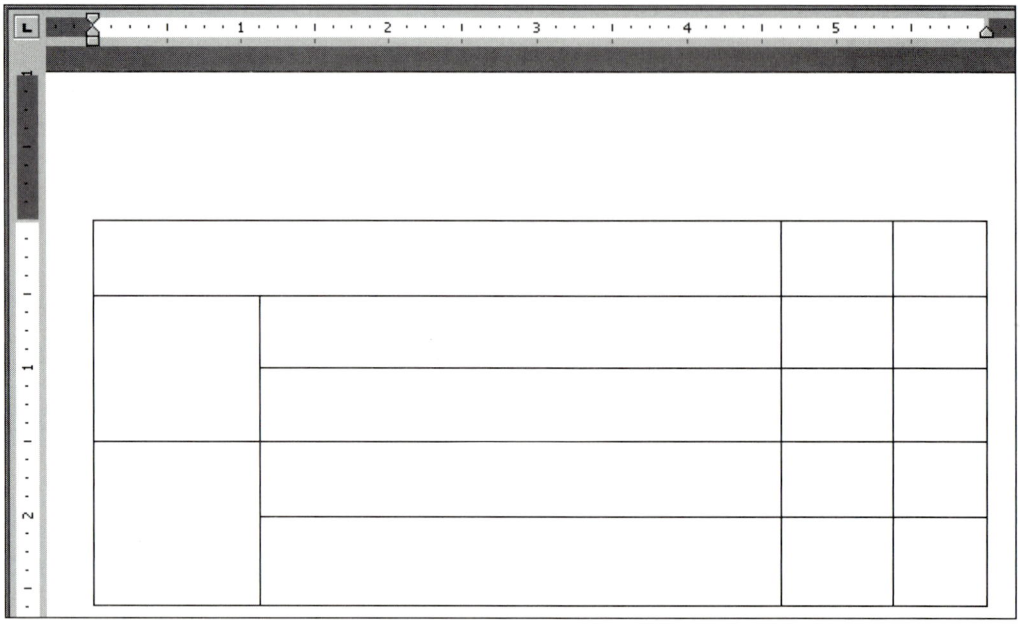

10. Click the **Eraser** button to deselect it.

11. Enter the table text illustrated in Figure 5-10.

12. Save the document as **Recycling Rate** followed by your initials and leave it open for the next Step-by-Step.

FIGURE 5-10
Text for Step-by-Step 5.9

Recycling Rate		2000	2002
PET	Soft drink bottles	48%	52%
	Vegetable oil bottles	12%	18%
HDPE	Milk jugs	29%	33%
	Bleach and laundry detergent bottles	14%	19%

Align Text Within Table Cells

The Tables and Borders toolbar displays several buttons you can use to align text within the cells. You can align text at the top, center, or bottom of a cell, as well as left or right. You can quickly change the direction of text in a table cell by clicking the Change Text Direction button. The direction of the text toggles between three text positions: top to bottom, bottom to top, and horizontal (the default position with which you began).

STEP-BY-STEP 5.10

1. Select the entire table. (*Hint:* Place the insertion point somewhere within the table, then open the **Table** menu, choose **Select**, and then choose **Table** in the submenu.)

2. Click the down arrow next to the **Align Top Left** button on the Tables and Borders toolbar. A box with nine alignment options is displayed. See Figure 5-11.

FIGURE 5-11
Cell Alignment options

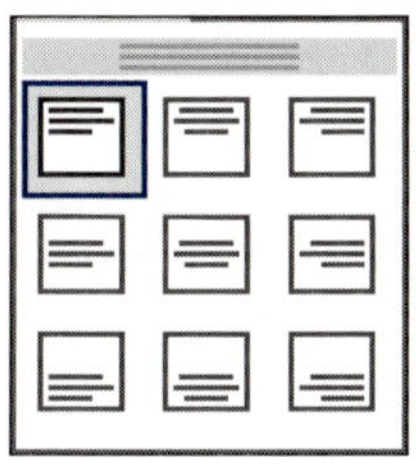

3. Select the **Align Center Left** option in the second row of options. (*Hint:* Point to the option and wait for the ScreenTip to display so you know you have the correct option.) The text in each cell is centered between the top and bottom boundaries of the cell.

4. Point to the cell *PET* and drag down to select it and the cell *HDPE*.

5. With both cells selected, click the **Change Text Direction** button on the Tables and Borders toolbar. The text rotates to the right and is displayed from top to bottom.

6. Click the **Change Text Direction** button again. The text rotates to the right and is now displayed from bottom to top.

STEP-BY-STEP 5.10 Continued

7. Notice that several of the buttons on the Formatting toolbar are altered to reflect the new text direction. Click the **Center** button on the Formatting toolbar. The text is centered between the top and bottom boundaries of the cells. Your document should now look like Figure 5-12.

Computer Concepts

You can also use the Draw Table tool to add rows or columns to an existing table and to split table cells.

8. Save the changes and leave the document open for the next Step-by-Step.

FIGURE 5-12
Document with text rotated and aligned

Recycling Rate		2000	2002
PET	Soft drink bottles	48%	52%
	Vegetable oil bottles	12%	18%
HDPE	Milk jugs	29%	33%
	Bleach and laundry detergent bottles	14%	19%

Format Borders and Shading in a Table

2-2.2.9-1 Borders and shading can greatly enhance the appearance of a table and even help to make the table easier to read. The default setting for tables is to print with a ½-point single-line border around all cells. Generally, this border will be appropriate for the tables you create. However, there may be occasions when you want to customize the border and add shading to some of the table cells. You may even want to remove the border completely. Word makes it easy to format borders and change the shading of cells in your table.

STEP-BY-STEP 5.11

1. Select the top row of cells. (*Hint:* Point to the left side of the first row. When the pointer changes to a right-pointing arrow, click.)

2-2.2.9-2

2. Click the down arrow next to the **Line Weight** button on the Tables and Borders toolbar. In the submenu, select **1 ½ pt**.

3. Click the **Outside Border** button on the Tables and Borders toolbar. The border line becomes heavier.

STEP-BY-STEP 5.11 Continued

2-2.2.9-3

4. With the row still selected, click the down arrow next to the **Shading Color** button on the Tables and Borders toolbar. If you have a color printer available, choose a light color. Select **Gray-10%** if you have a black and white printer. (*Hint:* Point to one of the shading options and wait for the ScreenTip to display so you know you have the correct option.)

5. Select the two cells at the left edge of the table (*PET* and *HDPE*). Repeat the shading color format. (*Hint:* Press **F4**.)

6. Click in the first cell, *Recycling Rate*, and center the text horizontally.

7. Select the last two columns (including the headings) and align the numbers at the right.

8. Save the changes and close the document.

Convert Text to a Table and AutoFormat

2-2.2.10-1

Assume that you've already created a multicolumn list using tab settings. You decide that you want to organize the data in a table because it will be easier to format. Do you have to key all the data again? The answer is no. Word can quickly convert text separated by paragraph marks, commas, tabs, or other characters into a table with cells.

When converting text to a table, Word determines the number of columns needed based on paragraphs, tabs, or commas in the text. When converting a table to text, Word inserts tabs to show where the column breaks are.

The AutoFormat feature provides several built-in table styles that include borders, background shading, and character formats. You can apply a table style by opening the Table menu and choosing Table AutoFormat. When you select a style in the dialog box, a preview area shows the effect of the style you select.

STEP-BY-STEP 5.12

1. Open **Step5-12** from the data files. Save the document as **Scores** followed by your initials.

2. Select the entire document. (*Hint:* Press **Ctrl + A**.)

STEP-BY-STEP 5.12 Continued

3. Open the **Table** menu and choose **Convert**. In the submenu, select **Text to Table**. The dialog box shown in Figure 5-13 is displayed.

FIGURE 5-13
Convert Text to Table dialog box

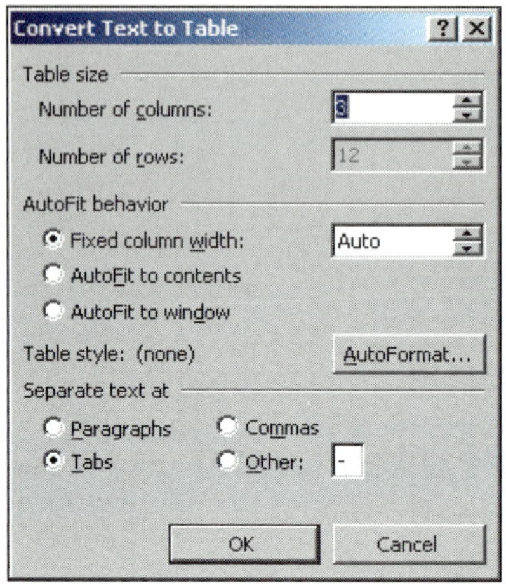

4. Under Table size, the number of columns should already be set to **3**. Under AutoFit behavior, select **AutoFit to contents**. Under Separate text at, make sure **Tabs** is selected. Click **OK**. Click anywhere in the window to deselect so you can see the revised table.

2-2.2.10-2 5. Position the insertion point in the table, then open the **Table** menu and click **Table AutoFormat**. The dialog box shown in Figure 5-14 is displayed.

FIGURE 5-14
Table AutoFormat dialog box

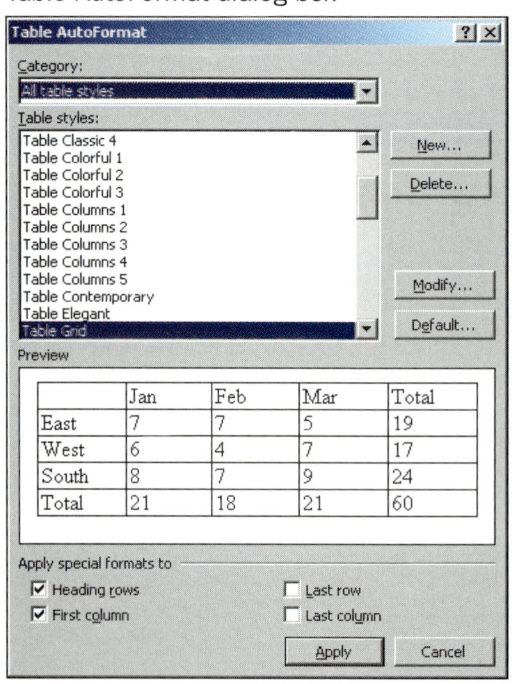

STEP-BY-STEP 5.12 Continued

6. Select **Table Colorful 2** in the Table styles list. Notice that the Preview box shows approximately how your table will be formatted. Click **Apply**.

7. With the insertion point still positioned in the table, center the table horizontally on the page by selecting the entire table and clicking the **Center** button on the Standard toolbar.

8. Save the changes and close the document.

Speech Recognition

If your computer has speech recognition capability, enable the Command mode. With the insertion point positioned within the table, say the commands to autoformat the table and position the table horizontally.

SUMMARY

In this lesson, you learned:

- The table feature in Word enables you to organize and arrange text and numbers easily.
- If you need to change the organization of information after you create a table and enter data, you can remove rows and columns.
- The AutoFit feature automatically adjusts the width of a column based on the contents of the cells in a column.
- Format fonts and text alignment in table cells the same way you apply those formats in other Word documents.
- The Draw Table tool and the Eraser tool are especially useful when you need to create a complex table. You can draw the table boundaries with the Draw Table tool much like you would draw a table on a sheet of paper. You can use the Eraser tool to remove cell boundaries.
- Borders and shading greatly enhance the appearance of a table and often make the table easier to read.
- Word will convert text to a table or a table to text.
- The AutoFormat feature automatically adds borders and shading to your table.

VOCABULARY *Review*

Define the following terms:

Cell	Merging cells	Splitting cells
Gridlines		

REVIEW *Questions*

TRUE/FALSE

Circle T if the statement is true or F if the statement is false.

T F 1. Table rows go across a page, and columns go down a page.

T F 2. You can choose to hide or display a table's gridlines.

T F 3. When you remove the boundary between two cells, you are splitting the cells.

T F 4. The AutoAdjust command automatically adjusts all column widths in a table.

T F 5. Word can create a table from text in which data is separated by paragraph marks, tabs, or commas.

FILL IN THE BLANK

Complete the following sentences by writing the correct word or words in the blanks provided.

1. A table consists of rows and columns of __________ to which you add text or graphics.
2. If you wanted to add a new row in the middle of a table beneath the row in which your insertion point is located, you would choose the __________ menu, click Insert, and then select Row Below.
3. Converting one cell into multiple cells is called __________ cells.
4. To create a complex table, use the __________ tool to position gridlines just where you want them.
5. The __________ feature automatically adds borders and shading to a table.

PROJECTS

PROJECT 5-1

1. Open **Project5-1** from the data files. Save the document as **Population** followed by your initials.
2. Position the insertion point in the last blank line of the document and use the **Insert Table** button to create a grid for a 6-row by 3-column table.

3. Complete the table by entering the data shown in Figure 5-15.

FIGURE 5-15
Data for Project 5-1 table

	1990	2000
18 – 24	30,388	28,513
25 – 34	52,697	44,248
45 – 54	27,157	40,347
55 – 64	23,864	25,890
65+	33,640	39,048

4. You realize you left out the data for the 35–44 age group. Insert a row in the proper location and key the following data: **35–44 42,802 50,938**

5. It would be helpful to see the percent change in population. Add a column to the right of the *2000* column and key the column heading **% Change** in the first row. Insert the following information in the cells of the new column:

   -6.2
   -16.0
   19.0
   48.6
   8.5
   16.0

6. Insert a new row above the first row of the table and merge all cells in it. Key the table title **Population by Age**. Center and boldface the first two rows of the table.

7. Use AutoFit to adjust column widths, then center the table in the page.

8. The data in the *% Change* column would look better if the decimal points were aligned. Right-align the numbers (but not the column head) in this column.

9. Remove all the borders in the table, then shade alternate rows of the data beginning with the *18–24* row.

10. Save your changes and close the document.

PROJECT 5-2

1. Open **Project5-2** from the data files. Save the document as **Orders** followed by your initials.
2. Use the **Draw Table** tool to edit the table as shown in Figure 5-16.

FIGURE 5-16
Revisions for table in Project 5-2

Customer						
Clothing	Item	Color	Size	Qty	Price	Total
	Lakeside Hat					
	Lakeside T-Shirt					
	Lakeside Sweatshirt					
Goodies	Red Hot Jam					
	Navel Oranges					
	Lakeside Crunch					
					Total	

3. Follow the steps below to edit the new table cells so they will look like the cells illustrated in Figure 5-17:
   A. Position the insertion point in the large empty cell just to the right of the *Customer* cell. Split this cell, using settings of 1 column and 4 rows.
   B. In the four new rows, key **Name, Address, City,** and **Phone**.
   C. Split the next large empty cell into 4 rows (and 1 column). Customers will write their names and addresses in these rows.

FIGURE 5-17
Revisions for new table cells in Project 5-2

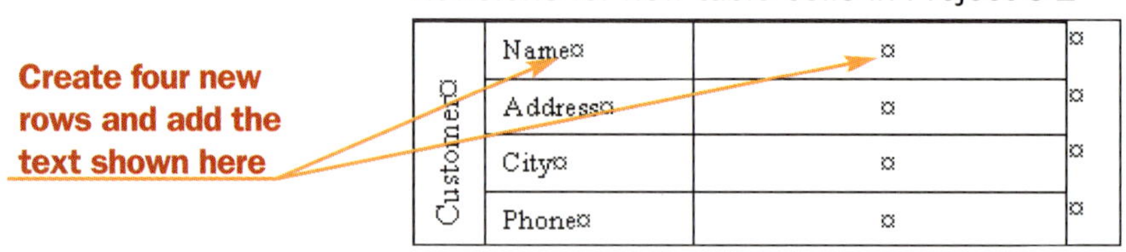

4. Center all text vertically in the table cells using the **Align Center Left** option.
5. Format the table using features you have learned in this lesson. You can remove or modify borders, add shading to emphasize portions of the form, and use other text formatting features such as bold, italic, and alignment to make the form easier to read.
6. Save your changes and close the document.

PROJECT 5-3

1. Open **Project5-3** from the data files. Save the document as **Hurricanes** followed by your initials. You have compiled the information in this document while doing research on hurricanes, and you decide you could format the information more clearly and attractively if you converted it to a table.

2. Select only the tabbed data (not the blank line or the source line) and convert the text to a table. Accept the suggested number of columns, select AutoFit to contents, and separate the text at tabs.

3. AutoFormat the table using the **Table Web3** format.

4. Insert a new row at the top of the table and merge all cells in it. Key the title **Costliest U.S. Hurricanes of the 20th Century**, and then press **Enter** and key (**In Billions**). Center and boldface the first two rows of the table.

5. Center the data in the *Category* column, and right-align the data in the *Damage* column.

6. You keyed the wrong year for Hurricane Andrew. Change the year for Andrew to **1992**.

7. You decide the first ten entries in the table give enough information about the destructive power of hurricanes. Delete the last two rows in the table.

8. Center the table horizontally.

9. Save your changes. Print and close the document.

WEB PROJECT

If you completed Project 5-1, you read a brief description of a change in demographics. What exactly are demographics? Using a Web search tool such as Ask Jeeves, find a definition of demographics and key it in Word. Then follow one or more links to find demographic data about your county or city. (The *City and County Data Book* at the University of Virginia is especially easy to use.) See if you can find out what percent of the population in your city is your age. You may also explore other interesting facts about your city or county such as number of births, how many children are in school, and so on. Below your definition of demographics, summarize in a table the demographic facts you have obtained about your city or county.

TEAMWORK PROJECT

If you completed Project 5-3, you learned how costly hurricanes can be in terms of property damage. The data shown in the Hurricanes table was compiled by the National Oceanic and Atmospheric Administration and, at the time of this writing, is current only through 1996. With a partner, see if you can update the table with more recent data.

1. Write down the years from 1997 to the last complete hurricane season (hurricane season begins in June and ends in November, so if you are working on this project before the end of November, do not include the current year in your list).

2. Split the years with your partner so that you each have half of them to research.

3. Using Web search tools or other research tools, try to locate a summary of hurricane damage for each year.

4. If any of the years you research total more dollar damage than the hurricanes shown in the Hurricanes table, insert new rows to add the data you have found.

CRITICAL *Thinking*

ACTIVITY 5-1

The owner of the stable where you ride horses has been complaining about the comings and goings of her part-time staff and unpaid helpers (of whom you are one). She'd like a way to keep track of names, phone numbers, what days and hours each worker is scheduled, and hourly salary (if any). Use what you have learned in this lesson to create a table that will help the stable owner organize the information about her staff. Key several fictitious entries in the table (including yourself) to test your solution.

LESSON 6

DESKTOP PUBLISHING

OBJECTIVES

Upon completion of this lesson, you should be able to:

- Format text in columns.
- Insert clip art and other graphics.
- Resize and position graphics.
- Format borders and shading.
- Create WordArt Objects.
- Use drawing tools.
- Insert and format text boxes.
- Use AutoShapes to Create Objects.
- Use templates, styles, and themes to increase the speed, efficiency, and quality of your work.
- Use AutoText to store pre-existing text entries.

Estimated Time: 1 hour

VOCABULARY

Banner
Clip art
Crop
Desktop publishing
Drawing canvas
Drawing objects
Graphics
Hard column break
Sizing handles
Style
Template
Text box
Theme
Thumbnails

Publishing a professional-looking newsletter or report could only be accomplished with the combined efforts of several people. Artists created the graphics and artwork, typesetters created the text, and designers completed the page layouts and prepared the pages of type for the printer. The process was often quite expensive. Today, with personal computers and inexpensive software, you can prepare attractive, professional-looking documents on your desktop computer. ***Desktop publishing*** is the process of using a computer to combine text and graphics to create an attractive document.

Word provides a number of features to make documents more attractive. You can format text in columns, import pictures, draw your own pictures, add borders and shading, and use WordArt to shape and rotate text.

Format Text in Columns

One common application for desktop publishing is newsletters. Newsletter text is often formatted in multiple columns. The text flows down one column and begins again in the next column if necessary. Usually, the heading (or title of the newsletter) is formatted as a single-column ***banner*** where the heading spreads the full width across the multiple newsletter-style columns.

It is easy to apply columns in Word, and there are a few different ways to do so. When you apply the column format, the columns are usually balanced so that the column lengths are approximately equal. There may be occasions, however, when you want to control where columns break. To adjust where a column ends, you can insert a ***hard column break***.

STEP-BY-STEP 6.1

1. If necessary, launch Word. Open **Step6-1** from the data files and save the document as **Newsletter** followed by your initials. If necessary, click **Show/Hide ¶** to display nonprinting characters.

2. Select the paragraph of text under the heading *PROTECTION FROM THE SUN*. Do not include the blank paragraph marks above or below the text in the selection.

3. Click the **Columns** button on the Standard toolbar. A grid displaying four columns appears.

4. Drag across the grid to select two columns. See Figure 6-1. When you release the mouse button, the selected text is formatted in two columns of equal width.

FIGURE 6-1
Columns grid

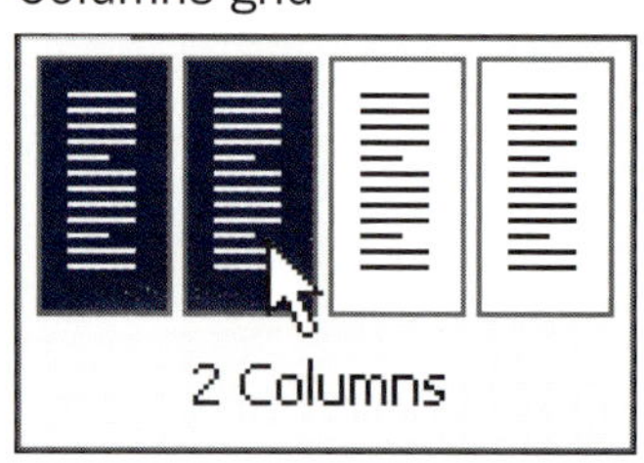

5. Select the three paragraphs of text under the heading *THE HEALTH RISKS OF LIVING ALONE*. Click the **Columns** button and select three columns in the grid, then release. The selected text is formatted in three columns of equal width.

6. Select the paragraph of text below the heading *HIKING AND BIKING ADVENTURES*.

7. Open the **Format** menu and choose **Columns**. The dialog box shown in Figure 6-2 is displayed.

STEP-BY-STEP 6.1 Continued

FIGURE 6-2
Columns dialog box

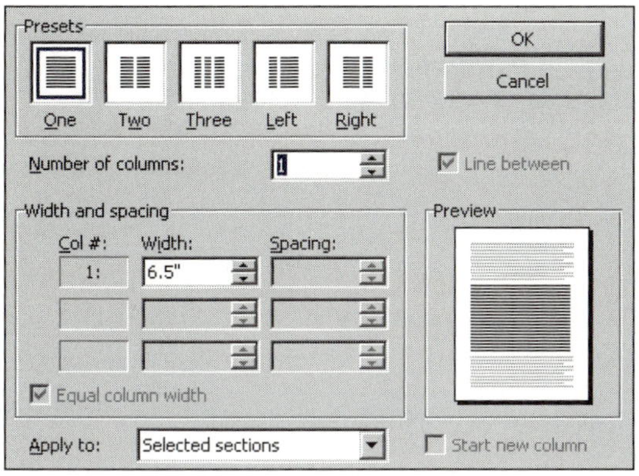

8. Select **Right** under Presets and turn on the option **Line between**. Word automatically adjusts the column widths under Width and spacing and updates the Preview.

9. Click **OK**. The text is formatted in two columns of unequal width, with a vertical line between the columns.

10. Position the insertion point in front of the third paragraph in *THE HEALTH RISKS OF LIVING ALONE*. The paragraph begins *Ironically,…*. Open the **Insert** menu, choose **Break**, then select **Column break** and click **OK**.

11. Position the insertion point in front of the second paragraph in the same article that begins *Studies show that….* Insert a column break.

12. Save the changes and leave the document open for the next Step-by-Step.

Insert a Graphic

You can use graphics to illustrate an idea presented in the document, to enhance the appearance of the document, or to make the document more functional. ***Graphics*** are items other than text and can include photos, borders, clip art, and drawing objects. ***Clip art*** is artwork that is ready to insert in a document. ***Drawing objects*** are Word tools that enable you to create your own artwork.

Speech Recognition

If your computer has speech recognition capability, enable the Command mode. With the text selected, say the commands to open the Format Columns dialog box and apply the column formats.

Insert Clip Art

2-2.2.11-2

Word has numerous clip art images and photos that are stored in the Office Collections folder. You can also access clip art that you have saved (in the My Collections folder). If you have an Internet connection open, you can search for clip art at the Microsoft Web site. Search results are displayed in the task pane as ***thumbnails***, which are miniature representations of a picture.

STEP-BY-STEP 6.2

1. Position the insertion point in front of the paragraph in the second article that begins *Doctors now believe....*

2-2.2.11-2 2. Open the **Insert** menu, choose **Picture**, and then select **Clip Art** from the submenu. The Insert Clip Art task pane is displayed. Compare your screen to Figure 6-3. Do not be concerned if your screen does not match exactly.

Did You Know?

You can leave the Insert Clip Art task pane open as you work so you can quickly access additional Clip Art images.

FIGURE 6-3
Insert Clip Art task pane

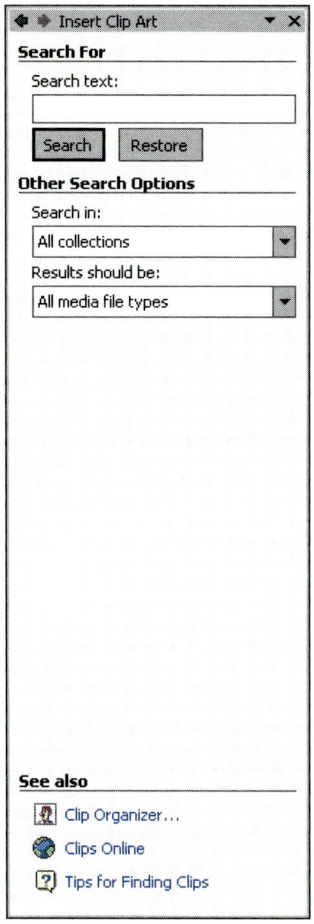

3. Select the text in the Search text text box and key **doctor**. If there is no text to be selected, just position the insertion point within the box.

Computer Concepts

You may find it easier to work with the graphics in a document by reducing the view of the document. For example, you can change the zoom of the document view to 75%.

STEP-BY-STEP 6.2 Continued

4. Specify where Word should search for clip art. Under Other Search Options, click the down arrow in the **Search in** list box. Double-click the option **Everywhere**. This toggles the selection of the option on or off. The option is selected when a checkmark is displayed in the box to the left of the option name. See Figure 6-4.

Computer Concepts

If there is a plus sign in front of the Everywhere option, click the plus sign to expand the list and display the option where clip art can be found. If there is a minus sign in front of the Everywhere option, as shown in Figure 6-4, the list of options is already expanded.

FIGURE 6-4
Options for specifying where to search for clip art

5. Click the **Search** button in the task pane. The results should display at least one clip art image as a thumbnail. See Figure 6-5.

FIGURE 6-5
Clip Art matching the search word *doctor*

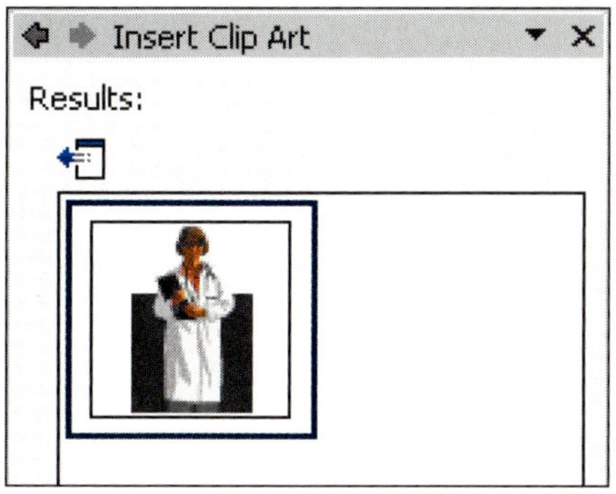

STEP-BY-STEP 6.2 Continued

6. Click the clip shown in Figure 6-5 (or any clip of a doctor) to insert the image in the document at the location of the insertion point.

7. Close the task pane.

8. Save the changes and leave the document open for the next Step-by-Step.

Insert a Picture from a File or a Symbol

2-2.2.11-1 You can also insert photos and clip art that are stored in other folders. This is called importing a picture. To insert a picture from a graphics file, position the insertion point where you want the picture inserted, open the Insert menu, choose Picture, and select From File in the submenu. When the Insert Picture dialog box opens, browse to locate and select the graphics file.

As you work with documents, you may encounter situations in which you need to enter a symbol that is not available to you from the keyboard or is not available or convenient to insert as clip art or a graphic. In these situations, you can utilize the existing set of symbols available to you in Microsoft Office.

> **Computer Concepts**
>
> If you click the down arrow on the right side of the clipart thumbnail, a shortcut menu will display and provide options for copying and pasting, deleting the clip from the Clip Organizer, copying the clip to a Collection folder, and so on.

STEP-BY-STEP 6.3

1. Position the insertion point in front of the paragraph beginning *Are you looking....*

2-2.2.11-1 2. Open the **Insert** menu, choose **Picture**, and then select **From File** in the submenu. The Insert Picture dialog box is displayed.

3. Locate the Lesson 6 data files in the Look in box. Select the file **Biking** and click **Insert**. The picture is inserted at the location of the insertion point, and the document wraps to a second page.

> **Hot Tip**
>
> To restore the settings from the previous search, click **Restore**.

2-2.1.4-1 4. Position your insertion point at the end of the last paragraph. Open the **Insert** menu and select **Symbol**.

5. Switch to the **Special Characters** tab if necessary and select **Copyright**. Click **Insert**. Click **Close**.

6. Click the **Undo Symbol** button.

7. Save the changes and leave the document open for the next Step-by-Step.

Resize and Position Graphics

2-2.2.12-1 Once you have inserted a graphic or picture in a document, there are many ways to manipulate the picture. To work with a graphic, you must click on it to select it. You will know it is selected when you see eight small squares on the border of the graphic. These squares are called ***sizing handles***. When a graphic is selected, you can cut, copy, paste, delete, and move it just as you would text.

Speech Recognition

If your computer has speech recognition capability, enable the Command mode and say the commands to insert the picture from a file. You can dictate all the commands necessary to open the dialog box, locate the file, and insert the file in the document.

Change the Size of a Graphic

2-2.2.12-2 The easiest way to change the size of a graphic is to drag one of the sizing handles. As you drag the sizing handle, you can see the effects of the change on your screen. If you want to change the size to exact measurements, you need to use the Format Picture command.

When you scale a graphic proportionally, you change all dimensions of the graphic (height and width) approximately equally. You can also scale a graphic just vertically or just horizontally, which distorts the image.

A text-wrapping format must be applied to the graphic before you can reposition it in your document. You can then move the graphic by dragging it to a new location.

STEP-BY-STEP 6.4

1. If necessary, turn on the display of the Ruler. (*Hint:* Open the **View** menu, and choose **Ruler**.)

2. Click on the clip art image of the doctor. When the picture is selected, the Picture toolbar shown in Figure 6-6 is displayed. Eight sizing handles appear on the outside border of the image. See Figure 6-7.

FIGURE 6-6
Picture toolbar

2-2.2.12-2

3. Point to the lower right corner of the image. When the pointer changes to a two-headed arrow, drag the corner sizing handle toward the center of the picture. When the picture is approximately 1 ¼ inches high and 1 ¼ inches wide, release the mouse. Use the rulers at the top and left edges of the document to judge the picture size.

STEP-BY-STEP 6.4 Continued

FIGURE 6-7
Picture with sizing handles

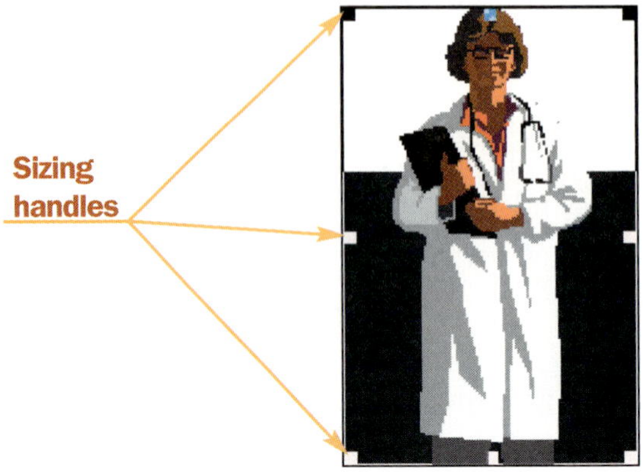

4. Save the changes and leave the document open for the next Step-by-Step.

Crop a Graphic

When you ***crop*** a graphic, you cut off portions of the graphic that you do not want to show. You might want to crop extra white space around an image or actually remove part of the image altogether.

STEP-BY-STEP 6.5

1. Click the biking clip art picture. The nonprinting border around the picture is displayed. Notice that there is excess white space on the right side and bottom of the picture.

2. Click the **Crop** button on the Picture toolbar. The pointer changes to a cropping box.

3. Position the cropping box on the sizing handle on the middle right of the picture. Then drag the sizing handle to the left to trim the white space. See Figure 6-8. When you release the mouse button, the portion of the picture you cropped is now gone.

> **Hot Tip**
>
> If the Picture toolbar is not displayed, open the **View** menu and choose **Toolbars**, then select **Picture**.

FIGURE 6-8
Cropping a picture

STEP-BY-STEP 6.5 Continued

4. Point to the sizing handle on the middle bottom of the picture and crop the white space at the bottom of the picture.

5. Click the **Crop** button to turn off the cropping feature.

6. Resize the picture so it is approximately 1 inch high and 1 inch wide. (*Hint:* Be sure to drag a corner handle so you will resize the image proportionately.)

7. Save the changes and leave the document open for the next Step-by-Step.

Wrap Text Around a Graphic

By default, Word inserts graphics in the line of text. This means that the graphic is positioned directly in the text at the insertion point. Instead of being in the line of text, however, you can format the text in the document to wrap around the graphic. By changing the wrapping style, you can drag and drop the graphic anywhere within the printable area of the page.

To create a tighter wrap around the graphic, you can edit the wrap points for the graphic. The wrap points identify the edge of the graphic. You can drag these wrap points to reposition them.

STEP-BY-STEP 6.6

1. If necessary, click on the biking picture to select it.

-2.2.12-3

2. Click the **Text Wrapping** button on the Picture toolbar. A drop-down list of wrapping options appears. Figure 6-9 provides a description of each of the options displayed in the drop-down list.

> **Computer Concepts**
>
> If the Picture toolbar is not displayed, make sure the picture is selected.

FIGURE 6-9
Text-wrapping options

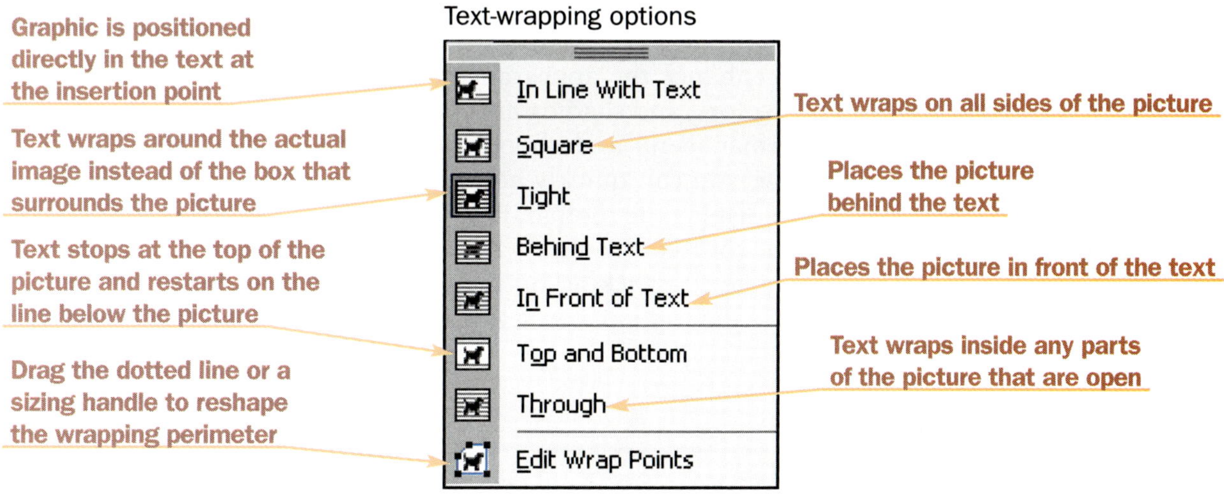

3. Select the **Square** option. The text now wraps along the right side and bottom of the picture.

STEP-BY-STEP 6.6 Continued

4. With the biking picture still selected, click the **Text Wrapping** button and then click **Edit Wrap Points**.

5. Point to the sizing handle on the bottom right of the picture and drag the handle to the left to create a diagonal line as shown in Figure 6-10. When you release the mouse button, the text shifts to the left along the diagonal line.

FIGURE 6-10
Editing the Wrap point of a picture

6. Point to the center of the picture. When the pointer changes to a four-headed arrow, drag the picture to the left so it aligns with the left margin.

7. Select the doctor picture, click the **Text Wrapping** button, and select the **Tight** option. The text wraps tightly around the actual image instead of the rectangle boundary of the image. The way the text wraps will depend on the clip art image you selected.

8. Drag the picture to the right side of the article.

9. Save the changes and leave the document open for the next Step-by-Step.

Computer Concepts

You cannot drag and drop a picture until after you have applied a text-wrapping style.

Format Borders and Shading

2-2.1.9-1

Borders and shading can help enhance the appearance of a document. Word offers many options for line styles, line weights, colors, and shading effects. To access these borders and shading features, you can open the Format menu and choose Borders and Shading to display the Borders and Shading dialog box. Or, you can quickly access most of the features by displaying the Borders and Shading toolbar. To display the toolbar, right click on any toolbar on your screen and choose Tables and Borders in the shortcut menu. A checkmark before the toolbar name indicates that the toolbar is already displayed. Clicking on the toolbar name will then turn off the shortcut menu and display or remove the toolbar you selected.

STEP-BY-STEP 6.7

1. Position the insertion point in the blank paragraph above the first line of text *PROTECTION FROM THE SUN.*

STEP-BY-STEP 6.7 Continued

2-2.1.9-2

2. Right-click on any toolbar and choose **Tables and Borders** in the shortcut menu to display the Tables and Borders toolbar. Click the down arrow on the **Line Weight** button on the Tables and Borders toolbar and select **3 pt**.

3. Click the down arrow on the **Border** button (the ScreenTip for this button probably says Outside Border) just to the left of the Shading Color button. Select **Top Border**.

4. Position the insertion point in the blank paragraph at the end of the document. Click the down arrow alongside the **Border** button and select **Bottom Border**.

5. Position the insertion point in the first heading *PROTECTION FROM THE SUN*.

2-2.1.9-3

6. Click the down arrow next to the **Shading Color** button on the Table and Borders toolbar and select the color **Tan**. (*Hint:* Point to a color in the color pallette and wait for the ScreenTip to display the name of the color.) A tan shade format is applied to the entire paragraph.

7. Position the insertion point in the second heading *THE HEALTH RISKS OF LIVING ALONE*, then click the **Shading Color** button. (Note that the color Tan is already selected and is showing on the Shading Color button.)

Speech Recognition

If your computer has speech recognition capability, enable the Command mode. With the insertion point positioned correctly, say the commands to access the toolbar buttons and select the shading color.

8. Repeat the format for the third heading *HIKING AND BIKING ADVENTURES*.

9. Close the Table and Borders toolbar by clicking the **Close** button in the top right corner.

10. Save the changes and leave the document open for the next Step-by-Step.

Create WordArt Objects

WordArt is a feature that enables you transform text into a graphic. You can create your own styles or you can choose from several predefined styles in the WordArt Gallery. When you create a WordArt object, the WordArt toolbar is displayed.

STEP-BY-STEP 6.8

1. Position the insertion point at the beginning of the document at the first paragraph mark.

2. Click the **Drawing** button on the Standard toolbar to display the Drawing toolbar. The Drawing toolbar is automatically docked at the bottom of your Word document window, above the Status bar.

3. Click the **Insert WordArt** button on the Drawing toolbar. The dialog box shown in Figure 6-11 is displayed.

STEP-BY-STEP 6.8 Continued

FIGURE 6-11
WordArt Gallery dialog box

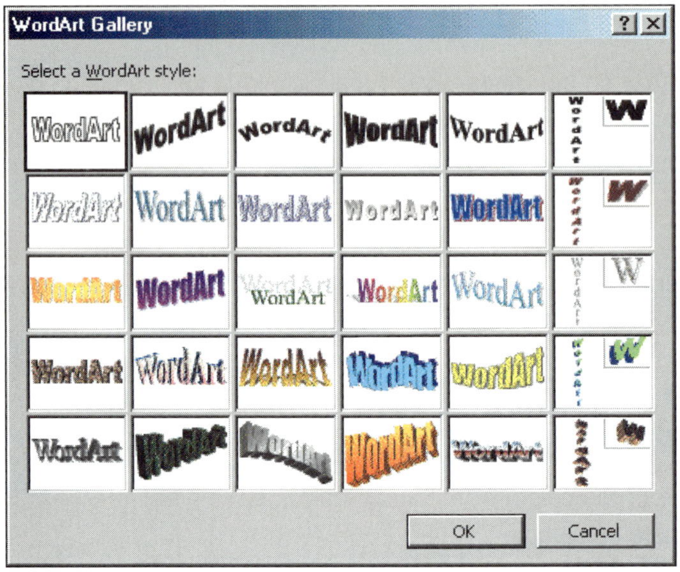

4. Select the fourth style in the second row, then click **OK**. The Edit WordArt Text dialog box shown in Figure 6-12 is opened.

FIGURE 6-12
Edit WordArt Text dialog box

5. Key **Health News** and click **OK**. Word formats the text as a WordArt object and positions the object in your document.

6. Click on the object to select it. Then, point to the sizing handle in the lower right corner and drag it to the right edge of the document. The WordArt object will expand to the width of the document, leaving a one-inch margin on the right.

7. With the object still selected, point to the object and right-click. Choose **Format WordArt** from the shortcut menu. If necessary, click the **Color and Lines** tab to display the dialog box shown in Figure 6-13.

STEP-BY-STEP 6.8 Continued

FIGURE 6-13
Format WordArt dialog box

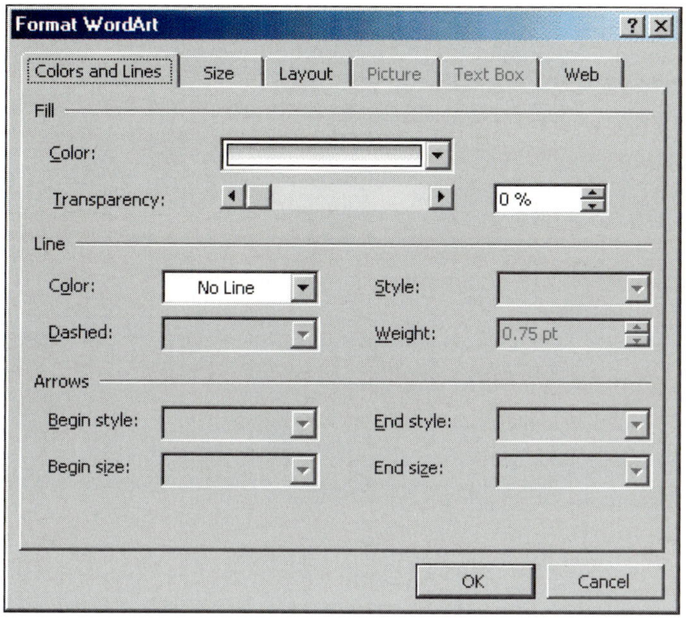

8. In the Color list box under Fill, click the down arrow to display a grid of colors. At the bottom of the grid, select **Fill Effects**. The Gradient tab in the Fill Effects dialog box is displayed.

9. For Color 1, select **Orange**. For Color 2, select **Tan**. Under Shading styles, select **Diagonal up**. Click **OK**. The Fill Effects dialog box closes, and the Format WordArt dialog box is still open.

10. In the Color list box under Line, select **Orange**. Click **OK**. The border lines and the fill colors for the WordArt object are formatted with the new colors.

11. With the WordArt object selected, click the **WordArt Shape** button on the WordArt toolbar. Choose a different shape. Notice that the shape changes but the text, fill color, and line colors remain unchanged. Explore other shapes and choose one that is appropriate for this newsletter.

12. Delete some of the blank lines under the WordArt object, and make other adjustments if necessary to fit the document on one page.

13. Save the changes and close the document.

Use Drawing Tools

Sometimes you may need to create your own artwork. For example, you may need to illustrate a map with directions. You can use the Drawing toolbar in Word to create drawing objects. When you insert a drawing object in Word, a ***drawing canvas*** displays. The drawing canvas helps you arrange your drawing and keep parts of your drawing together, while also providing a frame-like boundary between your drawing and the rest of the document.

2-2.2.14-1 Once you have drawn objects in your document, they can be manipulated in a variety of ways. As you place objects on the page, the most recent ones are placed on top—they are layered. You can select any object and choose to have it placed at the very back layer, the very front layer, or moved forward or backward one layer at a time. You can also select multiple objects and group them together to become one object that can be moved and manipulated as such.

Hot Tip

If you don't want the drawing canvas to display, press **Esc** after you select a drawing tool but before you begin drawing.

STEP-BY-STEP 6.9

1. Open a new document and, if necessary, display the Drawing toolbar.

2-2.2.13-1

2. Click the **Line** button on the Drawing toolbar. The pointer changes to a crosshair and the drawing canvas is displayed. Notice, too, that the Drawing Canvas toolbar is displayed. These toolbar buttons enable you to adjust the canvas size and fit the drawing within the drawing canvas. See Figure 6-14.

Did You Know?

You can format a background or border for the drawing canvas. You can also add a picture by choosing the floating wrapping style and then dragging the picture onto the drawing canvas.

FIGURE 6-14
Drawing Canvas and Drawing Canvas toolbar

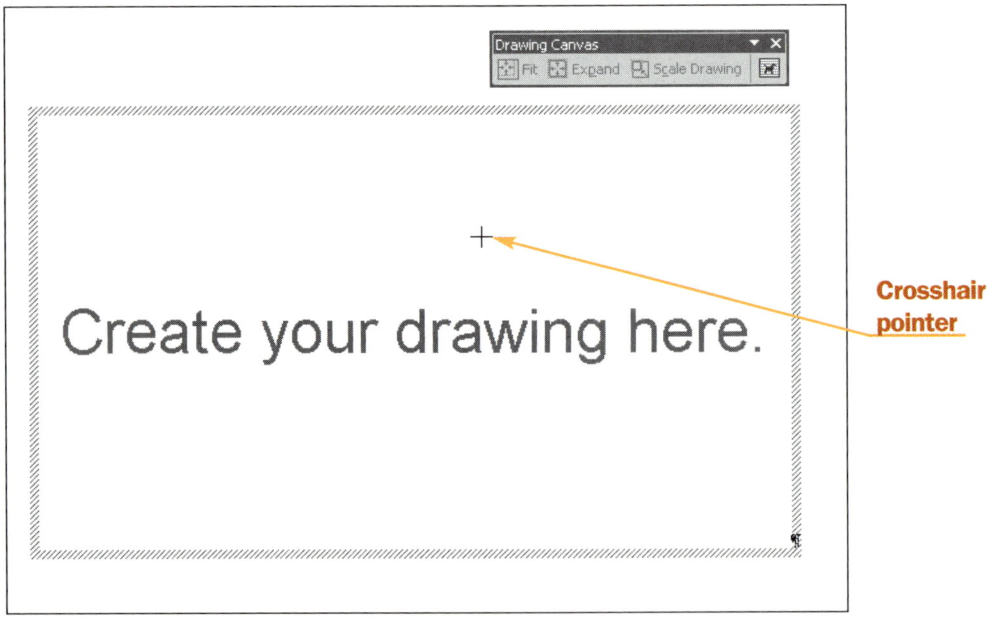

3. Point to the top left corner of the drawing canvas and drag the crosshair across the width of the canvas. Do not release the mouse button until the line is straight, even, and the length you want.

4. Click the **Line** button again and draw a second line, this time running diagonal across the drawing canvas.

STEP-BY-STEP 6.9 Continued

2-2.2.13-2 5. With the second line still selected (*Hint:* The sizing handles on each end of the line indicate that the line is selected.), click the **Line Style** button on the Drawing toolbar and select **3 pt** (the 3-pt single line, not the double line). The weight of the selected line is now heavier.

6. With the line still selected, click the down arrow next to the **Line Color** button on the Drawing toolbar. Select **Green**. The color of the selected line changes.

7. Click the **Rectangle** button on the Drawing toolbar. Position the crosshair in the middle of the screen and drag the crosshair down and to the right to create a box approximately one inch high and one inch wide. (This box should overlap the diagonal line at some point.)

> **Hot Tip**
>
> If the drawing canvas does not display, open the **Tools** menu, choose **Options**, select the **General** tab, and make sure there is a checkmark for the option **Automatically create drawing canvas when inserting AutoShapes**.

> **Computer Concepts**
>
> An object must be selected before you can choose an option from the Drawing toolbar. If the format you want to apply is dimmed, make sure the object you want to format is selected.

8. With the rectangle object still selected, click the down arrow to the right of the **Fill Color** button on the Drawing toolbar and select **Blue**. The rectangle is filled with the blue color.

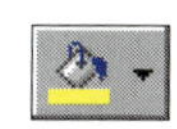

2-2.2.14-2 9. With the rectangle object still selected, open the **Draw** menu on the Drawing toolbar. Point to Order and select **Send Backward**. The rectangle is moved behind or under the diagonal line.

10. With the rectangle object still selected, hold down the **Ctrl** key and click on the diagonal line so that both the rectangle and the line are selected.

2-2.2.14-3 11. Open the **Draw** menu and click **Group**. This makes the rectangle and the line one object. Note how it can be moved and resized as a single object

> **Hot Tip**
>
> To create a perfect square, hold down **Shift** as you drag the crosshair, or just click once in the document without dragging.

12. With the object still selected, open the **Draw** menu and choose **Ungroup**. You do not need to save this document, but leave it open for the next Step-by-Step.

Insert and Format Text Boxes

A ***text box*** is a graphic that enables you to add text to your artwork. Because the text box is a graphic, you can resize and position it the same way you resize and reposition pictures and drawing objects. Within the text box, you can change the font and the alignment of the text.

STEP-BY-STEP 6.10

1. If necessary, display the Ruler. Click the **Text Box** button on the Drawing toolbar. 

2. Point anywhere on the screen and drag the crosshair to create a box approximately 1 inch wide and 1 inch high. When you release the mouse button, the insertion point will be inside the text box and the Text Box floating toolbar will appear. See Figure 6-15.

FIGURE 6-15
Text Box toolbar

3. Key your name inside the box. Select your name and change the font size and color (in the same manner that you would change any other text within the document).

4. If the box is too small to display all the text, drag a sizing handle on either the corner or side to make the box bigger. If the box is too high or too wide, drag a sizing handle to eliminate the excess white space.

5. Click inside the text box. Click the **Center** button on the Formatting toolbar to center the text.

6. If necessary, click on the text box to select it. Then point to a border (not the sizing handle) of the text box. When you see a four-headed arrow, drag the text box to position it under the second line you drew.

7. With the text box selected, click the down arrow next to the **Line Color** button on the Drawing toolbar. Select **No Line** in the submenu. Click outside the text box. The border is no longer visible.

8. Draw a tall, narrow text box (approximately 2 inches high and ½ inch wide).

9. Click the **Change Text Direction** button on the Text Box toolbar two times. 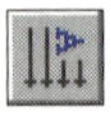

10. Key today's date.

11. You do not need to save the document, but leave it open for the next Step-by-Step.

Did You Know?

After you have clicked the **Text Box** button, if you just point to a single spot in your document and click, a text box will appear—the default size is 1 inch wide and 1 inch high. This is also true for inserting rectangles and circles. Remember that you cannot insert text in these objects without adding a text box inside of them.

Computer Concepts

When you click inside a text box, the text box displays a cross-hatched border. If you click directly on the text box border, the cross-hatched design will change to dots indicating that the text box is selected.

Hot Tip

To delete a text box, click the cross-hatched border until it turns into a border of small dots. Then press **Delete**.

Use AutoShapes to Create Objects

The AutoShape feature in Word enables you to create a variety of predesigned drawing objects. Stars, arrows, shapes, and callouts are among the AutoShape designs from which you can choose.

Create an AutoShape

You create an AutoShape the same way you create other drawing objects. Select the AutoShape that you want to draw. The pointer changes to a crosshair which you drag to the desired size of the AutoShape. When you create a callout, the AutoShape is automatically formatted as a text box so you can add text inside the object. You can resize and reposition AutoShapes in the same way you change the size and position of pictures and drawing objects.

STEP-BY-STEP 6.11

-2.2.13-2

1. Click the **AutoShapes** button on the Drawing toolbar. Select **Block Arrows** in the submenu, then select the first arrow option (**Right Arrow**).
2. Position the crosshair anywhere on the screen and drag it up and to the right to create the AutoShape object.
3. Point to the **AutoShape** arrow and right-click. Select **Add text** in the shortcut menu. An insertion point displays inside the AutoShape object.
4. Key the name of your school. Click the **Center** button on the Formatting toolbar to center the text.
5. If the AutoShape arrow is too small to display all of the text, drag a sizing handle on the corner or side of the AutoShape to make the arrow bigger. If the AutoShape arrow is too big, drag a sizing handle to eliminate the excess white space.
6. With the AutoShape arrow still selected, fill the object with any color you choose.
7. With the arrow still selected, position it in a different location in the document.
8. Click on the **AutoShapes** button and select **Callouts** in the submenu. Select the second option in the second row (**Line Callout 2**).
9. Position the crosshair anywhere in the document where there is space to create the callout. Drag to create the desired size for your callout object.
10. Key your address inside the callout box.
11. If the callout box is too small to display all of the text, drag a sizing handle to make the box bigger. If the callout box is too high or too wide, drag a sizing handle to eliminate the excess white space. You do not need to save this document, but leave it open for the next Step-by-Step.

Use Help to Learn How to Change an AutoShape

You decide you want the AutoShape arrow you drew to point in the opposite direction. Word makes it easy to change the AutoShape without creating a new AutoShape.

STEP-BY-STEP 6.12

1. If necessary, display the Office Assistant by opening the **Help** menu and choose **Show the Office Assistant**.
2. Click on the **Office Assistant**, key **autoshape**, and press **Enter**.
3. Click on **Change a shape to another shape**.
4. Read the information at the right. Leave the Help screen open so you can refer to it if needed as you work.
5. Change the AutoShape arrow to a left-pointing arrow. Close the Help screen when you are done changing the AutoShape.
6. You do not need to save this document, but leave it open for the next Step-by-Step.

Resize the Drawing Canvas

The drawing canvas is especially helpful if your drawing contains several shapes because it keeps your shapes together as one object. Now you will practice resizing the drawing canvas and using the drawing canvas to scale your drawing.

STEP-BY-STEP 6.13

1. If necessary, click in the center of the Drawing Canvas to display the toolbar shown in Figure 6-16. (*Hint:* If the toolbar does not display, right-click in the center of the Drawing Canvas and choose **Show Drawing Canvas Toolbar** in the shortcut menu.)

FIGURE 6-16
Drawing Canvas toolbar

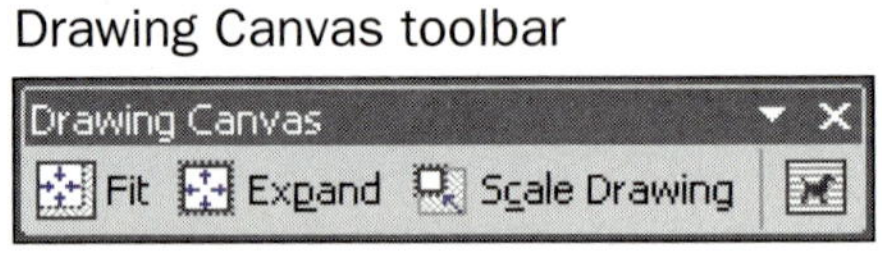

2. Drag one of the sizing handles to resize the drawing canvas. For example, drag a marker inward to eliminate excess white space around the drawing objects.
3. Click the **Fit** button on the Drawing Canvas toolbar. The boundary area of the drawing canvas automatically adjusts to fit the drawing objects and all excess space is eliminated.
4. Click the **Expand** button. The drawing canvas is enlarged in increments each time you click the expand button.

STEP-BY-STEP 6.13 Continued

5. Click the **Scale Drawing** button. The boundary of the drawing canvas changes to display eight sizing handles. Drag a corner handle to resize the drawing canvas just as you would resize a drawing object or a picture. The drawing objects are resized as a unit.
6. Click the **Text Wrapping** button on the Drawing Canvas toolbar and select the **Square** option. The text-wrapping format is applied to the canvas just as it is applied to any drawing object. You can reposition the drawing canvas, and all the objects will move as a unit.
7. Close the document without saving the changes.

IC³ 2-1.2.7-2

Templates

Every Word document is based on a template. A ***template*** is a file that contains document, paragraph, and character formats for documents that you create frequently. The template saves all standard text and formatting choices so all you need to do is enter the variable text. This can greatly increase the speed and efficiency of your work since you do not need to spend time setting up the details of the page. It can also increase the quality of your work since it can ensure that all documents you produce have the same settings and formats.

The default settings for the "blank" or new document margins and fonts are stored in this template. Depending on your Word installation, many types of document templates may be available to you.

IC³

STEP-BY-STEP 6.14

1. Open a new document in Word.
2. Click **New** on the File menu. This opens the New Document task pane.

2-1.2.7-1

3. In the New from template section, click **General Templates**.
4. In the Templates dialog box, switch to the **Letters & Faxes** tab, then select **Contemporary Letter** and click **OK**. This opens a new document that is already formatted in a letter style that has areas in which you can click to enter information.
5. Click in the upper right corner and enter your address.
6. Highlight *Company Name Here* and key a company name.
7. Click in the area below the date and key the following address:

   Josh O'Brien
   5020 Balsam Court
   Endicott, NY 13760

STEP-BY-STEP 6.14 Continued

8. Select **Sir or Madam** in the salutation line and key **Josh**.
9. Select the paragraph in the body of the letter and key **Thank you so much for agreeing to meet with me on September 30. I am really looking forward to discussing the possibility of combining our two businesses. I think we could make a great team!**
10. Click the line below *Sincerely* and key your name.
11. Click the line for your job title and press the **Delete** key.
12. Save your document as **Merger Letter**. Close the document, but leave Word open for the next Step-by-Step.

IC3 2-2.1.10-1

Styles

Another way in which you can quickly and easily change the appearance of a section of text is to apply a style. A ***style*** is a set of formatting characteristics that you can apply to text, tables, and lists in your document. When you apply a style, you apply a whole group of formats in one simple step.

For example, instead of taking three separate steps to format your title as 14 pt, Arial, bold, and center-aligned, you can achieve the same result in one step by applying a title style.

There are four general types of styles you can create and apply:

- A paragraph style controls all aspects of a paragraph's appearance, such as text alignment, tab stops, line spacing, and borders, and can include character formatting.
- A character style affects selected text within a paragraph, such as the font and size of text, and bold and italic formats.
- A table style provides a consistent look to borders, shading, alignment, and fonts in tables.
- A list style applies similar alignment, numbering or bullet characters, and fonts to lists.

You can create, view, and reapply styles from the Styles and Formatting task pane. Direct formatting that you apply is also stored in this pane so that you can quickly reapply it.

Styles are also included in templates. The blank document template contains a set of styles already created for you. You can also create your own styles and include them in a template. As you work in the document based upon that template, all of the styles associated with that template will then be available to you. This again can ensure consistency across multiple documents.

Did You Know?

All of the documents that were written to create this entire text were created by using a template containing a specific set of styles.

IC3

STEP-BY-STEP 6.15

1. Open a new blank document.

2. Open the **Format** menu and select **Styles and Formatting** to open the Styles and Formatting task pane. Note the styles that are already available to you.

2-2.1.10-2

3. In the Styles and Formatting task pane, click **New Style**.

4. In the Name box, key **TX**.

5. In the Style type box, select **Paragraph** if necessary.

6. In the Style based on box, select **Body Text** from the drop-down menu.

7. In the Style for following paragraph box, note that TX has already been selected. The style you are creating is the default style for the following paragraph. If this were a heading, you would likely want the following paragraph to be a paragraph style.

8. In the Formatting section, change the font style from Times New Roman to **Arial**. Leave all of the other Formatting options set as they are (based on the Body Text style). Click **OK**.

9. Key today's date in your document and press **Enter**.

2-2.1.10-3

10. Select **TX** from the Styles and Formatting task pane and key **This is an example of what you can do with a style.** Press **Enter**. (Note that the new paragraph is automatically formatted in the TX style.) You do not need to save your work, but leave the document open for the next Step-by-Step.

> **Hot Tip**
>
> For Help on an option, click the question mark, and then click the option.

> **Did You Know?**
>
> By selecting the **Add to template** check box in the New Style dialog box, the style you create will always be available with this template.

> **Hot Tip**
>
> If you want to use text that you've already formatted as the basis of a list style, paragraph style, or character style, select it, and then base the new style on the formatting and other properties applied to the selected text.

IC3

Themes

2-2.1.11-1

A ***theme*** is a way to maintain a consistent design in your document with elements such as fonts, graphics, colors, and backgrounds. Microsoft Office provides many preset themes that will give your documents a professional look. A theme can be applied to all pages or just to selected pages. If desired, you can apply different themes to each page in your document—although this is not typically done, for a theme brings uniformity and consistency to your document. If you apply a theme to all the pages in a document, then the theme is also applied to new pages as you create them. You can change the theme at any time and in any view. However, to apply a theme, the document must be displayed in the Normal view.

STEP-BY-STEP 6.16

2-2.1.11-2

1. With the document you created in the previous Step-by-Step open, open the **Format** menu and select **Theme**.

2. In the Theme dialog box, select **Spiral** from the Choose a Theme list box.

3. Click **OK** in the Theme dialog box. The theme is applied to your document. Note the many additional styles that have been added to the Styles and Formatting text box. Like a template, a theme has associated styles. You do not need to save your document, but leave it open for the next Step-by-Step.

Did You Know?

As you select different themes in the Theme dialog box the preview pane on the right will show examples of what the theme will look like in the document.

AutoComplete and AutoText

2-2.1.13-1

By now you have undoubtedly encountered Word's AutoComplete feature. This feature suggests the spelling for frequently used words and phrases. AutoComplete will fill in days of the week, months, salutations, and complimentary closings commonly used in letters. As you begin to key the first few characters of these frequently used words, Word suggest the entire spelling in a box on the screen (often referred to as a ScreenTip). You can accept the suggested spelling by pressing Enter. If you do not wish to accept the suggested spelling, continue keying and the Screen Tip will disappear.

What can you do about words or phrases that are common to your documents but are not included in the AutoComplete set of words? For this, Word provides AutoText. With AutoText you can create your own text entries which are then added to the AutoComplete set of words.

Note

AutoText entries must be at least five characters long if you want to insert the entry by using AutoComplete.

STEP-BY-STEP 6.17

1. With the document you created in the previous Step-by-Step open, open the **Tools** menu and select **AutoCorrect Options**.

2. Switch to the **AutoText** tab.

2-2.1.13-2 3. In the Enter AutoText entries here text box, key your full name.

4. Click **Add** and then click **OK**.

2-2.1.13-3 5. In the open document, begin to key your first name. After you have keyed the fourth letter in your name, the Screen Tip with your complete name will appear. Press **Enter** to accept the AutoComplete entry.

6. Press **Enter** to begin a new paragraph. Key the name of a company.

STEP-BY-STEP 6.17 Continued

7. Select the entire name of the company. Open the **Insert** menu, point to AutoText and select **New**.

8. In the Create AutoText dialog box, accept the name Word proposes or key a new one. (If you plan to insert the entry by using AutoComplete, make sure the name contains at least four characters because Word inserts an entry only after four characters have been typed.) Click **OK**.

9. Close the document without saving the changes.

Hot Tip

To store paragraph formatting with the entry, include the paragraph mark in the selection.

SUMMARY

In this lesson, you learned:

- Text can be arranged in a variety of multicolumn formats, all within the same document.
- Clip art and other pictures help to enhance the appearance and effectiveness of a document.
- When you format a picture for text wrapping, you can position the graphic anywhere on the page by dragging it to a new position.
- Borders and shading are also important tools for desktop publishing. You can choose from a variety of options for line styles, colors, and shading effects.
- WordArt enables you to convert text to a graphic. WordArt objects can be positioned and resized the same as pictures.
- You can create your own artwork using the drawing tools.
- Text boxes enable you to add text to your artwork. The text box can be resized and positioned the same as drawing objects. You can also format the text within the box.
- AutoShapes and callout designs help you make a professional-looking document.
- The drawing canvas helps you arrange, position, and resize your drawing objects. You can format and move the drawing canvas just as you format other objects.
- Microsoft Office features such as templates, styles, and themes can all be combined to increase the speed, efficiency, and quality of your work.
- AutoText can make entering repetitive phrases simple and easy.

VOCABULARY *Review*

Define the following terms:

Banner	Drawing objects	Template
Clip art	Graphics	Text box
Crop	Hard column break	Theme
Desktop publishing	Sizing handles	Thumbnails
Drawing canvas	Style	

REVIEW *Questions*

TRUE/FALSE

Circle T if the statement is true or F if the statement is false.

T F 1. When you create a document with columns, you can format the document's heading text in a single-column banner.

T F 2. Drawing objects are predrawn artwork ready to insert in a document.

T F 3. When you size a graphic proportionally, you change all the dimensions approximately equally.

T F 4. You will find drawing tools on the Formatting toolbar.

T F 5. To insert an AutoShape, select AutoShape on the Tools menu.

FILL IN THE BLANK

Complete the following sentences by writing the correct word or words in the blanks provided.

1. The process of using a computer to combine text and graphics is called ________.
2. ________ are small squares on the border of a graphic that let you know it is selected.
3. When you ________ a graphic, you remove a part of the graphic that you don't want to show.
4. You can select a text-wrapping option from the ________ toolbar.
5. The ________ helps you arrange and size your drawing objects.

PROJECTS

PROJECT 6-1

1. Open **Project6-1** from the data files. Save the document as **Garden News** followed by your initials.
2. Select the first two lines in the document. Apply a green shading to the selected headings. If necessary, select the text and change the font color to white. Note that if you choose a dark color, Word will automatically change the font color so it will display against the dark shading.
3. Position the insertion point in the *Fall Gardening* heading. Insert a 2 ¼-point border below the heading. Use the **Repeat** command to insert borders below the other two headings.
4. Position the insertion point at the beginning of the second paragraph below the *Fall Gardening* heading. Insert a clip art picture that relates to autumn. Resize the picture proportionately so it is about 1½ inches tall. Choose an appropriate text-wrapping option. Adjust the position of the picture so that the top of the picture lines up with the first line of the second paragraph.
5. Select the text (but not the blank line above the text) that describes the Annual Tree Sale. Apply a yellow shading to the selected text.
6. Position the insertion point at the beginning of the second paragraph under the *Gardening Today Spotlight* heading and insert the picture file **flower** from your data files. Crop the white space on the right side of the picture. Resize the picture to approximately 1 ½ inches high and 1 inch wide.
7. Apply a square text-wrapping option to the new picture. Move the picture to the right side of the page and position it so the top of the picture lines up with the first line of the second paragraph under the *Gardening Today Spotlight* heading.
8. Select the last paragraph in the document and apply the same green shading you used for the two headings at the top of the document. If necessary, change the font color to white.
9. Save your changes and close the document.

PROJECT 6-2

1. Open **Project6-2** from the data files. Save the document as **Creamery** followed by your initials.
2. Click to the left of the first word in the document. Then use the scroll bar to scroll down to locate the *2.00* price below the description of the *Mocha Delight* coffee. Hold down the **Shift** key and click to the right of the price to select everything in the document except the last paragraph and the blank line above it.
3. Format the selected text in two columns of equal width.
4. If the *THICK LIQUIDS* heading is at the bottom of the first column of text, insert a column break to move it (and any other text below it) to the next column.

5. The first column is now shorter than the second column. To fill up the empty space at the bottom of the first column, insert clip art relating to ice cream or create an appropriate drawing object in this space. Resize and position the graphic as necessary so it attractively fits in the space.

6. Create a WordArt title for the page using the words *The Creamery*. Position the WordArt graphic at the top of the page and center it horizontally. Apply the **Top and Bottom** text-wrap option to force the column text to move below the graphic. Modify the WordArt graphic as desired to change color or other formatting.

7. Save your changes and close the document.

PROJECT 6-3

1. Open a new document. Save it as **Map** followed by your initials.

2. Use the **Line**, **Rectangle**, and **Fill Color** drawing tools to create the lines and box illustrated in Figure 6-17. The Rulers on the edges of the screen are displayed in the figure to help you judge the size and position of the objects.

FIGURE 6-17
Drawing objects for Project 6-3

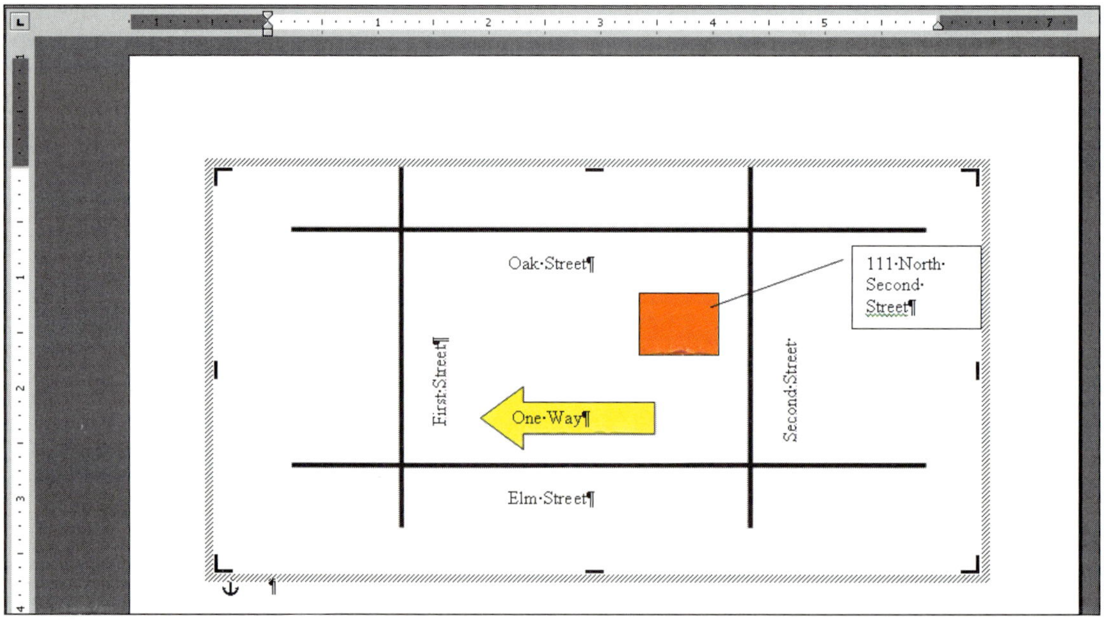

3. Fill the rectangle with the bright red color.

4. Create four text boxes for the street names:
   A. To create the First Street and Second Street text boxes, draw tall, narrow boxes. Then use the **Text Direction** button on the Text Box toolbar to change the direction of text in the text box.
   B. Remove the borders from the text boxes.

5. Use an **AutoShape** to create the One Way arrow in the map. Fill the AutoShape with the bright yellow color.

6. Create the callout that points out the exact address of the red rectangle.
7. Rescale the drawing object by resizing the drawing canvas so that the map fills the width of the page. Then apply the **Square** text-wrapping format and position the map in the center of the page horizontally.
8. Save your changes and close the document.

WEB PROJECT

Your aunt is a keen gardener who has mentioned more than once a fascination with "black" tulips. Use an Internet search tool to locate retail gardening sites on the Web that specialize in tulip bulbs. Gather information about the very dark tulip bulbs they call black tulips. Using the tools you learned about in this lesson (such as columns, banner headings, WordArt, and graphic images), create a flyer to promote this unique tulip bulb.

TEAMWORK PROJECT

In this lesson, you have learned some desktop publishing basics. Put your knowledge into practice by designing a newsletter for your class, school, or workplace. Follow these steps:

1. The class should divide into three or four groups.
2. Each group should brainstorm ideas for the layout of the newsletter, appropriate graphics, and what kinds of stories to use in the newsletter. Use features you have learned about in this lesson, such as borders, shading, columns, and WordArt, to make your newsletter design visually interesting and easy to read.
3. Each group should create a sample newsletter using its design. You need not write a number of real stories to fill up the spaces. Instead, write one paragraph of sample text and copy it as many times as necessary to show how text will appear in the newsletter.
4. As a class, compare the designs and discuss the strengths and weaknesses of each.

CRITICAL *Thinking*

ACTIVITY 6-1

You have created a drawing that contains a number of drawing objects. Although you have worked as carefully as you can, you cannot place some of the objects as precisely as you would like. Is there any way to move the objects in small increments without dragging them using the mouse? Is there any way to specify that your drawing object be positioned in a specific location? You would also like to align some of the objects precisely with one another. Is there any way to specify this kind of alignment for drawing objects?

Use the Help system in Word to find answers to these questions. Write a brief summary of what you learn.

LESSON 7

WORKING WITH POWERPOINT PRESENTATIONS

OBJECTIVES

Upon completion of this lesson, you should be able to:

- Open and save an existing presentation.
- Identify the parts of the PowerPoint screen.
- Navigate through a presentation.
- Apply a design template.
- Add slides.
- Add and edit text.
- Delete, copy, and rearrange slides.
- Use Help to get assistance.
- View the presentation in full-screen view.

Estimated Time: 1 hour

VOCABULARY

Clipboard
Normal view
Placeholders
Slide design
Slide layout
Slide Show view
Slide Sorter view

PowerPoint helps you create, edit, and manipulate professional-looking slides, transparencies, or on-screen presentations. You can also use PowerPoint to create speaker's notes and audience handouts. The presentations you create can include text, drawing objects, clip art, pictures, tables, charts, sound, and video clips.

Creating a presentation may seem like an overwhelming task, but PowerPoint provides many features that make that task easy and fun.

Open and Save an Existing Presentation

When you first start PowerPoint, the New Presentation task pane is displayed at the right. This task pane provides several options for opening an existing presentation or for creating a new presentation. The most recently opened presentations are displayed at the top of the task pane, but you can also search for additional files by using the open command.

STEP-BY-STEP 7.1

1. Start PowerPoint. A blank slide will open and a task pane similar to the one shown in Figure 7-1 is displayed.

2-1.2.1-1

FIGURE 7-1
New Presentation task pane

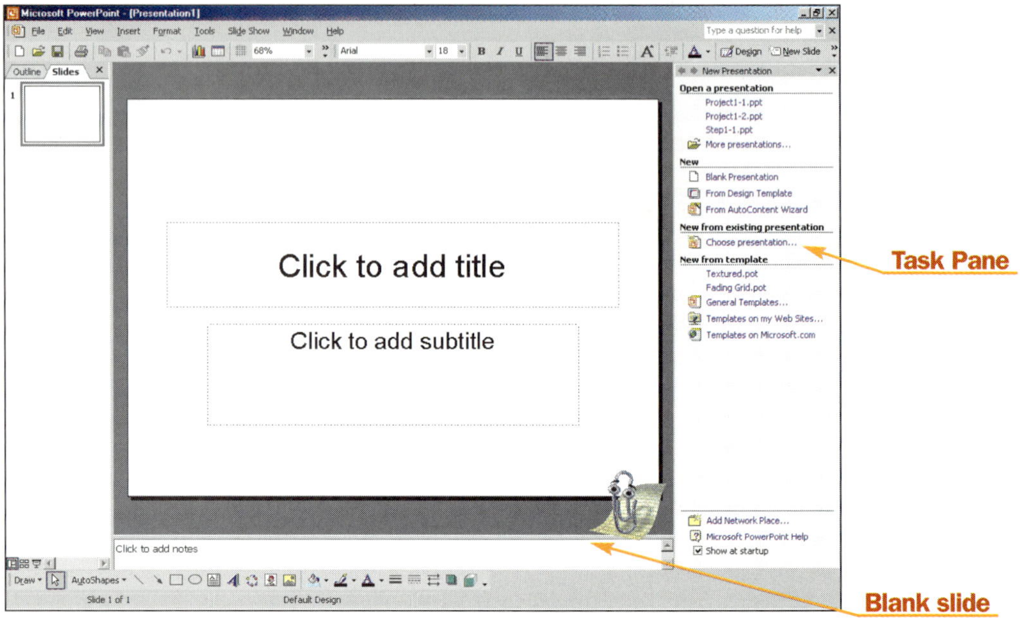

2. Under *Open a presentation* in the task pane, click the option **More presentations** to display the Open dialog box shown in Figure 7-2. Do not be concerned that your screen does not match the figure exactly.

FIGURE 7-2
Open dialog box

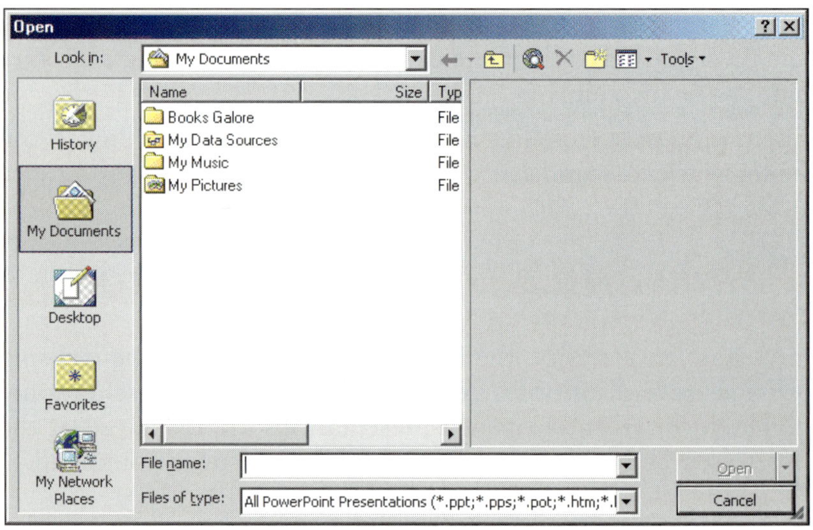

3. Locate and select the file **Step7-1** from the data files. Click **Open**.

STEP-BY-STEP 7.1 Continued

4. Save the presentation as **The 3Rs** followed by your initials. Leave the presentation open for the next Step-by-Step.

> **Did You Know?**
>
> You can save a presentation so it can be viewed using a Web browser. To save the presentation in HTML format, open the **File** menu and choose **Save as Web Page**.

Identify the Parts of the PowerPoint Screen

PowerPoint offers three different ways to view your presentation. When you first open a presentation, it will be displayed in one of three views. ***Normal view***, shown in Figure 7-3, displays three panes: the Outline pane, the Slide pane, and the Notes pane. You use the Outline pane to organize the content of your presentation. You can view the content of your presentation in outline format or in slide format. The Slide pane allows you to see the slide as it will appear in your presentation. You can click in the Notes pane and add notes and information to help you with your presentation.

FIGURE 7-3
Presentation displayed in Normal view

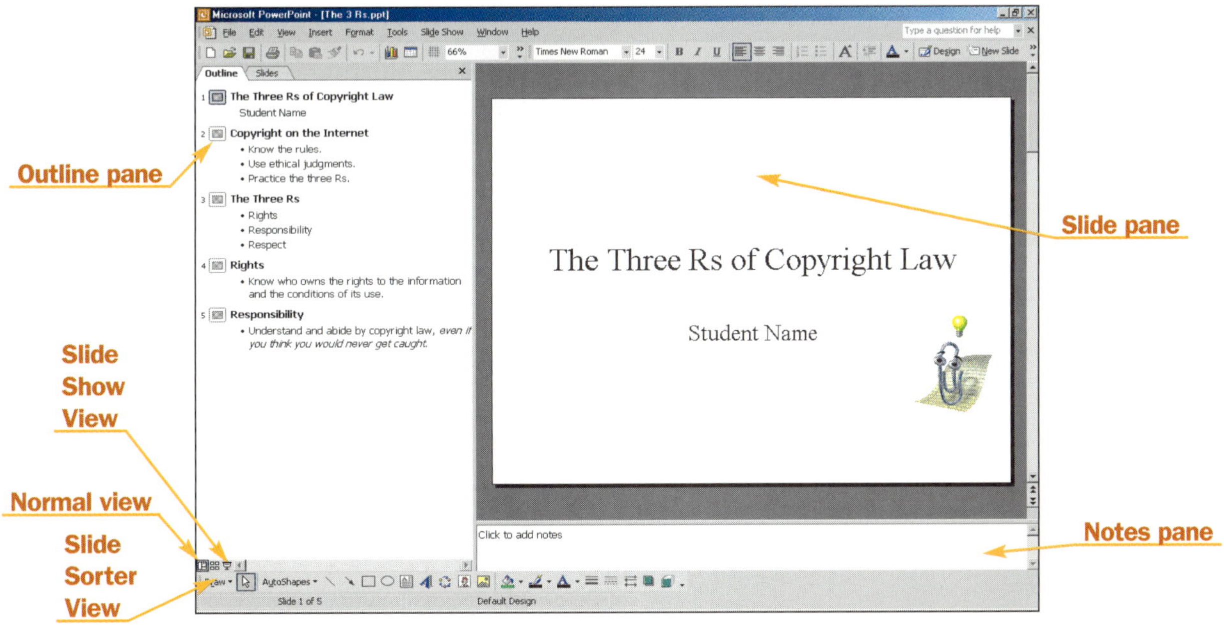

You can change the view by clicking the buttons at the lower left of the PowerPoint window. The other two views are ***Slide Sorter view*** and ***Slide Show view***. Slide Sorter view gives you an overall picture of your presentation by displaying your slides as thumbnails (miniature versions of each of the slides in the presentation). Slide Sorter view makes it easy to add and delete slides and change the order of the slides. In Slide Show view, the current slide fills the whole computer screen. You use this view when you present the show to your audience.

> **Hot Tip**
>
> To adjust the size of the panes in Normal view, point to the pane borders and, when the pointer changes to a double-headed arrow, drag the pane border.

STEP-BY-STEP 7.2

1. Compare your screen to Figure 7-3 and take time to identify the three panes on the screen. Notice that the current slide displayed in the slide pane is the first of five slides.

2. Look at the contents in the outline pane. If necessary, click the **Outline** tab to display all of the text contained on each of the five slides in the presentation.

3. In the Outline pane, click the **Slides** tab. The display changes to show thumbnail images of the slides.

4. In the Outline pane at the left, click anywhere on the thumbnail for the number 4 slide (*Rights*). The display in the Slide pane changes to show the fourth slide.

5. Click the **Slide Sorter View** button at the bottom of the screen. The display changes to show all the slides in the presentation as shown in Figure 7-4. Notice that the fourth slide has a blue border around it, indicating it is selected.

6. Click the **Normal View** button at the bottom of the screen to return to Normal view. You do not need to save the changes, but do leave the presentation open for the next Step-by-Step.

FIGURE 7-4
Presentation displayed in Slide Sorter view

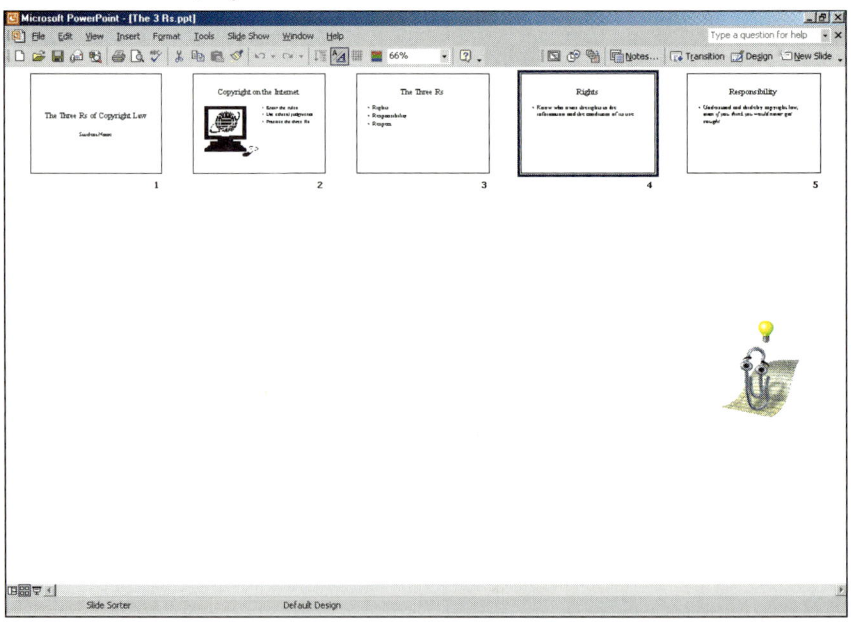

Navigate through a Presentation

You already know that you can move to a different slide by clicking on the slide text in the Outline pane. You can also use the scroll bar or shortcut keys to navigate through a presentation in Normal view.

STEP-BY-STEP 7.3

1. Click the **Next Slide** button at the bottom of the vertical scroll bar on the right. Each time you click the **Next Slide** button, the next slide in the presentation is displayed.

2. Click the **Previous Slide** button at the bottom of the vertical scroll bar. Each time you click the **Previous Slide** button, the previous slide in the presentation is displayed.

3. Press **Ctrl + End** to move to the last slide in the presentation. Notice that each time you move to a different slide, the thumbnail of that slide is selected in the Outline pane.

4. Press **PageUp** to move to the previous slide.

5. Press **PageDown** to move to the next slide.

6. Press **Ctrl + Home** to move to the first slide in the presentation.

7. Drag the scroll box down the vertical scroll bar. As you drag the box, a label to the left of the scroll bar shows the title and number of the slide. When you see *Slide: 3 of 5 The Three Rs*, as shown in Figure 7-5, release the mouse button. The third slide of the presentation is displayed.

8. Leave the presentation open for the next Step-by-Step.

> **Computer Concepts**
>
> If the Outline tab is selected in the Outline pane, the slide icon next to the slide number in the Outline pane changes to gray to indicate the current slide.

> **Speech Recognition**
>
> If your computer has speech recognition capability, enable the Command mode and say the commands to navigate through the presentation.

FIGURE 7-5
Slide label on scroll bar

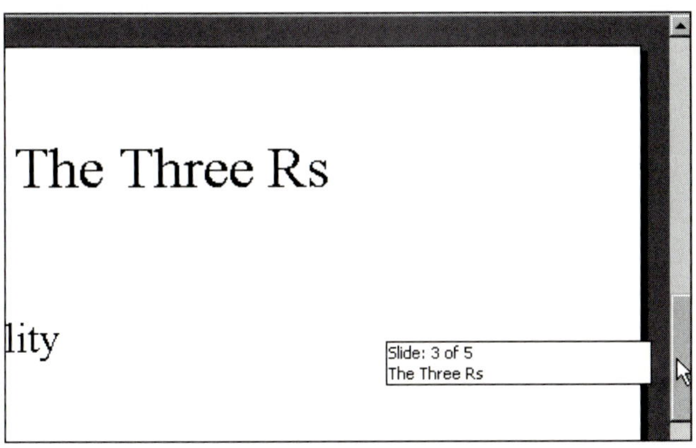

Apply a Design Template

You can easily give your presentation a professional look by applying a slide design. A ***slide design*** specifies a color scheme, text format, backgrounds, bullet styles, and graphics for all the slides in the presentation. PowerPoint provides several professionally designed templates from which you can choose. Each design template has a specific look and feel. When you apply a design template, each slide in the presentation has a consistent look. However, the content of your slides does not change.

Computer Concepts

The design template you choose for your presentation, if possible, should reflect the theme of the presentation topic. Moreover, the design should not detract from the message you want to deliver.

To apply a slide design template, open the Format menu and choose Slide Design. The Slide Design task pane will display, showing the template currently used in this presentation, recently used designs, and designs that are available for use.

If you like a slide design but you don't like the colors used in the design, you can easily change the color scheme of the design. PowerPoint offers several standard color schemes for each slide design. You can apply a new color scheme to all the slides or just to selected slides.

STEP-BY-STEP 7.4

1. Open the **Format** menu and choose **Slide Design**. The Slide Design task pane shown in Figure 7-6 is displayed at the right of your screen.

2. Under *Available For Use*, scroll down to view all the thumbnails for the available designs. Then, locate and click the design titled **Balance**. (*Hint:* The design has a brown background. When you point to the thumbnail of the slide design, a ScreenTip will display with the design name. The designs are organized alphabetically.) The slide design is applied to all slides and the new design appears in the Slide pane.

Speech Recognition

If your computer has speech recognition capability, enable the Command mode and say the commands to open the Slide Design task pane.

Hot Tip

You can apply a different slide design at any time to change the look of your presentation.

STEP-BY-STEP 7.4 Continued

FIGURE 7-6
Slide Design task pane

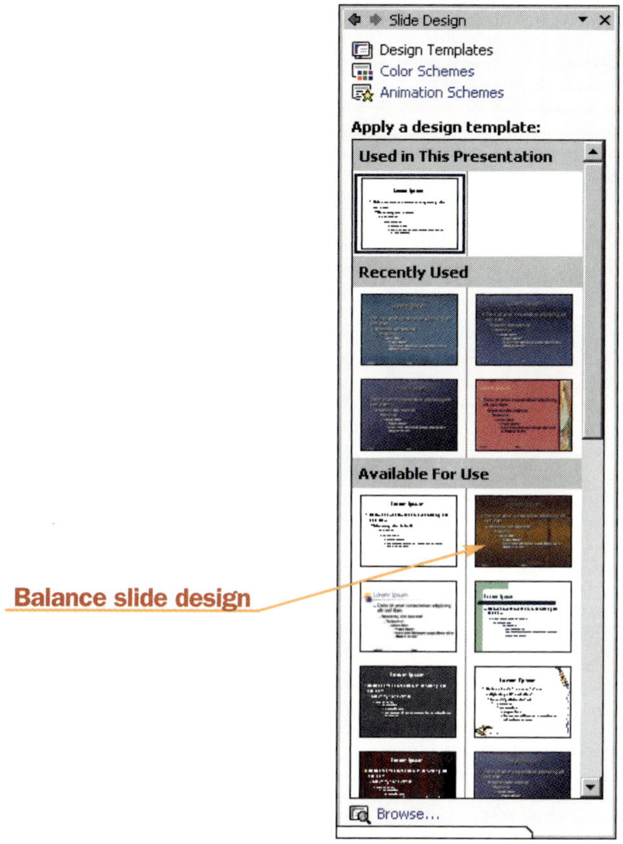

3. At the top of the task pane, click the link **Color Schemes**. Several color schemes are displayed in the task pane as shown in Figure 7-7.

STEP-BY-STEP 7.4 Continued

FIGURE 7-7
Task pane with color scheme options

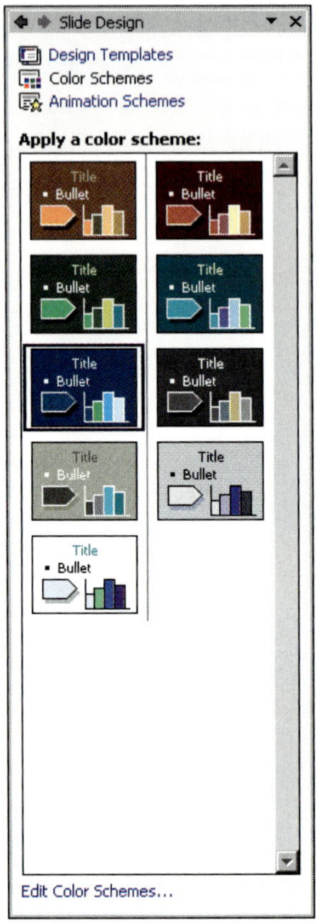

4. Click the down arrow on the right side of the first option. A drop-down menu with three options displays. Select **Show Large Previews**.

5. Use the scroll bar to view the color scheme options. Click some of the options to view the different color schemes. The new colors are applied to all the slides in the presentation, and the new colors appear in the Slide pane and in the Outline pane. Notice that not only does the background color change, but the text color also changes.

Extra Challenge

If you'd like to create your own color scheme, click the **Edit Color Schemes** link at the bottom of the Slide Design task pane. The Edit Color Scheme dialog box will display. If necessary, click the **Custom** tab, select the item you want to edit (such as Title text or Fills) and then click the **Change Color** button, select the new colors, and click **OK**. When you're done selecting the new colors, click **Apply** in the Edit Color Scheme dialog box.

STEP-BY-STEP 7.4 Continued

6. Select a color scheme that you prefer. Click the down arrow to display the drop-down menu, then select **Apply to All Slides**.

7. Save the changes. Leave the presentation open for the next Step-by-Step.

Add Slides

> **Computer Concepts**
>
> PowerPoint automatically adjusts the layout if you insert items that don't fit the original layout. For example, if you fill a text box with several lines of text and keep entering text, PowerPoint will reduce the font size as needed so all the text will fit inside the text box.

You can add new slides in Normal view or Slide Sorter view. In the next Step-by-Step, you will learn to add slides in both views.

To add a new slide, open the Insert menu and choose New Slide, or click the New Slide button on the Formatting toolbar.

When you add a slide, the design that you have already applied to the presentation is automatically applied to the new slide. The ***slide layout*** used in the previous slide is also applied. The slide layout refers to the way things are arranged on the slide. All but one of the layout options provide placeholders. The ***placeholders*** provide placement guides for adding text, pictures, tables, or charts. The placeholder will not print or display in the actual presentation.

You can resize and move the placeholders on the slide. You can even format the placeholders with fill colors and borders. And, if you do not use a placeholder, you can delete it.

STEP-BY-STEP 7.5

1. Go to the fourth slide in the presentation. (*Hint*: Use the scroll bar or click the #4 slide text in the Outline pane.)

2. Click the **New Slide** button on the Formatting toolbar. A new blank slide is created and placed after slide number 4. Notice that the Outline pane is updated to show that the new slide has been added.

3. Notice that the Slide Layout task pane shown in Figure 7-8 is now displayed at the right of your screen. The new blank slide is formatted with the same layout that was used for the number 4 slide. This layout is also selected under *Text Layouts* in the task pane. The ScreenTip in the task pane describes this layout as *Title and Text*.

STEP-BY-STEP 7.5 Continued

FIGURE 7-8
Slide Layout task pane

4. Select the **Title and 2 Column Text** option in the task pane. (*Hint:* It is directly to the right of the currently selected layout. When you point to the option, the ScreenTip will show the option name.) The slide layout for the new slide will change to display a text box for a title with two columns for text below.

5. Switch to Slide Sorter view. (*Hint:* Click the **Slide Sorter View** button at the bottom left corner of the screen.) Notice the new blank number 5 slide.

6. Click between slides number 3 and number 4 to position the insertion point between the two slides. The insertion point will be displayed as a long vertical line between the two slides.

7. Click the **New Slide** button on the toolbar. A new slide is created. You now have a total of seven slides in your presentation.

8. Save the changes and leave the presentation open for the next Step-by-Step.

Computer Concepts

Some placeholders for text automatically format a bullet at the beginning of each paragraph. The bullet color and symbol are formatted based on the design template. To remove the bullet, position the insertion point in the paragraph containing the bullet, and then click the **Bullet** button on the Formatting toolbar.

Add and Edit Text

To add text to a slide or to edit a slide, you must display the slide in Normal view. If the slide contains a placeholder for text, you simply click inside the placeholder and enter the text. If the slide does not have a placeholder for text, you can easily change the slide layout to accommodate text. When you add and edit text, the contents in the Outline pane are automatically updated.

STEP-BY-STEP 7.6

1. Double-click slide number **4** to open it in Normal view so you can add text. Notice that in the Outline pane, the #4 slide is selected. However, there is no text displayed for slide #4 or #6.
2. Click in the placeholder at the top of the slide that says *Click to add title*. Key **Respect**.
3. Click in the next placeholder that says *Click to add text* and key **Respect the people who invested the time and energy to develop and report the information**.
4. Click outside the placeholder to deselect it. Then press **Ctrl + Home** to move to the first slide.
5. Position the insertion point in front of the word *of* in the title. Press **Enter** to move the text to the next line.
6. Click **Student Name** to move to that placeholder. Select the words **Student Name** and replace the words with your first and last names.
7. Save the changes and leave the presentation open for the next Step-by-Step.

Speech Recognition

If your computer has speech recognition capability, click in the placeholder, enable Dictation mode, and dictate the text for the slides.

Computer Concepts

To remove a slide in Normal view, you must open the **Edit** menu and choose **Delete Slide**. To delete a slide in the Outline pane, click the slide icon to the right of the slide number to select the slide number and its contents, then press **Delete**.

Delete, Copy, and Rearrange Slides

You can delete slides in Normal view or Slide Sorter view. It is easy to delete multiple slides in Slide Sorter view, and this view also makes it easy to copy slides and rearrange the order of slides. You can use the Cut, Copy, and Paste commands to copy or move slides, or you can also use drag-and-drop editing.

When you use the Cut, Copy, and Paste commands, PowerPoint stores the slide content and design in the Clipboard. The ***Clipboard*** is a temporary storage place in your computer's memory. You send selected slides to the Clipboard by using the Cut or Copy commands. Then you can retrieve those contents by using the Paste command. The contents remain in the Clipboard until you copy or paste something new, or when you turn off your computer. You can paste Clipboard items as many times as you want.

Hot Tip

The shortcut keys for the Cut command are **Ctrl + X**. The shortcut keys for the Copy command are **Ctrl + C**. The shortcut keys for the Paste command are **Ctrl + V**. These are the same shortcut keys for performing these functions in other Microsoft Office applications.

Instead of using the Cut and Paste commands, you can rearrange one or more slides by using drag-and-drop editing. Select the slide(s) to be moved, then drag the slide(s) to the new location. When you release the mouse button, the slide(s) will be repositioned at the new location of the insertion point.

STEP-BY-STEP 7.7

1. Switch to Slide Sorter view.
2. Click slide number **6** to select it. Then press **Delete**. The slide is removed and the next slide numbers are revised to reflect the change.
3. Click slide number **3** to select it. Click the **Copy** button on the Standard toolbar. The slide content and design are copied to the Office Clipboard.
4. Position the insertion point after slide #6. Click the **Paste** button on the Standard toolbar.
5. The slides are out of order. The #4 slide should follow slide #6. Select the #4 slide and click the **Cut** button on the Standard toolbar. The #4 slide is removed and all subsequent slides are renumbered.
6. Position the insertion point between slide #5 and slide #6, then click the **Paste** button. The slides are rearranged and automatically renumbered.
7. Save the changes and leave the presentation open for the next Step-by-Step.

Hot Tip

You can select multiple slides before you move, copy, or delete. To select multiple slides in Slide Sorter view, click the first slide, hold down the **Ctrl** key, and click each additional slide to be included in the selection. Or, you can select a series of slides by clicking the first slide in the series and then holding down the **Shift** key while clicking the last slide in the series. All slides between and including the two slides you clicked will be selected.

Computer Concepts

If you do not know the function of a toolbar button, rest the mouse pointer on the button, but do not click it. After a few seconds, the name of the function appears in a ScreenTip. If you want more information about an option in a dialog box, click the **Help** button in the title bar of the dialog box, then click the option about which you want to display a ScreenTip.

Use Help to Learn How to Change the Slide Layout

As in other Office XP applications, the Office Assistant is available to assist you as you work in PowerPoint. The Office Assistant anticipates when you might need help, and it offers tips, solutions, instructions, and examples to help you work more efficiently.

If you have a specific question, you can go to the Office Assistant to search for help. To access Help for PowerPoint, you must have the application open. You can then ask the Office Assistant for information. If the Office Assistant is not displayed, you can access the tips, instructions, and examples in the Help menu.

STEP-BY-STEP 7.8

1. If the Office Assistant is not displayed on the screen, open the **Help** menu and choose **Show the Office Assistant**.
2. Click the **Office Assistant**. An Office Assistant dialog box similar to Figure 7-9 appears. Your dialog box will look different depending on the information last requested of the Office Assistant.

FIGURE 7-9
The Office Assistant dialog box

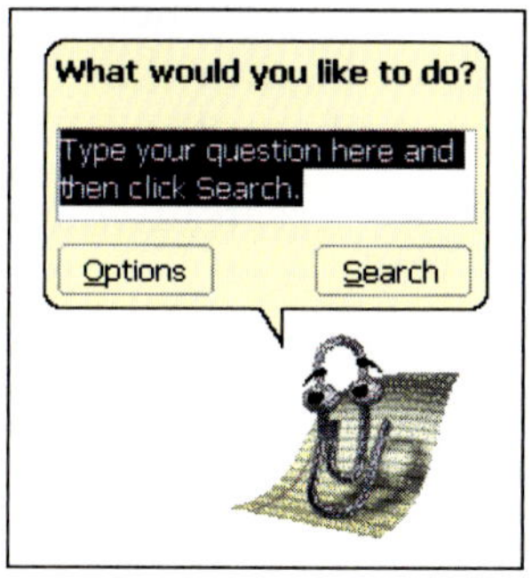

3. The text in the text box under *What would you like to do?* should already be selected. Key the following search text: **change slide layout**. As you begin to enter the new text, the selected text disappears.
4. Click **Search**. A list of topics that provide related information is displayed.
5. Click the topic **Apply a slide layout**. Read the information about the topic which displays in the right pane of the Help window.
6. Click the link **task pane**. A definition of the term *task pane* displays in a box on the screen. Click the link again to hide the definition.
7. Click the **PowerPoint** button in the taskbar to switch to the presentation or click any visible part of the PowerPoint window to make it the active window.
8. Go to the Normal view of slide #2 by either double-clicking it or by selecting it and then choosing **Normal view**.

Hot Tip

Sometimes the Office Assistant gets in the way. To move the Office Assistant, simply drag it to a new location on the screen.

STEP-BY-STEP 7.8 Continued

9. Using the information provided in the Help screen, change the layout of the slide so that the text is on the left side of the slide and the clip art image is on the right. (*Hint:* Click the slide layout to the left of the current design. The ScreenTip displays *Text & Clip Art*.)

10. Do not be concerned that the clip art image is now smaller. You will learn about resizing graphics in the next lesson. Save the changes and close the Help screen.

Did You Know?

You can change the way the Office Assistant provides help by right-clicking the **Office Assistant**, choosing **Options**, selecting the **Options** tab, and then making selections.

View the Presentation

Now that you have formatted and sequenced the slides in your presentation, you probably want to see what it will look like for your audience. You can see how it will look in full-screen view by choosing Slide Show View. As you view the presentation, you can click the left mouse button or press the spacebar to advance to the next file. You can also use the arrow keys or the PageUp and PageDown keys on the keyboard to advance forward or backward.

Computer Concepts

To display your speaker notes as you run the presentation, right click the screen in Slide Show view and then choose **Speaker Notes**.

When you move your mouse across the screen in Slide Show view, an arrow appears on the screen so you can point out parts of the slide. A triangle is displayed in the bottom left corner of the screen. When you click this triangle, a menu is displayed. Choosing Pen from this menu changes the mouse pointer to a pen. You can then draw or write on the screen. The pen marks overlay the slide and are temporary. They are automatically erased when you advance to the next slide.

STEP-BY-STEP 7.9

1. Go to slide #1 in Normal view.

2. Click the **Slide Show View** button in the lower left corner, just above the status bar. The first slide shows in full-screen view.

3. Click the left mouse button to advance to the next slide.

4. Explore using the arrow keys and the PageUp and PageDown keys to move from slide to slide.

Hot Tip

You can start the slide show on any slide by displaying or selecting the slide you want to begin with before switching to Slide Show view.

STEP-BY-STEP 7.9 Continued

5. Move the mouse pointer across the screen. When the triangle appears in the lower left corner, click it to display a menu. Choose **Pointer Options**, then choose **Pen**. Experiment writing on the screen with the pen, then advance to the next slide.

6. To end the slide show, press **Esc**. The current slide will display in Normal view. If you reach the end of the presentation, you can follow the screen directions and click to exit.

7. Click the application close box at the top right corner of the screen to close the presentation and the application.

Did You Know?

If you don't want a slide to appear when you run the presentation, you can hide the slide. Select the slide in Normal view or Slide Sorter view. Then open the **Slide Show** menu and choose **Hide Slide**. To restore the slide so it does display when you run the presentation, select the slide, open the **Slide Show** menu, and choose **Hide Slide** again to toggle the feature off.

SUMMARY

In this lesson, you learned:

- When you start PowerPoint, you can choose to create a new presentation or open an existing presentation.
- PowerPoint offers three different views to display a presentation. You work in either Normal view or Slide Sorter view as you create and edit your presentation. In Slide Show view, the current slide fills the full computer screen. You use this view when you present the show to your audience.
- In addition to using the Outline pane to move to a different slide, you can also use the scroll bar or shortcut keys to navigate through a presentation in Normal view.
- The slide design automatically formats slides with color schemes, bullet styles, and graphics. The slide design ensures that all slides in a presentation have a consistent look. You can apply a slide design at any time without affecting the contents of the slides.
- You can add a new slide in Normal view or Slide Sorter view. When you add a new slide, you must select a slide layout.
- To add or edit text, the slide must be displayed in Normal view. When you add text or edit text, the slide contents are automatically updated in the Outline pane.
- It is easy to delete, copy, and rearrange slides in Slide Sorter view. You can use the Cut, Copy, and Paste commands, or you can utilize drag-and-drop editing to rearrange the order of the slides.
- The Office Assistant anticipates when you might need help, and it offers tips, solutions, instructions, and examples to help you work more efficiently. If you have a specific question, you can use the Office Assistant to search for help.

Computer Concepts

If the Help screen is still open, it will also close automatically unless you have other Office applications open, in which case the Help screen will not close.

VOCABULARY*Review*

Define the following terms:

Clipboard
Normal view
Placeholders
Slide design
Slide layout
Slide Show view
Slide Sorter view

REVIEW*Questions*

TRUE/FALSE

Circle T if the statement is true or F if the statement is false.

T F 1. You can use the Outline pane to quickly navigate through a presentation.

T F 2. You can add new slides in Slide Show view.

T F 3. To move to the first slide in a presentation, you can press Ctrl + Home.

T F 4. To see your presentation as a slide show, you use Normal view.

T F 5. You can rearrange slides using either the Cut and Paste toolbar buttons or drag-and-drop editing.

FILL IN THE BLANK

Complete the following sentences by writing the correct word or words in the blanks provided.

1. To add text to a slide or to edit a slide, you must display the slide in ________ view.
2. ________ view displays a miniature version of each of the slides in the presentation.
3. A(n) ________ specifies a uniform color scheme, background, bullet style, text format, and graphics for a presentation.
4. ________ provide(s) guides for adding text, pictures, tables, and charts.
5. ________ view allows you to see slides in full view.

PROJECTS

PROJECT 7-1

1. Open **Project7-1** from the data files. Save the presentation as **Gettysburg** followed by your initials.
2. Change to Slide Sorter view. Move slide number 2 to the end of the presentation.
3. Change to Normal view and navigate to the first slide in the presentation.
4. Click in the title placeholder and position the insertion point in front of the word Gettysburg. Key **Battle of** and a space.
5. Click in the subtitle placeholder and key **Three Days in July**.
6. Move to slide number 3 (*Day 2—July 2*). Position the insertion point at the end of the last bullet item and press **Enter**. Key the final bullet point **34,000 Confederates vs. 33,000 Federals engaged.**
7. Choose and apply a slide design to the presentation.
8. Save your changes, view the presentation, and then close the presentation.

PROJECT 7-2

1. Open **Project7-2** from the data files. Save the presentation as **Searching** followed by your initials.
2. Change the color scheme of the current slide design to the scheme in the Color Scheme dialog box that has a purple title.
3. Change the layout of slide number 2 to **Title Only**.
4. Copy slide number 2 and paste the copy after slide number 3. Change the title text on this slide (slide number 4) to **Then, Choose a Tool.**
5. Add a slide at the end of the presentation with the Title and Text layout. In the title placeholder, key the title **Other Resources.**
6. Key the following items in the text placeholder:
   Resource lists
   Guides
   Clearinghouses
   Virtual libraries
7. Delete slide number 7.
8. Save your changes, view the presentation, and then close the presentation.

WEB PROJECT

In this lesson, you worked on a presentation that offered information on copyright law as it applies to using materials on the Internet. Use Web search tools to find out more about copyright violations that can happen when Internet users "borrow" materials from the Internet. What types of violations occur most frequently? What are the penalties for such violations? Add one or more slides to the The 3Rs presentation you worked on in the Step-by-Steps in this lesson to present the information you discover.

TEAMWORK PROJECT

One of the best uses of a PowerPoint presentation is to persuade an audience to adopt a particular point of view. With a partner, explore both sides of a specific issue. Follow these steps:

1. As a class, brainstorm some topic issues of interest to the entire class (such as a proposal for a new community park). Or, your instructor may have a list of issues already prepared.
2. Team members should gather information on the issue from surveys or research and then create a presentation to support their particular points of view.
3. If possible, present the slide shows for each issue and have the group vote on which is the most persuasive.

CRITICAL *Thinking*

ACTIVITY 7-1

You have applied a design template to a presentation. Several of the slides in the presentation need special emphasis so your audience will really pay attention. You wonder if you can change the color scheme for those particular slides. Can you do this in PowerPoint?

Use the Help files in PowerPoint to find the answer. Write a brief summary of what you learn.

LESSON 8

ENHANCING POWERPOINT PRESENTATIONS

OBJECTIVES

Upon completion of this lesson, you should be able to:

- Create a new presentation.
- Use the Slide Finder to copy slides from one presentation to another.
- Format text.
- Use Undo and Redo.
- Insert pictures.
- Check spelling and use AutoCorrect.

Estimated Time: 1 hour

VOCABULARY

Clip Organizer
Font
Points
Select text
Sizing handles

To create an effective presentation, you must consider all the text and graphics you enter on the slides. Changing the color of the text or changing the style for the text can make the slides easier to read. Adding pictures can help communicate your message and help your audience remember the information you present. It is also important, of course, to make sure you do not have any spelling errors in your slides.

Create a New Presentation

You have several options for creating a new presentation in PowerPoint:

- You can create a new blank presentation and apply a design template. The design template provides a preformatted slide design with colors, styles, and layouts. If you want to create a presentation without a preset design and without any existing content, you can create a new blank presentation. You can then apply your own design and slide layouts.
- You can choose the AutoContent Wizard to guide you through a series of questions about the presentation you want to create. Based upon your answers, the Wizard will organize ideas and create a presentation customized from your responses. You will not be instructed to use the AutoContent Wizard to create a presentation in this lesson, but you will have the opportunity to experiment with the feature in the Teamwork Project at the end of this lesson.

- PowerPoint provides several presentations when you choose General Templates in the New Presentation task pane. These presentations already contain content that was previously organized and formatted on slides. You can modify the content to customize the presentation for your needs.
- You can create a new presentation based on an existing presentation. All the slides from the existing presentation are opened in a new document. Save the new presentation with a new filename.

Computer Concepts

PowerPoint provides numerous design templates from which you can choose. Some of the templates are not installed during a typical installation. If you choose a design that is not installed, you may be able to open the design from the application CD.

You will not practice all of the options in this lesson, but you may want to experiment with the features on your own. Regardless of the way you create your presentation, PowerPoint provides placeholders for easy insertion of text, graphics, and other presentation elements.

STEP-BY-STEP 8.1

1. Start PowerPoint. Or, if PowerPoint is already open, display the New Presentation task pane. (*Hint:* Open the **View** menu and choose **Task Pane.** If the task pane is open but not showing the New Presentations options, click the down arrow in the title bar of the task pane and choose **New Presentation**.)
2. Click the link **From Design Template**. The Slide Design task pane is displayed. Select the **Ocean** template.
3. The slide pane shows a slide layout for a Title Slide. Click in the first placeholder and key **A New Country**. Press **Enter**, then key **A New Experience**.
4. Click in the second placeholder and key your first and last names.
5. Save the document as **Global Students** followed by your initials. Leave the document open for the next Step-by-Step.

Speech Recognition

If your computer has speech recognition capability, enable the Dictation mode. Then, dictate the title, click in the placeholder for the subtitle, and then dictate the subtitle.

Use the Slide Finder

The Slide Finder enables you to quickly find and copy slides from one presentation to another. You can copy selected slides one at a time or you can copy all of the slides at once. When slides are copied to a second presentation, they automatically adopt the format applied to the second presentation. You can access the Slide Finder either in Slide Sorter view or in Normal view.

STEP-BY-STEP 8.2

1. Switch to Slide Sorter view. The current slide is selected.

2. Open the **Insert** menu and choose **Slides from Files**. The Slide Finder dialog box shown in Figure 8-1 is displayed.

FIGURE 8-1
Slide Finder dialog box

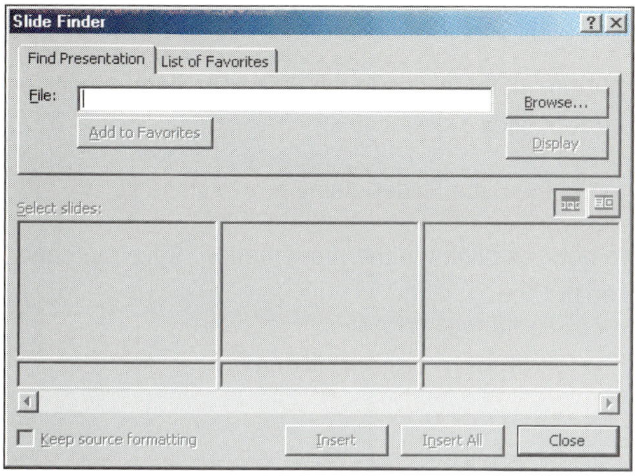

3. Click the **Browse** button in the dialog box. The Browse dialog box shown in Figure 8-2 is displayed. Locate and select the file **Step8-2a** in the data files.

FIGURE 8-2
Browse dialog box

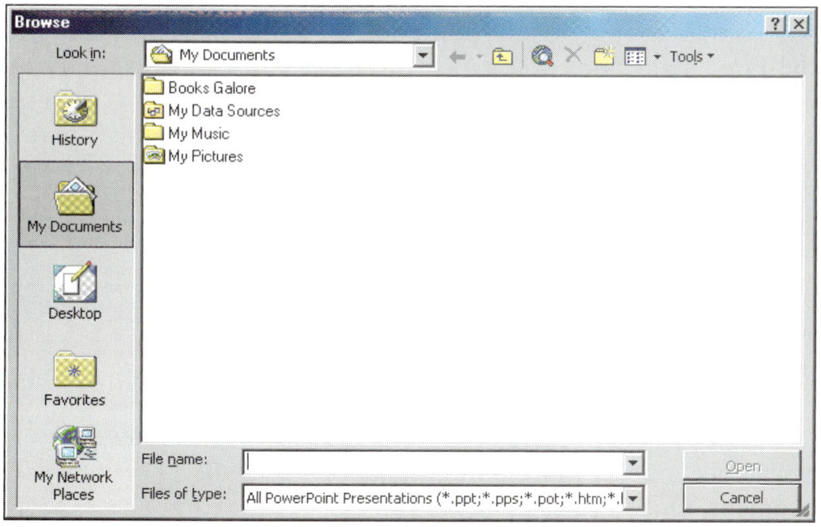

4. Click **Open** in the Browse dialog box. Miniature versions of the first three slides in the Step8-2a presentation are displayed at the bottom of the Slide Finder dialog box.

STEP-BY-STEP 8.2 Continued

5. Click slide number **2** to select it. Then click the **Insert** button. You can probably see that in the screen behind the dialog box, the slide is inserted into your *Global Students* presentation after the first slide. (You can also see that the inserted slide converts to the design template for the current presentation.)

6. The Slide Finder dialog box remains open. Click slide number **2** again to deselect it. Then click slide number **3** to select it, and click **Insert**.

7. Click the **Browse** button and locate and select the file **Step8-2b**. Click **Open**.

8. Click the **Insert All** button. All the slides in the Step8-2b file are inserted in the *Global Students* presentation after the current slide.

9. Click the **Close** button in the Slide Finder dialog box to close it.

10. Notice that there are now ten slides in the presentation. Save the changes and leave the document open for the next Step-by-Step.

Format Text

When you use a design template, the format of the text on each of the slides is predetermined. There may be occasions, however, when you want to alter the text format. You may want to change the ***font*** style or point size. A font is the general shape and style of a set of characters. Fonts are available in a variety of styles and sizes, and you can use multiple fonts in one document. The size of the font is measured in ***points***. The higher the point size is, the larger the font size is. One inch equals approximately 72 points.

You can quickly change font style and point size by using the Formatting toolbar. However, when you open the Font dialog box to change the font, you can also apply other font options such as color, outline, superscript, and shadow. The Font dialog box is also more useful if you want to make several font changes at one time or if you want to explore what options are available and what they would make the text look like.

Use Help to Learn about How to Select Text

To change the text, you must first select the text to be able to change the font, point size, or to apply any other text format such as boldface. When you ***select text***, you identify text or blocks of text for editing or formatting. You can select a single character, several characters, a word, a phrase, a sentence, one or more paragraphs, or even the entire document. Once you select text, you can delete it, replace it, change its appearance, move it, copy it, and so on.

Computer Concepts

You can leave Help screens open as you work with your presentation so you can reference the Help information quickly. Click the buttons in the taskbar to switch between the presentation document and the Help screens.

You can use the mouse or the keyboard to select text. In the next Step-by-Step we will go to the Help screens to learn more about how to select text. Instead of using the Office Assistant to get help, you will access Help by opening the PowerPoint Help dialog box.

STEP-BY-STEP 8.3

1. If the Office Assistant is displayed, point to the **Office Assistant** and right-click. Then choose **Options** in the shortcut menu. Clear the check box for Use the Office Assistant and click **OK**.

2. Open the **Help** menu and choose **Microsoft PowerPoint Help**. If necessary, click the **Show** button on the toolbar to display the Contents, Answer Wizard, and Index tabs.

3. If necessary, click the **Answer Wizard** tab to display the dialog box shown in Figure 8-3.

FIGURE 8-3
Answer Wizard in the Microsoft PowerPoint Help window

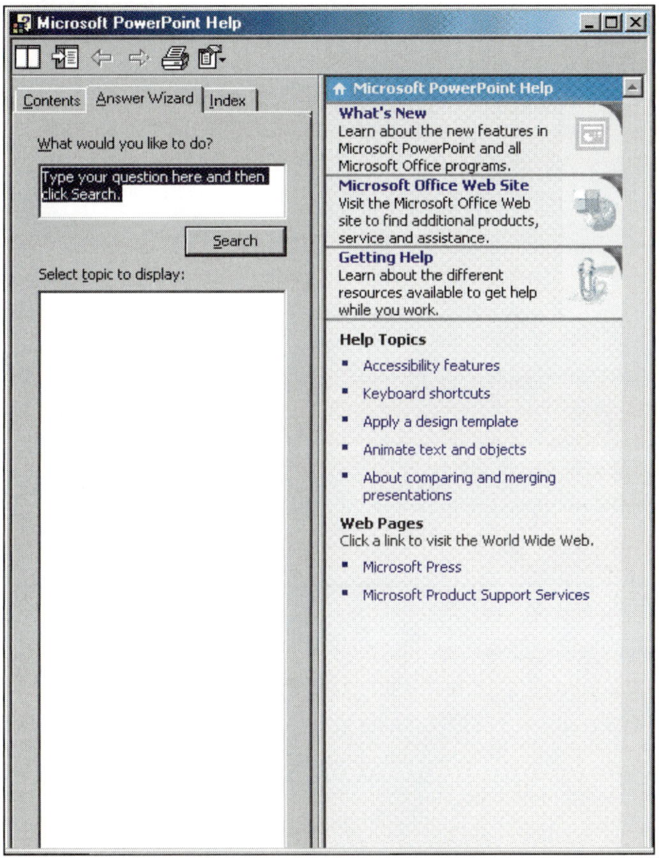

4. Click in the text box below *What would you like to do?* The text that is in that box is selected. With the text selected, key **select text**, then click **Search**.

5. Under *Select topic to display,* click the topic **Select text**. Read the information that appears at the right that details how to select a word, a paragraph, and all text on a slide.

6. Click in the text box under *What would you like to do?* Key **keyboard shortcuts**, and then click **Search**.

STEP-BY-STEP 8.3 Continued

7. A list of topics is displayed in the Select topic to display box. Select **Keyboard shortcuts**. In the list that appears at the right, click the link **Select text and objects**. The topic expands to display several keyboard shortcuts and a description of each. Read them all.

8. Study the list of keys in the Help screen. Then click the **Global Students button** in the taskbar to switch back to the presentation document. The Help screen will remain open, so you can refer to the list of keys and practice selecting text. When you're done practicing selecting text, close the Help screen.

Did You Know?

Serif typefaces (such as Times Roman) have embellishments or curls at the ends of the letters. Sans serif typefaces (such as Arial) have plain strokes with clear and simple curves. Serif typefaces are easiest to read and should be used when there are many words on a screen. Sans serif typefaces are usually heavier and bolder and should be used for titles and subtitles.

Change the Appearance of Text

You can change the appearance of the text in your presentation by changing the font style, the font size, and the font color. You can also add special emphasis by changing the text to italics, bold, or small capitals. However, using too many fonts or too many different formats generally makes the text harder to read. You want to use formats in moderation.

Did You Know?

You can position the insertion point in the Font size box, key the size, and press **Enter**. This method enables you to enter font sizes that do not appear in the list. However, there is a limit to the maximum and minimum size you can enter.

STEP-BY-STEP 8.4

1. Go to slide number 1 and display the slide in Normal view.

2. Triple-click the text in the first placeholder in the slide pane to select it *(A New Country A New Experience)*.

3. With the text selected, click the down arrow next to the **Font** box on the Formatting toolbar. Select **Arial** in the drop-down list.

4. With the text still selected, click the down arrow in the **Font Size** box on the Formatting toolbar. Scroll down and select **54** in the drop-down list. The selected text is enlarged to the bigger font size.

Hot Tip

To quickly increase the font size to the next increment in the Font Size box, select the text and press **Ctrl +]** (closing square bracket). Continue pressing the keys for additional increases. Press **Ctrl + [** (opening square bracket) to decrease the font size to the previous increment. This is quite helpful when you want to grow or shrink the text to fit within a specified area on the slide.

STEP-BY-STEP 8.4 Continued

5. With the text still selected, open the **Format** menu and choose **Font**. The dialog box shown in Figure 8-4 will display.

6. Click the down arrow in the box beneath Color. A box of color options is displayed. The set of colors shown here are all used in the template design and are, therefore, good choices.

7. Select the **gold** color. Then, click **OK** to close the Font dialog box.

8. Click anywhere on the slide to deselect the text so you can see the change in the font color. Do not save the changes, but leave the document open for the next Step-by-Step.

Computer Concepts

Too many font styles can make the slides difficult to read, and the mix of fonts can even be distracting. Limit your font styles to two.

Hot Tip

If the Redo button is not displayed on the Standard toolbar, you can click the **Toolbar Options** button at the right side of the toolbar. Then click the **Redo** button. The Redo button will appear on the toolbar until you close PowerPoint.

FIGURE 8-4
Font dialog box

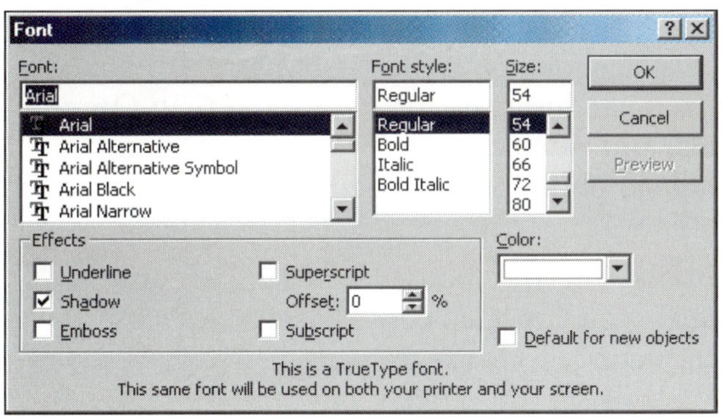

Use Undo and Redo

As you work with a presentation, you may accidentally change some text. Or you may change your mind and want to undo your edits. The Undo command will reverse one or more of your recent actions. You can keep choosing the Undo command to continue reversing actions. Or you can click the down arrow next to the Undo button on the Standard toolbar to see a drop-down list of your recent actions. When you choose an item in this list, all the actions listed above it will also be reversed.

There may be times when you want to redo an edit. The Redo command is similar to the Undo command. You use the Redo command to reverse an Undo action. As with the Undo command, when you click the down arrow next to the Redo button, a list of recent Undo actions appears. You can select one or more actions from the list that appears. When you save the document, the Undo and Redo lists are cleared.

STEP-BY-STEP 8.5

1. Click the **Undo** button on the Standard toolbar. The last edit—changing the text color—is reversed to its original color.

2. Click the down arrow next to the **Undo** button. The list of previous actions (*Font Size* and *Font*) is displayed in a drop-down list.

Speech Recognition

If your computer has speech recognition capability, enable the Command mode and say the command to save the document.

3. Click **Font** in the list. The font change and the font size change are both reversed.

4. Click the **Redo** button on the Standard toolbar. The last undo (changing the font) is reversed and the text is restored to Arial font.

5. Save the changes and leave the document open for the next Step-by-Step.

Insert Pictures

There may be times when you want to add clip art and graphics to your presentation. Often times, pictures help your audience remember your message. PowerPoint allows you to place pictures inside special graphic placeholders. When you insert a picture in a placeholder, the picture replaces the placeholder. You can insert pictures from the ***Clip Organizer*** (a wide variety of pictures, photographs, sounds, and video clips that you can insert in your documents). You can also insert a picture from a scanned photo or from a file.

When a clip art image is selected, eight small squares called ***sizing handles*** appear on the border of the graphic. When it is selected, you can cut, copy, paste, delete, move, and resize the picture. To resize the picture, drag a sizing handle. You will see the effects on the screen as you drag. If you drag a corner sizing handle, the picture will be resized proportionally.

Did You Know?

Sometimes photos, clip art, and graphics can be much more powerful than words. Can you think of a time when a picture was more meaningful than words?

STEP-BY-STEP 8.6

1. Go to slide number 2 and display it in Normal view. Notice that the slide layout includes title, content, and text. The content placeholder on the left displays six different icons as shown in Figure 8-5.

FIGURE 8-5
Placeholder for graphics content

2. Point to each of the icons to display the ScreenTip. Notice that you can insert tables, charts, clip art, pictures, diagrams or organization charts, and media clips.

3. Click the **Insert Clip Art** icon. A Select Picture dialog box similar to the one shown in Figure 8-6 is displayed. Do not be concerned if the clip art images in your dialog box are different.

FIGURE 8-6
Select Picture dialog box

STEP-BY-STEP 8.6 Continued

4. Click in the **Search text** box and key **globe**, then click **Search**. PowerPoint will search the Clip Organizer for all pictures related to this word. A dialog box will display images that match the word.

5. Click the picture of the image illustrated in Figure 8-7, or find one that is similar. You may need to scroll down through the pictures or even click the **Keep Looking** link at the bottom of the window.

Speech Recognition

If your computer has speech recognition capability, enable the Command mode and say the command to open the Select Picture dialog box. Then, say the commands to search for and insert the clip art image.

FIGURE 8-7
Search results

6. With the clip art image selected, click **OK**. The image is inserted in the slide and the Select Picture dialog box closes.

7. Eight sizing handles should appear around the picture, similar to Figure 8-8. Point to the sizing handle at the top left corner of the image. When the pointer changes to a two-headed arrow, drag the sizing handle up and to the left to make the picture bigger.

FIGURE 8-8
Selected picture with sizing handles

STEP-BY-STEP 8.6 Continued

8. Point to the center of the picture. The pointer will change to a four-headed arrow. If necessary, drag the picture to reposition it to the left of the bulleted list.

9. Save the changes and leave the document open for the next Step-by-Step.

Check Spelling and Use AutoCorrect

As you create a presentation, PowerPoint automatically checks for misspelled words. If the words you enter are not in PowerPoint's dictionary, the words will display with a wavy red line. The PowerPoint spellchecker makes it easy to correct spelling mistakes. However, you must also proofread all of your work, because the spellchecker will not identify all spelling errors. For example, if you use the word "too" instead of "two," the incorrect word will not be identified.

> **Did You Know?**
>
> You can add words to the AutoCorrect list during a spellcheck by clicking the **AutoCorrect** option in the Spelling and Grammar dialog box.

Sometimes you make the same spelling errors over and over. For example, you may frequently key "teh" instead of "the." The AutoCorrect feature in PowerPoint can automatically correct this error as you key text in a presentation. You can set the options for the AutoCorrect feature in the AutoCorrect dialog box.

STEP-BY-STEP 8.7

1. Go to slide number 7 in Normal view. Notice that there is a wavy red line under the word *Austrailia*.

2. Point to the word **Austrailia** and right-click. A shortcut menu is displayed and two correctly spelled words that are likely substitutes for the misspelled word are displayed at the top of the menu. See Figure 8-9.

FIGURE 8-9
Spelling shortcut menu

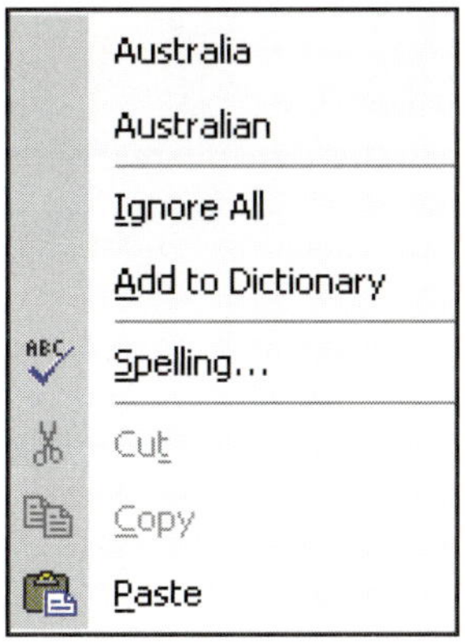

3. Click **Australia** in the shortcut menu. The correct spelling replaces the original spelling in the slide.

STEP-BY-STEP 8.7 Continued

4. Go to slide number 5 in Normal view. Position the insertion point in the second placeholder (*Click to add text*). Key the following three lines of text exactly as shown, pressing **Enter** at the end of each line. (*Note:* Watch carefully as you press the **Spacebar** after the word *foriegn*. Notice that PowerPoint automatically corrects the misspelled word.)

```
Study abroad.
Live with a host family.
Speak the foriegn language.
```

5. Save the changes and close the presentation. If the Help screens are still open, close them as well.

SUMMARY

In this lesson, you learned:

- PowerPoint offers several ways to create a new presentation including blank presentations and design templates, the AutoContent Wizard, presentations with content, and existing presentations.
- The Slide Finder enables you to quickly and easily find and copy one or more slides from one presentation to another.
- If you want to change the way text looks on a slide, you can select the text and apply different formats. For example, you can change the font style, font size, and font color.
- The Undo command allows you to reverse the last action. If desired, you can undo multiple actions at one time. The Redo command reverses an undo action.
- Pictures help to clarify the message of your presentation. Often times, pictures help your audience remember your message. PowerPoint makes it easy for you to add a picture to a slide.
- The Spelling and AutoCorrect features in PowerPoint make it easy to correct spelling and keyboarding errors.

VOCABULARY *Review*

Define the following terms:

Clip Organizer	Points	Sizing handles
Font	Select text	

REVIEW *Questions*

TRUE/FALSE

Circle T if the statement is true or F if the statement is false.

T F 1. To reposition a graphic or picture on a slide, the sizing handles must be displayed.

T F 2. PowerPoint automatically checks for misspelled words as you create a presentation.

T F 3. When you apply a design template to a slide, you cannot change the font of any text on the slide.

T F 4. When you insert a picture in a placeholder, the picture replaces the placeholder.

T F 5. The font dialog box provides many font options that are not available on the standard (default) toolbars.

FILL IN THE BLANK

Complete the following sentences by writing the correct word or words in the blanks provided.

1. The __________ enables you to copy slides from one presentation to another.
2. To change the font size of text, you must first __________ the text.
3. The __________ command will reverse one or more of your recent actions.
4. You can find pictures, photographs, sounds, and video clips in the __________.
5. The __________ feature in PowerPoint automatically corrects common spelling errors as you key them.

PROJECTS

PROJECT 8-1

1. If necessary, start PowerPoint. Create a new presentation with the **Stream** design template. Accept the Title Slide layout for the first slide. Save the presentation as **Refuge Inn** followed by your initials.

2. In the *title* placeholder, key **Refuge Inn.**

3. In the *subtitle* placeholder, key the following text exactly as shown: **Yuor Refuge from Stress.** PowerPoint will correct the misspelling for you.

4. You've thought of a better phrase for the subtitle. Click **Undo** to remove all but the first word.

5. Key **Island Retreat** as the new subtitle. The subtitle should now read *Your Island Retreat.*

6. Add a new slide and change the slide layout to Title and Text, if necessary. Key the title **About the Refuge Inn.** Key the following bullet items in the text placeholder:
   Family owned since 1952
   Double rooms, suites, and efficiencies
   Excellent restaurants nearby
   Hiking, boating, and biking in the Massassoit National Wildlife Refuge

7. Use the Slide Finder to open **Project8-1** from the data files. Insert slides 2, 3, and 4 to your presentation.

8. Add a Title and Text slide at the end of the presentation and key the title **Visit Us Soon!** Key the following bullet items on the slide:
   Open year round
   Packages available
   Call 555-555-4509 for more information

9. Save your changes and close the presentation.

PROJECT 8-2

1. Open **Project 8-2** from the data files and save the presentation as **Refuge Inn 2** followed by your initials.

2. If necessary, switch to Normal view. Beginning with slide number 1, review each slide and check for words with red, wavy underlines. Right-click the misspelled words and select the correct spellings. The name *Massassoit* is spelled correctly. (Choose **Ignore All** to remove wavy red underlines from all instances of the word.)

3. On slide number 1, format the title as Times New Roman, 48 pt., bold and change the color to pale yellow. Format the subtitle as Times New Roman and change its color to the same pale yellow as the title.

4. Format the title on each slide as Times New Roman, 48 pt. bold, and pale yellow. (*Hint:* If you learned how to use the Format Painter in Word, you can use it the same way in PowerPoint to complete this task quickly.)

5. Choose appropriate clip art pictures for slides 3 and 4. Resize and position the pictures as needed.

6. Save your changes and close the presentation.

WEB PROJECT

In this lesson, you created a presentation that offered information about studying abroad. The Web is a good place to locate more information on this subject. Use a search tool to find specific information about a student exchange or foreign study program. What countries can you visit in this program? What are the requirements for joining the program? How do you apply for the program? What courses of study are available? After completing your research, create a PowerPoint presentation that summarizes the information you have gathered.

TEAMWORK PROJECT

In the first two lessons of this unit, you have worked with fairly simple presentations. If you wanted to make a more complex presentation on a specific subject, you could use the AutoContent Wizard in PowerPoint to create the slides for you. With a partner, explore the AutoContent Wizard using these steps:

1. With your partner, begin the AutoContent Wizard. Select a presentation type from the list of all presentations. Choose a presentation type with a subject you know a little bit about, such as Selling Your Ideas or Communicating Bad News. It will also be helpful to imagine a particular situation that matches your presentation type. For example, if you choose the Communicating Bad News presentation, imagine that you and your teammate are the management team of a small company, and you each have to tell your employees that none of them will receive bonuses this year.
2. Answer the questions the Wizard asks you. If necessary, use the Help feature in PowerPoint to find out what options the Wizard is giving you.
3. After the presentation appears, examine the sample slide material in the outline pane. You will need to replace the sample text with your own text.
4. Replace the text as necessary to fit the situation you have imagined. Both partners should contribute in creating new text (you can alternate slides to share the work). Delete any unnecessary slides and add slides if necessary.
5. Run your presentation or make it available on your network.

CRITICAL *Thinking*

ACTIVITY 8-1

You have created a presentation of almost 30 slides and have applied a design template to all the slides. You really like the background and graphics of this design, but you think the font used throughout is not very attractive. You think a different font could give your presentation a more professional appearance. Is there an easier way to replace one font with another throughout an entire presentation?

Use the Help feature in PowerPoint to find the answer to this question. Write a brief report on what you learn.

LESSON 9

WORKING WITH VISUAL ELEMENTS

OBJECTIVES

Upon completion of this lesson, you should be able to:

- Apply animation schemes and preview animation.
- Create custom animation.
- Add sound effects to animations.
- Change the animation sequence.
- Format the animation timing.
- Modify an animation effect.
- Format slide transitions.
- Add animated clip art graphics and sound clips.
- Print the presentation.

Estimated Time: 1 hour

VOCABULARY

Animation
Animation schemes
Emphasis effect
Entrance effect
Exit effect
Sound effects
Transitions
Trigger

Adding special effects is the fun part of creating a presentation. PowerPoint offers several features to help you control the flow of information in your presentation. You can also use sound clips and animated clip art graphics to draw attention to the information and to hold the interest of your audience. However, these features must be used effectively if they are to enhance your presentation.

When you add ***animation***, you add special visuals or sound effects to text or an object. Animations add visual appeal and when used effectively, they can help keep the audience interested in your presentation. Without animation, text and objects automatically appear when a slide is displayed. However, when you add animation, you can determine how and when the text or graphics will appear on each slide. For example, you can have text fly in from the left, and you can have a picture zoom out from the center. As you format the animations, you can preview them to see how they work.

Apply Animation Schemes and Preview Animation

PowerPoint offers several ***animation schemes***, which are pre-designed sets of visual effects. To see the available animation scheme options, you must display the Animation Schemes task pane. The schemes are organized and listed in three categories: Subtle, Moderate, and Exciting.

An animation usually includes an effect for the slide title, bulleted lists and paragraphs of text, and objects on the slide. You can apply these animation schemes to selected slides or to all the slides in the presentation.

> **Computer Concepts**
>
> You can apply an animation scheme in Slide Sorter view, but you will not be able to preview the animation unless you are working in Normal view.

After you format animations, you can preview them for one slide or for the whole presentation. The AutoPreview option in the Animation task pane allows you to see a preview of animation effects automatically when you add or modify an effect. To see the preview again, you can click the Play button. When you preview a slide using the Play button in the Animation Schemes task pane, you do not need to click the mouse to ***trigger*** (start) the animation. However, the default trigger setting to start an animation in Slide Show view is to click the mouse. So, even though the animation played automatically in the preview, you may need to click the mouse button to trigger the animation in Slide Show view.

STEP-BY-STEP 9.1

1. Open **Step9-1** from the data files. Save the presentation as **3 Days** followed by your initials. If necessary, switch to Normal view.

2. Open the **Slide Show** menu and choose **Animation Schemes**. The Slide Design task pane shown in Figure 9-1 is displayed. Do not be concerned that your list under *Recently Used* does not match the list in the figure.

FIGURE 9-1
Slide Design task pane

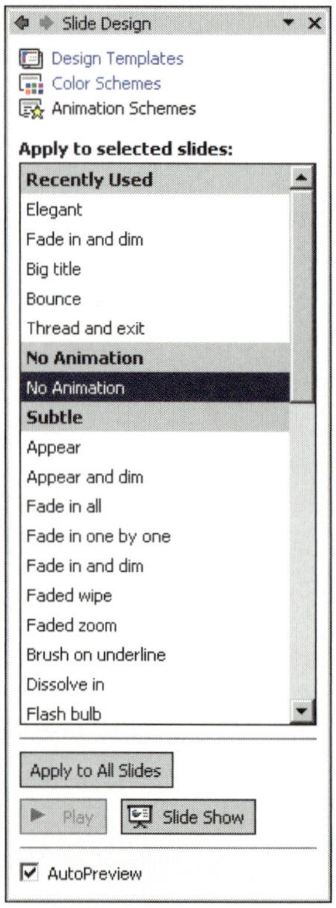

STEP-BY-STEP 9.1 Continued

3. Make sure the **AutoPreview** option at the bottom of the task pane is turned on. When it is turned on, the box will have a checkmark.

4. Scroll down to view the Moderate list and select **Zoom**. Because AutoPreview is turned on, you should see the animation in the slide pane as soon as you select the scheme. The animation scheme is applied to the first slide only.

> **Speech Recognition**
>
> If your computer has speech recognition capability, enable the Command mode and say the commands to display the Animation Schemes task pane.

5. Click the **Play** button at the bottom of the task pane to see the animation again. The Play button previews the current slide only.

6. Go to slide number 2 and apply the **Fade in one by one** scheme listed under *Subtle*.

7. Go to slide number 3 and select the **Zoom** scheme. (*Hint*: The scheme is now listed near the top of the task pane under *Recently Used*.)

8. Go to slide number 4. Explore the other schemes and apply a scheme of your choice.

9. Go to slide number 5 and select the **Big title** scheme under *Exciting*.

10. Click the **Apply to All Slides** button at the bottom of the task pane. The *Big title* scheme is applied to all slides in the presentation.

11. Go to slide number 1. Click the **Slide Show** button at the bottom of the task pane. Slide Show view launches, starting with the current slide. Click the mouse button to trigger each animation and then to advance to the next slide. Press **Esc** to end the slide show.

12. Save the changes and close the presentation.

> **Computer Concepts**
>
> To remove an animation scheme, select **No Animation** in the Slide Design task pane.

Create Custom Animations

Instead of using a preset animation scheme, you can apply custom animation to your PowerPoint presentation. You can select which text and objects you want to animate on each slide. However, if you want the effects applied to all slides, it would be easier to use an animation scheme. You can only apply custom animations to the text and objects on a single slide at a time, not to all slides in the presentation at once.

To apply custom animation, you must display the slide in Normal view. Then you display the Custom Animation task pane and select the effects you want. The effects options include Entrance, Emphasis, Exit, and Motion Path. All effects are organized in four categories: Basic, Subtle, Moderate, and Exciting.

To apply an effect, you must first select the text or object you want to format. The effects you can choose from appear in the Custom Animation list in the order you apply them. A green star in front of the item indicates that an ***entrance effect*** has been applied. An entrance effect controls how the text or object animates as it appears on the slide. A yellow star indicates an emphasis effect. An ***emphasis effect*** controls the animation effects after the text or object appears. A red star indicates an ***exit effect***. An exit effect controls the animation effects at the end of the animation sequence. To apply the same effect to multiple items, select all the items before choosing the effect.

> **Computer Concepts**
>
> If an animation scheme has been applied, you must remove the scheme before you can apply custom animations.

If you have several items on a slide, you can have a variety of animations applied. PowerPoint makes it easy to review the animations you have applied. All animated items are referenced on the slide with a number tag that indicates the sequence in which the animation effects will occur. However, this tag will not display in Slide Show view, and it will not print. When the Custom Animation task pane is displayed, the title for each animation appears in a list. An icon is displayed next to the title to represent the type of animation selected. If you click a title in the list, the settings for the start, color, and speed for that animation will display.

Apply an Entrance Effect

You can apply an entrance effect to help focus your audience's attention on a particular item on a slide. For example, you can apply an entrance effect to text in a bulleted list so that the list is introduced one bulleted item at a time. When this type of animation is applied, each bulleted item is tagged and listed separately in the Custom Animation list. However, in a bulleted list, only the first bulleted item appears in the list. The remaining bulleted items are collapsed and do not display unless you expand the list.

STEP-BY-STEP 9.2

1. Open **Step9-2** from the data files and save the presentation as **Exchange Student** followed by your initials.

2. Go to slide number 2. If necessary, switch to Normal view.

3. Open the **Slide Show** menu and choose **Custom Animation**. The task pane shown in Figure 9-2 is displayed. If necessary, turn on the **AutoPreview** option. Note that most of the options in the task pane are dimmed because no text or objects have been selected.

> **Speech Recognition**
>
> If your computer has speech recognition capability, enable the Command mode and say the commands to open the file and save it with a new name (and path if necessary).

STEP-BY-STEP 9.2 Continued

FIGURE 9-2
Custom Animation task pane

4. Click the clip art image on the slide to select it. Then click the **Add Effect** button in the task pane to display the menu shown in Figure 9-3.

FIGURE 9-3
Add Effect menu

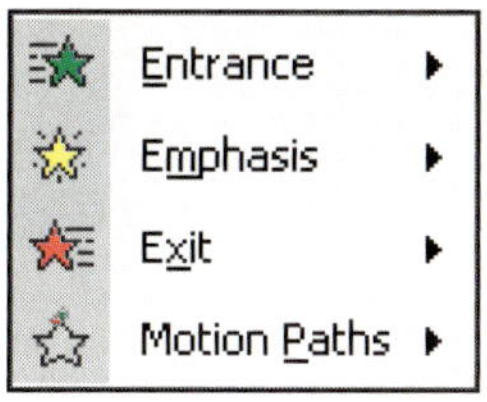

Hot Tip

You can also access the Custom Animation pane by clicking the down arrow at the top of the task pane and selecting **Custom Animation** in the drop-down list.

STEP-BY-STEP 9.2 Continued

5. Click **Entrance** to display a submenu similar to the one shown in Figure 9-4.

FIGURE 9-4
Entrance submenu

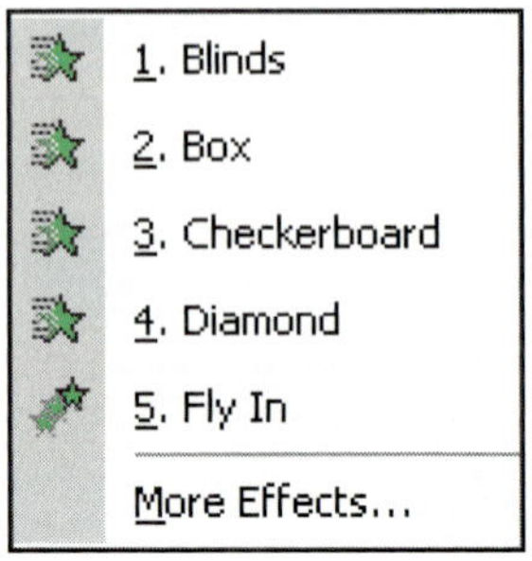

6. Click **More Effects** to display the Add Entrance Effect dialog box shown in Figure 9-5. Make sure that the **Preview Effect** option is turned on. Notice that the options display with green stars and that some of the stars reflect movement or a change in size.

FIGURE 9-5
Add Entrance Effect dialog box

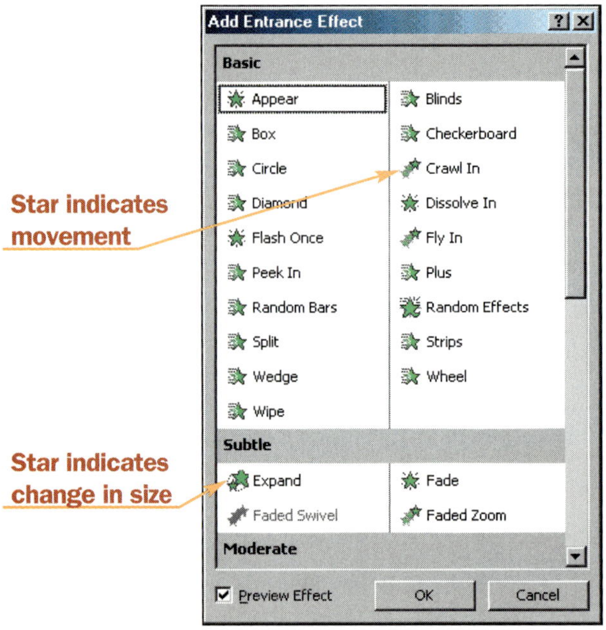

7. Point to the title bar in the dialog box and drag the box to the side of the screen so you can see the clip art graphic. Scroll down to the *Exciting* category and click **Pinwheel**. The animation will preview in the slide pane.

8. Click **OK** to apply the effect and close the dialog box. Notice that there is now a number tab (*1*) next to the clip art image on the slide. Also notice that the animated item is now displayed in the Custom Animation list in the task pane.

STEP-BY-STEP 9.2 Continued

9. Position the insertion point in the first bulleted item on the slide.

10. Click the **Add Effect** button in the task pane, select **Entrance**, and then select **More Effects**. Under *Moderate*, select **Stretch** and then click **OK**.

> **Computer Concepts**
>
> To remove an effect, select the animation item in the **Custom Animation** list and click the **Remove** button.

11. Notice that there are now three tags correlating the items on the slide to the Custom Animation list in the task pane. However, item number 3 (the second bulleted item in the text box) does not appear in the Custom Animation list, as is shown in Figure 9-6. Click the double arrows below the number 2 item in the list to expand the contents of the list.

12. Save the changes and leave the document open for the next Step-by-Step.

FIGURE 9-6
Custom Animation task pane with two items in the Custom Animation list

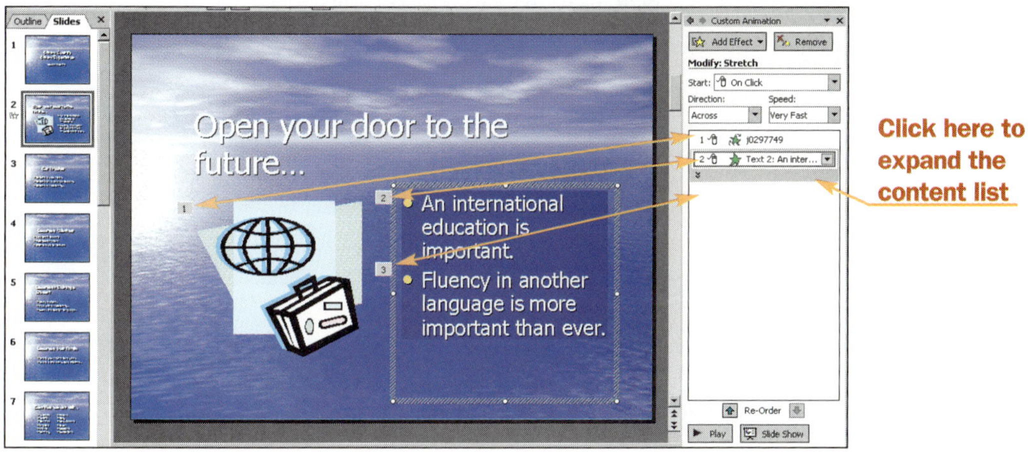

Apply an Emphasis Effect

You can also apply an emphasis effect to draw attention to text or an object on a slide. For example, you can create an animation that will change the fill color or font color of text. The procedures for applying an emphasis effect are the same as for applying an entrance effect. However, the effect options available for emphasis depend on whether you are applying the animation to an object or to text.

STEP-BY-STEP 9.3

1. Go to slide number 3 in Normal view.

2. Position the insertion point in the first bulleted item.

STEP-BY-STEP 9.3 Continued

3. Click the **Add Effect** button in the task pane, choose **Emphasis**, and then select **More Effects**. The Add Emphasis Effect dialog box shown in Figure 9-7 displays. If necessary, turn on the **Preview Effect** option.

FIGURE 9-7
Add Emphasis Effect dialog box

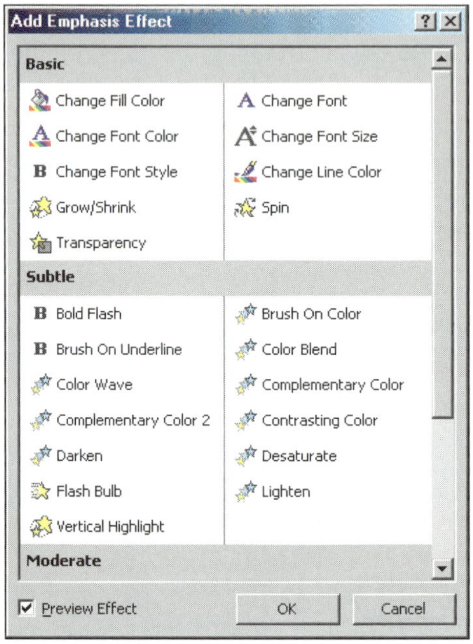

4. In the *Subtle* category, select **Color Wave** and then click **OK**. Notice that there are three animation tags on the slide.

5. Click the **Color** box in the task pane and select the **gold** color.

6. Save the changes and leave the presentation open for the next Step-by-Step.

Apply an Exit Effect

You can apply an exit effect to make text or objects leave the slide. For example, you can make text disappear very subtly by fading it away, or you can make an object disappear with a much more dramatic exit such as making it disappear quickly.

STEP-BY-STEP 9.4

1. Go to slide number 10 in Normal view.

2. Click the title **Global Students** to select it. Hold down **Shift** and click the subtitle containing the URL. Both items should be selected.

STEP-BY-STEP 9.4 Continued

3. Click the **Add Effect** button in the task pane, choose **Exit**, and then select **More Effects**. The Add Exit Effect dialog box shown in Figure 9-8 is displayed. If necessary, turn on the **Preview Effect** option.

> **Speech Recognition**
>
> If your computer has speech recognition capability, enable the Command mode and say the commands to navigate to slide number 10. (*Hint*: Say **Page Up** or **Page Down** to move from one slide to another in the Outline pane.)

FIGURE 9-8
Add Exit Effect dialog box

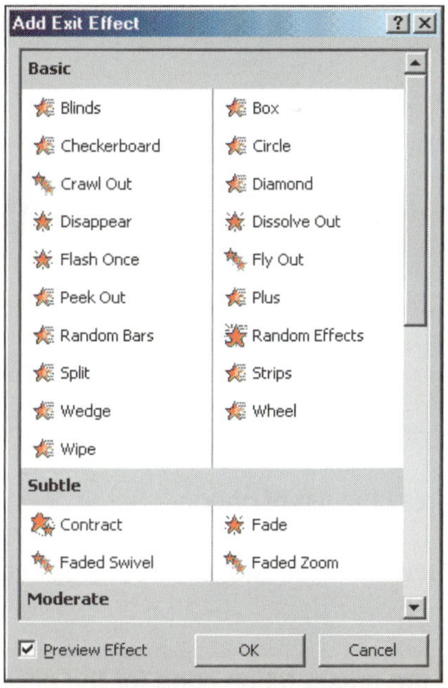

4. Under the Basic category, select **Peek Out**. Click **OK** to apply the effect and close the dialog box. Notice there are two number tags on the slide, but they both have the same number. This is because you applied the effect to both items at the same time.

5. Save the changes and leave the presentation open for the next Step-by-Step.

> **Extra Challenge**
>
> You can apply or draw a motion path effect to control where text or objects appear on a slide. Explore the Motion Path effect feature by first selecting some of the preset paths and then by drawing your own paths. To get more information about the feature, search the help screens for the key words *motion paths*.

Add a Sound Effect to an Animation

When you animate text and objects, you also have the option of adding ***sound effects*** to them. A sound effect is a recorded sound that can be added to animated text or objects on a PowerPoint slide. The sound can be stored in a file on your computer, a network, the Internet, or the Microsoft Clip Organizer. To add a sound effect, the text or object must already have an animation applied to it.

STEP-BY-STEP 9.5

1. The title and subtitle should still be selected in the slide pane and in the Custom Animation task pane.

2. Click the down arrow for the second selected item in the Custom Animation list and select **Effect Options**.

3. If necessary, click the **Effect** tab to display the Peek Out dialog box shown in Figure 9-9.

Hot Tip

If this is the first time sound effects have been applied on your computer, you may be prompted to install the Sound Effects feature. To complete the installation process, you will need the Microsoft Office XP CD-ROM.

FIGURE 9-9
Effect tab in the Peek Out dialog box

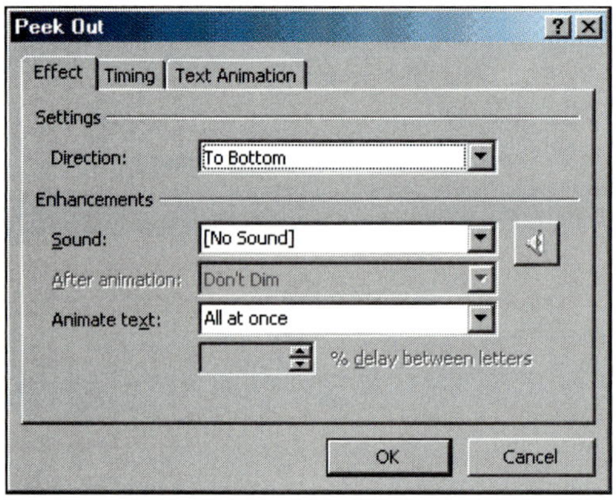

4. Click in the Sound box to display the list of options. Scroll down and select **Chime** and then click **OK**.

5. Click the **Play** button to preview the slide with the sound effect. Notice that both lines of text exit at the same time.

6. Save the changes and leave the presentation open for the next Step-by-Step.

Format the Animation Timing

As stated earlier, by default, animations are set to trigger when you click the mouse. However, the animation can be formatted to occur automatically. You can set timing options that will determine when the animation begins and the speed at which the animation occurs. You can even format the animation to repeat a specified number of times.

Hot Tip

To adjust the sound effect volume, click the speaker button in the Peek Out dialog box (Effect tab) and then drag the control button up or down to the desired setting.

STEP-BY-STEP 9.6

1. Click the task pane to deselect the items in the Custom Animation list, then click the URL item to select only that item.

STEP-BY-STEP 9.6 Continued

2. Click the down arrow next to the item in the task pane and select **Timing**. The Timing tab in the Peek Out dialog box is displayed. See Figure 9-10.

FIGURE 9-10
Timing tab in the Peek Out dialog box

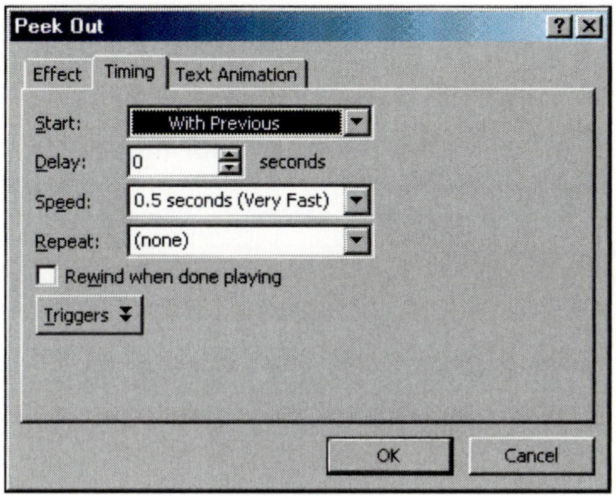

3. Click the **Start** box and select **After Previous**.

4. Click the **Delay** box and either key or select **1.5**.

5. Click the **Speed** box and select **3 seconds (Slow)**.

6. Click in the **Repeat** box and select **Until Next Click**. Then click **OK**.

7. Click the **Play** button to preview the new timing. Note that the URL animation will only repeat one time in the preview.

8. Click the **Slide Show** button to view the slide in full screen. Click to trigger the animation. First the title will exit very quickly with a sound effect. Then, 1.5 seconds later, the URL will exit a bit slower with a sound effect. The URL exit repeats, but the sound effect is not repeated. After the URL has exited a few times, click the mouse to end the animation.

9. Switch to Normal view. Save the changes and leave the presentation open for the next Step-by-Step.

Change the Animation Sequence

There may be times when you want to rearrange the order of animations after you apply the effects. You can change the order of your animations at any time by using the Custom Animation list in the task pane.

STEP-BY-STEP 9.7

1. Go to slide number 2 and click the **Play** button to preview the current sequence. Notice the order in which the text and object appear. The object appears before the bulleted list.

STEP-BY-STEP 9.7 Continued

2. Select item number **2** in the Custom Animation list.

3. Click the up arrow for the **Re-Order** buttons at the bottom of the task pane twice. Notice that order and numbers change in the task pane and the number tags on the slide also change.

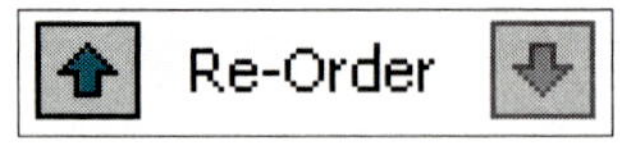

4. Click the **Play** button to preview the new sequence. The bulleted items now appear before the object.

5. Save the changes and leave the presentation open for the next Step-by-Step.

Modify an Animation Effect

When the animation involves movement, you can format the direction and/or the speed of the movement. When the animation involves a change in size, you can specify the percentage of the change in size, and you can also specify the speed for the change in size.

STEP-BY-STEP 9.8

1. Click the **Play** button to preview the current sequence. Notice the direction in which the bulleted list stretches across the slide.

2. If necessary, select item number **1** in the Custom Animation list.

3. Click the down arrow in the **Direction** box above the Custom Animation list in the task pane and select **From Left**.

4. Click the down arrow in the **Speed** box above the Custom Animation list in the task pane and select **Fast**.

5. Click the **Play** button to preview the new sequence.

6. Go to slide number 10. Select item number **1** in the Custom Animation list. Hold down **Shift** and select the second item in number 1. Then click the **Remove** button. All the animations from the slide (including the exit effects and the sound effect) are removed.

7. Save the changes and leave the presentation open for the next Step-by-Step.

Format Transitions

Slide ***transitions*** determine the changes in the display that occur as you move from one slide to another in Slide Show view. For example, you can format the transition so the current slide fades to black before the next slide is displayed. Or you can choose to have the next slide automatically appear after a designated number of seconds. You can even choose a sound effect that will play as the transition occurs. You can apply the transition choices to a single slide or to all the slides in the presentation. To apply a slide transition, you must work in the Slide Transition task pane.

STEP-BY-STEP 9.9

1. Open the **Slide Show** menu and choose **Slide Transition**. The Slide Transition task pane shown in Figure 9-11 is displayed. Make sure **AutoPreview** is turned on.

> **Hot Tip**
>
> You can also open the Slide Transition task pane by clicking the down-arrow at the top of the task pane and choosing **Slide Transition** in the menu.

FIGURE 9-11
Slide Transition task pane

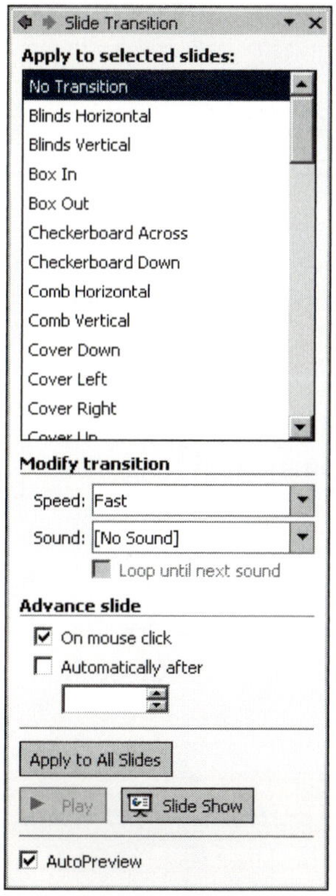

2. Under *Apply to selected slides*, scroll down and select **Strips Right-Down**.

3. Under *Modify transition*, in the Speed drop-down box, select **Medium**.

4. Under *Advance slide*, deselect **On Mouse Click**. Then, select **Automatically after**. In the box below, key or select **00.03**.

5. Click the **Apply to All** Slides button.

6. Go to slide number 1 and then click the **Slide Show** button to view the presentation in full screen. Each slide should automatically advance after three seconds.

7. Press **Esc** to exit the slide show. Save the changes and leave the presentation open for the next Step-by-Step.

Add Animated Clip Art Graphics and Sound Clips

Animated clip art, sound, and music add an extra dimension to a presentation. You can use sound and video at any point in a presentation to add emphasis or set the mood for the audience. Animated clip art graphics and sound clips are available in the Clip Organizer. You can also use clips from other sources.

Add an Animated Clip Art Graphic

You insert the animated clip art graphic where you want it to play during a slide show. The slide must be displayed in Normal view before you can insert the clip. The clip is inserted in the slide as an object and is displayed with a graphic. You can choose to have the animation play automatically when you move to the slide, or you can format the animation to play only when you click its image during the slide show.

STEP-BY-STEP 9.10

1. Go to slide number 10.
2. Open the **Insert** menu and choose **Movies and Sounds**. Select **Movie from Clip Organizer** in the submenu. Results similar to those shown in Figure 9-12 are displayed. Notice that each thumbnail displays a yellow star in the bottom right corner, indicating that the clip is animated.

Did You Know?

If you are connected to the Internet, you can search for available clips online by clicking the **Clips Online** link at the bottom of the task pane.

3. Point to the thumbnail showing the two computers and the globe (or find a similar clip) to preview the movie clip. When you see the down arrow for the thumbnail, click the arrow and then select **Preview/Properties** in the menu. Click the **Close** button in the Preview/Properties dialog box to close the preview.

Communication Skills

Individuals most likely to be promoted and succeed have something in common—they have good oral and written communication skills. The ability to make formal presentations is an increasingly important skill for many. In fact, communication skills can greatly enhance one's success in the classroom or on the job.

Many jobs require that an employee be able to organize, analyze, and communicate information. Moreover, employees are often called upon to formally present information. The audience may be as small as one or two persons, or it may be a much larger group. To deliver an effective presentation, you must possess the confidence to deliver the presentation competently.

STEP-BY-STEP 9.10 Continued

FIGURE 9-12
Task pane for inserting Movies from the Clip Organizer

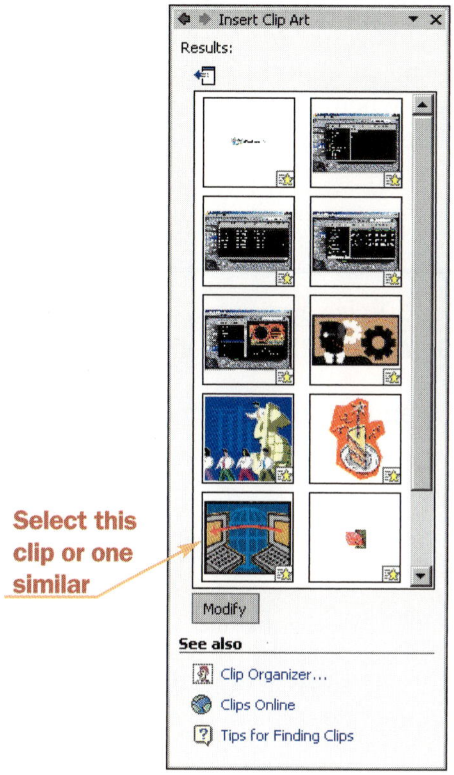

4. Click the thumbnail. The movie clip is inserted on the slide as an object.

5. Resize and reposition the clip at the bottom of the slide below the URL.

6. Open the **Slide Show** menu and choose **Slide Transition.**

7. In the task pane under *Advance slide*, deselect **Automatically after** so this last slide will not advance without a mouse click. If necessary, turn on the option **On mouse click.**

8. Click the **Slide Show** button to view the slide in full screen. Notice that the movie clip continues to play until you click the mouse button.

9. Press **Esc** to exit the slide show and return to Normal view. Save the changes and leave the presentation open for the next Step-by-Step.

Did You Know?

Web sites supported by various branches of the U.S. government are good sources of images, sounds, and video clips. Make sure the site allows you to use their multimedia materials.

Add a Sound or Music Clip

In addition to applying sound effects, you can also add a sound or music clip. Adding a sound or music clip is very similar to adding an animated graphic clip. You can add sound and music clips provided in the Clip Organizer or you can add sound or music from a file or CD audio track. The slide must be displayed in Normal view before you can insert the clip. The sound or music clip is represented on the slide by an icon. You can choose to have the clip play automatically, or you can set the option so the clip only plays when you click the object icon. If you do not want the sound clip icon to show during your slide show, you can hide it behind the movie clip.

STEP-BY-STEP 9.11

1. In Normal view, with Slide number 10 displayed, open the **Insert** menu and choose **Movies and Sounds**. Select **Sound from Clip Organizer** in the submenu.
2. Point to a thumbnail, click the down arrow, and preview the sound clip. When you find an appropriate clip, insert it in the document. When prompted to automatically play the sound in the slide show, click **Yes**.
3. Drag the sound clip icon to the bottom right corner of the slide.
4. Right-click the sound clip icon and choose **Custom Animation** in the shortcut menu.
5. Click the down arrow for the item in the **Custom Animation** list and select **Timing**. Click the down arrow in the **Repeat** box and select **Until Next Click**. Click **OK**.
6. Click the **Slide Show** button in the task pane to view the slide in full screen. The sound clip will continue to play until you click the mouse. Exit the slide show to return to Normal view.
7. If necessary, display the Drawing toolbar. Select the sound icon and click **Draw** on the Drawing toolbar. Choose **Order** in the pop-up menu, and then select **Send to Back**. Then, drag the icon to the middle of the movie clip image.
8. Save the changes and leave the presentation open for the next Step-by-Step.

Hot Tip

To edit or remove the sound clip, you will need to select the movie clip image, choose the **Order** command, and send that image to the back. Then you will see the sound icon.

Use Help to Learn about Ways to Print the Presentation

PowerPoint offers several options for printing your presentation. You can print the outline, individual slides, handouts, and more. The Help screens will allow you to learn about the available options.

STEP-BY-STEP 9.12

1. If the Office Assistant is not displayed, open the **Help** menu and choose **Show the Office Assistant**.

2. Click the **Office Assistant**. Key **print** in the text box, then click **Search**.

3. A list of topics is displayed. Select **About printing**.

4. Read the paragraph of text and then click the link **Outline, notes pages, and handouts**.

5. Read the paragraph about printing an outline.

6. If the Contents, Answer Wizard, and Index tabs are not displayed, click the **Show** button on the Help toolbar. **Note:** If you click the **Show** button and the Help panel displays without the tabs, click the **Options** button on the Help toolbar and then select **Show Tabs** in the menu.

7. Click the **Answer Wizard** tab if necessary. In the What would you like to do? box, key **print outline** and then click **Search**.

8. Read the steps for printing an outline. In Step 3, click the link **Print from Microsoft PowerPoint**.

9. Read the three steps and leave the Help screen open. Then click in the PowerPoint window.

10. Open the **File** menu and choose **Print Preview**. Click the down arrow in the **Print What** box on the Print Preview toolbar, and then select **Outline View**. The outline is displayed as it would print.

11. Click the **Close** button on the Print Preview toolbar.

12. Click the application close box to close the presentation and the Help screen. If other applications are open, the Help screen will not close.

SUMMARY

In this lesson, you learned:

- Animation effects help make your presentation more interesting. You can set effect options to control how text and objects appear on your slides.
- An animation scheme provides pre-designed sets of visual effects that can be applied to selected slides or to all slides in the presentation.
- You can preview animations for one slide or for the whole presentation using options that are available in the task pane.
- Custom animations enable you to select the text and objects you want to animate. You can apply effects that determine how text or objects enter, display, and exit the slide.
- Sound effects can be added to enhance the animation of text and objects.
- Timing options allow you to determine when the animation begins and the speed at which the animation occurs.

- Once animations are applied, you can rearrange the order in which animated text and objects appear.
- The slide transition affects how each new slide appears. You can apply transition settings to a single slide or to all the slides in the presentation.
- Animated clip art and sound or music clips can add a new dimension to a presentation. The clips can be formatted to play automatically or to play when clicked by the mouse.
- PowerPoint provides several options for printing a presentation, including the outline, notes pages, handouts, and transparencies.

VOCABULARY *Review*

Define the following terms:

Animation	Entrance effect	Transitions
Animation schemes	Exit effect	Trigger
Emphasis effect	Sound effects	

REVIEW *Questions*

TRUE/FALSE

Circle T if the statement is true or F if the statement is false.

T F 1. By default, animations are set to trigger when you click the mouse.

T F 2. To add a sound effect, the text or object must already have an animation applied to it.

T F 3. You can insert a sound effect from the Clip Organizer or from any other source of sound files.

T F 4. When you format a slide transition, it must be applied to all slides in the presentation.

T F 5. When you create custom animations, you can apply the effects to all slides in the presentation.

FILL IN THE BLANK

Complete the following sentences by writing the correct word or words in the blanks provided.

1. A(n) __________ effect controls the animation effects after the text or object appears.
2. A(n) __________ effect controls how the text animates as it appears on the slide.

3. A(n) ________ effect controls the animation effects at the end of the animation sequence.

4. A slide must be displayed in ________ view before you can insert an animated graphic or sound clip.

5. When you apply a(n) ________ to a slide or group of slides, the visual effects are already formatted.

PROJECTS

PROJECT 9-1

1. Open **Project9-1** from the data files. Save the presentation as **Rain Forest** followed by your initials.

2. In the *subtitle* placeholder on slide number 1, key **A Report by** and then key your name.

3. Go to slide number 2. Customize the animation for the bulleted list to enter the slide with a Peek In format from the bottom. Choose an appropriate speed for the Entrance effect. The text should appear on a mouse click.

4. Go to slide number 3. Customize the animation for the items on the slide as follows:
   A. Format an Emphasis effect so that the clip art image grows by 150%. The animation should start on a mouse click.
   B. Format an Entrance effect of your choice for the title. The animation should start after the animation for A.
   C. Format an Entrance effect of your choice for the bulleted list. The animation should start after the animation for B.

5. Go to slide number 4. Customize the animation for the bulleted list and the title as follows:
   A. Format an Exit effect so items in the bulleted list leave the slide with the Spiral Out effect.
   B. Set the speed at 2 seconds (Medium).
   C. Format an Exit effect so the title exits with the Stretchy effect.

6. Go to slide number 3. Change the order of the animation sequence so that the title is the first item in the animation sequence.

7. Preview the slide show from the beginning.

8. Save the changes and leave the presentation open for the next project.

PROJECT 9-2

Creating such a variety of effects from one slide to the next can be distracting. If you get too creative with animation features, your audience may have trouble focusing on the content of your presentation. In this project you will create a more consistent flow for all the slides in your presentation.

1. Save the presentation as **Rain Forest 2** followed by your initials.

2. Go to slide number 1 and insert an appropriate sound clip to play automatically. Position the sound icon in the lower right corner of the slide.

3. Apply an animation scheme of your choice to all slides in the presentation.

4. Choose an appropriate slide transition. Set the speed for the transition to medium. Format the slides to advance automatically after five seconds. Apply the transition formats to all slides in the presentation.

5. Preview the entire slide show and save the changes.

6. Display the presentation outline in Print Preview.

7. Close the presentation.

WEB PROJECT

In this lesson, you inserted animated objects and sound clips in your presentations. You can also insert video clips and movies in slides as objects. Video clips are short movies that play when you display the slide during a presentation. Suppose you intend to create a presentation about hurricanes and want to include a video of hurricane movement taken from space. Go to the NASA Web site (*www.nasa.gov* at the time this text was published) and navigate links to the multimedia video gallery. Locate a link that will show you videos of hurricanes. Choose a hurricane and then click the movie link for that hurricane. What type of "player" do you have to use to view the video? How large is the video file? Could you store a presentation that includes this video on a floppy disk? Play the video on your computer, if possible.

TEAMWORK PROJECT

The presentations you created in this lesson would work well as Web sites on the Internet. As with most other Office XP applications, PowerPoint presentations are easy to save as Web pages. In this project, explore with a teammate how to publish a PowerPoint presentation on the Web.

1. With your teammate, choose a topic for your Web presentation, or open one of the presentations you have created in this unit.

2. Both teammates should read the Help material in PowerPoint about creating Web presentations. There are two ways to prepare a presentation for Web viewing: You can save the presentation as a Web page or you can publish the presentation. Make sure you both understand the differences between these two ways of putting PowerPoint material on the Web.

3. One teammate should try publishing the presentation while the other should simply save the presentation as a Web page. Describe your experience to your teammate and compare the processes for both approaches. How does the process differ for each approach? Which approach gives you more control over the presentation's appearance on the Web? Which is easiest?

4. View your presentations in your browser and navigate the slides using the options available. After you have explored how a presentation would look on the Web, close your browser and your presentation.

CRITICAL *Thinking*

ACTIVITY 9-1

You have created a presentation to convince fellow citizens to support a local clean-up campaign. You have included as the last slide a list of several phone numbers and contact names for more information on the campaign. You anticipate that your audience will want to see this information a number of times during the presentation. It will be time-consuming to click through the slides each time to reach the last slide. PowerPoint offers several ways that you can jump directly to a specific slide during a presentation. Research this topic using Help and write a brief report discussing at least two methods of moving between slides. Create a short presentation to demonstrate the two methods.

LESSON 10

CREATING AND FORMATTING AN EXCEL WORKSHEET

OBJECTIVES

Upon completion of this lesson, you should be able to:

- Identify the parts of the Excel screen.
- Create and navigate through a worksheet.
- Use the AutoCorrect and AutoComplete features in Excel.
- Change column width and row height.
- Format the contents of a cell.
- Merge cells.
- Use the Undo and Redo features.
- AutoFormat the worksheet.

Estimated Time: 1 hr.

VOCABULARY

Active cell
Cell
Cell reference
Font
Merge
Range
Spreadsheet
Workbook
Worksheet

Excel is an electronic spreadsheet application designed to replace the tedious work of using pencils, paper, and calculators. A ***spreadsheet*** is the document that you use to store and work with data in Excel. The worksheet is a grid of rows and columns into which you can enter numbers, text, and formulas. The spreadsheet is used to gather, organize, and summarize text and numeric data. Generally, the spreadsheet is also used to perform calculations. In the past, people manually created ledgers that served the same function as today's electronic spreadsheets. So when changes were necessary, the process of making corrections to the ledger was painstaking. With an electronic spreadsheet, changes are relatively easy.

Identify the Parts of the Excel Screen

IC³ 2-1.2.1-1

When you first launch the Excel application, a blank ***worksheet*** is displayed. Excel refers to the spreadsheet as a worksheet. The new worksheet is titled *Book1*. This filename will remain until you choose Save As from the File menu and assign the document a new filename. The worksheet is always stored in a ***workbook*** which contains one or more worksheets. Excel has its own unique menus, screen parts, and toolbars. The mouse pointer displays as a thick plus sign when it is within the worksheet. When you move the pointer to a menu, it turns into an arrow.

The New Document task pane is also displayed. This task pane enables you to quickly open workbooks that you have recently accessed or to create a new workbook. After you open an existing workbook or create a new workbook, the task pane will disappear. If Excel is already launched, you can click the New button on the Standard toolbar to create a new blank worksheet.

The worksheet is divided into columns and rows. Columns of the worksheet appear vertically and are identified by letters at the top of the worksheet window. Rows appear horizontally and are identified by numbers on the left side of the worksheet window. The intersection of a single row and a single column is called a ***cell***. The ***cell reference*** identifies the column letter and row number (for example, A1 or B4).

Computer Concepts

You can open additional workbooks on top of the blank Book1. Thus, you can have multiple Excel documents open at the same time.

Computer Concepts

When you open a new workbook using the Blank Workbook option in the task pane, the document contains default settings to create a traditional printed worksheet. Default settings are preset options or variables. You can change the default settings as you work with the document.

STEP-BY-STEP 10.1

1. Start Excel.

2. Compare your screen with Figure 10-1.

FIGURE 10-1
Main Excel window

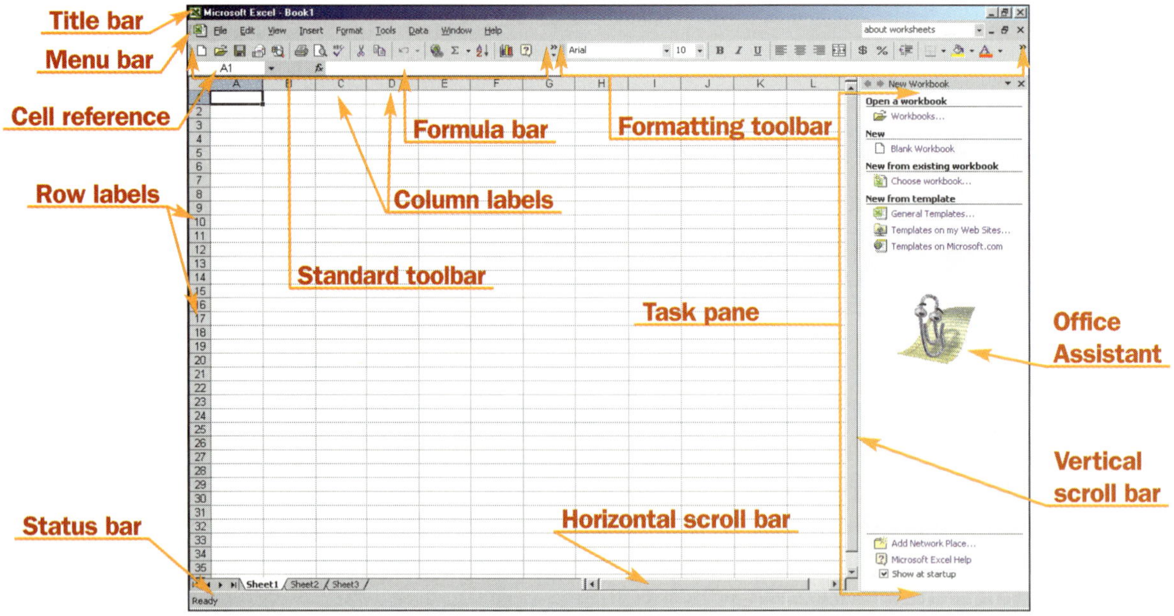

3. Note the various components of the Excel screen and their names. Leave the workbook open for the next Step-by-Step.

Create and Navigate through a Worksheet

2-1.3.1-2 To create a worksheet, you enter information into the cells. Before you can enter data into a cell, you must first select the cell. When the cell is selected, a dark border appears around the cell. You can select a cell using either the mouse or the keyboard. When a cell is selected, it is called the ***active cell***. The active cell is identified in the Name Box at the top of the worksheet screen. You can change the active cell by using the mouse or the keyboard.

Enter and Edit Data in a Worksheet

2-3.1.1-1 You enter data by keying text or numbers in the active cell and then either pressing Enter on the keyboard or clicking the Enter button (green checkmark) on the Formula Bar. You can also press Tab to enter the information and then move to the next cell. By default, Excel displays approximately eight characters in each cell. As you begin keying text, you will see the insertion point indicating where the next character of text will appear. When text is too long for a cell, it will spill over into the next cell—if the next cell is empty. If the next cell is not empty, the text that does not fit into the cell will not be displayed—but it is still contained within the cell.

2-3.1.2-1 You can edit, replace, or clear existing data in the worksheet cells. You can edit the data directly in the cell, or you can make the necessary changes to the cell contents in the Formula Bar. To replace cell contents, select the cell and key the new data. To clear the cell contents, select the cell and then press the Delete key or the Backspace key.

> **Hot Tip**
>
> If you choose not to enter the data you have keyed, you can press **ESC** or click the **Cancel** button (red X) in the Formula Bar.

STEP-BY-STEP 10.2

2-1.3.1-2 **1.** Click **Blank Workbook** in the New section of the task pane. A new workbook titled *Book2* is opened.

2-1.3.2-2 **2.** Click in cell **A3**. The cell is selected as shown in Figure 10-2.

FIGURE 10-2
Active cell in worksheet

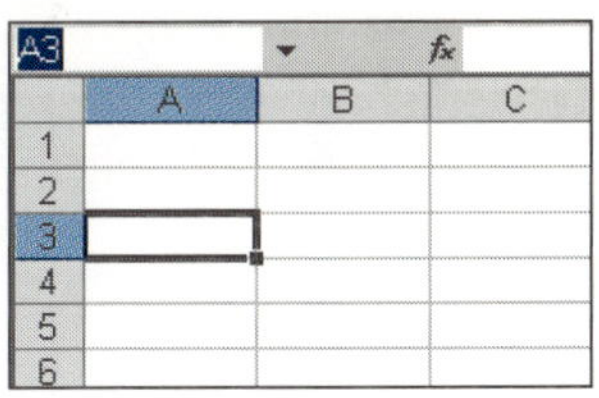

2-3.1.1-2 **3.** Key **Days**. Notice that the text you enter is displayed in the cell and in the Formula Bar.

4. Press **Tab**. The insertion point moves to the next cell in the third row, B3. Key **Cruise**.

5. Press **Tab** and key **Price**. Press **Tab** and key **Dates**. Press **Enter**. The insertion point moves to the first cell in the fourth row, A4. (The green checkmark in the Formula Bar only enters the data. It does not allow for the automatic movement to A4.)

> **Speech Recognition**
>
> If your computer has speech recognition capability, enable the Dictation mode and dictate the text and navigation commands to move from cell to cell and enter the data.

STEP-BY-STEP 10.2 Continued

2-3.1.2-3 **6.** Click in cell **A3**. It currently displays *Days* in the cell and in the Formula Bar. To edit the text in the Formula Bar, click in the **Formula Bar** and position the insertion point in front of the word *Days*. See Figure 10-3.

FIGURE 10-3
Insertion point positioned in the Formula Bar

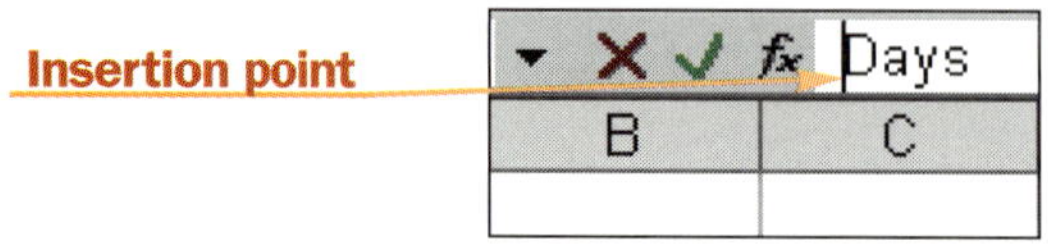

7. Key **#** and then press the **Spacebar**. Click the **Enter** button on the Formula Bar. The change is made in the Formula Bar and in cell A3.

2-3.1.2-2 **8.** Click in cell **B3**. It currently displays *Cruise*. Key **Destination** and press **Enter**. The contents of the cell are replaced with the new text you entered.

9. Click in cell **C3**. It currently displays *Price*. Press **F2**. Notice that the insertion point is now positioned at the end of the text in the cell.

10. Use the **Backspace** key to delete the existing text and key **Cost**, then press **Enter**. All the contents in the cell are replaced with the new text you entered, and the cell below, C4, becomes active.

2-3.1.1-3 **11.** Click in cell **A4**. Key **6** and press **Enter**. The cell below, A5, becomes active.

12. Key the following numbers, pressing **Enter** after each number. When you are done, your worksheet should look like Figure 10-4.

4

5

7

4

Did You Know?

You can choose to have text wrap within a cell in the same way text wraps within a word-processing document. The row height will automatically adjust to show all of the lines of text within the cell. To turn on the text wrap option, select the cell(s) and open the **Format** menu and choose **Cells**. Click the **Alignment** tab and turn on the **Wrap text** option.

Hot Tip

The Enter and Cancel buttons will not display in the Formula Bar unless you enter data in a cell or position the insertion point in the Formula Bar.

Speech Recognition

If your computer has speech recognition capability, turn on the Speak On Enter option to hear the value of the cell immediately after you enter data in each cell.

STEP-BY-STEP 10.2 Continued

FIGURE 10-4
Worksheet with data entered

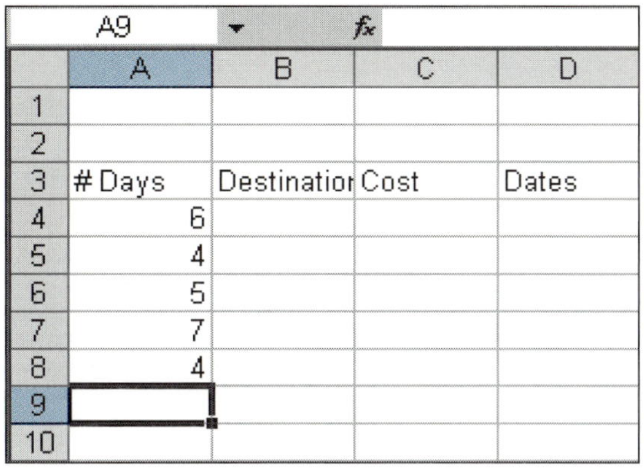

13. Edit the contents of cell A4. Double-click in the cell to display the insertion point. Then, change the contents to **7**, and press **Enter**.

14. Save the worksheet as **Cruises** followed by your initials. Leave the worksheet open for the next Step-by-Step.

Use Help to Find More Ways to Move the Insertion Point and Select Cells

You've already learned a few ways to position the insertion point and select cells. In the following Step-by-Step, you will use the Help feature to find a list of shortcut keys for navigating through a worksheet and selecting cells.

STEP-BY-STEP 10.3

1. Click the **Office Assistant**.

2. In the text box, key **shortcut keys** and then click **Search**.

3. When the Office Assistant displays a list of topics, select the topic **Keyboard shortcuts** (or something similar). The Help dialog box shown in Figure 10-5 suggests several topics. Your dialog box may not match exactly.

Hot Tip

You can also open the **Help** menu and choose **Microsoft Excel Help**, or click **F1**. You should then use the **Index** tab and its text box.

Hot Tip

To expand all the content at once, click the **Show All** link at the top of the list of topics. The link will then display Hide All. When you click the **Hide All** link, all the content will collapse at once.

STEP-BY-STEP 10.3 Continued

FIGURE 10-5
Microsoft Excel Help dialog box

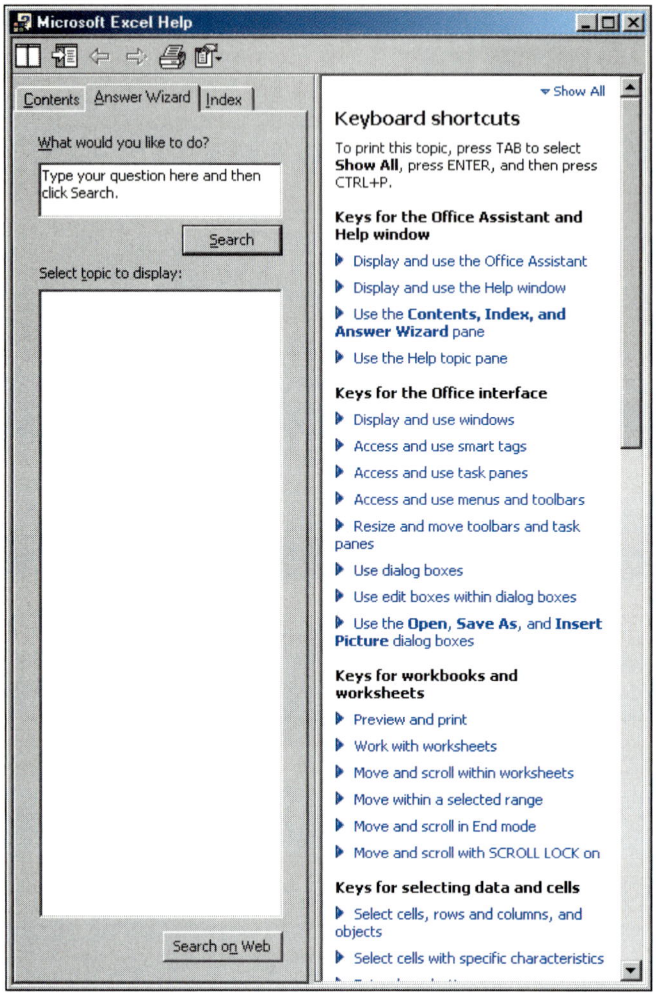

4. When you point to any of the topics in the list (a link), your mouse pointer will change to a hand. Notice there is a blue triangle just to the left of each link.

5. Click the link **Select cells, rows and columns, and objects**. The blue triangle just to the left of the link now points downward to indicate that the content is expanded.

6. Use the vertical scroll bar if necessary to see and read all of the shortcuts in the list.

7. Click the same link again to collapse the content. The blue triangle now points to the right.

8. Click the **Close** box on the Help dialog box. Leave the worksheet open for the next Step-by-Step.

Use the AutoCorrect and AutoComplete Features in Excel

The AutoCorrect feature in Excel corrects common mistakes as you enter data. For example, if you key *adn*, Excel will automatically change the text to read *and*. With the AutoComplete feature, Excel compares the first few characters you key in a cell with existing entries in the same column. If the characters match an existing entry, Excel proposes the existing entry. You can press Enter to accept the proposed entry.

STEP-BY-STEP 10.4

1. Click in cell **B4**. Key **Caribbean** and press **Enter**.
2. Key **Bahamas** and press **Enter**.
3. Key **C**. Notice that Excel suggests *Caribbean* because you entered it earlier in the column. Press **Enter** to accept the proposed text.
4. Key **Alaska** and press **Enter**.
5. Key **Belize adn**. Then look at the active cell as you press **Spacebar**. Excel automatically corrects the spelling of *and*. Key **Cozumel** and press **Enter**.
6. Save the changes and leave the worksheet open for the next Step-by-Step.

Change Column Width and Row Height

IC3 2-3.1.7-1 2-3.1.7-2

Sometimes the data you enter in a cell is wider than the column. When the data is too wide for the cell, Excel displays a series of number signs (####), cuts off the data, or allows the data to run outside of the column. You can widen the column in two ways. You can drag the right edge of the column heading to the desired size. Or, an alternative way to change the column width is to select the cells you want to change and then use the Column Width command. Through this method, you can specify the exact width, or you can let Excel find the best fit. Likewise, you can change the height of a row to meet the requirements of the data within the row.

> **Computer Concepts**
>
> You can also use the AutoFit Selection feature to reduce the width of a column to eliminate unnecessary white space in a column.

IC3 2-3.1.7-1

STEP-BY-STEP 10.5

1. Point to the boundary on the right side of the column heading B. When the pointer changes to a double-headed arrow, drag the boundary to the right about one-half inch to widen the column. See Figure 10-6.

STEP-BY-STEP 10.5 Continued

FIGURE 10-6
Dragging a column boundary to change the column width

Drag the column border to resize a column

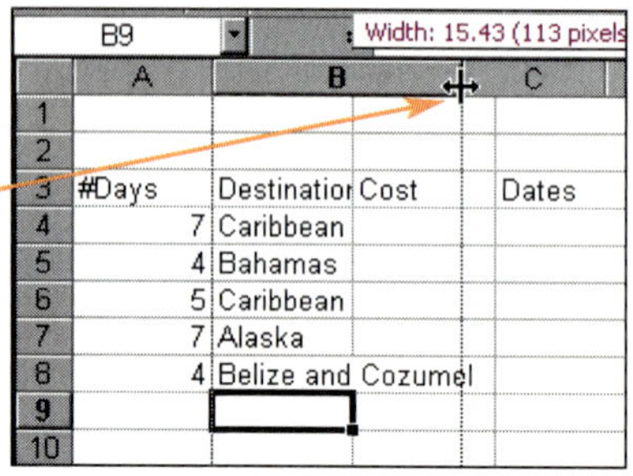

2. Click the column heading **B** to select the entire column.

2-3.1.8-1 3. Open the **Format** menu and choose **Column**, then select **AutoFit Selection** in the submenu. Excel automatically adjusts the cells in the column to fit the cell with the most content—in this case, *Belize and Cozumel.*

4. Click the row heading **3** to select the entire row.

2-3.1.7-2 5. Open the **Format** menu and choose **Row**. Select **Row Height** and change the height to **0.5**". Click **OK**.

6. Observe the change in row 3 and then click **Undo**.

7. Click anywhere in the worksheet to deselect the row. Save the changes and leave the worksheet open for the next Step-by-Step.

Hot Tip

You can also find the best fit by positioning the mouse pointer on the right edge of the column heading and double-clicking when the double-headed arrow appears.

Speech Recognition

If your computer has speech recognition capability, enable the Command mode and say the command to open the Format menu, choose the Column command, and select the AutoFit option.

Format the Contents of a Cell

2-3.1.2-4 Formatting the contents of a cell, like in other Windows applications, changes the way it appears. For example, you may want to change the alignment of the text or use commas in numbers to separate the thousands. To apply formats, you must first select the cell(s) containing the data to be formatted.

Computer Concepts

When you clear the contents of a cell, the formats applied to the contents of that cell are not removed. To remove the formats without removing the data, choose **Clear** from the Edit menu and select **Formats** in the submenu.

Change Fonts and Font Sizes and Align Text

The *font* is the design of the typeface in your document. Fonts are available in a variety of styles and sizes, and you can use multiple fonts in one document. The font size is a measurement in points that determines the height of the font. Bold, italic, underline, and color formats can also add emphasis to the contents of a cell.

Hot Tip

To change the font color, choose **Cells** from the Format menu, then click on the **Font** tab.

By default, Excel aligns text at the left of the cell and numbers at the right of the cell. However, you can change the alignment.

When you select a group of cells, the group is called a *range*. All cells in a range touch each other and form a rectangle. The range is identified by the cell in the upper left corner and the cell in the lower right corner, separated by a colon (for example, A1:D4).

Computer Concepts

After changing the font or font size, you may find it necessary to adjust the column width, even if you previously used the AutoFit feature.

STEP-BY-STEP 10.6

1. Click in cell **A3**, then drag to the right to select a range of cells containing the other three cells in the same row (B3, C3, and D3). The range A3:D3 is selected.
2. Click the **Italic** button on the Formatting toolbar. The text in each of the cells is formatted with the italic attribute.

3. With the cells still selected, click the down arrow at the right of the **Font** box on the Formatting toolbar. Scroll down and select **Times New Roman**.

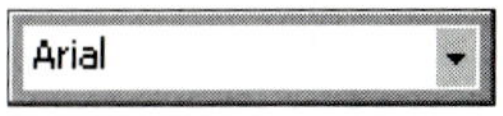

4. With the cells still selected, click the down arrow at the right of the **Font Size** box. Select **14**.
5. With the cells still selected, click the **Center** button on the Formatting toolbar. Each of the labels in the row is centered.

6. Click in cell **A4** and drag down to cell A8 to select a range of cells. Click the **Center** button.
7. Deselect the cells and save the changes. Leave the worksheet open for the next Step-by-Step.

Format Numbers and Dates

Generally, numbers are displayed with no formatting and are aligned at the right side of a cell. However, dates and times are automatically formatted in the default styles dd-mm-yy and hh:mm, respectively.

Format Painter

2-3.3.6-1

You can use the Format Painter to copy the format of a worksheet cell without copying the contents of the cell. For example, after formatting one cell as a date, you may format other cells for dates by painting the format. To paint a format, highlight a cell that has the format you want to use. Click the Format Painter button on the toolbar, and then highlight the range of cells that you would like to format in the same way.

STEP-BY-STEP 10.7

1. Click in cell **C4** and key **599**, then press **Enter**. Notice that the numbers are automatically aligned at the right edge of the cell.

STEP-BY-STEP 10.7 Continued

2. Key the following numbers, pressing **Enter** after each number:

   299

   399

   799

   299

3. Click in cell **C4** (*599*) and drag down to select the range C4:C8.

4. Open the **Format** menu and choose **Cells**. If necessary, click the **Number** tab to display the dialog box shown in Figure 10-7.

2-3.3.1-1 **FIGURE 10-7**
Number tab in the Format Cells dialog box

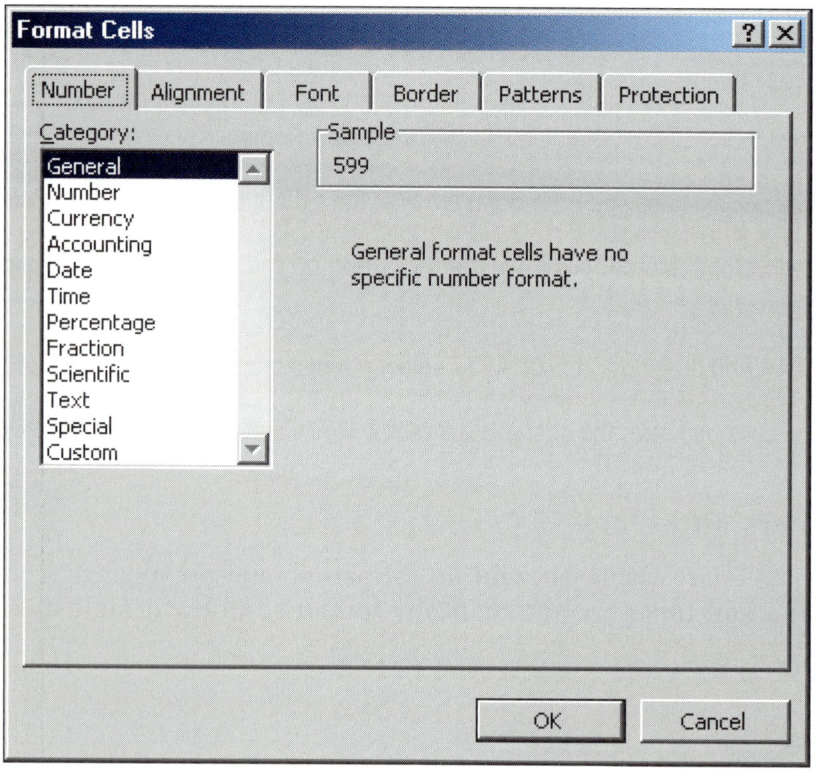

2-3.3.1-2 5. Under Category, select **Currency**. The dialog box changes to display the currency format options. See Figure 10-8.

> **Hot Tip**
>
> **Ctrl + 1** is a shortcut for accessing the Format Cells dialog box. You can also access the Cells dialog box by right-clicking an active cell or range and then selecting **Format Cells** in the shortcut menu.

STEP-BY-STEP 10.7 Continued

FIGURE 10-8
Currency format options in the Format Cells dialog box

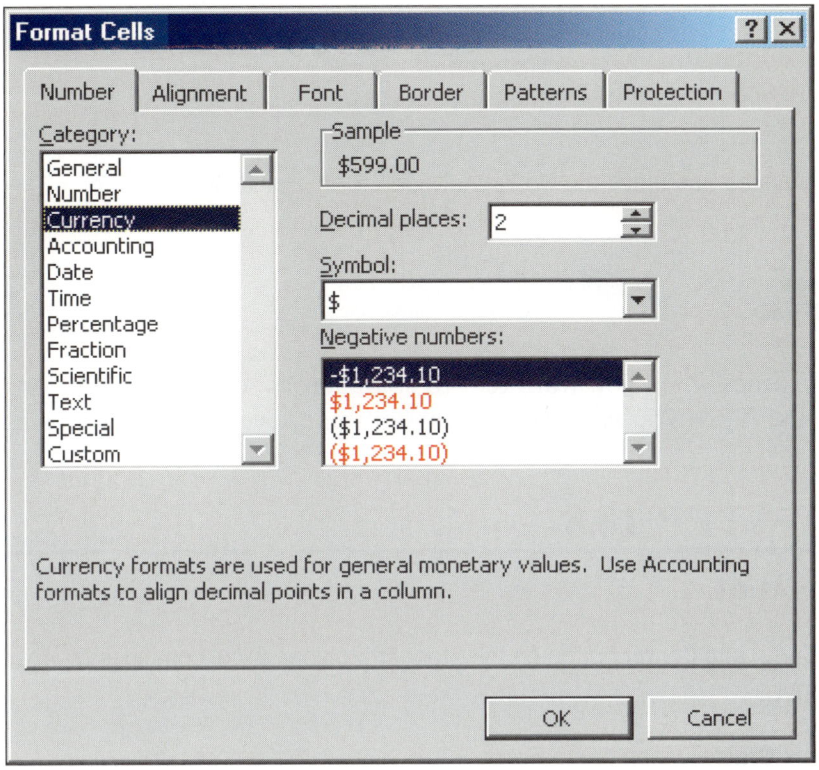

6. In the Decimal places box, click the down arrow until **0** is displayed. Click **OK**. The numbers are all formatted with dollar signs.

7. Click in cell **D4**. Key **March 3** and press **Enter**. Notice that Excel automatically changed the format to *3-Mar*.

8. Open the **Format** menu and choose **Cells**. Because you just accessed it, the Number tab should be displayed. If necessary, select the **Number** tab.

9. Under Category, select **Date**. Under Type, select **3/14/01** (not *3/14/2001). Click **OK**. The date format in cell D4 changes.

2-3.3.6-2 **10.** Click in cell **D4** if necessary. Click the **Format Painter** button on the toolbar.

11. Click in cell **D5** and drag down to cell **D9**. When you release the mouse button, the format from D4 will be copied to D5 through D9.

Did You Know?

2-1.2.5-3

You can magnify or reduce the view of the worksheet by using the **Zoom** button on the Standard toolbar. The default magnification is 100 percent. To get a closer view, select a larger percentage from the drop-down list or key in your own percentage and click **Enter**.

STEP-BY-STEP 10.7 Continued

12. Enter the following dates in cells D5 through D8, pressing **Enter** after each date:
    3/10
    3/18
    3/25
    3/31

13. Save the changes and leave the worksheet open for the next Step-by-Step.

Merge Cells

There will be times when you want text to span across several columns or rows. To do this, you can merge cells. When you ***merge*** cells, you combine several cells into a single cell.

STEP-BY-STEP 10.8

1. Select cells **A1:D1**.

2. Click the **Merge and Center** button on the Standard toolbar. Excel combines the four cells into a single cell (A1).

3. Key **La Croix Cruises**, then press **Enter**.

4. Click in cell **A1** to select it again. Change the font to **Times New Roman** and change the font size to **16**.

5. With the cell still selected, click the **Bold** button on the formatting toolbar.

6. With the cell still selected, click the down arrow to the right of the **Fill Color** button on the Formatting toolbar and select the color **Yellow**.

7. Deselect the cell and save the changes. Leave the worksheet open for the next Step-by-Step.

Use the Undo and Redo Features

2-1.3.7-1
2-1.3.7-2

If you make a mistake, or if you change your mind, you can use the Undo command to reverse your most recent changes. If you undo an action and then change your mind, you can reverse the undo action by using the Redo command. You can undo and redo multiple actions at one time by choosing from the Undo or Redo drop-down lists on the Standard toolbar. When you undo or redo an action from the drop-down list, Excel will also undo or redo all the actions listed above it on the list.

STEP-BY-STEP 10.9

1. Click in cell **A9**. Key **4** and press **Tab**.

2. Key **Baja Mexico** and press **Tab**.

3. Key **299** and press **Tab**.

4. Key **4/2** and press **Enter**.

2-1.3.7-1 5. Click the **Undo** button on the Standard toolbar. The date is removed.

6. Click the down arrow to the right of the **Undo** button. The Undo list, similar to that shown in Figure 10-9, is displayed.

> **Computer Concepts**
>
> There is a limit of 16 actions that you can undo and redo. Furthermore, the Undo and Redo actions are cleared from the drop-down list when you save the worksheet. Therefore, you should always undo an action as soon as you realize you have made a mistake.

FIGURE 10-9
Undo list

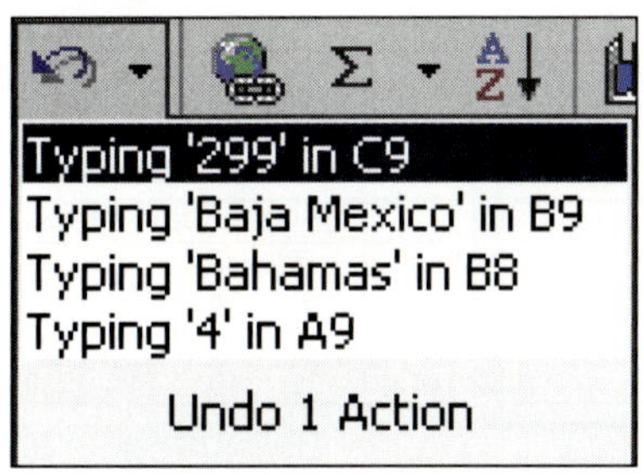

7. Click on the second action in the list (*Typing 'Baja Mexico' in B9*) to undo the last two actions. Cells B9 and C9 are empty now.

2-1.3.7-2 8. Click the down arrow to the right of the **Redo** button on the Standard toolbar to display the Redo list shown in Figure 10-10. Click on the third action in the list to redo all three. The content in Cells B9, C9, and D9 is restored.

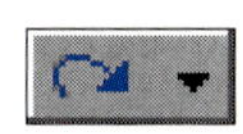

FIGURE 10-10
Redo list

9. Save the changes and leave the worksheet open for the next Step-by-Step.

> **Hot Tip**
>
> If the Redo button is not displayed on the Standard toolbar, click the **Toolbar Options** button (down arrow at the right side of the toolbar) and then click on the **Redo** button.

AutoFormat the Worksheet

2-3.3.5-1 Excel offers numerous AutoFormats that you can use to give your worksheet a professional look. These AutoFormats instantly format the entire worksheet with borders, shading, and data formatting. To apply an AutoFormat, you must first select the range to be formatted. The AutoFormat may override existing formats that you have applied. If desired, you can modify the formats that are applied.

STEP-BY-STEP 10.10

1. Select all the cells in the worksheet that contain data (A1:D9). (*Hint*: Click in the left corner of cell A1 and drag down to cell A9.)

2-3.3.5-2

2. Open the **Format** menu and choose **AutoFormat**. The dialog box shown in Figure 10-11 is displayed.

FIGURE 10-11
AutoFormat dialog box

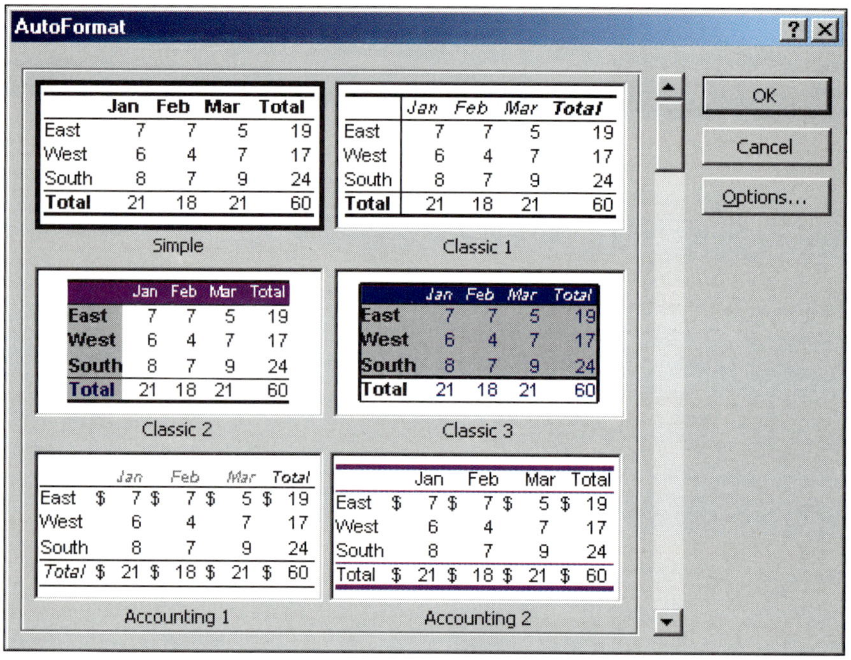

3. Scroll down and select the **Colorful 2** option. Click **OK**.
4. Select cells **A4:A9**, then click the **Center** button on the Formatting toolbar.
5. Click in cell **B3** and then click the **Center** button on the Formatting toolbar.
6. Deselect the cells and save the changes. Close the document.

SUMMARY

In this lesson, you learned:

- The Excel screen has its own unique screen parts, menus, and toolbars.
- To enter data in a cell, the cell must be selected. You can use the mouse or the keyboard to move from one cell to another.
- As you enter data, Excel will automatically correct some of your keyboarding errors. If the data you are entering matches characters of existing entries, Excel will propose the existing entry to save you time.
- There are several options for changing the column width. You can drag a column border, use the AutoFit feature, or specify an exact measurement.
- When you format the contents of a cell, you change the appearance of the text or numbers in the cell.
- If you want text to span across several rows or columns, you can merge the cells into a single cell.
- The Undo command reverses a previous action. The Redo command reverses an undo.
- You can quickly and easily give a worksheet a professional look by applying one of the autoformats available.

VOCABULARY *Review*

Define the following terms:

Active cell	Font	Spreadsheet
Cell	Merge	Workbook
Cell reference	Range	Worksheet

REVIEW *Questions*

TRUE/FALSE

Circle T if the statement is true or F if the statement is false.

T F 1. A worksheet is the same as a spreadsheet.

T F 2. Within the worksheet, the mouse pointer displays as a hand with a pointing finger.

T F 3. When data is too wide for a cell, the part of the data that will not fit is automatically deleted.

T F 4. By default, text aligns at the left of a cell.

T F 5. You use the Merge and Center button to allow text to span several columns.

FILL IN THE BLANK

Complete the following sentences by writing the correct word or words in the blanks provided.

1. The _________ identifies the column letter and row number.
2. The selected cell is called the _________ cell.
3. A selected group of cells is called a(n) _________.
4. The command you use to change a date format is _________.
5. To automatically apply shading, borders, and alignment options to selected cells in a worksheet, use the _________ feature.

PROJECTS

PROJECT 10-1

1. If necessary, launch Excel. If Excel is already launched, click the **New Button** on the Standard toolbar to create a new worksheet.
2. In cell A1, key **Running vs. Walking** and press **Enter.**
3. Beginning in cell A3, key the data shown below. If you would like, you can use AutoComplete to help you complete the entries, but you will then have to edit the entry to change *stroll* to **brisk** and **fast.** Do not be concerned if the columns are too narrow for the content. You will fix that in the next step.

Activity	Speed	Calories/Hour
Walking (stroll)	**2 mph**	**120**
Walking (brisk)	**3.5 mph**	**360**
Walking (fast)	**5 mph**	**480**
Jogging	**4 mph**	**600**
Running (moderate)	**10 mph**	**1020**

4. Save the worksheet as **Exercise** followed by your initials.
5. Adjust the column widths to display all text.
6. Merge and center cells A1:C1. Format the range of cells with a fill color of your choice.
7. Edit the speed for Jogging to 5 mph. In cell A1, change the word *vs.* to **versus.**
8. Undo the last change.
9. Format the text in cell A1 as **16-point bold.** Format the range A3:C3 as **12-point bold italic.** (Adjust cell widths as necessary after changing the text size.)
10. Select the cell range **B4:B8** and center the content.
11. Select the cell range **C4:C8** and apply the **Number** format with the 1000 separator and no decimal places.
12. Save the changes, then close the worksheet.

PROJECT 10-2

1. Open **Project10-2** from the data files. Save the spreadsheet as **Mensa Groups** followed by your initials.
2. Merge and center cells A1:D1.
3. Merge and center cells A2:D2.
4. Select the range **A1:C22** and apply the **List 2** AutoFormat.
5. Change the main heading text size to **12 point**.
6. Click in cell **A2**. Change the date format to the **March-01** style. Add the **bold** and **italic** formats and **center** the text in the cells.
7. Select the cell range **A4:C4** and add the **center**, **bold**, and **italic** formats.
8. Save your changes. Close the workbook.

WEB PROJECT

You have decided you would like to go on a bicycle tour of France. Use Web search tools to locate information on bicycle tours to France. (Your search expression should be similar to *"bicycle tours" AND France.*) Visit several sites to find information from a number of tour operators. Create a worksheet to store the results of your research. Your worksheet should record starting date, ending date, cost, the region of France the tour visits, and level of difficulty of the biking (if supplied). Format the worksheet as you learned in this lesson to make the information about each separate tour company easy to compare.

TEAMWORK PROJECT

Worksheets are excellent tools to organize information so you can make easy comparisons between sets of data. For this project, assume you need to set up a home office with new communications equipment. Because you're not yet sure of your budget, you need several price options for each piece of equipment. With a teammate, gather and organize information as follows:

1. Identify a list of at least 16 pieces of equipment that a state-of-the-art home office needs. Some of these may be a desktop computer, scanner, printer, fax (or all-in-one unit that includes scanning, copying, printing, and faxing functions), cordless phone, answering machine, and so on.
2. Create a worksheet to store the list of equipment you decide on. Create column headings for "Low End," Moderate," and "High End" so that you can store three prices for each equipment item.
3. Using computer catalogs or Web resources, find low-end, moderate, and high-end options for each equipment item. For example, low-end options for a copier would include 3 pages per minute and black and white copies. Moderate options for a copier would include 8 pages per minute and an automatic document feeder. High-end options would include 12 pages per minute, color copies, and zoom capability. Divide the research work so that you find information on half of the items and your teammate finds information on the other half. Key your results in one worksheet.

4. Format the worksheet so that you can clearly see all data you have entered. Apply AutoFormat to make the data more attractive and readable. Compare your worksheet with those of other teams to see what equipment items are considered most important for a home office.

CRITICAL *Thinking*

ACTIVITY 10-1

While formatting a worksheet, you have changed the default font in a few cell ranges from Arial to Times New Roman. Selecting each cell range is tedious, however. Is there a way you can select an entire worksheet and apply a new font to all cells at one time? Use the Help files in Excel to find the answer and then write a brief report on what you learn.

LESSON 11

ORGANIZING THE WORKSHEET

OBJECTIVES

Upon completion of this lesson, you should be able to:

- Insert and delete rows and columns.
- Clear and delete data.
- Copy and move data.
- Fill the same data in adjacent cells.
- Fill a data series in adjacent cells.
- Create multiple worksheets.
- Hide and unhide columns and rows.
- Freeze and unfreeze columns and rows.
- Sort data.
- Change the page setup.
- Print the worksheets.

Estimated Time: 1 hour

VOCABULARY

Ascending order
Clipboard
Descending order
Fill handle
Filling
Header row
Landscape orientation
Portrait orientation

Insert and Delete Rows and Columns

IC3 2-3.1.5-1

When you insert or delete a row or a column in Excel, it affects the entire worksheet. All existing data is shifted in some direction. For example, when you add a new column, the existing data shifts to the right. When you add a new row, the data shifts down a row. One of the beneficial features of Excel is that it automatically updates the cell references whenever you do this. If the data in one cell is dependent upon the data in another cell, when these cells are adjusted, Excel will keep straight what information is required where. When you delete rows and columns, the cells and all their contents are removed, and the cell references are also automatically updated.

To insert or delete multiple columns and rows in a single step, select the desired number of columns or rows before executing the command.

STEP-BY-STEP 11.1

1. Open file **Step11-1** from the data files. Save the worksheet as **Tallest Structures** followed by your initials. (*Note*: This spreadsheet contains data about the tallest towers and buildings built by man. This list is not intended to be an official list, and the data contained in the list may be inaccurate or out of date.)

2-3.1.5-3 2. Select any cell in column D. Open the **Edit** menu and choose **Delete**. The Delete dialog box shown in Figure 11-1 is displayed.

> **Extra Challenge**
>
> Explore the Internet for up-to-date information about the tallest buildings in the world. Look for details in your search about the standards used for measuring tall buildings, and use this information to evaluate your Internet sources to determine if the data is current, correct, and reliable.

FIGURE 11-1
Delete dialog box

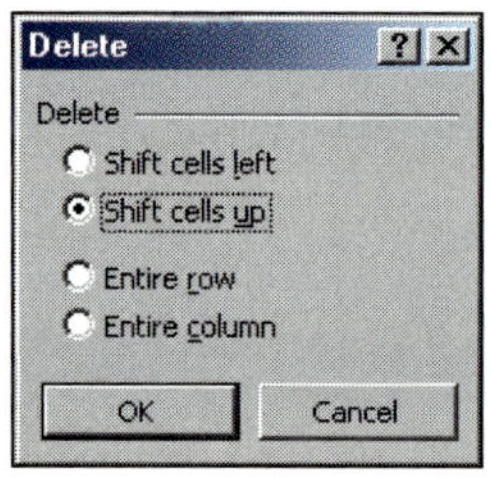

3. Select the option **Entire column** in the dialog box, then click **OK**. The column and all its contents are deleted from the worksheet. What was labeled *Column E* is now labeled *Column D*.

2-3.1.5-2 4. Click in any cell in Row 11. Open the **Insert** menu and choose **Rows**. A new row is inserted above the row you had selected and it becomes Row 11. The existing data shifts down, and the row labels are updated to reflect the change.

> **Speech Recognition**
>
> If your computer has speech recognition capability, enable the Command mode and dictate the commands to open the Delete dialog box and select the option.

5. Key the following information in the new row:

   Canadian National (CN) Tower

   TV/Tourist tower

   Toronto, Canada

   1,814

6. Click on the label for Row 12 and drag down to include Row 13 in the selection. Both rows should be selected.

7. Open the **Insert** menu and choose **Rows**. Two new rows are inserted above the selected rows.

STEP-BY-STEP 11.1 Continued

8. Key the following information in the new rows:

Ostankino Tower	**TV/Tourist tower**
Moscow, Russia	**1,772**
Oriental Pearl Tower	**TV tower**
Shanghai, China	**1,535**

9. Click on the label for Row 2. The whole row should be selected. Open the **Edit** menu and choose **Delete**. Because you selected the entire row before choosing the Delete command, the Delete dialog box does not display but the entire row is deleted.

10. Click on the column A label to select the entire column. Open the **Insert** menu and choose **Columns**. A new column is inserted to the left of what was column A—which is now *column B*. The new column is *column A* and is the active column.

11. Click in cell **A1**, then click the **Bold** button on the Formatting toolbar to turn on the bold format. Key **Ranking**, and then press **Enter**.

12. Save the changes and leave the workbook open for the next Step-by-Step.

Delete, Copy, and Move Data

Sometimes after entering data in a worksheet, you need to reorganize it. You may even want to remove some of the data and not replace it. Or, you may want to move or copy existing data from one location to another.

Clear and Delete Data

-1.3.3-1

The process for deleting data can be as simple as pressing the Delete or Backspace keys. When you delete the contents of a cell this way, the formats for the cell remain in the cell. Therefore, if you enter new data in the cell, the existing formats will apply to the new contents.

If you want to remove the contents and the formats, you need to clear the cell. Clearing the cell leaves a blank cell in the worksheet. You can clear the contents and the formats from the cell, clear just the contents, or clear just the formats.

-3.1.4-1

When you use the delete feature, you remove the cell entirely. With the delete feature, you have four options. You can delete an entire row or an entire column. Or you can delete just a single cell and then shift the cells to the left or shift the cells up. Likewise, you can insert a single cell and shift the surrounding cells to the right or down. However, use caution when using the shift feature. The results may misalign data in your rows and columns. If this happens, you can always Undo the deletion to return the data to its original position.

STEP-BY-STEP 11.2

-1.3.3-1

1. Click in cell **E9**. The cell currently displays *1,910*. Press the **Delete** key to remove the contents.

STEP-BY-STEP 11.2 Continued

2. With cell E9 still selected, key **1909** and press **Enter**. Notice that the cell contents are automatically centered within the cell and that the comma is automatically added because these formats remained after you deleted the original cell contents.

3. Click in cell **E6**. The cell currently displays *2,000*. Open the **Edit** menu and choose **Clear**. Select **Formats** in the submenu. The formats are removed from the cell, but the contents remain. Notice that the numbers align at the right, and the comma is removed.

4. Click the **Undo** button to reverse the action.

2-3.1.4-2 5. Click in cell **B13**. Open the **Insert** menu and choose **Cells**. The Insert dialog box is displayed. Select **Shift cells down** and then click **OK**. The contents in cells B13 through B21 are each shifted down one cell.

6. Shifting these cells made part of the Building column not align properly with the rest of the table. Click **Undo**.

2-3.1.4-3 7. Click in cell **C14**. Open the **Edit** menu and choose **Delete**. The Delete dialog box is displayed. Select **Shift cells left** and then click **OK**. The contents in cells D14 and E14 are shifted one cell to the left.

8. Notice that the city name is centered instead of left aligned. This is because the cell formats also shifted to the left. Click in cell **D14** and click the **Align Left** button to align the text consistently with the other data in the column.

9. Press **Tab** to move to cell E14, key **1,362**, and press **Enter**. Click the **Center** button if necessary to align the contents with the rest of the column.

10. Save the changes and leave the workbook open for the next Step-by-Step.

Copy and Move Data

2-1.3.5-1
2-3.1.2-4
Copying data saves you from having to key the same data into another location. The process, as in all Office applications, is easy. First, you must copy the data from one location. To copy the data, select it and then click the Copy button on the Standard toolbar. The data is placed in a temporary storage location in your computer's memory called the ***Clipboard***. Then, select the destination cell where you want to place the data, and paste the data into the new location. The data remains in the Clipboard. The Clipboard will hold up to 24 items. If you copy a 25th item, the very first item you placed in the Clipboard is deleted.

2-1.3.6-1 Moving data is similar to copying data, except you cut the data from one location and paste it in the destination location. When you move or copy all the data in a cell, the formats are also moved or copied. Unlike a word-processing table, if you move data to a cell that already has data in it, that data doesn't move to make room for the new data. If you don't want to lose information, you have to move data into empty cells; otherwise, the data in the destination cells will be replaced.

Did You Know?

If you want to add the same contents to multiple cells, you can select all the cells before you enter the content. After you key the content, press **Ctrl + Enter**. The content you keyed will then be entered into each of the selected cells.

STEP-BY-STEP 11.3

2-1.3.5-1 **1.** Click in cell **D2**. Click the **Copy** button on the Standard toolbar. The contents (*North Dakota, USA*) of the cell are copied to the Clipboard. Also, an animated border (a dotted-line marquee) is displayed around the selected cell as shown in Figure 11-2.

> **Hot Tip**
>
> If the Paste button is not displayed on the Standard toolbar, click the **Toolbar Options** button at the right end of the toolbar and then select the **Paste** button.

FIGURE 11-2
Marquee around a selected cell

Animated border (marquee)

2-1.3.6-1 **2.** Click in cell **D3**. Then click the **Paste** button on the Standard toolbar. The contents (*North Dakota, USA*) are pasted in the destination cell.

3. Press **Esc** to remove the marquee around the copied cell.

> **Hot Tip**
>
> If the Cut button is not displayed on the Standard toolbar, click the **Toolbar Options** button at the right end of the toolbar and then select the **Cut** button.

2-1.3.4-1 **4.** Click in cell **C5**. The cell currently displays *Radio tower*. Click the **Cut** button on the Standard toolbar. The contents of the cell are stored in the Clipboard and a marquee appears around the cell border.

5. Click in cell **C4**, then click the **Paste** button on the Standard toolbar. The contents from cell C5 are moved to cell C4.

> **Computer Concepts**
>
> You can copy or move multiple cells of data at the same time. First select the range, then click the **Copy** or **Cut** button. Select the first cell in the destination range and click the **Paste** button.

6. Save the changes and leave the workbook open for the next Step-by-Step.

Use the AutoFill Command to Enter Data

The AutoFill command is another time-saving feature that enables you to copy data from one cell to another. AutoFill also provides several options for entering certain kinds of data, such as months, days of the week, or a series of numbers.

Fill the Same Data in Adjacent Cells

Filling data is another method for copying data in a worksheet. It is faster than copying and pasting because filling requires only one step. However, the Fill command can only be used when the destination cells are adjacent to the original cell. You can fill data up or down in the same column, or right or left in the same row.

2-3.1.3-1 When you fill a cell, you can choose to copy the cell contents either with or without the formats. Therefore, this feature will save you even more time if you apply formats before using the Fill command.

STEP-BY-STEP 11.4

1. Click in cell **C7**. The cell currently displays *TV tower.*

2. Position your mouse pointer over the small square in the bottom right corner of the active cell. This square, shown in Figure 11-3, is called the ***fill handle***. When you point to the fill handle, the pointer changes to a bold plus sign.

FIGURE 11-3
Fill handle in a selected cell

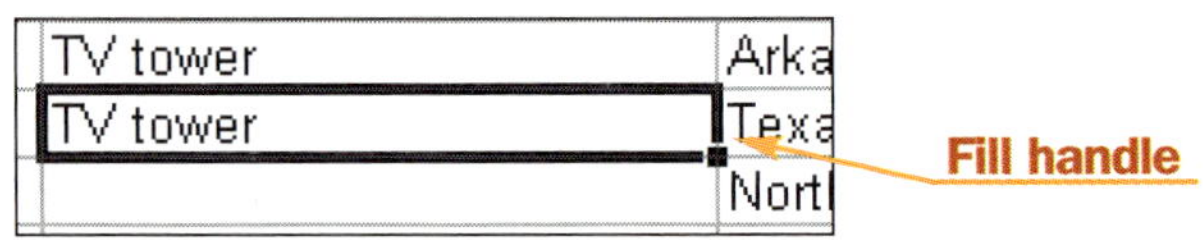

2-3.1.3-2

3. Drag the fill handle down to cell C9. The range of cells C7:C9 is selected. A ScreenTip similar to the one shown in Figure 11-4 displays the cell contents that will be copied to the range of cells.

FIGURE 11-4
Copying text to a range of cells

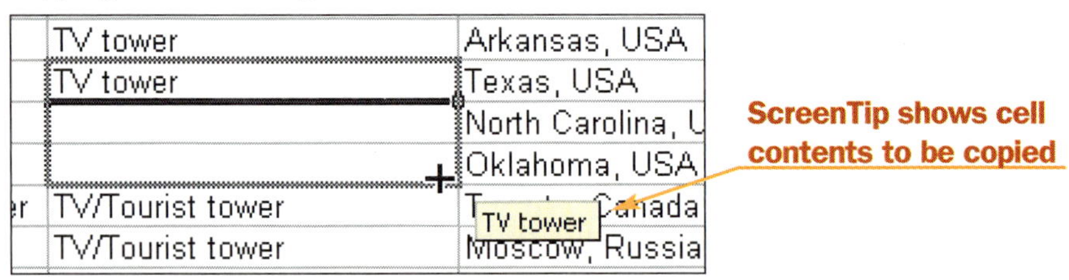

4. Release the mouse button, and the contents of C7 (*TV tower*) now appear in cells C8 and C9.

5. The AutoFill Options button displays next to the fill handle for cell C9. Point to the AutoFill Options button and the button will expand to show a down button. Click the down button to display the dialog box shown in Figure 11-5. Notice that you can choose to copy the content of the cells, fill the selected cells with formatting only, or fill the cells without the formatting.

FIGURE 11-5
AutoFill Options menu

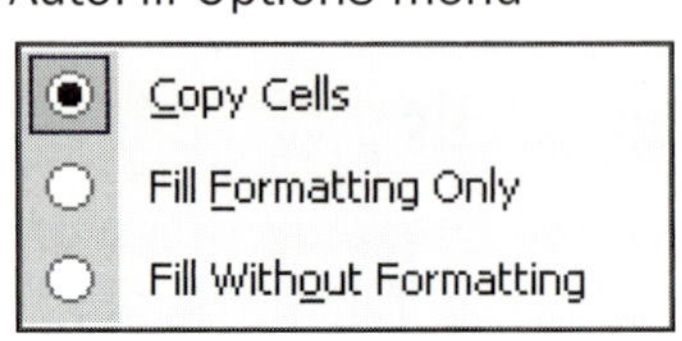

6. The Copy Cells option is already selected, and that is the option you want. Click outside the menu to close the menu without making any changes. Do not be concerned that the AutoFill Option button is still displayed.

STEP-BY-STEP 11.4 Continued

7. Click in cell **C6**, then point to the fill handle. Drag up to select cell C5. When you release, the cell contents from C6 (*TV tower*) are copied to cell C5.

8. Click in cell **C2** and fill the contents to Cell C3.

9. Deselect the cells and save the changes. Leave the workbook open for the next Step-by-Step.

Hot Tip

To quickly fill to the right, click in the destination cell and press the shortcut keys **Ctrl + R**. This copies the contents of the cell to the left. To quickly fill down, click in the destination cell and press the shortcut keys **Ctrl + D**. The contents of the cell above will be copied. To fill multiple cells, select the cell containing the contents, and then drag to create a range of cells before pressing the shortcut keys.

Use Help to Learn How to Fill Other Types of Data

You've already seen how Excel will fill adjacent cells with the same content. The fill command will also allow you to fill a series of numbers and increase or decrease the cell contents in increments based on the pattern of the original contents. You can use the Help screens to learn how to fill series of data.

Did You Know?

You can press **F1** to quickly access the Help screens. If the Office Assistant is displayed, you can enter your question in the text box. If the Office Assistant is turned off, the opening Help screen will display.

STEP-BY-STEP 11.5

1. If the Office Assistant is displayed, point to the Office Assistant and right-click. Then choose **Options** in the shortcut menu. Clear the check box for *Use the Office Assistant* and click **OK**.

2. Open the **Help** menu and choose **Microsoft Excel Help**. If necessary, click the **Show** button on the toolbar to display the Contents, Answer Wizard, and Index tabs.

3. Click the **Index** tab to display the dialog box shown in Figure 11-6.

STEP-BY-STEP 11.5 Continued

FIGURE 11-6
Index tab in Microsoft Excel Help

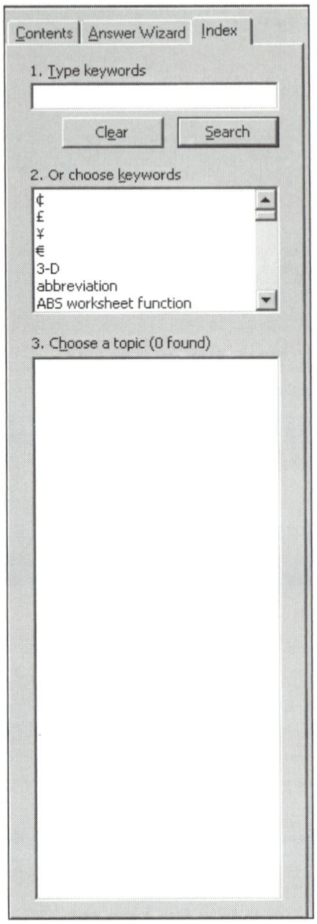

4. With the insertion point positioned in the text box below *1. Type keywords,* key **fill**. As you enter the text, the list in the section below (*2. Or choose keywords*) will scroll to display the keywords beginning with those characters.

5. Under *2. Or choose keywords*, double-click **fill** to open a list of topics. Under 3. *Choose a topic*, make sure the topic **About filling in data based on adjacent cells** is selected. Read the information in the first two paragraphs displayed at the right.

6. Scroll down if necessary so you can see all of the section with the heading *Fill in a series of numbers, dates, or other items.*

7. Read the information and look at the examples of series that can be extended. The examples illustrate that you can fill times, days of the week, months, quarters, and text. Notice, too, that if the initial selection includes the months January and April, the extended series will indicate a span of four months. July is the third month after April, and October is the third month after July.

8. Click the **Close** button in the top right corner of the screen to close the Help screens.

9. To turn the Office Assistant back on, open the **Help** menu and choose **Show the Office Assistant**. Leave the workbook open for the next Step-by-Step.

Fill a Data Series in Adjacent Cells

You can also use the fill feature to quickly fill in a series of numbers and dates. To fill in a series, a pattern must be established in the initial selection of cells. Then when you drag, the pattern is continued. When you drag the fill handle down or to the right, the series increases. However, if you drag the fill handle up or to the left, the series will decrease.

2-3.1.3-1

STEP-BY-STEP 11.6

1. Click cell **A2**. Key **1** and then press **Enter**.

2. Cell A3 is now the active cell. Key **2** and press **Enter**. You have now established a pattern where your numbers increase in increments of 1.

3. Select cells **A2** and **A3**, then click the **Center** button to center the cell contents.

2-3.1.3-3

4. With the cells still selected, point to the fill handle at the bottom of cell A3. When the pointer changes to a bold plus sign, drag down to cell A22 to select a range of cells. When you release the mouse button, Excel fills the cells with the numbers 3 through 21. The numbers are also centered within the cells.

5. Deselect the cells. Then, select cells **A2:A20** and press **Delete**.

6. Select cells **A21** and **A22**. Point to the fill handle at the bottom right corner of cell A22 and drag up to cell A2. The cells will fill with a series of numbers in decreasing order from 21 through 1.

7. Deselect the cells. Notice that in rows 5 and 6, the towers are exactly the same height. Click in cell **A6** and change the ranking from *5* to **4** and press **Enter**.

8. Save the changes and leave the workbook open for the next Step-by-Step.

Computer Concepts

If you click the **AutoFill Options** button, a new option called Fill Series will be available and selected in the menu. This option is now available because the original selected cells indicated a pattern.

Did You Know?

To continue selecting cells that are below the last visible row on the screen, hold down the mouse button as you reach the bottom (or top) of the screen. The worksheet will scroll and new rows will display.

Create Multiple Worksheets

Whenever you open a new worksheet in Excel, you automatically open a workbook with three sheets (or worksheets) in it. In Excel, the document you create is called a workbook, and each workbook contains the individual worksheets— just as a notebook contains many sheets of paper. To switch to a different worksheet, simply click on the worksheet tab at the bottom of the screen.

-3.1.6-1

Excel automatically assigns the name Sheet and a sequential number to each new worksheet. If desired, you can rename the worksheet. You can also add additional worksheets to a workbook or remove unnecessary ones.

STEP-BY-STEP 11.7

2-3.1.6-4 **1.** Click the **Sheet2** tab at the bottom of the screen as shown in Figure 11-7. A new blank worksheet is displayed.

FIGURE 11-7
Worksheet tabs

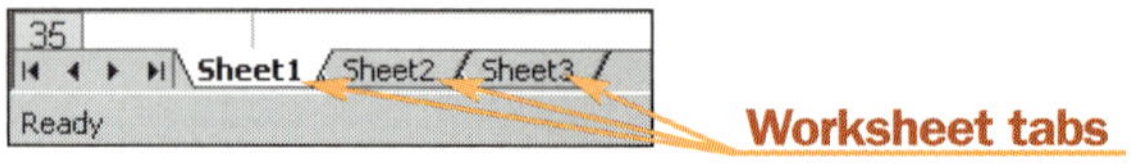

2-3.1.6-5 **2.** Double-click the **Sheet2** tab. The tab name is selected. Key **Buildings** and press **Enter**.

3. Double-click the **Sheet1** tab and rename the worksheet **Towers**.

4. Click on the **Buildings** worksheet tab to switch back to that worksheet.

> **Hot Tip**
>
> An alternative way to rename a worksheet is to right-click the worksheet tab, select **Rename** in the shortcut menu, key the new name, and press **Enter**.

5. Enter the data shown in Figure 11-8.

FIGURE 11-8
Data for Buildings worksheet

Building	Location	Height in Feet
Empire State Building	New York, USA	1,250
World Trade Center One	New York, USA	1,368
World Trade Center Two	New York, USA	1,362
Sears Tower	Illinois, USA	1,454
Bank of China Tower	Hong Kong, PRC	1,209
Central Plaza	Hong Kong, PRC	1,227
Petronas Tower 2	Kuala Lumpur, Malaysia	1,483
Petronas Tower 1	Kuala Lumpur, Malaysia	1,483
Jin Mao Building	Shanghai, PRC	1,379
The Centre	Hong Kong, PRC	1,149
Emirates Tower #1	Dubai, UAE	1,149

6. Center and bold the column headings and center the numbers in the third column. Select all three columns and then format the columns to AutoFit Selection.

2-3.1.6-3 **7.** Click the **Sheet3** tab. Click the **Edit** menu and select **Delete Sheet**. The unused sheet is deleted.

2-3.1.6-2 **8.** Open the **Insert** menu and select **Worksheet**. A new worksheet, automatically named Sheet4, is inserted.

> **Speech Recognition**
>
> If your computer has speech recognition capability, enable the Command mode and say the commands to select the column heading, then say the command to apply the bold and center formats.

9. Rename the new worksheet **Sheet3**.

10. Save the changes and leave the workbook open for the next Step-by-Step.

Hide and Unhide Columns and Rows

2-3.1.9-1 Hiding columns and rows temporarily removes them from display. This feature is especially helpful if you are working with a wide spreadsheet and you do not need to view all of the columns or rows. For example, you may need to see the first column and another column at the far right. You can hide the columns in the middle so you can view the two columns side by side. This feature is also helpful if you choose to print the worksheet, but you do not want all the content to show in the hard copy.

STEP-BY-STEP 11.8

1. Click in cell **D1** and label the column **Year Constructed**.
2. Click in cell **E1** and label the column **# Stories**.
3. If necessary, bold and center these headings, and autofit the column widths for selection.
4. Click the label for column B and drag to the right until both columns B and C are selected.
5. 2-3.1.9-2 Open the **Format** menu, choose **Column**, and then select **Hide** in the submenu. The selected columns are no longer visible on the screen.
6. Enter the data illustrated in Figure 11-9. Center the data in the columns. (*Note:* This list is not intended to be an official list, and the data contained in the list may be inaccurate or out of date.)

FIGURE 11-9
Data for Buildings worksheet

	A	D	E
1	**Building**	**Year Constructed**	**# Stories**
2	Empire State Building	1931	102
3	World Trade Center One	1972	110
4	World Trade Center Two	1973	110
5	Sears Tower	1973	110
6	Bank of China Tower	1989	70
7	Central Plaza	1992	78
8	Petronas Tower 2	1997	88
9	Petronas Tower 1	1997	88
10	Jin Mao Building	1997	88
11	The Centre	1998	73
12	Emirates Tower #1	1999	54

Enter the data in these two columns

7. 2-3.1.9-3 Select columns **A** and **D**. Open the **Format** menu, choose **Column**, and then select **Unhide** in the submenu. Columns B and C are now visible on the screen.
8. Save the changes and leave the workbook open for the next Step-by-Step.

Speech Recognition

If your computer has speech recognition capability, turn on the Speak On Enter feature so you can hear the value of the cell spoken immediately after you enter the data in each cell. Note that you can choose to have the computer read by rows or by columns.

Freeze Columns and Rows

Sometimes a worksheet becomes so large that you cannot view the entire worksheet on the screen. As you scroll to the bottom of the worksheet, column labels at the top of the worksheet disappear. As you scroll to the right, row labels at the left of the screen disappear. Freezing a column or row enables you to keep the column or row visible as you scroll. You can execute the Freeze command for all columns to the left of a selected column or all rows above a selected row. Or, you can execute the Freeze command around a specific cell, which will freeze the row(s) above the active cell and the column(s) to the left of the active cell.

STEP-BY-STEP 11.9

1. Click the **Towers** worksheet tab at the bottom of the screen to switch to that worksheet.
2. Click the column **C** label to select that column.
3. Open the **Window** menu and choose **Freeze Panes**.
4. Click the right scroll arrow on the horizontal scroll bar. Notice that as you scroll to the right, the first two columns do not move.
5. Open the **Window** menu and choose **Unfreeze Panes**.
6. Click in cell **B2**. Then open the **Window** menu and choose **Freeze Panes**. The row above the active cell and the column to the left of the active cell are now frozen.
7. Click the down arrow on the vertical scroll bar. Notice that the row with the column headings does not move.
8. Click the right arrow on the horizontal scroll bar. Notice that the first column with the ranking information does not move.
9. Open the **Window** menu and choose **Unfreeze Panes**. Leave the workbook open for the next Step-by-Step.

Sort Data

IC3 2-3.2.1-1

You can quickly sort data in a worksheet. To sort Excel data, you must indicate the column you want to base your sort on. The information in that column will be sorted, and all the data in corresponding rows will also move appropriately. Excel lets you sort alphabetically or numerically. ***Ascending order*** sorts alphabetically from A to Z or numerically from the lowest to the highest number. ***Descending order*** sorts alphabetically from Z to A or numerically from the highest to the lowest number.

Excel has two toolbar buttons (Sort Ascending and Sort Descending) that make sorting quick and easy. You simply click in the column you want to sort by and then click one of the sort buttons. Excel will automatically determine if you have a ***header row*** (headings at the top of your columns), and it will not include this row in the sort.

If you have a worksheet with multiple columns of data, you can base the sort on data in three different columns. For example, you can sort first by height, then by building name, and then by
2-3.2.2-1 city. When you want to sort by multiple criteria, you must open the Sort dialog box.

STEP-BY-STEP 11.10

1. Switch to the **Buildings** worksheet.

2-3.2.1-1

2. Click in any cell in column A. Then click the **Sort Ascending** button on the Standard toolbar. The building names are arranged in ascending alphabetical order, and the data in the other columns moves with the building name.

3. Click the **Sort Descending** button on the Standard toolbar. The building names are now arranged in descending alphabetical order, and the building data again moves with the building name.

2-3.2.2-1

4. Open the **Data** menu and choose **Sort**. All the data in the worksheet (except the headings) is selected and the dialog box shown in Figure 11-10 is displayed.

Hot Tip

If the Sort Descending button is not displayed on the Standard toolbar, click the **Toolbar Options** at the right side of the toolbar and then select the **Sort Descending** button.

FIGURE 11-10
Sort dialog box

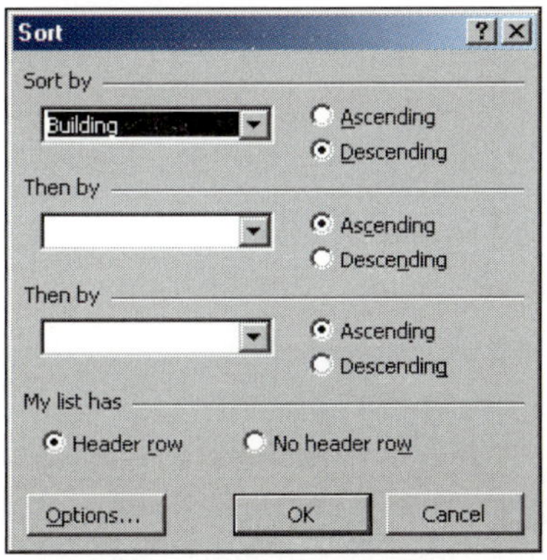

5. Select **Height in Feet** in the list box under *Sort by*. If necessary, select **Descending** at the right of the *Sort by* option.

6. Click the down arrow in the list box under the first *Then by* option. Select **Location** and then, if necessary, select **Ascending** at the right of the *Then by* option.

7. Click the down arrow in the list box under the second *Then by* option. Select **Building** and then, if necessary, select **Ascending** at the right of the *Then by* option.

8. Click **OK**. The worksheet data is rearranged from highest to lowest. If any two buildings are the same height, they are sorted in alphabetical order by the city. If the two buildings are in the same location, they are sorted in alphabetical order by building name.

9. Save the changes and leave the workbook open for the next Step-by-Step.

Print the Worksheet

Before you print the worksheet, you will want to look at it in Print Preview. Print Preview enables you to preview the worksheet on the screen to see what it will look like when it is printed. This can save you time and paper. If the worksheet does not display correctly on the page, you can make adjustments in the Page Setup dialog box.

Change the Page Setup

If the worksheet is large and the columns or rows wrap to a second page, you can sometimes fit the worksheet on one page by changing the page orientation. ***Portrait orientation*** formats the content of the document with the short edge of the page at the top. This is the default setting. You can change to ***landscape orientation*** in the Page Setup dialog box. Landscape orientation formats the document sideways with the long edge of the page at the top.

2-3.3.10-1 Another option for fitting the worksheet on one page is to turn on the Fit to command. This feature scales the worksheet up or down as necessary so it fits on the number of pages you designate.

> **Computer Concepts**
>
> The page setup settings apply to the current worksheet. They do not apply to all the worksheets in the workbook.

STEP-BY-STEP 11.11

1. Switch to the **Towers** worksheet.

2. Click the **Print Preview** button on the Standard toolbar. Notice that the *Height in Feet* column displays on page 2.

3. Click the **Close** button in the toolbar at the top of the screen to close Print Preview.

4. Open the **File** menu and choose **Page Setup**. If necessary, click the **Page** tab to display the dialog box shown in Figure 11-11.

FIGURE 11-11
Page tab in the Page Setup dialog box

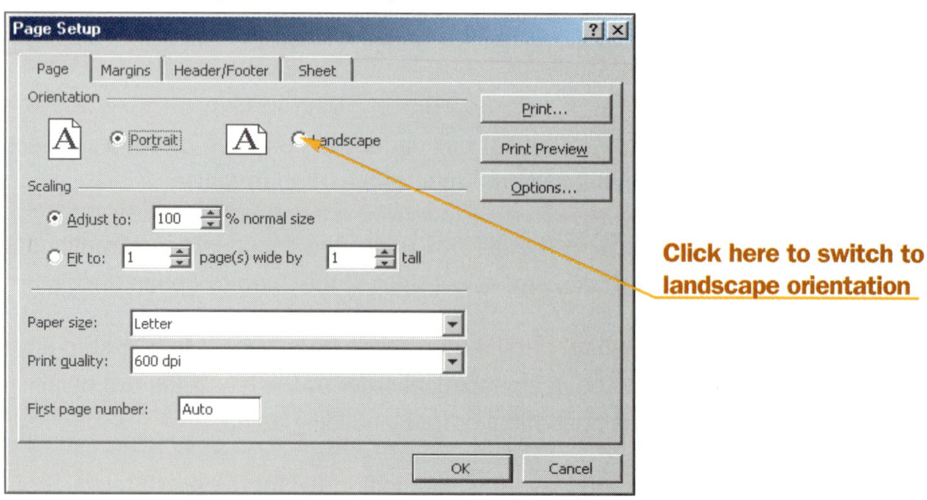

STEP-BY-STEP 11.11 Continued

5. Note that the Scaling is set at Adjust to 100% normal size by default. Click the **Print Preview** button to see how the Towers worksheet would appear when printed. Your screen should appear similar to Figure 11-12. Note that the last column of data is missing from the first printed page. (This is indicated in the worksheet itself by the dotted line between columns D and E.)

FIGURE 11-12
Worksheet in portrait orientation and normal size

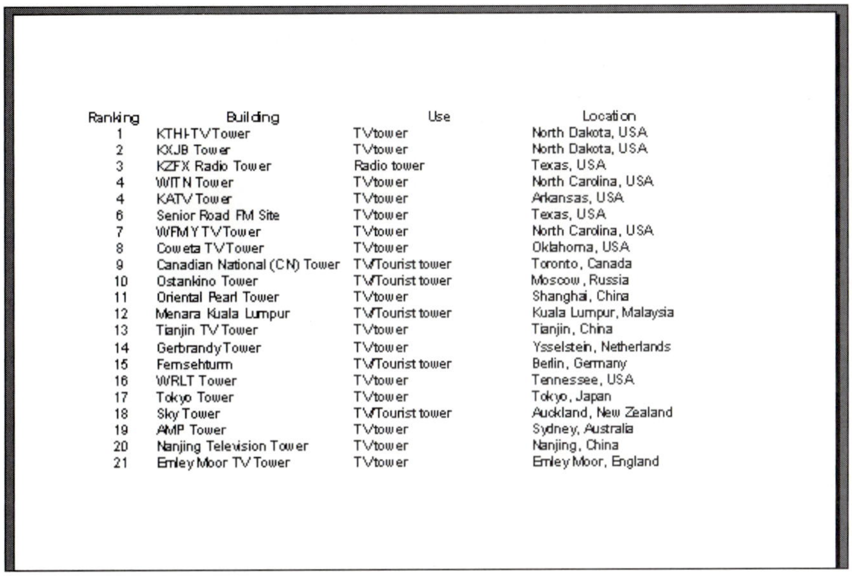

Ranking	Building	Use	Location
1	KTHI-TV Tower	TV tower	North Dakota, USA
2	KXJB Tower	TV tower	North Dakota, USA
3	KZFX Radio Tower	Radio tower	Texas, USA
4	WITN Tower	TV tower	North Carolina, USA
4	KATV Tower	TV tower	Arkansas, USA
6	Senior Road FM Site	TV tower	Texas, USA
7	WFMY TV Tower	TV tower	North Carolina, USA
8	Coweta TV Tower	TV tower	Oklahoma, USA
9	Canadian National (CN) Tower	TV/Tourist tower	Toronto, Canada
10	Ostankino Tower	TV/Tourist tower	Moscow, Russia
11	Oriental Pearl Tower	TV tower	Shanghai, China
12	Menara Kuala Lumpur	TV/Tourist tower	Kuala Lumpur, Malaysia
13	Tianjin TV Tower	TV tower	Tianjin, China
14	Gerbrandy Tower	TV tower	Ysselstein, Netherlands
15	Fernsehturm	TV/Tourist tower	Berlin, Germany
16	WRLT Tower	TV tower	Tennessee, USA
17	Tokyo Tower	TV tower	Tokyo, Japan
18	Sky Tower	TV/Tourist tower	Auckland, New Zealand
19	AMP Tower	TV tower	Sydney, Australia
20	Nanjing Television Tower	TV tower	Nanjing, China
21	Emley Moor TV Tower	TV tower	Emley Moor, England

6. Click the **Setup** button to return to the Page Setup dialog box.

-3.3.10-1 7. Under *Scaling*, turn on the *Fit to* option and accept the default settings of 1 page wide by 1 page tall.

8. Click **OK**. The dialog box closes and you return to the Print Preview screen as shown in Figure 11-13. Notice that the worksheet image is slightly smaller, but it all fits on one page in portrait orientation.

2-3.3.10-2 **FIGURE 11-13**
Worksheet in portrait orientation and scaled to fit

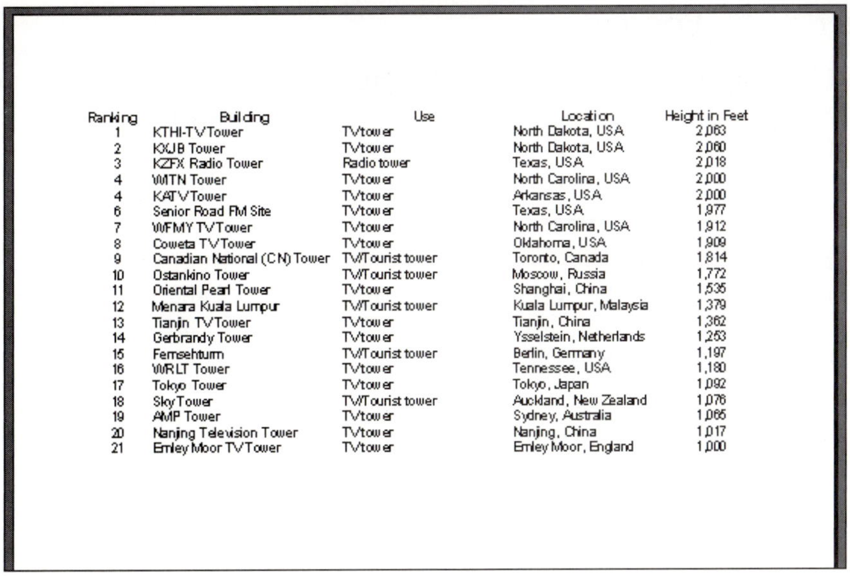

Ranking	Building	Use	Location	Height in Feet
1	KTHI-TV Tower	TV tower	North Dakota, USA	2,063
2	KXJB Tower	TV tower	North Dakota, USA	2,060
3	KZFX Radio Tower	Radio tower	Texas, USA	2,018
4	WITN Tower	TV tower	North Carolina, USA	2,000
4	KATV Tower	TV tower	Arkansas, USA	2,000
6	Senior Road FM Site	TV tower	Texas, USA	1,977
7	WFMY TV Tower	TV tower	North Carolina, USA	1,912
8	Coweta TV Tower	TV tower	Oklahoma, USA	1,909
9	Canadian National (CN) Tower	TV/Tourist tower	Toronto, Canada	1,814
10	Ostankino Tower	TV/Tourist tower	Moscow, Russia	1,772
11	Oriental Pearl Tower	TV tower	Shanghai, China	1,535
12	Menara Kuala Lumpur	TV/Tourist tower	Kuala Lumpur, Malaysia	1,379
13	Tianjin TV Tower	TV tower	Tianjin, China	1,362
14	Gerbrandy Tower	TV tower	Ysselstein, Netherlands	1,253
15	Fernsehturm	TV/Tourist tower	Berlin, Germany	1,197
16	WRLT Tower	TV tower	Tennessee, USA	1,180
17	Tokyo Tower	TV tower	Tokyo, Japan	1,092
18	Sky Tower	TV/Tourist tower	Auckland, New Zealand	1,076
19	AMP Tower	TV tower	Sydney, Australia	1,065
20	Nanjing Television Tower	TV tower	Nanjing, China	1,017
21	Emley Moor TV Tower	TV tower	Emley Moor, England	1,000

STEP-BY-STEP 11.11 Continued

9. Click the **Setup** button again. Under *Orientation*, select **Landscape**. Under *Scaling*, select **Adjust to** and change the percentage in the % normal size box to **100**.

10. Click the **Margins** tab to display the dialog box shown in Figure 11-14.

FIGURE 11-14
Margins tab in the Page Setup dialog box

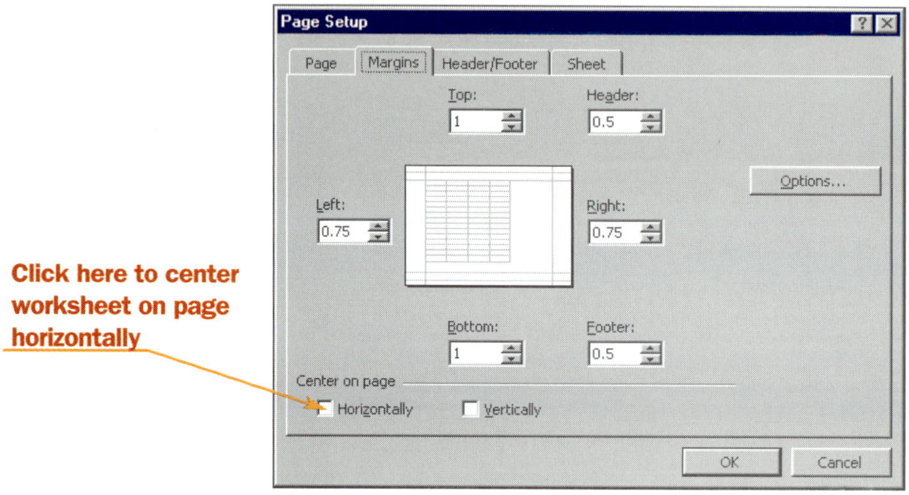

11. Under *Center on page* at the bottom of the dialog box, select **Horizontally**. Click **OK**. Notice that this time the preview of the worksheet shows the image in normal size. The page is turned sideways, and the columns are centered horizontally. Close the Print Preview screen.

12. Switch to the **Buildings** worksheet, change the page orientation to landscape, and center the worksheet horizontally on the page.

13. Save the changes and leave the workbook open for the next Step-by-Step.

Add a Header and a Footer

Headers and footers are a means of providing useful information on a printed worksheet. The header is text that is printed in the top margin of every worksheet page. The footer is text that is printed in the bottom margin of every page. Neither headers nor footers are displayed in the worksheet window. You must preview or print the worksheet to see them. Headers and footers are set up from the Page Setup dialog box.

IC³ 2-3.3.8-1 2-3.3.8-2

Among other things, headers and footers can include the date a worksheet was printed, the name of the person or company that created the worksheet, and the filename of the workbook. You can choose one of the standard (pre-made) headers or footers or you can create your own customized headers and footers. In Excel, formatting codes are used in headers and footers to represent the items you want to appear. With these you can insert dates, times, filenames, and page numbers automatically. By using the formatting codes instead of manually keying these items, the information is always updated automatically. For example, if you use the date and time formatting codes, whenever you print the worksheet, the date will reflect the current date and the time will be the exact time of the printing.

STEP-BY-STEP 11.12

1. Open the **File** menu and choose **Page Setup**.

2. Click the **Header/Footer** tab to display the dialog box shown in Figure 11-15.

FIGURE 11-15
Header/Footer tab in the Page Setup dialog box

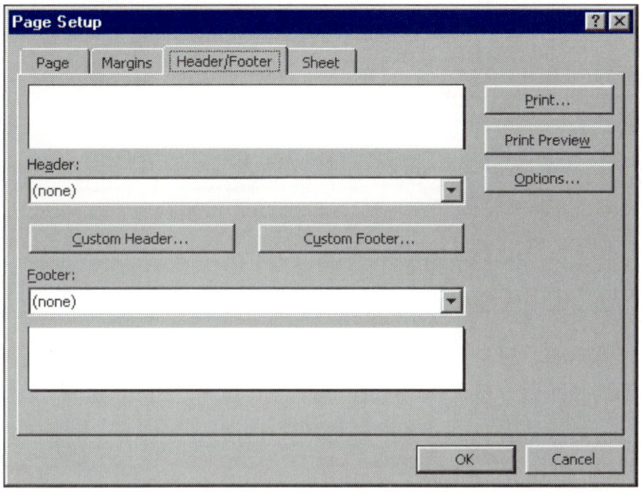

2-3.3.8-3 3. Open the **Footer** drop-down list, scroll down, and select **Tallest Structures.xls, Page 1**. An example of the footer appears in the lower portion of the dialog box.

4. None of the pre-made headers meets our needs, so we will create a custom header. Click the **Custom Header** button.

5. The cursor should be in the Left section. Click the **Sheet name** button. The &[Tab] formatting code appears.

6. Click in the **Right** section. Click the **Date** button. The &[Date] formatting code appears.

7. Click **OK**. The Page Setup dialog box now shows examples of both the header and the footer selected.

2-3.3.8-4 8. Click the **Print Preview** button. Your page should appear similar to Figure 11-16.

STEP-BY-STEP 11.12 Continued

FIGURE 11-16
Preview of worksheet with a header and a footer

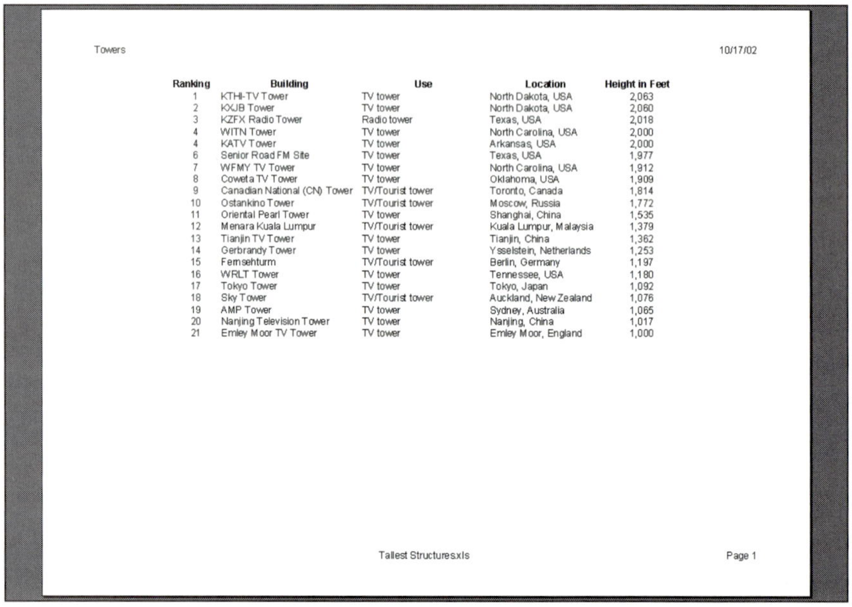

Towers 10/17/02

Ranking	Building	Use	Location	Height in Feet
1	KTHI-TV Tower	TV tower	North Dakota, USA	2,063
2	KXJB Tower	TV tower	North Dakota, USA	2,060
3	KZFX Radio Tower	Radio tower	Texas, USA	2,018
4	WITN Tower	TV tower	North Carolina, USA	2,000
4	KATV Tower	TV tower	Arkansas, USA	2,000
6	Senior Road FM Site	TV tower	Texas, USA	1,977
7	WFMY TV Tower	TV tower	North Carolina, USA	1,912
8	Coweta TV Tower	TV tower	Oklahoma, USA	1,909
9	Canadian National (CN) Tower	TV/Tourist tower	Toronto, Canada	1,814
10	Ostankino Tower	TV/Tourist tower	Moscow, Russia	1,772
11	Oriental Pearl Tower	TV tower	Shanghai, China	1,535
12	Menara Kuala Lumpur	TV/Tourist tower	Kuala Lumpur, Malaysia	1,379
13	Tianjin TV Tower	TV tower	Tianjin, China	1,362
14	Gerbrandy Tower	TV tower	Ysselstein, Netherlands	1,253
15	Fernsehturm	TV/Tourist tower	Berlin, Germany	1,197
16	WRLT Tower	TV tower	Tennessee, USA	1,180
17	Tokyo Tower	TV tower	Tokyo, Japan	1,092
18	Sky Tower	TV/Tourist tower	Auckland, New Zealand	1,076
19	AMP Tower	TV tower	Sydney, Australia	1,065
20	Nanjing Television Tower	TV tower	Nanjing, China	1,017
21	Emley Moor TV Tower	TV tower	Emley Moor, England	1,000

Tallest Structures.xls Page 1

9. Click the **Close** button to close Print Preview and return to the worksheet.

10. Save the changes and leave the workbook open for the next Step-by-Step.

Print the Worksheets

2-3.3.9-1 When you click the Print button on the Standard toolbar, Excel prints the active worksheet with the default print settings. If you want to change any of the print options, you need to open the Print dialog box. If you don't want to print the entire worksheet, you can select the range you want to print. Open the File menu and choose Print Area, and then select Set Print Area in the submenu.

2-3.3.7-1 When the worksheet is more than one page in length, Excel determines where to break the page and begin a new one. If you don't like where Excel has split the data between pages, you can create your own page break by dragging the page break to a new location. You can also insert a manual page break in a location of your choice.

STEP-BY-STEP 11.13

You are going to print your Towers worksheet, but you want to explore the options of printing it as two pages—one page with the top ten buildings and the second page with the remaining buildings—or just printing the top ten buildings in the list.

1. Click in cell **A12**.

2-3.3.7-2

2. Open the **Insert** menu and select **Page Break**. A dotted line appears above row 12 indicating a page break.

STEP-BY-STEP 11.13 Continued

2-3.3.7-3 **3.** Open the **File** menu and select **Print Preview**. Your first page will appear as shown in Figure 11-17.

FIGURE 11-17
Print preview of worksheet with manual page break inserted.

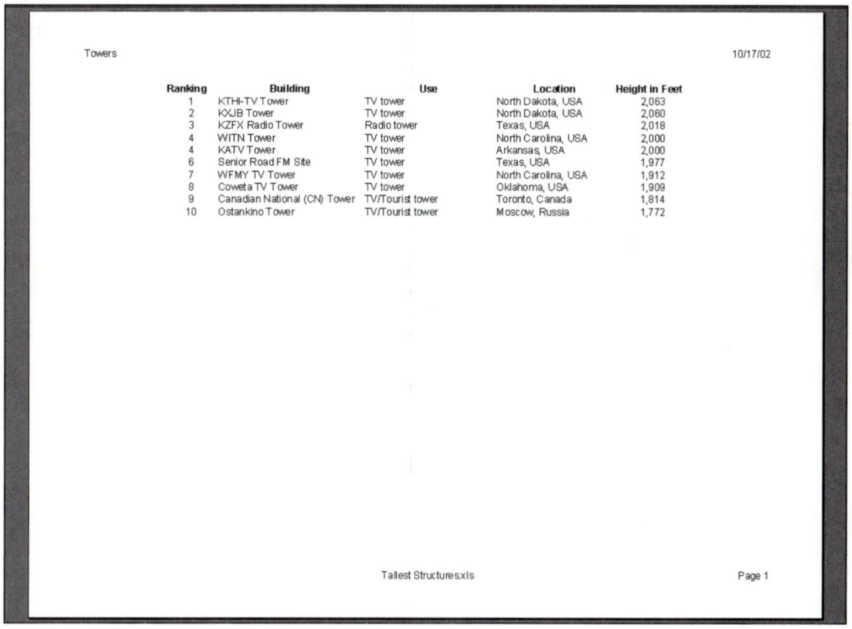

Towers 10/17/02

Ranking	Building	Use	Location	Height in Feet
1	KTHI-TV Tower	TV tower	North Dakota, USA	2,063
2	KXJB Tower	TV tower	North Dakota, USA	2,060
3	KZFX Radio Tower	Radio tower	Texas, USA	2,018
4	WITN Tower	TV tower	North Carolina, USA	2,000
4	KATV Tower	TV tower	Arkansas, USA	2,000
6	Senior Road FM Site	TV tower	Texas, USA	1,977
7	WFMY TV Tower	TV tower	North Carolina, USA	1,912
8	Coweta TV Tower	TV tower	Oklahoma, USA	1,909
9	Canadian National (CN) Tower	TV/Tourist tower	Toronto, Canada	1,814
10	Ostankino Tower	TV/Tourist tower	Moscow, Russia	1,772

Tallest Structures.xls Page 1

4. Select the **Next** button to see the second page.

5. You decide that you prefer to keep all of the information on one page. Click the **Close** button to return to the worksheet.

6. With cell A12 still selected, open the **Insert** menu and select **Remove Page Break**.

7. Select the range of cells from **A1** through **E11**. This is all of the information for the top ten buildings in the list.

2-3.3.9-2 **8.** Open the **File** menu, select **Print Area**, and then select **Set Print Area** in the submenu. Click anywhere in the worksheet and notice that the area you had selected now has a dotted line around it to indicate the print area.

9. Open the **File** menu and select **Print Preview**. Your preview screen should appear similar to Figure 11-18.

2-3.3.9-3

FIGURE 11-18
Preview of a defined print area

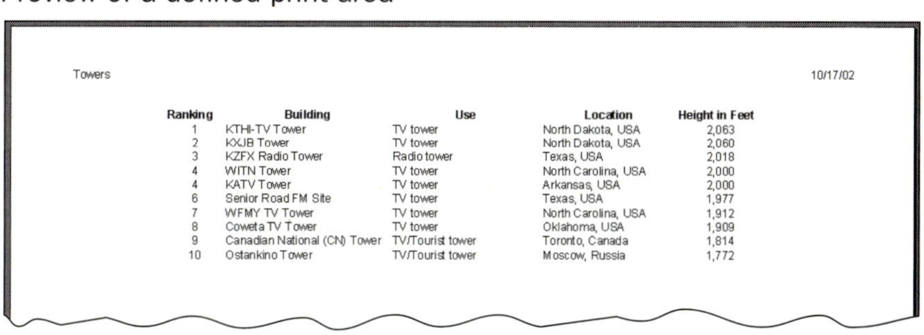

Towers 10/17/02

Ranking	Building	Use	Location	Height in Feet
1	KTHI-TV Tower	TV tower	North Dakota, USA	2,063
2	KXJB Tower	TV tower	North Dakota, USA	2,060
3	KZFX Radio Tower	Radio tower	Texas, USA	2,018
4	WITN Tower	TV tower	North Carolina, USA	2,000
4	KATV Tower	TV tower	Arkansas, USA	2,000
6	Senior Road FM Site	TV tower	Texas, USA	1,977
7	WFMY TV Tower	TV tower	North Carolina, USA	1,912
8	Coweta TV Tower	TV tower	Oklahoma, USA	1,909
9	Canadian National (CN) Tower	TV/Tourist tower	Toronto, Canada	1,814
10	Ostankino Tower	TV/Tourist tower	Moscow, Russia	1,772

STEP-BY-STEP 11.13 Continued

10. Close Print Preview and return to the worksheet. You decide it would still be best to print the entire worksheet. Open the **File** menu, select **Print Area**, and then select **Clear Print Area** in the submenu.

11. Open the **File** menu and choose **Print** to display the Print dialog box.

12. Under *Print what*, select **Entire workbook** as shown in Figure 11-19. Your dialog box will probably not match exactly.

FIGURE 11-19
Print dialog box

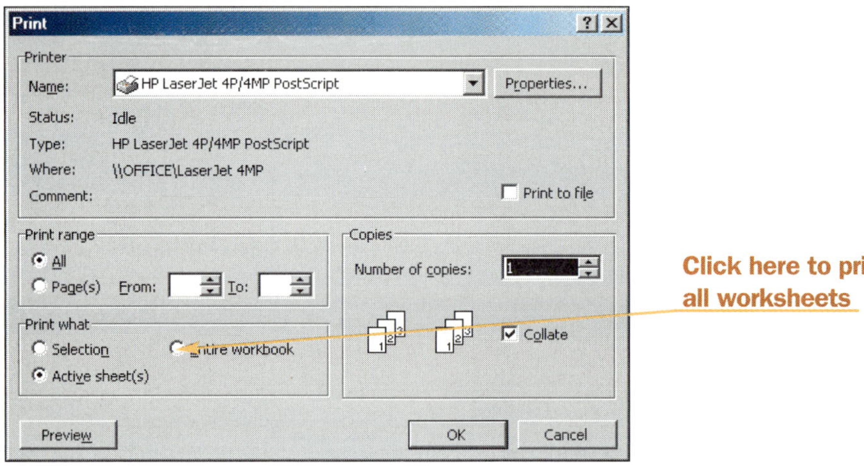

13. If you are permitted to print, click **OK** to print both worksheets in the workbook. If you are not permitted to print, click **Cancel** to close the Print dialog box.

14. Save your changes and leave the workbook open for the next Step-by-Step.

> **Did You Know?**
>
> The options available in the Print dialog box vary according to the type of printer available.

Additional Options for Viewing Worksheet Data

We have discussed a number of ways in which you can work with the data within your worksheet—both while looking at it in the worksheet as well as when printing the worksheet. There are, however, a number of other options. You can specify borders and shading to be applied to specific cells. You can apply styles to your cells. In addition to aligning your cell data to the left, right, or center, you can choose to wrap the text within selected cells or to rotate the text within the cell.

There are also a few options that directly affect how the worksheet will appear when printed. You can set gridlines to appear in the printed page, and you can specify that certain rows or columns be repeated on each printed page.

2-3.3.2-1

Cell Borders and Shading

A worksheet is often divided into areas that visually keep related information together. Borders (lines that appear around cells) and shading can help to create these visually distinct areas of the worksheet. Shading (also known as a pattern) can be used to add emphasis to a specific region on the worksheet. They can be used independently or in conjunction with one another. The way in which your worksheet will be used should guide you when deciding what cell borders or shading will be most helpful. For example, will the worksheet be printed in black and white or will it always be used online? Do you need to emphasize a specific row or column of data? You should always evaluate the borders and shading that you apply to determine whether they make the data easier to read and understand.

STEP-BY-STEP 11.14

1. Select cells **A1** through **E1**.
2. Open the **Format** menu and select **Cells**.
3. In the Format Cells dialog box, click on the **Border** tab.
4. Choose **None** in the *Presets* section if necessary.
5. In the *Line, Style* section, select the double line and then select **Blue** from the drop-down color palette.

2-3.3.2-2

6. In the *Border* section, choose the bottom horizontal line. The double blue line will appear in the preview box. Click **OK**. This border separates the headings from the data.
7. Select cells **A2** through **E11**.
8. Open the **Format** menu and select **Cells**. Click on the **Patterns** tab.

2-3.3.2-3

9. Select the light blue color and click **OK**. Deselect the range to see the pattern applied. This sets the top ten buildings in the list apart for the rest.
10. Save your changes and leave the workbook open for the next Step-by-Step.

Gridlines

-3.3.11-2

By now you have probably noticed that the gridlines which you see in the worksheet do not appear in the printed worksheet. If you want certain lines to appear in the printed worksheet, you need to add borders, as discussed in the previous section. The borders you specify will be placed in the locations of the current gridlines. But what if you just want to print all of the gridlines as they appear in the on-screen worksheet? Or what if you do not want to see the gridlines in the on-screen worksheet? You can handle both of these situations by turning the gridlines on or off.

To remove gridlines from the on-screen worksheet, open the Tools menu, select Options, and then choose the View tab. In the Window options section, deselect Gridlines, and then click OK. The gridlines will no longer appear on the screen—although the cells still exist and any borders you have placed will still be present.

To add gridlines to the printed document, open the Page Setup dialog box, choose the Sheet tab, and then select Gridlines in the Print section.

:-3.3.11-1

STEP-BY-STEP 11.15

1. Open the **File** menu and select **Page Setup**.

2. In the Page Setup dialog box, select the **Sheet** tab.

2-3.3.11-3

3. In the *Print* section, select the **Gridlines** option.

4. Click the **Print Preview** button. Your worksheet should appear similar to the one shown in Figure 11-20.

2-3.3.11-4

FIGURE 11-20
Preview of worksheet with gridlines applied

Ranking	Building	Use	Location	Height in Feet
1	KTHI-TV Tower	TV tower	North Dakota, USA	2,063
2	KXJB Tower	TV tower	North Dakota, USA	2,060
3	KZFX Radio Tower	Radio tower	Texas, USA	2,018
4	WITN Tower	TV tower	North Carolina, USA	2,000
4	KATV Tower	TV tower	Arkansas, USA	2,000
6	Senior Road FM Site	TV tower	Texas, USA	1,977
7	WFMY TV Tower	TV tower	North Carolina, USA	1,912
8	Coweta TV Tower	TV tower	Oklahoma, USA	1,909
9	Canadian National (CN) Tower	TV/Tourist tower	Toronto, Canada	1,814
10	Ostankino Tower	TV/Tourist tower	Moscow, Russia	1,772
11	Oriental Pearl Tower	TV tower	Shanghai, China	1,535
12	Menara Kuala Lumpur	TV/Tourist tower	Kuala Lumpur, Malaysia	1,379
13	Tianjin TV Tower	TV tower	Tianjin, China	1,362
14	Gerbrandy Tower	TV tower	Ysselstein, Netherlands	1,253
15	Femsehturm	TV/Tourist tower	Berlin, Germany	1,197
16	WRLT Tower	TV tower	Tennessee, USA	1,180
17	Tokyo Tower	TV tower	Tokyo, Japan	1,092
18	Sky Tower	TV/Tourist tower	Auckland, New Zealand	1,076
19	AMP Tower	TV tower	Sydney, Australia	1,065
20	Nanjing Television Tower	TV tower	Nanjing, China	1,017
21	Emley Moor TV Tower	TV tower	Emley Moor, England	1,000

5. You decide that the worksheet appears better without the gridlines. Click the **Setup** button to return to the Page Setup dialog box.

6. Deselect the **Gridlines** option and click **OK**.

7. Close the print preview. Leave the worksheet open for the next Step-by-Step.

Create and Apply Styles

2-3.3.4-1

A style is a grouping of information about cell formatting. This information is saved together as a style so that it can be used over and over again. A style can include up to six format attributes (the same attributes that are available from within the Format Cells dialog box): number, font, alignment, border, pattern, and protection. Once you have saved this information, you can apply it to a specific cell or to a range of cells to achieve consistency and to save yourself a great deal of time. Excel has six predefined styles. By default, the predefined Normal style is applied to each cell whenever you start a new worksheet.

Styles can be created in two ways:

- By using an example of a cell that has the formats you want associated with the style
- By choosing formats from the Style dialog box and selecting the format you want to associate with the style

Cell Alignment

In Lesson 10 we discussed basic cell alignment in that we talked about center-, left-, and right-aligning the content of a cell in reference to its horizontal position within the cell. There are several other options, however, for aligning cells. There are additional horizontal positions including centering across selected cells, justifying the content of a cell, and distributing the content. You can adjust the alignment of the content of a cell vertically as well. Your choices for vertical alignment are top, center, bottom, justified, and distributed.

If you examine the Alignment tab of the Format Cells dialog box, you will also find some other interesting choices such as changing the orientation of text within a cell, setting the content
2-3.3.3-1 to shrink to fit within the cell, or allowing the text to wrap to new lines within the cell if it doesn't fit on one line.

STEP-BY-STEP 11.16

1. Select cell **A1**.
2. Open the **Format** menu and select **Style**.

2-3.3.4-2
3. Key **Column Heading** in the Style name text box.
4. Click the **Modify** button. This opens the Format Cells dialog box with which you are, by now, familiar.
5. On the Number tab, verify that **General** is selected.
6. Click the **Alignment** tab. Set the Horizontal position to **Left**, and the Vertical position to **Bottom**.

2-3.3.3-3
7. In the *Orientation* section of the Alignment tab, drag the text indicator to **45** Degrees.

2-3.3.3-2
8. In the *Text control* section of the Alignment tab, select **Wrap text**.
9. Click the **Font** tab. Change the Size to **12** and the Color to **Blue**.
10. Leave the Border, Pattern, and Protection tabs unchanged. Click **OK**.
11. In the Style dialog box, click **Add**. Notice that the text in A1 has changed to the new settings, but you can't read it because the cell is not tall enough.
12. Open the **Format** menu, select **Row**, and select **Height** in the submenu. Set the row height to **55**.
13. Open the **Format** menu, select **Column**, and select **Width** in the submenu. Set the column width to **10**.
14. Select **B1** through **E1**.
15. Open the **Format** menu and select **Style**.

2-3.3.4-3
16. Select **Column Heading** from the drop-down Style name list box. Click **OK**. The style you created is applied to each of the cells in your selection. Note how the text wrapping worked in the last column.
17. Save your changes and leave the workbook open for the next Step-by-Step.

Repeating Rows and Columns

2-3.3.12-1
2-3.3.12-4 When we inserted the page break after the first ten buildings in the Tallest Structures worksheet in Step-by-Step 11.13, you may have noticed that the second page did not have any headings. If you truly had been making the decision whether to print the worksheet as two pages, this would have likely contributed to your decision to return to one page. But it is possible to have a worksheet continue from one page to the next and to have any necessary row or column headings repeated. These repeated headings will appear on each and every printed page.

While this is not really necessary for the worksheets we have been using in this lesson—they easily fit on one page—you will find this tool to be extremely helpful as you learn to work with Excel and begin creating and using larger worksheets. A page with a lot of data is not very useful if you do not know what the data represents. You need to repeat the table headings so that the data has meaning and is understandable to all who read it.

STEP-BY-STEP 11.17

1. Select cell **A12**.
2. Open the **Insert** menu and select **Page Break**.
3. Open the **File** menu and select **Page Setup**.
4. 2-3.3.12-2 Switch to the **Sheet** tab. In the *Print titles* section, select the **Collapse Dialog** button at the end of the text box next to *Rows to repeat at top*. This will temporarily collapse the Page Setup dialog box so that you can select the rows to repeat from within the worksheet.
5. Select row **1**. Note that the formula for row 1 is inserted into the dialog box.
6. Click the **Expand Dialog** button to see the entire Page Setup dialog box and then click **Print Preview**. The first page of your worksheet appears just as it would have regardless of your settings for a repeated heading row.
7. Click the **Next** button. Your screen should appear similar to Figure 11-21.

IC³ 2-3.3.12-3

STEP-BY-STEP 11.17 Continued

FIGURE 11-21
Second page of the worksheet with header row repeated

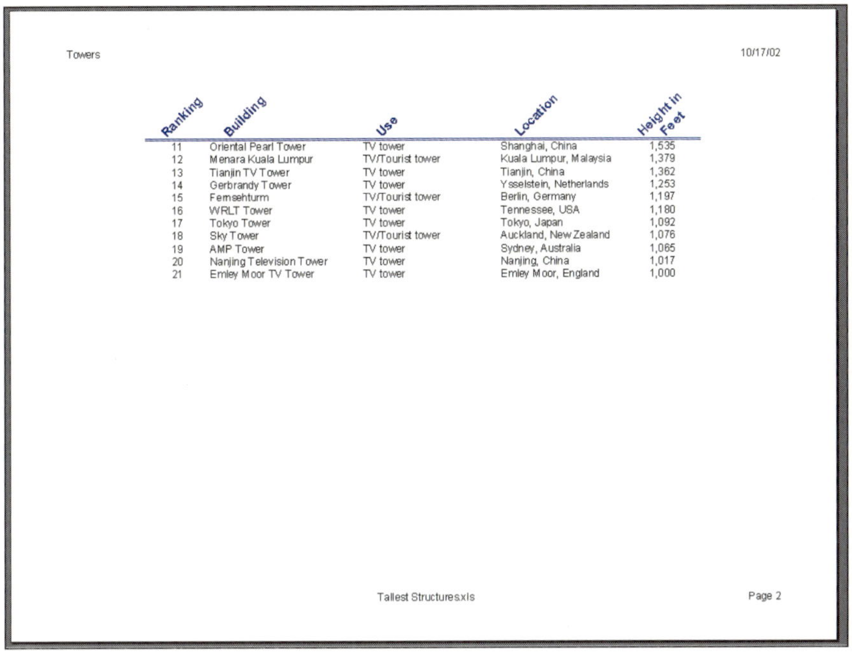

Towers 10/17/02

Ranking	Building	Use	Location	Height in Feet
11	Oriental Pearl Tower	TV tower	Shanghai, China	1,535
12	Menara Kuala Lumpur	TV/Tourist tower	Kuala Lumpur, Malaysia	1,379
13	Tianjin TV Tower	TV tower	Tianjin, China	1,362
14	Gerbrandy Tower	TV tower	Ysselstein, Netherlands	1,253
15	Fernsehturm	TV/Tourist tower	Berlin, Germany	1,197
16	WRLT Tower	TV tower	Tennessee, USA	1,180
17	Tokyo Tower	TV tower	Tokyo, Japan	1,092
18	Sky Tower	TV/Tourist tower	Auckland, New Zealand	1,076
19	AMP Tower	TV tower	Sydney, Australia	1,065
20	Nanjing Television Tower	TV tower	Nanjing, China	1,017
21	Emley Moor TV Tower	TV tower	Emley Moor, England	1,000

Tallest Structures.xls Page 2

8. Close the Print Preview screen.

9. Even with the addition of the header row to the second page, you decide that you would still prefer to keep all of the data on one page. Open the **Insert** menu and select **Remove Page Break**.

10. Save your changes and close the workbook.

SUMMARY

In this lesson, you learned:

- When you insert or delete rows and columns, all existing data is shifted up, down, left, or right.
- To reorganize a worksheet, you can delete, copy, or move the data.
- The AutoFill command enables you to copy data from one cell to another or enter certain kinds of data such as months, days of the week, or a series of numbers.
- You can add one or several worksheets to a workbook, and you can rename each worksheet.
- Hiding columns and rows temporarily removes them from the display. This can be helpful when you are working with a wide spreadsheet or you do not need to view all of the columns or rows.
- Freezing a column or row enables you to keep the column and row labels visible as you scroll through a worksheet.

- The sort feature provides options for organizing worksheet data numerically or alphabetically. You can sort the data based on a single column, or you can sort the data based on multiple criteria.
- Before you print, you can preview the worksheet on the screen to see what it will look like when it is printed. You can change the page orientation or use the Fit to feature to fit all the data on one page.
- You can choose to print the active worksheet only, or you can choose to print all worksheets in the workbook.

VOCABULARY *Review*

Define the following terms:

Ascending order	Fill handle	Landscape orientation
Clipboard	Filling	Portrait orientation
Descending order	Header row	

REVIEW *Questions*

TRUE/FALSE

Circle T if the statement is true or F if the statement is false.

T F 1. When you fill a cell, you can choose to copy the cell contents either with or without the formats.

T F 2. Using the Delete key will remove both text and formats from a cell.

T F 3. Hiding columns and rows temporarily removes them from display.

T F 4. A workbook can only contain a maximum of three worksheets.

T F 5. Excel usually decides where to break pages when printing a worksheet.

FILL IN THE BLANK

Complete the following sentences by writing the correct word or words in the blanks provided.

1. After you click the Copy button to copy the contents of a cell, the cell is surrounded by a(n) __________ border.
2. The __________ command enables you to copy data from one cell to a number of cells above, below, to the left, or to the right.
3. A collection of related worksheets is called a(n) __________.

4. ________ a column or row enables you to keep the column or row visible as you scroll.

5. To sort from the largest number to the smallest, you would sort in ________ order.

PROJECTS

PROJECT 11-1

1. Open **Project11-1** from the data files. Save the worksheet as **Classes** followed by your initials.
2. Rename *Sheet1* as **Languages**. Rename *Sheet2* in the workbook as **Fitness**.
3. Switch to the **Languages** worksheet. Select the cell range **A4:F9** and AutoFit the column width to selection.
4. Someone has mistakenly formatted the class numbers with 1000s separators. Use the **Clear** command on the **Edit** menu to clear only the formats from these cells. Then center the values again.
5. Copy the cell range **A1:F4**. Switch to the **Fitness** worksheet. With cell **A1** selected, paste the copied cells.
6. Enter the following fitness class information:

Class	Class #	Winter	Spring	Summer	Fall
Low Impact Aerobics	5105	10	12	15	9
Bench Step Aerobics	5100	9	11	14	12
Combo Aerobics	5290	8	11	13	11
Nautilus	5309	13	14	18	15
Beginning Yoga	4380	10	9	8	7
Tai Chi Chuan	4300	11	9	8	12

7. Switch to the **Languages** worksheet. Insert a new column to the left of column B. The new column will be very wide since it defaults to the width of the column before it. Do not be concerned. You will adjust the width later. In cell B4, enter the column heading **Fee**.
8. Click in cell **B5** and enter the value **120**. Format this value as currency with zero decimal places and center the value in the cell.
9. Fill cells B6:B9 with the value in cell B5. Select the cell range **B5:B9** and AutoFit the column to selection.
10. Insert a row above row 8. Insert the following information in the new row:

German for Beginners	$120	7044	18	17	19	15

11. Switch to the Fitness worksheet. Insert a new column to the left of column B and enter the column heading **Fee**.
12. The fee for all **fitness** classes is $95. Enter that value in cell B5. Format the cell for Currency with 0 decimal places. Then fill the value in the cell range B6:B10. Select the cell range **A5:B10** and AutoFit the column to selection.
13. Select the range **C5:G10** and center the values.

14. Center both worksheets horizontally on the page. Preview each worksheet in Print Preview.

15. Save your changes. If you are permitted to print, print both worksheets in the workbook. Close the workbook.

PROJECT 11-2

1. Open **Project11-2** from the data files. Save the presentation as **Tutoring** followed by your initials.

2. Click in cell **G1** and key **September**. Use the AutoFill handle to automatically fill cells H1:J1 with the month names **October**, **November**, and **December**. Select the cell range **A1:J15** and adjust column widths to display the content.

3. You decide that last names should come first in this worksheet:
   A. Insert a new column to the left of column A.
   B. Select all data in column C (the *Last Name* column) and move it into the new column A. Adjust the width of column A to display all data.
   C. Delete the now empty column C.

4. To make it easier to find information about specific students, sort the data in the worksheet. Use the **Sort** dialog box and specify a sort by last name and then by first name, both in ascending order.

5. Harris Patrick has decided not to continue in the tutoring program. Delete the row that contains his data.

6. Hide the *Rate* column.

7. Click in cell **C1** and freeze panes. Then scroll horizontally so you can easily see how many hours each student is committed to per month.

8. Unfreeze panes and preview the worksheet. Even with the *Rate* column hidden, the data will not all fit on one page.

9. Change the orientation to landscape and center the worksheet horizontally on the page.

10. Unhide the *Rate* column.

11. Check the worksheet in Print Preview. If you have permission to print, print the worksheet.

12. Save your changes and close the workbook.

WEB PROJECT

You need to give a talk about earthquake hazards. Use Web search tools to locate information about damage caused by earthquakes. Create a worksheet to hold the information you locate. Use one worksheet in the workbook to hold information on five or six large U.S. earthquakes and another sheet to hold information on several large earthquakes elsewhere in the world. Your worksheets should record the date, magnitude, and location of the quake, property damage (if you can find it), and persons killed or injured in the quake. Sort the data you find by date or magnitude.

TEAMWORK PROJECT

With a partner, explore voting statistics for your state in Presidential elections from 1980 through the most recent Presidential election. Follow these steps:

1. Create a worksheet to hold your data. In column A, key **1980** in one cell and then **1984** in the cell below it. Use AutoFill to add the remaining Presidential election years up to and including the most recent Presidential election.
2. Create columns for **Republican**, **Democrat**, and **Independent** candidates.
3. Using an almanac or Web search tools, find information on the popular vote for Republican, Democrat, and Independent candidates for your state in each election. If there is more than one Independent candidate, add together all the votes for all Independent candidates. Collect data from 1980 through the most current Presidential election. Divide the research assignment evenly so that both you and your partner gather the data.
4. Add a column to your worksheet and title it **Winning Party**. Insert the political party of the President who won each election. Use the fill command to insert parties if the same party won two or more consecutive presidential elections. What party won most often in the years you studied?

CRITICAL *Thinking*

ACTIVITY 11-1

You have created a very large worksheet. You would like to be able to work in several parts of the worksheet simultaneously and be able to scroll in each part. You discover you cannot scroll in each part if you simply freeze panes. Is there another way to create panes in a worksheet that would allow you to scroll in each pane independently? Use the Help files in Excel to discover the answer to this question and then write a brief description of what you learn.

LESSON 12

CREATING WORKSHEET FORMULAS

OBJECTIVES

Upon completion of this lesson, you should be able to:

- Understand formulas.
- Create a formula.
- Identify and correct formula errors.
- Use the AutoSum feature.
- Use the AutoFill command to enter formulas.
- Use absolute cell references.
- Audit formulas on the worksheet.

Estimated Time: 1 hour

VOCABULARY

Absolute cell reference
Argument
Dependent cells
Formulas
Function formula
Mixed cell reference
Operand
Operator
Order of evaluation
Precedent cells
Relative cell references

One of the primary uses of a spreadsheet is to solve problems that involve numbers. The worksheet is often used to complete complex and repetitious calculations accurately, quickly, and easily. Instead of using a calculator to perform mathematical calculations, Excel will perform the calculations for you.

Understand Formulas

IC³ 2-3.2.3-1

The equations used to calculate values in a cell are known as ***formulas***. A formula uses numbers and cell references to perform calculations such as addition, subtraction, multiplication, and division. A formula consists of two components: an ***operand*** and an ***operator***. The operand is a number or cell reference. The operator is a symbol that tells Excel what mathematical operation to perform with the operands. For example, in the formula =B5+6, the operands are B5 and 6; the operator is the plus sign. Figure 12-1 lists some of the mathematical operators used in Excel.

IC3 2-3.2.3-2

FIGURE 12-1
Operators used in Excel

Mathematical Operation	Operator
Addition	+ (plus sign)
Subtraction	— (minus sign)
Multiplication	* (asterisk)
Division	/ (forward slash)
Percent	% (percent sign)

All formulas begin with the equal sign. This tells Excel that you are entering a formula instead of a numeric value.

A formula can be as simple as a single cell reference. For example, if you enter the formula =B3 in cell C4, the cell will display the same contents as cell B3. If you then change the value in cell B3, cell C4 will automatically be updated to reflect the change.

Formulas containing more than one operator are called complex formulas. For example, the formula =A4*B5+10 will perform both multiplication and addition. The sequence used to calculate the value of a formula is called the ***order of evaluation.*** Figure 12-2 provides examples to illustrate the order of evaluation.

FIGURE 12-2
Examples of order of evaluation

Formula	Result
=6+4*4	6+16=22
+6*4+2	24+2=26
=6-4/2	6-2=4
=6/2+4	3+4=7
=(6+4)*4	10*4=40
=(6*4)-(10/2)	24-5=19

Formulas are evaluated as follows:

- Multiplication and division are performed before addition or subtraction.
- Calculations are performed from the left side of the formula to the right side.
- You can change the order of evaluation by using parentheses. Calculations enclosed in parentheses are performed first.

IC3 2-3.2.3-3

Did You Know?

You can find all the mathematical operator symbols on the number keypad.

Create a Formula

There are two ways to enter a cell address into a formula. You can key the cell address or you can point to the cell. When entering the cell reference, the column letter can be keyed in either uppercase or lowercase. In the Step-by-Steps in this text, the column letters you must key are shown in lowercase. As you enter the cell references, Excel color-codes the borders around the cells and the cell references in the formula.

> **Computer Concepts**
>
> When creating formulas, there must be a closing parenthesis for every opening parenthesis. Otherwise, Excel will display an error message when you enter the formula.

The formula is displayed in the Formula Bar as you enter it in the cell. However, once you press Enter or click the Enter button on the Formula Bar, the result of the formula will display in the cell. To see the formula, you must click in the cell and then view the formula in the Formula Bar.

STEP-BY-STEP 12.1

IC3

1. Open **Step12-1** from the data files. Save the workbook as **Regional Sales** followed by your initials.

2-3.2.3-4

2. Click in cell **E3**. Key **=b3+c3+d3**. Compare your screen to Figure 12-3. Notice that each cell you referenced in the formula is selected with a color, and the color matches the color of the cell reference in the formula. Also, notice that the formula is displayed in the cell and in the Formula Bar.

> **Speech Recognition**
>
> If your computer has speech recognition capability, enable the Command mode and say the commands to open and save the file.

FIGURE 12-3
Entering a formula in a cell

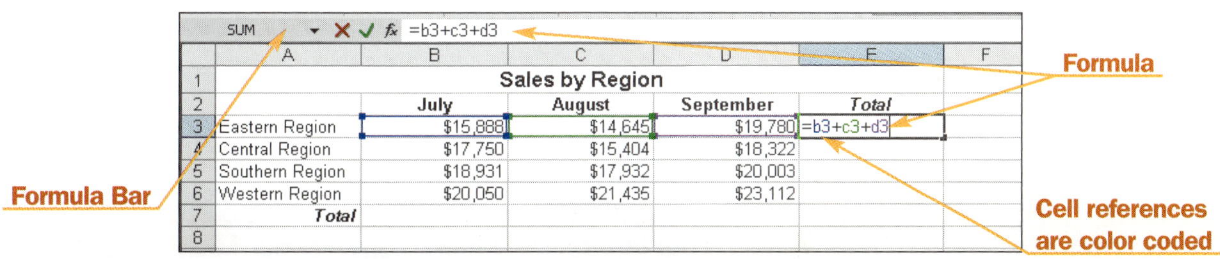

3. Press **Enter** or click the **Enter** button on the Formula Bar. The result of the formula $50,313 is displayed in cell E3.

4. Click in cell **E3**. Compare your screen with Figure 12-4. Notice that the formula is still displayed in the Formula Bar.

FIGURE 12-4
Result of a formula displayed in a cell

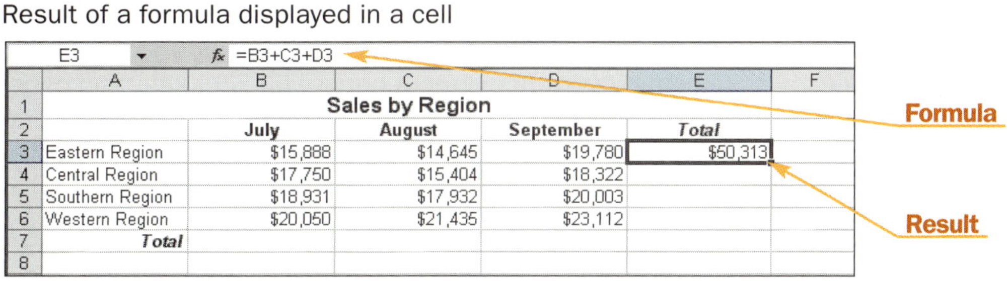

STEP-BY-STEP 12.1 Continued

5. Click in cell **E4**. Key **=**. Then click in cell **B4**. Notice that the cell reference B4 now displays following the = in both the Formula Bar and in cell E4.

2-3.2.3-4

6. Key **+** and then click in cell **C4**. Key **+** and click in cell **D4**. Both the cell and the Formula Bar now display the formula *=B4+C4+D4*.

7. Press **Enter** or click the **Enter** button on the Formula Bar. The result *$51,476* is displayed in cell E4.

8. Double-click in cell **B4**. Change the amount to **16,750**.

9. Press **Enter** or click the **Enter** button on the Formula Bar. Notice that the result in cell E4 changes to *$50,476* to reflect the change.

10. Save the changes and leave the workbook open for the next Step-by-Step.

Computer Concepts

Cell references are used in formulas rather than the actual value in the cell. That way, if the value in the cell changes, the formula does not need to be updated.

Historically Speaking

Imagine driving from Michigan to Georgia and needing five different currencies for your trip. To purchase items during your journey, you must convert your Michigan dollars to Ohio marks, Kentucky pounds, Tennessee lira, and Georgia francs. Not only would it be inconvenient, it would also be costly. Each time you converted the money, the money changers would charge you a fee. This is what tourists traditionally experienced when they traveled in Europe. Each time they entered a different country, they had to convert their money to that country's currency.

In January 1999, 11 European countries embraced one currency unit—the euro. The transition to the euro occurred over a three-year period and gradually came to be in general use. The euro was first introduced in electronic trading—business transactions completed without cash. In January 2002, euro notes and coins started circulating.

The changeover to a single currency affects banks, businesses, and consumers. The euro symbol now appears in banks, on financial statements, and on retail price tags. Office XP provides full support for entering, displaying, and printing the euro symbol and for working with values in euro currency.

Identify and Correct Formula Errors

C3
-3.2.8-1

When Excel cannot properly perform a calculation, an error value will display in the cell where you entered the formula. The error may exist because the cell contains text instead of a numeric value. An error value will display if the cell referenced in the formula contains an error or if a formula tries to divide by zero. An error value will also display if the cell is not wide enough to display the result.

> **Did You Know?**
>
> Excel has an AutoCorrect feature that automatically checks a formula for common keyboarding mistakes. Sometimes Excel is able to identify the error. If so, a suggested correction appears in an alert box.

Use Help to Learn How to Troubleshoot Formulas and Error Values

If an error value displayed in your worksheet, would you know what to do to correct the problem? You can go to the Help screens to learn about how to troubleshoot the error.

STEP-BY-STEP 12.2

1. Click in cell **E5**. Enter the following formula: **=a5+c5+d5**.
2. Press **Enter** or click the **Enter** button on the Formula Bar. *#VALUE!* is displayed in cell E5. This is the error value. Excel cannot perform the calculation because cell A5 does not contain a numeric value.
3. Open the **Help** menu and choose **Microsoft Excel Help**. If the Office Assistant is displayed, point to the Office Assistant and right-click. Then choose **Options** in the shortcut menu. Clear the check box for *Use the Office Assistant* and click **OK**. Then open the **Help** menu and choose **Microsoft Excel Help**.
4. If necessary, click the **Show** button on the toolbar to display the Contents, Answer Wizard, and Index tabs.
5. If necessary, click the **Contents** tab to display a dialog box similar to the one shown in Figure 12-5. (*Hint:* If you click a plus symbol, the list will expand to display another level of topics.)

STEP-BY-STEP 12.2 Continued

FIGURE 12-5
Contents tab in Microsoft Excel Help

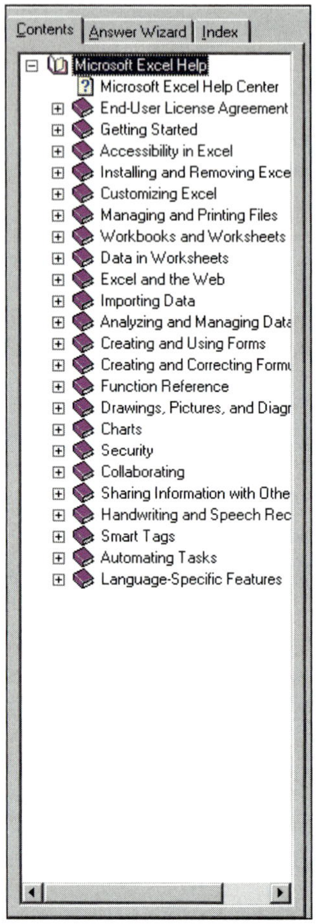

6. Click the plus sign (**+**) to the left of the topic *Creating* and *Correcting Formulas*. The list of topics expands to show a new list of subtopics.

7. Click the **plus** sign to the left of the subtopic *Correcting Formulas*. Then select the subtopic **Find and correct errors in formulas**.

8. The topic information is displayed in the pane at the right. Click the link **Correct an error value, such as #NAME?**. The topic is expanded.

> **Did You Know?**
>
> If the entire topic title is not displayed in the Contents pane, you can point to the topic title and a ScreenTip displaying the entire title will appear.

9. Click the link **#VALUE**. Read the information about why the error message is displayed, then follow the suggested steps:

   a. Click in cell **E5** in the worksheet.

   b. Point to the Trace Error button that is displayed to the left of the cell.

   c. A ScreenTip displays, showing *A value used in the formula is of the wrong data type.*

   d. Click the down arrow on the **Trace Error** button to display the menu shown in Figure 12-6.

STEP-BY-STEP 12.2 Continued

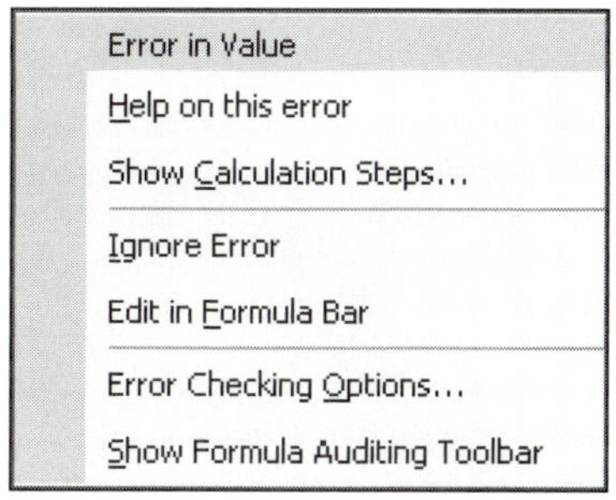

FIGURE 12-6
Error menu

e. Select **Show Calculation Steps**. The Evaluate Formula dialog box shown in Figure 12-7 is displayed. Now you can clearly see that the problem is that you are trying to add text (*Southern Region*) with numbers.

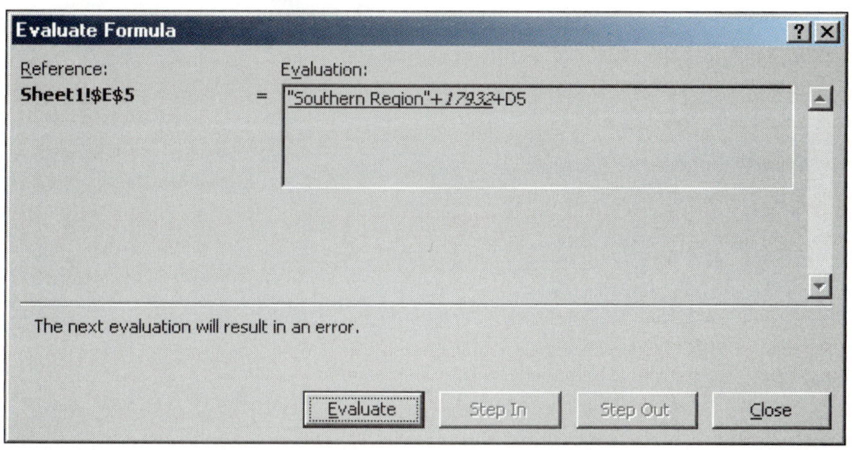

FIGURE 12-7
Evaluate Formula dialog box

10. Click the **Close** button in the Evaluate Formula dialog box and then close the Help dialog box. Leave the workbook open for the next Step-by-Step.

Common Errors

There are a number of common errors that occur—and common causes for those errors. Table 12-1 lists these common errors, their typical causes, and some possible solutions.

2-3.2.8-2

TABLE 12-1
Common errors, their causes, and solutions

ERROR	TYPICAL CAUSE/SOLUTION
#####	Occurs when the column is not wide enough or if a negative date is entered. If the column is not wide enough, widen the column or change the number format so that the number will fit within the column. Negative dates usually occur when there is an incorrect formula calculating a date. Check and correct your date formula.

TABLE 12-1 Continued
Common errors, their causes, and solutions

ERROR	TYPICAL CAUSE/SOLUTION
#VALUE!	Occurs when the wrong type of argument or operand is used. It could result from entering text when a formula requires a number of a logical value such as TRUE or FALSE. Trace the error to determine which of these is the cause and correct it.
#DIV/0!	Occurs when a number is divided by zero. Most often caused by using a cell reference to a blank cell or to a cell that contains zero. Trace the error and correct the reference.
#NAME?	Occurs when Excel doesn't recognize text in a formula. This is most often caused by using a function that is part of the Analysis Toolpak add-in without the add-in being loaded. To resolve this, install and load the Analysis Toolpak add-in. Can also be caused by using a name that doesn't exist. To resolve this, make sure the name exists. On the Insert menu, point to Name, and then click Define. If the name is not listed, add the name by using the Define command.
#N/A	Occurs when a value is not available to a function or formula. This can be caused by missing data or by referencing a cell that contains #N/A instead of data (you can use this as a placeholder for data that is not yet available). Trace the error and replace the missing data with a real value. Can also be caused by giving an inappropriate value for a lookup. To resolve this, make sure the lookup_value argument is the correct type of value—for example, a value or a cell reference, but not a range reference.
#REF!	Occurs when a cell reference is not valid. Often caused by deleting cells referred to by other formulas or pasting moved cells over cells referred to by other formulas. To correct this error, trace the error and then change the formulas. Or, if you notice the error right after deleting or pasting cells, restore the cells on the worksheet by clicking Undo immediately after you delete or paste cells which caused the error. This can also be caused by running a link to a program that is not running. To resolve the error in this case, start the program to which the worksheet is trying to link.
#NUM!	Occurs with invalid numeric values in a formula or function. This can be caused by using an unacceptable argument in a function that requires a numeric argument. To correct this, make sure the arguments used in the function are numbers. For example, even if the value you want to enter is $1,000, enter 1000 in the formula. This error can also be caused by using a worksheet function that iterates, such as IRR or RATE, and the function cannot find a result. To resolve the error in this case, use a different starting value for the worksheet function or change the number of times Microsoft Excel iterates formulas.
#NULL!	Occurs when you specify an intersection of two areas that do not intersect. The intersection operator is a space between references. Typically caused by an incorrect range operator. Trace the error and make sure that the correct range operators are used. To refer to a contiguous range of cells, use a colon (:) to separate the reference to the first cell in the range from the reference to the last cell in the range. For example, SUM(A1:A10) refers to the range from cell A1 to cell A10 inclusive. To refer to two areas that don't intersect, use the union operator, the comma (,). For example, if the formula sums two ranges, make sure a comma separates the two ranges (SUM(A1:A10,C1:C10)).

Edit a Formula

You can choose from three methods to edit a formula: 1) you can double-click the cell and then edit the formula in the cell, 2) you can select the cell, press F2, and then edit the formula in
2-3.2.6-1 the cell, or 3) you can select the cell and then edit the formula in the Formula Bar.

STEP-BY-STEP 12.3

1. Double-click cell **E5**.

2-3.2.6-2

2. Change the cell reference from *A5* to **b5**. Press **Enter** or click the **Enter** button on the Formula Bar. The result *($56,866)* displays in cell E5.

3. Save the changes and leave the workbook open for the next Step-by-Step.

Use the AutoSum Feature

Although it is easy to enter a formula, if the formula consists of several cells, it could take you a long time to enter all the cell references. A shortcut for entering cell references is to identify a range of cells. For example, B5:D5 includes the cells B5, C5 and D5.

The AutoSum feature enables you to quickly identify a range of cells and enter a formula. When you use the AutoSum button, Excel scans the worksheet to determine the most logical col-
2-3.2.7-1 umn or row of adjacent cells containing numbers to sum. Excel identifies those cells as a range. For example, if the active cell is E7 and there are numbers in cells A7 through D7, Excel will identify the range A7 through D7.

After identifying the range of cells, the AutoSum feature creates a `function formula` to calculate the sum of the range. A ***function formula*** is a special formula that names a function instead of using operators to calculate a result. In this case, the function is SUM. The SUM function formula is the most frequently used type of function formula. Figure 12-8 illustrates the parts of the SUM function formula. A function contains three parts—the equal sign, the function name, and the arguments. The equal sign tells Excel that a formula follows. The function name tells Excel what to do with the data. The ***argument*** is a value, cell reference, range, or text that acts as an operand in a function formula. The argument is enclosed in parentheses after the function name. You will learn about other function formulas in the next lesson.

FIGURE 12-8
Parts of a function formula

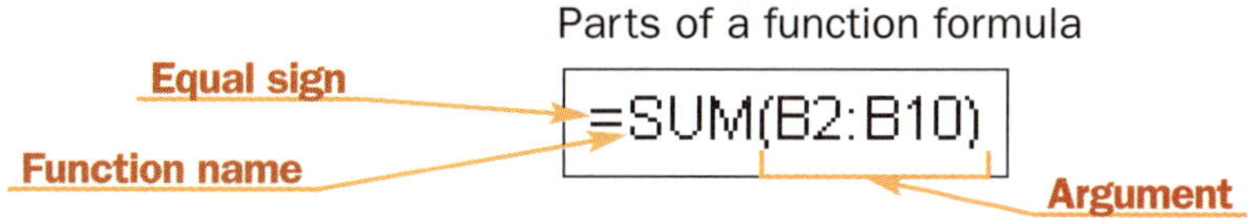

Sometimes Excel does not identify the correct range when you use the AutoSum feature. To identify a different range of cells, drag to select the desired cell range. Then click Enter to display the sum in the cell.

2-3.2.7-2

STEP-BY-STEP 12.4

1. With cell **E6** selected, click the **AutoSum** button on the Standard toolbar. Excel displays a marquee (an animated border) around the cell range E3:E5 and proposes the formula *=SUM(E3:E5)*. A ScreenTip also displays showing that the formula involves adding numbers. See Figure 12-9.

FIGURE 12-9
Proposed AutoSum formula

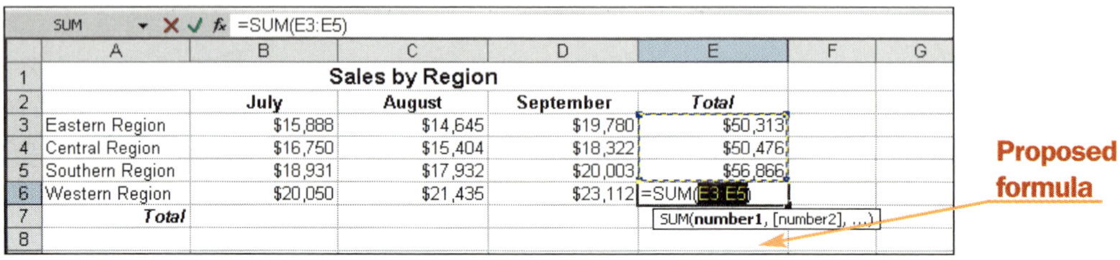

2. Click in cell **B6** and drag to select cells C6 and D6. Excel places a marquee around the new range B6:D6. The proposed formula changes to *=SUM(B6:D6)* to reflect the cell references in the new selection.

3. Press **Enter** or click the **Enter** button on the Formula Bar to accept the new formula. The result *$64,597* is displayed in cell E6.

4. Click in cell **B7**. Click the **AutoSum** button and, since it is correctly summing the cell range B3:B6, press **Enter** or click the **Enter** button on the Formula Bar. The result *$71,619* displays in cell B7.

5. Use the **AutoSum** button to enter a formula to calculate the column totals in cells C7, D7, and E7.

6. Insert a new row between the Central Region and Southern Region. Key the following information in the new row. Notice that as you enter the new data, Excel automatically adjusts the results in cells B8, C8, and D8.

   Midwest Region 14505 16112 17341

7. Click in cell **B8**. Look at the formula in the Formula Bar. Notice that Excel automatically updated the range in the formula. The formula now shows the range B3:B7 instead of B3:B6.

8. Click in cell **E5**, then click the **AutoSum** button. Change the range in the formula to **b5:d5**. Then press **Enter** or click the **Enter** button on the Formula Bar. (Notice that the value in cell E8 changes to reflect the new total added in the column.)

Speech Recognition

If your computer has speech recognition capability, enable the Command mode. Then position the insertion point in the designated cell and say the command to calculate the total using the AutoSum feature. Say **Enter** to accept the proposed formula.

Computer Concepts

When you insert or delete a new row or column that affects a range of cells identified in a formula, Excel will automatically update the range in the formula to reflect the change(s) in the range.

Computer Concepts

Note that the value in cell E8 did not change until you entered a new value in cell E5. This is because the formula calculated the range E3:E7. However, if the formula in cell E8 had instead calculated the range B7:D7, the value in cell E8 would have been adjusted at the same time cells B8, C8, and D8 changed.

STEP-BY-STEP 12.4 Continued

9. Notice that there is a triangle in the top left corner of cell E5. Click in the cell, and then point to the Trace Error button that displays to the left. The ScreenTip indicates that the formula in this cell differs from the formulas in this area of the spreadsheet. If you click in any of the other cells in the column, you will see that most of the formulas use plus signs instead of the sum feature to calculate the total. The formula in cell C5 is, however, accurate.

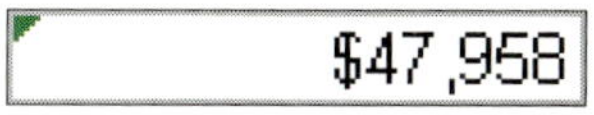

10. Compare your screen to Figure 12-10. If necessary, edit the formulas to correct any errors. When the values in your worksheet match those illustrated in Figure 12-10, save the changes and close the workbook.

Hot Tip

To quickly preview the sum of a range of cells, select the range of cells. The sum is displayed in the status bar at the bottom of the screen.

FIGURE 12-10
Completed worksheet

E20 fx

	A	B	C	D	E	F
1			Sales by Region			
2		**July**	**August**	**September**	***Total***	
3	Eastern Region	$15,888	$14,645	$19,780	$50,313	
4	Central Region	$16,750	$15,404	$18,322	$50,476	
5	Midwest Region	$14,505	$16,112	$17,341	$47,958	
6	Southern Region	$18,931	$17,932	$20,003	$56,866	
7	Western Region	$20,050	$21,435	$23,112	$64,597	
8	***Total***	$86,124	$85,528	$98,558	$270,210	
9						

Use the AutoFill Command to Enter Formulas

In Lesson 11, you learned how AutoFill can copy data to adjacent cells or fill a range of cells with a data series such as numbers 1 through 10. You can also use AutoFill to copy formulas. You can fill formulas up, down, left, and right.

IC3 -3.2.10-1

By default, when you create formulas, the cell references are formatted as ***relative cell references***. That means when the formula is copied to another cell, the cell references will be adjusted relative to the formula's new location. This automatic adjustment is helpful when you need to repeat the same formula for several columns or rows.

STEP-BY-STEP 12.5

1. Open **Step12-5** from the data files. Save the workbook as **Mileage Report** followed by your initials.

2. Click in cell **D3**. Enter the formula **=c3-b3**. Press **Enter** or click the **Enter** button in the Formula Bar. The result *81* displays in cell D3.

3. Click in cell **D3**. Point to the fill handle in the lower-right corner of cell D3. When the pointer changes to a bold plus sign, drag down to cell D7. The results of the formula display in each of the selected cells.

4. Click in cell **D4**. Notice the formula in the Formula Bar displays *=C4-B4*.

STEP-BY-STEP 12.5 Continued

5. Click in cell **D5**. Notice the formula in the Formula Bar displays *=C5-B5*.

6. Save the changes and leave the worksheet open for the next Step-by-Step.

IC3 2-3.2.10-1

Use Absolute Cell References

There are times, though, when you don't want the cell reference to change when the formula is moved or copied to a new cell. For example, you may be calculating expenses for auto mileage. The number of miles should always be multiplied times a fixed amount that represents the cost per mile. To create this formula, you format an absolute cell reference. An ***absolute cell reference*** does not change when the formula is copied or moved to a new location.

To create an absolute cell reference, you insert a dollar sign ($) before the column letter and/or the row number of the cell reference you want to stay the same. To illustrate, =A1 is a formula with an absolute reference.

IC3 2-3.2.10-3

A cell reference that contains both relative and absolute references is called a ***mixed cell reference***. For example, you can have an absolute column reference and a relative row reference. Or, you can have a relative column reference and an absolute row reference. To illustrate, =$A1 is a formula with a mixed cell reference. The column reference is absolute and the row reference is relative. When formulas with mixed cell references are copied or moved, the row or column references that are preceded by a dollar sign will not change. However, the row or column references that are not preceded by a dollar sign will adjust relative to the cell to which they are moved.

Hot Tip

Another method for creating an absolute cell reference is to key the cell reference and then press **F4**. This toggles the display of a dollar sign in front of the column letter and/or the row number. When you press **F4** once, Excel will insert a dollar sign in front of the column letter and another dollar sign in front of the row number. If you press **F4** a second time, Excel will insert a dollar sign in front of the row reference only. If you press **F4** a third time, Excel will insert a dollar sign in front of the column reference only.

IC3 2-3.2.10-2

STEP-BY-STEP 12.6

1. Click in cell **E3**. Enter the formula **=d3*c10**.

2. Press **Enter** or click the **Enter** button on the Formula Bar. Excel multiplied the value in cell D3 (*81*) times the value in cell C10 (*$0.33*). The result is *$26.73*.

3. Click in cell **E3**. Drag the fill handle down to cell E7. The results display in each of the selected cells.

4. Click in cell **E4**. Notice the formula in the Formula Bar displays *=D4*C10*. When you filled the formula down, Excel automatically changed the cell references for D3 in the original formula. However, because the cell reference for C10 was absolute, Excel did not change that cell reference.

5. Click in cell **E8**. Click the **AutoSum** button, then press **Enter** or click the **Enter** button on the Formula Bar.

6. Save the changes and keep the workbook open for the next Step-by-Step.

Audit Formulas on the Worksheet

Because Excel performs the calculations, spreadsheet users (even experienced ones) often assume that the results in the worksheet are accurate. However, the results are only accurate if the user has entered accurate data and correct formulas. Therefore, data and formulas should be checked to ensure the accuracy of the results.

If your worksheet contains several formulas, it would be a tedious task to click each cell in order to view and proofread each formula. Fortunately, there is an easier way to display formulas. Simply hold down Ctrl and press the single left quotation mark (generally located in the upper-left corner of the keyboard). You can also display formulas in a worksheet by opening the Tools menu and choosing Options. Then click the View tab and turn on Formulas under Window options.

Likewise, it could be very time-consuming to verify all the cell references in the formulas. The Formula Audit toolbar offers some tools that make it easy to trace these cell references and display both ***precedent cells*** and ***dependent cells***. The cells that provide data to a formula are called precedents. Formulas that reference a particular cell are called dependents.

STEP-BY-STEP 12.7

1. Press **Ctrl +** ‘ (single left quotation mark). The number formats are removed from the cells, and the formulas display instead of the results.

2. Compare your worksheet with the one illustrated in Figure 12-11. If your formulas do not match those in the figure, click the cell and edit the formula. If the Formula Auditing toolbar is displayed, drag it to the side. You will use it later.

FIGURE 12-11
Worksheet with formulas displayed

E9 ▾ *fx*

	A	B	C	D	E
1			JULY MILEAGE REPORT		
2	Date	Odometer Start	Odometer End	Total Miles	Expense
3	36708	78541	78622	=C3-B3	=D3*C10
4	36709	78904	78991	=C4-B4	=D4*C10
5	36714	79106	79165	=C5-B5	=D5*C10
6	36715	80155	80352	=C6-B6	=D6*C10
7	36716	80394	80457	=C7-B7	=D7*C10
8	Total				=SUM(E3:E7)
9					
10		Cost per mile	0.33		
11					

3. Click in cell **E8**. The cells referenced in the formula are highlighted.

4. Press **Ctrl +** ‘ to hide the formulas and display the results.

5. If necessary, display the Formula Auditing toolbar shown in Figure 12-12. Open the **View** menu, choose **Toolbars**, and select **Formula Auditing**.

FIGURE 12-12
Formula Auditing toolbar

STEP-BY-STEP 12.7 Continued

6. Click cell **D7**. Then click the **Trace Precedents** button on the Formula Auditing toolbar. An arrow displays through cells B7 and C7 to trace the cells that provide data to the formula.

7. Click in cell **C10**. Click the **Trace Dependents** button on the Formula Auditing toolbar. Several arrows display pointing to the cells in column E that depend on the data in cell C10.

8. Compare your worksheet with the one illustrated in Figure 12-13.

FIGURE 12-13
Arrows show precedents for cell D7 and dependents for cell C10

	A	B	C	D	E	F
1	JULY MILEAGE REPORT					
2	Date	Odometer Start	Odometer End	Total Miles	Expense	
3	1-Jul	78,541	78,622	81	$26.73	
4	2-Jul	78,904	78,991	87	$28.71	
5	7-Jul	79,106	79,165	59	$19.47	
6	8-Jul	80,155	80,352	197	$65.01	
7	9-Jul	80,394	80,457	63	$20.79	
8	Total				$160.71	
9						
10		Cost per mile	$0.33			
11						

9. Click the **Remove All Arrows** button on the Formula Auditing toolbar to remove the arrows from the worksheet.

10. Close the workbook. Click **Yes** if you are prompted to save changes.

Speech Recognition

If your computer has speech recognition capability, enable the Command mode. Position the Insertion point in the designated cells and then say the commands to trace the precedents and dependents.

SUMMARY

In this lesson, you learned:

- One of the primary uses for Excel spreadsheets is to perform calculations. Formulas are equations with numbers, cell references, and operators that tell Excel how to perform the calculations.
- All formulas begin with =. To enter the cell references in a formula, you can key the cell address or you can point and click the cell you want to reference.
- If Excel cannot perform a calculation, an error value will display. The Trace Error button will display and can help guide you in troubleshooting the problem. Then, you can edit the formula directly in the cell or in the Formula Bar.
- The AutoSum feature enables you to quickly identify a range of cells and enter a formula.
- The AutoFill feature enables you to quickly copy formulas to adjacent cells. The cell references are adjusted relative to the formula's new location.

- If you do not want the cell reference to change when the formula is moved or copied to a new location, the cell reference must be formatted as an absolute cell reference.
- Displaying formulas in the worksheet can make it easier to view and proofread the formulas.
- Tracing the precedents and dependents of a formula make proofing formulas quicker and easier.

VOCABULARY *Review*

Define the following terms:

Absolute cell reference	Function formula	Order of evaluation
Argument	Mixed cell reference	Precedent cells
Dependent cells	Operand	Relative cell reference
Formulas	Operator	

REVIEW *Questions*

TRUE/FALSE

Circle T if the statement is true or F if the statement is false.

T F 1. A formula must consist of more than one cell reference.

T F 2. You can enter a cell reference in either uppercase or lowercase.

T F 3. If you do not include a closing parenthesis in a formula, Excel will display an error message.

T F 4. You can only fill formulas down.

T F 5. An absolute cell reference will automatically adjust when moved or copied.

FILL IN THE BLANK

Complete the following sentences by writing the correct word or words in the blanks provided.

1. A complex formula consists of two components: a(n) __________ and a(n) __________.
2. The __________ determine(s) the sequence calculations are performed in a complex formula.
3. The __________ feature enables you to quickly find the total of a range of cells.
4. Cell references that contain both relative and absolute references are called __________.
5. __________ provide data to a formula.

PROJECTS

PROJECT 12-1

1. Open **Project12-1** from the data files. Save the workbook as **Deer** followed by your initials.
2. Click in cell **G6** and create a formula that will add the numbers for all four days of the survey.
3. Use **Fill** to copy the formula to the cell range G7:G14.
4. Click in cell **H6** and create a formula that will divide the total in cell G6 by the square miles value in cell B6. (*Hint*: The operator for division is / (forward slash). Format the cell with the Number format using one decimal place.)
5. Use **Fill** to copy the formula to the cell range H7:H14.
6. The Division of Wildlife in your state suggests that for deer herds to remain healthy, there should be no more than 25 deer per square mile. Find out how the deer herds in your state county parks compare with this suggested density by calculating the percent over or under for each park:
   A. Click in cell **I6** and type the formula **=h6/25**. Format the resulting value as a Percentage with no decimal places.
   B. Fill down the formula in each cell in the range I7:I14.
   C. Which parks meet the suggested density figures (are under 100%)? Which parks have a serious overpopulation problem (are over 130%)?
7. Check your formulas by displaying all the formulas in the worksheet.
8. Hide the formulas again. Save the changes and close the workbook.

PROJECT 12-2

1. Open **Project12-2** from data files. Save the workbook as **Pies** followed by your initials.
2. Click in cell **E6** and create a formula that will multiply the total number of deep-dish apple pies by the price for all fruit pies in cell C5. (*Hint*: The formula should include an absolute cell reference for cell C5.)
3. Use **Fill** to copy the formula for the other fruit pies.
4. In cells D11 and E11, use **AutoSum** to sum the total number of fruit pies and the fruit pie revenue.
5. Using the same procedure, calculate revenues and subtotals for the remaining pie categories.
6. In cell D33, create a formula that will add each of the subtotal values in the D column (cells D11, D17, D24, and D31).
7. In cell E33, create a formula that will add each of the subtotal revenue values in the E column (cells E11, E17, E24, and E31).
8. In cells D35 and E35, create formulas to subtract last year's numbers and revenues from the Grand Total amounts for this year. Is Melissa gaining or losing business?

9. Change the price for Tropical Treats to **$15.00**. How did the change impact Melissa's gain/loss?

10. Save the changes and close the workbook.

WEB PROJECT

You plan to visit Europe in the coming summer and would like to know what kind of exchange rate you can expect when changing dollars to euros. Search the Web for a site that gives a current exchange rate for euros. Then create a worksheet that contains a cell in which to type a dollar amount, a cell that contains the current euro exchange rate, and a cell that will display the result of the calculation to convert dollars to euros.

TEAMWORK PROJECT

At some time in your future, you will probably consider the purchase of a car, either new or used. It is easy to overlook the fact that there are other expenses associated with a car besides the initial purchase price. With a partner, explore the costs of buying, running, and maintaining a car in this project. Follow these steps:

1. With your teammate, decide what kind of car you want to purchase. It can be either new or used.

2. Establish the expenses you expect to be associated with the car. For example, you will have the purchase price, insurance, regular fill-ups of gasoline, and regular maintenance. Divide this list of expenses with your partner.

3. Find a representative price for your car in a newspaper or on a Web site. You can locate insurance information on the Web or by calling car insurance agencies. Establish an average price per gallon of gas. Ask friends or family about yearly regular maintenance costs such as tune-ups, new tires, oil changes, and so on.

4. Create a worksheet to store the data you gather. In part of the worksheet, figure out approximately how many gallons of gas your car might use in 12 months and add that sum to the values you have established for purchase, car insurance, and regular maintenance.

5. How much do you figure it will cost you to purchase and use your automobile for a year?

CRITICAL *Thinking*

ACTIVITY 12-1

Open a new worksheet. In cell B2, key **25**. Press **Enter** and key **30**. Press **Enter** and key **35**. Press **Enter** and key **40**. Suppose you wanted to add up these numbers and then multiply the total by **2**.

In cell D2, key the following formula: **=b2+b3+b4+b5*2**. In cell D3, key the following formula: **=(b2+b3+b4+b5)*2**.

Are the values in cells D2 and D3 the same? Why not? Write a brief report to explain why the formula results are different.

LESSON 13

USING FUNCTION FORMULAS

OBJECTIVES

Upon completion of this lesson, you should be able to:

- Understand function formulas.
- Use the Average and Sum functions.
- Use the Count function.
- Use the Minimum and Maximum functions.
- Use the Now functions.
- Use logical functions.

Estimated Time: 1 hour

VOCABULARY

Logical functions
Mathematical functions
Statistical functions
Trigonometric functions

Understand Function Formulas

IC³ 2-3.2.4-1

Excel has more than 300 built-in functions for performing calculations. In fact, you have already used one of Excel's built-in mathematical and trigonometric functions—the SUM function. ***Mathematical*** and ***trigonometric functions*** perform calculations that you could do using a scientific calculator. When you used the AutoSum button, Excel used the SUM function to calculate the results. ***Statistical functions*** are functions that describe large quantities of data. For example, a statistical function can determine the average of a range of data.

2-3.2.4-2

Table 13-1 describes some of the most common mathematical and statistical functions.

TABLE 13-1
Common Excel functions

MATHEMATICAL AND TRIGONOMETRIC FUNCTIONS	
=PRODUCT	Multiplies values in the specified cells
=ROUND	Rounds the value to the nearest value in one of two ways: with the specified number of decimal places or to the nearest whole number
=ROUNDUP	Rounds the value up to the next higher positive value (or the next lower negative value) with the number of specified decimal places
=ROUNDDOWN	Rounds the value down to the next lower positive value (or to the next higher negative value) with the number of specified decimal places
=SUM	Adds the values in the specified range of cells
STATISTICAL FUNCTIONS	
=AVERAGE	Totals the range of cells and then divides the total by the number of entries in the specified range
=COUNT	Counts the number of cells with values in the specified range
=MAX	Displays the maximum value within the specified range of cells
=MEDIAN	Displays the middle value in the specified range of cells
=MIN	Displays the minimum value within the specified range of cells

Figure 13-1 illustrates an example of a formula containing an Average function. The equal sign tells Excel that a formula follows. The function name AVERAGE tells Excel to calculate an average of the three cells included in the argument—B4, B6, and B8.

FIGURE 13-1
Average function formula

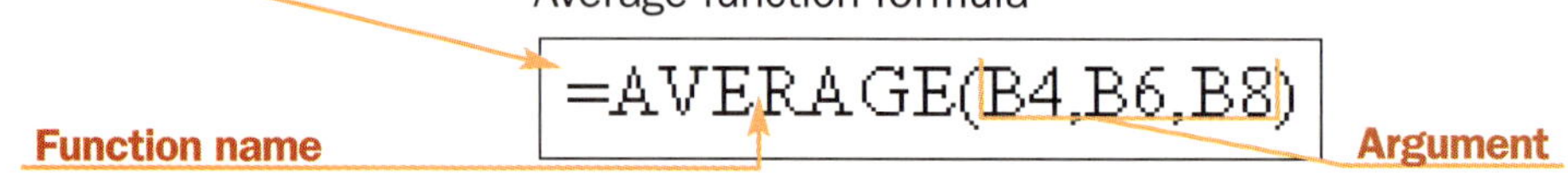

There are several methods for entering functions in the worksheet. If you know the function name and argument, you can key an equal sign, the function name, and the argument. Or, if you want help entering the formula, you can use the Insert Function button and the Function Arguments dialog box to guide you through the process of building a formula that contains a function.

> **Computer Concepts**
> When the function formula contains more than one argument, commas are used to separate the arguments.

Use the Average and Sum Functions

The Average function is a statistical function. It displays the average of the range identified in the argument. For example, the function =AVERAGE(B2,G2) calculates the average of the values contained in cells B2 and G2. As you already know, the Sum function is a mathematical function. If you used the Sum function instead of the average function, the total (instead of the average) of the values contained in cells B2 and G2 would be calculated.

Did You Know?

It is not necessary to key the function name in all caps.

STEP-BY-STEP 13.1

1. Open **Step13-1** from the data files. Save the workbook as **Weather** followed by your initials.

2-3.2.4-3

2. You want to calculate the average low temperature for the week. Click in cell **B13**. Key **=average(b2:b8)**. This formula tells Excel to calculate the average of the values in the cell range B2:B8.

Speech Recognition

If your computer has speech recognition capability, enable the Command mode and say the commands to open the file and then save it with a new filename.

3. Press **Enter** or click the **Enter** button on the Formula Bar. The result *9* is displayed in cell B13.

2-3.2.4-3

4. Now you want to calculate the average high temperature for the week. Click in cell **D13**. Click the **Insert Function** button on the Formula Bar. An Insert Function dialog box similar to the one shown in Figure 13-2 is displayed. Do not be concerned if your dialog box looks a little different.

FIGURE 13-2
Insert Function dialog box

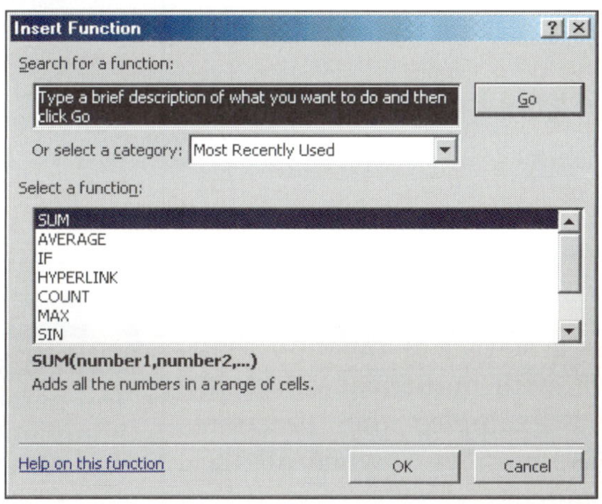

5. In the *Search for a function* box, key **calculate average** and click **Go**. The display of options under *Select a Function* changes and **AVERAGE** is already selected. Notice that a brief explanation of the Average function is displayed at the bottom of the dialog box.

Hot Tip

If you do not know which category to choose from, click the down arrow in the **Or select a category:** list box and then select **All**. The complete list of function names will display.

STEP-BY-STEP 13.1 Continued

6. Click **OK**. The Function Arguments dialog box shown in Figure 13-3 is displayed. Notice that Excel identified the range D10:D12 in the Number 1 text box. Also, Excel proposes a formula with the AVERAGE function in the Formula Bar. The result *25* is displayed at the bottom of the Function Arguments dialog box.

FIGURE 13-3
Function Arguments dialog box

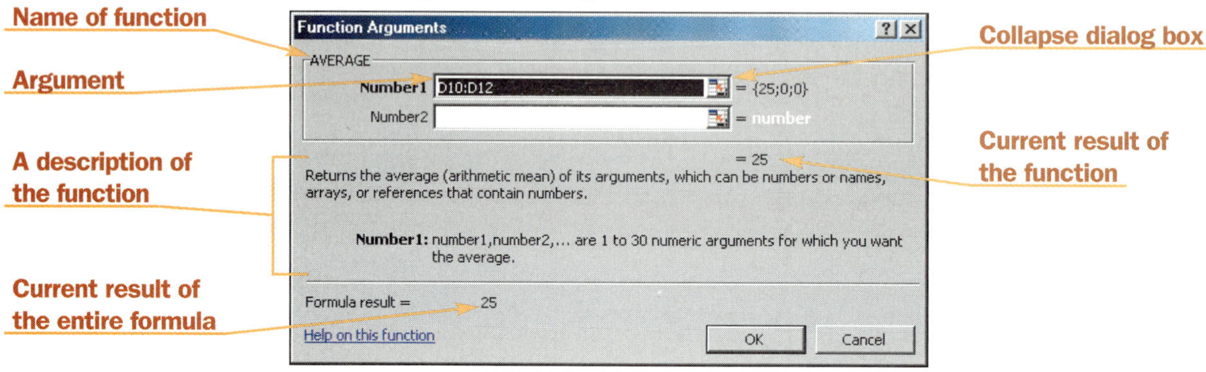

7. The range in the Number 1 text box is not correct. Click in the text box and change the range to **d2:d8**. Notice the result at the bottom of the dialog box now displays *24*.

8. Click **OK**. The result *24* is displayed in cell D13.

9. Save the changes and leave the workbook open for the next Step-by-Step.

Computer Concepts

The Insert Function dialog box makes it easy for you to browse through all of the available functions to choose the one you want. Furthermore, when you select a function, a brief explanation of that function is displayed. If you want help on the function, click the link at the bottom of the dialog box.

Use the Count Function

The Count function is a statistical function that displays the number of cells with numerical values in the argument range. For example, the function =COUNT(B4:B10) displays the number 7 when all the cells in the range contain a numeric value.

You can edit a range of cells in the Function Arguments dialog box by selecting the cells. Although the intent of the Function Arguments dialog box is to guide you in creating formulas, the dialog box can get in the way when you are creating the formula. That is why the collapse and expand features are available in the Function Arguments dialog box. They allow you to minimize and maximize the dialog box as you work with it.

Computer Concepts

The purpose of the Function Arguments dialog box is to help you construct a function formula.

Hot Tip

You can also use the Formula Palette to edit functions in existing formulas.

STEP-BY-STEP 13.2

> **Speech Recognition**
>
> If your computer has speech recognition capability, enable the Command mode and say the commands to navigate to the specified cells.

1. Click in cell **B12**.

2. Click the **Insert Function** button to display the Insert Function dialog box. Under *Select a function*, select **COUNT**.

3. Click **OK**. The Function Arguments dialog box is displayed. Because you chose a different function, the information looks slightly different. The text boxes are now labeled *Value 1* and *Value 2*. Excel proposes the range B10:B11 in the Value 1 text box and the result is *1*. The range, however, is not correct.

4. Click the **Collapse Dialog** button at the right side of the Value 1 text box. The dialog box minimizes so that you only see its title bar and the range of cells. (see Figure 13-4). The proposed formula is still displayed in the Formula Bar.

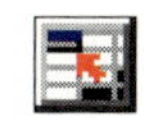

FIGURE 13-4
Minimized Function Arguments dialog box

5. If necessary, drag the minimized dialog box out of the way and then select the range **B2:B8**. The formula in the dialog box is updated and now shows the new range you selected. Notice, too, that the formula in the Formula Bar is also updated.

6. Click the **Expand Dialog** button at the right side of the Function Arguments title bar, or press **Enter**. The dialog box is maximized. Notice that the Value 1 text box now displays the range *B2:B8*.

7. Click **OK**. The result *7* is displayed in cell B12.

8. Click in cell **B16**. Click the **Insert Function** button and select **SUM** under *Select a function*. Click **OK**.

9. The Function Arguments dialog box displays. The range in the Number 1 text box is not correct. Minimize the Function Arguments dialog box. Click in cell **F2** and drag to select the range **F2:F8**. Then maximize the dialog box and click **OK**. The result *12* displays in cell B16.

10. Save the changes and leave the workbook open for the next Step-by-Step.

Use the Minimum and Maximum Functions

The Minimum (MIN) and Maximum (MAX) functions are also statistical functions. The MIN function displays the smallest number contained in the range identified in the argument. The MAX function displays the largest number contained in the range identified in the argument.

STEP-BY-STEP 13.3

1. Click in cell **B14**. Click the **Insert Function** button to display the Insert Function dialog box.
2. In the *Search for a function* box, key **minimum**. Under *Select a function*, select **MIN** if necessary and click **OK**.
3. Collapse the Function Arguments dialog box and then select the range **B2:B8**.
4. Expand the dialog box and then click **OK**. The result *–2* is displayed in cell B14.
5. Click in cell **B15**. Click the **Insert Function** button to display the Insert Function dialog box.
6. Under *Select a function*, select **MAX** and click **OK**.
7. Collapse the dialog box and select the range **D2:D8**.
8. Expand the dialog box and click **OK**. The result *30* is displayed in cell B15.
9. Save the changes and leave the workbook open for the next Step-by-Step.

Use the Now Function

Sometimes you may want to insert the current date or the current time in a cell. The Now function is a Date and Time function you can use to enter the current date and time. You can then format the results in the desired date format. When you format the results, you can choose to show the date and time, just the date, or just the time.

> **Did You Know?**
>
> You can also display the Insert Function dialog box by opening the **Insert** menu and choosing **Function**.

If you want to enter just the current date or just the current time, you can save time by using shortcut keys. The shortcut to enter the current date is Ctrl + ; (semicolon). The shortcut to enter the current time is Ctrl + Shift + ; (semicolon).

STEP-BY-STEP 13.4

1. Click in cell **B17**. Click the **Insert Function** button. The Insert Function dialog box is displayed.
2. In the *Search for a function* box, key **date and time** and click **Go**. NOW is highlighted under *Select a function*.
3. Press **Enter** or click **OK**. The Function Arguments dialog box is displayed.
4. Click **OK**. The current date and time are displayed in cell B17. Notice that the time is based on the 24-hour clock.

> **Speech Recognition**
>
> If your computer has speech recognition capability, say the command to open the Insert menu, then say the command to choose the Function command. Continue to say the commands to select the options in the Insert Function dialog box and in the Function Arguments dialog box.

STEP-BY-STEP 13.4 Continued

5. With cell B17 still selected, open the **Format** menu and choose **Cells**. Select the **Number** tab and, under *Category,* select **Time**. Under *Type*, select **1:30 PM**.

6. Click **OK**. Now only the time is displayed. The current time based on the 12-hour clock is displayed, followed by either AM or PM.

7. With cell B17 still selected, open the **Format** menu and choose **Cells**. The Number tab should already be displayed. Under *Category*, select **Date**, and under *Type*, select **3/14/01**. Click **OK**. The result in the cell changes to display only the current date.

8. Click in cell **B18**. Hold down **Ctrl** and **Shift**, then press **;**. Press **Enter**. The current time based on the 12-hour clock is displayed.

9. Save the changes and leave the workbook open for the next Step-by-Step.

Computer Concepts

When you use the NOW function, the format for the date or time will display depending on the cell formats. The date and time are not updated continuously, but they will be updated when you perform a calculation in the worksheet and also when the worksheet is reopened.

Computer Concepts

When you use the shortcut keys to enter the current time or current date, they are entered as absolute values. In other words, the values will not change when other calculations are performed or when the worksheet is reopened.

Use Logical Functions

One of the most powerful and useful features of spreadsheets is their ability to perform different calculations based on changing values. ***Logical functions*** are special functions that display predetermined text or values when certain conditions exist. You can use logical functions either to see whether a condition is true or false or to check for multiple conditions.

Use the IF Function

The most used logical function is the IF function. You can use the IF function to determine whether a condition is true or false. If the condition is true, a value (such as the text YES) is given. If the condition is false, a value (such as the text NO) is displayed.

An example of a formula containing an IF function is illustrated in Figure 13-5. The IF function has three parts: the logical test, the IF function, and the value.

The logical test can include operators or qualifiers that help to evaluate the range of numbers or results. In Table 13-2, the logical test is B2>100.

FIGURE 13-5
Formula with a logical function

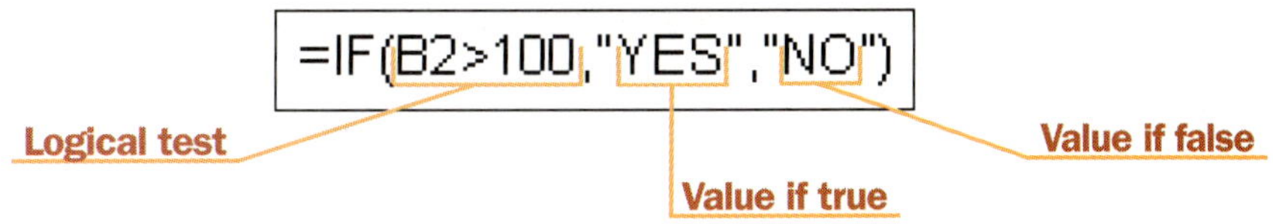

Table 13-2 describes some of the qualifiers you can use for a logical test.

TABLE 13-2
Qualifiers for a logical text

LOGICAL TEST QUALIFIERS	
=	Equal to (or the same as)
>	Greater than
<	Less than
>=	Greater than or equal to
<=	Less than or equal to
<>	Not equal to

The second part of the IF function is called value if true. It contains values or functions that result when the logic test is true. For example, in the IF function illustrated in Figure 13-5, if the logical test is true, then the text *YES* will result.

The value if false is the third part of the IF function. It contains values or functions that result when the logic test is false. For example, in the IF function illustrated in Figure 13-5, if the logical test is false, then the text *NO* will result.

In the next Step-by-Step, you will use the IF function to determine whether the daily low temperatures were below the normal low and whether the daily high temperatures were above the normal high.

STEP-BY-STEP 13.5

1. Click in cell **C2**. Click the **Insert Function** button to display the Insert Function dialog box.
2. Under *Select a function*, select **IF**. Click **OK**. The Function Arguments dialog box shown in Figure 13-6 is displayed. It looks different than the previous function dialog boxes because the IF function requires different information.

FIGURE 13-6
Function Arguments for the IF function

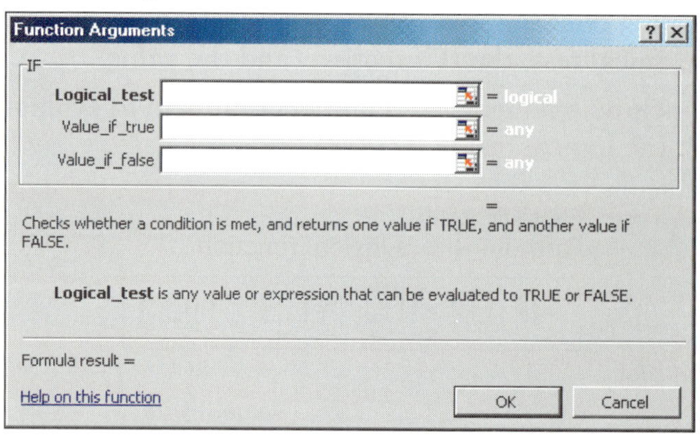

STEP-BY-STEP 13.5 Continued

3. In the *Logical_test* text box, key **b2<b10**. This logical test determines whether the value in cell B2 is lower than the value in cell B10 (the normal low temperature). Remember you learned in Lesson 3 that the dollar signs indicate that the column and row references are absolute.

4. Click in the *Value_if_true* box and key **YES**. This tells Excel to enter the text *YES* when the logical test is true.

5. Click in the *Value_if_false* box. Notice that Excel put quotes around the word *YES* in the box above. Key **NO**. This tells Excel to enter the text *NO* when the logical test is false.

6. Click **OK**. Excel determines that the value in cell B2 is not below the normal low temperature; therefore, the result displayed in the cell is *NO*.

> **Computer Concepts**
>
> If you do not enter a value in the Value_if_true box, Excel will display the result *TRUE*. If you do not enter a value in the Value_if_false box, Excel will display the result *FALSE*.

7. Fill down the function from cell C2 through C8.

8. Click in cell **E2**. Click the **Insert Function** button, then select **IF** under *Select a function* and click **OK**.

9. In the *Logical_test* text box, key **d2>d10**. In the *Value_if_true* text box, key **YES**. In the *Value_if_false* text box, key **NO**. This formula tells Excel to determine whether the value in cell D2 is greater than the value in cell D10 (the normal high temperature).

10. Click **OK**. The value *NO* is displayed in cell E2.

11. Fill down the formula from cell E2 through E8. Deselect the cells.

12. Save the changes and leave the workbook open for the next Step-by-Step.

> **Did You Know?**
>
> You can click the down arrow to the right of the Function button to display other functions you have used.

Use Help to Learn about Other Logic Functions

The IF function is just one example of a logic function. The Help screens can help you learn about some of the other logic functions that Excel provides.

STEP-BY-STEP 13.6

1. Open the **Help** menu and choose **Microsoft Excel Help**. If the Office Assistant is displayed, point to the **Office Assistant** and right-click. Then, choose **Options** in the shortcut menu. Clear the check box for **Use the Office Assistant** and click **OK**. Then, open the **Help** menu and choose **Microsoft Excel Help**.

2. If necessary, click the **Show** button on the toolbar to display the Contents, Answer Wizard, and Index tabs.

STEP-BY-STEP 13.6 Continued

3. If necessary, click the **Answer Wizard** tab to display the dialog box shown in Figure 13-7.

FIGURE 13-7
Answer Wizard tab of the Help screen

4. In the *What would you like to do?* text box, key **learn more about logical functions**. Then click **Search**.

5. Under *Select topic to display*, select **AND worksheet function**.

Computer Concepts

The examples of functions presented in this lesson are very simple. As you can see by reviewing the topics related to logical functions in the Help screens, function formulas can perform very complex calculations that would be extremely difficult to perform manually.

STEP-BY-STEP 13.6 Continued

6. Click the link **See Also** displayed at the top of the information at the right. The Topics Found dialog box shown in Figure 13-8 is displayed.

FIGURE 13-8
Topics Found dialog box

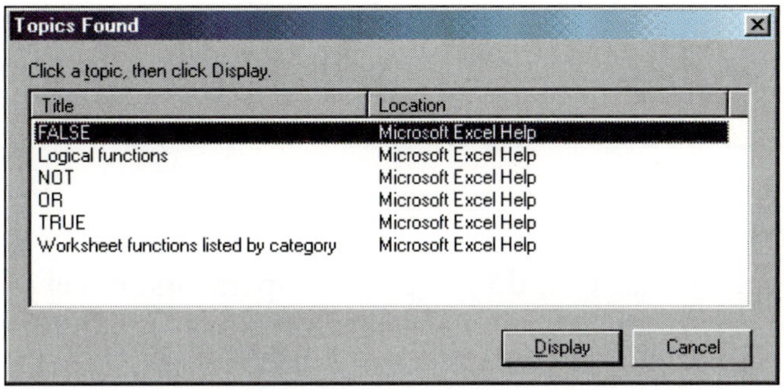

7. Select **Logical functions**, then click **Display** in the dialog box.

8. Click any one of the links to read about a logical function available in Excel.

9. Click the **Back** button on the Help toolbar to go back to the previous Help screen. If desired, click another link under the topic *Logical Functions* to read about another logical function available in Excel.

10. Close the Help screens and leave the workbook open for the next Step-by-Step.

Combining Functions and Formulas

2-3.2.5-1 In Lesson 12 we discussed how to build worksheet formulas and the variety of operators that can be used. In this lesson, we have looked at specific function formulas. What might not be readily apparent, however, is that you can combine these two types of formulas to create specific formulas that are required to analyze your data.

STEP-BY-STEP 13.7

1. Select cell **D15**.

2. Key **Avg Low & High:**. Press **Enter**.

3. Select cell **E15**.

2-3.2.5-2 4. Key **=(average(b2:b8)+average(d2:d8))/2**. Press **Enter**.

5. Select cell **D16**.

6. Key **Avg of Median:**. Press **Enter**.

STEP-BY-STEP 13.7 Continued

7. Select cell **E16**.

2-3.2.5-3

8. Key =**(average(median(b2:b8),median(d2:d8))**. Press **Enter**.

9. Save your changes to the worksheet and then close the workbook.

SUMMARY

In this lesson, you learned:

- Functions are special formulas that do not require operators. Excel provides more than 300 built-in functions to help you perform mathematical and trigonometric, statistical, and logical functions.
- The Average function displays the average of the range identified in the argument. The Sum function totals the values in the specified range of cells.
- The Count function displays the number of cells with numerical values in the argument range.
- The Minimum and Maximum functions display the smallest or the largest number contained in the range identified in the argument.
- The Now function can be used to enter the current date and/or current time.
- Logical functions are used to display text or values when certain conditions exist. The most used logical function is the If function.

VOCABULARY *Review*

Define the following terms:

Logical functions	Statistical functions	Trigonometric functions
Mathematical functions		

REVIEW *Questions*

TRUE/FALSE

Circle T if the statement is true or F if the statement is false.

T F 1. A function contains two parts: the function name and the arguments.

T F 2. When entering a function name, you must use all capital letters.

T F 3. The Function Argument dialog box displays only when you have an error in a function formula.

T F 4. To enter the current date in a worksheet cell, use the Now function.

T F 5. The If function has three parts: the logical test, the value if true, and the value if false.

FILL IN THE BLANK

Complete the following sentences by writing the correct word or words in the blanks provided.

1. __________ functions are used to describe large quantities of data.
2. If you wanted to display the smallest number contained in a range of cells, you would choose the __________ function.
3. The __________ function displays the number of cells with numerical values in the argument range.
4. To quickly enter the current time in a cell, use the shortcut keys __________.
5. __________ functions are used to display text or values when certain conditions exist.

PROJECTS

PROJECT 13-1

1. Open **Project13-1** from the data files. Save the workbook as **Grades** followed by your initials.
2. In cell B4, use a function to display the current date in the format 3/14/01.
3. In cell F7, use a function to average the test scores in cells B7:E7. Format the resulting value with no decimal places. Fill the formula down to average the tests for the remaining classes.
4. You want to keep track of your current grade in each class in column G. If your test average is above 90, you will receive an "A." If it is not above 90, you will receive a "B." (You're a very good student!). Use the IF function to display your current grades as follows:
   A. The logical test for the IF function is **f7>90**.
   B. The value if true is "A."
   C. The value if false is "B."
5. Fill the formula down for the other classes and then center the grades in column G. In what classes are you currently receiving an "A?"
6. Save your changes and close the workbook.

PROJECT 13-2

1. Open **Project13-2** from the data files. Save the workbook as **Birds** followed by your initials.
2. In cell J6, use a function to sum the number of blue jays observed at all stations. Fill the formula down to sum the totals for the other bird species.
3. In cell A25, enter **Species Counted** and boldface the text.
4. In cell B25, use the Count function to total the number of species observed at Station 1. (*Hint*: Your count should equal *14*.) Fill the formula across to count the number of species observed at each of the other stations, but do not fill the formula into column J. Boldface cell range B25:I25.
5. The Audubon Society would like to know if too many birds of any one species are visiting each station and, therefore, driving other birds away. In cell A27, key **Maximum Counted** and boldface the text.
6. In cell B27, use a formula to find the maximum number of birds counted at Station 1. Fill the formula across for all stations and boldface the values.
7. The Society would also like to know the minimum number of birds counted. Low numbers of individual species could indicate stress in the bird population. In cell A29, key **Minimum Counted** and boldface the text.
8. In cell B29, use a formula to find the minimum number of birds counted at Station 1. Fill the formula across for all stations and boldface the values.
9. Save your changes and close the workbook.

WEB PROJECT

In this lesson, you worked with some representative weather data to learn how to analyze the data using statistical and logical functions. Use Web search tools to locate information on the weather in your area. Choose any month and find the actual high and low temperatures and precipitation amounts (in rain or snow) for that month. Record the temperatures and precipitation amounts in a worksheet. Locate information on normal high temperatures, low temperatures, and monthly precipitation amounts for your area and record those on your worksheet. Use functions to analyze the data you have gathered. During the month you chose, were the temperatures in your area higher or lower than normal? How many days recorded precipitation? Was the precipitation amount higher or lower than normal for the month?

TEAMWORK PROJECT

As you have learned in this lesson, functions can help you analyze data in a number of ways. Excel includes hundreds of functions to help you with financial, statistical, mathematical, and other problems. In this project, explore two functions of your choice with a teammate to learn how they can be applied to specific data analysis situations. Make sure your functions are not covered in this or the previous lesson. Follow these steps:

1. In a blank Excel worksheet, open the Insert Function dialog box. Review the functions in each category to find two you are interested in exploring with your teammate. (Your functions should come from two different categories.)

2. Read the Microsoft Excel Help files for the functions you have chosen to find out what kind of data the function can analyze and what kinds of information you must supply as arguments for the functions.
3. Construct worksheets containing data appropriate for each function and then use the functions to analyze the data.
4. After you are sure you are using the function correctly, make a team presentation to share what you have learned about your functions.

CRITICAL *Thinking*

ACTIVITY 13-1

You want to buy a used car that costs $5,000. You can scrape up $2,000 of the total, but you will need to borrow the rest of the money. Your uncle has offered to loan you the additional money at a modest 5% interest per year, but only if you can pay the money back in four years. He has agreed to let you make a payment once a year for the four years.

Create a worksheet that contains the following information:

Rate	5%
Nper (number of payments)	4
PV (principal)	$3000

Using Excel's PMT function, plug in the information shown above from your worksheet to find out how much you will have to pay your uncle each year if you accept the loan. (The yearly payment will appear in red and in parentheses in the cell where you insert the PMT function.)

LESSON 14

USING THE WORKSHEET TO COMMUNICATE INFORMATION

OBJECTIVES

Upon completion of this lesson, you should be able to:

- Apply conditional formats.
- Insert a cell comment.
- Insert a picture in a worksheet.
- Resize and position pictures.
- Create a chart.
- Edit chart data.
- Edit chart formats and options.

Estimated Time: 1 hour

VOCABULARY

Cell comment
Chart
Clip art
Conditional formats
Embedded chart
Sizing handles

Excel comes with a number of tools that can help you communicate worksheet data more effectively. Features such as formats, comments, pictures, and charts can help to enhance the information contained in a worksheet. The features are easy to use and often make the worksheet more useful.

Apply Conditional Formats

Conditional formats are built-in format features in Excel which apply various formats to cell contents when certain conditions are met. These special formats make it easy for you to monitor worksheet results. For example, you may want to bring attention to values that fall below a minimum requirement or flag a date that indicates a passed deadline. The format is applied only when the value meets specified conditions. If the value changes, the format will also change. To illustrate, if the minimum requirement for inventory falls below 500, the value in the cell will be formatted in a red format. When the value for inventory rises above the minimum requirement, the red format is removed.

STEP-BY-STEP 14.1

1. Open file **Step14-1** from the data files. Save the workbook as **Quality Control** followed by your initials.

2. Select the range **D4:D8**.

3. Open the **Format** menu and choose **Conditional Formatting**. The dialog box shown in Figure 14-1 is displayed.

FIGURE 14-1
Conditional Formatting dialog box

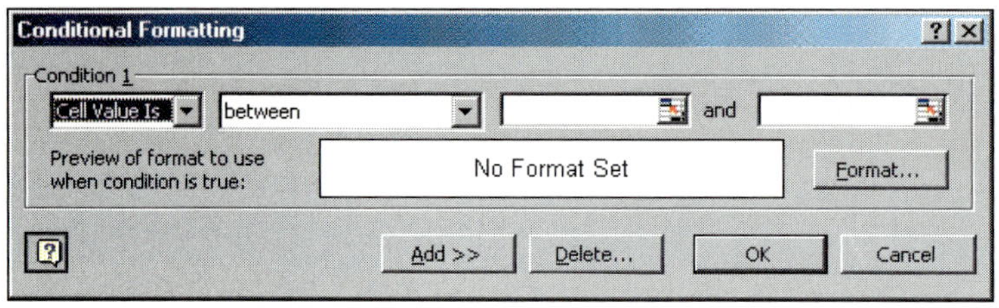

4. The first text box displays *Cell Value Is*. This condition is correct. Click in the second text box and then select **greater than** in the drop-down list.

5. Click in the third text box and key **3.00%**.

6. Click the **Format** button in the dialog box. The Format Cells dialog box shown in Figure 14-2 is displayed.

FIGURE 14-2
Format Cells dialog box

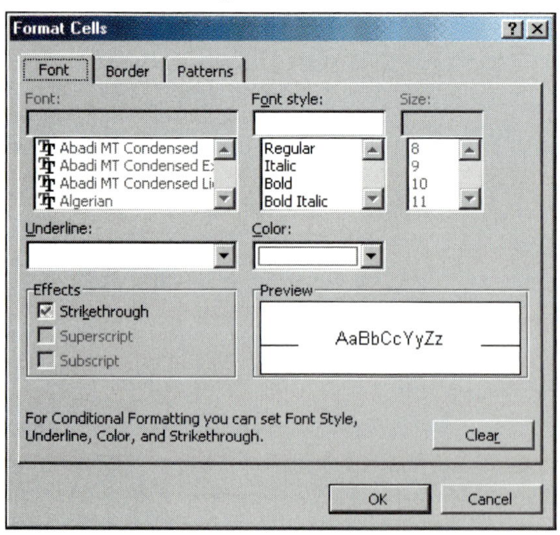

7. Click the down arrow in the list box under *Color*. Select the color **Red**.

8. Click **OK** to close the Format Cells dialog box. Then click **OK** to close the Conditional Formatting dialog box.

STEP-BY-STEP 14.1 Continued

9. Click outside the selected range. Notice that only one of the values in the % *Defective* column exceeds the 3.00% limit you set.

10. Click in cell **C4**, key **7**, and press **Enter**. Now that the percentage in cell D4 exceeds the limit, the font color for that value changes to red.

11. Save the changes and close the workbook.

> **Hot Tip**
>
> If you point to a color in the color palette, a ScreenTip will display with the name of the color.

Insert a Cell Comment

A ***cell comment*** is a message that helps explain the information contained in the cell. Cell comments can be used to help you remember details about the data, or they can be used to help others understand the data.

When you insert a comment, Excel creates a text box and inserts a user name. The user name is the same as the user information provided in the General sheet in the Tools Options dialog box. A red triangle (note indicator) appears in the corner of the cell to indicate that it contains a comment. However, this triangle will not print when you print the worksheet.

When you point to a cell with a note indicator, the comment will display in a ScreenTip. If necessary, you can edit or delete the cell comment.

STEP-BY-STEP 14.2

1. Open **Step14-2** from the data files. Save the workbook as **News** followed by your initials.

2. With the insertion point positioned in cell A1, open the **Insert** menu and choose **Comment**. The comment box shown in Figure 14-3 is displayed.

FIGURE 14-3
Cell Comment text box

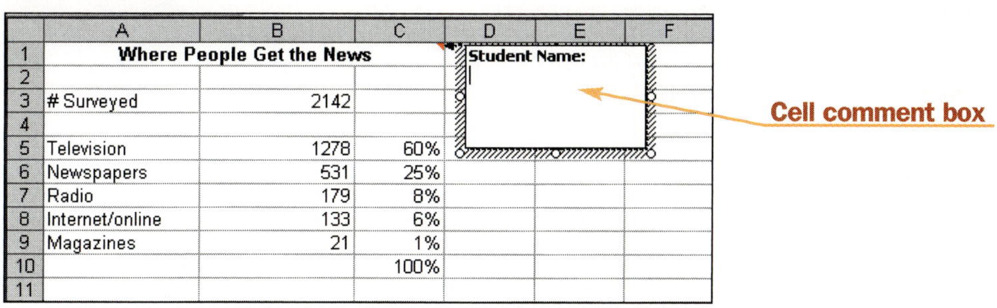

3. Key **Overall findings have a margin of error of plus or minus 3.6%.**

4. Click anywhere outside the cell comment text box to close the display. Notice that a red triangle appears in the top right corner of cell A1. This mark indicates that the cell contains a comment.

STEP-BY-STEP 14.2 Continued

5. Click in cell **C10** and insert the comment **Total may not add up to 100% due to rounding.**

6. Click anywhere outside the cell comment text box to close the display.

7. Point to cell A1 and rest the mouse pointer over the cell. The cell comment text box will display next to the cell.

8. With the cell comment still displayed, right-click to display a shortcut menu. Choose **Edit Comment** from the shortcut menu. The cell comment text box is selected and the insertion point appears in it.

9. Edit the text in the cell comment text box to read **3.8%** instead of *3.6%*. Then click outside the comment box.

10. Point to cell **C10** and right-click. Choose **Delete Comment** from the shortcut menu. The comment box and the red triangle are removed.

11. Save the changes and leave the workbook open for the next Step-by-Step.

Hot Tip

You can also insert a comment by right-clicking on the desired cell and then choosing **Insert Comment** from the shortcut menu.

Did You Know?

If the text box is not large enough to display your comment, you can resize the cell comment text box by pointing to a corner sizing handle. When the pointer changes to a two-headed arrow, drag the sizing handle to enlarge the box.

Speech Recognition

If your computer has speech recognition capability, enable the Dictation mode and dictate the comment.

Computer Concepts

To print the comments with the worksheet, choose **Page Setup** from the File menu. Click the **Sheet** tab and choose one of the options in the Comments box.

Insert Images in a Worksheet

Adding a picture to your worksheet can make it more visually appealing. For example, you can add a company logo or a photograph related to the worksheet data. You can also insert images from the Office Clip Gallery or use the drawing toolbar to insert drawn objects into the worksheet.

Insert a Clip Art Image

2-3.4.1-1

Pictures can help communicate worksheet data. ***Clip art*** is pictures and other artwork that is ready to insert in a worksheet. Excel has numerous clip art images and photos that are stored in the Clip Art folder. You can also insert picture files from other sources or from scanned images.

STEP-BY-STEP 14.3

1. Click in cell **A11**.

2-3.4.1-1

2. Open the **Insert** menu and choose **Picture**, then select **Clip Art** from the submenu. The Insert Clip Art task pane similar to that shown in Figure 14-4 is displayed.

STEP-BY-STEP 14.3 Continued

FIGURE 14-4
Insert Clip Art task pane

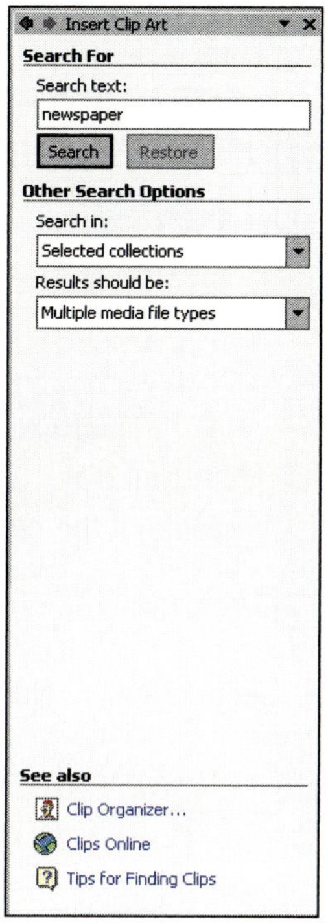

3. Click in the *Search text* text box and key **computer**, then click **Search** or press **Enter**. Excel will search the Clip Art gallery for all pictures related to this keyword.

4. Select a picture of a computer (or other picture related to the contents of the worksheet, such as TV, newspaper, Internet, and so forth). (*Note:* If you can't find a picture related to a computer, click the **Modify** button at the bottom of the task pane and search for keywords *TV*, *radio*, *Internet*, and so forth until you find a picture that fits with the content of the worksheet.)

5. Click the picture to insert it in the worksheet.

6. Close the task pane. If the Picture toolbar is in the way, dock it at the top, bottom, or side of the screen.

7. Save the changes and leave the workbook open for the next Step-by-Step.

Hot Tip

If the Add Clips to Organizer dialog box appears, click **Later** in order to proceed with these steps.

Did You Know?

If your computer has an Internet connection, you can click the link **Clips Online** at the bottom of the Insert Clip Art task pane and locate images on the Web.

Did You Know?

You can leave the Insert Clip Art task pane open as you work so you can quickly access additional clip art images. If you know you might use a clip art image again, add it to the Favorites folder in the Clip Organizer to save time in finding it again.

Insert Drawn Objects

2-3.4.2-1

Just as with other Microsoft Office applications, you can use the Drawing toolbar within Excel to insert a variety of drawn objects into your worksheet. These can be used to draw attention to specific data or just for added effect like a clip art image.

STEP-BY-STEP 14.4

1. If the Drawing toolbar is not visible, open the **View** menu, point to **Toolbars**, and select **Drawing** from the submenu.
2. Click **Oval** on the Drawing toolbar.
3. 2-3.4.2-3 Move your cursor (which is now shaped like a crosshair) to near the top left corner of 100% in cell C10. Click and drag until the oval shape surrounds 100%, then release the mouse button. This creates a solid oval shape which blocks the value in the cell.
4. Right-click on the oval and select **Format AutoShape**.
5. In the Colors and Lines tab, in the Fill section, select **No Fill** as the Color. In the Line section, change the Color to **red**. Click **OK**.
6. Click **Arrow** on the Drawing toolbar.
7. 2-3.4.2-2 Move the crosshair to the right of the oval, approximately one-half inch away. Click and drag towards the oval. Release the mouse button when the line is touching the oval.
8. Save your changes and leave the worksheet open for the next Step-by-Step.

Resize and Position Images

2-3.4.1-2

Once you have inserted a picture or drawing in a worksheet, there are many ways to manipulate the image. To work with the image, you must click it to select it. You will know it is selected when you see eight small circles on the border of the graphic. These circles are called ***sizing handles***. Once an image is selected, you can resize it and reposition it.

> **Computer Concepts**
>
> Resizing and repositioning pictures in Excel is the same as resizing and repositioning pictures, text boxes, and other objects in other Office applications.

The easiest way to change the size of an image is to drag one of the sizing handles. As you drag the sizing handle, you can see the effects of the change on your screen. When you resize an image proportionally, you change all dimensions of the graphic approximately equally. You can also resize an image just vertically or just horizontally, but that will distort the image.

STEP-BY-STEP 14.5

2-3.4.1-2

1. If necessary, click the picture you selected to display the sizing handles. Eight sizing handles appear on the outside border of the image as shown in Figure 14-5.

FIGURE 14-5
Worksheet with picture selected

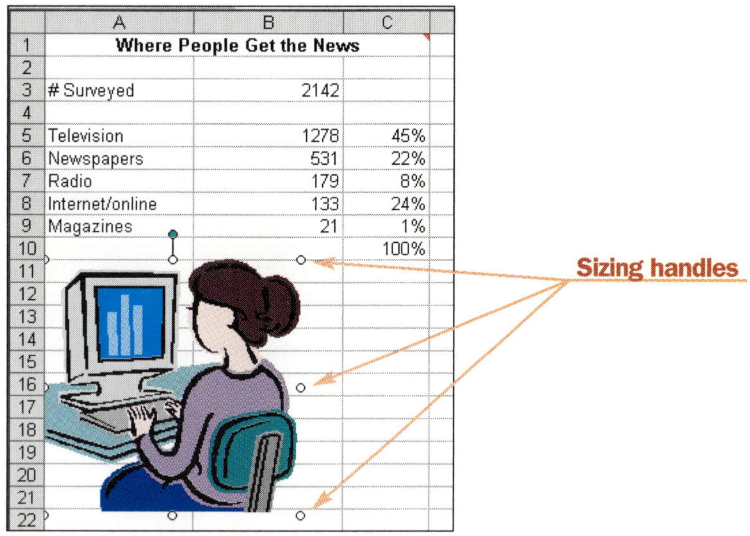

2. Point to the sizing handle in the lower right corner of the picture. When the pointer changes to a two-headed arrow, drag the sizing handle up and to the left. When the bottom picture border extends down to cell B16, release the mouse button.

3. Point to the center of the picture. When the pointer changes to a four-headed arrow, drag the picture to the right to center it under the columns of data.

4. Select the oval you drew in the previous Step-by-Step.

2-3.4.2-4

5. Drag the oval up so that it surrounds 44% in cell C5.

6. Select the arrow you drew and drag it up alongside the oval.

2-3.4.2-4

7. With the arrow still selected, point to the right sizing handle and drag to the right to enlarge the arrow. Click somewhere else within the worksheet to deselect the arrow.

8. Save the changes and leave the workbook open for the next Step-by-Step.

Create a Chart

2-3.4.3-1

A ***chart*** is a graphic representation of your worksheet data. Charts help to make the data more interesting and easier to read and understand. Before you can create a chart, you must decide what type of chart you want to create. Excel provides several options for chart types. The chart type you select will depend on the data you want to represent. Table 14-1 lists some of the Excel chart types and a description of the types of data you can illustrate with each chart.

2-3.4.4-1

TABLE 14-1
Chart types

Area chart	Effective for emphasizing trends because it illustrates the magnitude of change over time.
Bar chart	Helpful when you want to make comparisons among individual items.
Column chart	Useful in showing changes over a period of time, or for making comparisons among individual items.
Doughnut chart	Similar to a pie chart in that it shows comparisons between the whole and the parts. However, a doughnut chart enables you to show more than one set of data.
Line chart	Illustrates trends in data at equal intervals.
Pie chart	Compares the sizes of portions as they relate to a whole unit, and it illustrates that the parts total 100 percent. Effective when there is only one set of data.
Scatter chart	Illustrates scientific data, and it specifically shows uneven intervals – or clusters – of data.

After you decide which chart type you want to create, you must decide which chart options you want to use. To do this, you must first understand the parts of a chart. Figure 14-6 describes the parts of a chart. Take time to study this illustration and become familiar with the various parts.

2-3.4.3-3
2-3.4.5-1

FIGURE 14-6
Parts of a chart

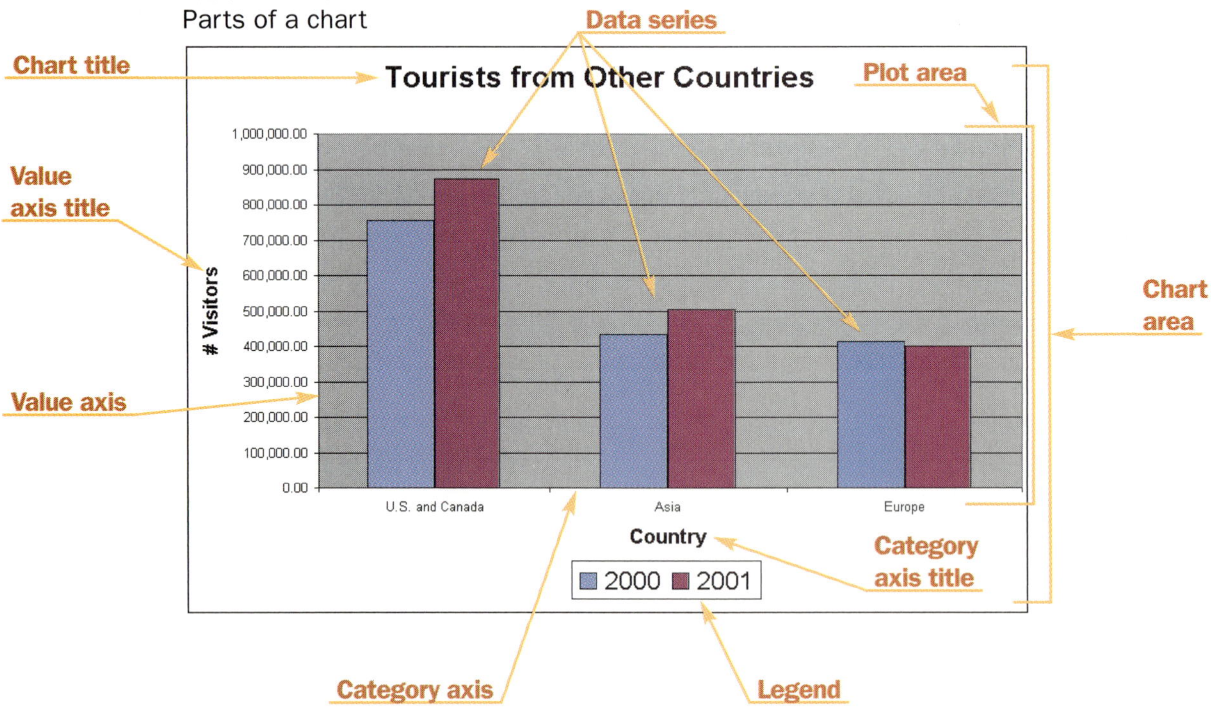

Use the Chart Wizard to Create a Chart

The Chart Wizard in Excel makes it easy for you to create professional-looking charts. The Chart Wizard will ask you questions about several chart options. You can create the chart on a separate sheet, or you can create the chart on the worksheet that has the data you want to chart. If the chart will not fit on the same sheet with the data or if you want to create more than one chart from the same data, you will probably want to create the chart on a separate sheet. An ***embedded chart*** is a chart created on the same sheet as the data used in the chart. One advantage of embedding a chart on the same page as the data is that the data and the chart can be viewed at the same time.

Computer Concepts

With the exception of the pie and doughnut type charts, all chart types have a horizontal and a vertical axis.

Before you begin the Chart Wizard, you must first select the data you want to be represented in the chart. You do not always need all the worksheet data to create the chart, so you need to select the range of cells that you want to illustrate in the chart before you use the Wizard.

STEP-BY-STEP 14.6

1. Select the range **A5:B9**.

2-3.4.3-2 2. Click the **Chart Wizard** button on the Standard toolbar. The dialog box shown in Figure 14-7 is displayed.

2-3.4.4-2 3. Under *Chart type*, select **Pie**, then select the second chart sub-type in the first row (Pie with a 3-D visual effect).

4. Click and hold the **Press and Hold to View Sample** button in the dialog box. A preview of the chart is displayed.

Speech Recognition

If your computer has speech recognition capability, enable the Command mode and say the command to start the Chart Wizard. Then, say the commands to navigate through the steps in the Chart Wizard and select the options. Use the keyboard to enter chart and axis titles.

FIGURE 14-7
Chart Wizard—Step 1 of 4—Chart Type dialog box

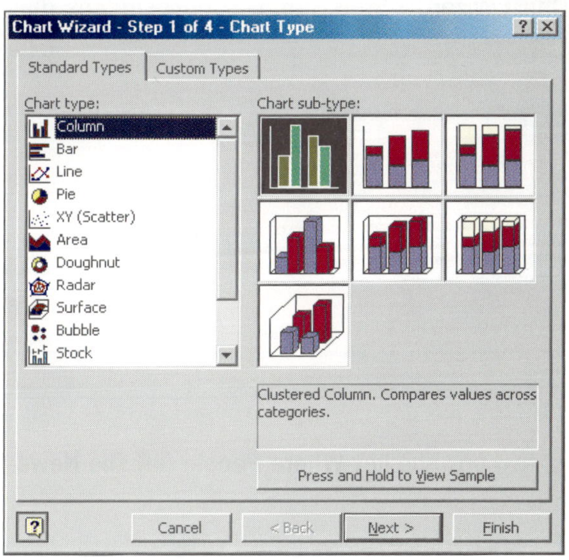

STEP-BY-STEP 14.6 Continued

5. Release the button and click **Next**. The dialog box shown in Figure 14-8 is displayed. A preview of the chart is shown in the Chart Source Data dialog box. Notice also that the data range you selected is displayed in the Data range text box.

Hot Tip

Click the **Back** button to return to the previous Chart Wizard dialog box if, for instance, you want to make a change to a previous selection.

FIGURE 14-8
Chart Wizard—Step 2 of 4—Chart Source Data dialog box

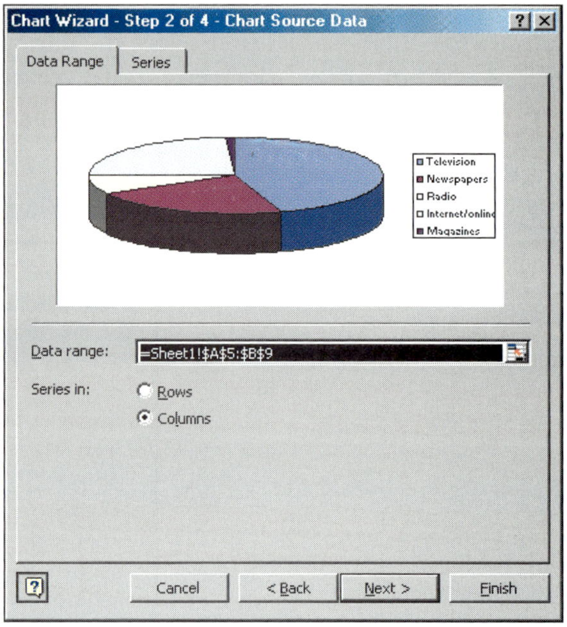

6. Click the **Next** button to display the dialog box in Figure 14-9.

FIGURE 14-9
Chart Wizard—Step 3 of 4—Chart Options dialog box

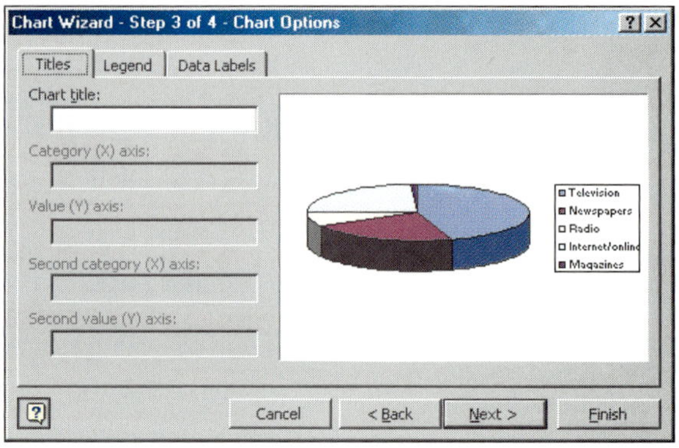

7. Click in the Chart title: text box and key **Where People Get the News**.

STEP-BY-STEP 14.6 Continued

8. Click the **Data Labels** tab to change the dialog box options. Under *Label Contains*, select the option **Percentage**. The preview of the chart is updated to show the labels. Compare your screen to Figure 14-10.

FIGURE 14-10
Data Labels tab in Step 3 of 4—Chart Options dialog box

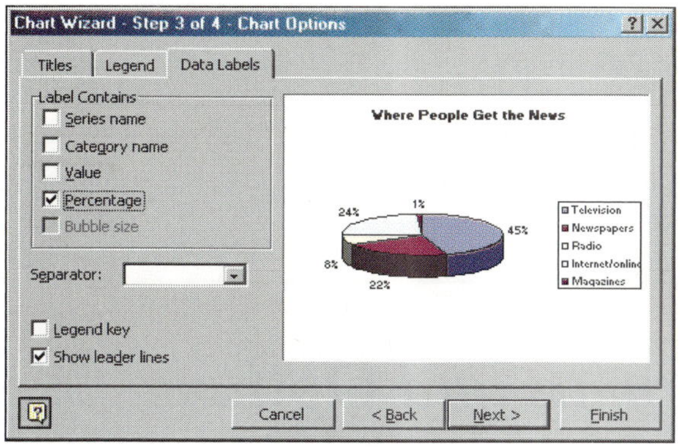

9. Click **Next**. The dialog box shown in Figure 14-11 is displayed.

FIGURE 14-11
Chart Wizard—Step 4 of 4—Chart Location dialog box

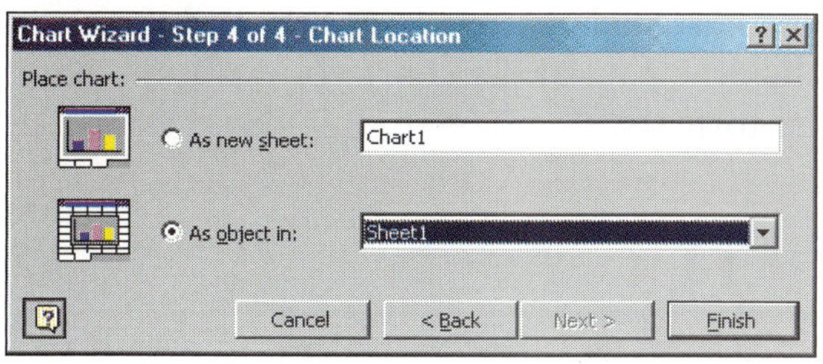

10. Select the **As new sheet** option to place the chart on a sheet by itself. The new sheet will be named *Chart1*.

11. Click **Finish** in the Chart Wizard dialog box. The wizard closes and the chart is displayed in a new sheet in the workbook.

12. Save the changes and leave the workbook open for the next Step-by-Step.

Hot Tip

You can create an instant chart by selecting the data you want to chart and then pressing **F11**. A two-dimensional column chart is created. However, notice that there are no chart or axis titles in this chart.

Edit Chart Data

There may be occasions when the data used to create the chart changes—after the chart has been created. Fortunately, you do not need to create a new chart. When you edit the data in the worksheet, Excel will automatically update the chart to reflect the changes.

STEP-BY-STEP 14.7

1. Notice that the chart currently displays *24%* for Internet/online.

2. Click the **Sheet1** tab to switch to the worksheet containing the data for the chart.

3. Click cell **B8** and key **555**, then press **Enter**. The value in cell C8 is updated from *24%* to *25%*.

> **Hot Tip**
>
> If you point over a data series in a chart, Excel displays the related worksheet data in a ScreenTip.

4. Click the **Chart1** tab. Notice that the chart has also been updated and it now shows *25%* for Internet/online. (Also note that the other percentages changed accordingly.)

5. Save the changes and close the workbook.

Edit Chart Formats and Options

You've already seen that you can easily update chart data, even after the chart is created. But can you change the chart options after you create a chart?

Edit Chart Formats

Many of the parts of the chart such as the chart title and the axis titles are positioned on the chart in a text box. If you click the part of the chart you want to change, the text box will display and then you can change the formats.

STEP-BY-STEP 14.8

2-3.4.5-2

1. Open file **Step14-8** from the data files. Save the workbook as **Demographics** followed by your initials.

2. You do not want the information from column C included in the chart, so hide column C. Then select the range **A2:E7**.

2-3.4.4-2

3. Click the **Chart Wizard** button. Under *Chart type:*, select **Bar**. Under *Chart sub-type:*, select the first option in the second row (Clustered bar with a 3-D visual effect).

4. Click **Next**. For *Series in:*, Columns is the correct option.

5. Click **Next**. If necessary, click the **Titles** tab to display the Titles sheet. In the *Chart title* text box, key **Centerville Demographics**. In the *Category (X) axis* text box, key **Year**. In the *Value (Z) axis* text box, key **Census Count**.

> **Computer Concepts**
>
> The value Z axis is used for three-dimensional charts.

6. Click **Next**. Leave the option *As object in:* selected. Then click **Finish**. The chart is displayed below the worksheet data. Do not be concerned if the chart overlaps some of the worksheet data.

STEP-BY-STEP 14.8 Continued

7. Point to any white area in the chart. When a ScreenTip displays *Chart Area*, click and drag the chart down to the bottom left corner just below the worksheet data.

8. Click the chart title. The text box surrounding the title is displayed.

9. With the text box selected, click the down arrow in the *Font Size* box on the Formatting toolbar and select **14** (or a font size not already selected). The text box is resized to accommodate the new font size.

> **Did You Know?**
>
> The chart is an object, just like a clip art image or a graphic. You can resize the chart by dragging a sizing handle. Be sure to drag a corner handle if you want to resize the chart proportionally.

10. Right-click the category axis title *Year*. Select **Format Axis Title** in the shortcut menu. The Format Axis Title dialog box is displayed.

11. If necessary, click the **Font** tab. Change the font size to **12** and click **OK**.

12. Right-click the value axis title *Census Count*. **Select Format Axis Title** in the shortcut menu. From the Format Axis Title dialog box, change the font size to **12**.

13. Save the changes and leave the workbook open for the next Step-by-Step.

Edit Chart Options

The Chart Options command enables you to change many of the chart features. For example, you can change the text in the chart title, or you can change the position of the legend.

2-3.4.5-2

STEP-BY-STEP 14.9

1. If necessary, click the chart to select it. (*Hint:* It is selected when you see the eight sizing handles around the border of the chart.)

2. With the chart selected, open the **Chart** menu and choose **Chart Options**. The Chart Options dialog box shown in Figure 14-12 is displayed.

FIGURE 14-12
Chart Options dialog box

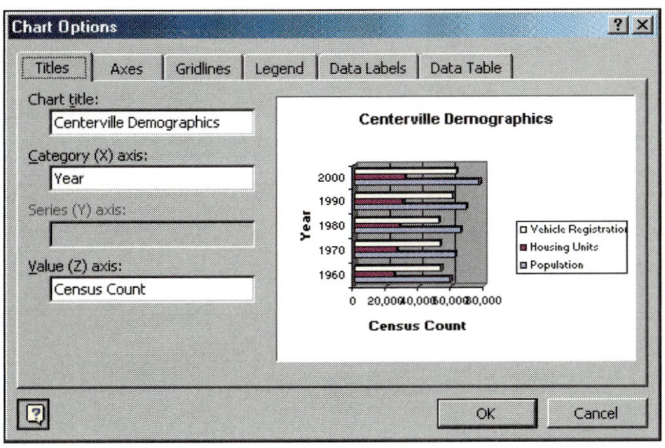

STEP-BY-STEP 14.9 Continued

3. Click the **Legend** tab. Select **Bottom** in the Placement section. The preview in the dialog box now shows the legend below the chart.

4. Click the **Titles** tab. Under *Chart title:*, change the title in the text box to **Centerville Growth Trends**.

5. Click **OK**. The chart title is changed, and the legend is repositioned at the bottom of the chart.

6. Save the changes and leave the workbook open for the next Step-by-Step.

Change the Chart Type

2-3.4.4-2

Now that you have created a bar chart and edited some of the chart parts, you realize a bar chart is not the best chart type for displaying the demographic data. A line graphic would be more effective for illustrating trends in data. Fortunately, you can change the chart type easily—and without starting over!

STEP-BY-STEP 14.10

1. With the chart selected, open the **Chart** menu and choose **Chart Type**. The Chart Type dialog box opens.

2-3.4.4-2

2. Under *Chart type:*, select **Line**. Under *Chart sub-type:*, the first option in the second row is already selected.

3. Click **OK**. The bar chart is converted to a line chart.

4. Save the changes and leave the workbook open for the next Step-by-Step.

Use Help to Learn How to Change an Embedded Chart to a Chart Sheet

You decide the chart would be much easier to read if it were enlarged. However, there is no room to expand the chart when it is embedded on the worksheet. Go to the Help screens to see whether you can move the embedded chart to a new chart sheet.

STEP-BY-STEP 14.11

1. Click in the *Ask a Question* box at the right side of the menu bar and key **move an embedded chart**. Then press **Enter**.

2. In the list of topics, click **Place a chart on a worksheet or on its own chart sheet**.

3. Read the information displayed in the screen.

4. Close the Help screen.

Speech Recognition

If your computer has speech recognition capability, enable the Command mode and say the commands to open the Chart Type dialog box and select the new chart type. Then say the command to save the changes.

STEP-BY-STEP 14.11 Continued

5. With the chart selected, open the **Chart** menu and choose **Location**. Select **As new sheet** in the Chart Location dialog box. Click **OK**.

6. Right-click the axis title *Census Count*, then choose **Format Axis Title** in the shortcut menu. When the Format Axis Title dialog box is displayed, click the **Alignment** tab.

> **Hot Tip**
>
> If the chart is not displayed full screen, open the **View** menu, choose **Zoom**, and select **100%** under *Magnification* in the Zoom dialog box.

7. The dialog box shown in Figure 14-13 is displayed. In the Orientation box, point to the red diamond and drag it up to the top of the radius. When the Degrees box displays **90**, release and click **OK** to close the Format Axis Title dialog box.

FIGURE 14-13
Alignment tab in the Format Axis Title dialog box

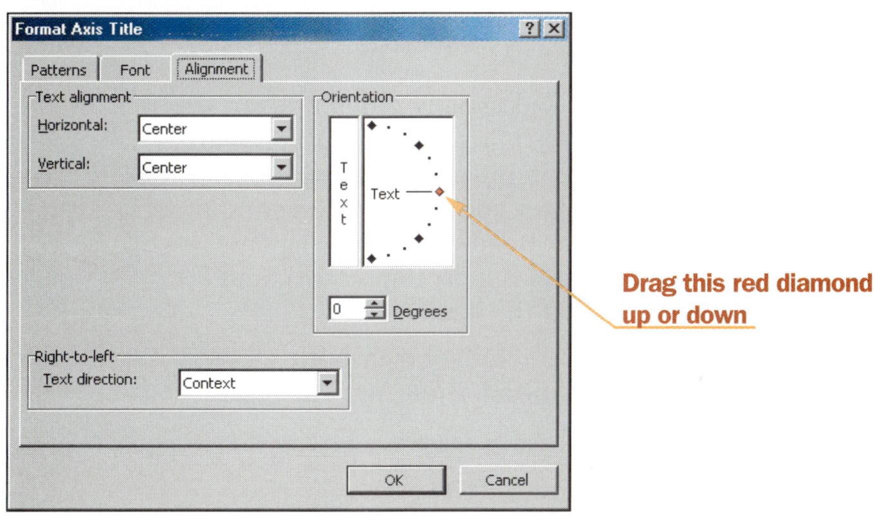

8. Right-click the axis title *Year*, then choose **Format Axis Title** in the shortcut menu. Again, drag the red diamond in the Orientation box until the Degrees box displays **0**. Click **OK**.

9. Click the **Sheet1** tab and unhide column C. Deselect the cells.

10. Save the changes and close the workbook.

Interpreting Worksheet and Chart Data

Worksheets and charts can be an excellent means of conveying information. But they can also be confusing or misleading if they are not set up correctly. As you continue your work with worksheets, you will become more comfortable with interpreting the data within in them and more adept at analyzing charts created from them.

Draw Logical Conclusions from Worksheets

As we discussed in Lesson 12, the results of a worksheet are only accurate if correct data and formulas have been entered. Auditing your worksheet is one way to verify your results. If you are certain of the accuracy of the content of the worksheet, then the next questions are: What does this worksheet tell me? What logical conclusions can I draw from it?

IC3 2-3.2.9-1 2-3.2.9-2

Obviously a worksheet can contain a great deal of information. The easiest way to summarize that information is to use the tools within Excel to obtain the information required. For example, if you want to know the average of a set of values, you would use the AVERAGE function. When using tools such as this, you can be certain of the results. But there are other ways in which you can draw conclusions from the worksheet. For example, you may notice in a column that the values are continually increasing. If this column is a chronological listing of your company's sales, you could conclude that there is a trend—that your company's sales are increasing each year. On the other hand, if this same column was not a chronological listing of sales, but rather a listing of sales by region, it is not logical to interpret a trend. If the regions are listed alphabetically, it does not make sense to conclude that the sales are higher because a region's name appears later in the alphabet.

Interpret Graphical Data

IC3 2-3.4.6-1

As you recall, Excel provides many different chart types that you can choose from to display data. But what use are these charts? Again, like the worksheets themselves, you must be careful to ensure that the data within them is accurate and that the values represented in the charts are correctly labeled. If the values and their representation are correct, charts are extremely useful for spotting and interpreting trends, summarizing data, highlighting the most important data (or, at least, the data that you feel is most important), and for making facts clear that would perhaps not be clear when looking at the worksheet.

In all cases, you must carefully weigh both where values within a worksheet or chart are coming from as well as what each value actually represents.

SUMMARY

In this lesson, you learned:

- Conditional formats help you monitor worksheet results because you can apply various formats to cell contents when certain conditions are met.
- Cell comments can be added to the worksheet to help the creator and other users understand the data contained in the worksheet.
- Not only do pictures enhance the appearance of the worksheet, they also help to communicate the worksheet data.
- Clip art can be repositioned and resized as needed in a worksheet for an attractive presentation.
- A chart displays the worksheet data visually and often helps the audience understand and interpret the information more clearly.
- When the worksheet data is changed, the chart is automatically updated to reflect those changes.
- Chart formats, options, and types can be changed at any time, even after the chart has been created.

VOCABULARY *Review*

Define the following terms:

Cell comment	Clip art	Embedded chart
Chart	Conditional formats	Sizing handles

REVIEW *Questions*

TRUE/FALSE

Circle T if the statement is true or F if the statement is false.

T F 1. The red triangle that indicates a comment is inserted in a cell will also show when the worksheet is printed.

T F 2. Once you create a chart using the chart wizard, you cannot edit the chart.

T F 3. All chart types can be used to graph any kind of data.

T F 4. If the data changes after the chart is created, you must create a new chart.

T F 5. You can reposition a chart easily by dragging the selected chart to another section of the worksheet.

FILL IN THE BLANK

Complete the following sentences by writing the correct word or words in the blanks provided.

1. To emphasize data in a cell when certain conditions are met, you can apply __________.
2. You know a picture is selected when you see the __________ on the border of the graphic.
3. A chart created on the same sheet with the data is called a(n) __________ chart.
4. To change the position of a chart label, select the chart and then choose __________ from the Chart menu.
5. To change a column chart to a bar chart, you would select the column chart and then choose __________ from the Chart menu.

PROJECTS

PROJECT 14-1

1. Open **Project14-1** from the data files. Save the workbook as **Reorders** followed by your initials.

2. In cell K7, insert a formula to subtract the Current Inventory value in cell J7 from the Beginning Inventory value in cell E7.

3. Apply conditional formatting to cell K7 as follows:
   A. In the Conditional Formatting dialog box, specify the condition *Cell Value Is* less than **5**.
   B. Click the **Format** button. On the Font tab, select **Bold**.
   C. Click the **Patterns** tab. Select the pink color that is the first color in the fifth row from the top of the color palette.

4. Fill the formula and conditional formatting down through cell K16.

5. Sales figures are in for the fourth quarter of the year. Insert the following values, beginning in cell I7, to see what items must be reordered immediately (i.e., any items with fewer than 5 left in inventory).

   15

   17

   18

   8

   10

   18

   5

   8

   8

   5

6. Insert the following comment in cell B14: **This item discontinued; no reorder.**

7. Insert a clip art picture relating to sports, exercise, or recreation. Resize the picture so that it will fit in the first five rows of the worksheet to the left of the title information.

8. Save your changes. Close the workbook.

PROJECT 14-2

1. Open **Project14-2** from the data files. Save the workbook as **Tree Sale** followed by your initials.

2. Use the Chart Wizard to chart the data in cell range A5:E12 as follows:
   A. In the Step 1 of 4 dialog box, select the first column chart in the second row of chart options (Clustered column with a 3-D visual effect).
   B. In the Step 2 of 4 dialog box, select the **Rows** option to chart the data by rows.
   C. In the Step 3 of 4 dialog box, key the Value (Z) axis label **Total Sales.** Click the **Legend** tab and select the **Bottom** placement option.
   D. In the Step 4 of 4 dialog box, accept the default option to embed the chart on the same sheet.

3. Position the chart so that it is below the worksheet data. Enlarge the chart if space permits, but do not make the chart wider than the last column of data.

4. Rotate the Value (Z) axis label (*Total Sales*) to **90** degrees so it reads from bottom to top and change its point size to **10**.
5. You have just noticed an error in the data. Change the value for Tulip poplar in Week 1 to **$4,150** and observe the change in the chart.
6. You have decided that this chart would look better on a sheet by itself. Move the chart to a new sheet.
7. Display the Chart Options dialog box and add the title **Fall Tree Sale** to the chart. Change the title point size to **16**.
8. Click the legend and increase the size of the legend text to **12** point.
9. Save your changes. Close the workbook.

WEB PROJECT

With the increasing popularity of the Internet as a source of sales revenue, many retailers and other merchandisers are offering a wide variety of products for sale online. Online sales have increased greatly over the past several years. Using Web search tools, locate information about online sales for at least two recent years. (*Hint:* Target your search for news articles and current events.) Try to find specific information on categories such as books, music, apparel, computers and peripherals, toys, and so on. Record the sales figures you find in a worksheet and then chart the data.

TEAMWORK PROJECT

Increasing entertainment options have led some people to wonder if the era of mass-market professional sports is on the wane. Do people still go out to the ballgame, or do they stay at home watching satellite TV, playing video games, or surfing the Internet? With a teammate, track attendance figures for several professional sports franchises to see if you can identify a trend. Follow these steps:

1. With your teammate, choose a professional sport that you both want to research, such as baseball, basketball, football, or hockey. Select five teams from large and small cities.
2. Using Web search tools or other sources of information, locate the season attendance figures for your five teams for the previous five years (or as many as you can find).
3. Record your data in a worksheet and then chart the data. Do you see a pattern of rising or decreasing attendance for the teams you chose?

CRITICAL *Thinking*

ACTIVITY 14-1

You have created a three-dimensional pie chart with a number of slices. Some of them are hard to see because the three-dimensional chart is rather flat. Can you tilt the chart in any way so you can see the pie slices better? Use the Help files in Excel to find the answer and then write a summary on what you learned.

WORKING WITH ACCESS DATABASES

OBJECTIVES

Upon completion of this lesson, you should be able to:

- Identify the parts of the Access screen.
- Understand the purpose of the database objects.
- Create a table using a wizard.
- Enter records in datasheet view.
- Change the column width in datasheet view.
- Add and delete fields in Design view.
- Change field properties.

Estimated Time: 1 hour

VOCABULARY

Cell
Database
Datasheet view
Design view
Entry
Field
Field name
Field properties
Primary key
Record
Wizard

A ***database*** is a collection of related information organized for rapid search and retrieval. Databases can contain all types of data from an address list to schedules for a soccer tournament. Access is the Microsoft Office database program that enables you to organize and manipulate data in many ways.

You might wonder what the difference is between a spreadsheet and a database. Actually, they are very similar. Like spreadsheets, databases are composed of rows and columns. Both enable you to organize, sort, and calculate the data. Although a spreadsheet is great for calculating data, a database offers much more comprehensive functions for manipulating the data. Access is a powerful program that offers many features, most of which are beyond the scope of this course. The lessons in this unit will introduce you to some of the basic features for entering, organizing, and reporting data in Access. Then as you continue to learn and use Microsoft Office, you will have the building blocks you need for utilizing this powerful program.

Identify the Parts of the Access Screen

IC³ 2-1.2.1-1

The Access screen is similar to other Office XP applications—displaying a title bar, a menu bar, and a status bar. Unlike Word and Excel, Access does not have a standard document view. The Access screen changes based on the features you are using as you work with the database. Furthermore, many of the menu options and toolbar buttons are unique to Access.

2-1.2.1-1

STEP-BY-STEP 15.1

1. Launch Access. The Microsoft Access window and the New File task pane shown in Figure 15-1 are displayed. Do not be concerned that the files listed in the Open a file section of your task pane are different.

FIGURE 15-1
Microsoft Access window with the New File task pane

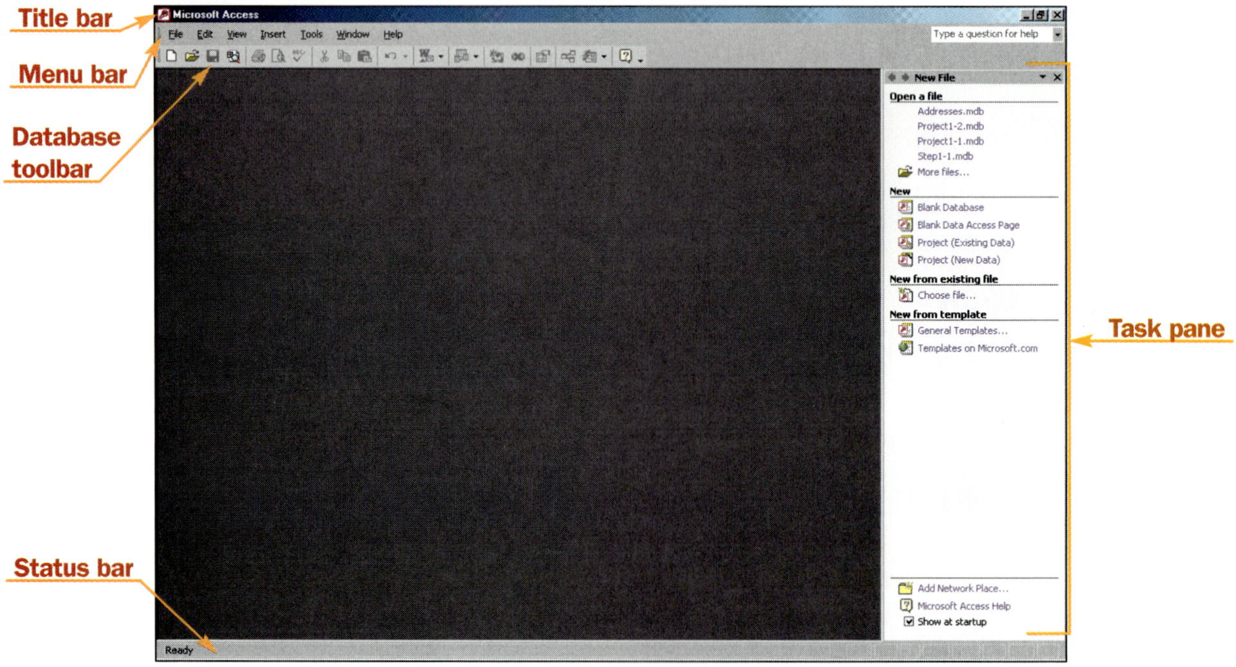

2. In the task pane, under *Open a file*, select **More Files** (or just **Files**).

3. The Open dialog box shown in Figure 15-2 is displayed. Do not be concerned if the folders displayed in your dialog box are different.

Did You Know?

The files listed above More Files at the top of the task pane in Access are the documents most recently accessed.

STEP-BY-STEP 15.1 Continued

FIGURE 15-2
Open dialog box

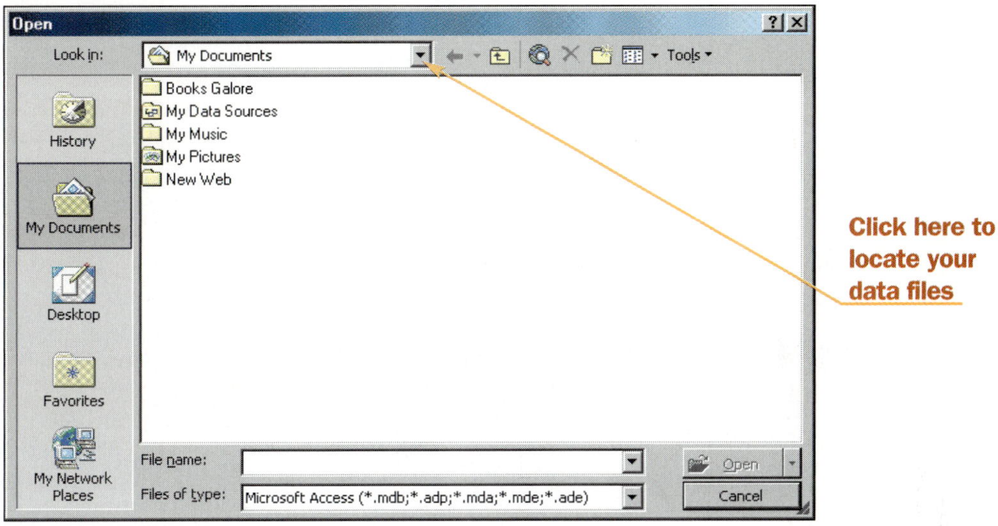

4. Locate and open the file **Step15-1** from the data files. The Step15-1: Database window, similar to that shown in Figure 15-3, is displayed. Compare your screen with Figure 15-3 and identify the parts of the Access screen to familiarize yourself with the program.

FIGURE 15-3
Step 15-1: Database window displayed

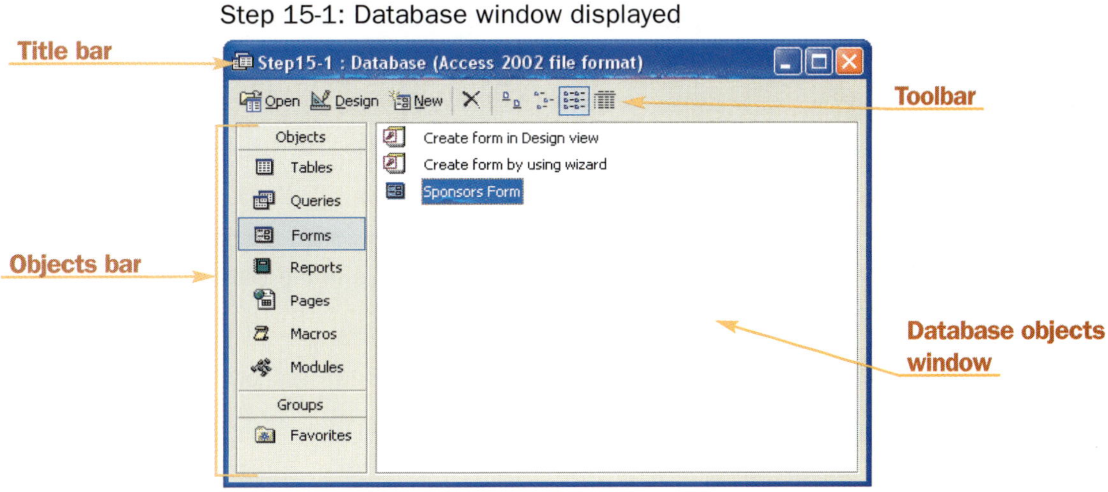

5. Leave the database open for the next Step-by-Step.

Understand the Purpose of the Database Objects

Notice that the Objects bar displays several objects: Tables, Queries, Forms, Reports, Pages, Macros, and Modules. These objects work together to help you organize and report the information that you store in the database. Every database file contains each of these objects. Tables are the primary objects in the database, and each of the objects and everything you do in a database relies on the data stored in the tables. A database can contain multiple tables.

The following list describes the purpose of each of the objects. You will learn to create tables in this lesson, and you will learn to create queries, forms, and reports in Lessons 16 and 17. Although you will not learn how to create pages, macros, or modules in the scope of this course, the following explanations help to describe the potential of the features that are available to you in Access.

- Tables –Tables store data in columns and rows. All database information is stored in tables, and all other database objects rely on the existence of the table(s).
- Queries – A query is a way to ask question about the information stored in the table. Access searches for and retrieves data from the database table(s) to answer your question.
- Forms – Forms make it easy for you to enter data into a table.
- Pages – Pages enable you to design other database objects so they can be published on the Web.
- Macros – Macros enable you to perform a series of operations with a single command.
- Modules – Modules enable you to perform more complex operations that cannot be completed with macros.

Computer Concepts

In all other lessons in this unit, you have saved learner data files using a new file name. However, you can only use the Save As command for naming and saving parts of an Access database. You cannot use the File Save As command to save the entire database under a new name. To rename an Access file, double-click on **My Computer** on the desktop. Then locate and select the filename, open the **File** menu, and choose **Rename**. Another alternative is to open the **Tools** menu, choose **Database Utilities**, and select the **Compact and Repair Database** command. You can then locate the existing database file that you want to rename and assign it a new name. If desired, you can save the file in a new location.

STEP-BY-STEP 15.2

1. Select **Tables** on the Objects bar if necessary. The Sponsors table in the Database objects window will already be selected.

2. Click the **Open** button in the Database window toolbar. The Sponsors: Table shown in Figure 15-4 is displayed.

FIGURE 15-4
Sponsors: Table

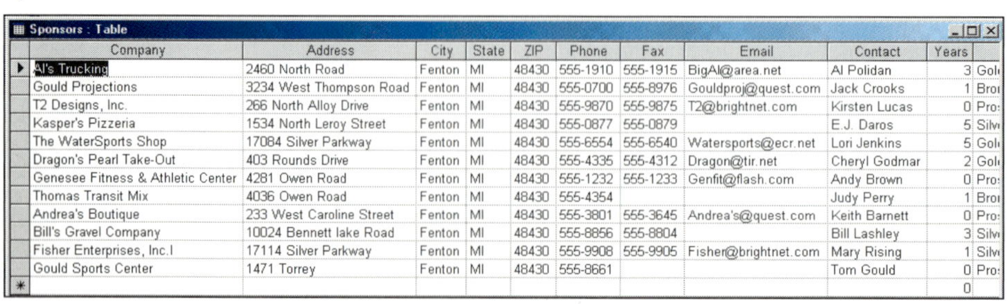

Sponsors : Table

Company	Address	City	State	ZIP	Phone	Fax	Email	Contact	Years	
Al's Trucking	2460 North Road	Fenton	MI	48430	555-1910	555-1915	BigAl@area.net	Al Polidan	3	Gol
Gould Projections	3234 West Thompson Road	Fenton	MI	48430	555-0700	555-8976	Gouldproj@quest.com	Jack Crooks	1	Bro
T2 Designs, Inc.	266 North Alloy Drive	Fenton	MI	48430	555-9870	555-9875	T2@brightnet.com	Kirsten Lucas	0	Pro
Kasper's Pizzeria	1534 North Leroy Street	Fenton	MI	48430	555-0877	555-0879		E.J. Daros	5	Silv
The WaterSports Shop	17084 Silver Parkway	Fenton	MI	48430	555-6554	555-6540	Watersports@ecr.net	Lori Jenkins	5	Gol
Dragon's Pearl Take-Out	403 Rounds Drive	Fenton	MI	48430	555-4335	555-4312	Dragon@tir.net	Cheryl Godmar	2	Gol
Genesee Fitness & Athletic Center	4281 Owen Road	Fenton	MI	48430	555-1232	555-1233	Genfit@flash.com	Andy Brown	0	Pro
Thomas Transit Mix	4036 Owen Road	Fenton	MI	48430	555-4354			Judy Perry	1	Bro
Andrea's Boutique	233 West Caroline Street	Fenton	MI	48430	555-3801	555-3645	Andrea's@quest.com	Keith Barnett	0	Pro
Bill's Gravel Company	10024 Bennett lake Road	Fenton	MI	48430	555-8856	555-8804		Bill Lashley	3	Silv
Fisher Enterprises, Inc.l	17114 Silver Parkway	Fenton	MI	48430	555-9908	555-9905	Fisher@brightnet.com	Mary Rising	1	Silv
Gould Sports Center	1471 Torrey	Fenton	MI	48430	555-8661			Tom Gould	0	Pro
*									0	

STEP-BY-STEP 15.2 Continued

3. Click the right arrow on the horizontal scroll bar (at the bottom of the screen) to view the columns to the right. This table provides data about companies that currently provide sponsorship for a club as well as companies that potentially could become sponsors.

4. Open the **File** menu and choose **Close** to close the table. The Database window is visible again.

5. Click **Queries** on the Objects bar. There is one query object named *Prospective Sponsors Query*, and it should already be selected.

6. Double-click the query object to open it. This query locates and displays the companies that are considered to be prospective sponsors. The information comes from the Sponsors table.

> **Did You Know?**
>
> You can also close the table by clicking the close box in the top right corner of the Sponsors: Table title bar. Be sure you click the table close box and not the Access application close box, which is at the top right side of the Microsoft Access title bar.

7. Open the **File** menu and choose **Close** to close the query. The Database window is still displayed.

8. Click **Forms** on the Objects bar. There is one form object named *Sponsors Form*, and it should already be selected.

9. Double-click the form object to open it. This form makes it easy to enter information about each of the club sponsors. When you enter information in this form, the information is stored in the Sponsors table. Open the **File** menu and choose **Close** to close the form. The database window is still displayed.

10. Click **Reports** on the Objects bar. There is one report object named *Prospective Sponsors Report*, and it should already be selected.

11. Double-click the report object to open it. The report displays the data contained in the Prospective Sponsors Query.

> **Speech Recognition**
>
> If your computer has speech recognition capability, enable the Command mode and say the commands to open and close the database objects.

12. Open the **File** menu and choose **Close** to close the report, then open the **File** menu again and choose **Close** to close the Database window. Leave Access open for the next Step-by-Step.

Create a Table

When you create a new database, the first object you need to create is a table. It is the primary object because it contains the data. You can create as many tables as you need to store the information. An Access table contains fields and records. A ***field*** is a single piece of database information, such as a first name, a last name, or a telephone number. A ***record*** is a group of related fields in a database, such as all the information about the person, including first and last name, address, postal code, telephone number, and so forth.

When you create a table in Access, you will be prompted to create a primary key. The ***primary key*** uniquely identifies each record in a table. The primary key tells Access how your records will be sorted, and it prevents duplicate entries. For example, you may have a student ID number, and no other student has exactly the same number as you.

You can display the table in Datasheet view or in Design view. ***Datasheet view*** displays the table data in a row-and-column format. ***Design view*** displays the field names and what kind of values you can enter in each field. It is in Design view that you can define or modify the field formats.

If this sounds like a lot to remember, do not be concerned. Access provides a wizard that simplifies the task of creating and entering data in the table.

Create a Table Using a Wizard

When you create a table using a ***wizard***, you respond to a series of questions about how you want to set up the table. The wizard guides you through the process and formats the table based on your answers.

STEP-BY-STEP 15.3

1. Click the **New** button in the Database toolbar. The New File task pane displays at the right.

2. In the task pane under *New*, select **Blank Database**. A File New Database dialog box similar to the one shown in Figure 15-5 is displayed. Your dialog box may look different.

FIGURE 15-5
File New Database dialog box

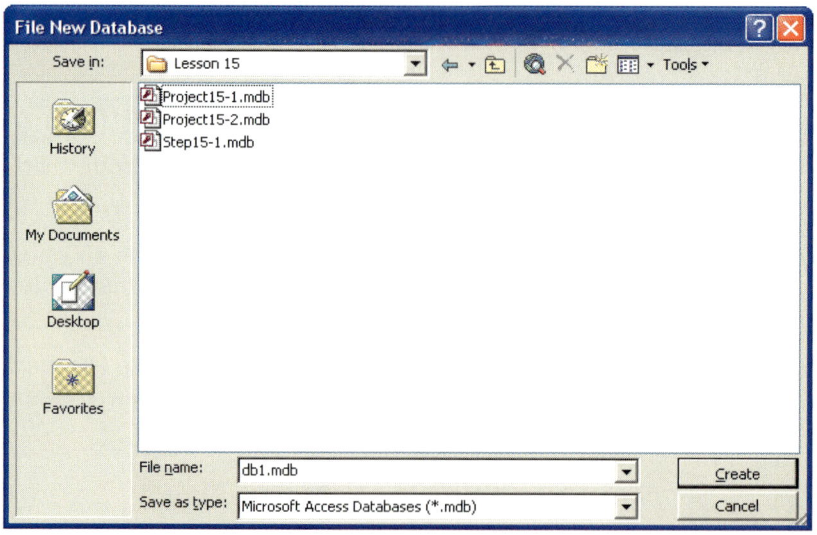

STEP-BY-STEP 15.3 Continued

3. Locate the folder where you save your documents. Then delete the proposed file name in the File name: box and key **Addresses** followed by your initials. Click **Create**. A new database window like the one shown in Figure 15-6 is displayed.

FIGURE 15-6
Addresses: Database window

4. Double-click **Create table by using wizard**. The Table Wizard dialog box opens. Select **Personal** to display the dialog box shown in Figure 15-7.

FIGURE 15-7
Table Wizard dialog box

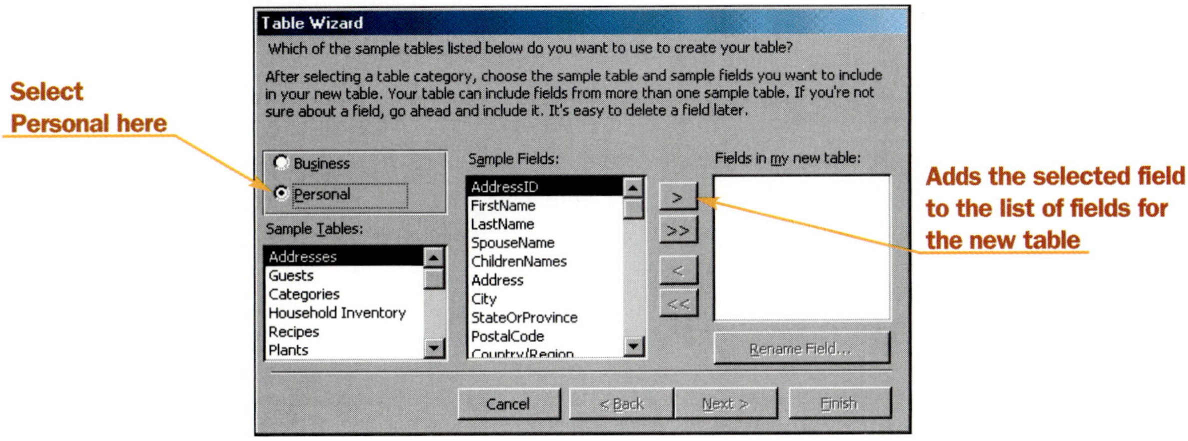

STEP-BY-STEP 15.3 Continued

5. Identify the fields to be included in the table. In the Sample Fields list, select **FirstName.** Then click the single right arrow to add the field in the Fields in my new table list.

6. Using the same procedure, select the following fields in the Sample Fields list and add them to the Fields in my new table list.

   LastName

   Address

   City

   StateOrProvince

   PostalCode

   Country/Region

7. Click **Next**. The wizard will ask you to name your table. The proposed name *Addresses* is displayed, and this name is appropriate. This step of the wizard also asks if you want the wizard to set a primary key for you. The answer *Yes, set a primary key for me.* is already selected. Click **Next** to accept the settings on this page of the wizard.

8. The wizard then asks what you want to do after the wizard creates your table. If necessary, select **Enter data directly into the table**. and click **Finish**.

9. The table is created and the columns display the field names. Because there are no records entered in the table, a single blank row is displayed. See Figure 15-8.

Computer Concepts

A default setting tells Access 2002 to save files in the Access 2000 file format. A file in Access 2000 file format can be opened in both Access 2000 and Access 2002. You can choose to save your Access files in Access 2002 file format, but then you will be able to open those files only with Access 2002. To change the default setting, an Access file must be open. Open the **Tools** menu, choose **Options**, and then click the **Advanced** tab. In the Default File Format box, select the desired Access file format.

Did You Know?

If you click the right double arrows, all the fields are added to Fields in my new table. If you click the left single arrow, the selected field will be removed from Fields in my new table list. If you click the double left arrows, all the fields will be removed from the Fields in my new table list.

FIGURE 15-8
Addresses: Table displayed in Datasheet view

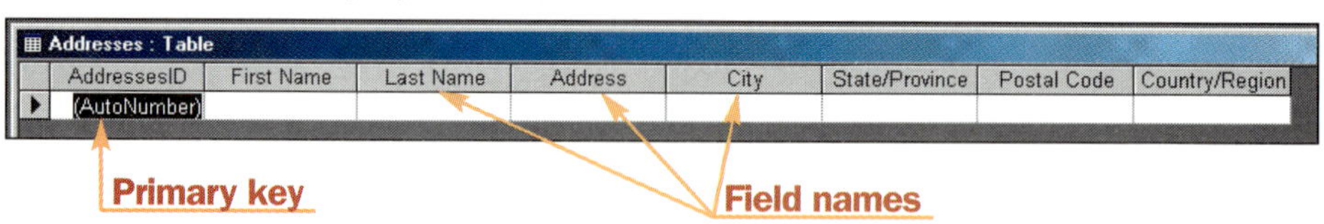

10. Notice that in the first row in the *AddressesID* field, *(AutoNumber)* is displayed. This field contains the primary key, and Access will automatically number each record that you enter.

11. Click the **Save** button on the Database toolbar and leave the table open for the next Step-by-Step.

Enter Records in Datasheet View

The Addresses table is currently displayed in Datasheet view. In this view, the table display is similar to a spreadsheet. The intersection of a row and a column is called a ***cell***. Fields appear as columns, and each column has a ***field name***. The field name is a label that helps you identify the fields. Each row in the table contains one single record of the entire database.

Speech Recognition

If your computer has speech recognition capability, enable the Command mode and say the commands to navigate through the table.

When you enter data into a cell, it is called an ***entry***. To move from one cell to another, you can use the mouse to click in a cell. You can also use the keyboard to navigate in a table. Table 15-1 describes the keys you can use to move around in a table in Datasheet view.

TABLE 15-1
Keys for navigating in Datasheet view

KEY	DESCRIPTION
Enter, Tab, or right arrow	Moves the insertion point to the next field.
Left arrow or Shift + Tab	Moves the insertion point to the previous field.
Home	Moves the insertion point to the first field in the current record.
End	Moves the insertion point to the last field in the current record.
Up arrow	Moves the insertion point up one record and stays in the same field.
Down arrow	Moves the insertion point down one record and stays in the same field.
Page Up	Moves the insertion point up one screen.
Page Down	Moves the insertion point down one screen.

STEP-BY-STEP 15.4

1. Enter the first record. Click in the first empty cell (the *First Name* field), and key **Jaimey**. Notice that as you enter the text in the first field, Access automatically assigns the primary key *1* in the *AddressesID* field.

2. Press **Tab** to move to the next field, and complete the entry by entering the following information in the respective fields:

   Last Name **McGuirk**
   Address **610 Brae Burn**
   City **Mansfield**
   State/Province **OH**
   Postal Code **44907-9122**
   Country/Region **USA**

STEP-BY-STEP 15.4 Continued

3. Press **Tab** twice to move to the *First Name* field in the next row. Enter the following data for two more records:

First Name	**Jesse**
Last Name	**Bain**
Address	**288 Silvercrest Drive**
City	**Lexington**
State/Province	**OH**
Postal Code	**44904-9007**
Country/Region	**USA**
First Name	**Matt**
Last Name	**Smith**
Address	**4645 Rule Road**
City	**Bellville**
State/Province	**OH**
Postal Code	**44813-0987**
Country/Region	**USA**

4. Click the **Save** button to save the changes and leave the database open for the next Step-by-Step.

Modify a Table

Although it is usually easier to change your table design before you enter data, you can refine the design at any time. You can modify the table in Datasheet view or Design view.

Use Help to Learn How to Change the Column Width

The default column widths are often too wide or too narrow for the data in the table. This is the case with your database. The Address field is not wide enough to display all the text in the street address, and there's a lot of white space in the StateOrProvince field. Go to the Help screens to learn how to adjust the column width.

STEP-BY-STEP 15.5

1. In the Ask a Question text box, key **change column width** and then press **Enter**.

2. When the list of topics displays, select the link **Resize a column or row.** If you do not see this topic, click the **See more...** link.

3. Under Step 2 in the Help screen, click the link **Resize a column** to expand the content. Study the illustration and read the information about dragging the right edge of the column to change the column width. Be sure to read the note at the bottom of the screen about undoing the changes to the width of columns.

STEP-BY-STEP 15.5 Continued

4. Click the **Close** box on the Help window to close the Help screen.

5. Point to the right edge of the Address column. The pointer changes to a two-headed arrow as illustrated in the Help screen. Drag the column border to the right to increase the width of the column. Continue to drag the column border until you get the correct width so that the complete address for all entries is visible.

6. Point to the right edge of the *State/Province* column and drag the border to the left to decrease the width of the column so there is no wasted space in that column. Do not be concerned that the entire field name does not display after you resize the column width.

> **Did You Know?**
>
> You can leave the Help screen open and click the database button in the taskbar to return to the database. That way you can quickly switch to the Help screen if you need to refer to it again as you work with the database.

7. Point to the field name *First Name*. When a down arrow displays, click and drag to the right until all the columns in the table are selected.

8. Open the **Format** menu and choose **Column Width**. The dialog box shown in Figure 15-9 is displayed.

FIGURE 15-9
Column Width dialog box

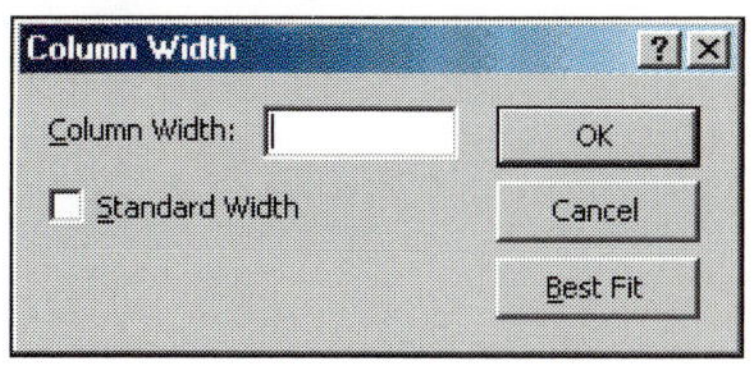

9. Click **Best Fit**. Notice that the width of each column is adjusted to accommodate the contents within the column, including the field name at the top of each column.

10. Save the changes and leave the database open for the next Step-by-Step.

Add and Delete Fields in Design View

Often, after you create a table and enter data, you decide you want to add or delete fields. You can add fields in either Datasheet view or Design view. Design view, however, provides toolbar buttons that make the task easier.

STEP-BY-STEP 15.6

1. Click the **View** button on the Table Datasheet toolbar. The table is displayed in Design view as shown in Figure 15-10.

STEP-BY-STEP 15.6 Continued

FIGURE 15-10
Addresses: Table displayed in Design view

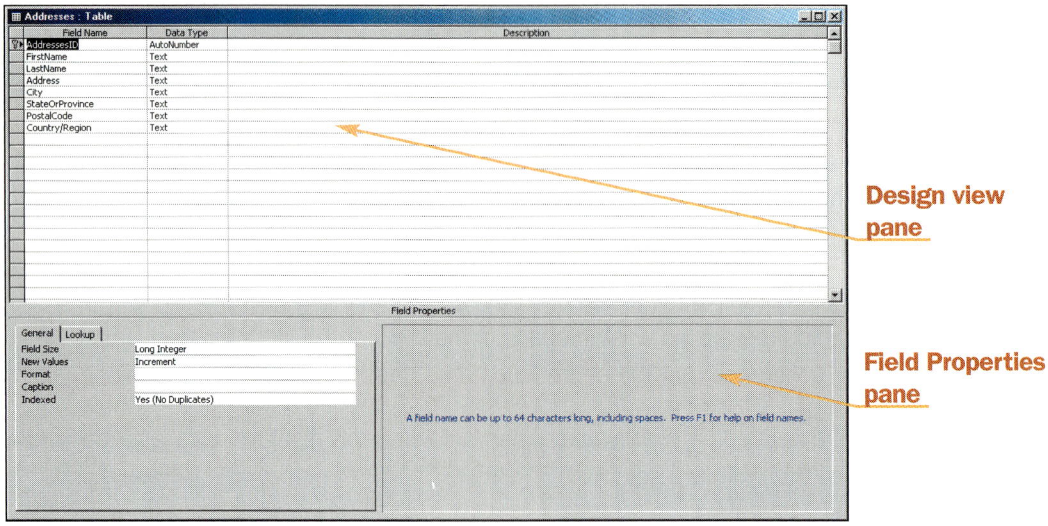

2. Click in the first blank row directly below the field name *Country/Region*.

3. Key **Birthdate** and press **Enter**. The new field is entered.

4. Click the **Country/Region** field. A right-pointing arrow displays to the left of the field name. This arrow indicates that the row is the current row.

5. Click the **Insert Rows** button on the toolbar. A new row is inserted above the selected row.

6. Key **e-mail** and then press **Enter**.

7. Select the row containing the *Country/Region* field. Click the **Delete Rows** button on the toolbar.

8. When prompted to delete the field and all the data in the field, click **Yes**. The field and all the data entered in the field are removed from the table.

9. Save the changes and leave the database open for the next Step-by-Step.

Computer Concepts

The View button is a toggle button. This means when you're viewing the table one way, the button changes to make it easy to switch quickly to the other view. So, when the table is in Datasheet view, the View button shows Design view. If you click the View button, the table switches to Design view and the View button now indicates Datasheet view. The View button makes it very easy to switch between these two ways of viewing the table.

Speech Recognition

If your computer has speech recognition capability, enable the Command mode and say the toolbar button name to insert the new row.

Computer Concepts

Use caution when deleting rows in Design view. Once you confirm the deletion, you cannot undo the deletion.

Change Field Properties

In Design view, you can specify the data type for each field. For example, you can specify text, numbers, currency, and even Yes/No. The default data type for a field is regular text, which is appropriate for most of the fields in your table. However, when users enter data for the Birthdate field, you may want to specify that the data type be formatted to hold date and time data instead of text.

When you select a data type, a dialog box displays several options for field properties. ***Field properties*** are specifications that allow you to customize the data type settings. The field properties available depend on the data type selected. One of the most common field properties is field size. The default field size is 50 characters, but you can specify that the field allow up to 255 characters. Another common field property is format. The format specifies how you want Access to display numbers, dates, times, and text.

STEP-BY-STEP 15.7

1. Your database should still be displayed in Design view. Click in the **Data Type** cell next to the field *Birthdate*. The current data type is Text, and when you click in the cell, a down arrow will display.

2. Click the down arrow to display the options shown in Figure 15-11 and then select **Date/Time**.

FIGURE 15-11
Data Type options

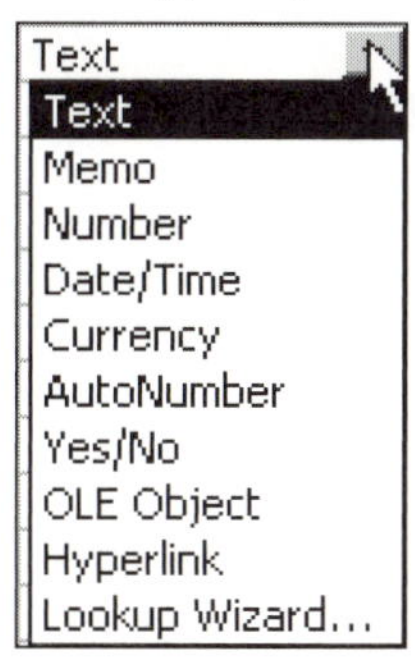

3. Notice that the Field Properties that are displayed in the pane at the bottom of the Design view window change to show the values for the Date/Time data type.

4. In the Field Properties pane at the bottom of the window, click in the text box next to *Format*. When the down arrow displays, click it to display the list of options shown in Figure 15-12.

FIGURE 15-12
Date/Time format options

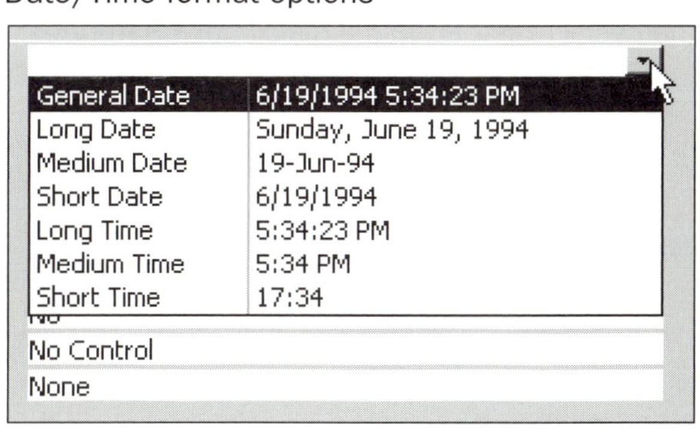

STEP-BY-STEP 15.7 Continued

5. Select **Short Date**.

6. In the Design view pane, click in the **Data Type** cell for the *StateOrProvince* field. The data type is set for Text.

7. Click in the **Field Size** text box in the Field Properties pane. The field size is currently set at *20*. Change the field size to **2**. This will require that the user use two-letter state abbreviations when entering the state name in the table.

> **Hot Tip**
>
> Press **F6** to move the insertion point between the Field Properties pane and the Design view pane.

8. Click the **View** button on the toolbar to switch to Datasheet view. When prompted to save the changes, click **Yes**. When prompted that data may be lost, click **Yes** to continue.

9. Enter the following data in the *Birthdate* and *e-mail* fields. Notice that as you enter the birthdate data, Access will automatically format the date using the short date format you specified.

First Name	e-mail	Birthdate
Jaimey	**JMcGuirk@ nets.com**	**March 13, 1978**
Jesse	**JBain@ LFSC.com**	**April 11, 1979**
Matt	**MSmith@ qry.com**	**June 18, 1980**

10. Enter the following new record. Remember that as you enter the state name, Access will not permit you to enter more than two characters. You will need to enter the two-letter state abbreviation for Ohio.

First Name	**Kelsey**
Last Name	**Erwin**
Address	**2038 Leiter Road**
City	**Lucas**
State/Province	**Ohio**
Postal Code	**44843-9880**
e-mail	**KErwin@csfa.com**
Birthdate	**October 6, 1979**

11. Format the *e-mail* and *Birthdate* columns width for best fit. (*Hint*: Open the **Format** menu, choose **Column Width**, and then select **Best Fit** in the dialog box.) Save the changes.

12. Open the **File** menu and choose **Close**. The Datasheet objects window is displayed. Notice that your Addresses table is now displayed as an object in the Database objects window.

13. Open the **File** menu and choose **Close** to close the database file.

> **Computer Concepts**
>
> Access offers several other ways to create a table. You can create a table in Datasheet view or you can use the Table Wizard.

SUMMARY

In this lesson, you learned:

- Many parts of the Access screen are similar to other Office XP applications. However, Access also has several different toolbar buttons and menus to perform tasks unique to Access.
- Database objects work together to help you organize and report the information stored in the database.
- Tables are the primary objects in a database. All other objects are based on data stored in tables.
- You use Datasheet view to enter records in a table.
- A table can be modified after it is created, even after data records have been entered into it. You can edit a table in Datasheet view or in Design view.
- In Design view, you can specify the data type for each field. The field properties are specifications that allow you to customize the data type settings. Text is the default field property for a cell.

VOCABULARY *Review*

Define the following terms:

Cell	Entry	Primary key
Database	Field	Record
Datasheet view	Field name	Wizard
Design view	Field properties	

REVIEW *Questions*

TRUE/FALSE

Circle T if the statement is true or F if the statement is false.

T F 1. All database information is stored in tables.

T F 2. You cannot add or delete fields after you have entered data in a table.

T F 3. Tables are the primary objects in a database because they store the data.

T F 4. Databases are similar to spreadsheets.

T F 5. Unlike Excel, you cannot adjust Access column widths.

FILL IN THE BLANK

Complete the following sentences by writing the correct word or words in the blanks provided.

1. A(n) ________ is a single piece of information in a database, such as a first name, a last name, or a telephone number.
2. ________ view displays the table data in a row-and-column format.
3. The ________ uniquely identifies each record in a table.
4. ________ are specifications that allow you to customize a field beyond choosing a data type.
5. A(n) ________ is a group of related fields, such as all the information about an employee.

PROJECTS

PROJECT 15-1

1. Open **Project15-1** from the data files. This database stores membership information and the current video collection of the Oak Creek Film Society (OCFS), a club for lovers of classic films.
2. Notice that this database contains two tables: Collection and Members. Open the **Collection** table to see the films the OCFS has collected so far.
3. Close the table and click the **Forms** object in the Objects bar. Open the **Members** form to see the form used to insert member data.
4. Close the form and click the **Queries** object in the Objects bar. Double-click the **Suspense** query to see the films in the collection that belong to the *Suspense* category. Close the query.
5. You need to create a new table for the database to store information on special events that the OCFS sponsors. Create a new table using the wizard:
   A. Select the **Business** category if necessary and then select the sample table **Events.**
   B. Add the following sample fields to your new table: **EventName, Location, StartDate,** and **EventDescription.**
   C. Accept the table name **Events**.
   D. Let the wizard set a primary key for you.
   E. There is no relationship between this new table and existing tables. So, when prompted about the relationship, simply click **Next.**
   F. When prompted about what you want to do after the wizard creates the table, select **Enter data directly into the table**, if necessary, and click **Finish**.
6. Enter the following data in Datasheet view:

Event Name	Location	Start Date	Event Description
Holiday Classics	**Odeon Theatre**	**12/15/02**	**Christmas theme**
Horror Classics	**Odeon Theatre**	**1/17/03**	**Horror theme**
Hitchcock Classics	**Odeon Theatre**	**2/22/03**	**Suspense theme**

7. You decide your table needs some modifications. With the **Events** table open, switch to Design view.

8. The *EventDescription* field doesn't add much to the table because the subject of each event is clear from the event name. Delete the **EventDescription** field and all contents.

9. It would be helpful to see the time for each event. Insert a new field following the *StartDate* field named **Start Time** with the Date/Time data type. Specify the **Medium Time** field property.

10. Each event includes clips from classic films. Insert a new field named **Films** following the *StartTime* field. Because each event includes more than one film, change the field size for the Films field to **200**.

11. Save your changes to the design and return to Datasheet view. Insert the following data in the new fields.

Event	Start Time	Films
Holiday Classics	**7:00 PM**	**A Christmas Story, A Christmas Carol**
Horror Classics	**7:00 PM**	**Dracula, Frankenstein**
Hitchcock Classics	**6:30 PM**	**The Birds, Vertigo**

12. Add one more event with the following information. Note that all three movies fit in the *Films* field now that you have changed the field size.

Event:	**Spoofing the Classics**
Location:	**Odeon Theatre**
Start Date:	**3/17/03**
Start Time:	**4:00 PM**
Films:	**The Pink Panther, Young Frankenstein, Dr. Strangelove**

13. Adjust the column widths to display all text in the fields. Save your changes.

14. Close the Events table and the Project15-1 database.

PROJECT 15-2

1. Open **Project15-2** from the data files. This database stores statistics for the Pistons Softball Team.

2. Open the **Stats** table and switch to Design view. Notice that the default value for the Number Data Type is *0*. That explains why the last row in the table shows zeros when the table is displayed in Datasheet view.

3. Add the following new fields after the *HP* field:

Field Name	Data Type	Description
SOL	**Number**	**Strike out looking**
SOS	**Number**	**Strike out swinging**
OBE	**Number**	**On by error**
SACF	**Number**	**Sacrifice fly**

4. Save your changes. Switch to Datasheet view and update the existing records by entering the following data in the new fields:

Player	SOL	SOS	OBE	SACF
Reardon	3	8	7	6
Erwin	6	6	4	2
Caulfield	4	8	13	10
Chen	8	12	1	3
Winters	1	11	8	1

5. Switch to Design view and change the format for the date/time data type in the *Joined* field to **Short Date.**

6. Select the entire table and format the column widths for best fit.

7. Save the changes to your database. Close the Stats table and the Project 15-2 database.

WEB PROJECT

Films of all types are such popular forms of entertainment that many sites on the Internet are dedicated to film information. A good source of information about movies is the Internet Movie Database. Think of a movie you have seen recently (or one you saw in the past that still interests you). Use a Web search tool to locate the current URL of the Internet Movie Database. If that site is not available, locate a site that provides movie information. Use the search box on the home page to key the name of the movie and then display information about the movie. If you were going to create your own database about films you like, what fields would you use to store the information?

TEAMWORK PROJECT

Databases are ideal for storing statistics such as those of sports teams. With a partner, create a database to record stats for a sports team. Follow these steps:

1. With your teammate, choose a team for further study.

2. Collect the statistics you will need for your database. Some of the pieces of information you might collect would be players' names, number of games, and statistics for each game. Divide up the players and/or games with your teammate so you each have half the work to do.

3. Create a database to store the data you collect.

CRITICAL *Thinking*

ACTIVITY 15-1

You want to insert two new fields in a database. One field—named Notes—will hold complete sentences of text. In some cases, the sentences are fairly lengthy. The other field, named Values, has to hold numbers containing decimals. However, it is important that these numbers are not rounded off during calculations. What data types and field properties will you need to specify in order to display data properly in these new fields? Experiment in Access to find the answers, and then check your answers using the Access Help screens.

LESSON 16

EDITING RECORDS AND USING FORMS

OBJECTIVES

Upon completion of this lesson, you should be able to:

- Edit records in Datasheet view.
- Add and delete records in Datasheet view.
- Cut, copy, and paste data in Datasheet view.
- Change the datasheet layout.
- Hide columns in a table.
- Create a form.
- Enter and edit data in a form.

Estimated Time: 1 hour

VOCABULARY

Clipboard

Field selector

Record selector

Edit Records in Datasheet View

It is common for data to change after you've entered it in your database. For example, people move, so you have to change their addresses and probably their phone numbers. Access provides several navigation features that make it easy for you to move around in a datasheet table so you can make necessary edits. These features are especially useful when you're working in large databases. Figure 16-1 shows the navigation buttons that are displayed at the bottom of a table shown in Datasheet view.

FIGURE 16-1
Navigation buttons

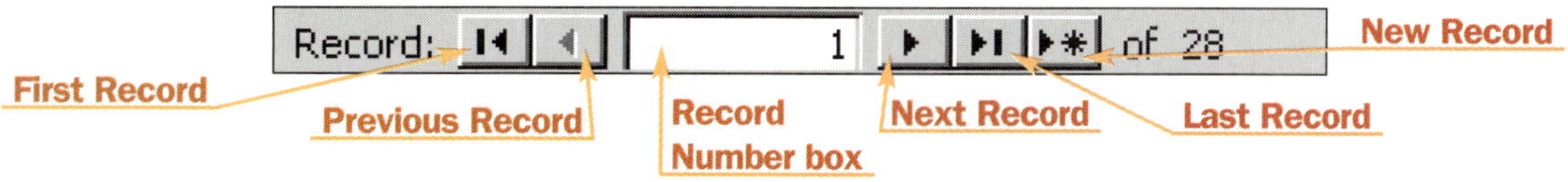

If you make a mistake adding or editing data, you can choose the Undo command to reverse your last action. As soon as you begin editing another record, however, the Undo command is no longer available.

STEP-BY-STEP 16.1

1. If necessary, launch Access and then open the file **Step16-1** from the data files.

2. If necessary, click **Tables** in the Objects bar, and then double-click the **Classics** table in the Database objects window to open the table. The table is displayed in Datasheet view.

3. The first cell in the table *(ID number 1)* is selected. The right-pointing arrow to the left of the first row indicates that this is the current row.

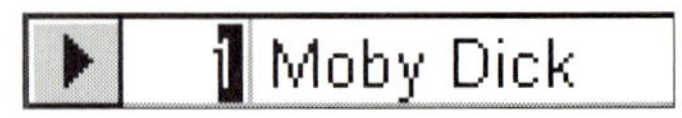

4. Click the **Next Record** button in the bottom left corner of the screen. The selection moves to the ID number 2 in the second row in the table.

5. Click the **Previous Record** button. Notice that even though the selection changes rows, the selection remains in the same field – *ID*.

6. Select the number **1** in the Record Number box and key **22**. Press **Enter** (or **Tab**). The selection moves to the ID **22** in the twenty-second row in the table.

7. Press **Tab** twice to position the insertion point in the *Author First* field in the same row. Key **James** to change the entry. Notice that a pencil displays at the left edge of the row, indicating that the record is being edited.

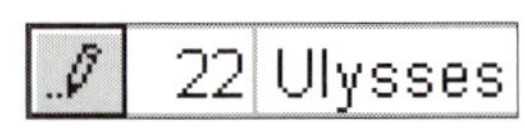

8. Click the **Next Record** button. The selection (or insertion point) moves to the next row in the table. Notice that the selection stays in the *Author First* field. Also notice that the pencil is no longer displayed to the left of row 22. This is because when you pressed Next Record, the edit was completed. (This is true whether you press a navigation button, press the **Enter** key, use the **Tab** key to move to the next row, use the arrow keys, or the mouse. As soon as you move out of the row, the entry is completed.)

> **Computer Concepts**
>
> When you edit a record in Datasheet view, Access automatically saves the changes to the record.

9. Click the **First Record** button. The insertion point moves to the *Author First* field in the first row in the table.

10. Click the **Last Record** button. The insertion point moves to the *Author First* field in the last row in the table.

11. Press **Tab** twice to move to the *Cover* field in the same row. Key **Paperback** to replace the current entry.

12. Click the **Previous Record** button to move to the row above. Key **Paperback** to replace the entry. Press **Tab** (or **Enter**).

13. The change was not necessary. Click the **Undo** button on the toolbar. The action is reversed and the cell should display *Hardcover*. Leave the database open for the next Step-by-Step.

> **Did You Know?**
>
> You can also execute the Undo command by pressing **Ctrl + Z** or opening the **Edit** menu and choosing **Undo**.

Add and Delete Records in Datasheet View

To add a record, you must enter the data in the blank row at the end of the table. To delete a record, you must first select the record. To select a record, point to the ***record selector***, which is the box located at the left edge of each row. You use the record selector to select the row. When you see a right-pointing arrow in the record selector, you can click, and the entire row is selected. You can select more than one record by dragging down several rows. This means you can delete multiple rows at once.

After a record is selected, you can press the Delete key to remove the data. Access will display a message box to ask you if you are sure about the deletion. Once you've deleted a record, you cannot use the Undo command to restore it.

Hot Tip

You can also select multiple, consecutive records by selecting the first record, holding down the **Shift** key, and then clicking on the last record. All the fields in between the first selected record and the last record will be selected.

STEP-BY-STEP 16.2

1. Click the **New Record** button. The insertion point is positioned in the first available blank row at the end of the table.

2. Press **Tab** to move to the *Title* field. Access will automatically insert an ID number for the primary key when you begin to enter data. Enter the following data for the new record:

Title:	**Crime and Punishment**
Author First:	**Fyodor**
Author Last:	**Dostoyevsky**
Cover:	**Hardcover**
# Pages:	**499**
Publisher:	**HarperCollins Publishers, Inc.**
Price:	**6.99**

3. Point to the left of the *ID* field 26. (The record is fourth from the bottom in the table.) When the pointer changes to a right-pointing arrow, click to select the entire row.

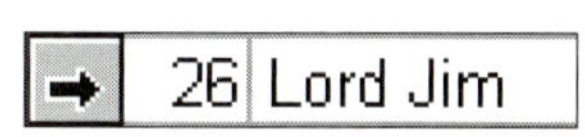

4. Press **Delete**. When prompted to confirm the deletion of the record, click **Yes**. The record is deleted from the table. Leave the database open for the next Step-by-Step.

Cut, Copy, and Paste Data in Datasheet View

Selected data can be copied or moved from one location in an Access table to a new location within the same table, or to a different table. The Copy command duplicates the data in a new location. The Cut and Paste commands relocate selected data.

When you use the Cut, Copy, and Paste commands, Access stores the selected text in the Clipboard. The ***Clipboard*** is a temporary storage place in your computer's memory. You send selected contents of your database to the Clipboard by using the Cut or Copy commands. Then you can retrieve those contents by using the Paste command. Pasting the contents of the Clipboard does not delete the contents from the Clipboard. Therefore, you can paste Clipboard items as many times as you want. When you turn off the computer, the Clipboard contents are lost.

As items are added to the Clipboard, the items are displayed as icons of the application (i.e., the Access icon or the Excel icon) in the Clipboard task pane. Along with the icon there is a thumbnail of the copied graphic or copied text. The Clipboard will store up to 24 items. The newest entry is always added to the top of the gallery. When you copy or cut a 25th item, the first item you placed in the Clipboard is deleted.

Computer Concepts

You can access the Cut, Copy, and Paste commands by clicking the appropriate buttons on the toolbar. You can also access the commands by right-clicking on the selected data to display a shortcut menu and then choosing the desired command from the menu.

Hot Tip

As in all Office applications, the shortcut keys for Cut are **Ctrl + X**; for Copy, **Ctrl + C**; and for Paste, **Ctrl + V**. The Cut, Copy, and Paste commands can also be found on the Edit menu. There are Copy, Cut, and Paste buttons on the Standard toolbar.

Computer Concepts

When you cut data from a table, you will get a warning about deleting the record. However, when you cut data, the data is stored in the Clipboard. Thus, if you change your mind and want to restore the data, you can paste the data in the table. When you paste data in a table, the data will overwrite the existing data.

STEP-BY-STEP 16.3

1. Open the **Edit** menu and choose **Office Clipboard**.

2. Click the **Clear All** button in the Clipboard task pane to clear the contents of the Clipboard. (If you have not copied or cut any items, the Clipboard will already be cleared and this step will not be necessary. Your Clear All button will be greyed out and not available.) Your Clipboard task pane should now look like the one shown in Figure 16-2.

Speech Recognition

If your computer has speech recognition capability, enable the Command mode and say the command to display the Office Clipboard task pane, then say the command to clear all the contents on the Clipboard.

STEP-BY-STEP 16.3 Continued

FIGURE 16-2
Empty Clipboard task pane

3. Go to record 7 (*Oliver Twist*) and select the entire row.

4. Click the **Copy** button on the toolbar to copy the record data to the Clipboard. An Access icon and the first portion of the text is added to the Clipboard task pane to indicate contents from an Access database are stored in the Clipboard.

5. Go to record 12 (*Wuthering Heights*) and select the entire row. Then click the **Copy** button to copy the record data to the Clipboard. A second Access icon is added to the Clipboard task pane to indicate another item is stored in the Clipboard.

6. Click the **New Record** button. The new row is selected.

7. Click the first object at the top of the list (*Wuthering Heights*) in the Clipboard toolbar. The contents of the object are pasted into the new record row. Notice that the contents still remain in the Clipboard.

8. Click the **New Record** button. Paste the contents of the second object (*Oliver Twist*) in the new record row. Then, close the Clipboard task pane.

Speech Recognition

If your computer has speech recognition capability, enable the Command mode and say the commands to navigate in the table in Datasheet view. Note that the commands you can use include Up, Down, Left, Right, Page Down, Page Up, Home, End, and New Record.

STEP-BY-STEP 16.3 Continued

9. Edit the fields in the Oliver Twist record (31) as follows: Change *Paperback* to **Hardcover**, change the page count to **325**, and change the price to **4.99**. Press **Enter**.

10. Edit the fields in the Wuthering Heights record (30) as follows: Change *Hardcover* to **Paperback**, change the page count to **225**, and change the price to **3.49**. Press **Enter**. Leave the database open for the next Step-by-Step.

Change the Datasheet Layout

If you want to rearrange the fields in Datasheet view, you can drag them to a new location. To select a field, point to the field name at the top of the column. The box containing the field name is also a ***field selector***. You use the field selector to select the column. When you see a down-pointing arrow in the field selector, click, and the entire column is selected. After you select the field, point to the field selector and drag the selection to the new location. As you drag, a vertical bar will follow the mouse pointer to indicate where the field will be moved. When you release the mouse button, the field is inserted in its new location.

STEP-BY-STEP 16.4

1. Scroll to the right until the *Cover* column, the *# Pages* column, the *Publisher* column, and the *Price* column are all visible on the screen.

2. Point to the field name *Cover*. When the pointer changes to a down-pointing arrow, click and drag to the right to select the *Cover* and *# Pages* columns.

3. Release the mouse button when the two columns are selected. Then point to either of the field names and drag the columns to the right. As you drag, a bold vertical line will display. When that vertical line is positioned on the border between the *Publisher* column and the *Price* column as shown in Figure 16-3, release the mouse button.

FIGURE 16-3
Dragging columns to a new location

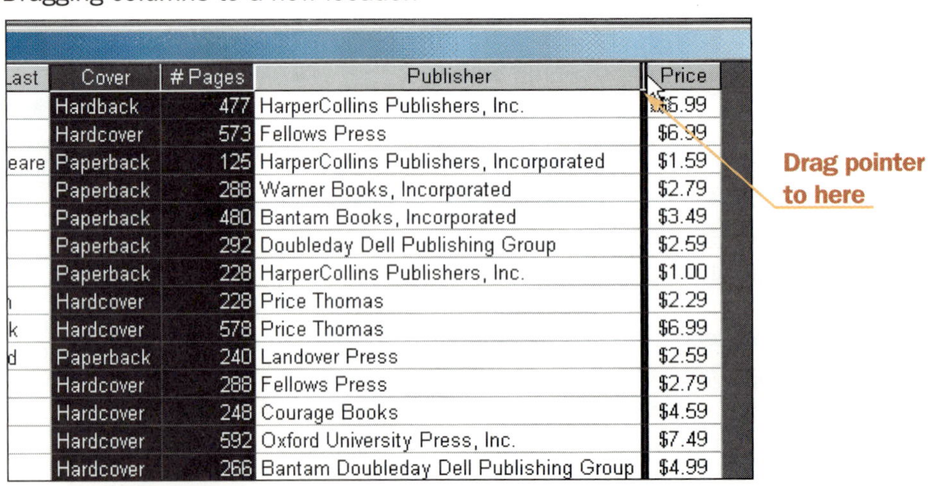

STEP-BY-STEP 16.4 Continued

4. Click anywhere in the table to deselect the columns. The two columns are moved and now display after the *Publisher* column and before the *Price* column.

5. Compare your screen to Figure 16-4. If the columns are not in the correct order, try again. Select the column(s) you need to move and drag it to the new location. Leave the database open for the next Step-by-Step.

FIGURE 16-4
Table with columns rearranged

ID	Title	Author First	Author Last	Publisher	Cover	# Pages	Price
1	Moby Dick	Herman	Melville	HarperCollins Publishers, Inc.	Hardback	477	$5.99
2	Little Women	Louisa	Alcott	Fellows Press	Hardcover	573	$6.99
3	Romeo & Juliet	William	Shakespeare	HarperCollins Publishers, Incorporated	Paperback	125	$1.59
4	To Kill a Mockingbird	Harper	Lee	Warner Books, Incorporated	Paperback	288	$2.79
5	Uncle Tom's Cabin	Harriet	Stowe	Bantam Books, Incorporated	Paperback	480	$4.59
6	The Adventures of Huckleberry Finn	Mark	Twain	Doubleday Dell Publishing Group	Paperback	292	$2.59
7	Oliver Twist	Charles	Dickens	HarperCollins Publishers, Inc.	Paperback	228	$1.00
8	The Scarlet Letter	Nathaniel	Hawthorn	Price Thomas	Hardcover	228	$2.29
9	The Grapes of Wrath	John	Steinbeck	Price Thomas	Hardcover	578	$6.99
10	The Great Gatsby	F. Scott	Fitzgerald	Landover Press	Paperback	240	$2.59
11	Pride and Prejudice	Jane	Austen	Fellows Press	Hardcover	288	$2.79

Use Help to Learn How to Hide Columns

When all the columns in a table cannot display on the screen at one time, you must scroll horizontally to view all the columns. This can make it difficult to enter data in Datasheet view because you cannot see all of the fields.

If you completed the lessons in the Excel unit, you learned to hide columns in a spreadsheet. Go to the Help screens to see if you can hide columns in an Access table as well.

STEP-BY-STEP 16.5

1. Click the **Office Assistant**, or open the **Help** menu and choose **Microsoft Access Help**.

2. In the text box, key **hide columns** and then press **Enter** or click **Search**.

> **Hot Tip**
>
> The shortcut for accessing the Help command is **F1**.

3. When the assistant displays a list of topics, select the topic **Show or hide columns in a datasheet**.

4. Read the directions for hiding a column. Be sure to also read about how to show hidden columns.

5. Click the **Classics: Table** button in the taskbar to view the database table.

6. Hide the *Author First*, *Author Last*, *Publisher*, and *Cover* columns.

7. Only four columns should now display. Compare your screen with Figure 16-5. You should see only four fields displayed in the table.

> **Did You Know?**
>
> If the Office Assistant is in the way, point to the Office Assistant and drag it to the side of the screen. To turn off the display of the Office Assistant, right-click, and choose **Hide** in the shortcut menu.

STEP-BY-STEP 16.5 Continued

FIGURE 16-5
Table with columns hidden

ID	Title	# Pages	Price
1	Moby Dick	477	$5.99
2	Little Women	573	$6.99
3	Romeo & Juliet	125	$1.59
4	To Kill a Mockingbird	288	$2.79
5	Uncle Tom's Cabin	480	$3.49
6	The Adventures of Huckleberry Finn	292	$2.59
7	Oliver Twist	228	$1.00
8	The Scarlet Letter	228	$2.29
9	The Grapes of Wrath	578	$6.99
10	The Great Gatsby	240	$2.59
11	Pride and Prejudice	288	$2.79
12	Wuthering Heights	248	$4.59

8. Edit the following records as follows:

Record 5:	Uncle Tom's Cabin	Change the price to **$4.59**
Record 14:	My Antonia	Change the price to **$6.99**
Record 16:	Great Expectations	Change the price to **$5.99**

9. To unhide the columns, open the **Format** menu and choose **Unhide Columns**. The Unhide Columns dialog box shown in Figure 16-6 will display.

FIGURE 16-6
Unhide Columns dialog box

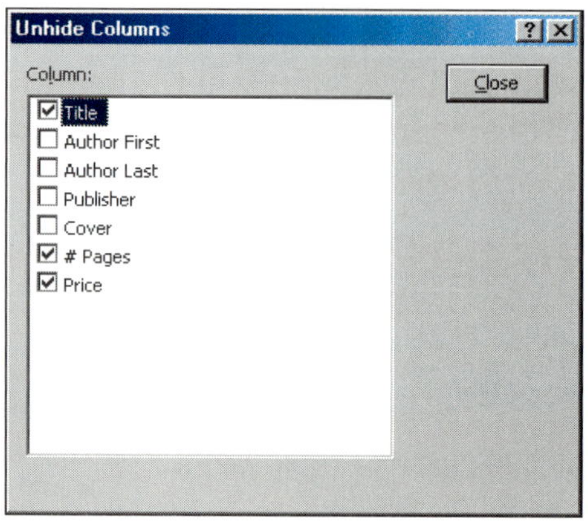

10. The boxes without checkmarks indicate the columns that are currently hidden. Click each of the empty boxes to select them. (You may notice the columns reappearing in the database behind the dialog box as you check them.) When all the boxes in the dialog box have checkmarks, click the **Close** button in the dialog box.

11. Open the **File** menu and choose **Close** to close the table. When prompted to save the changes to the layout of the table, click **Yes**.

> **Hot Tip**
>
> If you can't remember all the steps for a certain task, click the **Microsoft Access Help** button in the taskbar and review the information presented in the Help screen. Then switch back to the database and complete the task.

12. Click the **Microsoft Access Help** button in the task bar and then close the Help window. Leave the database open for the next Step-by-Step.

Create a Form

Access offers another way to enter data in a table. You can create a data-entry form. A form offers a more convenient way to enter and view records. When you create a form, you are adding a new object to the database. Although you can create a form manually, the Form Wizard makes the process easier. The wizard asks you questions and formats the form according to your preferences.

STEP-BY-STEP 16.6

1. Click **Forms** in the Objects bar.
2. Double-click **Create form by using wizard** in the Database Objects window. The Form Wizard dialog box shown in Figure 16-7 is displayed.

FIGURE 16-7
Form Wizard dialog box

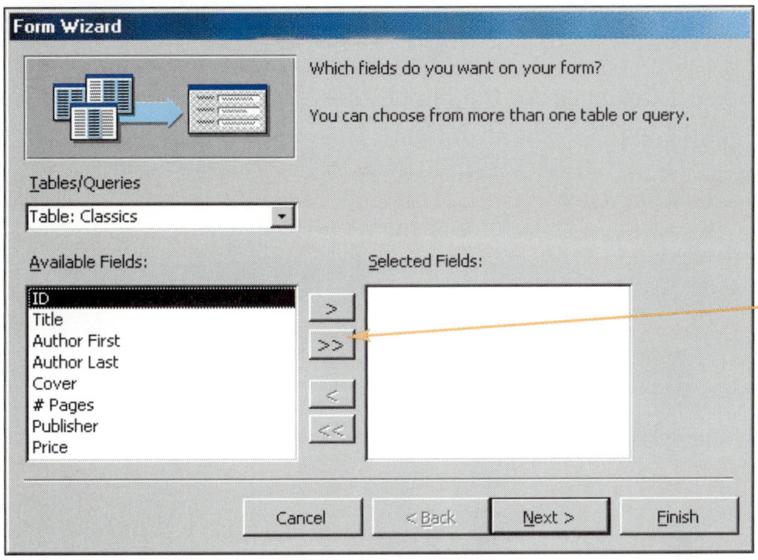

3. Notice that *Table: Classics* is already selected under *Table/Queries*. Also notice that all the fields available in the table are listed under *Available Fields*.
4. You need to identify the fields you want on your form. Click the double arrows button (**>>**). All of the field names are displayed in the Selected Fields list. This tells Access to include all the fields in the form.
5. Click the **Next** button. The Form Wizard dialog box changes so you can select a layout for the form, as shown in Figure 16-8.

STEP-BY-STEP 16.6 Continued

FIGURE 16-8
Selecting a layout for a form

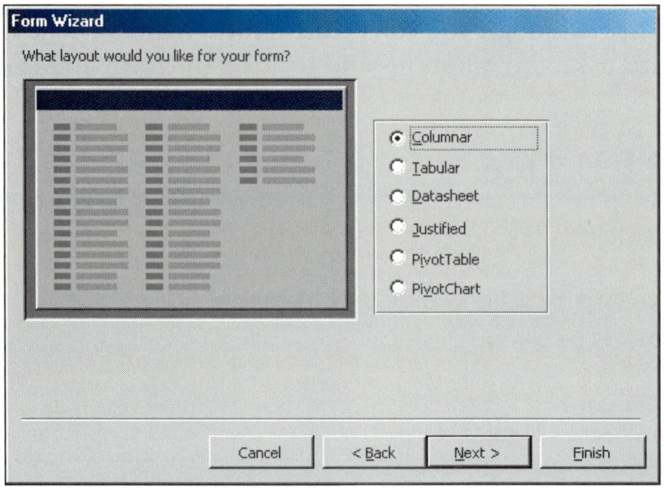

6. If necessary, select **Columnar** for the layout, then click **Next**. The dialog box changes so you can select a style for the form, as shown in Figure 16-9.

FIGURE 16-9
Choosing a style for a form

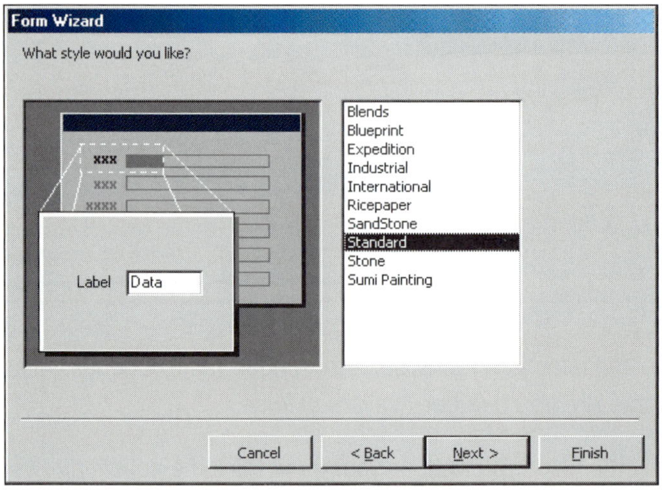

7. If necessary, select the **Standard** style. The preview box shows you what this form style looks like.

8. Select some of the other styles to see what they look like. Then select **Stone** and click **Next**. The final Form Wizard dialog box changes so you can create a title for the form, as shown in Figure 16-10.

STEP-BY-STEP 16.6 Continued

FIGURE 16-10
Creating a title for a form

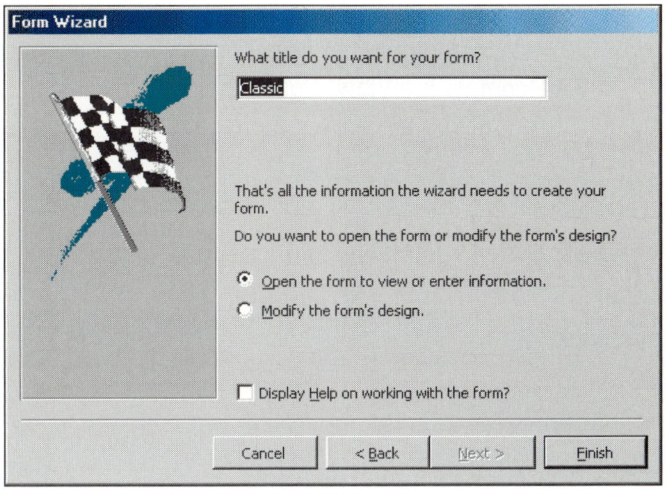

9. Key **Classic Books**.

10. If necessary, click the **Open the form to view or enter information.** option to select it. Then click **Finish**. Access creates and displays the form similar to that shown in Figure 16-11. Notice that data from the first record is displayed in the form. Leave the form and the database open for the next Step-by-Step.

FIGURE 16-11
Customized form

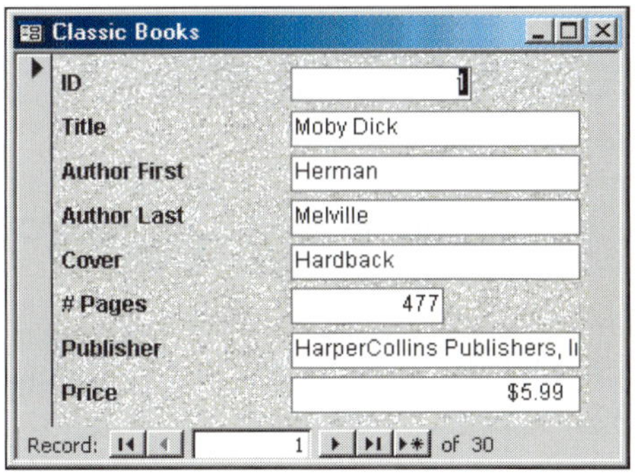

Enter and Edit Data in a Form

Entering data in a form is similar to entering data in a table in Datasheet view. You use the same keys to move the insertion point among the fields. Furthermore, the same navigation buttons are available at the bottom of the form. To add a new record, go to the blank record at the end of the database or click the New Record button. To edit an existing record, display the record and make the changes in the fields of the form.

STEP-BY-STEP 16.7

1. Click the **New Record** button at the bottom of the form. A new form is displayed with labels, but there is no data entered in the form.

2. Press **Tab** to position the insertion point in the field *Title*. Access will assign an ID number when you begin to enter data. Key **A Room with a View**. Notice that the Pencil icon is displayed at the top left corner of the form, indicating that you are editing the record.

3. Press **Tab** and key **E. M.**

4. Press **Tab** and enter the following information into the form:

Author Last:	**Forster**
Cover:	**Paperback**
# Pages:	**355**
Publisher:	**Bagshot Press**
Price:	**5.99**

5. Press **Enter** (or **Tab**). A new blank form is displayed.

6. Select the number **32** in the Record Number box, key **8**, and press **Enter**. A form containing the data for the eighth record is displayed.

7. The author's last name is misspelled. It should be Hawthorne. Click in the *Author Last* field, position the insertion point at the end of the entry, and key the letter **e**.

> **Speech Recognition**
>
> If your computer has speech recognition capability, enable the Dictation mode, position the insertion point in the field, and dictate the entry. Or, enable the Command mode and say the commands to navigate from one field to another.

8. Open the **File** menu and choose **Close**. Notice that the Database objects window displays the new form *Classic Books* in the list of objects.

9. Click the **Tables** button in the Objects bar, then double-click the **Classics** table to open it.

10. Scroll down to the end of the table. Notice that the new record has been added to the table. Go to record 8. Notice that the name Hawthorne has been corrected.

11. Close the table and the Database.

> **Computer Concepts**
>
> When you enter or edit a record in form view, Access automatically updates the records in the table.

SUMMARY

In this lesson, you learned:

- Access provides several navigation buttons to make it easy for you to move around in a table. If you make a mistake adding or editing data, you can choose the Undo command to reverse your last action.

- You can add and delete records in a table while working in Datasheet view. New records are added at the end of the table. To delete a record, you must first select the entire row containing the record.
- Selected data can be copied or moved from one location in an Access table to a new location within the same table, or to a different table.
- The Clipboard task pane displays copied and cut items, and it also enables you to paste items.
- To rearrange database fields in Datasheet view, you must select the columns containing the fields and then drag them to a new location.
- If you have several fields in a table, you can hide some of the columns so you can display the fields with which you need to work. You can unhide these columns when you are done.
- The Form Wizard helps you create a professional-looking, customized form for entering data.
- Entering and editing data in a form is similar to entering and editing data in a table in Datasheet view. You use the same navigation buttons to move from one record to another.

VOCABULARY *Review*

Define the following terms:

Clipboard | Field selector | Record selector

REVIEW *Questions*

TRUE/FALSE

Circle T if the statement is true or F if the statement is false.

T F 1. You can use the Undo command any time after you have entered a record to reverse changes.

T F 2. You must add new records at the end of the table.

T F 3. You cannot save changes to the datasheet layout.

T F 4. A form makes it easy to enter new data into a table.

T F 5. You use the same navigation controls in a form as you use in a datasheet.

FILL IN THE BLANK

Complete the following sentences by writing the correct word or words in the blanks provided.

1. To go to record 35 in a database, you would key 35 in the __________ box and then press Enter.
2. The box at the left edge of a row is called the __________.

3. The box containing the field name is called the ________.

4. The easiest way to create a new form is to use the ________.

5. To insert new data in a form, click the ________ button to display a blank form.

PROJECTS

PROJECT 16-1

1. Open **Project16-1** from the data files. Open the **Collection** table.
2. Hide the *Year*, *Length*, *MPAA*, and *Director* columns.
3. Make the following corrections to the data in the table:
   A. Go to record 20 (*King Solomon's Mines*) and change the *Category* field to **Adventure**.
   B. Go to record 24 (*The Haunting*). You think the title of this film is incorrect. It should be *The Haunting of Hill House*. Key **of Hill House** in the *Title* field.
   C. Whoops, you were wrong. That was the title of the book, not the film. Your original title was correct after all. Click **Undo** to return the title to *The Haunting*.
   D. Go to record 26 (*Casablanca*) and scroll, if necessary, so you can see the *Awards* field. To save space, you are not including the word *Best* for all Academy Awards. Delete the word *Best* and the space that follows in this field.
4. Unhide the hidden columns.
5. You need to add several films that were acquired for recent events. (You do not have to enter a number in the *ID* field; Access will supply a number automatically when you key an entry in the *Title* field.)

Title:	**Vertigo**	Title:	**Dr. Strangelove**
Year:	**1958**	Year:	**1964**
Length:	**128**	Length:	**93**
MPAA:	**NR**	MPAA:	**NR**
Color/BW:	**Color**	Color/BW:	**BW**
Director:	**Hitchcock**	Director:	**Kubrick**
Category:	**Suspense**	Category:	**Comedy**
Actor:	**James Stewart**	Actor:	**Peter Sellers, George C. Scott**
Actress:	**Kim Novak**		

6. You have another new film to add. To save time, copy record 29 (*Star Wars*) and paste it in a new record. Change the title to **The Empire Strikes Back**, the year to **1980**, the Length to **124**, and the Director to **Kershner**. Remove *Alec Guinness* from the list in the *Actor* field and add **Billy Dee Williams** to the list. Delete the existing text in the *Award* field and then enter **Special Effects**.
7. You have discovered that the 1969 version of Hamlet is damaged. Delete this record (14) from the table.
8. Move the *Category* column to the right of the *Title* column.

9. Close the table and save changes when prompted.

10. Exit the database.

PROJECT 16-2

1. Open **Project16-2** from the data files.

2. Select **Forms** in the Objects bar. Use the **Form Wizard** and the following information to create a new form using the Members table: select **all fields**, the **Columnar** format, and the **Sumi Painting** style. Finish using the Form Wizard by naming the form **OCFS Members**.

3. Add a new record using the form. (You do not need to enter a number in the *Member ID* field. Simply press **Enter** or **Tab**. Access will add the Member ID automatically after you key an entry in the *First Name* field.)
   First Name: **Sam**
   Last Name: **Martin**
   Address: **Old Ferry Rd**
   City: **Oak Creek**
   State: **OH**
   Zip: **43211**
   Phone: **555-1216**

4. Go to record 8 and change Judith Schuyler's phone number to **555-5005**.

5. Go to record 14. Brian Tannenbaum has moved. Change his street address to **7140 Cascade Street** and leave all other information the same.

6. Close the form and the database.

WEB PROJECT

Every year, financial publications create lists of the richest people in this country and the world. Use Web search tools to find the most recent list of wealthy Americans. Record each person's wealth ranking, first name, last name, and current wealth for each of the first ten people listed. Also record the current job title, if any, and how each person achieved his or her current wealth if you can easily determine this information. (For example, William Gates acquired his wealth through ownership of Microsoft stock.) Create a database to store your information. You'll want to cite your references, so be sure to include a resources field where you can record the Web site(s) where you found the information. If you identify any other items you want to record, modify the database structure and add the information.

TEAMWORK PROJECT

Create a roster for your computer class or workgroup to record the names, addresses, phone numbers, e-mail addresses, and other information about your classmates or co-workers. Follow these steps:

1. With a teammate, determine what information you want to gather and organize.

2. Divide the names of your classmates or co-workers so that each of you will gather information for half the group.

3. After you have gathered the information, create a new database and a table with the fields you identified in Step 1. Then use the Form Wizard to create a form to make data entry easier. Select the options you think will present the information you've collected in the best way, and give your form a relevant title.

4. Enter the information into the form.

CRITICAL *Thinking*

ACTIVITY 16-1

You want to create new records using data from some fields in other records. For example, you want to use a company name from one record, a city from another record, and a product from a third record. It would be tedious to copy and paste all three records and then delete the material you don't need. Is there any way to copy only a single field entry to the Clipboard and then paste it into a new record? Experiment with an Access table and the Clipboard. Use the Help screens if you're unable to figure it out. Write a brief report about what you discover.

ORDERING AND FINDING DATA AND CREATING REPORTS AND MAILING LABELS

OBJECTIVES

Upon completion of this lesson, you should be able to:

- Sort data in Datasheet view.
- Find and replace data in Datasheet view.
- Create a query.
- Create a report.
- Create mailing labels.

Estimated Time: 1 hour

VOCABULARY

Ascending order
Descending order
Landscape orientation
Orientation
Portrait orientation
Query
Report

As the amount of data in a database increases, it becomes more difficult to manage records and find information. Access has several useful features that help you work with larger databases. These features help you order the data, find the data, and summarize and report the data.

In this lesson, you will work with the same database you edited in the previous lesson. However, instead of opening the file you saved in Lesson 16, you will start again by opening a new data file created for this lesson. This ensures that the database file you are working with matches the illustrations and examples presented in this lesson.

Sort Data in Datasheet View

Often you will want records in a database to appear in a specific order so you can access data easier and more quickly. Databases often contain numerous records. Access provides toolbar buttons that will help you sort the records in a table quickly. You can sort text and numbers in either ascending or descending order. ***Ascending order*** sorts alphabetically from A to Z and numerically from the lowest to the highest number. ***Descending order*** sorts alphabetically from Z to A and numerically from the highest to the lowest number.

Unfortunately, the Undo command is not available after you perform a sort. However, if you change your mind after sorting data, you can open the Records menu and choose Remove Filter/Sort.

STEP-BY-STEP 17.1

1. Open the file **Step17-1** from the data files.

2. Click **Tables** in the Objects bar, then double-click **Classics** in the list of objects to open the table.

3. Click in any row in the field *Title*.

4. Click the **Sort Ascending** button on the toolbar. The records in the table are rearranged and placed in alphabetical order from A to Z by book title.

> **Speech Recognition**
>
> If your computer has speech recognition cabability, enable the Command mode and say the command to open the data file.

5. Open the **Records** menu and choose **Remove Filter/Sort**. The records are returned to the original order.

6. If necessary, scroll to the right and click in any row in the *Price* field.

7. Click the **Sort Descending** button on the toolbar. The records are rearranged in numerical order with the highest priced book listed first.

8. Click in any row in the *Author Last* field, then click the **Sort Ascending** button. The records are arranged in alphabetical order from A to Z by the author's last name. Leave the database open for the next Step-by-Step.

Find and Replace Data in Datasheet View

There may be occasions when you need to locate a particular value, one record, or a group of records in a database. Locating this data can be simple if the database is not large. However, if the database is quite large, finding a particular record or value can be tedious.

Use Help to Learn about Scrolling in a Datasheet or Form

If your database is not large, you may find it more expedient to locate data by scrolling in a datasheet or form. Go to the Help screens to learn more about scrolling in order to locate a specific record.

STEP-BY-STEP 17.2

1. Open the **Help** menu and choose **Microsoft Access Help**. If the Office Assistant is displayed, point to the Office Assistant and right-click. Then choose **Options** in the shortcut menu. Clear the check box for Use the Office Assistant and click **OK**. Then, open the **Help** menu and choose **Microsoft Access Help**.

2. If necessary, click the **Show** button on the toolbar to display the Contents, Answer Wizard, and Index tabs.

STEP-BY-STEP 17.2 Continued

3. If necessary, click the **Contents** tab to display a dialog box similar to the one shown in Figure 17-1. Do not be concerned if your dialog box looks different.

FIGURE 17-1
Contents tab in Microsoft Access Help

4. If necessary, click all minus signs so that your screen matches the dialog box in Figure 17-1.

5. Click the plus sign next to **Working with Data**. Then click the plus sign next to the subtopic **Finding, Sorting, and Grouping Data**. Then select the plus sign next to the subtopic **Finding and Replacing Data**. Another list of subtopics is displayed.

6. Click the topic **Find a record in a datasheet or form**.

Computer Concepts

If you click the plus (+) sign next to a topic, the topic will expand to show a list of subtopics. If you click a minus (–) sign next to a topic, the list of subtopics will collapse so that only the topic above the current level is displayed.

7. Click the link **Find a specific record by scrolling in a datasheet or form** to expand the topic. Click the links for **Datasheet view** and **continuous form** to display the definitions of those terms. Click a second time to hide the definitions. Read all of the information. If you don't know the meaning of a term, click it to read its definition.

STEP-BY-STEP 17.2 Continued

8. Click the **Classics: Table** button in the taskbar to view the database table.

9. Use the scroll bars to practice scrolling. Then scroll and locate the following book titles:

   The Great Gatsby

   Little Women

   A Tale of Two Cities

   Dr. Jekyll and Mr. Hyde

10. Click the **Microsoft Help** button in the taskbar and then close the Help screens. Leave the database open for the next Step-by-Step.

Did You Know?

If you have a Microsoft IntelliMouse or Microsoft IntelliMouse Explorer, you can also use the wheel on the mouse to scroll. The wheel eliminates the need to click buttons and scroll bars on the screen.

Speech Recognition

If your computer has speech recognition cabability, enable the Command mode and say the commands to scroll through the database records.

Hot Tip

To turn the display of the Office Assistant back on, open the **Help** menu and choose **Show the Office Assistant**.

Use the Find Command

Let's assume that you want to see if there are any books about Huckleberry Finn included in the database. You could sort the records in alphabetical order by title and then scroll down through the list to look for the title. However, if the database had hundreds, or even thousands of records, this method could be time-consuming. The Find Command provides a much faster way for you to locate specific records or find certain values within fields quickly.

STEP-BY-STEP 17.3

1. Position the insertion point in the first row in the *Title* field. Be careful, though, not to select any text in a cell.

2. Open the **Edit** menu and choose **Find**. The Find and Replace dialog box shown in Figure 17-2 is displayed. Do not be concerned if your dialog box does not match exactly.

Did You Know?

If you only want to search a specific section of the table, you can select the section before you execute the Find command. Access will look for the search text only in the selected cells.

Hot Tip

The shortcut keys for displaying the Find dialog box are **Ctrl + F**.

STEP-BY-STEP 17.3 Continued

FIGURE 17-2
Find and Replace dialog box

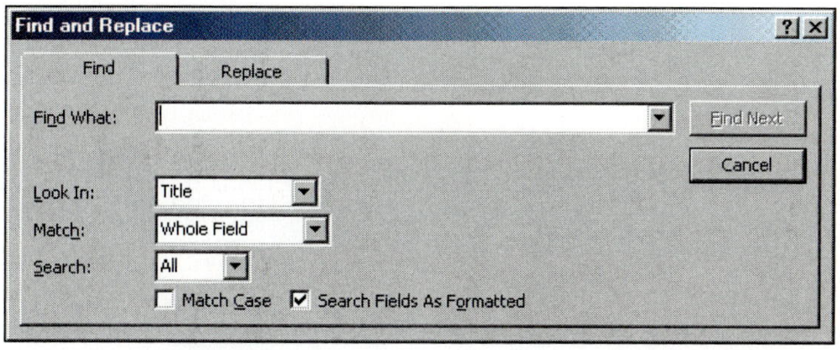

3. With the insertion point already positioned in the Find What text box, key **Huckleberry Finn**. If there is already text in the box, it will be replaced when you key the new search text.

4. Notice that *Title* is displayed in the Look In box. This option is correct as is. It tells Access to look for all occurrences in the *Title* column.

> **Hot Tip**
>
> If you want Access to search the entire database, select the name of the database table in the Look In box.

5. Change the options, if necessary, to match those illustrated in Figure 17-3:
   a. Click the down arrow in the **Match** box and select **Any Part of Field**. Access will locate any book title that has the words *Huckleberry* and *Finn* in it.
   b. If necessary, select **All** in the Search box.
   c. The *Match Case* and *Search Fields As Formatted* options should not be selected. If they are selected, point to the option and click once to uncheck the box and turn the option off. When these options are turned off, Access ignores capitalization and data formats when searching for matching text.

> **Speech Recognition**
>
> If your computer has speech recognition cabability, enable the Command mode and say the commands to change the options in the Find and Replace dialog box.

FIGURE 17-3
Completed Find and Replace dialog box

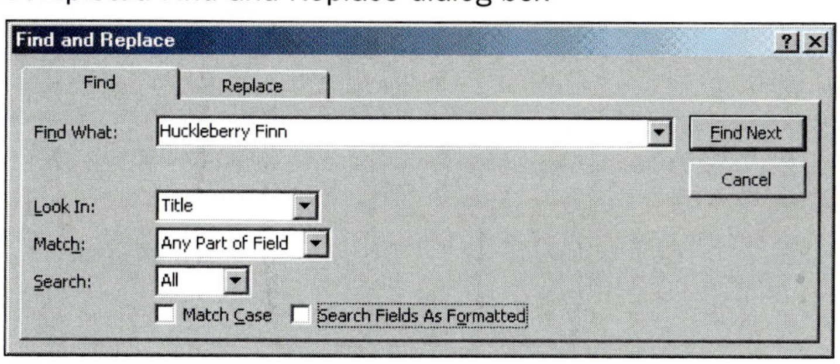

STEP-BY-STEP 17.3 Continued

6. Click the **Find Next** button in the dialog box. Access scrolls to the first record that matches the search criteria and highlights the book title in the *Title* field. See Figure 17-4.

FIGURE 17-4
Search text located in Classics table

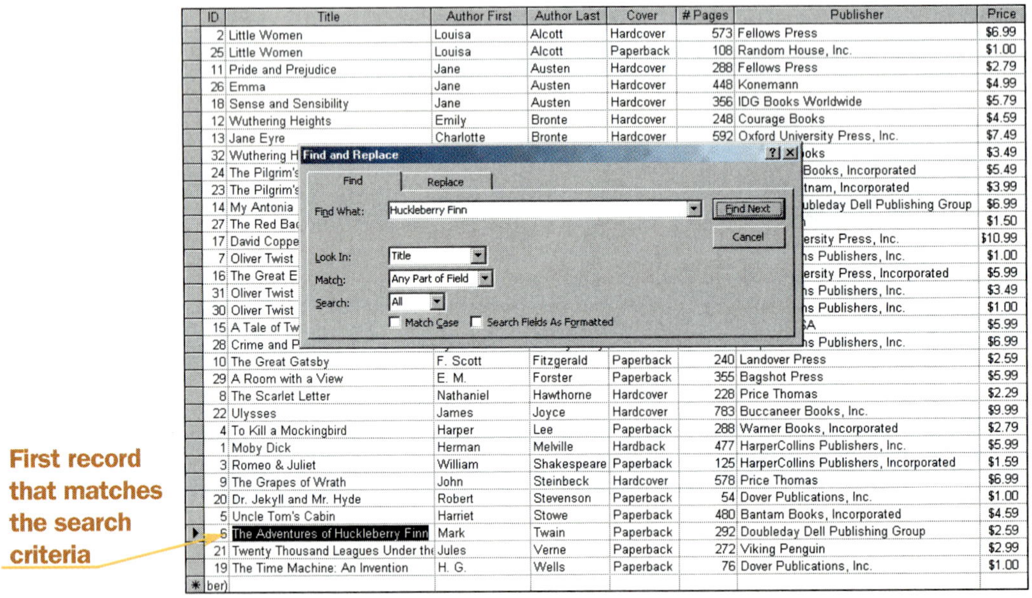

7. Click the **Find Next** button again. A message displays indicating that there are no more occurrences of the search text.

8. Click **OK** in the message box to close the message. Then click the **Cancel** button in the Find and Replace dialog box. Leave the database open for the next Step-by-Step.

Hot Tip

You can use the shortcut keys **Shift + F4** to execute the Find command without opening the Find and Replace dialog box. Access will search for the text and values that were entered in the Find What box for the last search.

Use the Replace Command

If you are working with a large database and you want to replace existing data with new data, the task can be tedious. However, like the Find command, the Replace command makes the task easy. The Replace command locates the search text and replaces it with new text that you specify. For example, in the Classics database there is no consistency in the spelling of the word Incorporated. Sometimes it is spelled out completely, and sometimes it is abbreviated (Inc.). You can search for all the occurrences when the word is abbreviated and then automatically replace those abbreviations with the complete spelling.

STEP-BY-STEP 17.4

1. Click in the first row in the *Publisher* field.

2. Open the **Edit** menu and choose **Find**. Click the **Replace** tab to display the dialog box shown in Figure 17-5.

> **Hot Tip**
>
> The shortcut keys for displaying the Replace dialog box are **Ctrl + H**.

FIGURE 17-5
Replace tab in the Find and Replace dialog box

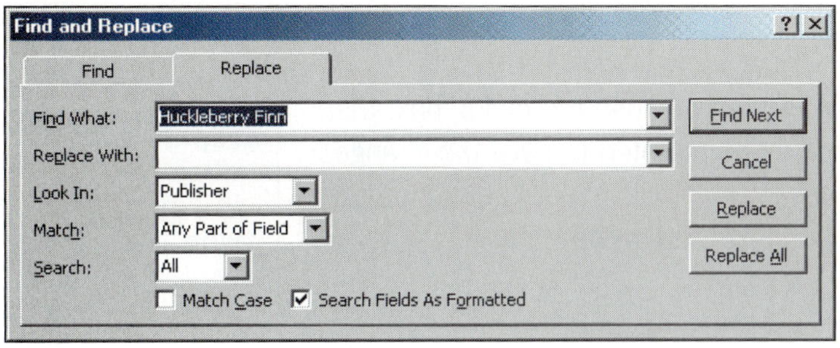

3. Notice that the Find What box still contains the text from your last search. Key **Inc.** to replace the old search text.

4. Click in the **Replace With** box to select it and key **Incorporated**.

5. The Look In box should display *Publisher*. The Match box should display *Any Part of Field*. The Search box should display *All*.

6. Click the **Find Next** button. Access selects the entry *Random House, Inc.* in the second record in the *Publisher* column because it contains the abbreviation *Inc.* Do not be concerned that the entire entry is selected.

7. Click the **Replace** button in the dialog box.

> **Computer Concepts**
>
> If you change your mind about a replacement, you can use the Undo command to reverse the action. Remember, you must choose the **Undo** command before editing another record.

> **Computer Concepts**
>
> There may be times when you do not want to replace the selected text. On those occasions, simply click the **Find Next** button to go to the next occurrence. No changes are made unless you click the **Replace** button.

8. If necessary, click the up arrow in the vertical scroll bar so you can see the second record in the *Publisher* column. Notice that *Inc.* was replaced with *Incorporated*, but the remaining text in the entry (*Random House,*) did not change.

9. Notice, too, that the next occurrence of *Inc.* is selected. When you pressed the **Replace** button in Step 7, Access automatically replaced the appropriate text and performed the Find Next function.

STEP-BY-STEP 17.4 Continued

10. Click the **Replace All** button. A message is displayed warning that you will not be able to undo the replace operation. Click **Yes**. Access replaces all occurrences of *Inc.* with *Incorporated* throughout the column.

11. Scroll up and down to view all the entries in the column. Notice that there are no more abbreviations for *Incorporated*.

12. Click the **Cancel** button to close the dialog box, then close the table. When prompted to save the changes to the design of the table, click **Yes**. Leave the database open for the next Step-by-Step.

> **Computer Concepts**
>
> When you use the Replace option, you can view each change and confirm the replacements individually. You should use the Replace All option only when you are confident about making all the replacements without reviewing them first. You can use the Match Case option to aid in preventing inadvertent replacements. Match Case allows you to be more specific in what you replace, and you won't need to approve each replacement individually.

Create a Query

Although the Find command provides an easy way to find data, you may need to locate multiple records, all containing the same values. If you have a large database, and several records contain the value you are searching for, this is another task that can be tedious. In this case, you can use a ***query***, which enables you to locate multiple records matching a specified criteria. Remember, you learned in Lesson 15 that Query is one of the database objects displayed in the Objects bar. The query provides a way for you to ask a question about the information stored in a database table(s). Access searches for and retrieves data from the table(s) to answer your question.

To illustrate, consider the following example. Suppose you just read a book by Charles Dickens. You really enjoyed the book and you would like to read another book authored by him. You could locate the books by Charles Dickens one at a time in the Classics database by using the Find command. But a query makes your task easier, and also creates a list of the titles for you.

When you create a query, you must identify all the fields for which you want to display information. For example, you might want only the title and the author name to display. The order in which you select the fields will be the order in which the information is displayed in the query results.

STEP-BY-STEP 17.5

1. Click the **Queries** button on the Objects bar. The query objects are displayed in the Database objects window. Note that there are currently no query objects for this database.

2. Double-click **Create query in Design View**. The Show Table dialog box shown in Figure 17-6 is displayed.

STEP-BY-STEP 17.5 Continued

FIGURE 17-6
Show Table dialog box

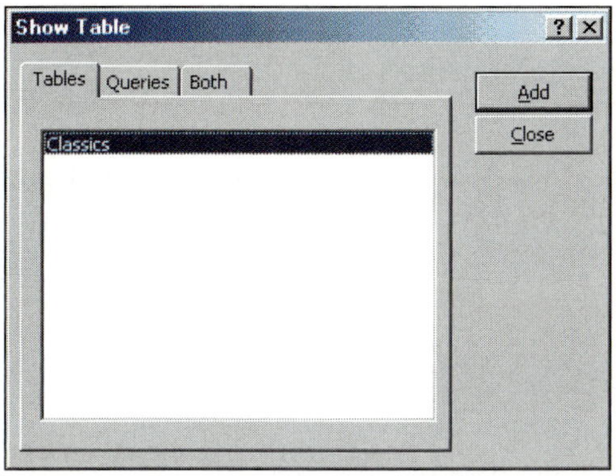

3. Click the **Add** button in the dialog box. This adds the fields from the selected table (*Classics*) to your new query.

4. Click the **Close** button in the dialog box to close the Show Table dialog box. The fields available from the *Classics* table are listed in a dialog box and the query grid shown in Figure 17-7 is displayed.

FIGURE 17-7
Query window

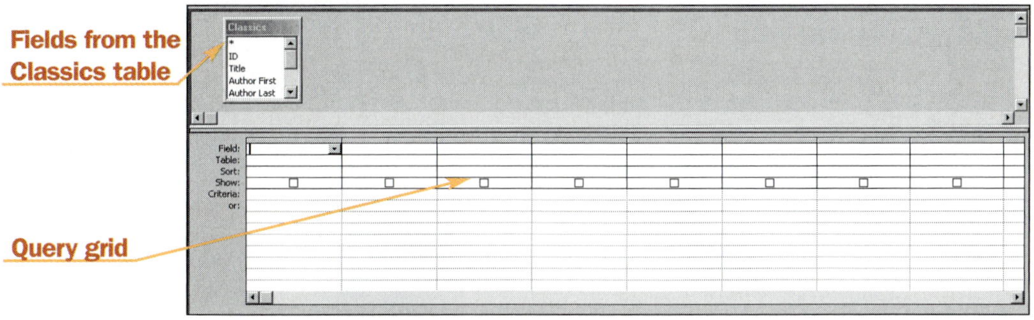

5. In the query grid, click the down arrow in the first column next to *Field*. Choose **Author Last** from the drop-down list.

6. Click in the first column next to *Criteria*. Key **Dickens** and press **Enter**. This tells Access to display any records written by authors with the last name *Dickens*. Access places quotations around the text.

7. Click in the second column next to *Field*, click the down arrow, and then select **Title** from the drop-down list. Your screen should match Figure 17-8.

> **Computer Concepts**
>
> Because databases often include more than one table, you can choose the table you want to use for the query. In this case, the database has only one table—*Classics*—and it is already selected.

STEP-BY-STEP 17.5 Continued

FIGURE 17-8
Completed query grid

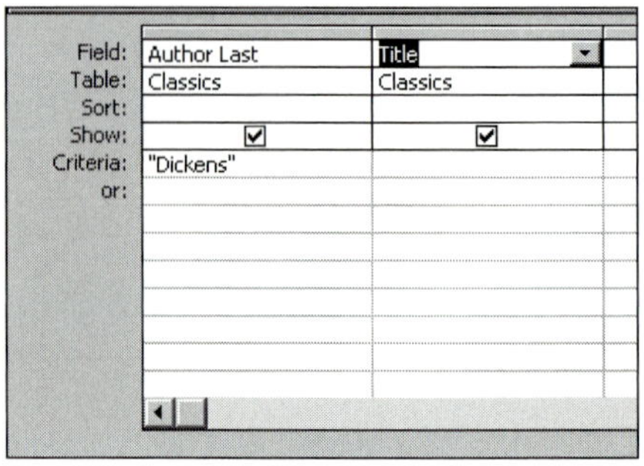

8. Click the **Save** button on the toolbar. Because the query has not yet been saved, the Save As dialog box is displayed. Key **Dickens Query** and click **OK**.

9. Open the **File** menu and choose **Close**. The query Design view is closed and the Datasheet window is displayed. The Dickens Query is in the list of Query objects.

Hot Tip

You can also double-click the query object to open it.

10. Select **Dickens Query** in the list of objects and then click the **Open** button in the Datasheet window. The results of the query are displayed as illustrated in Figure 17-9.

FIGURE 17-9
Dickens Query

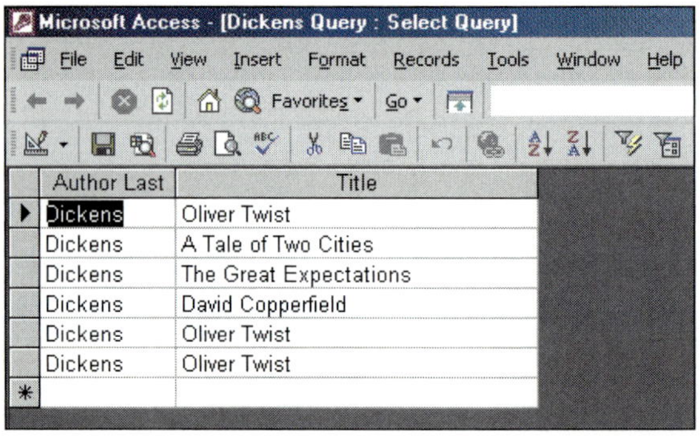

11. Close the query. Leave the database open for the next Step-by-Step.

Did You Know?

You can save a table, form, or query as a Web page. Choose **Save As HTML** on the File menu. This command will start the Publish to the Web Wizard. Follow the steps through the wizard to create your Web page.

Create a Report

You can print a database in Datasheet view, but when you do, all of the data contained in the database is printed. This can be very cumbersome if the database is large or if you only need certain information from the database. A ***report*** is a database object which allows you to organize, summarize, and print all or a portion of the data in a database. You can create a report based on a table or a query.

Although you can prepare a report manually, the Report Wizard provides an easy and fast way to design and create a report. The wizard will ask you questions about which data you want to include in the report and how you want to format that data. Most of the format options that the wizard will present are beyond the scope of this lesson. More than likely, when the options are presented in the wizard dialog boxes, you can ignore most of them.

One of the format options you will apply in the report is page orientation. The ***orientation*** determines how the report will print on the page. ***Landscape orientation*** formats the report with the long edge of the page at the top. ***Portrait orientation*** formats the report with the short edge of the page at the top.

STEP-BY-STEP 17.6

1. Click the **Reports** button on the Object bar. The report objects are displayed in the Database objects window. There are currently no reports to display for this database.

2. Double-click **Create report by using wizard**. The Report Wizard dialog box shown in Figure 17-10 is displayed. If necessary, click the down arrow in the text box under *Tables/Queries* and select **Table:Classics**.

FIGURE 17-10
Report Wizard dialog box

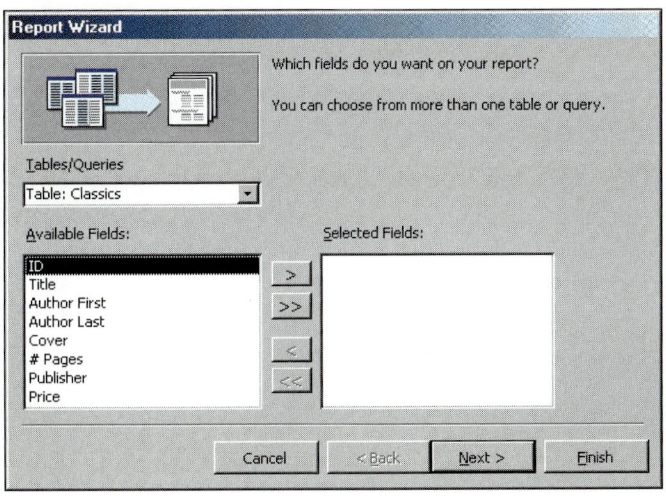

3. Choose the field names to be included in the report:
   a. Select **Author First**, then click **>** to move the field name to *Selected Fields*. The field name is displayed under *Selected Fields*.
   b. Select **Author Last** and then click **>**.
   c. Select **Title**, then click **>**.
   d. Select **Price** and then click **>**.

STEP-BY-STEP 17.6 Continued

4. Then click the **Next** button. The dialog box shown in Figure 17-11 is displayed, and it offers options for grouping a report by fields. With this report, these options are not needed.

FIGURE 17-11
Grouping level options

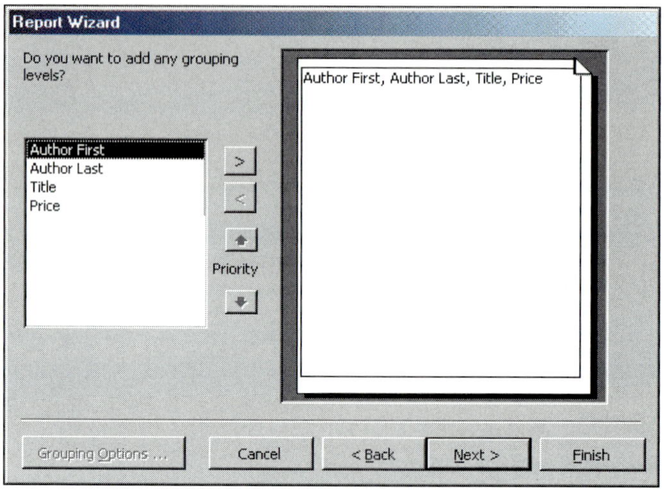

5. Click the **Next** button. The dialog box shown in Figure 17-12 is displayed, and it offers options for the sort order of the records. Click the down arrow in the first box and select **Author Last**. Click the down arrow in the second box and select **Title**. Leave the order at the default setting Ascending. If there are two or more books by the same author, the titles will be ordered first by author last name, then by the book title.

FIGURE 17-12
Sort order options

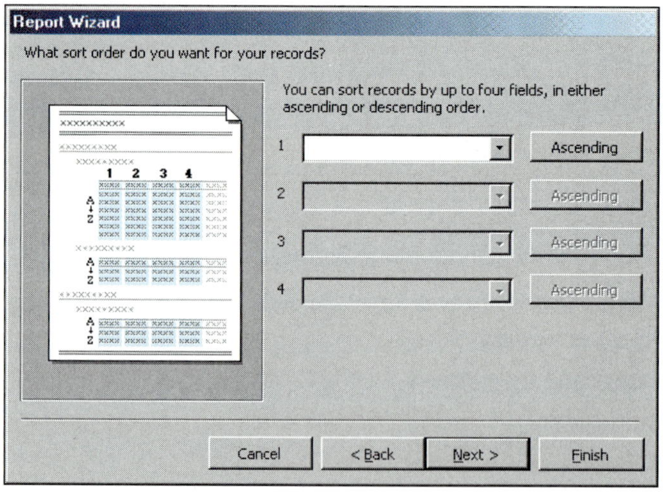

6. Click the **Next** button. The next dialog box, shown in Figure 17-13, offers options for layout and orientation. If it is not already selected, click the **Tabular** option. Then select the **Landscape** option under *Orientation*. Notice that the option to adjust the field width to fit all fields on a page is selected.

STEP-BY-STEP 17.6 Continued

FIGURE 17-13
Layout and orientation options

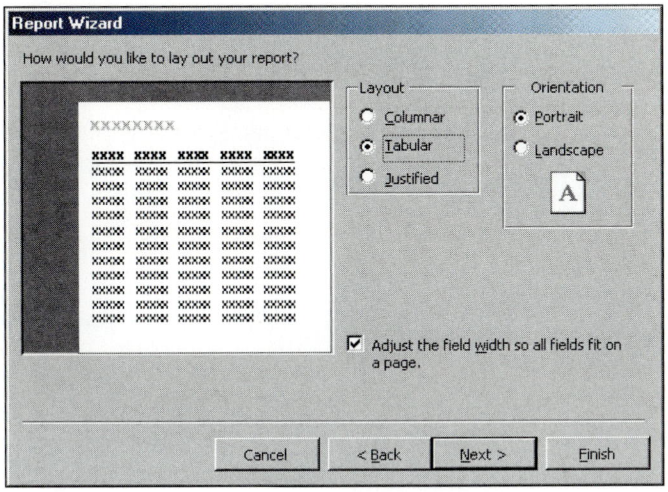

7. Click the **Next** button. The dialog box shown in Figure 17-14 is displayed, and it offers options for styles. Your dialog box may have a different style selected. Select the **Casual** style.

FIGURE 17-14
Style options

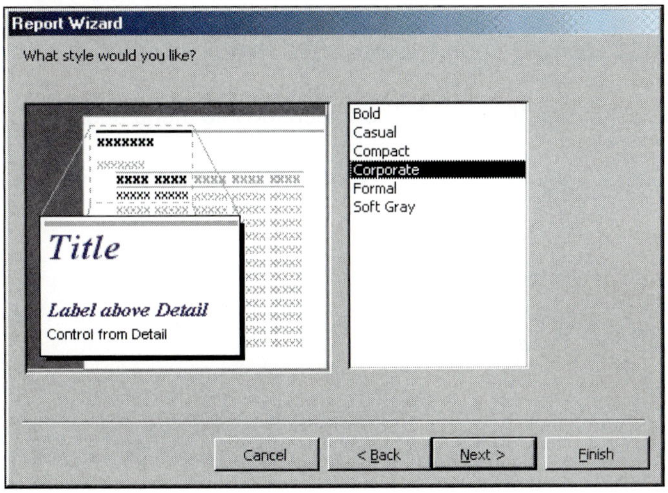

8. Click the **Next** button. The last dialog box for the Report Wizard shown in Figure 17-15 asks you what title you want to use for the report. The title currently displayed is *Classics* because that is the name of the table. Change the title to **Classic Books**.

STEP-BY-STEP 17.6 Continued

FIGURE 17-15
Title dialog box

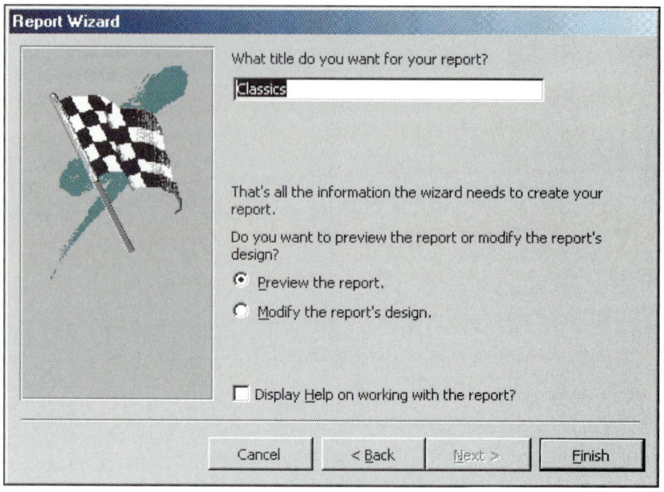

9. If necessary, click the option **Preview the report** to select it. Then click the **Finish** button. A preview of the report is displayed in Print Preview.

10. Click the down arrow to the right of the **Zoom** box on the Standard toolbar and select **75%**. The preview of the report is reduced. If necessary, reduce the zoom more so you can see the entire page.

11. Click the **Close** button on the Print Preview toolbar. The report is displayed in Design view.

12. Click the **Save** button to save the report. Then open the **File** menu and choose **Close** to close the report.

13. Notice that the Classic Books report is listed in the Database objects Reports window. Close the database.

Create Mailing Labels

Because databases often contain data regarding names and addresses, it is common to create mailing labels based on the database information. For example, if you maintain your friends' names and addresses in a database file, you can quickly print labels to mail greeting cards. You can print labels for selected friends or for the entire database. In the next Step-by-Step, you will use the report feature to create mailing labels. You will create a new report using a different wizard.

STEP-BY-STEP 17.7

1. Open **Step17-7** from the data files.

2. If necessary, click the **Reports** button on the Object bar. There are no reports to display for this database.

STEP-BY-STEP 17.7 Continued

3. If necessary, click the **New** button in the Database objects toolbar. The New Report dialog box is displayed.

4. Select **Label Wizard**. Click the down arrow in the list box below and select **Mailing List**. When your dialog box looks like the one illustrated in Figure 17-16, click **OK**.

FIGURE 17-16
New Report dialog box

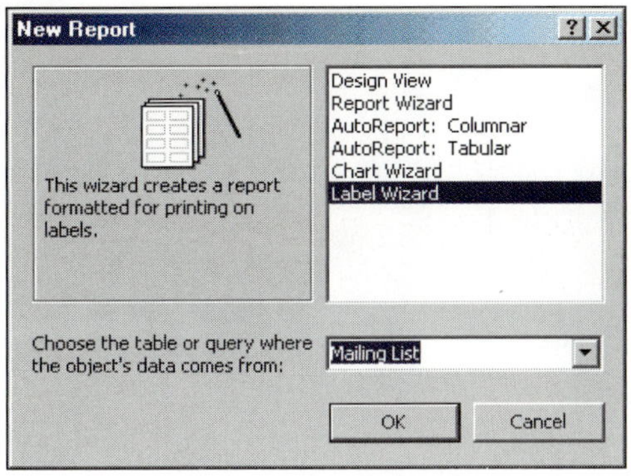

5. The Label Wizard dialog box is displayed. If necessary, select **Sheet feed** under *Label Type*. And, if necessary, select **Avery** in the Filter by manufacturer list box. Scroll down in the first list box above and select Product number **3110** (or another product number with three labels across and no larger than 1 ¼" × 2 ⅜").

6. When your dialog box looks like Figure 17-17, click **Next**.

FIGURE 17-17
Label Wizard dialog box displaying selected label options

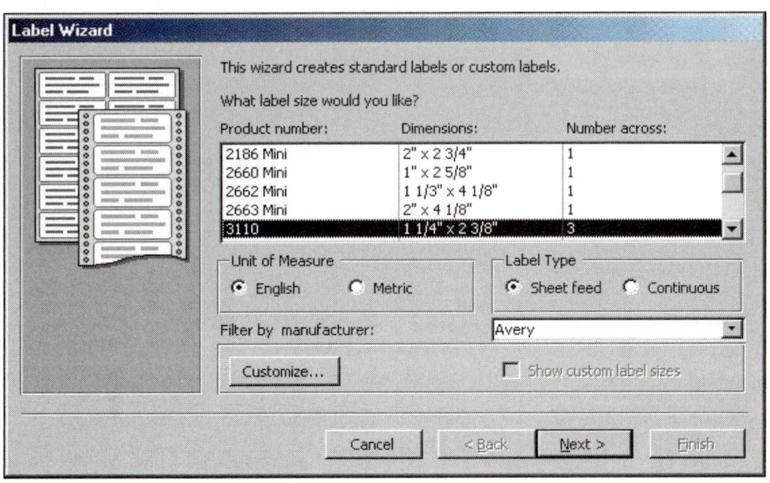

7. The next step in the wizard is to describe the text appearance on the mailing label. If necessary, change the Font size to **10**. If necessary, change the other options so your dialog box looks like the one shown in Figure 17-18. Then, click **Next**.

STEP-BY-STEP 17.7 Continued

FIGURE 17-18
Label Wizard dialog box displaying selected font options

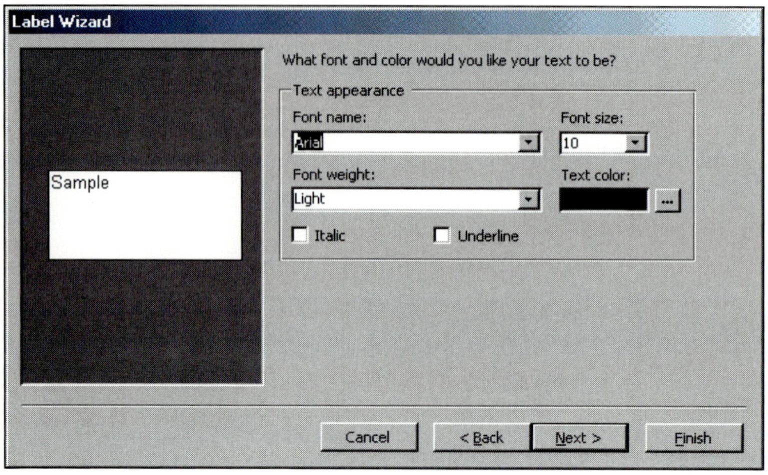

8. The next step in the wizard is to choose the fields. From the Available Fields list, construct a prototype (a sample) for the labels. Select the fields as shown in Figure 17-19. (*Hint:* Select the field name from the Available Fields list, and then click **>**. Leave a blank space between fields, and press **Enter** to move to the next line. It is not necessary to key a comma after the field *City*.) When your dialog box looks like Figure 17-19, click **Next**.

FIGURE 17-19
Label Wizard dialog box displaying a prototype label

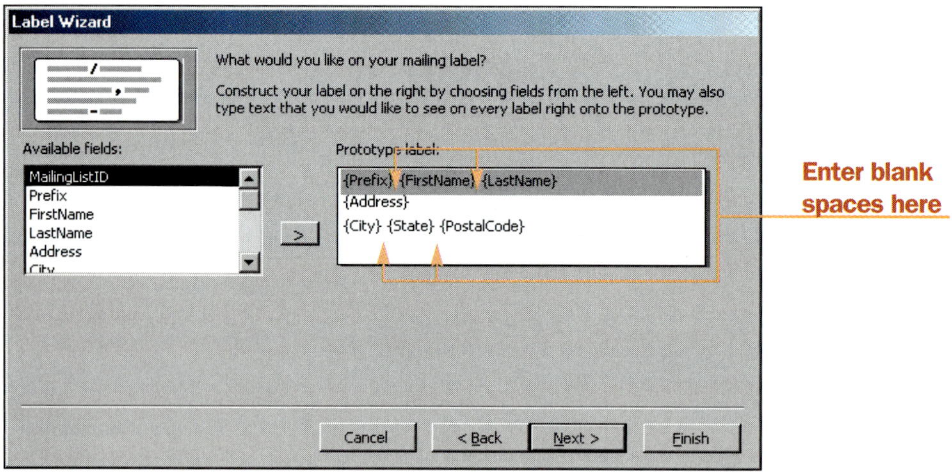

9. The next step in the wizard is to sort the labels. Scroll down and select the **PostalCode** field from the Available Fields list and then click **>**. The field name is moved to the Sort by list. When your dialog box looks like Figure 17-20, click **Next**.

STEP-BY-STEP 17.7 Continued

FIGURE 17-20
Label Wizard dialog box displaying the selected sort options

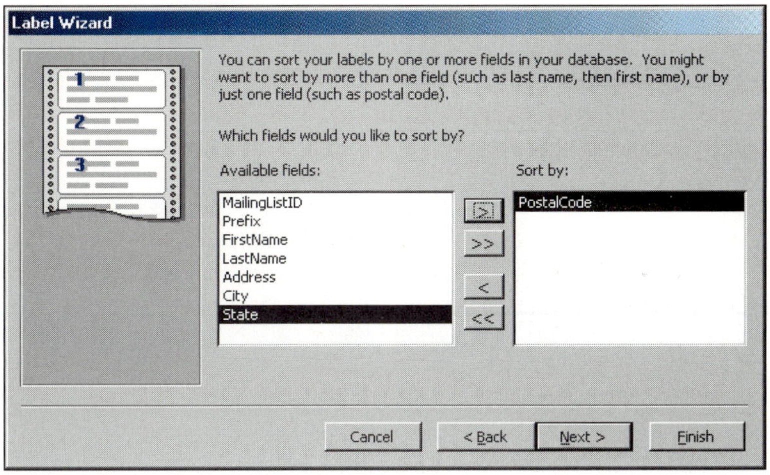

10. The last step in the wizard is to name the report. You can assign a name to the report if desired, but the proposed name *Labels Mailing List* is good. Click **Finish**. If you get a message indicating that some data may not be displayed, click **OK**. The labels are displayed as they will print. If you were printing the labels, you would put the label sheets in your printer and choose the command to print.

11. Open the **File** menu and choose **Close** to close the report. Notice that the Labels Mailing List report is listed in the Database objects Reports window. Close the database.

SUMMARY

In this lesson, you learned:

- You can sort records in Datasheet view in either ascending or descending order.
- The Find command can save you time looking for records and specific values in a table. The Replace command can save you time finding and replacing specific text.
- You can create a query to find records that match specified criteria. Access searches for and retrieves data from the table(s) that match the criteria you identify.
- A report allows you to organize, summarize, and print all or a portion of the data in a database. You can choose a wizard to guide you through the process in creating and formatting a report.
- When you want to create mailing labels, you create a report object and you use the Label wizard.

VOCABULARY *Review*

Define the following terms:

Ascending order	Orientation	Query
Descending order	Portrait orientation	Report
Landscape orientation		

REVIEW *Questions*

TRUE/FALSE

Circle T if the statement is true or F if the statement is false.

T F 1. If you change your mind after you sort data, you can choose the Undo command to return the data to its original order.

T F 2. You can use the Find command to locate specific data in a particular field or anywhere in the table.

T F 3. The Replace command replaces existing data with new data.

T F 4. You can use the Find command to make a list of multiple records that match specific criteria.

T F 5. The Report Wizard guides you through the process of organizing and summarizing data in a database.

FILL IN THE BLANK

Complete the following sentences by writing the correct word or words in the blanks provided.

1. If you have several records in a database, you can easily locate data you are searching for by using the __________ command.

2. If you want to sort data with the most recent date at the top of the list, you would choose __________ order.

3. A(n) __________ enables you to locate multiple records, all matching the same criteria.

4. __________ orientation prints the report with the long edge of the page at the top.

5. You can base a report on either a(n) __________ or a(n) __________.

PROJECTS

PROJECT 17-1

1. Open **Project17-1** from the data files. Open the **Members** table.
2. You want to make sure that you added a new member to the database. Find the record for *Sam Martin.*
3. Oak Creek is growing rapidly and has earned another zip code. Find all the 43210 zip codes in the table and change them to **43213**.
4. You would like to have a list of member names and phone numbers to hand out to all members. Create a report as follows:
   A. Start the Report Wizard and choose the **Members** table.
   B. Select only the **First Name, Last Name,** and **Phone** fields.
   C. Do not group the report.
   D. Sort the report by **Last Name** in ascending order.
   E. Use the **Tabular** format and **Portrait** orientation.
   F. Choose the **Bold** style.
   G. Name the report **Members Phone List** and preview the report.
5. Close the preview, and then close the database.

PROJECT 17-2

1. Open **Project17-2** database, and then open the **Collection** table.
2. Sort the table by **Category** in ascending order. How many adventure films do you have in the collection?
3. Sort the table by **Length** in descending order. What is the longest film in the collection?
4. Close the table without saving design changes.
5. For an upcoming society meeting, you want to see the titles, directors, and lengths of all foreign films in the collection. Follow these steps to create your query:
   A. Create a new query in Design view using the **Collection** table.
   B. Add the **Category**, **Title**, **Director**, and **Length** fields to the query, in that order.
   C. In the Category Criteria box, key **Foreign.**
   D. Save the query as **Foreign Query.**
6. Open the query. How many foreign titles do you have in the collection? Close the query results.
7. You are considering doing a special event on several directors. Create a report that will show you what films you have by each director. Follow these steps to create the report:
   A. Create a new report using the Report Wizard based on the **Collection** table. Select the **Director, Title,** and **Year** fields for the report, in that order.
   B. Do not add any grouping levels.
   C. Sort the report by **Director.**
   D. Choose the **Columnar** layout and **Portrait** orientation.
   E. Use the **Compact** style.
   F. Name the report **Directors Report** and preview the report.

8. Close the preview and then close the database.

WEB PROJECT

Use Web search tools to find information on the worst natural disasters of the twentieth century in the United States. These disasters can include earthquakes, tornadoes, hurricanes, winter storms, and so on. Create categories for each type of disaster you identify. Try to find as much information about the disasters as you can: injuries, deaths, property damage, location of the disaster, date and time of the disaster, and so on. Create a database table to store the information you find. Sort the data to find the most injuries and the greatest property damage. Create a query that locates all natural disasters in a particular state, such as California. Create a report from selected data in your table.

TEAMWORK PROJECT

If you have completed any of the Web Projects in this unit, you have visited a number of sites and employed a number of useful tools such as search engines, directories, and almanacs. With the help of a partner, create a database table to store data on some of the tools you have used and sites you have visited. If you have not completed any of the Web Projects, you can still explore the Web now on your own to try out various search tools and locate interesting and useful sites. Or, if you do not have Web access, create a database that stores reference materials you use regularly in your classes, such as encyclopedias, dictionaries, almanacs, and so on. Then create a report from your data.

Follow these steps:

1. With your teammate, make a list of the Web search tools (or other reference materials) you have used in this course. You can categorize them as search engines, directories, or other online resources. Record the URLs of these various resources, and make a few notes about what type of information you can get from each search tool. Create a database table to store the information.

2. Create another table to store information on various sites (or articles) you have visited. Record the URL of the site and what type of data you found there. Have your teammate help you remember the sites.

3. Create a report for each table so that you will have a hard copy of useful tools and sites.

CRITICAL *Thinking*

ACTIVITY 17-1

Creating a query isn't the only way you can display specific records in a database. You can use what is called a filter. Open the **Project17-1** database and then open the **Collection** table. Click in any Category field that reads *Shakespeare*. Click the toolbar button just to the right of the Sort Descending button. What happens to the table?

Use the Help files in Access to find out what kind of a filter you just applied. How do you redisplay all the records in the table?

LESSON 18

WORKING WITH OUTLOOK

OBJECTIVES

Upon completion of this lesson, you should be able to:

- Identify the parts of the Outlook screen.
- Schedule and manage appointments.
- Create and manage contacts.
- Organize and manage tasks.
- Send and receive e-mail.

Estimated Time: 1 hour

VOCABULARY

Ascending order
Contacts
Descending order
Event
Field
Form
Item

Microsoft Outlook is a program that can help you organize your appointments, addresses, tasks, and e-mail messages. Outlook stores information in folders. Each Outlook folder can organize different types of information and makes it easy for you to store many kinds of personal and business information and then display it at the touch of a button. A particular piece of information stored in an Outlook folder is called an ***item.***

IC³ 2-1.2.1-1

Identify the Parts of the Outlook Screen

When you launch Outlook, a screen similar to the one shown in Figure 18-1 is displayed. Like other Office programs, Outlook displays both a menu bar and the Standard toolbar. You can display or hide toolbars by opening the View menu, choosing Toolbars, and then selecting the toolbar name. The Preview Pane enables you to preview the content of any item. You can display or hide the Preview Pane by opening the View menu and choosing Preview Pane. You will learn more about each part of the window in this lesson.

Hot Tip

Your Outlook Bar may display different icons than shown in Figure 18-1. You can customize the Outlook Bar by adding or removing shortcut icons. To add a new shortcut, right-click the background of the Outlook Bar, choose **Outlook Bar Shortcut**, and in the Add to Outlook Bar dialog box select the folder you want to add. To delete a shortcut, right-click the shortcut and choose **Remove from Outlook Bar**.

FIGURE 18-1
The Outlook window

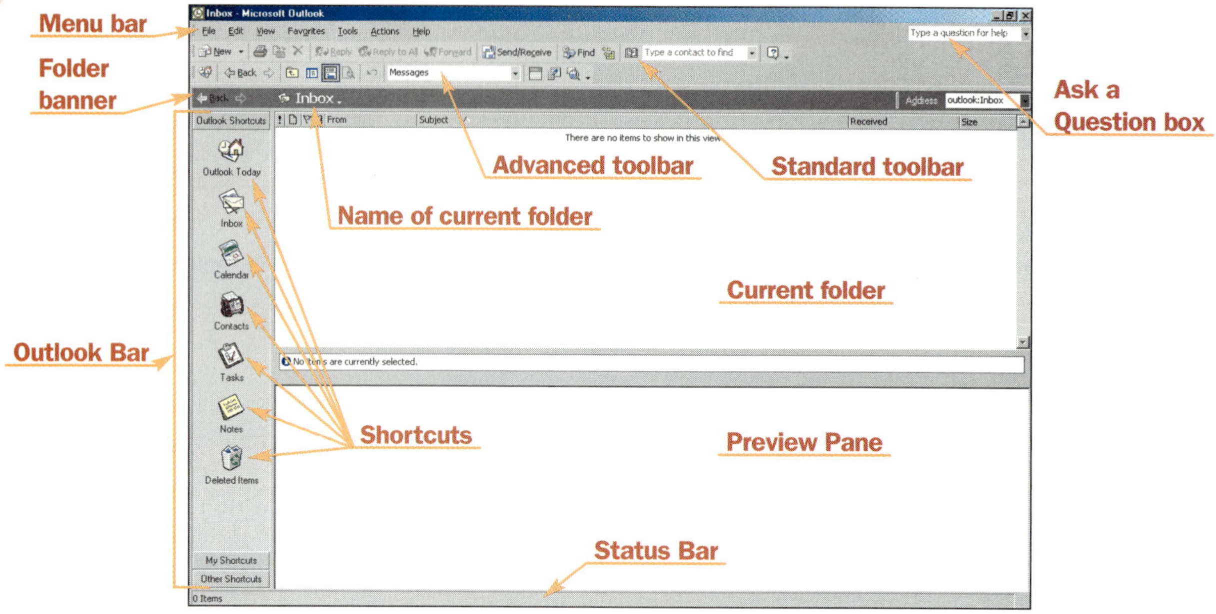

There are different Outlook folders, and you use each one to perform a different function. The name of the current Outlook folder appears in the folder banner, which is the shaded area located at the top of the window. Figure 18-1 shows the Inbox folder. If your current folder isn't the Inbox folder, your screen will display a different folder.

Table 18-1 lists some of the Outlook folders and how you use them. You can quickly access different folders using the shortcuts in the Outlook Bar at the left of the window. To select what displays in the Outlook window, you can change the view settings for each file folder.

TABLE 18-1
Outlook folders and their functions

OUTLOOK BAR SHORTCUT/ FOLDER NAME	USE THIS FOLDER TO
Inbox	Send, receive, and organize e-mail messages.
Calendar	Schedule appointments, meetings, and events.
Contacts	Store information such as names, addresses, phone numbers, and e-mail addresses.
Outlook Today	Get an overview of some of your current Outlook information.
Tasks	Create lists of things you need to do.
Deleted Items	Store items you have deleted from other folders.

You will not use all of Outlook's folders in this lesson, but in the following Step-by-Step you will take a short tour of Outlook by opening several Outlook folders. Most Outlook folders can be customized to display information in a folder in a number of different ways. When you open a folder, you will see the view that was used the last time that folder was opened.

STEP-BY-STEP 18.1

1. Launch Outlook. If your computer is on a network, you may be prompted to enter your profile name and a password when launching Outlook. If a dialog box appears asking you to make Outlook your default program for e-mail, Calendar and Contacts, click **No**.

2. Click the **Calendar** shortcut in the Outlook Bar. This folder contains features that help you set up appointments and meetings. If no one has entered any meetings in Outlook yet, this folder will be empty.

3. Click the **Contacts** shortcut in the Outlook Bar. This folder stores information about personal and business contacts. If no one has entered any contacts in Outlook yet, this folder will be empty.

4. Click the **Tasks** shortcut in the Outlook Bar. This folder displays a grid in which you can enter information about tasks you want to accomplish. If no one has yet entered any tasks in Outlook, this folder will be empty.

5. Click the **Deleted Items** shortcut. The Deleted Items folder opens. Any time you delete items from other folders, the items are stored here until you delete them permanently. If no one has deleted any items in Outlook, this folder will be empty.

6. Click the **Calendar** shortcut again to return to the Calendar folder. Leave this folder open for the next Step-by-Step.

Computer Concepts

Clicking the **Outlook Today** shortcut in the Outlook Bar will show you all tasks and appointments for the current day. It will also indicate how many new e-mail messages you have. You can set this page to be the opening page when you launch Outlook.

Hot Tip

You can quickly launch Outlook by clicking the **Outlook** button on the Windows taskbar.

Computer Concepts

AutoArchive is a default feature that automatically clears out old and expired items from folders, such as old e-mails or expired meetings scheduled on the calendar. If a dialog box appears asking you to archive deleted files, check with your instructor regarding what your response should be.

Hot Tip

You can also change folders by opening the **View** menu, choosing **Folder List**, and then selecting the folder name in the Folder List. Or, Open the **View** menu, choose **Go To**, select **Folder**, and then select the folder name.

Hot Tip

You can also open a folder by clicking the folder name in the folder banner to display a list of folder names. To go to a folder on the list, just click the folder name.

Schedule and Manage Appointments

The Calendar folder shown in Figure 18-2 contains three separate areas that help you create and keep track of appointments. You can use the Appointment Book to create and display your appointments. The Date Navigator helps you to locate and display dates in the past or future. The TaskPad displays items from your Tasks list.

FIGURE 18-2
Calendar Folder

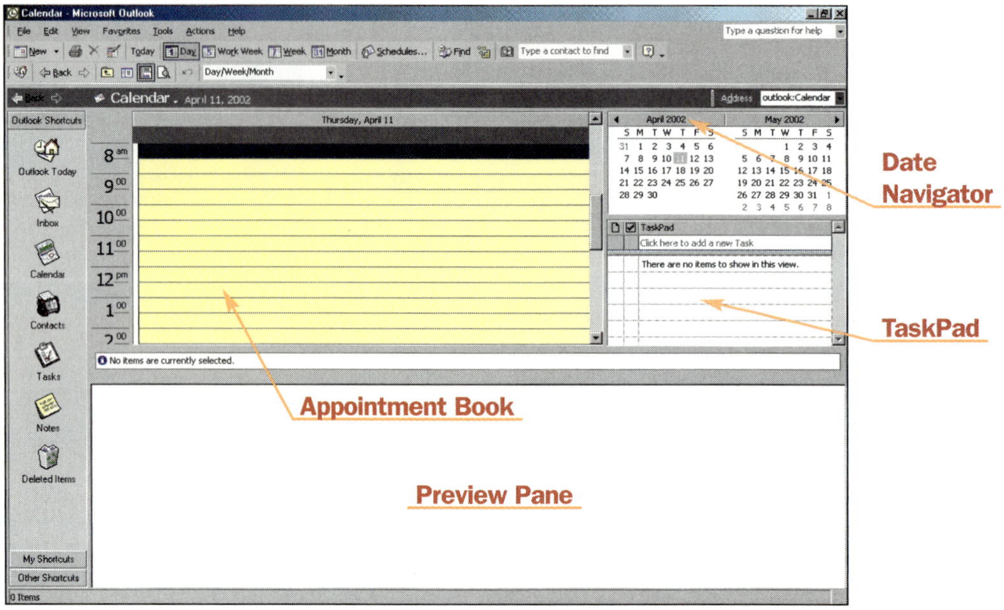

Schedule an Appointment

To schedule an appointment, display the day of the appointment and then select New Appointment from the Actions menu. Outlook provides a ***form*** with preset controls to help you enter the right information for your appointment. For example, there are controls for subject, location, start time, and end time. Each piece of information in the form is called a ***field***. After you save and close the form, the appointment appears in the Appointment Book.

You can view the contents of an item in the Preview Pane without opening the item. However, to edit the item, you must first open the item and make the changes in a form. To open the item, double-click the item.

Did You Know?

While working in Outlook, you can view and work with files or folders saved on local or network disks in Outlook. Click **Other Shortcuts** at the bottom of the Outlook Bar to display shortcuts to My Computer, My Documents, and Favorites. When you click one of these shortcuts, Outlook displays the files and folders similar to the way they are displayed in Microsoft Windows Explorer except that, in Outlook, more information is displayed and there are more ways to view the contents of a folder. You can also use Outlook to view Web pages so you don't have to leave Outlook and open your browser. For example, you can go to a Web page from a link in an e-mail.

STEP-BY-STEP 18.2

1. If necessary, open the **View** menu and choose **Preview Pane** to display the Preview Pane of the Calendar folder.

2. In the Date Navigator, click the date that is one week from today. The date at the top of the Appointment Book changes to that date.

3. Click the **New Appointment** button on the Standard Toolbar. The Untitled - Appointment form opens.

4. The insertion point is positioned in the Subject text box. Key **Dr. Savin** in this text box.

5. Click in the **Location** text box. Notice that the dialog box title bar now displays *Dr. Savin - Appointment*. Key **Lakeside Medical**.

6. Notice that the date you selected is already entered in the first set of Start Time and End Time list boxes. Click in the second Start Time list box (it currently displays *8:00 AM*) to display the drop-down list, and select **10:00 AM**.

7. Outlook always assumes your appointment will take half an hour. Change the length of the appointment by clicking the down arrow of the second End Time list box and selecting **11:00 AM (1 hour)**. Your form box should now look like the one shown in Figure 18-3.

> **Hot Tip**
>
> You can also right-click at the time for the appointment and select **New Appointment** from the shortcut menu or double-click at the appointment time to display the dialog box. You can also open the **Actions** menu and choose **New Appointment**.

> **Computer Concepts**
>
> Notice that the reminder option is checked. Outlook will remind you of your appointment with a sound effect. You can select the reminder sound and specify how far ahead of the appointment Outlook should remind you.

FIGURE 18-3
Completed Appointment form

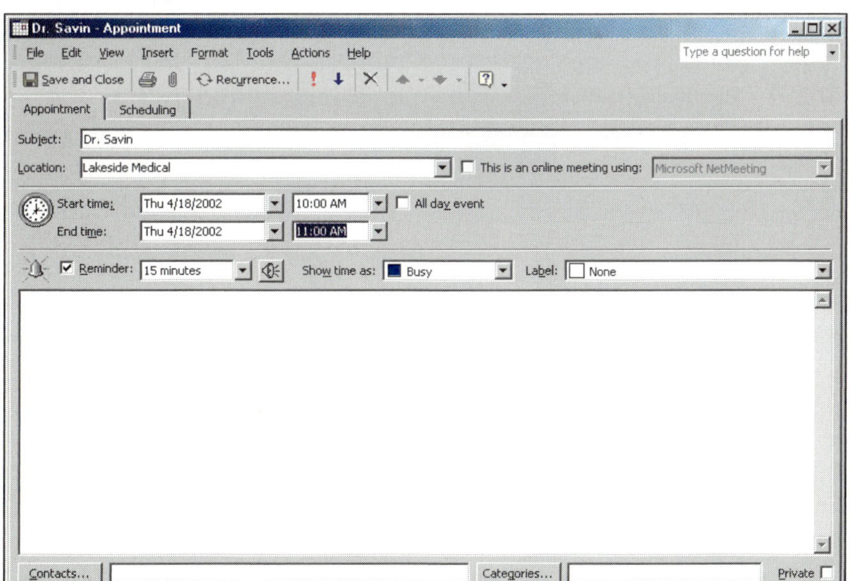

STEP-BY-STEP 18.2 Continued

8. Click the **Save and Close** button at the top of the form to save the appointment information and close the form. The appointment is displayed in your Appointment Book. The bell symbol indicates that you will receive an audible reminder about the appointment.

Schedule Recurring Appointments

Some appointments occur repeatedly, such as a weekly club meeting or a monthly board meeting. You can designate these appointments as recurring. You simply indicate how frequently the meeting will occur, and Outook will set up all the appointments within the time period specified.

STEP-BY-STEP 18.3

1. Open the **Actions** menu and choose **New Recurring Appointment**. The Appointment Recurrence form is displayed.

2. Under *Appointment time*, set the Start time at **7:00 PM** and the End time at **9:00 PM (2 hours)**.

3. In the left side of the Recurrence pattern section, select **Monthly**. Then select the second option on the right beginning with the word *The*. Select **second** in the first text box and select **Tuesday** in the second text box.

4. Compare your form with the completed form shown in Figure 18-4 to make sure you have selected all the correct options. Make any necessary changes. Note that your dates will be different than those shown in the figure.

> **Speech Recognition**
>
> If your computer has speech recognition capability, enable the Command mode and say the commands to open the Appointment Recurrence form and schedule the appointments.

FIGURE 18-4
Completed Appointment Recurrence form

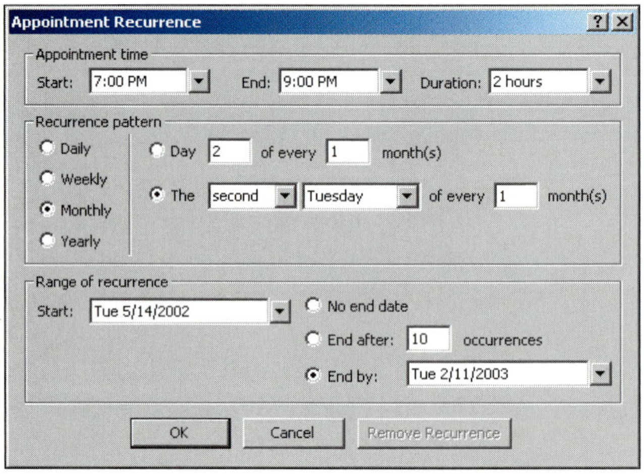

STEP-BY-STEP 18.3 Continued

5. Click **OK** to save the recurrence information. The Untitled – Appointment form is still displayed, and the appointment has not yet been saved. For the subject for the recurring meeting, enter **Club Board Meeting**. For the location, enter **Community Center**.

6. Click the **Save and Close** button to save the recurring appointment information and close the form.

7. Notice that the second Tuesday of each month from this point forward is highlighted in the Date Navigator. Click that highlighted date in the Date Navigator to display the appointments for that date. Scroll down to 7:00 PM in the Appointment Book. Notice that the monthly meeting at the Community Center is scheduled. If you check the second Tuesday for any upcoming month, the meeting is scheduled from 7:00 to 9:00 PM. Leave the Calendar folder open for the next Step-by-Step.

Use Help to Learn How to Schedule an Event

Appointments usually take place on a specific day at a specific time. You can also, however, schedule an event. An ***event*** is a scheduled item in the Outlook calendar that lasts 24 hours or longer. Examples of events are vacations, or an annual event that occurs every year, such as a birthday or anniversary. You can use Microsoft Outlook Help to learn how to create an event in the Appointment Book.

STEP-BY-STEP 18.4

1. Click the **Office Assistant** or open the **Help** menu and choose **Microsoft Outlook Help**. Key **create an event** in the text box and click the **Search** button.

2. If necessary, click the **Create an all-day event** link to display a Help window about scheduling an all-day event.

3. Read the information on scheduling an event. Close the Help window and then use what you have learned to schedule an event the day after your appointment with Dr. Savin. Key **Jobs Fair** for the subject of the event and **Wilson Center** as the location of the event. Save and close the form.

4. Notice that the all-day event appears at the top of the Appointment Book. Leave the Calendar folder open for the next Step-by-Step.

Did You Know?

You can also quickly access Help screens by entering your search text in the Ask a Question box and then pressing **Enter**.

Change Views and Delete Appointments

All Outlook folders allow you to change your view of the items in the folder. Different views can show you more detail about the items or help you focus on a specific kind of item stored in the folder. For example, you can view the active appointments, the recurring appointments, or the events in your calendar.

In the Calendar folder, you can also change the view of your current appointments and events using the four view buttons on the Standard toolbar. Click these buttons to view your appointments by day, by work week (Monday through Friday), by week (Monday through Sunday), or by month.

You can delete an appointment if you no longer need it. Deleted items are automatically moved to the Deleted Items folder and will stay in that folder until deleted permanently. If you change your mind about a deletion, you can retrieve the item from the Deleted Items folder.

STEP-BY-STEP 18.5

1. Open the **View** menu and choose **Current View**. Select **Active Appointments** in the submenu. Your appointments display in a grid so you can easily see all of them at once.

2. Open the **View** menu, choose **Current View**, and then select **Day/Week/Month** to return to the previous view.

3. Click the **Month** button on the Standard toolbar. A monthly calendar displays with your appointments listed on the appropriate days. Click the **Day** button to return to the previous view where you can see the Date Navigator and the TaskPad.

4. Use the Date Navigator to go to the day on which you have an appointment with Dr. Savin. (*Hint:* The date is highlighted.) Click the appointment with Dr. Savin and then click the **Delete** button on the Standard toolbar. The appointment is moved to the Deleted Items folder.

5. Move to the next day and click the jobs fair event name at the top of the Appointment Book. Click the **Delete** button to remove the event.

6. Delete the recurring monthly board meeting. When you click the Delete button, the dialog box shown in Figure 18-5 will display. Select the option **Delete the series.** and then click **OK**. Leave Outlook open for the next Step-by-Step.

FIGURE 18-5
Confirm Delete dialog box

Create and Manage Contacts

The ***Contacts*** folder allows you to store many kinds of information about people you work with or communicate with on a regular basis. As you insert information about a contact, Outlook creates an address card for that contact. Outlook arranges the address cards in alphabetical order so you can easily locate each one. Figure 18-6 shows two address cards in the Contacts folder.

FIGURE 18-6
Business and personal contacts in the Contacts folder

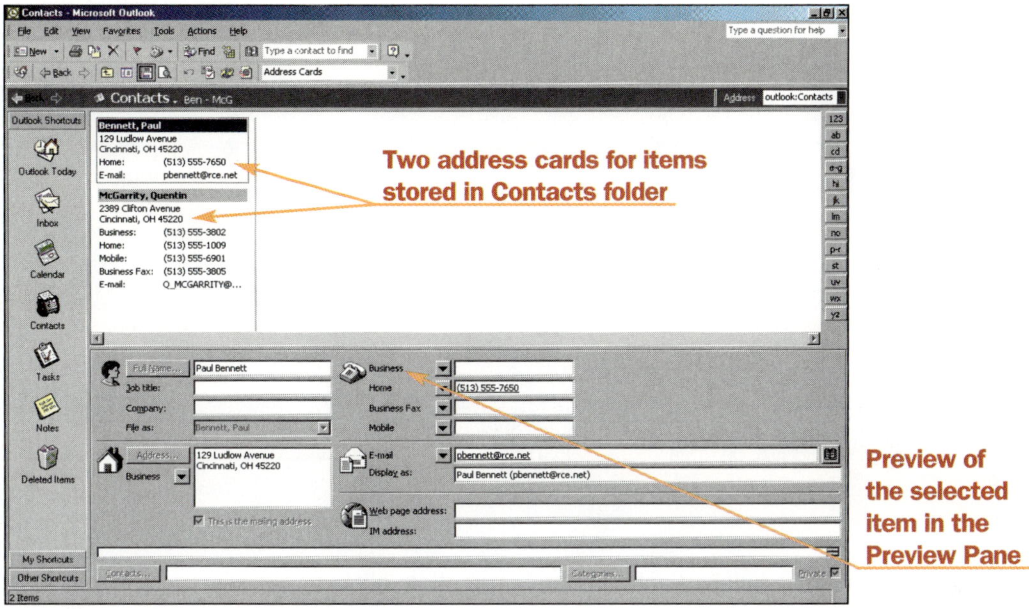

Add a New Contact

To add a new contact, choose New Contact from the Actions menu. Outlook displays a dialog box with a number of tabs. You can fill in as much or as little information on these tabs as you like. After you complete the dialog box, Outlook adds a new address card to the Contacts folder.

STEP-BY-STEP 18.6

1. Click the **Contacts** shortcut to open the Contacts folder.
2. Open the **View** menu, choose **Current View**, and select **Address Cards** on the submenu, if necessary.
3. Open the **Actions** menu and choose **New Contact**. The Untitled - Contact form opens.
4. Click in the Full Name text box and key **Jane Treadway**. This is the way the contact will be filed in the Contacts folder.
5. Press **Tab** to move the insertion point to the next text box. Notice the dialog box name changes to Jane Treadway – Contact and the File as text box below automatically fills in *Treadway, Jane*. Key **Office Manager** in the Job title text box.
6. Press **Tab** to go to the next text box and key **Williston Associates**.
7. Click in the Address text box and key the address shown in Figure 18-7. Then key the remaining information shown in the figure.

Hot Tip

You can also double-click in any blank space in the **Contacts** folder (not the Preview Pane) to display the Untitled – Contact form or you can click the **New** button on the Standard toolbar.

STEP-BY-STEP 18.6 Continued

FIGURE 18-7
Contact information for Jane Treadway

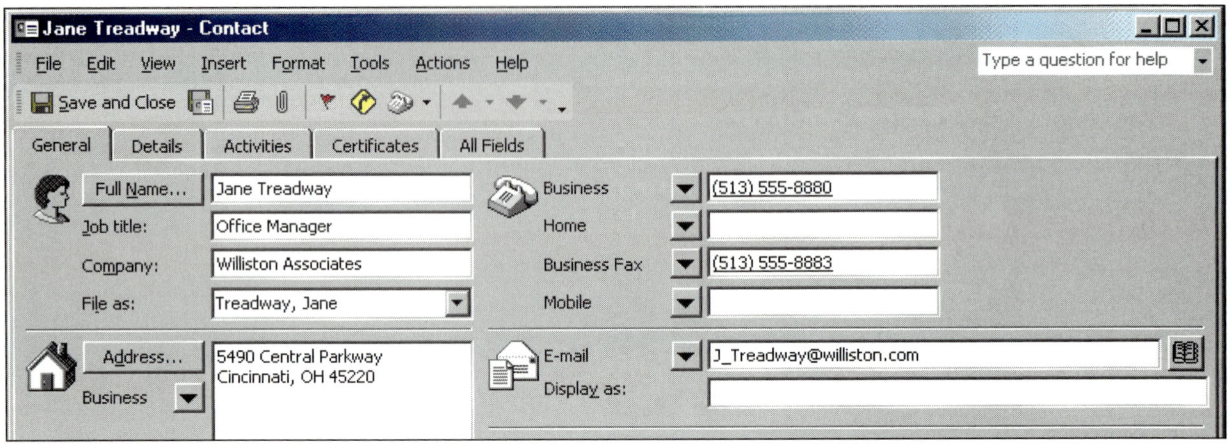

8. When you have finished entering the information, click the **Save and Close** button. If you are prompted to designate the contact as a Small Business Customer Manager contact, click **No**. The form closes and the contact information appears in the Contacts folder.

> **Hot Tip**
>
> If you click the **Full Name** button in the Untitled – Contact dialog box, a Check Full Name form will display. This form will help you complete all the necessary information including title, first, middle, and last names, and a suffix if applicable.

9. Add another contact from Williston Associates:
   a. Open the **Actions** menu and choose **New Contact from Same Company**. The Williston Associates – Contact form is displayed, with the business address and business phone and fax numbers already entered.
   b. Enter the name **Penny Cantin**. Penny's job title is **Marketing Manager**. Her e-mail address is **P_Cantin@williston.com**.
   c. Click the **Save and Close** button. If prompted to designate the contact as a Small Business Customer Manager contact, click **No**.

10. Notice that as the new contact is entered, Outlook places the address cards in alphabetical order by last name. Leave the Contacts folder open for the next Step-by-Step.

Change Views and Delete Address Cards

You might wonder why Jane Treadway's and Penny Cantin's job title and company name information do not display on their address card. The Address Card view does not show these details. To see all the information you insert for your contacts, you need to use the Detailed Address Cards view.

You can easily remove an address card from the contacts list. In the next Step-by-Step, you will remove one of the contacts you added.

STEP-BY-STEP 18.7

1. Open the **View** menu and choose **Current View**. Select **Detailed Address Cards** in the submenu. You can now see all information on the address cards.

2. Open the **View** menu and choose **Current View**. Select **Address Cards** to return to the original view.

3. Click the address card for **Penny Cantin** to select it. The bar behind the name changes to a color to indicate it is the active card. (If this contact is the first one in the list, it may already be selected.)

4. Click the **Delete** button on the Standard toolbar to remove the contact. Leave Outlook open for the next Step-by-Step.

Organize and Manage Tasks

The Tasks folder helps you organize things you have to do. You can use the Tasks list as you would a to-do list. You can add tasks, reorganize them if one task suddenly becomes more important than another, and cross each task off as you finish it.

Tasks are displayed in a grid, as shown in Figure 18-8. Depending on the view you are working in, you have a number of columns of information about each task. In Figure 18-8, the Subject and Due Date columns tell you the name of each task and the day it should be completed.

> **Computer Concepts**
>
> You can also enter a new task by opening the **Actions** menu and choosing **New Task** or by clicking the **New Task** button on the Standard toolbar to open the Untitled - Task dialog box. You enter all task information in the dialog box and then click **Save and Close** to add the task to the list.

FIGURE 18-8
Tasks folder with three tasks displayed

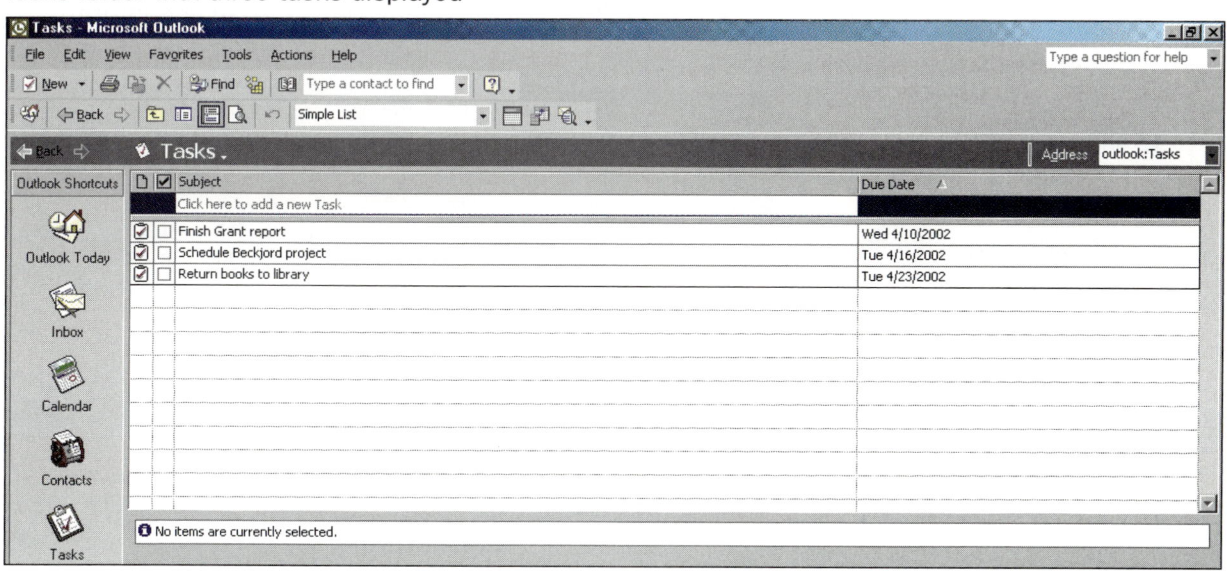

Add and Work with Tasks

The easiest way to add a new task is to display the Tasks folder and click in the box that reads *Click here to add a new Task*. When you do, the Subject box becomes active so you can key the name of the task you want to add. Press Tab to move to the next column, just as you would when entering text in a worksheet or a table, and enter the information required in that column.

As you enter each task, Outlook keeps your tasks in order by due date. You can sort the tasks to display them in a different order. ***Ascending order*** sorts alphabetically from A to Z and numerically from the lowest to the highest number. ***Descending order*** sorts alphabetically from Z to A and numerically from the highest to the lowest number. The Subject column header will display a triangle pointing either upward or downard, indicating the sort order.

To sort the tasks, click the heading of the column you want to sort by. For example, to sort tasks by name, click the Subject column header.

STEP-BY-STEP 18.8

1. In the Outlook Bar, click the **Tasks** shortcut to open the Tasks folder.
2. Open the **View** menu, choose **Current View**, and then select **Simple List** from the submenu, if necessary.
3. Click in the box that reads **Click here to add a new Task**. Key **Return books to library** and then press **Tab**. Key the date that is two weeks from today's date and press **Enter**. Outlook will automatically add the day of the week to your date.
4. The Subject box is currently selected so you can enter another task. Key **Schedule Beckjord project** and then press **Tab**. Key the date that is one week from today's date and press **Enter**.
5. Add another new task: Key **Finish Grant report** and then press **Tab**. Key tomorrow's date and press **Enter**.
6. The tasks are currently displayed in chronological order by due date. To display the tasks in alphabetical order by subject, click the **Subject** column header. The tasks are listed in ascending order and the *Finish Grant report* task now appears at the top of the list. Notice that the *Subject* column header displays a triangle pointing upward.
7. Click the **Subject** column header again, and the tasks are listed in descending order and the *Finish Grant report* task appears at the bottom of the list. Notice that the *Subject* column header displays a triangle pointing downward.
8. To display the tasks in order by due date, click the **Due Date** column header. Notice that the tasks appear in descending date order and a triangle pointing downward displays in the column header.

Computer Concepts

You can double-click on a task to open the task form and display details about the task. You can use this form to enter information about the status of the task, the number of hours worked, mileage, billing information, and so forth.

Did You Know?

If you switch to the Calendar after entering tasks, you will see your tasks in the TaskPad.

STEP-BY-STEP 18.8 Continued

9. Click the **Due Date** column header again to display the tasks in ascending date order. Leave the Tasks folder open for the next Step-by-Step.

> **Hot Tip**
>
> You can format a reminder so Outlook will display a message to remind you when the task is due. Double-click the task to open the task form. Then check the reminder option and select a date and time.

Marking Tasks as Complete and Deleting Tasks

After you have completed a task, you mark it as complete by clicking in the check box to the left of the task name. A checkmark appears in the check box and the rest of the task information is crossed out.

You can leave a completed task in the task list or you can remove the task from the list. To remove the task, select it and click the Delete button on the Standard toolbar. You can remove several tasks at one time even if they are not located next to each other in the task list. To do so, select the first task, hold down the Ctrl key, and then click the other tasks you want to delete. If the tasks you want to delete are all grouped together, select the first task, hold down the Shift key and then select the last task in the group of tasks. All tasks in between the first and last tasks are then selected. Regardless of how you select the tasks, click the Delete button to delete them. Like all other Outlook items, deleted tasks go to the Deleted Items folder.

STEP-BY-STEP 18.9

1. You have returned your books to the library. Click in the empty check box to the left of the task name. A checkmark appears in the check box, and the task name and due date are crossed out.
2. Mark each task as complete.
3. Click the last task in the list. Hold down **Ctrl** and click the first task in the list. Both tasks are selected.
4. Click the first task in the list. It should now be the only selected task. Press **Shift** and click the last task to select all of them.
5. Click the **Delete** button on the Standard toolbar to remove all tasks. Leave Outlook open for the next Step-by-Step.

Send and Receive E-Mail

If your computer is set up to handle e-mail, you can use the Inbox folder in Outlook to send and receive e-mail messages. An advantage to using Outlook as your e-mail application is that, as you create messages, you have easy access to the other Outlook folders. You can quickly address the message to someone on your contacts list, check your calendar to make sure you are available for a meeting, or add a task to your task list when a message requests further action.

> **Computer Concepts**
>
> Before you can use Outlook for e-mail, you must have a mail account with an ISP (Internet Service Provider), and Outlook must be configured to send and receive e-mail.

Receiving E-Mail

When Outlook launches, it sends a request to your mail server to find out if you have any messages waiting. If you do, Outlook receives them and displays them in the Inbox folder. The top half of the Inbox folder displays message headers for any new messages. The message header tells you who sent the message, the subject of the message, and the date and time your server received it. The bottom half of the Inbox displays the actual text of the message. If you have a number of messages, you can read each one by clicking its message header to display the message text in the bottom part of the Inbox.

> **Computer Concepts**
>
> E-mail attachments can contain viruses. Never download or open files from people you don't know. And, most importantly, be sure to keep your anti-virus software up to date.

If you are already working in Outlook, you can check your e-mail at any time. Open the Inbox folder and click the Send/Receive button on the Standard toolbar. After you have finished reading your messages, you can delete them by selecting each message header and clicking the Delete button on the Standard toolbar.

Sending E-Mail

Sending e-mail is as easy as clicking a few buttons and keying your message text. If you want to send a message to a contact stored in the Contacts folder, click the To button. A dialog box opens to allow you to select a contact name. Because you have already stored the e-mail address for that contact in the Contacts folder, you do not have to rekey the address. The contact's name appears in the To text box, and the message will automatically be sent to the e-mail address you previously stored. If you want to send a copy of the message to another person, enter that person's e-mail address in the Cc text box. If an e-mail address is not in your address book, you can also type it in the To or the Cc box.

> **Computer Concepts**
>
> The Instant Messaging feature in Outlook enables you to send messages in real time. In other words, you can send and receive messages while you and the contact are both logged on. In order for the Instant Messaging feature to work, both people must be logged onto the Internet. Each contact must have an Instant Messaging account and you must enter the contact's Instant Messaging address into the IM text box in the General tab of the Contact form.

It is good e-mail etiquette to include a subject for your mail message. The subject should be brief, yet it should be descriptive enough to tell the recipient what the message is about. Then key your message.

After you have entered the addresses, subject, and text of your message, just click the Send button in the message window to send the e-mail message. In the next Step-by-Step, you will practice creating an e-mail message, but you will not send it. You can perform the steps even if you do not have an ISP (Internet Service Provider) or if your ISP information is not entered in Outlook.

STEP-BY-STEP 18.10

1. Click the **Inbox** shortcut in the Outlook Bar, or open the **View** menu, choose **Go To**, and select **Inbox** to open the Inbox folder. In the Inbox folder, click the **New Mail Message** button. The Untitled Message – Microsoft Word form shown in Figure 18-9 appears.

STEP-BY-STEP 18.10 Continued

FIGURE 18-9
New Message form

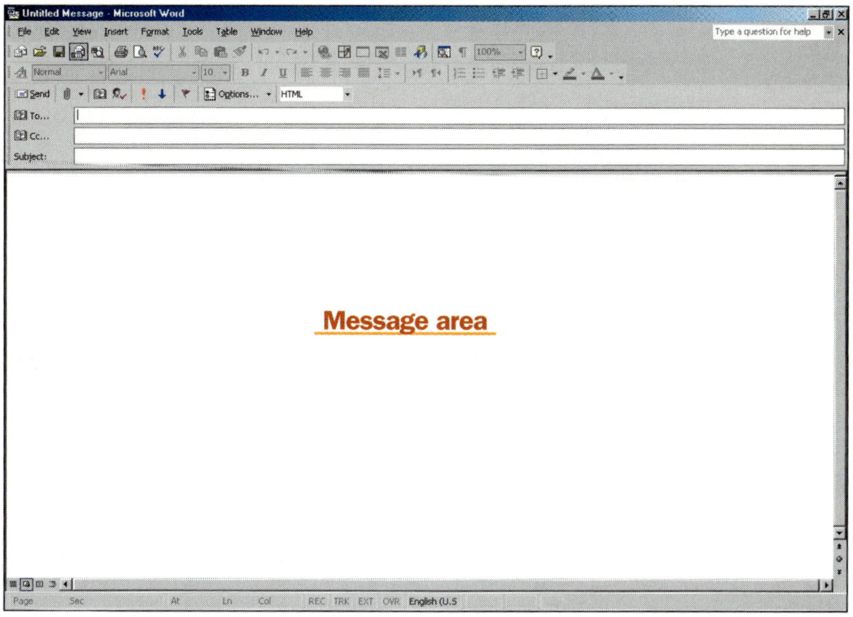

2. You will send a message to Jane Treadway, the contact you added earlier. Click the **To...** button to open the Select Names dialog box.

3. Jane Treadway's name should appear in the Name list at the left side of the Select Names dialog box. Click her name to select it, and then click the **To ->** button to add the name to the Message Recipients list. Your Select Names dialog box should look similar to the one shown in Figure 18-10. However, you may have additional contacts listed. Do not be concerned if yours looks different.

> **Hot Tip**
>
> If your screen does not match Figure 18-9, you may not have Word selected as your e-mail editor. To choose this option, open the **Tools** menu, choose **Options**, click the **Mail Format** tab, and turn on **Use Microsoft Word to edit e-mail messages**.

STEP-BY-STEP 18.10 Continued

FIGURE 18-10
Contact name added to the Message Recipients list

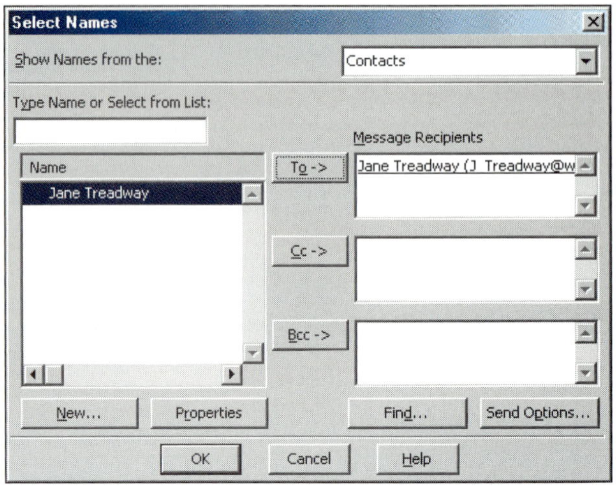

4. Click **OK** to close the dialog box. Jane Treadway's name now appears in the To... box in the message window.

5. Click in the **Subject** text box and key **Product Info**.

6. Click in the message area. As soon as you do, the title of the window changes to *Product Info – Message - Microsoft Word*.

7. Key the following message:

   Hi Jane,

   I will have the information you asked for later today. I need to contact a sales rep for the latest figures.

8. Press **Enter** twice and key your name to sign the e-mail.

9. Open the **File** menu and choose **Save As**. Save the message with the name **Treadway Message**. Click the **Save** button.

10. Close the message window by clicking the application close button in the title bar (at the top right corner of the screen). Remember, you are not actually sending this message to the recipient.

11. When prompted to save the draft of this message, click **No**.

Hot Tip

You can insert more than one name in the Message Recipients list for the To... box. The message will go to all the names on the list at the same time. Add people you would like to receive a copy of this e-mail to the Cc... list. If you want someone to receive a copy of the e-mail without letting the other message recipients know who else is receiving the e-mail, add them to the Bcc (blind copy) list.

Speech Recognition

If your computer has speech recognition capability, enable the Dictation mode and dictate the message.

STEP-BY-STEP 18.10 Continued

12. Switch to the Contacts folder and delete the Jane Treadway contact from the Contacts folder.

13. Close Outlook.

> **Computer Concepts**
>
> By default, Outlook saves the file in html format unless you've selected Word as your e-mail editor. If Word is your editor, Outlook saves the files in Word format and you can use the spellcheck and grammar checking features to help you proofread your document. However, if you've formatted for plain text, the file will be saved as a text file.

SUMMARY

In this lesson, you learned:

- The Outlook window changes depending on which folder is open. The Outlook Bar displays shortcuts that give you quick access to each of the Outlook folders.
- Each Outlook folder has a number of views you can use to display the information.
- The Calendar folder lets you schedule appointments and events. A form makes it easy for you to enter information about your appointments. Each piece of information is called a field.
- Each appointment and event you schedule is displayed in the Appointment Book.
- You can use the Date Navigator to select the day of the appointment.
- The Contacts folder is designed to store information about business and personal contacts with whom you communicate with often.
- You create address cards that hold information such as name, address, phone number, e-mail address, and so on. Address cards are listed in alphabetical order in the Contacts folder.
- The Tasks folder supplies a grid in which you store information about tasks you must complete.
- You can sort the tasks to see them in different orders.
- After you have completed a task, you can mark it as completed or delete it.
- The Inbox folder is an e-mail application you can use to send and receive e-mail messages.

VOCABULARY *Review*

Define the following terms:

Ascending order	Event	Form
Contacts	Field	Item
Descending order		

REVIEW *Questions*

TRUE/FALSE

Circle T if the statement is true or F if the statement is false.

T F 1. Each Outlook folder organizes a different type of information.

T F 2. Each piece of information in a form is called a field.

T F 3. As you add contacts, Outlook arranges them in alphabetical order.

T F 4. You can sort tasks by subject or by due date.

T F 5. To preview the contents of an item, you must open the form for the item.

FILL IN THE BLANK

Complete the following sentences by writing the correct word or words in the blanks provided.

1. The ________ contains shortcuts you can click to open folders.
2. The ________ helps you to locate and display calendar dates in the past or future.
3. A(n) ________ is a scheduled item in the Outlook calendar that lasts 24 hours or longer.
4. Use the ________ folder to organize things you have to do.
5. A(n) ________ contains a set of controls in which you enter a piece of information to be stored in an item.

PROJECTS

PROJECT 18-1

1. If necessary, launch Outlook. Open the **Calendar** folder. Enter the following appointments and events:
   - A. A week from tomorrow, you have an appointment with R. Golding, a career counselor, in Rhodes Hall. The appointment is at 10:00 AM and should last an hour and a half.
   - B. Your brother Dave's birthday is three days from today. Schedule the birthday as an event.
   - C. Your family will get together at 7:00 PM on that day for a celebration. You expect this celebration to last about two hours.
   - D. You promised your friend Marian that you would go to the library with her to do some research. She wants to go next Tuesday at 9:00 AM and stay two hours.
   - E. You've been elected to the board for a volunteer group in your community. The board meets the first Monday of each month. Schedule a recurring appointment for six months.
2. Click the **Month** view button to see all of your appointments.

3. Open the **Contacts** folder. Enter and save the following personal and business contacts. Use your own city or town, state, and zip code for the addresses.

Full Name:	Marian Teodorescu	Full Name:	Rose Golding
Job Title:		Job Title:	Career Counselor
Company:		Company:	Careers Plus
Address:	18 Baldwin Way	Address:	451 Rhodes Hall
Business Phone:		Business Phone:	555-8825
Home Phone:	555-9834	Home Phone:	
E-mail:	teodorm@netlink.com	E-mail:	rgolding@careers.org

4. Leave Outlook open for the next Project.

PROJECT 18-2

1. Open the **Tasks** folder. Enter the following tasks:
   - **A.** Buy a present for your brother Dave by the day before his birthday. (Check the Calendar if you need to remember what day Dave's birthday is.)
   - **B.** Complete your resume, due a week from today.
   - **C.** You need a new printer cartridge to print your resume. Get one by the day after tomorrow.
   - **D.** You need to confirm your trip to the library with Marian for research within three days.
2. Sort the tasks by subject. Then sort them in descending date order. Sort them again in ascending date order.
3. Switch to Calendar view to see your tasks in the TaskPad.
4. Open the **Inbox** folder. Create the following e-mail messages:
   - **A.** Create a message to Marian to confirm that you will be going to the library with her next Tuesday. (Hint: Remember to click the **To...** button in the new message window to locate her name in your contacts list.) The subject of the message should be **Library Research**. Key your name at the end of the message. Save the message as **Marian** and do not send it.
   - **B.** Create a message to Ms. Golding to confirm your appointment with her at 10:00 next week (use your Calendar to find the exact date and use it in your message). The subject of the message should be **Confirm Meeting**. Thank her for taking the time to see you. Key your name at the end of the message. Save the message as **Confirm Meeting** and do not send it.
5. You have confirmed your trip to the library with Marian and bought a new printer cartridge. In the Tasks folder, mark these tasks as complete.
6. Go back through all the Outlook folders and delete all the items you added in Project 18-1 and Project 18-2.
7. Close Outlook.

WEB PROJECT

Individuals who use e-mail for frequent communication are often annoyed by unwanted e-mail called spam. Spam is unsolicited e-mail messages that can be obnoxious, offensive, and a waste of your time. Some countries have laws against spam. Your Internet service provider may try to block spam before it reaches your mailbox. However, you may still be inconvenienced by junk e-mail.

Using some of the search engines you have used in this course, research the topic "spam" to learn ways you can stop spam. Write a brief summary of your findings.

TEAMWORK PROJECT

You probably noticed when you created e-mail messages in this lesson that your e-mails looked plain and boring. While you don't want your e-mails to be distracting or silly (particularly if you are sending them to business contacts), you can still add some visual interest. Two Outlook features can provide a more professional appearance for your e-mails: stationery and a signature. With a partner, use the following steps to explore these Outlook features:

1. Using the Help feature in Outlook, one teammate should research "stationery" and the other teammate should research "e-mail signatures."
2. Using what you learned from the Help files, set a new default stationery and create an e-mail signature file. Open new e-mail messages to see your stationery and signature in place.
3. If you have e-mail capability, send a message to your teammate so he or she can see how the message looks when it is received by Outlook.
4. After you have finished experimenting with these features, remove the e-mail signature and the stationery formats that you applied. (Use the Help files in Outlook to help you restore default settings.)

CRITICAL*Thinking*

ACTIVITY 18-1

The Outlook Today folder displays an overview of some of your current Outlook information. The folder displays a summary of your appointments, a list of your tasks, and a list of new e-mail messages. You can use Outlook Today as your starting point when you work in Outlook. Use the Help feature to learn how to make Outlook Today your default page.

KEY APPLICATIONS

REVIEW *Questions*

TRUE/FALSE

Circle T if the statement is true or F if the statement is false.

T F 1. In Word, to manually move text to a new page, you can insert a hard page break.

T F 2. Alignment refers to the white space between the edge of the paper and the text.

T F 3. If you need to create a complex table in Word, you should use the Draw Table tool.

T F 4. As you create a presentation, PowerPoint automatically checks for and corrects misspelled words.

T F 5. When you use Slide Finder, you must choose to insert all slides.

T F 6. When data is too wide to fit in a cell, Excel displays a series of asterisks (*****).

T F 7. You can easily change a column chart to a bar chart if you wish.

T F 8. Databases and spreadsheets are very similar in structure.

T F 9. You can insert a new record anywhere in an Access table.

T F 10. Conditional formatting is used to show negative numbers in a worksheet.

MATCHING

Match the correct term in Column 1 to its description in Column 2.

	Column 1		Column 2
___	1. Absolute cell reference	A.	Small squares surrounding a graphic or object, indicating that it is selected
___	2. AutoComplete	B.	A file that contains formatting and text that you can customize to create a new document similar to, but slightly different from, the original
___	3. Clip Organizer	C.	An object that allows you to select, format, and print only specific fields from a table
___	4. Workbook	D.	Collection of pictures, photographs, sounds, and videos
___	5. Template	E.	Determines the changes in the display that occur as you move from one slide to another in Slide Show view
___	6. Slide transition	F.	An object that allows you to locate multiple records matching specified criteria
___	7. Query	G.	Cell reference that does not change when moved
___	8. Argument	H.	Word suggests the spelling of frequently used words
___	9. Sizing handles	I.	A collection of related worksheets
___	10. Report	J.	A value, cell reference, range, or text that acts as an operand in a function formula

PROJECTS

PROJECT 1

1. Start Word and open **Project1** from the data files. Save the document as **Refuge** followed by your initials.
2. Change the page orientation to landscape. Then position the insertion point in the blank line at the top of the document and specify three columns.
3. Position the insertion point in the second blank line below the heading *National Wildlife Refuge* and insert an appropriate clip art image for the topic. Resize the picture to be about 2 inches high. Center the picture, but do not wrap text around it.

4. Insert a 3-point blue-gray border below the *National Wildlife Refuge* heading. Use **Repeat** to insert the same border for the first blank paragraph beneath the clip art picture.

5. Create a WordArt heading for the first column of text using the word **Massassoit**. Size the graphic so it is as wide as the column. Move the WordArt graphic to the top of the first column and wrap text above and below it. Adjust the graphic if necessary so that it is at the top of the column, with the blank line and the words *National Wildlife Refuge* below it. Change the color of the graphic if desired to coordinate with the clip art picture.

6. Use drag-and-drop to move the first paragraph of text (the description of the National Wildlife Refuge System) to the last blank line in the document.

7. Use bullets to format the entries beneath the *Wildlife and Ecosystem*, *Public Use*, and *Safety Information* headings. (*Hint:* Align the bullet with the left edge of the column, if necessary, by opening the Bullets and Numbering dialog box and clicking the **Customize** button. Then change the Bullet position indent to **0** and the Text position indent to **0.25**.)

8. Under the *Wildlife and Ecosystem* heading, delete the bullet that reads *Do not remove any plant life from the Refuge*. Then, in the bullet that reads *Do not remove any animals from the Refuge*, use **Overtype** to replace the word *animals* with **species**.

9. You're pretty sure you misspelled Lyme when keying information about ticks and Lyme disease. Find the word *Lime* and replace it with **Lyme**.

10. Find the list of unusual bird visitors to the Refuge in column 3. Select these bird names and insert a left-aligned tab at approximately 1½" on the Ruler above the column. This tab should line up the second column of names.

11. Use **Find** to locate the phrase *Enjoy all wildlife from a distance*, and then use a light shade of blue to emphasize the entire sentence.

12. Insert another appropriate picture that fits the content. Resize the picture to be about 1 inch square. Wrap text around the picture and move it to the end of the document so that the last paragraph of text wraps around it. Make sure the picture aligns at the bottom with the last line of text and with the right edge of the column.

13. Create a footer with the current date left aligned (make sure the date will update automatically).

14. Preview the document to see if any changes need to be made in the layout. If necessary, resize pictures and the WordArt graphic to fit all text on one page. Insert column breaks if any headings fall at the bottoms of columns.

15. Save your changes and close the document.

PROJECT 2

1. Start PowerPoint and open **Project2** from the data files. Save the presentation as **Everest** followed by your initials.

2. Apply the **Mountain Top** design template.

3. On slide #1, click to the left of the first word in the title placeholder. Key **Mt. Everest:** and then press **Enter.**

4. Change the font of the title to **Times New Roman 54 pt.** Change the size of the font for the author of the quote (**—Ed Viesturs**) to **24 pt** and **Italic.**

5. Change the titles of the remaining slides in the presentation to **Times New Roman 54 pt.**

6. Change the layout of slide 6 to **Title and 2-Column Text.** In the new right-hand column, key the following text:
   First ascent by an American: Whittaker, 1963
   First ascent by an American woman: Allison, 1988

7. Go to slide #1 and then run the presentation. After you have finished viewing the slides, save your changes, close the presentation, and close PowerPoint.

PROJECT 3

1. Start Access. Open **Project3** from the data files, and then open the **Specimens** table.

2. Several people have recently asked you some specific questions about the zoo's specimens. Use the sort feature to find the answers to these questions:
   A. How many Reptile specimens does the zoo have?
   B. Does the zoo have any ring-tailed lemurs and, if so, how many?
   C. What species has the largest population? (*Hint*: Sort in the Number field in descending order and then find the common name at the top of the table.)
   D. Sort in ascending order on the ID field to return the table to its original order.

3. You want to know how many members of the Carnivora order the zoo currently has. Create a query in Design view as follows:
   A. Add the **Order**, **Common Name**, **Species Name**, and **Number** fields to the query.
   B. In the Order column, click in the **Criteria** box and key **Carnivora.**
   C. Save the query as **Carnivores Query** and close it.

4. Open the **Carnivores Query.** How many different species does the zoo have? How many carnivores are there altogether? Close the query.

5. Create a report to show all the animals in each group. Follow these steps:
   A. Start the Report Wizard and select the **Specimens** table for the report.
   B. Select the **Group, Common Name, Endangered,** and **Number** fields for the report.
   C. In the next dialog box, select **Group** and then click the > button to group the records by this field.
   D. In the next dialog box, choose to sort by **Common Name.**
   E. Choose the **Stepped** layout and the **Compact** style.
   F. Name the report **Animals by Group** and preview the report. Use the navigation controls at the bottom of the report to view the second page of the report.

6. Close the preview window, then close the database and Access.

SIMULATION

You volunteer at the local Rails-to-Trails organization which converts old, unused railroad beds into trails for public use. These trails can be used for a variety of activities including walking, biking, running, and in-line skating. You have been asked to complete several jobs that will help distribute information about rail-trails in your area.

JOB 1

You are always being asked about rail-trails in neighboring states. You have decided to prepare a fact sheet about current and projected trails in the five-state area.

1. Start Excel and open **Job1** from the data files. Save the workbook as **Trail Miles** followed by your initials.
2. Widen columns as necessary to display all information.
3. Apply the **Number** format with the 1000 separator and zero decimals to the number values.
4. Insert a row above row 4. In cell B4, enter the heading **Open**. Merge and center this data over cells B4 and C4. In cell D4, enter the heading **Projected**. Merge and center this data over cells D4 and E4.
5. In cell A12, key **Totals**. In cells B12:E12, total the numbers of trails and miles.
6. Sort the data in ascending order by state.
7. Apply the **List 2** AutoFormat to the worksheet. Then center the two lines in the title.
8. Save your changes. Close the workbook and exit Excel.

JOB 2

A new section of a popular rail-trail is about to open for use. In this Job, you will create a press release giving general information about rail-trails.

1. Open **Job2a** from the data files folder. Save the document as **Press Release** followed by your initials.
2. Check spelling and grammar in the document and make all changes. You would like to use the phrase "rail-trail" rather than "rail trail" throughout. Use Replace to locate any instances of rail trail and change them to rail-trail.
3. Apply **Arial bold 11-point** font to *Press Release*, *For Immediate Release*, *Contact*, *Date*, *Headline*, and *Body*.

4. Apply **10% gray** shading to the *Press Release*, *For Immediate Release*, and *Date* paragraphs. Position the insertion point following *Contact:*, press the **Spacebar**, and key **Diane Twining**. Insert a left tab at the 4.25-inch mark so that Diane Twining is close to the right margin.

5. Insert the current date (it should not updated automatically) after the tab symbol following *Date*.

6. Select the *Headline* paragraph and the first line of the Body and set a left tab at 0.75 inches. Position the insertion point following the tab symbol in the Headline paragraph and key the headline **Little Miami Scenic Trail Open to Springfield.**

7. In the first Body paragraph, set a hanging indent at 0.75 inches so all text aligns with the first word of the body text. Apply a left indent of 0.75 inches to the remaining body paragraphs.

8. Open **Job2b** and select the map graphic by clicking on any of the lines in the map. When white handles appear around the graphic, copy it to the Clipboard. Return to the **Press Release** document and paste the map in the document. Move it to the right side of the second paragraph of body text.

9. Insert a centered page number at the bottom of each page. Preview the document.

10. Save your changes and close the document. Close the Job1b document and exit Word.

LIVING ONLINE

Unit

Part 1 Networks and the Internet

Estimated Time for Unit: 10 hours

LIVING ONLINE

Part 1 Networks and the Internet

Lesson 1
Understanding Network Concepts

3-1.1.1, 3-1.1.2, 3-1.1.3, 3-1.1.4, 3-1.1.5, 3-1.1.6, 3-1.2.1, 3-1.2.5

Lesson 2
What Is the Internet?

3-1.1.1, 3-1.2.2, 3-1.2.3, 3-1.2.4, 3-2.3.4, 3-3.1.1, 3-3.1.2, 3-3.1.3, 3-3.1.4, 3-3.1.5, 3-3.1.6, 3-3.2.1, 3-3.2.2, 3-3.2.3, 3-4.1.1, 3-4.1.2, 3-4.1.3, 3-4.1.4, 3-4.1.5

Lesson 3
Using the Internet

3-2.1.1, 3-2.1.2, 3-2.1.3, 3-2.1.4, 3-2.1.5, 3-2.1.6, 3-2.2.1, 3-2.2.2, 3-2.2.3, 3-2.2.4, 3-2.2.5, 3-2.2.6, 3-2.2.7, 3-2.2.8, 3-2.2.9, 3-2.2.10, 3-2.2.11, 3-2.2.12, 3-2.2.13, 3-2.2.14, 3-2.2.15, 3-2.2.16, 3-2.3.1, 3-2.3.2, 3-2.3.5, 3-3.2.4, 3-3.2.5, 3-3.2.6, 3-3.2.7, 3-3.2.8, 3-3.2.9, 3-3.2.10, 3-4.3.3

Lesson 4
Researching on the Internet

3-2.3.3, 3-3.1.6, 3-3.2.3, 3-3.3.1, 3-3.3.2, 3-3.3.3, 3-3.3.4, 3-3.3.5, 3-3.3.6, 3-3.3.7

Lesson 5
Evaluating Electronic Information

3-3.3.7, 3-4.3.1, 3-4.3.4, 3-4.3.6

Lesson 6
Exploring Technological Issues

3-1.1.1, 3-4.2.1, 3-4.2.2, 3-4.2.3, 3-4.2.4, 3-4.2.5, 3-4.2.6, 3-4.2.7, 3-4.2.8, 3-4.2.9, 3-4.2.10, 3-4.2.11, 3-4.3.2, 3-4.3.3, 3-4.3.5

LESSON 1

UNDERSTANDING NETWORK CONCEPTS

OBJECTIVES

Upon completion of this lesson, you should be able to:

- Describe a network.
- Explain the benefits of a network.
- List and describe the types of networks.
- Explain the advantages and disadvantages of networked computing.
- List and describe communications media.
- Describe communications hardware.
- Describe communications software.
- Describe the different network topologies.
- Describe network architecture.
- Describe network protocols.

Estimated Time: 1.5 hours

VOCABULARY

Bus topology
Client/server network
Clients
Communications channel
Data communications
Ethernet
Local area network (LAN)
Modem
Network
Peer-to-peer
Ring topology
Server
Star topology
TCP/IP
Token ring
Topology
Transmission media
Wide area network (WAN)

As companies grow and purchase more computers, they often find it advantageous to connect those computers through a network. This allows users to share software applications and to share hardware devices such as printers, scanners, and so forth.

Introducing Networks

IC³ 3-1.1.1-1

When most people think of networks, they envision something fairly complicated. At the lowest level, networks are not that complex. In fact, a ***network*** is simply a group of two or more computers linked together. As the size of a network increases and more and more devices are added, the installation and management does become more technical. Even so, the concept of networking and the terminology remain basically the same regardless of size.

In this lesson we discuss local area networks (LANs) and wide area networks (WANs). The primary difference between the two is that a LAN is generally confined to a limited geographical area, whereas a WAN covers a large geographical area. Most WANs are made up of several connected LANs.

Most organizations today rely on computers and the data stored on the computer. Many times they find they need to transmit that data from one location to another. The transmission of data from one location to another is known as ***data communications***. To transmit that data requires the following components, as illustrated in Figure 1-1.

- A sending device, which is generally a computer
- A communications device, such as a ***modem***, that converts the computer signal into signals supported by the communications channel
- A communications channel or path, such as telephone lines or cable, over which the signals are sent
- A receiving device that accepts the incoming signal, which is generally a computer
- Communications software

FIGURE 1-1
Communications components

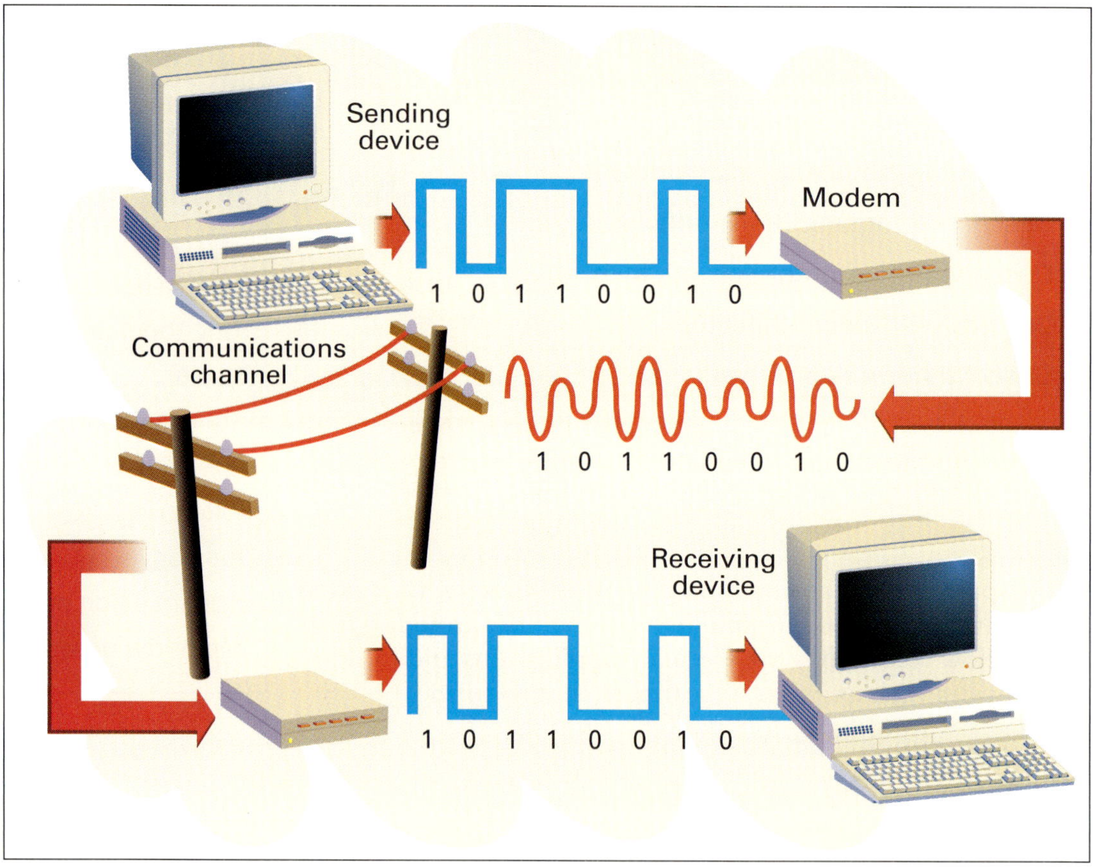

IC3
3-1.1.1-2
3-1.1.2-2
3-1.1.3-1

Most networks have at least one server and many clients. A server is a computer that manages network resources, and a client is a computer on the network that relies on the server for resources.

Network Benefits

To consider the topic of network benefits, you might first think about the biggest network of all, the Internet. Think about some of the changes that have occurred in our society because of the Internet. Perhaps the most profound of all of these changes is electronic mail. A network provides almost instant communication and e-mail messages are delivered almost immediately. Other benefits include the following:

- 3-1.1.2-1 3-1.1.2-2 *Information sharing:* Authorized users can use other computers on the network to access and share information and data. This could include special group projects, databases, and so forth.
- 3-1.1.5-2 *Hardware sharing:* No longer is it necessary to purchase a printer or a scanner or other frequently used peripherals for each computer. Instead, one device connected to a network can serve the needs of many users.
- 3-1.1.5-1 *Software sharing:* Instead of purchasing and installing a software program on every single computer, it can be installed on just the server. All of the users can then access the program from one central location. This also saves companies money because they purchase a site license for the number of users. This is much less expensive than purchasing individual software packages.
- 3-1.1.5-3 *Collaborative environment:* Enables users to work together on group projects by combining the power and capabilities of diverse equipment.

Communications Media

3-1.2.1-1 3-1.2.1-2 3-1.2.1-3 To transfer data from one computer to another requires some type of link through which the data can be transmitted. This link is known as the ***communications channel***. The worldwide telephone network is an important player in this channel. The telephone system is actually a collection of the world's telephone networks, including cellular, local, long-distance, and communications satellite networks. Although it was originally designed to handle voice communications, it's now used to transmit data, including fax transmissions, computer-to-computer communications such as e-mail, and live video from the Web.

3-1.1.1-2 3-1.1.4-1 3-1.1.4-3 At one end of the communications channel, you have a sending device, such as a computer or fax machine. A communications device, such as a modem, connected to the sending device converts the signal from the sender to a format that transmits over a standard dial-up telephone line or a dedicated line. A dial-up line provides a "temporary" connection, meaning each time a call is placed, the telephone company selects the line to transmit it over. A dedicated line, on the other hand, provides a permanent or constant connection between the sending and receiving communications devices. The transmission is moved or "switched" from one wire or frequency to another. A switch is a device located at the telephone company's central office that establishes a link between a sender and receiver of data communications. At the receiving end, another modem converts the signal back into a format that the receiving device can understand.

To send the data through the channel requires some type of ***transmission media***, which may be either physical or wireless.

Physical Media

Several types of physical media are used to transmit data. These include the following:

- *Twisted-pair cable:* This is the least expensive type of cable and is the same type used for many telephone systems. It consists of two independently insulated copper wires twisted around one another. One of the wires carries the signal and the other wire is grounded to absorb signal interference. See Figure 1-2.

FIGURE 1-2
Twisted pair cable

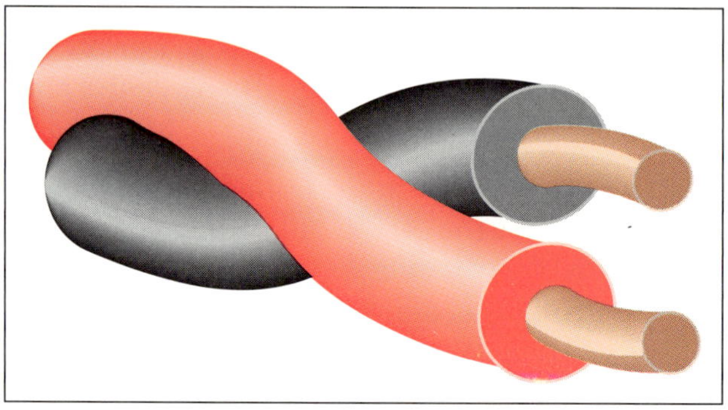

- *Coaxial cable:* Coaxial cabling is the primary type of cabling used by the cable television industry and it is also widely used for computer networks. Because the cable is heavily shielded, it is much less prone to interference than twisted-pair cable. However, it is more expensive than twisted-pair. See Figure 1-3.

FIGURE 1-3
Coaxial cable

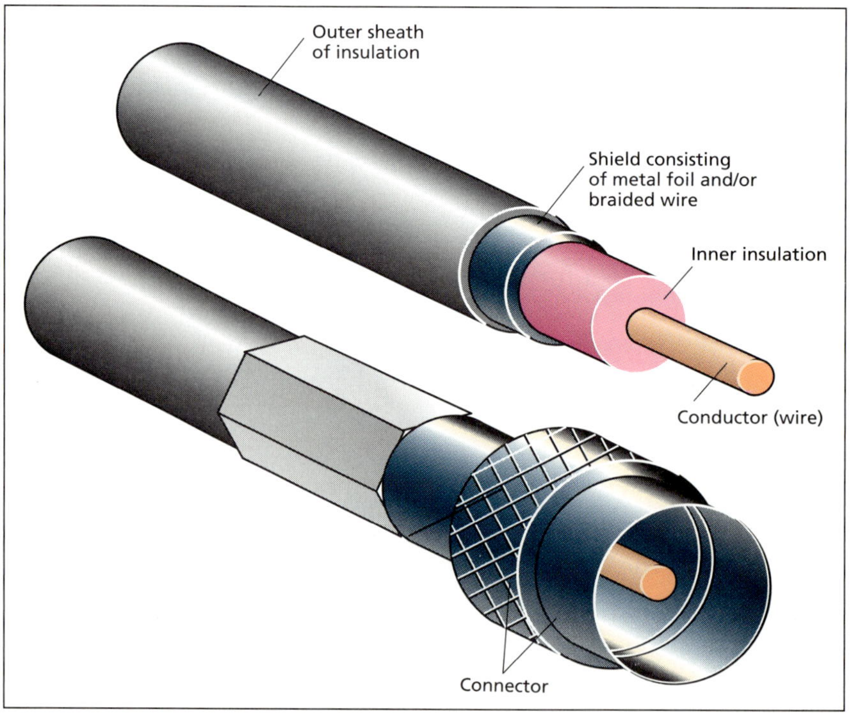

- *Fiber-optic cable:* Fiber-optic cable is made from thin, flexible glass tubing. Fiber optics has several advantages over traditional metal communications line. The bandwidth is much greater, so it can carry more data; it is much lighter than metal wires and is much less susceptible to interference. The main disadvantage of fiber optics is that it is fragile and expensive. See Figure 1-4.

Did You Know?

Telephone companies are continually replacing traditional telephone lines with fiber-optic cables. In the future, almost all communications will use fiber optics.

FIGURE 1-4
Fiber-optic cable

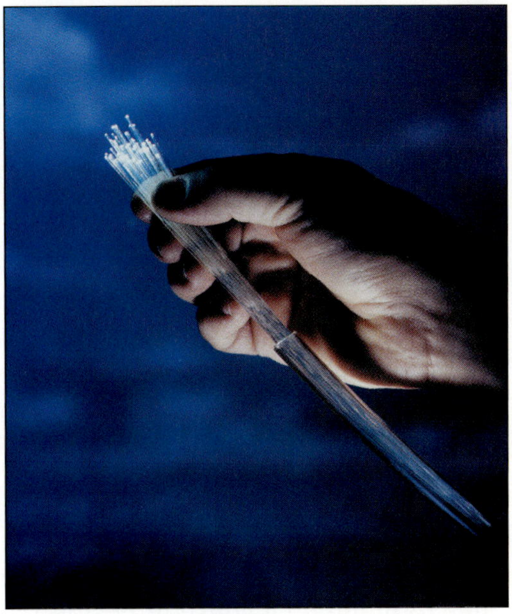

Wireless Media

Just like physical media, several wireless options are also available:

- *Radio signals:* Transmissions using radio signals require line of sight; that is, the signal travels in a straight line from one source to the other. For radio transmission, you need a transmitter to send the signal and a receiver to accept the signal.

- *Microwaves:* A microwave signal is sent through space in the form of electromagnetic waves. Just like radio signals, they must also be sent in straight lines from one microwave station to another. To avoid interference, most microwave stations are built on mountain-tops or placed on the top of large buildings. See Figure 1-5.

FIGURE 1-5
Microwave tower

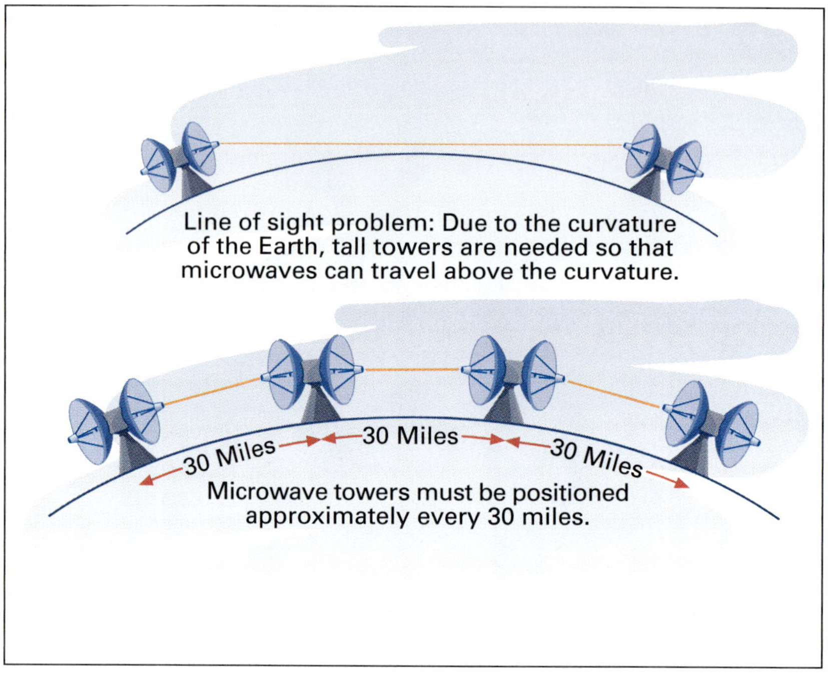

- ***Satellites:*** Communication satellites are placed in orbit 22,300 feet above the surface of the earth. This allows the satellite to maintain a constant position above one point on the earth's surface by rotating at the same speed of the earth. The satellite contains equipment that receives the transmission, amplifies it, and sends it back to earth. See Figure 1-6.

FIGURE 1-6
Satellites

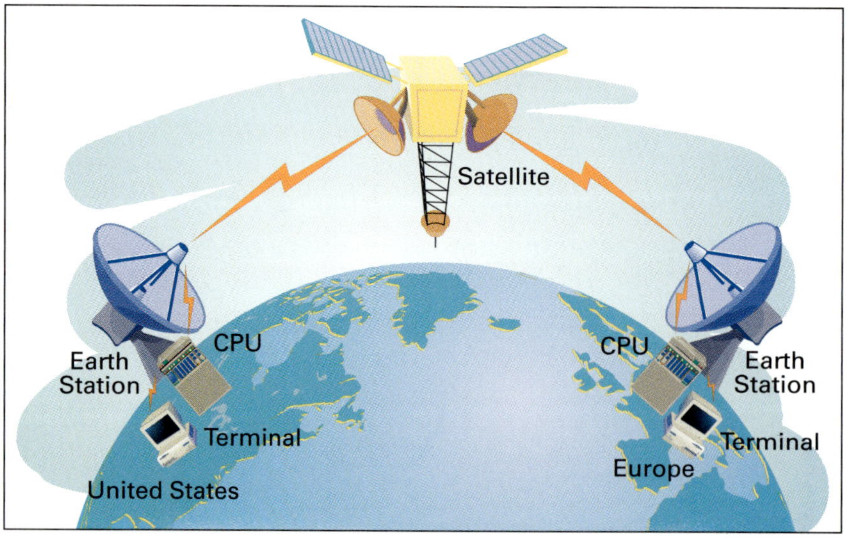

The type of communications media an organization may select to use within a network is determined by several different factors: the type of network, the size of the network, and the cost.

Network Hardware

Most networks consist of a network server and computer clients. In addition to the server and the client, there are two other categories of network hardware: communication devices and devices that connect the network cabling and amplify the signal.

Communications Hardware

Communications hardware devices facilitate the transmitting and receiving of data. When we think about communications hardware, the first thing that generally comes to mind is the desktop computer and modem. However, all types of other devices send and receive data. Some examples are large computers such as supercomputers, mainframe computers, and minicomputers; handheld and laptop computers; and even fax machines and digital cameras. Two of the more commonly used transmitting devices for personal use are as follows:

3-1.1.4-2

- *Modem:* The word MODEM is an acronym for modulate-demodulate, which means to convert analog signals to digital and vice versa. This device enables a computer to transmit data over telephone lines. Computer information is stored digitally, whereas information sent over telephone lines is transmitted in the form of analog waves. Both the sending and receiving users must have a modem. See Figure 1-7.

FIGURE 1-7
Computer with modem attached

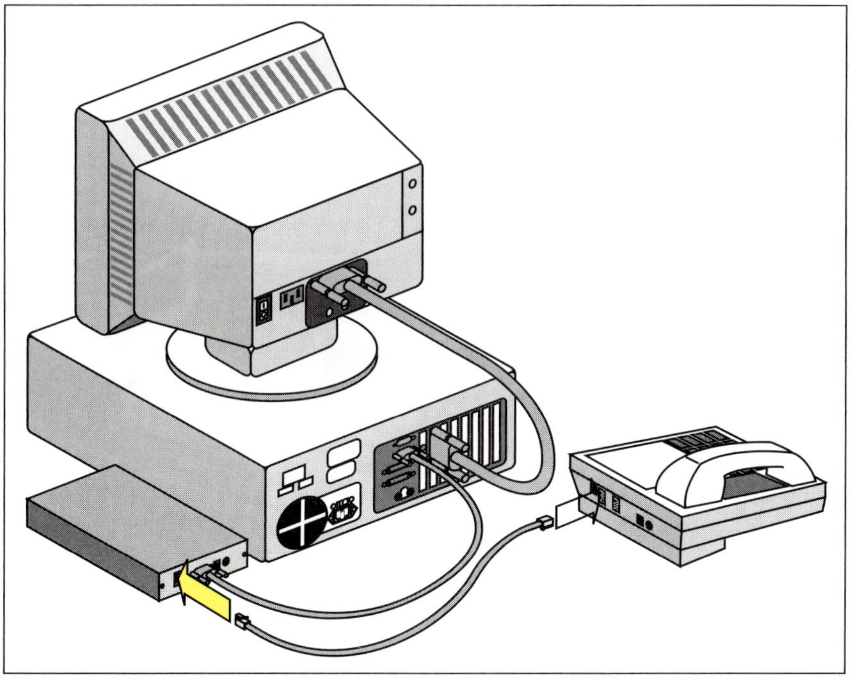

- *Cable modem:* A cable modem uses coaxial cable to send and receive data. This is the same type of cable used for cable TV. The bandwidth, which determines the amount of data that can be sent at one time, is much greater with a cable modem. A cable modem can be connected directly to your computer or connected to a set-top box used with your television. With a set-top box, you can access and surf the Web from your TV.

Network Transmission Hardware

Modems work well for personal computers and a small one- or two-person office. However, when it comes to transmitting data across LANs and WANs, the devices are considerably different. Some of the more widely used of these devices are as follows:

- *Network interface cards (NICs):* This is an add-on card for either a desktop PC or a laptop computer. Each computer on a network must have a NIC. This card enables and controls the sending and receiving of data between the PCs in a LAN.
- *Hub:* You may have heard the word hub applied to airports. Travelers make connections through various hubs to go from one location to another. In data transmission, a hub works similarly. It is a hub or junction where data arrives from one or more directions and is forwarded out in one or more other directions. Hubs contain ports for connecting computers and other devices. The number of ports on the hub determines the number of computers that can be connected to a hub. See Figure 1-8.

FIGURE 1-8
Computers connected to a hub

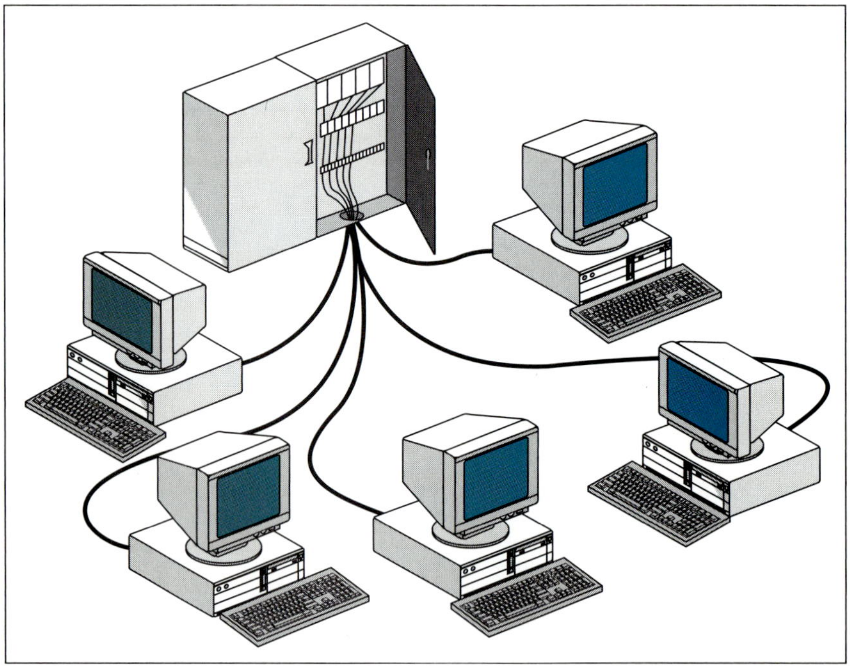

IC3 3-1.1.1-2

- *Bridge:* A bridge is a special computer that connects one LAN to another LAN. Both networks must use the same protocol, or set of rules. Think about the bridge as a device that determines if your message is going to the LAN within your building or to the building across the street.
- *Gateway:* A gateway is a combination of software and hardware that links two different types of networks that use different protocols. For instance, gateways between electronic mail systems permit users on different systems to exchange messages.

IC3 3-1.1.1-2

- *Router:* A router is like a traffic policeman—this intelligent device directs network traffic. When you send data through a network, it is divided into small packets. All packets don't travel the same route; instead one may go in one direction and another in a different direction. When the packets reach their final destination, they are reassembled into the original message. A router connects multiple networks and determines the fastest available path to send these packets of data on their way to their correct destination. And, just like our traffic policeman, in the event of a partial network failure, the router can redirect the traffic over alternate paths.

Internet

For definitions of networking terminology, visit *www.datacom.textron.com* and then search for "glossary."

Types of Networks

Many types of networks exist, but the most common types are ***local area networks (LANs)*** and ***wide area networks (WANs)***. As explained earlier, a LAN is generally confined to a limited geographical area and a WAN covers a wide geographical area.

Local Area Networks

Most LANs connect personal computers, workstations, and other devices such as printers, scanners, or other devices. There are two popular types of LANs—client/server and peer-to-peer. The basic difference is how the data and information is stored.

3-1.1.3-1
3-1.1.3-2

- ***Client/server network:*** This is a type of architecture in which one or more computers on the network acts as a ***server***. The server manages network resources. Depending on the size of the network, there may be several different servers. For instance, there may be a print server to manage the printing and a database server to manage a large database. In most instances, the server(s) is a high-speed computer with lots of storage space. The network operating system software and network versions of software applications are stored on the server. All of the other computers on the network are called ***clients***. They share the server resources. See Figure 1-9.

FIGURE 1-9
Client/server network

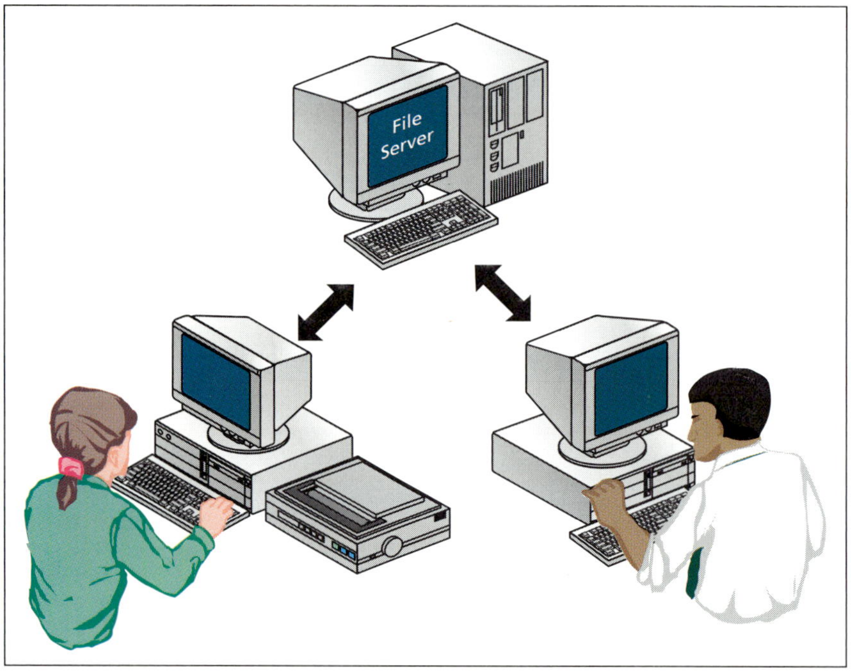

- *Peer-to-peer:* In this type of architecture, all of the computers on a network are equal. There is no computer designated as the server. People on the network each determines what files on their computer they will share with others on the network. This type of network is much easier to set up and manage. Many small offices use peer-to-peer. See Figure 1-10.

FIGURE 1-10
Peer-to-peer network

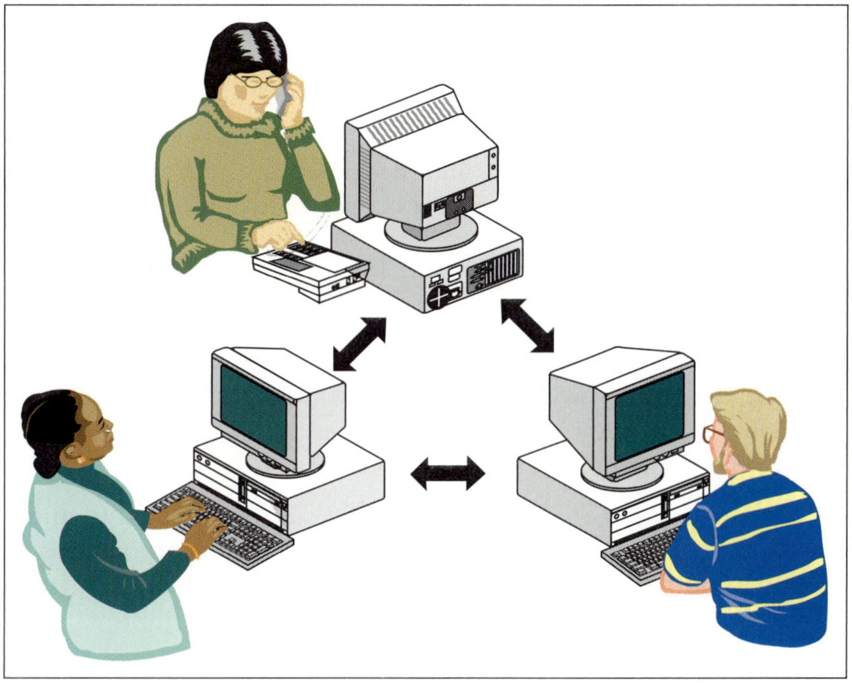

Ethics in Technology

RISKS OF NETWORKED COMPUTING

The security of a computer network is challenged every day by equipment malfunctions, system failures, computer hackers, and virus attacks.

IC3
3-1.1.6-1
3-1.1.6-2

Equipment malfunctions and system failures can be caused by a number of things, including natural disasters such as floods or storms, fires, and electrical disturbances, such as a brownout or blackout. Server malfunctions or failures mean users lose access (at least temporarily) to network resources, such as printers and drives, and information.

Computer hackers and viruses represent a great risk to networked environments. People who break into computer systems are called hackers. They break into systems to steal services and information, such as credit card numbers, test data, and even national security data, or to harm a company or organization they don't like or support, or sometimes just for the thrill of being able to do it. People create computer viruses and infect other computers for some of the same reasons. Viruses are very dangerous to networked computers—they're usually designed to sabotage files that are shared.

Wide Area Networks

A WAN covers a large geographical network. This area may be as large as a state or a country or even the world, since the largest WAN is the Internet. Most WANs consist of two or more LANs and are connected by routers. Communications channels can include telephone systems, satellites, microwaves, or any combination of these.

IC3 3-1.2.5-1

Two variations on a WAN are intranets and extranets. An intranet is designed for the exclusive use of people within an organization. Many businesses have implemented intranets within their own organizations on which they make available files such as handbooks and employee manuals, newsletters, and employment forms.

IC3 3-1.2.5-2

An extranet is similar to an intranet, but it allows specified users outside of the organization to access internal information systems. Like the Internet, intranets and extranets utilize and support Web technologies, such as hyperlinks and Web pages coded in hypertext markup language (HTML).

Network Topologies

Networks can be designed using a variety of configurations. These configurations are referred to as topologies. A ***topology*** is simply the geometric arrangement of how the network is set up and connected. There are three basic topologies.

- ***Bus topology:*** Within this type of topology, all devices are connected to and share a master cable. This master cable is called the bus or backbone. There is no one host computer. Data can be transmitted in both directions, from one device to another. This type of network is relatively easy to install and inexpensive. See Figure 1-11.

FIGURE 1-11
Bus topology

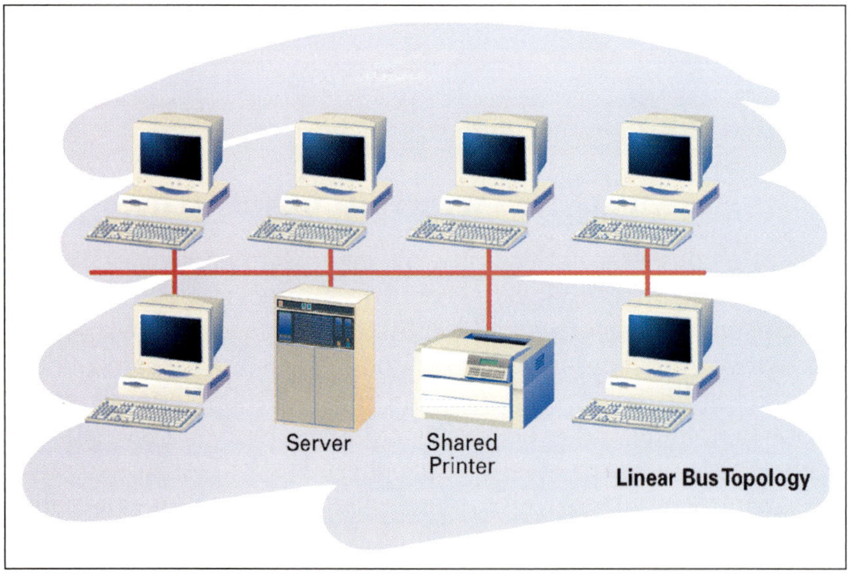

- ***Ring topology:*** A ring topology is somewhat similar to a bus. However, the devices are connected in a circle instead of a line. Each computer within the circle is connected to an adjoining device on either side. Data travels from device to device around the ring. This type of topology is more difficult to install and manage and more expensive. However, it does provide for faster transmission speeds and can span large distances. See Figure 1-12.

FIGURE 1-12
Ring topology

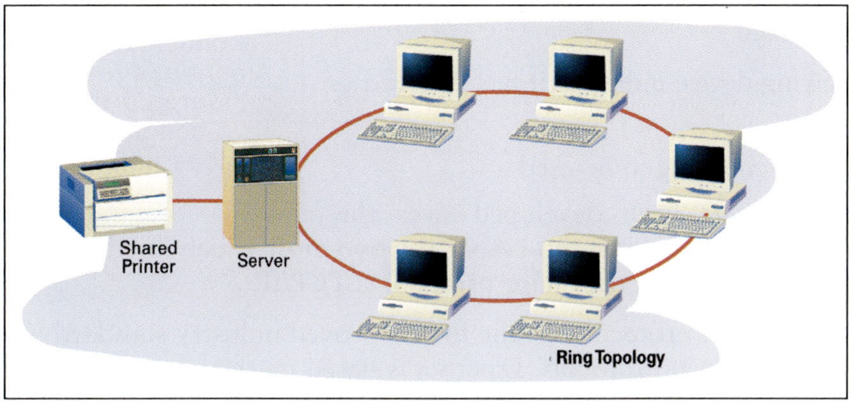

- ***Star topology:*** Within a star topology, all devices are connected to a central hub or computer. All data that transfer from one computer to another must pass through the hub. Star networks are relatively easy to install and manage, but bottlenecks can occur because all data must pass through the hub. This type of network requires more cabling than the other types. See Figure 1-13.

FIGURE 1-13
Star topology

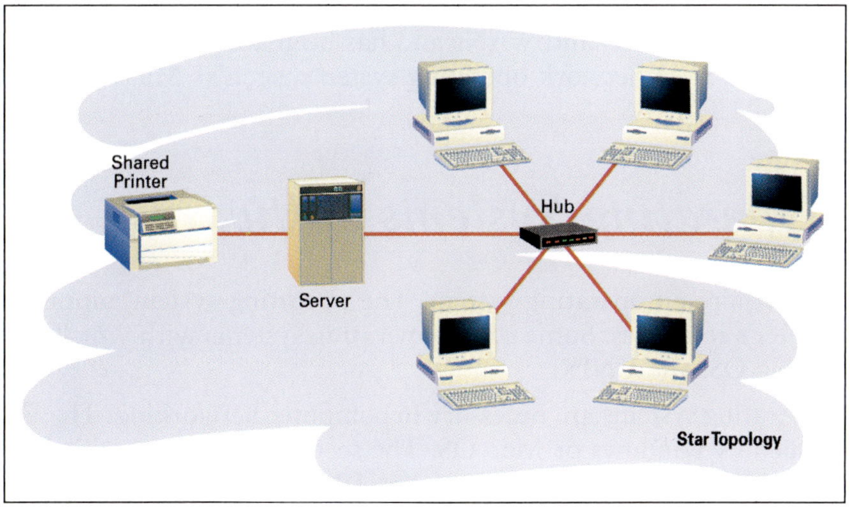

These topologies can also be mixed or combined to perform hybrid topologies.

Communications Protocols

A protocol is simply an agreed-on set of rules and procedures for transmitting data between two or more devices. Some of the features determined by the protocol are as follows:

- How the sending device indicates it has finished sending the message
- How the receiving device indicates it has received the message
- The type of error checking to be used

> **Hot Tip**
>
> Looking for that perfect career? Then you might want to check out Information Technology (IT). A study by the Information Technology Association of America reveals 346,000 IT jobs are currently vacant in U.S. companies, leaving 1 in 10 jobs unfilled.

Many protocols have been developed over the years. However, within networking and LANs, the two most widely used protocols are Ethernet and token ring. On the Internet, the major protocol is TCP/IP.

- ***Ethernet:*** The ***Ethernet*** protocol was the first approved industry standard protocol. It is one of the most popular LAN protocols. Ethernet is based on the bus topology, but can work with the star topology as well. It supports data transfer rates of up to 10 megabits per second (Mbps). There are two new Ethernet versions. The first is called Fast Ethernet and supports data transfer rates of 100 Mbps. The second is called Gigabit Ethernet and supports data transfer rates of 1,000 megabits, or 1 gigabit, per second.
- ***Token ring:*** The second most widely used LAN protocol is called ***token ring***. Within this type of network, all of the computers are arranged in a circle. A token, which is a special signal, travels around the ring. To send a message, a computer on the ring catches the token, attaches a message to it, and then lets it continue to travel around the network.
- ***TCP/IP:*** TCP/IP is the acronym for Transmission Control Protocol/Internet Protocol. This protocol is used by both LANs and WANs and has been adopted as a standard to connect hosts on the Internet. Even network operating systems, such as Microsoft NT or Novell Netware, support TCP/IP.

Network Operating Systems Software

All computers require an operating system. The operating system, among other functions, manages the computer's resources. Some of the operating systems with which you may be familiar are Windows, Mac OS, and UNIX.

Two types of operating systems are necessary in computer networking. The first is the desktop operating system, such as Windows or Mac OS. The second is the networking operating system. Some desktop operating systems, such as Windows, UNIX, and the Mac OS, have built-in networking functions. These functions work adequately within a very limited environment. To really utilize a network, however, full function network operating systems (NOS) software is required.

Network operating systems run on the server and provide features such as administration, file, print, communications, security, database, management, and other services to personal computer clients.

SUMMARY

In this lesson, you learned:

- A network is a group of two or more computers linked together.
- A local area network is generally confined to a limited geographical area.
- A wide area network is made up of several connected local area networks.
- Data communications is the transmission of data from one location to another.
- The Internet is the biggest network of all.
- You can use a network for information sharing, hardware sharing, software sharing, and as a collaborative environment.
- The link through which data is transmitted is the communications channel.
- Transmission media can be either physical or wireless.
- Physical media includes twisted-pair cable, coaxial cable, and fiber optic cable.
- Wireless media includes radio signals, microwaves, and satellites.
- Most networks consist of a network server and computer clients.
- A modem is a type of communications device.
- Network interface cards enable the sending and receiving of data between the PCs in a LAN.
- A hub is a device that controls the incoming and forwarding of data.
- A bridge connects one LAN to another.
- A gateway links two different types of networks.
- A router directs the Internet or LAN traffic.
- The two popular types of LANs are the client/server network and peer-to-peer.
- Network topologies include bus, ring, and star.
- A protocol is an agreed-on set of rules and procedures for transmitting data between two or more devices.
- The Ethernet protocol is one of the most popular LAN protocols.
- Token ring is the second most widely used LAN protocol.
- TCP/IP is a protocol used by both LANs and WANs to connect to the Internet.
- All computers require an operating system.
- Networks require network operating systems.

VOCABULARY *Review*

Define the following terms:

Bus topology	Local area network (LAN)	Star topology
Client/server network	Modem	TCP/IP
Clients	Network	Token ring
Communications channel	Peer-to-peer	Topology
Data communications	Ring topology	Transmission media
Ethernet	Server	Wide area network (WAN)

REVIEW *Questions*

MULTIPLE CHOICE

Select the best response for the following statements.

1. A _________ is confined to a limited geographical area.
   A. wide area network
   B. local area network
   C. tiny area network
   D. metropolitan area network

2. The least expensive type of physical communications media is _________.
   A. twisted-pair cable
   B. fiber optics cable
   C. coaxial cable
   D. radio signals

3. A _________ changes analog signals to digital signals and digital signals to analog.
   A. satellite
   B. NIC
   C. bridge
   D. modem

4. A _________ is a combination of software and hardware that links two different types of networks.
   A. hub
   B. bridge
   C. gateway
   D. router

5. A geometric arrangement of a network is called a _________.
   A. bridge
   B. WAN
   C. LAN
   D. topology

TRUE/FALSE

Circle T if the statement is true or F if the statement is false.

T F 1. Within a bus topology, all devices are connected to a master cable.

T F 2. A protocol is a type of topology.

T F 3. Token ring is the most widely used LAN protocol.

T F 4. Satellites orbit the earth.

T F 5. Software sharing is one of the benefits of networking.

FILL IN THE BLANK

Complete the following sentences by writing the correct word or words in the blanks provided.

1. The least expensive type of cable is __________.
2. __________ signals must be sent in straight lines.
3. Fiber optic cable is made from __________.
4. An add-on card that allows a computer to connect to a network is called a(n) __________.
5. The __________ protocol was the first approved industry standard protocol.

PROJECTS

PROJECT 1-1

Keep a record of the different types of data communications devices you use in a day or week. For instance, did you use the telephone, the computer, a fax machine, and so forth? Create a graph illustrating your data.

PROJECT 1-2

Your work supervisor has asked you to prepare a proposal for a new copier for the office. You are to work with several of your co-workers. However, it is difficult for everyone to get together at the same time. Write a report, giving a short overview of the proposal you have been assigned to prepare and an explanation of how using a computer network would help your group accomplish its goal.

WEB PROJECT

Two of the most popular networking operating systems are Microsoft NT and Novell Netware. Search the Web for information on both of these network operating systems. Prepare a report and chart comparing the features of these two NOSs.

TEAMWORK PROJECT

Your supervisor is pleased with the research you have completed on the copier proposal. She would now like for you and two or three of your co-workers to put together a proposal for a network for the company. You should determine the type of network, what devices should be on the network, what network operating system to use, and what communications media to use. She has requested a brief description of why you selected each item.

CRITICAL *Thinking*

ACTIVITY 1-1

As a result of computers and networks, more and more people are working from home. These people are called telecommuters. Prepare a paper describing some jobs you think people could do at home. Then add two paragraphs: one on the advantages of working at home and a second on the disadvantages of working at home.

ACTIVITY 1-2

The goal for this project is to describe an existing network. Interview someone you know who works with a network. Find out what kind of network he or she uses and for what purposes. Prepare a presentation that highlights the information you obtained from the interview.

LESSON 2

WHAT IS THE INTERNET?

OBJECTIVES

Upon completion of this lesson you should be able to:

- Explain the origin of the Internet.
- Explain how to connect to the Internet.
- Explain how the Internet works.
- Identify different types of Web sites and describe the different elements of a Web site.
- List the major features of the Internet and explain what they do.

Estimated Time: 1.5 hours

VOCABULARY

Domain name
Electronic mail
File transfer protocol (FTP)
Hypertext markup language (HTML)
Hypertext transfer protocol (HTTP)
Newsgroup
Uniform Resource Locator (URL)
USENET
World Wide Web

IC3 3-3.2.3-3

Each day millions of people "surf," or explore, the information superhighway. The "information superhighway" refers to the Internet. It is compared to a highway system because it functions much like a network of interstate highways. People use the Internet to research information, to shop, to go to school, to communicate with family and friends, to read the daily paper, to make airplane reservations, and so forth. They use the Internet at work and at home. Anyone with access to the Internet can connect with and communicate with anyone else in the world.

Evolution of the Internet

IC3 3-1.2.2-1

The Internet is a worldwide network of smaller networks that allow for the exchange of data, information, and e-mail messages. Even though no one person or organization can claim credit for the Internet, we can trace its early origins to the 1960s and the U.S. Department of Defense. The birth of the Internet is closely tied to a networking project started by a governmental division called the Advanced Research Projects Agency (ARPA). The goal was to create a network that would allow scientists to share information on military and scientific research.

The original name for the Internet was ARPANET. In 1969 ARPANET was a wide area network with four main host node computers. A host node is any computer directly connected to the network. These computers were located at the University of California at Santa Barbara, the University of California at Los Angeles, the Stanford Research Institute, and the University of Utah.

Over the next several years, the Internet grew steadily but quietly. Some interesting details are as follows:

- The addition of e-mail in 1972 spurred some growth.
- 3-1.1.1-3 By 1989 more than 100,000 host computers were linked to ARPANET.
- In 1990 ARPANET ceased to exist, but few noticed because its functions continued.
- The real growth began when the World Wide Web came into being in 1992.
- The thousands of interconnected networks were called an Inter-Net-Network and became known as the Internet, or a network of smaller networks including small company LANs, 3-1.2.2-2 Internet service providers, and online services.
- In 1993 the world's first browser, Mosaic, was released. A browser is a graphical interface for the Internet. Mosaic made it so easy to access the Internet that there was a 340% growth rate in this one year.
- The Internet is still growing at an unprecedented rate.

How Computing and the Internet Impact Society

3-4.1.1-1 Computers and the Internet have had dramatic effects on how we live, learn, and work. For example, the nature of many jobs has changed because of computer usage and the Internet. Time-consuming, labor-intensive communications tasks that used to require the use of face-to-face meetings, telephone calls, faxes, or paging through printed materials is now performed quickly and efficiently using Internet browsers and e-mail. Human resource managers and recruiters, for example, no longer have to sift through stacks of resumes to find qualified job candidates. They can now search for job candidates using online resources, allowing them to focus on resumes that most closely match the job requirements. In some cases, they can even conduct interviews online via e-mail correspondence.

3-4.1.1-2 3-4.1.2-1 Information technology has also facilitated changes in the way many organizations go about their business. Libraries, for example, have replaced their card catalogs with computer files that users can access 24-hours-a-day via the Internet. Shopping for many products—especially those for which quality and fit are standardized and customers do not need to see or feel something before they buy—is rapidly shifting to Internet retailers and wholesalers that can offer lower cost and quicker service. Schools use computers and the Internet to supplement traditional classroom teaching, to facilitate collaborative projects such as homework and university research, and to provide online educational services that students can take without ever leaving their homes or workplaces.

3-4.1.3-1 3-4.1.3-2 The use of computers and the Internet in American homes has spread quickly among all demographic groups and across geographic regions. It has been spurred by increasing computer usage in schools and workplaces. By 2002, more than two-thirds of Americans used computers, and more than 150 million Americans, nearly 60% of the population, used the Internet at home, work, or school. Usage levels among children were even higher. Common uses at home include e-mail, operating home offices, managing household budgets and financial planning, obtaining information on products and services, making online purchases, playing games, and searching for health information.

3-4.1.4-1 3-4.1.4-2 Computer technology also operates behind the scenes in many daily activities. When people insert a bankcard into an ATM or swipe a credit card at the store, computers read coded information to allow them to access accounts and keep track of transactions. So-called "smart cards" even store real-time information right on the card. Cars use computers embedded in various components to keep them running smoothly and performing efficiently based on their owners' driving habits. Computer automation in factories speeds up work and raises quality standards as interconnected production processes, many performed by computerized robots, are constantly monitored and fine-tuned to avoid bottlenecks and maximize efficiency.

IC3 3-4.1.5-1 3-4.1.5-3

The benefits of computers and the Internet are so numerous and widespread that they're value is incalculable. Businesses have automated record-keeping tasks that used to require countless man-hours, freeing workers for more productive activities. Marketers instantaneously send information via the Internet to prospective customers anywhere in the world, incurring no incremental cost beyond maintaining a Web site and e-mail list. Buyers comparison shop products and services offered by dozens or even hundreds of possible sellers, all without making a single phone call.

IC3 3-4.1.5-2

For people who are disabled or disadvantaged, computers and the Internet give them opportunities they've never known. Voice recognition and speech synthesis technology open up vast sources of information and opportunities for communication for the blind or verbally disabled. People who have difficulty moving around physically can now conduct many activities via the Internet that previously would not have been possible. For anyone and everyone, computers and the Internet are creating new opportunities every day—to manage investments, to learn and research, to keep in touch with distant friends and family members, to stay informed about political developments and make views known to government officials, and to nurture relationships that bridge and break down national, ethnic, and cultural barriers in an increasingly interconnected world.

IC3 3-1.2.3-2

Accessing the Internet

Before you can even begin to surf the Net you have to be connected. If you connect to the Internet from an office or academic setting, you are probably connecting through a local area network (LAN). You connect to the Internet using a network interface card (NIC). This is a special card inside your computer that allows the computer to be networked. A direct connection is made from the LAN to a high-speed connection line, most likely leased from the local telephone company. See Figure 2-1.

FIGURE 2-1
Ways to access the Internet

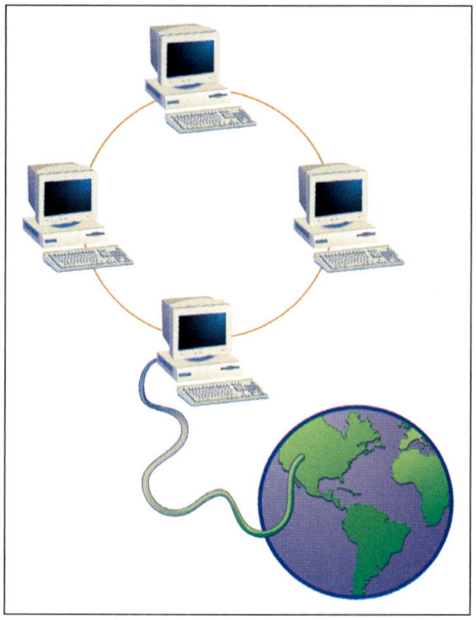

3-1.2.4-1 For the home user, the most common type of Internet connection is with a modem and a telephone line. Signals transmitted across a normal telephone line are analog or continuous. A modem is a device that converts the computer's digital signal into an analog signal, therefore allowing data to be sent from one computer to another.

Getting connected to the Internet is fairly simple, but there are a few steps you need to take:

3-1.2.3-1
3-1.2.3-2

- **Step 1:** Locate an Internet service provider (ISP) or an online service. There are thousands of Internet service providers. Most are small local companies. Their service is primarily a connection or "on ramp" to the Internet. Online services are large national and international companies. Four of the largest online services are America Online, Prodigy, CompuServe, and MSN. Generally, the local ISP is less expensive, but many people use the online services because of the additional information and services they offer.
- **Step 2:** Once you find an ISP, you must install some type of telecommunications software. This software enables your computer to connect to another computer. Most likely your ISP or online service company will provide this software.
- 3-1.1.1-3 **Step 3:** You will need to install a software application called a Web browser in order to surf the Web. The Web is one component of the Internet (see later in this lesson). Two of the most popular browsers are Netscape's Navigator and Microsoft's Internet Explorer.

You've contracted with your ISP and you've installed your software. It's now time to connect to the Internet. This is the easy part. You give instructions to your computer to dial a local telephone number. This number connects you to your ISP's computer, which in turn connects you to the Internet. You're online with the world. See Figure 2-2.

FIGURE 2-2
Modem and telephone connection

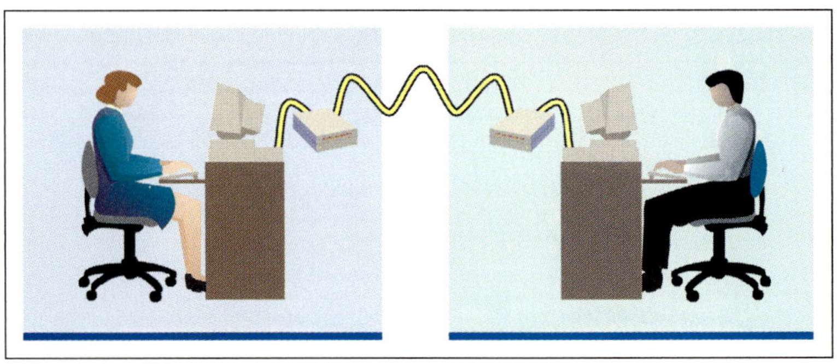

Other Types of Connections

3-1.2.4-1 Many people are happy with their Internet telephone connection, but some want more speed and are willing to pay for it. They may choose to use high-speed digital lines such as ISDN (Integrated Services Digital Network) or DSL (Digital Subscriber Lines). With ISDN and DSL, special hardware allows data transmission at far greater speeds than the standard phone wiring.

Another high-speed option is the cable modem. This type of modem also connects to your computer, but it uses a network interface card. Instead of using a telephone line as a transmission media to connect to the ISP, coaxial cable is used. This is the same type of cable used for cable TV.

Finally, a third way to connect to the Internet is using your television and WebTV. Most WebTV products consist of a set-top box that connects to your telephone line and television. It makes a connection to the Internet via your telephone service and then converts the downloaded Web pages to a format that can be displayed on your TV.

How Does the Internet Work?

First of all, the Internet is transitory, ever changing, reshaping, and remolding itself. It is a loose association of thousands of networks and millions of computers across the world that all work together to share information. The beauty of this network of networks is that all brands, models, and makes of computers can communicate with each other. This is called interoperability.

So how do we communicate across the Internet? Think about our postal service. If you want to send someone a letter anywhere in the world, you can do that—as long as you know the address. The Internet works in a similar fashion. From your computer, you can connect with any other networked computer anywhere in the world—as long as you know the address.

3-1.2.2-1

Computers on the Internet communicate with each other using a set of protocols known as TCP/IP, or Transmission Control Protocol and Internet Protocol. A protocol is a standard format for transferring data between two devices. TCP/IP is the agreed-on international standard for transmitting data. It is considered the language of the Internet. The TCP protocol enables two host computers to establish a connection and exchange data. A host computer is simply a computer that you access remotely. The IP protocol works with the addressing scheme. It allows you to enter an address and sends it to another computer; from there the TCP protocol takes over. Returning to our postal service analogy, this is similar to what happens when you take a letter to the post office. You deliver the letter to the post office and then the post office takes over. See Figure 2-3.

FIGURE 2-3
Data travels the Internet

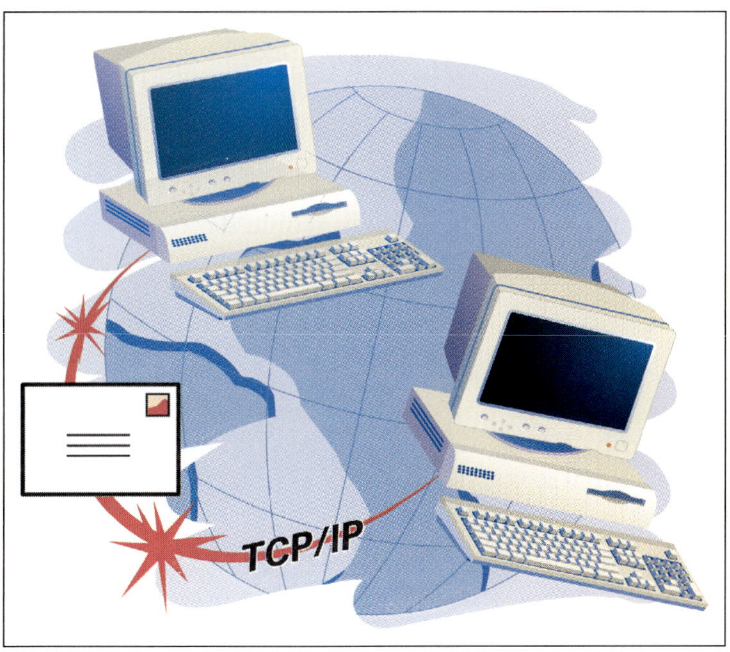

Postal addresses usually contain numbers and street names. Likewise, when we access another computer on the Internet, we are accessing it via a number. However, we don't have to remember or type in that number. Instead we can type in the ***domain name***. The domain name identifies a site on the Internet. An example of a domain name is *www.microsoft.com*. If we want to access the Microsoft Corporation's computers that are connected to the Internet, we start our browser and type the domain name.

Major Features of the Internet

So far in this lesson, we've discussed the Internet. The Internet, however, is made up of many services. Some of the more popular of these services include the World Wide Web, e-mail, chat, mailing lists, FTP, and Newsgroups.

> **Internet**
>
> There are hundreds or even thousands of online tutorials to help you become more familiar with Internet features. You can find several tutorials at *www.northernwebs.com*. Topics covered include learning while you surf, offline operations and file downloading, configuring e-mail and news readers, FTP, and myths of the Internet.

The World Wide Web

IC3 3-1.1.1-2

Many people use the terms ***World Wide Web***, or Web for short, and Internet interchangeably. In reality, they're actually two different things. The Web is a subset or an application that makes use of the Internet.

IC3 3-1.1.1-3

It consists of a collection of electronic files, referred to as Web pages, which contain information and built-in hyperlinks. When you click a hyperlink, you are transferred to another electronic file. A series of related Web pages is referred to as a Web site. There are thousands (if not millions) of Web sites functioning on the Web.

IC3 3-3.1.5-1 3-3.1.6-1 3-1.1.6-2

Businesses have Web sites where they can advertise and sell products and services, provide information to investors, or post job openings. The Web sites for schools, universities, and other educational institutions often list course offerings, supply electronic enrollment forms, and even offer distance-learning opportunities. And there are a multitude of sites hosted by businesses, professional and non-profit associations, churches, medical organizations, and so forth which exist solely to provide information. In addition, there are a number of Web sites designed to access data from electronic databases that are stored on a server. For example, when you purchase something online from a company, all the information about that item, including its identification number, price, description, measurements or weight (if applicable), and delivery options, comes from a database of the company's products. Your local library stores data on books, videos, newspapers, and journals in an electronic database that you can access through the library's Web site anytime of the day.

The Web actually began in March 1989 when Tim Berners-Lee, who works with a European organization known as Cern, wrote a small computer program for his own personal use. This text-based program permitted pages to be linked through a formatting process known as hypertext markup language (HTML). Clicking a linked word transfers you from one computer to another. You do not have to type the Web site address. This was a step forward, but it is not the catalyst that made the Web what it is today.

The number of people using the Web greatly increased in 1993. This increase occurred when Marc Andreessen, working for the National Center for Supercomputing Applications at the University of Illinois, released Mosaic. Mosaic was the first graphical browser. See Figure 2-4.

FIGURE 2-4
Mosaic Web site

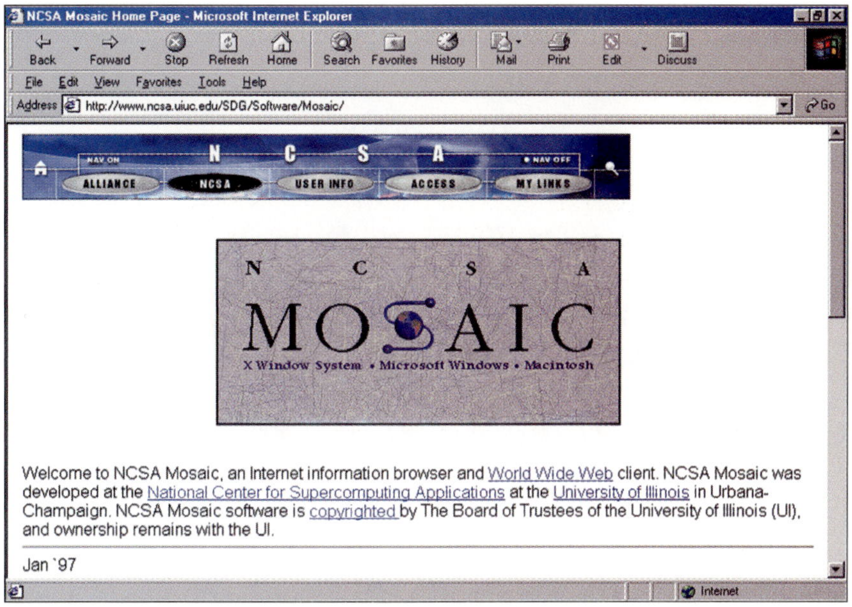

In 1994 Andreessen co-founded Netscape Communications. With the introduction of Mosaic and the Web browsers that followed, the Web became a communications tool for a much wider audience. Currently, two of the most popular Web browsers are Internet Explorer and Netscape Navigator. As a result of these enhancements, the Web is one of the most popular services available on the Internet.

Web Protocols—HTTP

The Web has its own underlying protocols. One protocol is known as HTTP, or ***hypertext transfer protocol.*** This protocol, or standard, defines how messages are formatted and transmitted. You can send and receive Web pages over the Internet because Web servers and browsers both understand HTTP. For instance, when you enter a Web site address in your browser, this sends an HTTP command to the Web server to tell it to locate and transmit the requested Web page. A Web server is a computer that contains Web pages. By installing special software, any computer can become a Web server. Every Web server has its own IP address and most have a domain name. The domain name identifies the IP address.

3-3.2.1-1

The Web site address is commonly referred to as the ***URL***, or ***Uniform Resource Locator***. Every Web page on the Internet has its own unique address. The first part of the address indicates what protocol to use, and the second part specifies the IP address or the domain name where the resource is located. For example, in the URL *www.hamsterdance.com*, the http protocol indicates that this is a Web page and the domain name is *hamsterdance*. See Figure 2-5. The *.com* at the end of the name indicates that this is a commercial organization or business. See Table 2-1 for other domain abbreviations.

FIGURE 2-5
Hamsterdance

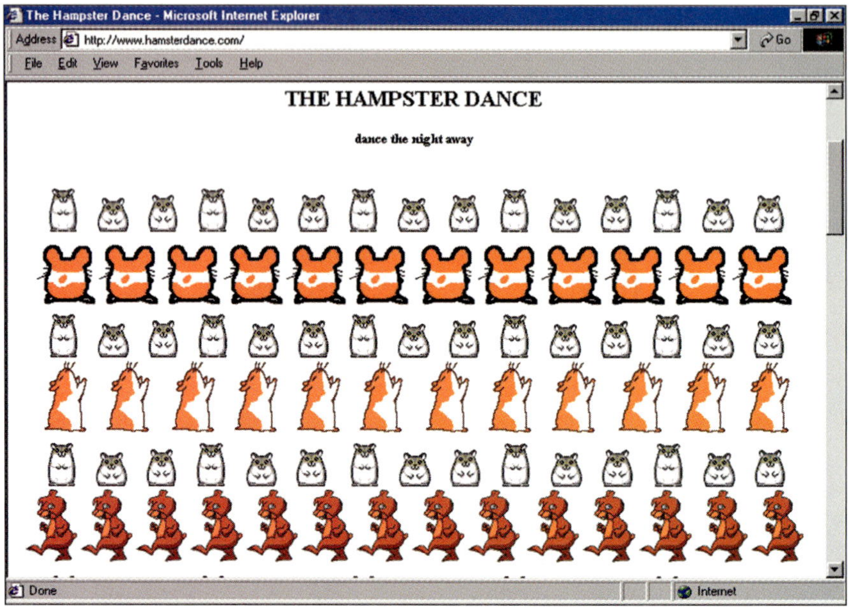

TABLE 2-1
Domain names

DOMAIN ABBREVIATION	TYPE OF ORGANIZATION
edu	Educational institutions
com	Commercial businesses, companies, and organizations
gov	Government institutions, such as the IRS
mil	Military organizations, such as the army
net	Network provider org Nonprofit organization

Web Protocols—HTML

A second protocol or standard that controls how the World Wide Web works is ***HTML***, or ***hypertext markup language***. This protocol determines how Web pages are formatted and displayed and allows the users to exchange text, images, sound, video, and multimedia files. Hypertext is a link to another location. The location can be within the same document, in another document on the same Web server, or on a Web server on the other side of the world. You click on the link and are transported to the location.

Hot Tip

Have you ever had a burning desire to know just exactly how something works? For instance, have you wondered how a cell phone works? Or what happens to your body when you drink all of that caffeine? Or how nuclear energy works? Or what the name WD-40 stands for? You can find the answers to all of these questions at *www.howstuffworks.com/*.

A Web page is nothing more than an ordinary text page coded with HTML markup tags and then displayed within a browser. Markup tags consist of set text commands that are interpreted by the browser. Different browsers may format and display the HTML markup tags differently. Altogether, three items determine the look of a Web page:

- The type and version of the browser displaying the Web page
- The actual HTML markup tags used to code the page
- The user's monitor and monitor resolution

STEP-BY-STEP 2.1

1. Start your Web browser.

3-3.2.2-1 2. In the Address box, key **www.weather.com**, and press **Enter**.

3-3.2.3-1 3. Notice that the Web page contains text that is underlined. The underlined text also changes color when you hover the mouse pointer on it. These are hyperlinks. Pictures and graphics can also be hyperlinks. You can tell that a picture or graphic is a hyperlink if the mouse pointer changes to the shape of a hand with a pointing finger when you hover the mouse pointer on it. Click a link of your choice to go to a different Web page.

3-3.2.3-2 4. Locate the graphic that says **The Weather Channel**. If you don't see this graphic, position your mouse pointer on another picture or graphic hyperlink. Click the hyperlink to jump to another Web page. Clicking links allows you to navigate from Web page to Web page. In other words, you're "surfing" the Web!

3-3.1.4-1 5. Notice the bar at the top of the Web page. It should have links for "Home," "Travel," "My Weather," etc. These represent Web site navigation tools. You can also use buttons, such as the Back and Forward buttons, on the toolbar of your browser to navigate a Web site. Click one of the links in the navigation bar. Click additional links to search for other weather-related information. When you are done, close your browser.

Electronic Mail

3-1.1.1-3 Another popular service on the Internet is ***electronic mail***, or e-mail. In its simplest form, e-mail is an electronic message sent from one computer to another. Anyone with an e-mail account can send a message to anyone else who has an e-mail account. In addition to sending a message, you can include attachments such as pictures or documents. You can also forward messages to other people who have e-mail accounts.

When you send postal mail to someone, you must know the address. The same thing is true for e-mail. An e-mail address consists of three parts:

- The user name of the individual
- The "@" symbol
- The user's domain name

For instance, Mary Smith's e-mail address could be msmith@AOL.com.

To send an e-mail, you must have an e-mail program. This is generally supplied by your ISP. Many different e-mail programs are available. You'll learn more about e-mail in Lesson 3.

Chat Rooms

You can call someone through the Internet and "talk" to them the way you do on the phone, only you are writing and reading on your computer rather than talking and listening with a phone in your hand. You are using the computer to create real-time communication between yourself and another user or a group of users. To participate in a chat, you enter a virtual chat room. Once a chat has been initiated, users enter text by typing on the keyboard, and the message appears on the monitor of the other participants.

Did You Know?

Did you know there are Web sites where you can "Ask an expert" an educational question you may have—from the arts to law to health? One of the more popular educational "Ask an Expert" Web sites is located at *www.askanexpert.com/*. At this Web site, you can communicate with professionals such as astronauts, a fireplace expert, a nanny expert, and a public relations expert—just to name a few.

IC3 3-3.1.1-1 3-3.1.1-2

Mailing Lists

A mailing list is a group of people with a shared interest. Their e-mail addresses are collected into a group, and this group is identified by a single name. Whenever you send a message, everyone on the list receives a copy. Some mailing lists are called LISTSERVs, named after a mailing list software program. There are mailing lists for every imaginable topic. Many professional groups and associations utilize mailing lists as an effective way of communicating with members and potential members. You can subscribe to a mailing list just as you would subscribe to a magazine. A list owner is the person who manages the list.

Ethics in Technology

ELECTRONIC MAIL: RULES OF ETIQUETTE

Electronic mail (e-mail) is a popular feature of the Internet. It is easy to understand and simple to use. It is also easy to abuse and easy to give someone the wrong impression of what you are trying to say.

When we communicate face to face with someone, our visual cues indicate much of what we are trying to express. We smile, cry, wrinkle our nose. If we are communicating via telephone, our voice inflections can indicate our emotions. But this is not so for e-mail. It is a totally different communications medium.

There are no set rules, but some of the following may help you with your e-mail:

IC3 3-2.3.4-1

- Be polite. Avoid jokes and emotions (series of characters that represent an emotion, such as surprised— : - 0) in professional and business-related e-mails. The person(s) reading the e-mail may not understand them or misinterpret them.
- Limit each message to a single subject.
- Keep your message short and to the point.
- Remember that your message can become a permanent part of someone's records.
- Remember that e-mail sent through company networks is not private.

Mailing Lists Features

There are several variations of mailing lists, such as the following:

- Announcements are one type of mailing list. For example, you could subscribe to the IBM mailing list and receive announcements of new products.
- A discussion list is another type of list. Members use this type of list to ask questions and share information on a particular topic. For instance, let's assume you belong to a mailing list for word processing. You want to include a special feature within your document, but you're not sure how to do this. You can send your question to the list members. Most likely, if the list is an active list, you will receive several responses to your question.
- Some lists are public lists and some are closed or private lists. With a public list, anyone can subscribe. A private list limits subscribers to members of a particular organization or group.
- Some mailing lists have a summary or digest version. Instead of receiving each individual message posted to the list, the list manager or list owner groups the postings. Generally this is for a designated time period, such as a day or a week. Then the postings are sent as a batch to all subscribers.

Hot Tip

Interested in going to high school online? In Florida, you can do just that. The online high school started in 1996. Thousands of students are now attending the online high school. Students attending the online school can earn a high school diploma. There is no tuition charge for students living in Florida. You can check out a list of other virtual high schools at *www.vhs. ucsc.edu/vhs/casestudies.htm*.

Internet

Like to play games? If so, you can play all types of games online—from board games to role-playing games. Check out the GameSpot Web site at *www.gamespot.com*.

Technology Careers

WEB DEVELOPER

A Web developer can wear many hats. With the ever-expanding and changing Internet, skill requirements can change daily.

As a Web developer, you will need some technical skills including programming. Some of the more common programming languages are C++, Java, and CGI. You will need a strong background in database development. Oracle and SQL are two of the most widely used database interfaces. Some other requirements may include using Active Server Pages, JavaScript, and Perl.

Employment opportunities in this field are increasing each day as more and more companies develop a Web presence. Depending on the size and location of the company, salaries can range from $25,000 to more than $100,000 a year. Education requirements vary—from certifications with only a high school diploma to a master's degree in information technology.

Before you start subscribing to mailing lists, do your homework. Many of these lists produce a huge volume of e-mail messages. You could end up receiving hundreds or even thousands of messages a day.

Newsgroups

3-3.1.2-1

A ***newsgroup*** is a discussion forum or a type of bulletin board. Each "board" is dedicated to discussion on a particular topic. The difference between a newsgroup and a mailing list is that with a newsgroup you can select the topics you want to read. These messages are stored on a news server, which is a computer that contains the necessary newsgroup software.

3-3.1.2-2

A worldwide network of computers called ***USENET*** facilitates the transmission of messages among the news servers. The news servers utilize the Network News Transport Protocol (NNTP) to connect with other USENET news servers. This protocol also makes it possible to distribute messages to anyone using a newsreader.

To find groups and participate in discussions that interest you, you need a newsreader. This software enables you to read messages and to post your message to a newsgroup. Many e-mail programs contain a newsreader. If your e-mail program does not contain a newsreader or you want one with more features, many are available for download through the Internet.

3-3.1.3-1
3-3.1.3-2

Some newsgroups are moderated, meaning any messages or information sent to the group are first read and reviewed by a moderator. The moderator determines whether the information is appropriate and relevant and, in some cases, may edit the material before posting to the group.

There are over 50,000 different newsgroups, and the number is increasing each day. These newsgroups are easy to navigate because they are organized by subject into hierarchies. There are eight major subject headings. See Table 2-2. Each subject hierarchy is broken down into subcategories, and there are hundreds of alternative hierarchies.

TABLE 2-2
Subject hierarchies

HIERARCHY ABBREVIATION	DESCRIPTION	EXAMPLE
comp	Computer science and computer-related topics	comp.infosystems
humanities	Fine arts, literature discussions	humanities, classics
misc	Anything that doesn't fit within the other categories	misc.jobs
news	USENET information	news.announce
rec	Recreational topics	rec.music.info
talk	Discussions and debates on controversial subjects	talk.environment
sci	Scientific discussions and research	sci.energy
soc	Social issues	soc.culture

File Transfer Protocol

At one time or another, you may have been on the Internet and tried to access a special feature such as an audio file. You receive a message that a plug-in is required. A plug-in is an add-on software application that adds a specific feature to your Web browser or other programs. You click on a link and the plug-in is downloaded or transmitted to your computer.

You most likely have just used ***file transfer protocol*** (FTP). This is an Internet standard that allows users to download and upload files to and from other computers on the Internet.

> **Internet**
>
> Need some help with public speaking? This Web site has public speaking presentation tips. Check it out at *www.homebusinessmag.com*.

Many FTP servers are connected to the Internet. Some of these require user IDs and passwords. Others permit anonymous FTP access. This means that anyone can upload and download files from the server. The files on the server can be any type of file. Some examples are software updates for your printer, a revised instruction manual, or a new program that is being tested.

Many people use FTP servers to store compressed or zipped files that they want to share with someone else. Using a compression program reduces the size of a file so it can be downloaded and/or uploaded more quickly. For this type of activity, it is generally easier to use a stand-alone application program. One of the more popular stand-alone programs is WS_FTP. This program is free to students and educational institutions. The remote computer to which you are transferring a file must also have FTP available.

SUMMARY

In this lesson, you learned:

- No one person or organization can claim credit for the Internet.
- Origins of the Internet can be traced to the U.S. Department of Defense. The original name for the Internet was ARPANET.
- Mosaic was the Internet's first graphical interface.
- To connect to the Internet from a business or academic setting, you probably have a direct connection via a local area network and a network interface card. For the home user, the most common type of Internet connection is with a modem and telephone line.
- To connect to the Internet, you need an Internet connection, telecommunications software, and a browser.
- Other types of Internet connections include ISDN, DSL, cable modem, and WebTV.
- Interoperability means that all brands, models, and makes of computers can communicate with each other.
- A protocol is a standard format for transferring data between two devices. TCP/IP is the agreed-on international standard for transmitting data.
- The domain name identifies a site on the Internet.
- The Web is an application that makes use of the Internet. Other features of the Internet include electronic mail, chat rooms, mailing lists, and newsgroups.
- Web pages can be linked through hypertext.
- Microsoft's Internet Explorer and Netscape's Navigator are two of the most popular Web browsers.
- The HTTP protocol defines how Web messages are formatted and transmitted.

- The Web site address is referred to as the URL, or Uniform Resource Locator. Every Web page on the Internet has its own unique address.
- A Web page is coded with HTML markup tags. HTML is another protocol that controls how Web pages are formatted and displayed.

VOCABULARY *Review*

Define the following terms:

Domain name	Hypertext transfer protocol (HTTP)	USENET
Electronic mail	Newsgroup	World Wide Web
File transfer protocol (FTP)	Uniform Resource Locator (URL)	
Hypertext markup language (HTML)		

REVIEW *Questions*

MULTIPLE CHOICE

Select the best response for the following statements.

1. A(n) ________ is any computer directly connected to a network.
   A. newsreader
   B. host node
   C. domain name
   D. URL

2. The process of all makes and models of computers being able to communicate with each other is called ________.
   A. services
   B. ISDN
   C. interoperability
   D. Internetwork

3. The first graphical browser was named ________.
   A. Internet Explorer
   B. Navigator
   C. Avatar
   D. Mosaic

4. If you wanted to send someone a message on the Internet, you would use ________.
   A. e-mail
   B. a newsreader
   C. a chat room
   D. a list manager

5. A virtual world is a type of ________ program.
   A. e-mail
   B. chat
   C. newsgroup
   D. FTP

TRUE/FALSE

Circle T if the statement is true or F if the statement is false.

T F 1. Educational institutions normally use the ".aca" domain name.

T F 2. A mailing list owner manages virtual chat rooms.

T F 3. ISDN is a high-speed connection to the Internet.

T F 4. You must use a modem to communicate over a regular telephone line.

T F 5. TCP/IP is called the language of the Internet.

FILL IN THE BLANK

Complete the following sentences by writing the correct word or words in the blanks provided.

1. An e-mail address consists of ________ parts.
2. An announcement list is a type of ________ list.
3. The original name for the Internet was ________.
4. ________ software enables your computer to connect to another computer.
5. A(n) ________ modem uses coaxial cable.

PROJECTS

PROJECT 2-1

Visit the National Zoo at *www.si.edu/natzoo/*. Tour the Web site. Use your word-processing software and write a summary of this Web site. Include the following topics: (1) information on the Web Cams and what animals you could view; (2) description of the elephant demo; and (3) description of the audio tours. What is your overall opinion about this site?

PROJECT 2-2

In this lesson, several Internet features were described. Which one of these features would you most likely use and why? List each of the features and use a ranking scale of 1 to 5 (1 means you would probably never use this feature and 5 that you would definitely use it). Prepare a report that explains your rankings. Explain why you ranked each feature as you did.

WEB PROJECT

Internet etiquette is a very important topic for someone who uses the Internet for e-mail, newsgroups, and other Internet features. Do an Internet search and see what additional information you can find on Internet etiquette. Prepare a report on your findings. If available, use a presentation program to deliver your report. Here are some URLs to get you started:

www.iwillfollow.com/email.htm

www.dtcc.edu/cs/rfc1855.html

www.albion.com/netiquette/

www.fau.edu/netiquette/netiquette.html

TEAMWORK PROJECT

You and your teammates work for a company that currently has no Internet connection. Your manager has asked you and your "co-workers" to prepare a presentation that would convince the president of the company that an Internet connection would be a vital enhancement to the company's operations. You and your team should gather information and statistics and present your findings in either a written report or a slideshow presentation.

CRITICAL *Thinking*

ACTIVITY 2-1

Do you think the government will ever be able to regulate the Internet? That is, will any agency ever be able to control and limit what someone puts online? Use your word-processing program and write a page on your thoughts on this issue.

LESSON 3

Using the Internet

OBJECTIVES

Upon completion of this lesson, you should be able to:

- Describe a browser.
- Understand browser terminology.
- Understand how to use a browser to surf the Internet.
- Understand and use browser features.
- Understand e-mail features.
- Use e-mail features.

Estimated Time: 1.5 hours

VOCABULARY

Address bar
Address book
Browser
Electronic mail
Home page
Uniform Resource Locator (URL)
Web server

What Is a Browser?

A ***browser*** is the software program that you use to retrieve documents from the World Wide Web (WWW or Web) and to display them in a readable format. The Web is the graphical portion of the Internet. The browser functions as an interface between you and the Internet. Using a browser, you can display both text and images. Newer versions of most browsers can also support multimedia information, including sound and video.

The browser sends a message to the ***Web server*** to retrieve your requested Web page. Then the browser renders the HTML code to display the page. HTML, or hypertext markup language, is the language used to create documents for the WWW. You navigate through the Web by using your mouse to point and click on hyperlinked words and images.

Two popular browsers are Microsoft Internet Explorer and Netscape Communicator. See Figures 3-1 and 3-2.

FIGURE 3-1
Internet Explorer

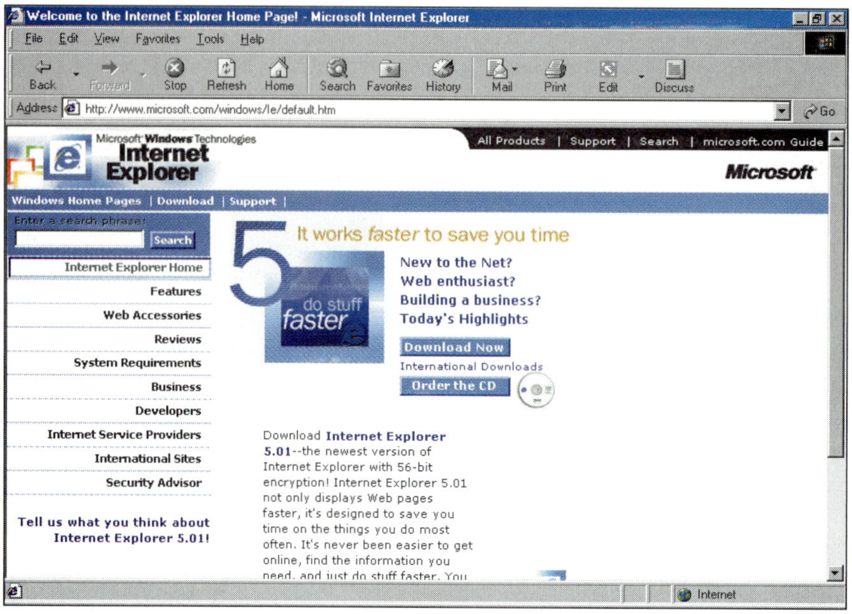

FIGURE 3-2
Netscape Communicator

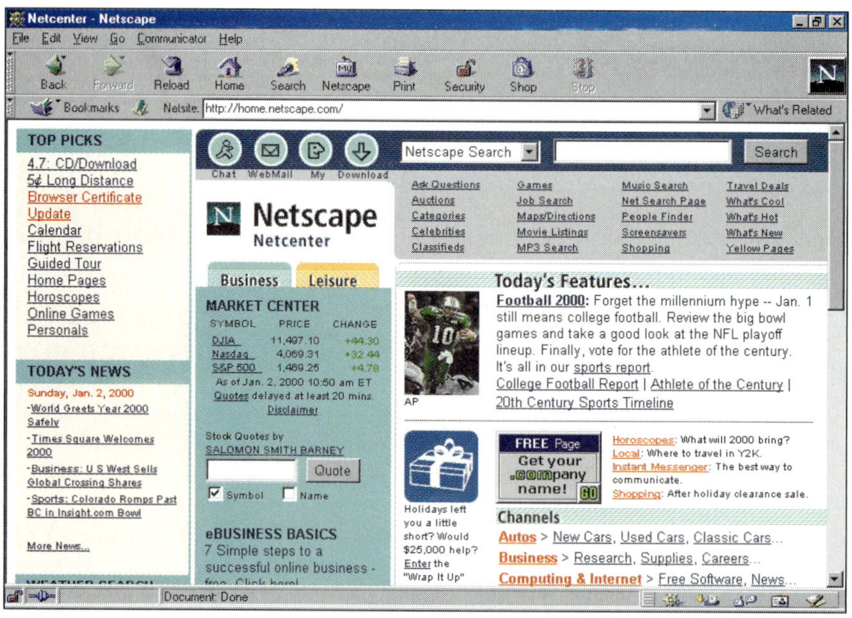

Both these browsers have very similar features, but the menu options to select these features may be somewhat different. The major differences between the two browsers are primarily within some special built-in tools. These tools include programs for mail, chat, viewing and listening to multimedia, and so forth.

Browser Terminology

Understanding the parts of the browser window is the key to using a browser effectively. See Figure 3-3. Table 3-1 contains a definition of each part of the screen.

FIGURE 3-3
Browser window terminology

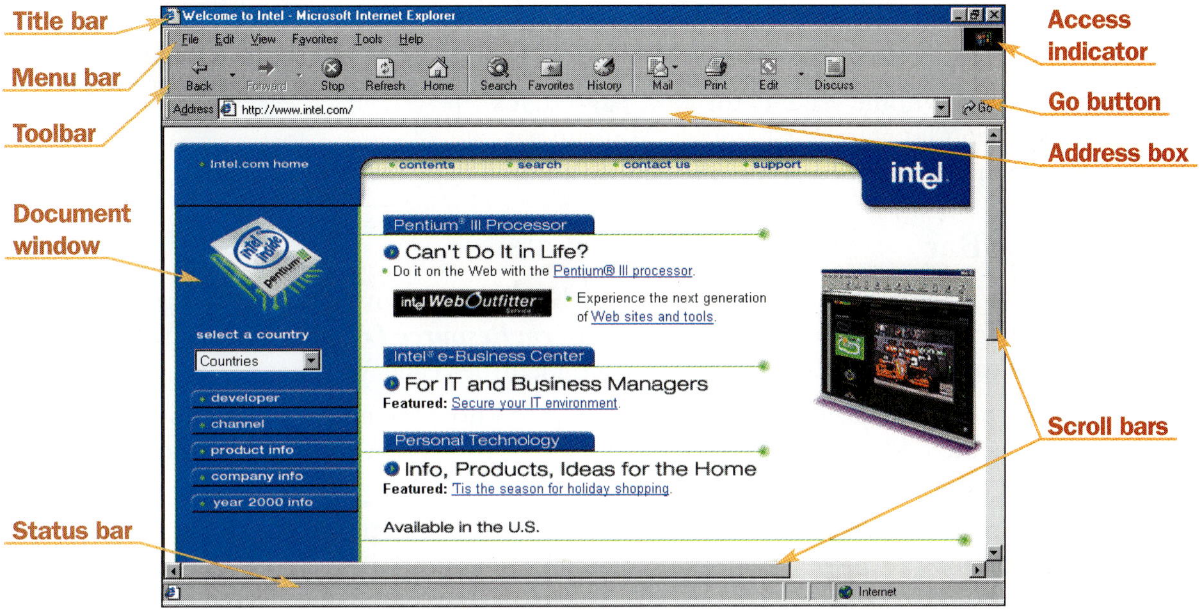

TABLE 3-1
Parts of the browser window

ITEM	DEFINITION
Title bar	The bar at the top of the window that contains the name of the document.
Menu bar	Contains menu names that you can click to display various commands and options.
Toolbar	Contains icons for single-click access to most commonly used menu commands.
Address bar	Contains the URL, or address, of the active Web page; also where you enter the location for the Web page you want to visit.
Go button	Connects you to the address displayed in the Address bar.
Document window	Displays the active Web page.
Status bar	Located at the bottom of the browser window; shows the progress of Web page transactions.
Access indicator	A small picture in the upper right corner of the browser; when animated, it means your browser is accessing data from a remote computer.
Scroll bars	Vertical and horizontal scroll bars; let you scroll vertically and horizontally if the Web page is too long or wide to fit within one screen.

Browser Basics

> **Did You Know?**
>
> Many people create a custom home page. If you have access to the Internet and can upload your own Web page, you may want to create a page with hyperlinks you visit frequently.

In this lesson it is assumed you have an Internet connection—either dial-in or direct connection. To connect to the Internet, you first launch your Web browser. In most instances, you can double-click the browser icon located on your computer's desktop. If the icon is not available, open the browser from the Start menu.

IC3 3-3.2.4-1 When your browser is installed, a default home page is selected. The home page is the first page that's displayed when you launch your browser. You can easily change your home page. Most people choose a home page they want to view frequently.

The Address Bar

The *address bar* is located near the top of the browser window. This bar contains the address of the current page. This address is called the ***Uniform Resource Locator (URL)***. The URL tells the browser where to locate the page. A unique URL identifies each Web page.

If you want to visit a specific Web site, you need to know the address. This address bar is also where you enter the address of the Web site you wish to visit. After you key the URL, you can press Enter to go to the Web site.

Once you are at a Web site, you can use a variety of navigation tools to get to the information you are searching for.

IC3 STEP-BY-STEP 3.1

1. Launch your Internet browser. The first page you see is your home page.

3-3.2.4-1

2. In the address bar, key the following URL: **www.whitehouse.gov**. This takes you to the home page of the White House for the U.S. president.

3-3.2.4-2

3. You can navigate through the pages of the site using a number of navigation tools:

3-3.2.5-1

   a. Notice the list of links on the left side of the home page. Click one of your choice and review the information on the page you jumped to. Click the **Home** link to return to the home page.

   b. Notice the links across the top of the page. Click the **Kids Only** link. Review the information on the page, and then click the **Back** button on your browser's toolbar.

STEP-BY-STEP 3.1 Continued

c. Click the **Site Map** link at the top of the page. You are jumped to a page that illustrates in outline form the various Web pages contained within the site, as shown in Figure 3-4.

FIGURE 3-4
Site map page at *www.whitehouse.gov*

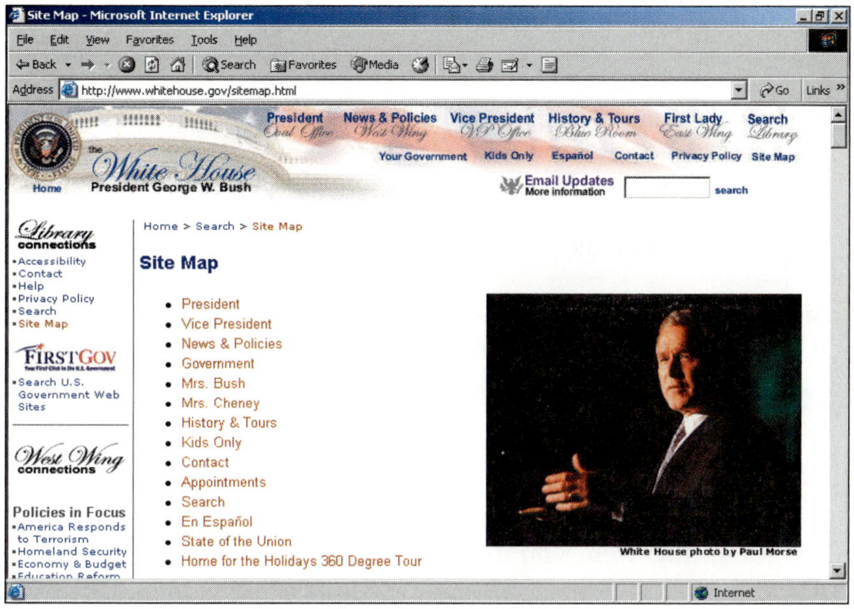

d. You should see a "search" box on the Site Map page. In the box, key **"George Washington"**. Be sure to key the opening and closing quotation marks as shown.

3-3.2.5-2 **e.** Click a link in the search results list to find more information on George Washington. If necessary, click additional links on the pages to find more detailed information on the first president. This is referred to as "drilling down" in a Web site to find information. Try to find a page that includes both text and images.

4. Review the information you find, and keep this Web page open for the next Step-by-Step.

Favorites and Bookmarks

3-3.2.6-1 3-3.2.6-2 The Web has so much to offer that it's very likely you are going to find some sites you really like and wish to return to often. It's easy to keep these sites just a mouse click away by adding them to your Favorites (Internet Explorer) or Bookmark (Communicator) list.

To add a site to your list of sites:

- Go to the site you want to add.
- For Internet Explorer, on the Favorites menu, click Add to Favorites. For Communicator, click Bookmarks, and choose Add Bookmark.
- To revisit any of the Favorites or Bookmarks, just click the Favorites or Bookmarks button, and then select the shortcut to the site.

3-3.2.7-1 As your list begins to grow, you can organize it by creating folders. You can organize by topics in much the same way you would organize files in a file drawer.

STEP-BY-STEP 3.2

3-3.2.6-1
1. You should have a Web page on George Washington open in your browser. Highlight the page's URL in the address bar, and then add the site to your Favorites or Bookmarks. The Web page should now appear in your Favorites or Bookmarks list.

3-3.2.7-1
2. Create a folder named **George Washington** in your Favorites or Bookmarks list.

3-3.2.7-2
3. Drag the Web page you saved to your list to the **George Washington** folder.
4. Go back to the home page for the *www.whitehouse.gov* site.

3-3.2.6-2
5. Open your **George Washington** Favorites or Bookmarks folder, and then click the link for the George Washington Web page you saved. Remain in this screen for the next Step-by-Step.

Working with Web Pages

As you view pages on the Web, you'll find a lot of things you'd like to save to a computer disk so that you can refer to them later without having to connect to the Internet. Browsers have features that enable you to save a complete Web page or any part of a Web page. This includes text, images, or hyperlinks.

Ethics in Technology

INTERNET SECURITY

3-4.3.3-1
3-4.3.3-2

If you've surfed the Internet recently, you know you can purchase just about any item you want—from a Mercedes Benz to Uncle Bill's Jam and Jellies. You can have the items shipped to you and pay for it when it arrives or you can use a credit card. The question is how safe you feel about transmitting credit card and other financial information over the Internet.

When you provide your credit card number, it travels through several computers before it reaches its final destination. To ensure that your credit card number is not easily stolen, companies use a technology called encryption. This encryption software acts similarly to the cable converter box on your television. The data is scrambled with a secret code so no one can interpret it while it is being transmitted. When the data reaches its destination, the same software unscrambles the information.

Not all Web sites use security measures. One way to identify a secure site is to check the status bar at the bottom of your Web browser. There you will see a small icon—usually a lock. When the lock is closed, it indicates the site is using security technology.

3-3.2.8-1 3-3.2.8-2 3-3.2.8-3 3-3.2.8-4

You can save the contents of an entire Web site to disk. With the site open in your browser, you simply use the browser's Save As command. Most browsers give you options for saving, such as saving the entire Web site, including graphics, links, and text; or saving it in htm/html only format, where you see "placeholders" for graphic links; or saving it as a text file where only the text is saved.

3-3.2.8-5

Once you've saved the site, you can open it from disk. The application in which you open it depends on the save options you chose. For example, if you chose to save it as a text file, you can open it in your word-processing program. If you chose to save it in htm/html only format, you can open it in your word-processing program, in an html editing program, or in your browser. Note that you don't have to be connected to the Internet in order to open the site file in your browser.

STEP-BY-STEP 3.3

1. Your favorite or bookmarked George Washington Web page should be open in your browser. On the File menu, select **Save As**.

3-3.2.8-1 3-3.2.8-2 3-3.2.8-3 3-3.2.8-4

2. In the dialog box, select a location on disk to save the Web page using the different save options available in your browser. Be sure to use different filenames that identify each save option; for example, *George Washington HTML Only*, *George Washington Text*, and so forth.

3-3.2.8-5

3. Close your browser. Experiment with opening the different versions of the Web site. Use your word processor to open each version.

3-3.2.9-1 3-3.2.9-2 3-3.2.9-3

You can also copy and save specific elements of a Web page to disk and use in a new document or file. For example, you might want to save a photographic image to disk, or a paragraph of text. You can then open these in other applications or paste them into new files, such as a word-processing document, where you can edit and manipulate them as desired.

3-3.2.10-1 3-3.2.10-2

Or maybe you just want to print a copy of a Web page. You can do that directly from your browser. Most browsers provide previewing and page setup options that enable you to control how the Web page prints.

STEP-BY-STEP 3.4

1. Start your browser and open your favorite or bookmarked George Washington Web page.

3-3.2.9-1 3-3.2.9-2

2. Highlight a paragraph of text, and then select the **Copy** command on your browser's Edit menu.

3. Open your word-processing program and paste the paragraph in a new blank document. Save the file with a name of your choice.

3-3.2.9-3

4. Go back to the Web page in your browser. Right-click a photo or graphic image, and choose the command to save the picture. Select a format for the image and the location to which you want to save it.

5. Open a drawing or graphics program, and then open the image you saved from the Web page.

6. Close all open files, and return to your browser.

STEP-BY-STEP 3.4 Continued

3-3.2.10-2 7. Preview the Web page in your browser. Then, open the dialog box containing page setup options. You might want to change the orientation or margins of the Web page, or even add a header or footer to it.

3-3.2.10-1 8. When you have completed changing the page setup options, print the Web page. Then, close your browser.

E-Mail

E-mail, or ***electronic mail***, is one of the most popular services on the Internet. You can use e-mail to stay in touch with your family and friends, conduct business, and send attachments such as text and image files. You can even check your e-mail when you're on vacation or a business trip.

3-2.1.1-1 E-mail is not that different from regular mail. Actually, it's very similar. You have a message, an address, and a carrier that figures out how to get it from one location to another. Most of the time, e-mail travels much faster than regular mail (sometimes referred to as "snail mail"). When you send someone an e-mail message, it is broken down into small chunks called packets. These packets travel independently from server to server. You might think of each packet as a separate page within a letter. When the packets reach their final destination, they are recombined into their original format. This process enables the message to travel much faster. In fact, some messages can travel thousands of miles in less than a minute.

Browsers usually come with a built-in e-mail program. For example, Outlook Express is the name of Internet Explorer's program. See Figure 3-5.

FIGURE 3-5
Outlook Express

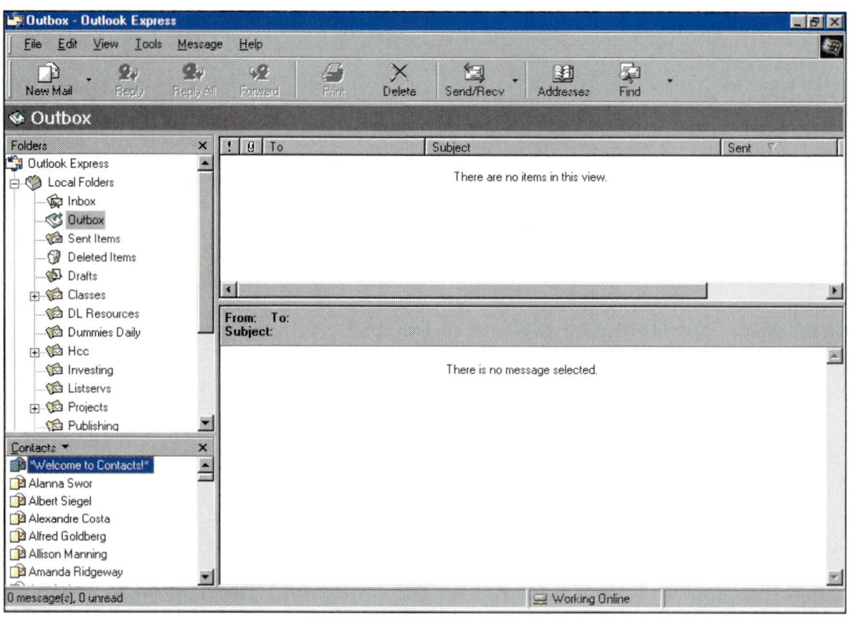

E-mail Addresses

IC3
You send and receive e-mail through an e-mail address. Every e-mail user has a unique e-mail
address. An e-mail address consists of the user name, followed by the @ symbol, followed by the
3-2.1.2-1 user's domain name. Examples of domain names include *.com* for commercial institutions or
3-2.1.2-2 businesses, *.edu* for educational institutions, *.gov* for government offices, *.net* for network gate-
3-2.1.4-1 ways, and *.org* for organizations. The domain name can help you identify the affiliation of an
3-2.1.4-2 e-mail addressee. For example, the e-mail address for the president of the United States is
3-2.1.4-3 *president@whitehouse.gov*.

Creating a Message

IC3
Regardless of the e-mail program used, all e-mail messages contain certain standard ele-
ments, as shown in Figure 3-6. The header contains information on the address(es) of the
3-2.1.3-1 receiver(s). The header also has CC and BCC fields, where you can enter e-mail addresses for
3-2.1.3-2 individuals who are to receive a "carbon copy" of the message or who are to be "blind" copied,
3-2.1.3-3 meaning the primary addressee does not see that others are copied on the message. You can man-
3-2.2.15-1 ually key in e-mail addresses, or you can insert them from your address book. An ***address book***
3-2.2.15-3 is an electronic list of your contacts that works in conjunction with your e-mail program. Once
you enter an e-mail address in your address book, all you have to do is click the name and the
address is inserted automatically in the header of your message. This eliminates the possibility of
keying in the wrong e-mail address

FIGURE 3-6
Standard elements in an e-mail message

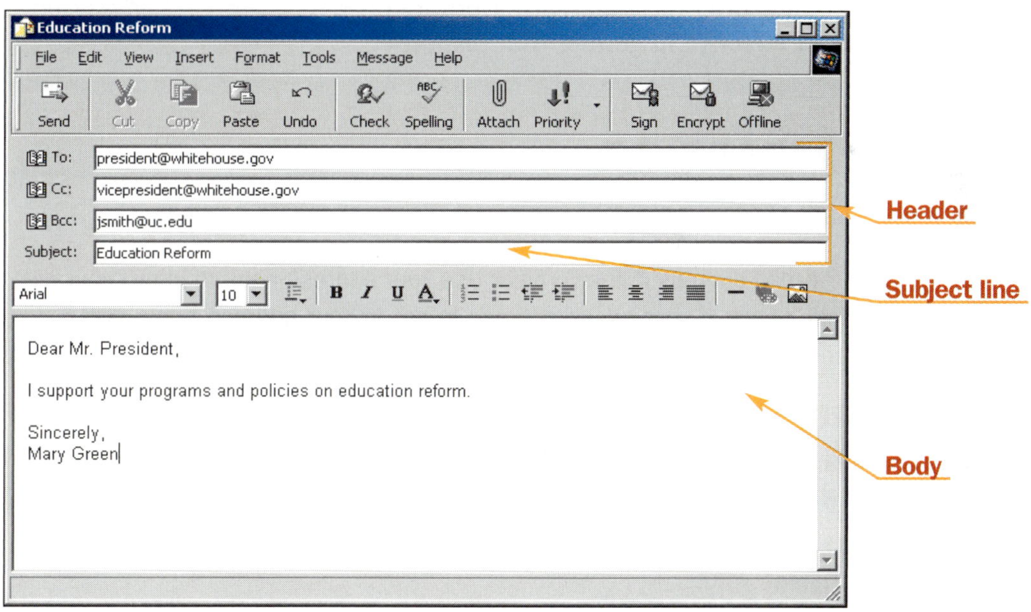

IC3
The subject field in the header section contains a brief description of the content of the mes-
sage. The body contains the text of the message.
3-2.1.3-4
3-2.1.3-5

3-2.1.6-1
3-2.1.6-2

If you send a copy of a file attached to your e-mail message, you should also see a field or icon in the header section to indicate that the message has an attachment. You can attach just about any kind of file to an e-mail message—word-processing documents, pictures or graphics files, sound files, and video files. Sending files as attachments is an easy way to transfer data from one computer to another. The addressee can then open the attachment and view it on their computer, save it to disk (referred to as downloading), or delete it.

Writing Professional E-mail Messages

3-2.3.1-1
3-2.3.1-2
3-2.3.1-3
3-2.3.5-1

E-mail has become a prevalent form of communication for both personal and business users. While it can be informal in nature—much like a telephone conversation—e-mail communication should be courteous and professional, especially among business users. E-mail messages can be printed and saved, so they can serve as "written proof" of what has transpired, much like a signed letter or other official document. It's important to proofread your messages before sending them. Most e-mail programs have spell checkers that can help identify spelling and grammatical mistakes. Be very careful about using emoticons, humor, and jokes in your messages. They can easily be misunderstood and misinterpreted. Keep your messages short and to the point. If you're soliciting a response from the receiver of the message, you'll find that a brief message with a pointed list of questions is most effective in getting that response.

Did You Know?

3-2.2.16-1

Most e-mail programs come with a variety of features and options that let you customize the look and feel of the program. For example, you can create a "signature" that's automatically applied to the e-mails you send. You can block messages from certain people by adding their e-mail addresses to a "blocked senders" list. You can change the format of the message text or apply a stationery design to messages you send.

STEP-BY-STEP 3.5

3-2.2.1-1

1. If necessary, start your e-mail program and choose to create a new message.

3-2.2.2-1
3-2.2.15-2

2. Enter your e-mail address in the To field. Use your address book to insert your own e-mail address in the CC field. (*Note*: If your e-mail address in not in your address book, add it now.) For the subject line, enter **George Washington Information**.

3-2.2.2-1

3. For the body of the message, key the following:

   Here is some information on the first president of the United States. Please review and let me know if you have any questions.

   Thanks,

   [Your Name]

3-2.2.3-1

4. Attach the file containing the paragraph of text that you copied from your favorite or bookmarked George Washington Web page in Step-by-Step 3.4.

3-2.2.5-1

5. Send the e-mail message and attachment. Remain in this screen for the next Step-by-Step.

Working with Messages You Receive

3-2.2.9-2

When you receive an e-mail message, you have a number of options on what you can do with it. You can send a reply to the message, forward the message to someone else, save the message to a specified location, or delete the message. Before you can perform an action on a message, you must first select it.

3-2.1.5-1
3-2.2.12-2
3-2.3.2-1
3-2.3.2-2
3-2.3.2-3

- *Replying to a message.* You can reply to an e-mail message in one of two ways. Click the Reply or Reply All button, key your reply message, and then send the message. With this type of reply, the original message is included along with your reply message. This type of reply is appropriate when you're answering a question or responding to specifics in the original message. Or, you can create a new mail message in response to a message. With this type of reply, only the text of your reply message is included, unless you copy text from the original e-mail message and paste it into the new message. If you copy information from another e-mail message, the > character often precedes each line of the copied information to identify that it came from another source. Some e-mail programs automatically apply default formats to text that you paste into a message. In this case, you might want to apply your own formatting options, such as changing the font color, to identify that the material came from a different source. When you reply to an e-mail message, the recipient(s) normally sees the letters "Re" preceding the text in the subject line to indicate that it's a reply message.

3-2.1.5-3
3-2.2.14-2

- *Forwarding a message.* This is similar to replying to a message. Forwarding messages helps cut down on the time you spend keying messages from scratch. It's also a quick way to share information with a number of people. When you forward a message, the recipient(s) normally sees the letters "Fw" preceding the text in the subject line to identify it as a message that's being forwarded.

3-2.2.10-1
3-2.2.8-1
3-2.2.8-2

- *Saving a message.* You can save an e-mail message in various formats (including text and html formats) to disk so that you can open and read it later. You can also save and organize e-mail messages in folders within your e-mail program. In Outlook Express, for example, you can create folders within your local folders (Inbox, Outbox, Sent Items, Deleted Items) to further organize your messages. To copy or move a message into a folder, simply right-click the message, select the Move to Folder or Copy to Folder option, and then select the folder to which you want to move or copy in the dialog box that opens.

3-2.2.11-1

- *Deleting a message.* You can delete an e-mail message easily by selecting it and then pressing the Delete key or clicking the Delete button on the e-mail program's toolbar. In some e-mail programs, this moves the message into a "deleted mail" storage area. To delete it permanently, you must delete it from this location.

STEP-BY-STEP 3.6

3-2.2.5-1

1. To complete this exercise, you must have sent yourself an e-mail as instructed in Step-by-Step 3.5. From your inbox, select the *George Washington Information* e-mail message to view it.

3-2.2.3-2

2. Open the attachment. An attachment is usually identified by an icon of a paper clip. Click the paper clip icon and then click the attachment. It should open in your word processor.

STEP-BY-STEP 3.6 Continued

3-2.2.3-3 **3.** You can save the attachment to disk from within the application in which you opened it. Or, you can save it from the e-mail message. Close the attachment file and return to your e-mail program. Make sure the e-mail message is selected in your inbox. Click the paper clip icon and then choose to save the attachment. Save it to a location on disk.

3-2.2.12-1
3-2.2.12-2 **4.** Reply to the e-mail message. Make sure the e-mail message is selected in your inbox, and click the **Reply** button. The original sender's e-mail address (yours!) should automatically appear in the "To" field. In the subject line, you should see "Re" to indicate that you're sending a reply. Close the e-mail message without saving or sending.

3-2.2.13-1
3-2.2.13-2 **5.** Click the **Reply All** button. The original sender's e-mail address should automatically appear in the "To" field. The e-mail addresses of anyone else who received the e-mail should automatically appear in the "To" field as well or in the "CC" field if they were copied on the original e-mail.

6. Key in the following text for your reply:

Thanks. I'll let you know if I have any questions.

[Your Name]

7. Send the e-mail.

8. Now, forward the e-mail to yourself and someone in your address book. Select the e-mail message in your inbox, and click the **Forward** button.

3-2.2.14-1
3-2.2.14-2 **9.** Insert the e-mail addresses in the "To" field. Notice the "Fw" in the subject line. The recipient will be able to identify the message as one that's being forwarded.

3-2.2.4-1 **10.** Delete the attachment by selecting it in the Attach field and pressing the **Delete** key.

11. Forward the e-mail by clicking the **Send** button.

3-2.2.10-1 **12.** Save the original *George Washington Information* e-mail message to disk. Select the message in your inbox. Open the **File** menu and select **Save As**. In the Save Message As dialog box, select the location you want to save the file to, enter a new name for the message if desired, select the format you want to save the message in, and click **Save**. Remain in this screen for the next Step-by-Step.

Organizing and Managing E-mail

3-2.2.6-1
3-2.2.6-2
3-2.2.7-1
Most e-mail programs give you a number of options for managing and organizing e-mail messages. You can sort e-mail according to the name of the sender, by subject, or by the date received. You can use the search feature to find e-mail messages from a certain person or received on a certain date. You can organize mail into different folders that you create within your e-mail program. For example, you might have a folder for personal correspondence and, within that folder, you might have individual folders for your personal contacts.

STEP-BY-STEP 3.7

3-2.2.7-1 1. You should now have several versions of the *George Washington Information* e-mail message in your inbox. Use the sort feature to sort the messages by the Subject field.

3-2.2.6-1 3-2.2.6-2 2. Search your inbox messages for the messages from yourself. Then, search your inbox for the message that you forwarded (see Steps 8 and 9 in Step-by-Step 3.6). For the searching options, make sure you key "Fw" in the subject line field. This will find all messages that have been forwarded.

3. Create a new folder at the same level as your inbox folder and name it **George Washington**.

3-2.2.8-1 3-2.2.9-2 4. Right-click any one of the *George Washington Information* e-mail messages in your inbox. On the shortcut menu, click **Move to Folder** and select the **George Washington** folder. The message is removed from the inbox and placed in the George Washington folder.

3-2.2.8-2 5. Right-click another of the *George Washington Information* e-mail messages in your inbox. On the shortcut menu, click **Copy to Folder** and select the **George Washington** folder. A copy of the message remains in the inbox and is also placed in the George Washington folder.

3-2.2.9-1 3-2.2.11-1 6. Select all the *George Washington Information* e-mail messages in your inbox by selecting one, holding down the **Ctrl** key, and clicking the others. Click the **Delete** button on the toolbar or press the **Delete** key to delete the messages from your inbox.

7. Close your e-mail program when you are done.

Ethics in Technology

E-MAIL/E-ACHES

3-2.3.5-1 Although e-mail is one of the more popular services of the Internet, its widespread use has ushered in a number of problems. One of the most nagging problems is simply the overflow of e-mail messages many users find in their inboxes. Like your telephone number, your e-mail address can get into the address books of marketers and newsgroups, enabling them to send you many unwanted e-mails, or "spam," as these messages are commonly called.

3-2.1.5-1 3-2.1.5-2 3-2.3.5-1 3-2.3.5-2 E-mail communication can also lead to confusion and misinterpretation. Receivers are often guilty of not thoroughly reading an e-mail message before they reply, or they may not use the "Reply All" option correctly. It's important to pay close attention to who your messages and replies are going to. You don't want to automatically reply to all addressees if the content of the message is not relevant to all of them, but you also need to be sure to reply to all parties who have an interest in your reply.

SUMMARY

In this lesson, you learned:

- A browser is a software program you use to retrieve documents from the World Wide Web.
- Two popular browsers are Microsoft's Internet Explorer and Netscape's Communicator.

- Your home page is the first page that's displayed when you launch your browser.
- Internet Explorer's address bar and Communicator's location bar are located near the top of the browser window.
- The address of a Web site is called the Uniform Resource Locator (URL).
- The row of buttons at the top of the browser is the toolbar.
- For sites you will return to often, you can add them to your Favorites and Bookmarks.
- When viewing pages on the Internet, you can copy and save text, hyperlinks, images, and entire Web pages.
- E-mail is one of the most popular services on the Internet. The address book is where you keep a list of your e-mail contacts. You can organize your e-mail into folders.

VOCABULARY *Review*

Define the following terms:

Address bar	Electronic mail	Uniform Resource Locator (URL)
Address book	Home page	Web server
Browser		

REVIEW *Questions*

MULTIPLE CHOICE

Select the best response for the following statements.

1. A software program used to retrieve documents from the WWW is called a ________.
   A. packet
   B. home page
   C. browser
   D. Web server

2. An URL is the ________.
   A. Web site address
   B. same as the location bar
   C. same as the address bar
   D. toolbar

3. Which of the following is *not* a navigation tool you might find at a Web site?
   A. bookmark
   B. site map
   C. navigation bar
   D. search box

4. To save an image from a Web page document to your computer, _________.
   - **A.** move the mouse pointer over the image and left-click
   - **B.** move the mouse pointer over the image and right-click
   - **C.** double-click the image
   - **D.** select the image

5. When e-mail messages are sent over the Internet, they are broken down into _________.
   - **A.** pieces
   - **B.** packets
   - **C.** messages
   - **D.** contacts

TRUE/FALSE

Circle T if the statement is true or F if the statement is false.

T F 1. The home page is the first page that's displayed when you launch your browser.

T F 2. You can save an entire Web site to disk.

T F 3. The Favorites list contains URLs that you want to block from anyone to visit.

T F 4. E-mail attachments must be small files in text format only.

T F 5. You can view saved Web pages offline.

FILL IN THE BLANK

Complete the following sentences by writing the correct word or words in the blanks provided.

1. In e-mail, use the _________ to keep a list of contacts.
2. A(n) _________ is the program you use to retrieve documents from the Web.
3. You can apply _________ as a background design for your e-mail messages.
4. To ensure that credit card numbers are not easily stolen, companies use a technology called _________ to scramble the data.
5. The language used to create documents on the WWW is called _________.

PROJECTS

PROJECT 3-1

1. Start your browser and connect to the Web.
2. Search for a weather-related Web site and find the weather report for your city (or a large city close by).
3. Save the Web site to disk.
4. From your browser, print the Web page containing the weather forecast for your city.
5. Select the text on the Web page and copy it to a blank document in your word processor.

6. Format the text as you desire. Add a title to the document that identifies the Web site and URL from which the information came.
7. Save the document with a filename of your choice. Then, print a copy of the document.
8. Close your browser and any other open files.

PROJECT 3-2

1. Start your e-mail program.
2. Create an e-mail message to send to a contact in your address book and copy it to yourself. Write a message that relates to the weather document you created in Project 3-1.
3. Attach the weather document you created in Project 3-1 and send the message.
4. Create a folder at the same level as your inbox folder and name it **Weather**. When you receive the weather message, copy it to the **Weather** folder.
5. Delete the weather message from your inbox.
6. Close your e-mail program.

WEB PROJECT

At the Web site of Sierra Multimedia Productions, located at *222.sierramm.com*, you will find a free Windows-based presentation called *Interactive Guide to the Internet*. The presentation provides information on how to use the Internet. It runs on the user's desktop as a stand-alone application and is aimed at beginners. Launch your browser and locate this Web site. Download the presentation and review it on your computer.

TEAMWORK PROJECT

There are a number of Web sites where you can establish a free e-mail account. The URLs for some of these are as follows:

www.hotmail.com

www.usa.net

www.yahoo.com

www.myownemail.com

You and your teammates should investigate the Web sites listed here and any other free e-mail sites you can locate. Prepare a report on which e-mail program is the best and why it is the best. Be sure to include a list of features and options available with each program.

CRITICAL *Thinking*

ACTIVITY 3-1

Access Microsoft's Encarta Learning zone at *learn.msn.com*. Browse the site, and make note of links you click. Prepare a report on why you might save this site to your bookmarks or favorites.

LESSON 4

RESEARCHING ON THE INTERNET

OBJECTIVES

Upon completion of this lesson, you should be able to:

- List some reasons for searching the Internet.
- Describe different search approaches.
- Define a search engine.
- Explain how search engines work.
- Identify some of the more popular search engines.
- Describe the subject directory search approach.
- Describe some search tips and tricks.

Estimated Time: 1.5 hours

VOCABULARY

Boolean logic
Hits
Hyperlinks
Keywords
Math symbols
Related search
Search engine
Spider
Subject directories
Wildcard character

The Internet contains a wealth of information. In fact, you can find information on just about any topic you can imagine. The problem is that the Internet contains so much information, it can be difficult to locate just what you need. In this lesson, you learn how to conduct searches on the Internet that get you to the information you need.

The Key to a Successful Search

We live in the information age, and the amount of information continues to grow at a fast rate. To conduct an effective online search on a particular topic can be a real challenge. One can easily be overwhelmed by the overabundance of raw data. With the right tools, however, the task becomes easier. One key to a successful Internet search is an understanding of the many tools available. Certain tools are more suitable for some purposes than others.

When searching online, there are two basic tools that you can use for finding information: search engines and subject directories. You use a search engine to search for keywords. You use a directory to find specialized topics. The primary difference between these two search tools is that people assemble directories and search engines are automated.

IC3 3-3.3.1-1

It's important to understand that no single Web tool indexes or organizes the whole Web. When using an online search tool, you are searching and viewing data extracted from the Web. This data has been placed into the search engine's database. It is the database that is searched—not the Web itself. This is one of the reasons why you get different results when you use different search engines.

Why Search the Internet?

You might ask yourself, "Why would I want to search the Internet? What's out there that can help me?" Reasons why people search the Internet are many. The following are just a few examples:

- You need to do some research for that paper due in your continuing education class next week.
- Your grandfather is losing his hearing and has asked you to help him find some information on hearing aids.
- You plan to take a trip to Mexico this summer and would like to get information on some of the best places to stay.

As you can see from these illustrations, there can be hundreds of reasons why you might want to conduct an Internet search. See Figure 4-1.

FIGURE 4-1
Searching the Internet

Introducing Search Engines

3-3.3.2-1 A ***search engine*** is a software program. There are hundreds of search engines throughout the Internet. Each search engine may work a little differently, but most of them have some common search features. For example, all search engines support keyword searches. Although keyword searches may not be the most effective way to search, this is the search method most individuals use.

Some search engines support an additional enhancement called concept-based searching. The search engine tries to determine what you mean and returns hits on Web sites that relate to the keywords. ***Hits*** are the number of returns or Web sites based on your keywords. If you search for "video games," the search engine may also return hits on sites that contain Nintendo and Playstation. One of the best-known search engines using concept-based searching is Excite. Its search engine uses ICE (intelligent concept extraction) to learn about word relationships.

Another feature supported by some search engines is stemming. When you search for a word, the search engine also includes the "stem" of the word. For example, you enter the search word "play," and you may also get back results for plays, playing, and player.

Keyword Searches

Keyword searches let you search for keywords within a Web document. The Web page author can specify these ***keywords*** using meta tags within the Web page document. Meta tags are special tags embedded within the Web page document. They do not affect how the page displays. Many search engines use these tags to create the index. For example, if your Web site is about Nintendo 64, your meta tag may look something like this:

<meta name="keywords" content="Nintendo 64, Mario, James Bond, Donkey Kong">

Ethics in Technology

SPAMMING

3-2.3.3-1 3-2.3.3-2 You may have heard of spam. No—it's not the luncheon meat that comes in a can. We're talking about Internet spam. Internet spam has several definitions. It is defined as electronic junk mail or junk newsgroup postings, or even unsolicited e-mail. This unsolicited e-mail is most likely some type of advertising or get-rich scheme, similar to the junk mail you or your family receive almost every day. With traditional junk mail, however, the people who send the mail pay a fee to distribute their materials.

Spam, in contrast, is similar to receiving a postage-due letter. Even though you don't pay the postage as it arrives in your electronic mailbox, you are still paying for it indirectly. The charges are in the form of disk space, connect time, or even long-distance Net connections.

3-2.3.3-3 Spam is not illegal yet, but several groups are trying to stop it. Several states are attempting to pass laws banning the sending of unsolicited e-mail. You can limit spam in a number of ways. Several services exist to which you can submit a complaint or report about a spam provider. There are also many spam-blocking and filtering services, as well as services and programs that hide your e-mail address from potential spammers. Visit *spam.abuse.net* to learn more.

3-3.3.4-1 What if the Web page author doesn't specify meta tags? Then the search engine evaluates the document and indexes "significant" words. Depending on the search engine, significant words may be those words mentioned at the beginning of a document or words that are repeated several times throughout the document.

To search using keywords, the process is as follows:

- You launch your Web browser and go to a search engine Web site.
- You submit an online form to the search engine. This form contains your keywords. These keywords describe the information you are trying to locate.
- The search engine matches as many keywords as possible by searching its own database. A database is a collection of organized information.
- The search engine then returns a list of ***hyperlinks*** to Web site addresses where the keywords are found. You click the hyperlinks to view the Web sites.
- If you are unable to find the information for which you are searching within these hyperlinked sites, you can revise your keywords and submit a new request.

3-3.3.1-1 So how does a search engine find all of those Web sites? To answer the question requires an overview of the search engine's three main parts:

- 3-3.1.6-1 The search engine program or software itself is the main component. This program searches through the millions of records stored in its database.
- 3-3.3.2-2 The second part is a ***spider***, or crawler. The spider is a search engine robot that searches the Internet for the keywords. It feeds the pages it finds to the search engine. It is called a spider because it crawls the Web continually, examining Web sites and finding and looking for links. Every month or so, it may return to a previous Web site to look for changes.
- The third part of the search engine is the index or indexer. When the spider finds a page, it submits it to the index. Once a Web page is indexed, it then becomes available to anyone using that search engine.

Some search engines claim to index all words, even the articles "a," "an," and "the." Other search engines index all words, except articles and stop words such as "www," "but," "or," "nor," "for," "so," or "yet." Some of the search engines index all words without reference to capitalization. Other engines differentiate uppercase from lowercase.

Did You Know?

Some search engines such as AltaVista can translate your search results into another language.

When you use a keyword search, you may find that the number of hits you receive are in the thousands or even millions. Hits are the number of returns on your keywords. Each hit is linked to the URL, which is the Web site address.

In some searches, you might receive thousands of hits. Trying to find information in such a large list can be a bit overwhelming. However, if you examine the page a little more closely, you will discover that each hit has a relevance rating percentage assigned, beginning with

100%. See Figure 4-2. As you move down the list of hits, the relevant number becomes less. This indicates that the site does not contain all of the search words or contains only one or two instances of the keywords. At this point, you have several options:

- You can click on any of the links and review the information at that site.
- You can redefine your keywords.
- You can use another search engine.

FIGURE 4-2
Hits for a search of video games using Infoseek

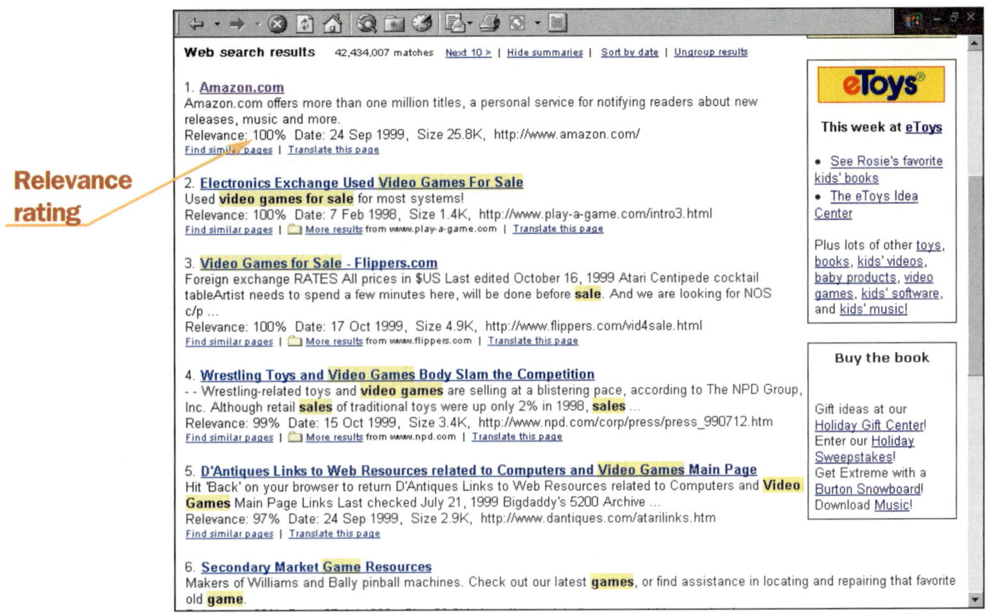

Net Business

SEARCH ENGINE OPTIMIZATION

3-3.3.2-3
3-3.3.7-3

When Web site developers register their sites with search engines, they normally provide a list of keywords that will help get their site on a user's search results list. Web sites can often improve their rankings (or where they appear in the list) by employing cutting-edge Web marketing technology. For example, there are a number of organizations that offer search engine optimization services to Web site operators. These services might include an in-depth analysis of keywords that people will use in search engines, design of banner ads and buttons to be placed on the Web site of a search engine, etc.

In addition, for a fee, you might use a service (such as Wordtracker) to find out all the keywords that people use to find products or services similar to yours, then make sure those keywords appear in your Web page.

There are also a number of "pay-per-click" search engines operating online. With this type of search engine, Web site owners bid on keywords. When a person uses the keywords in a search, the links in the search results list appear in order from highest to lowest bid on the keywords. The owner of the Web site pays the search engine the per-click fee only when someone clicks the link to the site.

Using another search engine might be your best choice. It is impossible for any one search engine to index every page on the Web. Also, each search engine has its own personal algorithm that it uses to index Web sites. An algorithm is a formula or set of steps for solving a particular problem. Therefore, using a different engine may provide a totally different list of hits. There are many popular search engine sites, and you may need to try several before you find the information you are seeking. See Table 4-1 for a list of some popular search engines.

TABLE 4-1
Search engines

SEARCH ENGINE	URL
Lycos	*www.lycos.com*
Yahoo!	*www.yahoo.com*
AltaVista	*www.altavista.com*
Google	*www.google.com*
Infoseek	*www.infoseek.com*
Excite	*www.excite.com*
WebCrawler	*www.webcrawler.com*
AlltheWeb	*www.alltheweb.com*
Northern Light	*www.northernlight.com*

IC³

STEP-BY-STEP 4.1

1. Launch your browser and go to **www.lycos.com**.

3-3.3.3-1

2. In the search box, enter the keywords **cookie recipes** and press **Enter**.

3. The page that opens should give you an indication of the number of hits the search engine found. Browse through the page. Click links if you'd like to find more information on cookie recipes.

4. When you are done, close your browser.

Specialty Search Engines

Specialty search engines, sometimes called category-oriented search tools, generally focus on a particular topic. If you know you are looking for information in a particular format, your best bet is to search a site that specializes in indexing and retrieving that information. Here are some examples:

- You're looking up a former classmate or a long-lost cousin; try the Switchboard Web site at *www.switchboard.com* or Yahoo's people search at *people.yahoo.com*.
- You want to download a shareware game called Renegade Racers; try the Shareware Web site at *www.shareware.com*.

- You want to do a little online jewelry shopping; try Catalog City at *www.catalogcity.com* or Bottom Dollar at *www.bottomdollar.com*.
- Perhaps you're a sports fan and want to find out about the latest happenings in the wrestling world; try Sports Search at *www.sportsearch.com*.
- Are you thinking about your future and what careers options you may have? Try CareerPath at *www.careerpath.com* to find a database of over 250,000 jobs.

These are just a few examples of the many hundreds of specialty Web sites. If you are looking for a particular information source, but are not sure where to look, try the Beaucoup Web site at *www.beaucoup.com*. This site contains links to more than 3,000 specialty search engines. See Figure 4-3. For a super search, you can also enter keywords at this site and search 10 different search engines at one time. Some specialty search engines are listed in Table 4-2.

Hot Tip

Some search engines automatically include plurals; others do not. To be on the safe side, include the plural. For example, if you're searching for squirrels, use the keyword *squirrels*.

Internet

For education purposes, one of the best subject guides is the WWW Virtual Library. The VL is the oldest subject directory on the Web. This site is considered to have the highest quality guides to particular sections of the Internet. You can find the Virtual Library at *www.vlib.org*.

FIGURE 4-3
Beaucoup Web site

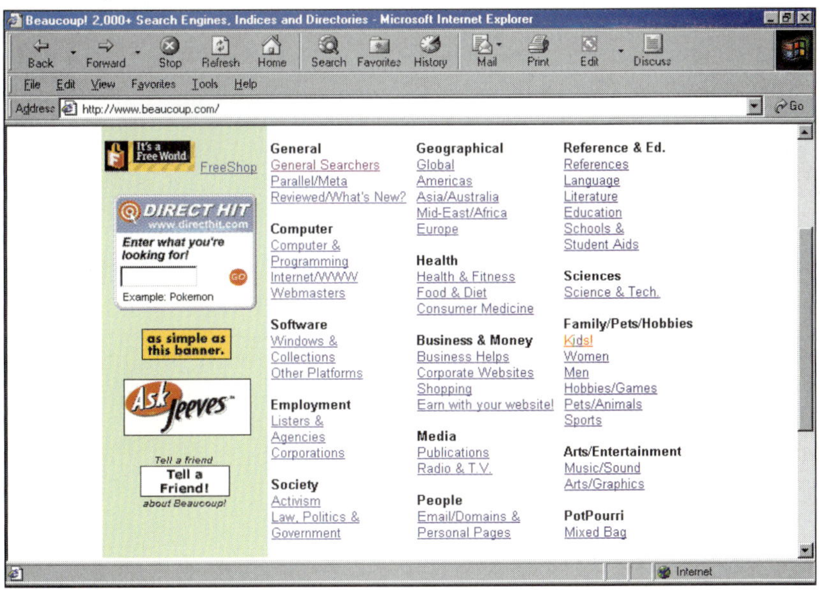

TABLE 4-2
Specialty search engines

MAPS AND TRAVEL INFORMATION	PEOPLE AND COMPANIES	COMPANIES AND CAREERS	WORLD DATA
Microsoft's *www.expedia.com*	PeopleSite at *www.peoplesite.com*	Arthur's Job Base at *www.ajb.com*	World Health Organization at *www.who.int*
MapQuest at *www.mapquest.com*	Yellow Pages at *www.yellow.com*	Monster Job Bank at *www.monster.com*	CIA World Factbook at *www.odci.gov/cia/publications/factbook*
Hotel Lodging Rooms at *www.irsus.com/rooms.htm*		Career Resource Center at *www.careers.org*	World Bank at *www.worldbank.org*
Great Outdoors at *www.gorp.com*			

Multimedia Search Engines

Are you interested in finding graphics, video clips, animation, and even MP3 music files? Then a multimedia search engine is probably the best way to go. For music and MP3, you might want to try the Lycos search engine at *mp3.lycos.com/*, *www.savvysearch.com/*, or *www.audiofind.com*. MP3 is a file format that allows audio compression at near-CD quality.

Corbis at *www.corbis.com/* boasts of "The world's largest collection of fine art and photography." AltaVista at *www.altavista.com* has a special tab for images, audio, and video. Or try Ditto, the visual search engine at *www.ditto.com,* to search for pictures, photographs, and artwork.

Subject Directory Searching

Earlier in this lesson we indicated that the primary difference between a search engine and a directory is that people assemble directories. Subject experts carefully check the Web sites to make sure they meet a particular set of standards. Then the URL for the Web site is added to the database.

Most ***subject directories*** are organized by subject categories, with a collection of links to Internet resources. These resources are arranged by subject and then displayed in a series of menus. To access a particular topic, you start from the top and "drill down" through the different levels—going from the general to the specific. This is similar to a traditional card catalog or the telephone yellow pages.

Let's say you have been asked to prepare a report on ancient Greek sculpture. You can use a search engine and keywords to try to locate information, or you can use a subject directory search tool. One of the better educational directory Web sites is the Encyclopedia Britannica, located at *www.britannica.com*. See Figure 4-4.

FIGURE 4-4
Britannica Web site

Subject directory searches often provide a more guided approach than entering keywords into a search engine. Additional benefits of directories are as follows:

- They are easy to use.
- You're not searching the entire Web.
- The Web sites have been handpicked and evaluated.
- Most links include some type of description.
- They produce better quality hits on searches for common items.

See Table 4-3 for a list of some other popular subject directories.

TABLE 4-3
Subject directories

DIRECTORY NAME	URL	DESCRIPTION
The Librarian's Index	*www.lii.org*	High quality; compiled by public librarians
Yahoo	*www.yahoo.com*	Very large subject directory
Galaxy	*www.galaxy.com*	Good annotations; good quality

Tools and Techniques for Searching the Web

As the Internet continues to expand and more and more pages are added, effective searching requires new approaches and strategies. Remember that the more specific your search, the more likely you will find what you want. Tell the search engine precisely what it is you're searching for. To find relevant information, you must use a variety of tools and techniques.

Phrase Searching

If you want to search for words that must appear next to each other, than phrase searching is your best choice. A phrase is entered using double quotation marks and only matches those words that appear adjacent to each other and in the order in which you specify.

If you are searching for more than one phrase, you can separate multiple phrases or proper names with a comma. For example, if you were searching for baseball cards, enter the phrase "baseball cards" in double quotes. The results will contain Web sites with the words "baseball cards" adjacent to each other. Without the quotes, the search engine would find Web pages that contain the words baseball and cards anywhere within each page. To find Mickey Mantle baseball cards, you would enter "baseball cards", "Mickey Mantle." It is always a good idea to capitalize proper nouns because some search engines distinguish between upper- and lowercase letters. On the other hand, if you capitalize a common noun such as Bread, you will get fewer returns than if you typed in *bread*.

Search Engine Math

You can use ***math symbols*** to enter a formula to filter out unwanted listings. For example:

- Put a plus sign (+) before words that must appear (also called an inclusion operator).
- Put a minus sign (-) before words that you do not want to appear (also called an exclusion operator).
- Words without qualifiers need not appear, but are still involved in sorting your search.

You're making cookies for a party and would like to try some new recipes. Your search words are +cookie+recipes. Only pages that contained both words would appear in your results. Now let's suppose that you want recipes for chocolate cookies. Your search words are +cookie+recipe+chocolate. This would display pages with all three words.

To take this a step further, you don't like coconut. So you don't want any recipes that contain the word *coconut*. You will find that the minus (-) symbol is helpful for reducing the number of unrelated results. You would write your search phrase as +cookie+recipe+chocolate-coconut. This tells the search engine to find pages that contain cookie, recipe, and chocolate and then to remove any pages that contain the word coconut. To extend this idea and to get chocolate cookie recipes without coconut and honey, your search phrase would be +cookie+recipe+chocolate-coconut-honey. Simply begin subtracting terms you know are not of interest, and you should get better results. You will find that almost all of the major search engines support search engine math. You can also use math symbols with most directories.

Boolean Searching

Recall that when you search for a topic on the Internet, you are not going from server to server and viewing documents on that server. Instead you are searching databases. ***Boolean logic*** is another way that you can search databases. This works on a similar principle as search engine math, but has a little more power. Boolean logic consists of three logical operators:

- AND
- NOT
- OR

Returning to our cookie example, you're interested in a relationship between cookies and recipes. So you may search for "cookies AND recipes." The more terms you combine with AND,
3-3.3.5-1 the fewer returns you will receive. Or you want chocolate cookie recipes without coconut. You
3-3.3.6-1 would search for "cookies AND recipes AND chocolate NOT coconut."

OR logic is most commonly used to search for similar terms or concepts. For example, you search for "cookies AND recipes OR chocolate" to retrieve results containing one term or the other or both. The more terms you combine in a search with OR logic, the more results you will receive from your search.

Some search engines assist you with your logical search through the use of forms. For example, clicking on the HotBot search engine's Advanced Search tab brings up a form. Using this form, you can specify the language, words, and phrases to include and to omit, and even specify a time period. See Figure 4-5. Keep in mind that some search engines do not support Boolean logic.

FIGURE 4-5
HotBot's advanced search form

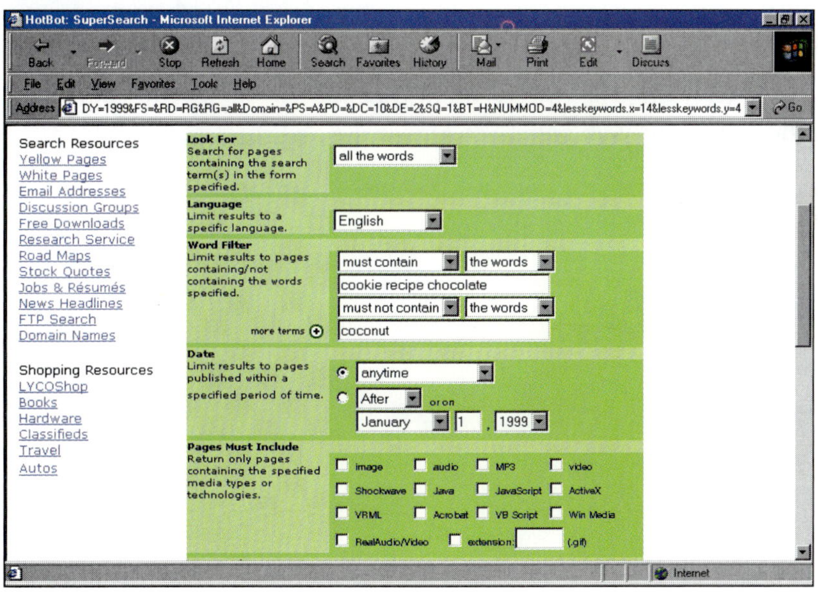

STEP-BY-STEP 4.2

1. Launch your browser and go to one of the search engines listed in Table 4-1.

3-3.3.5-2 2. In the search box, enter **cookies AND recipes AND chocolate AND coconut**, and press **Enter**.

3. Note the number of hits the search engine finds. Go back to the home page of the search engine.

STEP-BY-STEP 4.2 Continued

4. In the search box, enter **cookies AND recipes AND chocolate NOT coconut**, and press **Enter**.

5. Again, note the number of hits; it's probably fewer than in the first search.

6. When you are done, close your browser.

Wildcard Searching

The * symbol, or asterisk, is considered a ***wildcard character***. If you don't know the spelling of a word or you want to search plurals or variations of a word, use the wildcard character. For example, you want to search for "baseball cards and Nolan Ryan," but you're not sure how to spell Nolan. You can construct you search using a wildcard—"baseball cards" and "N* Ryan." Some search engines only permit the * at the end of the word; with others you can put the * at the end or beginning. Some search engines do not support wildcard searches.

Title Searching

When a Web page author creates a Web page, the Web page generally contains an HTML title. The title is entered between title tags, such as

<Title>Learn the Net: An Internet Guide and Tutorial</Title>

When you go to a Web site, the title is what appears on the title bar at the top of the Web page. See Figure 4-6.

> **Note**
>
> IC3 3-3.1.4-1
>
> Notice the advertisement at the top of the Web page shown in Figure 4-6. This is referred to as a banner ad. Mori Luggage & Gifts paid the Web site owner to display this ad.

FIGURE 4-6
Learn the Net—title bar example

Many of the major search engines allow you to search within the HTML document for the title of a Web page. If you did a title search for "Internet Tutorial," then most likely one of your results or hits would be the page shown in Figure 4-6. Not all search engines support title searches.

Other Search Features

3-3.2.3-4

Another feature provided by several search engines is a ***related search***. These are preprogrammed queries or questions suggested by the search engine that often lead to other Web pages containing similar information. A related search can dramatically improve your odds of finding the information you are seeking. Several search engines offer this feature, although they may use different terminology. You may see terms such as "similar pages," "related pages," or "more pages like this." WebCrawler uses "similar pages." See Figure 4-7. All of these terms basically mean the same thing.

FIGURE 4-7
WebCrawler uses the term "Similar Pages"

SUMMARY

In this lesson you learned:

- Two basic tools you can use for finding information are search engines and directories.
- People assemble directories, and search engines are automated.
- A search engine is a software program.
- Most search engines support keyword searches.
- Concept-based searching occurs when the search engine returns hits that relate to keywords.
- Stemming relates to the search engine finding variations of the word.

- Meta tags are special tags embedded in a Web page; many search engines use the tags to create their index.
- Keywords describe the information you are trying to locate.
- A search engine has three main parts: the search engine software, a robot that searches for keywords, and an index.
- Stop words such as *www*, *but*, *or*, and *so forth* are not indexed by many search engines.
- The URL is the same as the Web site address.
- A relevance rating percentage indicates how close a site matches keywords.
- Specialized search engines focus on a particular topic.
- Multimedia search engines focus on video, animation, graphics, and music.
- Subject directories are organized by subject categories.
- Use double quotation marks around a set of words for phrase searching.
- Use the plus and minus sign for inclusion and exclusion of words within a search.
- Boolean searches use the three logical operators OR, AND, and NOT.
- The * symbol is used for wildcard searching.
- Some search engines support title searching.
- A related search is a preprogrammed question suggested by the search engine.

VOCABULARY *Review*

Define the following terms:

Boolean logic	Math symbols	Spider
Hits	Related search	Subject directories
Hyperlinks	Search engine	Wildcard character
Keywords		

REVIEW *Questions*

MULTIPLE CHOICE

Select the best repsonse for the following statements.

1. There are ________ basic tools that you can use for finding information on the Internet.
   A. one
   B. two
   C. three
   D. four

2. __________ occurs when the search engine includes other variations of the keyword.
   A. Concepts
   B. Stemming
   C. Meta tags
   D. Natural language

3. The __________ is a search engine robot that roams the Internet looking for keywords.
   A. index
   B. searcher
   C. spider
   D. wart hog

4. The __________ indicates the Web site address.
   A. search box
   B. hit
   C. indexer
   D. URL

5. If you were looking for video and music resources, you might use a __________ search engine.
   A. multimedia
   B. sports
   C. phrase
   D. spider

TRUE/FALSE

Circle T if the statement is true or F if the statement is false.

T F 1. It is easy to find information on the Internet.

T F 2. Keywords describe the information you are trying to locate.

T F 3. The lower the relevance rating percentage, the more likely your search terms are included.

T F 4. The Britannica Web site is a search engine.

T F 5. Boolean searches and math symbol searches are identical.

FILL IN THE BLANK

Complete the following sentences by writing the correct word or words in the blanks provided.

1. The __________ is a symbol for a wildcard character.

2. A preprogrammed query is a(n) __________.

3. Web pages for __________ directories are reviewed by people.

4. A(n) __________ search engine charges the Web site owner only when someone clicks the link to the Web site.

5. A Web author uses __________ tags to specify keywords within a Web page document.

PROJECTS

PROJECT 4-1

1. Use search engine math symbols to conduct searches for the following:
   A. Carnivals and circuses in Canada, but not in Vancouver.
   B. Skateboards and roller blades in Florida.
2. Conduct searches for the same topics using Boolean logic.
3. Prepare a short report that describes the differences in search results using these two search methods.

PROJECT 4-2

Use your favorite search engine to conduct a Boolean search for information about your two favorite bands. Create a one-page report. Include within the report what search engine you used and why, how many sites you found, and how you were able to narrow the search.

WEB PROJECT

You have been asked to prepare a presentation on the history of McDonald's. Use the search techniques that you think are best to find information on the Web for your presentation.

TEAMWORK PROJECT

You and your teammates are to select a type of insect and provide information about the life and habits of the insect. Create a "Search Strategy" form that you can use to search the Internet. Within the form, list possible search tools and ways in which to search. Include the URLs for any suggested search engines or directory Web sites.

CRITICAL *Thinking*

ACTIVITY 4-1

IC³ 3-3.2.3-4

Select a topic of your choice to research on the Web. Try to be as specific as possible in the topic you choose; for example, "Olympic gold medalists" or "national parks in the Eastern United States." Search for information using three different search engines. Refer to Table 4-1 for a list of some popular search engines. Be sure to use exactly the same search techniques (such as keywords, Boolean operators, or related searches). Create a table with a separate column for each search engine. Then under the column headings, list the top 10 sites that the search engine locates. Determine which engine provided you with the highest-quality results.

LESSON 5

EVALUATING ELECTRONIC INFORMATION

OBJECTIVES

Upon completion of this lesson, you should be able to:

- Identify reasons for evaluating Internet resources.
- Identify criteria for evaluating electronic information.
- Describe software piracy.
- Identify Internet resources.
- Understand the rules of copyright.
- Cite Internet resources appropriately.
- Explore other legal and ethical issues concerning information you obtain from the Internet.

Estimated Time: 1.5 hours

VOCABULARY

Copyright
Currency
Navigation
Public domain
Shareware

Information is only as good as the source. Anyone, anywhere, can put anything on the Internet. It may be true; it may not be true. How can you determine if the information is legitimate? Developing the ability to evaluate information critically on the Internet is a very important skill today in this information age!

Evaluating Information Found on the Internet

IC3 3-3.3.7-1

The Internet provides opportunities for students, teachers, scholars, and anyone needing information to find it from all over the world. It is fairly easy to locate information and to publish it electronically. However, because anyone can put information on the Internet, it is not always accurate or reliable. Anyone using information obtained from the Internet needs to develop skills to evaluate what they find.

Hot Tip

The Internet epitomizes the concept of *caveat lector:* Let the reader beware.

Viewing a Page

The pages on the Web have so many different looks. Some pages are full with pictures, sounds, animations, links, and information. Some are very exciting; others may be just plain. Sometimes the appearance of the page alone may draw you to a site and, after reading it, you realize it is not the site you need.

Following are some questions you may want to ask when you open a Web page:

- Did the page take a long time to load?
- Are the graphics on the page related to the site?
- Are the sections on the page labeled?
- Who wrote the information on this page?
- How can you communicate with the author?
- When was the page last updated?
- Are there appropriate links to other Web pages?
- Is it easy to follow links?
- Can you tell what the page is about from its title?
- Is the information useful to you?
- How old is the information?
- Does any of the information contradict information you found someplace else?
- Did the author use words like *always, never, best, worst*?
- Do you think the author knows the information he or she is sharing?

These questions represent just a start at evaluating electronic information.

Did You Know?

Links that are no longer active are called *dead links*.

Ethics in Technology

RESTRICTING INTERNET ACCESS

IC3 3-4.3.1-1

In various situations, people might want to block access to specific Internet sites or to sites that contain certain content. For instance, parents often want to prevent their children from visiting sites with adult-oriented material. Or companies might want to deny their employees access to online shopping and entertainment sites that are not business-related.

IC3 3-4.3.1-2

There are several tools to restrict site access. A low-tech solution is to simply have someone oversee computer users and what is on their monitors. At the other end of the spectrum, there are software programs that can be installed on a computer or network that will automatically block access to user-specified sites or to sites with specified content.

Determining Authorship

IC3 3-3.3.7-2

A well-developed resource identifies its author and/or producer. You will be given enough information to be able to determine whether the originator is a reliable source. What expertise or authority does the author have that qualifies him or her to distribute this information? If you don't see this information, use the BACK button to see whether another part of the file contains this information. Look especially for a name and e-mail address of the person who created or maintains the information. You can always contact him or her for information regarding credentials and expertise.

If the information regarding the author is not visible, a search by the author's name using a search engine may provide the information regarding the author. It may also lead to other information by the same author. If an e-mail address is visible, use it to request information regarding the author.

The domain portion of the URL will also give you information concerning the appropriateness of the site for your area of study. Examples:

- .edu for educational or research information
- .gov for government resources
- .com for commercial products or commercially sponsored sites
- .org for nonprofit organizations
- .mil for military branches

Ethics in Technology

SOFTWARE PIRACY

One of the biggest problems facing the computer industry today is software piracy, the illegal copying or use of programs. Copying software is very easy. Some people believe it is all right to copy software and use it for free. They think software is too expensive. And it can be. Some low-level software costs less than $25, but more specialized software can cost hundreds, even thousands of dollars! When users copy the software, they are only giving up access to documentation and tech support; so they decide it is worth it to copy it illegally.

You, too, may ask, "What is the big deal about copying software?" Remember, developing a software program is an expensive process that takes highly trained programmers hundreds of hours to develop.

Shareware, free software that can be used for a given period of time, is also being abused. Many people use it with no intention of purchasing it. You will probably be surprised to know that not only individual users copy software illegally—so do businesses. Billions of dollars are lost every year as a result of pirated software.

Software can be pirated in many ways. Of course, the easiest is to copy from the original disks. Software can also be copied from the server of a network and over an e-mail system.

The Copyright Act of 1976 was passed to govern software piracy. In 1983, a Software Piracy and Counterfeiting Amendment was added. It is no longer a misdemeanor to copy software illegally—it is a felony.

Evaluating Content

Is the purpose of this Web site stated? Is the information accurate? Is the information in-depth enough? Has the information been reviewed? Don't take any information presented on
3-3.3.7-2 the Internet at face value. The source of the information should be clearly stated whether it is original or borrowed from somewhere else. Make sure you understand the agenda of the site's owner. Is it trying to sell a product or service? Is it trying to influence public opinion? As you read through the information, pay close attention to determine whether the content covers a specific time period or an aspect of a topic or whether it is more broad. Check other resources, such as books or journals at the local library, that contain similar information.

Is Content Timely?

A very important consideration of an effective site is its ***currency***, which refers to the age of the information, how long it has been posted, and how often it is updated. Some sites need to be updated more often than others to reflect changes in the kind of information. Medical or technological information needs to be updated more often than historical information. Out-of-date information may not give you the results you need.

Most sites on the Internet have numerous links that will take you to additional sites of similar information. Sometimes, however, it is not information you can use. Decide whether the site
3-3.3.7-3 you plan to use has useful information or whether it is just a site that links you to more and more sites. Does the site contain dead links—links that are no longer active? Also, determine whether the links go only to other pages within the site. This will help you assess the objectivity of the information on the site.

The style of writing and the language used can reveal information about the quality of the site. If the style is objective, the chances are the information is worthy of your attention. However, if it is opinionated and subjective, you may want to give second thought to using it. Ideas and opinions supported by references are additional signs of the value of the site.

The overall layout of the page is also important. The page should be free of spelling and grammatical errors. Even if the page appears to contain valuable information, misspelled words and incorrect grammar usage tend to bias a reader regarding the validity of the information.

Navigating the Site

Navigation is the ability to move through a site. Being able to move quickly through the links on a Web site is a very important element. Having the information laid out in a logical design so you can locate what you need easily adds to the efficiency of the site. The consistency of the layout from page to page adds to the ability to navigate easily. The first page of a Web site indicates how the site is organized and the options available.

Moving through a site is done by clicking on the links on the page. Some pages consist of many links; others may only contain a few. Regardless, the links should

- be easy to identify.
- be grouped logically.
- be pertinent to the subject of the original page.

There should be a link on each page that will take you back to the home page and one that will allow you to e-mail the author.

Types of Internet Resources

The types of electronic resources include the following:

- journals and journal articles
- magazines and magazine articles
- newspapers and newspaper articles
- e-mail
- mailing lists
- commercial sites
- organizational sites
- subject-based sites

Some of these are presented in complete form; others are only portions of the document. Regardless of the type, the site should give information concerning

- the identification of the publisher.
- article reviewer information.
- special hardware requirements.
- availability of older copies of the article, newspaper, or journal.
- the currency of the site.

Search Engines

Search engines are programs written to query and retrieve information stored in a database. They differ from database to database and depend on the information stored in the database itself. Examples of search engines are AltaVista, Excite, Yahoo, and Google. If you used one of the many search engines available to locate information on the Internet, you need to know

- how the search engine decides the order in which it returns information requested. The top spaces (the first sites listed) are sold to advertisers by the search engines. Therefore, the first sites listed are not always the best sites or the most accurate and reliable.
- how the search engine searches for information and how often the information is updated.

Understanding Rules of Copyright

IC³ 3-4.3.4-1

For the most part, information displayed on an Internet site is easy to copy. Often you can highlight whatever text or graphics that you want to copy, hit the "copy" command, and then paste it onto another document. Or you can print out an entire page that's displayed on the monitor. The ease with which information can be copied, however, does not mean that users have a legal right to do so. Internet publications can claim the same legal protection as books, newspapers, CDs, movies, and other forms that are protected by copyright rules.

IC³ 3-4.3.4-2

Most sites have copyright information. ***Copyright*** is the exclusive right, granted by law for a certain number of years, to make and dispose of literary, musical, or artistic work. Even if the copyright notice isn't displayed prominently on the page, someone wrote or is responsible for the creation of whatever appears on a page. This means that you cannot use the information as your own. You must give credit to the person who created the work.

IC³ 3-4.3.4-2 3-4.3.4-4

If Internet content, such as music files, is copyrighted, it cannot be copied without the copyright holder's permission. To do so is a violation of copyright laws. It can lead to criminal charges for theft as well as civil lawsuits for monetary damages.

IC³ 3-4.3.4-3

Copyright law does provide certain exceptions to the general prohibition against copying. If copyright protection has lapsed on certain material, then it is deemed to be in the ***public domain*** and is available for anyone to copy. Also, the law allows for the fair use of properly identified copyrighted material that is merely a small part of a larger research project, for instance, or cited as part of a critique or review.

Technology Careers

INTERNET WEB DESIGNER/WEBMASTER

Every page on the Internet was designed by someone. Today, that someone is called a Web designer. The way a page looks on the Internet is the responsibility of the Web designer. The overall goal of the Web designer is to design and create a page that is efficient and appealing.

Each page on the Internet has to be maintained and kept up-to-date. The Webmaster is responsible for this task. A typical Webmaster manages a Web site. That usually includes creating content, adapting existing content in a user-friendly format, creating and maintaining a logical structure, and running the Web server software.

Not so long ago, both of these functions were the responsibility of the Webmaster. However, with today's growing technology in hardware and software, these tasks are becoming more and more specialized and therefore performed by more than one person. Webmasters and Web designers can work in any organization that has a Web site. Such organizations include educational institutions, museums, libraries, government agencies, and of course, businesses.

A person working in either of these capacities needs to have skills in graphic design, HTML language, Web design software programs, general programming, and the ability to adapt to new Web technology as it evolves.

An associate or bachelor's degree in computer science or graphic design is usually required. However, because the field is relatively new, many employers will accept persons with extensive experience in graphic design combined with computer skills.

The starting salary for a Webmaster or Web designer will vary depending on location and experience. The average salary can vary from $20,000 to $36,000.

Citing Internet Resources

Internet resources used in reports must be cited. You must give proper credit to any information you include in your report that is not your original thought. This will also provide the reader of the document with choices for additional research. It will also allow the information to be retrieved again. You can find general guidelines for citing electronic sources in the *MLA Handbook for Writers of Research Papers*, published by the Modern Language Association. *The Chicago Manual of Style* is another source for this information.

Here are some samples of citing Internet resources as suggested in the *MLA Handbook for Writers of Research Papers:*

- *Online journal article:* Author's last name, first initial. (date of publication or "NO DATE" if unavailable). Title of article or section used [Number of paragraphs]. Title of complete work. [Form, such as HTTP, CD-ROM, E-MAIL]. Available: complete URL [date of access].

> **Internet**
>
> For information concerning using MLA style for citing sources, visit *www.mla.org*.

- *Online magazine article:* Author's last name, first initial. (date of publication). Title of article. [Number of paragraphs]. Title of work. [Form] Available: complete URL [date of access].
- *Web sites:* Name of site [date]. Title of document [Form] Available: complete URL [date of access]
- *E-mail:* Author's last name, first name (author's e-mail address) (date). Subject. Receiver of e-mail (receiver's e-mail address).

Remember, anyone can put information on the Internet. Evaluate any resources that you choose to use carefully to ensure you have a high-quality resource that could really be of value to you.

Internet Detective

There is an on-line tutorial on evaluating the quality of the information you locate on the Internet. It gives specific information regarding evaluating electronic resources. You can access the Internet Detective by visiting *www.sosig.ac.uk/desire/internet-detective.html*. You can surf though the pages of this site. Your instructor may give you additional directions for using this site.

Evaluation Survey

You can use the information discussed in this lesson to construct a survey to evaluate electronic resources. See Figure 5-1.

FIGURE 5-1
Survey form

CRITERIA FOR EVALUATING ELECTRONIC RESOURCES

1. Can you identify the author of the page?	Yes ______	No ______
2. Is an e-mail address listed?	Yes ______	No ______
3. Can you access the site in a reasonable time?	Yes ______	No ______
4. Is the text on the screen legible?	Yes ______	No ______
5. Are the commands and directions easy to follow?	Yes ______	No ______
6. Is the information current?	Yes ______	No ______
7. When you perform a search, do you get what you expect?	Yes ______	No ______
8. Are instructions clearly visible?	Yes ______	No ______
9. Is the information updated regularly?	Yes ______	No ______

10. Make any comment here you would like concerning the site.

____

____

Identify a site on the Internet and use the survey to evaluate it. You may select a site such as a magazine article of interest to you, the White House, or any topic on which you may want to gather information.

Other Legal and Ethical Issues

3-4.3.6-1 The ease of obtaining information from the Internet and of publishing information on it can contribute to other legal problems as well. Just because information is obtained from an Internet site does not mean that someone can copy it and claim it as their own, even non-copyrighted information. That's plagiarism. The Internet does not relieve an author of responsibility for acknowledging and identifying the source of borrowed material.

3-4.3.6-2 Likewise, the Internet does not relieve anyone of the burden of ensuring that information they publish is true. If someone publishes information about another person or organization and it is not true, they can be sued for libel and forced to pay compensation for any damage they caused. The Internet makes widespread publication of information easy. It also creates the potential for huge damages if the information turns out to be false.

IC3 3-4.3.6-3 The free flow of information via the Internet also creates opportunities for criminals to gather personal information, acquire credit, and conduct transactions using false identities. Identity theft, as it is called, is a growing problem that can cause big headaches for unsuspecting victims. Other criminal problems that the Internet has been feeding include making sexual advances to minors, posting anonymous threats, and circulating rumors to manipulate stock prices. All are made easier by the Internet, but they are just as illegal and just as wrong.

IC3 3-4.3.6-4 And not all improper activities that make use of the Internet are necessarily illegal. Pranks, hoaxes, and making unfair use of free-trial "shareware" software may not be against the law, but they can still cause harm to innocent people—often more harm than their perpetrators might realize. The Internet is a powerful tool, for good and ill, which needs to be handled with care.

SUMMARY

In this lesson, you learned:

- The criteria for evaluating Internet resources include authorship, content, copyright information, navigation, and quality control.
- There are various types of Internet resources including electronic journals, magazines, newspapers, Web sites, and e-mail messages.
- Internet publications and Web site content can claim the same legal protection as books, newspapers, CDs, movies, and other forms that are protected by copyright law.
- It is very important to cite any information that you use from the Internet. The MLA style is widely used for citing electronic resources.

VOCABULARY *Review*

Define the following terms:

Copyright	Navigation	Shareware
Currency	Public domain	

REVIEW *Questions*

MULTIPLE CHOICE

Select the best response for the following statements.

1. _________ is the illegal copying or use of software.
   A. Piracy
   B. Webmastering
   C. Counterfeiting
   D. Surfing

2. __________ refers to the age of information.
   A. Date
   B. Infancy
   C. Currency
   D. Dead link

3. .Edu, .gov, .org, and .com are examples of the __________ portion of an URL.
   A. name
   B. domain
   C. ending
   D. handle

4. __________ is the exclusive right, granted by law for a certain number of years, to make and dispose of literary, musical, or artistic work.
   A. Copyright
   B. Security
   C. Privacy
   D. Resource

5. __________ is the ability to move through a site.
   A. Linking
   B. Grouping
   C. Citing
   D. Navigation

TRUE/FALSE

Circle T if the statement is true or F if the statement is false.

T F 1. It can be assumed that all information found on the Internet is accurate.

T F 2. The age of an article will affect its usefulness to a user.

T F 3. Everyone who puts information on the Internet is an authority on the particular subject.

T F 4. Shareware is free software that can be used for a given period of time.

T F 5. Spelling and grammatical errors on a Web page may affect a user's opinion of a site.

FILL IN THE BLANK

Complete the following sentences by writing the correct word or words in the blanks provided.

1. __________ refers to the age of the article.

2. All sites should have the __________ address of the author so the user can make contact.

3. Some information on the Internet is classified as __________, which means it can be used without citation.

4. __________ refers to the ability to move through a site.

5. A(n) __________ is responsible for managing and maintaining a Web site.

PROJECTS

PROJECT 5-1

Search the Internet for Web sites containing information on Olympic gold medalists. In the results list, pick at least two sites that you think might contain useful information. Using the survey form shown in Figure 5-1, evaluate each site. Write a 100-word report on your evaluation of the sites. Be sure to include the URL of the site and elaborate on what you found in answer to each of the survey questions.

PROJECT 5-2

Go to the Web site for the White House (*www.whitehouse.gov*). Review the section in the lesson on navigation, and then evaluate the navigation system and tools at the White House Web site. You'll want to click links on various pages. Write a 100-word report that explains the site's system for navigating. Be sure to mention any problems you had in getting around the site.

WEB PROJECT

Choose a topic to research on the Internet. Print the first two sites that you find. Using the information you studied in this lesson, critique the two sites and write a report of your findings.

TEAMWORK PROJECT

Your supervisor has informed you that she has contracted the services of a Web designer to create a Web page for your video/multimedia store. However, she would like to be able to talk intelligently with the Web designer when telling him or her exactly what she wants on the Web page. She has asked you and the other part-time employee to work together to provide her with samples of Web pages for five video/multimedia stores. She also wants you to provide her with a critique of each page.

CRITICAL *Thinking*

ACTIVITY 5-1

You want to design a Web site on a topic of your choice. Sketch out a design for the home page of the Web site. Review the evaluation criteria discussed in this lesson and make sure your Web site follows the criteria.

LESSON 6

EXPLORING SECURITY AND PRIVACY ISSUES

OBJECTIVES

Upon completion of this lesson, you should be able to:

- Identify types of computer crimes.
- Identify the "work" of hackers.
- Identify computer viruses.
- Describe how privacy is invaded because of computer use.
- Identify various security measures.
- Identify computer-related laws.

Estimated Time: 1.5 hours

VOCABULARY

Biometric security measures
Computer crime
Computer fraud
Data diddling
Hacking
Logic bomb
Time bomb
Trojan horse
Virus
Worm

As the use of computers has grown in volume and importance, protecting computer systems and the information they hold has become increasingly important. This lesson explores the many issues regarding the risks of computing and the measures you can take to minimize those risks.

Safeguarding Hardware and Data

One ever-present threat to a computer system is an electrical power failure. Electricity not only provides the power to operate a computer, but it also is the medium by which data is stored.

IC3 3-4.2.2-1 3-4.2.2-2

Computers are vulnerable both to power surges, or spikes in the electric current, and to power outages. Lightning can trigger either condition, for example. A power spike can corrupt computer hardware, rendering it inoperable and making any stored information inaccessible. A power outage can wipe out any data that has not been properly saved.

IC3 3-4.2.2-3 3-4.2.6-1

To safeguard computer systems against power outages, electric cords should be secured so that they cannot be accidentally disconnected. Another option is to install an uninterruptible power source, usually a battery that kicks in if the normal current is interrupted. Surge suppressors, which plug into electric outlets, can protect against power spikes. They wear out over time, though, and need to be monitored and replaced as necessary. To safeguard data as it is being entered, active files should be saved frequently. Some programs do this automatically; others require users to do it manually.

IC3
3-4.2.5-1
3-4.2.7-1
3-4.2.7-2
3-4.2.7-3

Even saved data can be lost or corrupted by equipment failure, software viruses or hackers, fire or flood, or power irregularities. So it is essential to back up important files regularly. Backing up files entails saving them to removable disks or some other independent storage device that can be used to restore data in the event that the primary system becomes inaccessible. Backup procedures should place a priority on files that would be difficult or impossible to replace or reconstruct if they were ever lost, such as users' data files. Secure backup procedures used by large organizations include a regular schedule for backing up designated files, and a means of storing backup files off site so that they'll survive intact if the main system is destroyed either by natural disaster or by criminal acts.

Types of Computer Crimes

A well-planned data backup system can help ward off or minimize the risks of computer crimes affecting you. But what is a ***computer crime***? It is a criminal act committed through the use of a computer, for example, getting into someone else's system and changing information or creating a computer virus and causing it to damage information on others' computers. It can also involve the theft of a computer and any equipment associated with the computer.

IC3
3-4.2.1-1

Computer crime is a bigger problem than most people realize. Billions of dollars every year are lost to corporations because of this often undetected, and therefore unpunished, crime. Computer crimes have increased since data communications and computer networks have become popular. Many computer crimes consist of stealing and damaging information and stealing actual computer equipment. Other types of computer crimes can include the following:

- unauthorized use of a computer
- infection of a computer by a malicious program (a virus)
- harassment and stalking on the computer
- theft of computer equipment
- copyright violations of software
- copyright violations of information found on the Internet

Hot Tip

The FBI's National Crime Information Center has a division for computer crimes.

Computer Fraud

Computer fraud is conduct that involves the manipulation of a computer or computer data in order to obtain money, property, or value dishonestly or to cause loss. Examples of computer fraud include stealing money from bank accounts and stealing information from other people's computers for gain.

Managers and supervisors in companies should be aware of certain signs that may be indicators of computer fraud:

- Low staff morale: Unhappy staff members may decide the company owes them.
- Unusual work patterns.
- Staff members who appear to be living beyond their income.

Did You Know?

The first computer crime, electronic embezzlement, was committed in 1958.

Computer Hacking

3-4.2.11-1

Computer ***hacking*** involves invading someone else's computer, usually for personal gain or just the satisfaction of invading someone else's computer. Hackers are usually computer experts who enjoy having the power to invade someone else's privacy. They can steal money, or change or damage data stored on a computer.

3-4.2.11-2

It is estimated that hacking causes millions of dollars of damage each year. There have been several high-profile cases of hacking in the United States.

Computer Viruses

3-4.2.10-1
3-4.2.10-2

A ***virus*** is a program that has been written, usually by a hacker, to cause corruption of data on a computer. The virus is attached to an executable file (like a program file) and spreads from one file to another once the program is executed. A virus can cause major damage to a computer's data or it can do something as minor as display messages on your screen. There are different variations of viruses.

- A ***worm*** makes many copies of itself, resulting in the consumption of system resources that slows down or actually halts tasks. Worms don't have to attach themselves to other files.
- A ***time bomb*** is a virus that does not cause its damage until a certain date or until the system has been booted a certain number of times.
- A ***logic bomb*** is a virus triggered by the appearance or disappearance of specified data.
- A ***trojan horse*** is a virus that does something different from what it is expected to do. It may look like it is doing one thing while in actuality it is doing something quite opposite (usually something disastrous).

In order to protect your computer against virus damage:

-4.2.10-3

- Use antivirus software. This software should always run on your computer and should be updated regularly.
- Be careful in opening e-mail attachments. It is a good idea to save them to disk before reading them so you can scan them.
- Don't access files copied from floppy disks or downloaded from the Internet without scanning them first. See Figure 6-1.

FIGURE 6-1
Scanning a file for potential virus

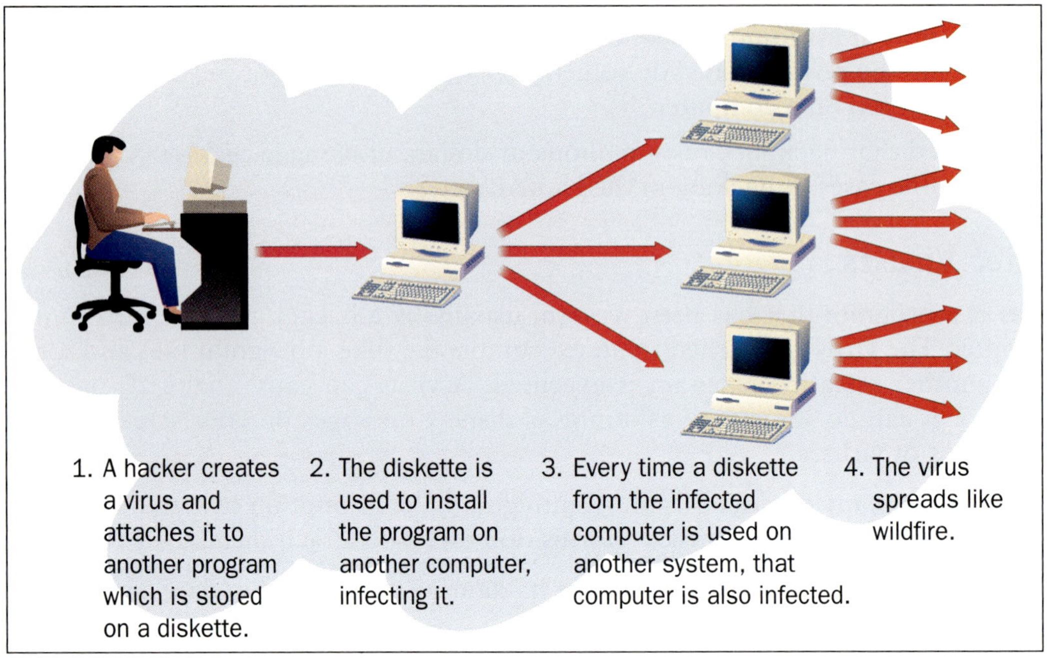

Other Computer Crimes

Theft of computer time is also a crime committed regularly on the job. This crime is committed when an employee uses a company's computer for personal use such as running a small side business, keeping records of an outside organization, or keeping personal records. While you are working these types of tasks, you are not being as productive as you could be for your employer.

Using the information you see on someone else's screen or printout to profit unfairly is theft of output.

Changing data before it is entered into the computer or after it has been entered into the computer is called ***data diddling***. Anyone who is involved with creating, recording, encoding, and checking data can change data.

Privacy

The amount of personal information available on each of us is astonishing. You would probably be very upset to know the extent to which this information is available and to whom it is available. There are many companies who gather information to create databases and sell or trade this information to others.

Any time you submit information on the Internet, it is possible for this information to be gathered by many persons and used for various situations. Information can also be gathered from online data regarding school, banking, hospitals, insurance, and any other information supplied for such everyday activities.

Much of the information gathered and sold results in your name being added to mailing lists. These lists are used by companies for marketing purposes. Junk e-mails are used for the same purpose. Information regarding one's credit history is also available to be sold.

IC3 3-4.2.9-1 If you work for a company that provides you with e-mail, you should know that the information you send is available to the company; it is the company's property. It can be accessed from backup copies made by the system.

IC3 3-4.2.9-1 3-4.2.9-2 Since any information gathered from (or documents created on) a company's computer system is company property and not an individual worker's personal property, they normally have no right to personal privacy regarding those things. The company has a right to access them and use them for its legitimate purposes. If the company monitors its Internet logs, for instance, and discovers that an employee has been spending a lot of time visiting Web sites that bear no relation to work-related duties, it can discipline the employee. Likewise, if an employee uses a company computer in a way that harms the company—contracting a computer virus through unauthorized activities, for example, or allowing hackers into the company's system—he or she can be disciplined or fired.

Security

Computer security is necessary in order to keep hardware, software, and data safe from harm or destruction. Some risks to computers are natural causes, some are accidents, and some are intentional. It is not always evident that some type of computer crime or intrusion has occurred. Therefore, it is necessary that safeguards for each type of risk be put into place. It is the responsibility of a company or an individual to protect their data.

Technology Careers

SYSTEM ANALYST

A system analyst works with the user to develop information systems. They plan and design new systems, recommend changes to existing systems, and participate in implementing changes. They are also responsible for writing manuals for the programs as well as external documentation. The system analyst is responsible for making sure that all users understand and can use the system effectively as well as keeping management informed.

This position requires a good technical knowledge of the computer. The system analyst should be up-to-date in the advances in the computer science field, good with details, and comfortable dealing with difficult people. Effective teaching skills are imperative because the analyst will have to teach the system to the users. A system analyst should be a "people person" because they work with a lot of users. They have to be self-motivated, a team worker, and a good listener. Many system analysts begin as programmers and work their way up to system analysts. However, having a four-year degree in computer science will enhance chances of obtaining a higher-paying beginning position. Having a certification, which requires five years of experience as an analyst and passing an exam, will also enhance chances of a higher-paying job.

A system analyst in a big firm can make anywhere from $47,000 to $60,000. In a small firm they can make anywhere from $38,000 to $50,000. These ranges vary based on location and size of the number of users on the system.

The best way to protect data is to effectively control the access to it. If unauthorized persons gain access to data, they may obtain valuable information or trade secrets. Perhaps worse, they might change data so that it provides misleading information or destroy data outright so that no one can use it.

3-4.2.5-2 The most common form of restricting access to data is the use of passwords. See Figure 6-2. Users may need a password in order to log on to a computer system or to specific parts of it. Companies often establish password-protected locations on hard drives and networks so that certain people have access to certain areas but not to others. In order to maintain secure passwords, they should be changed frequently so that people who no longer need access are locked out again.

3-4.2.11-4 It's important for all users to maintain password security in order to keep out unauthorized users, hackers, and other computer criminals. They should not reveal a password to anyone without authorization. They should inform the appropriate people if they discover that someone knows passwords they shouldn't know. They should avoid using the same or similar passwords for other applications or Internet accounts.

FIGURE 6-2
Passwords are used to protect against unauthorized use

3-4.2.1-2
3-4.2.11-3
3-4.2.11-4
3-1.1.1-2

Other security measures include the following:

- Making security a priority; maintain and enforce security measures.
- Electronic identification cards to gain access to certain areas within a building or department.
- Firewalls, which consist of special hardware and software, protect individual companies' networks from external networks. A firewall would allow users inside the organization the ability to access computers outside of their organization but keep outside users from accessing their computers.
- Use antivirus software to protect data on your computer.
- Institute a very selective hiring process that includes careful screening of potential employees. Do not keep employees on staff who refuse to follow security rules. This measure will prevent internal theft or sabotage.
- Regularly backing up data and storing it offsite.
- Employing ***biometric security measures***, which examine a fingerprint, a voice pattern, or the iris or retina of the eye. These must match the entry that was originally stored in the system for an employee. This method of security is usually used when high-level security is required. See Figure 6-3.

FIGURE 6-3
Biometric security measures

Internet Security

The security and privacy of personal information on the Internet is improving all the time. It is still necessary, however, to take precautions to protect both personal and business-related information. Many Web sites and online accounts require the use of passwords. Typically, users choose their own passwords for their accounts, and they tend to use passwords that are easy to remember. Problems can arise, however, if passwords become known to unauthorized persons. There are a number of useful strategies for keeping passwords secure.

IC3 3-4.3.2-1

First, use different passwords for different accounts and purposes, not the same password or ones that are easy to guess. For example, say someone uses their telephone number or street address as a password on all of their Internet accounts because it's easy to remember. Unauthorized users might quickly gain access through a bit of trial and error, using information that's readily available in any telephone directory. In other instances, corporate spies have devised online scams using e-mail contests to elicit passwords from employees of target companies. Once the spies know those passwords, they then use them to break into companies' internal computer networks, because they know that a large number of employees are lazy and will have used their internal security passwords to enter the phony e-mail contest.

IC3 3-4.2.8-1

Other password security strategies include changing passwords frequently (particularly if you suspect someone knows them), using word and number combinations rather than just words, and avoiding the use of obvious passwords or password hints.

IC3 3-4.3.3-1 3-4.3.3-2

Another common security concern on the Internet is credit card information. Because the Internet makes transactions so quick and easy, credit card numbers that fall into the wrong hands can cause lots of headaches for cardholders very quickly. Although there are effective encryption technologies to keep credit card numbers secure, you can make yours even more secure by following simple precautions. Only purchase from Internet sites that you know are reputable and trustworthy. Read and understand online companies' privacy and consumer-protection policies before you buy. Be sure that any credit card information is transmitted in a secured, encrypted mode.

IC3 3-4.3.5-1 3-4.3.5-2

Of course, credit card information isn't the only personal information that you may want to protect. The same precautions ought to be taken whenever you are asked to disclose anything about yourself that you don't want made known generally or given to market research companies.

Ethics in Technology

THE TEN COMMANDMENTS FOR COMPUTER ETHICS

1. Thou shalt not use a computer to harm other people.
2. Thou shalt not interfere with other people's computer work.
3. Thou shalt not snoop around in other people's files.
4. Thou shalt not use a computer to steal.
5. Thou shalt not use a computer to bear false witness.
6. Thou shalt not use or copy software for which you have not paid.
7. Thou shalt not use other people's computer resources without authorization.
8. Thou shalt not appropriate other people's intellectual output.
9. Thou shalt think about the social consequences of the program you write.
10. Thou shalt use a computer in ways that show consideration and respect.

Keep in mind that any information you give out can quickly end up in places you never dreamed of. Disclose only what you think is legitimately necessary for the intended purpose. Don't give out personal information to unknown parties. Use code names when appropriate to protect your identity and personal security.

Maintaining a Safe Working Environment

IC3 3-4.2.3-1

A safe working environment is important for the people who work with computers as well as for the computers themselves. As with any type of electrical equipment, computer systems pose various potential hazards. Wires need to be out of the way so people don't trip over them and so they do not impede movement in the event of an emergency. Power cords must be properly installed and insulated so they do not pose a fire hazard, and the power supply and distribution must be adequate to avoid overloads. Equipment also has to be ventilated and cooled to prevent excessive heat buildup.

IC3 3-4.2.4-1 3-4.2.4-2 3-4.2.4-3

Computer operators need to take precautions to avoid chronic physical maladies such as repetitive motion injuries, eyestrain, and back problems that can arise over time. Use of ergonomic furniture, good posture, proper workstation layout, and changing positions periodically throughout the day are all effective ways to minimize these types of injuries. Eyestrain can be avoided or minimized by using a high-resolution monitor, adequate and properly positioned lighting, and taking regular breaks to allow eye muscles to relax.

Protection for Technology Injuries

In the rise of computer crimes and other technology issues, many laws have been passed in an effort to assist those injured by these offenses. However, many of the offenses are difficult to prove. Here is a list of some of the laws that protect users.

- The Copyright Act of 1976: Protects the developers of software.
- Computer Matching & Privacy Protection Act, 1988: Regulates how federal data can be used to determine whether an individual is entitled to federal benefits.
- Electronic Communication Privacy Act, 1986: Prohibits the interception of data communications.
- Computer Fraud and Abuse Act, 1986: Prohibits individuals without authorization from knowingly accessing a company computer to obtain records from financial communications.
- Software Piracy and Counterfeiting Amendment of 1983.
- Many states have individual laws governing computer crimes in their states.

SUMMARY

In this lesson, you learned:

- Computer crime has become a major problem, costing companies billions of dollars annually.
- Computer fraud is conduct that involves the manipulation of a computer or computer data for dishonest profit.
- Computer hacking involves invading someone else's computer for personal gain. Sometimes it is done for financial gain and sometimes just as a prank.

- A computer virus is a program that has been written to cause corruption of data on a computer. There are different variations of viruses. These include worms, time bombs, logic bombs, and trojan horses.
- To protect yourself against viruses, install and keep an antivirus program running on your computer. Be sure to update it regularly.
- E-mail attachments can contain viruses. It is a good idea to save any message to disk if you are not familiar with the sender. After saving it to a disk, you can scan it for viruses.
- Personal privacy has been invaded by the computer. Information about our personal lives is freely available.
- Other computer crimes include theft of computer time, data diddling, and using information from another person's screen or printouts.
- Companies purchase personal information obtained on the Internet to sell to various companies for marketing purposes.
- Computer security is necessary in order to keep hardware, software, and data safe from harm or destruction.
- The best way to protect data is to control access to the data. The most common way to control access to data is to use passwords.
- Laws have been passed in an effort to assist those who have been injured by computer crimes and offenses.

VOCABULARY *Review*

Define the following terms:

Biometric security measures	Hacking	Trojan horse
Computer crime	Logic bomb	Virus
Computer fraud	Time bomb	Worm
Data diddling		

REVIEW *Questions*

MULTIPLE CHOICE

Select the best response for the following statements.

1. __________ is a criminal act that is committed through the use of a computer.
   - A. Hacking
   - B. Privacy
   - C. Copyright
   - D. Biometrics

2. __________ invade other people's computers.
   A. Hackers
   B. Programmers
   C. Trojan horses
   D. System analysts

3. A(n) __________ is a program that has been written to cause corruption of data on a computer.
   A. shareware
   B. virus
   C. antivirus software
   D. biometric

4. __________ control access to computer data.
   A. Passwords
   B. Hackers
   C. Trojan horses
   D. Worms

5. A virus that does not cause its damage until a certain date is called a(n) __________.
   A. worm
   B. time bomb
   C. antivirus software
   D. logic bomb

TRUE/FALSE

Circle T if the statement is true or F if the statement is false.

T F 1. A computer crime involves crimes committed through the use of a computer.

T F 2. A computer crime may involve the theft of a computer and any equipment associated with the computer.

T F 3. Hackers only invade other people's computers for fun.

T F 4. Laws to police computer use are difficult to enforce.

T F 5. Worms, time bombs, logic bombs, and trojan horses are variations of viruses.

FILL IN THE BLANK

Complete the following sentences by writing the correct word or words in the blanks provided.

1. Mailing lists are sold to various companies for __________ purposes.

2. __________ software should always be running on a program in order to protect it from viruses.

3. __________ security measures involve examining a fingerprint, a voice pattern, or the iris or retina of the eye.

4. The first computer crime was electronic __________.

5. Changing data before or after it's been entered in a computer is called data __________.

PROJECTS

PROJECT 6-1

Many colleges and universities have formal statements regarding the ethical use of their computer systems. Use the Internet or contact a local college or university to obtain a copy of such a statement. After reading it carefully, rewrite it to include any additional rules you believe should be included.

PROJECT 6-2

Computer crimes have been responsible for the loss of millions of dollars. Some crimes result in more loss than others. Use the Internet and other resources to locate information on lost revenue due to the top five computer crimes. If you have access to spreadsheet software, prepare this information in a spreadsheet and perform formulas that will not only add the totals, but also display the percentage of each crime's portion. Some keywords that may be helpful are *computer crimes*, *computer crime costs*, *hackers*, *viruses*, and *software piracy*. Use various search engines to research each term.

WEB PROJECTS

The Global Information Infrastructure Awards are designed to recognize innovation and excellence in the use of the Internet. This organization is also responsible for promoting responsible use of the Internet. Search the Internet using a search engine for information on the awards. Look for information on organizations that have won the awards. Write a report on an organization and what it won an award for.

TEAMWORK PROJECT

The video store you work at has been having problems lately with viruses. Your supervisor has asked you and the other part-time employee to do some research to find out what steps to take to reduce the chances of this continuing. Include in your report the names of software programs that could be used and information on how to train employees to avoid this problem.

CRITICAL *Thinking*

ACTIVITY 6-1

Use the Internet and other resources to identify early security measures that were used to protect computers and computer data. Describe how these measures counteracted the intrusions made. Then, visit the Web sites of some companies that make computer security devices such as *www.pcguardian.com*. Write a report of your findings.

LIVING ONLINE

REVIEW *Questions*

TRUE/FALSE

Circle T if the statement is true or F if the statement is false.

T F 1. A LAN is generally confined to a limited geographical area.

T F 2. The Internet is an example of a LAN.

T F 3. Satellites and microwave signals are examples of physical transmission media.

T F 4. ARPANET was the name of the first Web browser.

T F 5. Computers on the Internet communicate with each other using TCP/IP.

T F 6. Government agencies typically use the "irs" domain name.

T F 7. A newsgroup is an Internet-supported discussion forum.

T F 8. The home page is the first Web page displayed when you launch your browser.

T F 9. You can save only text on a Web page to disk.

T F 10. Google, Lycos, and Infoseek are examples of search engines.

MATCHING

Match the description in Column 2 to the correct term in Column 1.

Column 1	Column 2
___ 1. Keywords	A. A computer program written to cause corruption of data on a computer.
___ 2. Shareware	B. A computer program that makes copies of itself resulting in the corruption of system resources that slows down or actually halts tasks.
___ 3. Hits	C. Process of invading someone else's computer, usually for personal gain or just for the fun of it.
___ 4. Hacking	D. Changing data before it is entered into a computer or after it has been entered.
___ 5. Virus	E. The exclusive right, granted by law for a certain number of years, to make and dispose of literary, musical, or artistic work.
___ 6. Spider	F. Material that is available for anyone to copy because it's copyright protection has lapsed or does not exist.
___ 7. Worm	G. Free software that can be used for a given period of time.
___ 8. Public domain	H. Words on a Web page that are specified in searches.
___ 9. Copyright	I. Search engine robot that searches the Internet for keywords.
___ 10. Data diddling	J. The number of returns you get on a search of the Web.

PROJECTS

PROJECT 1

1. Start your Web browser and create a Favorites or Bookmarks folder. Give the folder a name of your choice, such as "Project 1 Sites."
2. Use a search engine of your choice to find information on the following topics:
   A. Popular Web browsers
   B. Shareware games
   C. Domain names
   D. Free e-mail providers

3. Save the most informative Web sites to your Favorites or Bookmarks folder.
4. Copy pertinent information on each topic to a word-processing document.
5. Save the documents with filenames of your choice, and then print the documents. Close all open files.

PROJECT 2

1. Start your e-mail program.
2. In your word processor, format one of the documents you saved in Project 1 (or format a different document if you didn't complete Project 1), and then save and close it.
3. Send an e-mail to yourself and attach the document.
4. Create a folder in your e-mail program to contain the e-mail message you sent in Step 3.
5. When you receive the e-mail message, move it to the new folder.
6. Open the attached file and print a copy. Then, close all open programs.

PROJECT 3

1. Go to one of the favorite or bookmarked Web sites you found in Project 1.
2. Evaluate the Web site using the criteria listed in Figure 5-1 in Lesson 5.
3. Prepare a 150-word report on the design and quality of content you found at this site. Be sure to touch on all the criteria listed in Figure 5-1.

SIMULATION

JOB 1

You are the systems manager for a small company. The company is housed in a two-story building with 10 standalone computers and two printers on each floor. The owner has suggested that you look into designing a networked environment. Your first step is to research the two types of LANs—client/server and peer-to-peer. Prepare a report in which you describe in detail the design of each type of network, and then make a recommendation on which you think would be best for your company.

JOB 2

The human resource manager at your company has asked you to help him write a section for the employee handbook on computer security and Internet use. He wants you to provide information on the following:

- Backing up data
- Using passwords to access company computers
- The company's policy on employee use of the Internet

You might search the Web for example employee handbooks to see how other companies address these issues. Or, interview the human resource managers of some local companies and ask them about their policies on these issues.

APPENDIX

IC^3 INTERNET AND COMPUTING CORE CERTIFICATION OBJECTIVES

IC^3—Module 1: Computing Fundamentals

STANDARDIZED CODING NUMBER	OBJECTIVES & SKILL SETS	PERFORMANCE BASED	LESSON NUMBER & PAGE NUMBER	EXERCISE NUMBER
Domain 1.0: Computer Hardware	*This domain includes the knowledge and skills required to identify different types of computers, the components of a personal computer (including internal components such as microprocessors) and how these components work together. The domain also includes the knowledge and skills relating to computer storage as it applies to hardware components like floppy and hard disks and performance as it applies to processor speed and memory.*			
Objective 1.1	**Identify different types of computers, how computers work (process information) and how individual computers fit into larger systems**			
IC^3-1 1.1.1	Identify different types of computers (mainframe, minicomputer, microcomputers, laptop computers)	no	Lesson 1: 5, 8	
IC^3-1 1.1.2	Identify different types of microcomputers (PC, Macintosh, workstation)	no	Lesson 1: 8	
IC^3-1 1.1.3	Identify the role of the central processing unit	no	Lesson 2: 23, 24	
IC^3-1 1.1.4	Identify how the speed of the microprocessor is measured	no	Lesson 4: 62	

*Skill must be covered in "hands-on" exercise, lab, or assessment.
Key: SBS=Step-by-Step PR=Project CT=Critical Thinking

STANDARDIZED CODING NUMBER	OBJECTIVES & SKILL SETS	PERFORMANCE BASED *	LESSON NUMBER & PAGE NUMBER	EXERCISE NUMBER
IC^3-1 1.1.5	Identify the role of different types of memory (RAM, ROM, hard or floppy disk storage)	no	Lesson 2: 25, 27 Lesson 3: 47	
IC^3-1 1.1.6	Identify the flow of information between storage devices (such as floppy or hard disks) to the microprocessor and RAM	no	Lesson 1: 14 Lesson 2: 21, 25	
IC^3-1 1.1.7	Identify how the flow of information within a computer works in relation to everyday computer operations including (1) starting or "booting" the computer, (2) starting a computer application, (3) creating documents (such as a word-processing file) and (4) saving and closing files	no	Lesson 2: 26 Lesson 4: 63	SBS 4.1
IC^3-1 1.1.8	Identify how information is transferred from one computer to another	no	Lesson 5: 73	
IC^3-1 1.1.9	Identify how large systems work (centralized data processing and storage)	no	Lesson 1: 4	
IC^3-1 1.1.10	Identify how computers integrate into larger systems (terminals or microcomputers connected to mini or mainframe systems, networks or the Internet)	no	Lesson 1: 9	
IC^3-1 1.1.11	Identify how computers share resources	no	Lesson 1: 11	
Objective 1.2	**Identify the function of computer hardware components and common problems associated with individual components**			
IC^3-1 1.2.1	Identify external components (monitor, mouse, keyboard, etc.)	no	Lesson 3: 42	
IC^3-1 1.2.2	Identify internal components (microprocessor, video card, etc.)	no	Lesson 2: 24	
IC^3-1 1.2.3	Identify input devices (keyboard, mouse, joystick, microphone, etc.)	no	Lesson 3: 39 Lesson 8: 134	
IC^3-1 1.2.4	Identify output devices (monitor, printer, speakers, etc.)	no	Lesson 3: 42, 43	

STANDARDIZED CODING NUMBER	OBJECTIVES & SKILL SETS	PERFORMANCE BASED	LESSON NUMBER & PAGE NUMBER	EXERCISE NUMBER
IC^3-1 1.2.5	Identify storage devices (hard disk, CD ROM, floppy)	no	Lesson 3: 47, 49	
IC^3-1 1.2.6	Identify ports used to connect input and output devices to a computer	no	Lesson 3: 46	
IC^3-1 1.2.7	Identify and be able to solve common problems associated with computer components	no	Lesson 2: 24	
Objective 1.3	**Identify issues relating to computer performance and how it is affected by different components of the computer**			
IC^3-1 1.3.1	Identify microprocessor speed and how it affects performance	no	Lesson 2: 24	
IC^3-1 1.3.2	Identify how the amount of RAM in a computer affects performance	no	Lesson 2: 26	
IC^3-1 1.3.3	Identify how storage devices affect performance	no	Lesson 3: 48	
IC^3-1 1.3.4	Identify other factors that affect performance (video capacity, network or modem connection speed, etc.)	no	Lesson 2: 26	
Objective 1.4	**Identify the factors that go into a decision on how to purchase a computer or select a computer for work or school**			
IC^3-1 1.4.1	Identify when large systems (such as mini or mainframe computers) are more appropriate for a particular job than a microcomputer	no	Lesson 1: 8	
IC^3-1 1.4.2	Identify how to select the right type of computer (PC, Macintosh, workstation) based on the purpose for which the computer will be used	no	Lesson 1: 8	
IC^3-1 1.4.3	Identify how to decide between a desktop or laptop/notebook computer	no	Lesson 1: 9	
IC^3-1 1.4.4	Identify hardware considerations (processor speed, hard disk size, monitor type, etc.)	no	Lesson 1: 8	

*Skill must be covered in "hands-on" exercise, lab, or assessment.
Key: SBS=Step-by-Step PR=Project CT=Critical Thinking

STANDARDIZED CODING NUMBER	OBJECTIVES & SKILL SETS	PERFORMANCE BASED *	LESSON NUMBER & PAGE NUMBER	EXERCISE NUMBER
IC^3-1 1.4.5	Identify software considerations (operating system, pre-packaged applications and utilities, etc.)	no	Lesson 1: 9	
IC^3-1 1.4.6	Identify integration considerations (network connection or modem, how the computer will interact with larger systems such as networks and the Internet)	no	Lesson 6: 102	
IC^3-1 1.4.7	Identify how price is impacted by different hardware, software and integration factors	no	Lesson 1: 9	
IC^3-1 1.4.8	Warranties, support agreements and other considerations for buying a computer	no	Lesson 1: 8	
Domain 2.0: Computer Software	*This domain includes the knowledge and skills required to identify how software works, software categories such as operating systems, applications and utilities, popular products in each category, and which application is best used for a specific purpose*			
Objective 2.1	**Identify how software works and how software and hardware work together to perform computing tasks**			
IC^3-1 2.1.1	Identify how data is input into a computer (via keyboard, mouse, scanner, microphone, etc.)	no	Lesson 3: 36	
IC^3-1 2.1.2	Identify how data is transformed from analog to digital formats	no	Lesson 3: 42	
IC^3-1 2.1.3	Identify how users interact with software by giving commands	no	Lesson 3: 38, 40	
IC^3-1 2.1.4	Identify how software applies rules (algorithms) to process data	no	Lesson 4: 55	
IC^3-1 2.1.5	Identify how software outputs the result of data processing to output devices such as a monitor or printer	no	Lesson 4: 57	
IC^3-1 2.1.6	Identify problems in software code (bugs) and how they are identified and fixed as part of the software development process	no	Lesson 4: 58	

STANDARDIZED CODING NUMBER	OBJECTIVES & SKILL SETS	PERFORMANCE BASED	LESSON NUMBER & PAGE NUMBER	EXERCISE NUMBER
Objective 2.2	**Identify different types of software, the tasks for which each type of software is most suited, and the popular programs in each software category**			
IC³-1 2.2.1	Operating systems (including the ability to identify products such as DOS, Microsoft® Windows®, Macintosh® OS and UNIX as operating systems)	no	Lesson 4: 56, 60, 61	
IC³-1 2.2.2	Word processors (including the ability to identify products such as Microsoft Word® or WordPerfect® as word processors)	no	Lesson 6: 99, 100	
IC³-1 2.2.3	Spreadsheet programs (including the ability to identify products such as Microsoft Excel® or Lotus® 1-2-3® as spreadsheet programs)	no	Lesson 6: 101	
IC³-1 2.2.4	Presentation programs (including the ability to identify products such as Microsoft PowerPoint® as a presentation program)	no	Lesson 4: 56	
IC³-1 2.2.5	Database programs (including the ability to identify products such as Microsoft Access® as a database program)	no	Lesson 6: 101	
IC³-1 2.2.6	Graphics programs	no	Lesson 4: 56	
IC³-1 2.2.7	Multimedia programs	no	Lesson 4: 56	
IC³-1 2.2.8	Electronic mail programs	no	Lesson 6: 103	
IC³-1 2.2.9	Web browsers (including the ability to identify products such as Microsoft Internet Explorer® or Netscape® Navigator® as browser programs)	no	Lesson 1: 14 Lesson 6: 99, 103	
IC³-1 2.2.10	Utility programs (including the ability to identify different categories of utility software such as compression programs, virus detectors, and disk-maintenance programs.	no	Lesson 4: 57, 58	
IC³-1 2.2.11	Specialized personal software (such as contact management or financial software)	no	Lesson 4: 56	

*Skill must be covered in "hands-on" exercise, lab, or assessment.
Key: SBS=Step-by-Step PR=Project CT=Critical Thinking

STANDARDIZED CODING NUMBER	OBJECTIVES & SKILL SETS	PERFORMANCE BASED *	LESSON NUMBER & PAGE NUMBER	EXERCISE NUMBER
IC^3-1 2.2.12	Custom mini- or mainframe software (to automate schools, hospitals, banks, etc.)	no	Lesson 6: 95	
IC^3-1 2.2.13	Identify products frequently sold together as software "suites"	no	Lesson 4: 56, 69	
IC^3-1 2.2.14	Identify problems that can arise if the wrong software product is used for a particular application	no	Lesson 4: 56	
Domain 3.0: Using an Operating System	*This domain includes the knowledge and skills required to perform the most frequently used functions of an operating system. Elements include the ability to install and run software, control the workspace (desktop), perform file management and change system settings (display, date and time settings, etc.). For purposes of this domain, the operating system covered is Windows, the most popular PC operating system, with consideration of some elements of DOS as they impact an understanding of Windows.*			
Objective 3.1	**Identify what an operating system is and how it works**			
IC^3-1 3.1.1	Identify the purpose of an operating system	no	Lesson 4: 57	
IC^3-1 3.1.2	Identify character-based operating systems (DOS)	no	Lesson 4: 61	
IC^3-1 3.1.3	Identify graphical-user-interface operating systems (Windows)	no	Lesson 5: 71, 72	
IC^3-1 3.1.4	Identify different versions of Windows	no	Lesson 4: 56, 61, 62, 63 Lesson 8: 128, 130	SBS 8.1
IC^3-1 3.1.5	Identify non-Windows operating systems	no	Lesson 4: 63	
IC^3-1 3.1.6	Identify the capabilities and limitations imposed by the operating system	no	Lesson 4: 56, 62	
Objective 3.2	**Be able to manipulate and control the Windows desktop, files and disks**			
IC^3-1 3.2.1	Identify elements of the Windows desktop and of different types of windows	no	Lesson 8: 133	

STANDARDIZED CODING NUMBER	OBJECTIVES & SKILL SETS	PERFORMANCE BASED	LESSON NUMBER & PAGE NUMBER	EXERCISE NUMBER
IC^3-1 3.2.2	Manipulate windows (maximize, minimize, close)	yes	Lesson 5: 73, 80 Lesson 9: 145 Lesson 11: 182	SBS 5.1
IC^3-1 3.2.3	Shut down and restart the computer	yes	Lesson 5: 72 Lesson 8: 137, 139 Lesson 13: 228	SBS 8.3
IC^3-1 3.2.4	Use the Windows Start menu and Taskbar	yes	Lesson 8: 131, 132, 137 Lesson 11: 181	SBS 8.2
IC^3-1 3.2.5	Add a shortcut to the Start menu	yes	Lesson 8: 132 Lesson 14: 245	SBS 14.1
IC^3-1 3.2.6	Switch between open windows/programs	yes	Lesson 8: 128, 137 Lesson 9: 153	SBS 8.2
IC^3-1 3.2.7	Use Online Help	yes	Lesson 5: 89 Lesson 10: 159, 160, 162, 166	SBS 10.1, 10.4
IC^3-1 3.2.8	Create, delete, move and modify desktop folders	yes	Lesson 5: 76, 82	SBS 5.3
IC^3-1 3.2.9	Create, delete, move and modify desktop icons	yes	Lesson 14: 245, 246, 248	SBS 14.1, 14.2, 14.5
IC^3-1 3.2.10	Start the Windows Explorer/File Manager	yes	Lesson 14: 249, 251	SBS 14.7
IC^3-1 3.2.11	Identify the directory/folder structure used to organize and store files	no	Lesson 14: 250, 251, 252	
IC^3-1 3.2.12	Change directory and file views	yes	Lesson 14: 254	SBS 14.8
IC^3-1 3.2.13	Create, move, copy and delete a directory/folder	yes	Lesson 5: 76, 82 Lesson 14: 256	SBS 5.3 SBS 14.10
IC^3-1 3.2.14	Select one or more files	yes	Lesson 5: 83, 88	SBS 5.7

*Skill must be covered in "hands-on" exercise, lab, or assessment.

Key: SBS=Step-by-Step PR=Project CT=Critical Thinking

STANDARDIZED CODING NUMBER	OBJECTIVES & SKILL SETS	PERFORMANCE BASED *	LESSON NUMBER & PAGE NUMBER	EXERCISE NUMBER
IC^3-1 3.2.15	Move, copy, delete and rename a file	yes	Lesson 13: 234 Lesson 14: 256	SBS 13.12 SBS 14.10
IC^3-1 3.2.16	Display and identify file properties	yes	Lesson 13: 228, 229, 230	SBS 13.10
IC^3-1 3.2.17	Find files	yes	Lesson 13: 230, 231	SBS 13.11
IC^3-1 3.2.18	Format a floppy disk	yes	Lesson 13: 213, 214	SBS 13.1
IC^3-1 3.2.19	Identify precautions one should take when manipulating files	no	Lesson 13: 231	
IC^3-1 3.2.20	Solve common problems associated with working with files	no	Lesson 13: 232	
Objective 3.3	**Be able to change system settings and install software**			
IC^3-1 3.3.1	Display control panels	yes	Lesson 11: 183	SBS 11.1
IC^3-1 3.3.2	Identify different control panel functions	no	Lesson 9: 154 Lesson 11: 182	
IC^3-1 3.3.3	Change date/time settings	yes	Lesson 13: 228	SBS 13.9
IC^3-1 3.3.4	Change display settings	yes	Lesson 11: 181, 184	SBS 11.1
IC^3-1 3.3.5	Identify precautions one should take when changing system settings	no	Lesson 4: 63 Lesson 14: 252	
IC^3-1 3.3.6	Solve common problems associated with changing operating system settings	no	Lesson 4: 62	
IC^3-1 3.3.7	Install software	yes	Lesson 4: 56, 63	SBS 4.1
IC^3-1 3.3.8	Identify installed applications	no	Lesson 4: 56	
IC^3-1 3.3.9	Start installed applications	yes	Lesson 4: 63	SBS 4.1

IC^3—Module 2: Key Applications

STANDARDIZED CODING NUMBER	OBJECTIVES & SKILL SETS	PERFORMANCE BASED	LESSON NUMBER & PAGE NUMBER	EXERCISE NUMBER
Domain 1.0: Common Program Functions	*This domain includes the knowledge and skills required to perform functions common to all Microsoft Windows applications with an emphasis on the common functionality between the two Microsoft Office applications, Microsoft Word and Excel. Elements include the ability to start and exit either the Word or Excel application, modify the display of toolbars and other on-screen elements, use online help, and perform file management, editing, formatting and printing functions common to Word, Excel and most Windows applications. ICVs are encouraged to demonstrate that these common functions are similar between Word and Excel and also common to Windows applications other than these two.*			
Objective 1.1	**Be able to start and exit a Windows application and utilize sources of online help**			
IC^3-2 1.1.1	Start a Windows application	yes	Lesson 1: 4, 5	SBS 1.1
IC^3-2 1.1.2	Exit a Windows application	yes	Lesson 1: 11	SBS 1.5
IC^3-2 1.1.3	Identify and prioritize help resources (online, documentation, help desk, etc.)	no	Lesson 1: 13	
IC^3-2 1.1.4	Access online help	yes	Lesson 1: 14	SBS 1.7
IC^3-2 1.1.5	Use help search functionality	yes	Lesson 1: 14 Lesson 2: 33	SBS 1.7 SBS 2.6

*Skill must be covered in "hands-on" exercise, lab, or assessment.
Key: SBS=Step-by-Step PR=Project CT=Critical Thinking

STANDARDIZED CODING NUMBER	OBJECTIVES & SKILL SETS	PERFORMANCE BASED *	LESSON NUMBER & PAGE NUMBER	EXERCISE NUMBER
IC³-2 1.1.6	Access Internet-based help functionality	yes	Lesson 1: 15	SBS 1.8
Objective 1.2	**Identify common on-screen elements of Windows applications, change application settings and manage files within an application**			
IC³-2 1.2.1	Identify on-screen elements common to Windows applications (pull-down menus, toolbars, scroll bars, titlebar, status bar, application window, document windows, mouse pointer, etc.)	no	Lesson 1: 4 Lesson 2: 28 Lesson 7: 132, 133 Lesson 10: 187, 188 Lesson 15: 289, 290 Lesson 18: 343	SBS 2.1 SBS 7.1 SBS 10.1 SBS 15.1
IC³-2 1.2.2	Display or hide toolbars	yes	Lesson 2: 28	SBS 2.1
IC³-2 1.2.3	Switch between open documents	yes	Lesson 2: 29	SBS 2.2
IC³-2 1.2.4	Change views	yes	Lesson 2: 34	SBS 2.7
IC³-2 1.2.5	Change magnification level	yes	Lesson 4: 66 Lesson 10: 197	SBS 4.6
IC³-2 1.2.6	Create new files	yes	Lesson 2: 27, 29	SBS 2.1
IC³-2 1.2.7	Create new files based on pre-existing templates	yes	Lesson 6: 121	SBS 6.14
IC³-2 1.2.8	Open files	yes	Lesson 1: 6, 7	SBS 1.2
IC³-2 1.2.9	Save files	yes	Lesson 1: 8, 9 Lesson 2: 30	SBS 1.3 SBS 2.3
IC³-2 1.2.10	Save files in different locations, names, file formats	yes	Lesson 1: 6, 8, 9	SBS 1.3
IC³-2 1.2.11	Identify and solve common problems relating to working with files (identify why files cannot be opened, resolve file incompatibility issues, etc.)	no	Lesson 1: 11, 12	
Objective 1.3	**Perform common editing and formatting functions**			
IC³-2 1.3.1	Navigate around open files with scroll bars, keyboard shortcuts, or the Go To command	yes	Lesson 2: 31, 32 Lesson 10: 189	SBS 2.4 SBS 10.2

STANDARDIZED CODING NUMBER	OBJECTIVES & SKILL SETS	PERFORMANCE BASED	LESSON NUMBER & PAGE NUMBER	EXERCISE NUMBER
IC^3-2 1.3.2	Select information	yes	Lesson 3: 43, 44 Lesson 10: 189	SBS 3.5 SBS 10.2
IC^3-2 1.3.3	Clear selected information	yes	Lesson 3: 40 Lesson 11: 207	SBS 3.2 SBS 11.2
IC^3-2 1.3.4	Cut selected information	yes	Lesson 3: 46, 48 Lesson 11: 209	SBS 3.7 SBS 11.3
IC^3-2 1.3.5	Copy selected information	yes	Lesson 3: 46, 48 Lesson 11: 208, 209	SBS 3.7 SBS 11.3
IC^3-2 1.3.6	Paste cut or copied information	yes	Lesson 3: 46, 48 Lesson 11: 208, 209	SBS 3.7 SBS 11.3
IC^3-2 1.3.7	Use the Undo, Redo and Repeat commands	yes	Lesson 3: 42 Lesson 10: 198, 199	SBS 3.4 SBS 10.9
IC^3-2 1.3.8	Find information	yes	Lesson 3: 51	SBS 3.11
IC^3-2 1.3.9	Replace information	yes	Lesson 3: 51, 52	SBS 3.12
IC^3-2 1.3.10	Check spelling	yes	Lesson 4: 68	SBS 4.7
IC^3-2 1.3.11	Change fonts	yes	Lesson 4: 60	SBS 4.1
IC^3-2 1.3.12	Bold, underline, italicize text	yes	Lesson 4: 60	SBS 4.1
IC^3-2 1.3.13	Change text color	yes	Lesson 4: 60, 61	SBS 4.1
IC^3-2 1.3.14	Apply text effects (superscript, subscript, etc.)	yes	Lesson 4: 60, 61	SBS 4.1
IC^3-2 1.3.15	Change text orientation (left, right, center, justify)	yes	Lesson 4: 61, 62	SBS 4.2
Objective 1.4	**Perform common printing functions**			
IC^3-2 1.4.1	Set margins		Lesson 4: 63	SBS 4.3
IC^3-2 1.4.2	Change paper size and orientation	yes	Lesson 4: 62, 63	SBS 4.3

*Skill must be covered in "hands-on" exercise, lab, or assessment.
Key: SBS=Step-by-Step PR=Project CT=Critical Thinking

STANDARDIZED CODING NUMBER	OBJECTIVES & SKILL SETS	PERFORMANCE BASED *	LESSON NUMBER & PAGE NUMBER	EXERCISE NUMBER
IC^3-2 1.4.3	Preview a file before printing	yes	Lesson 4: 64	SBS 4.4
IC^3-2 1.4.4	Print files	yes	Lesson 1: 10	SBS 1.4
IC^3-2 1.4.5	Use common printing options (number of pages, number of copies, printer, etc.)	yes	Lesson 1: 10	SBS 1.4
IC^3-2 1.4.6	Identify and solve common problems associated with printing	no	Lesson 4: 67	
Domain 2.0: Word Processing Functions	*This domain includes the knowledge and skills required to perform functions specific to creating documents with a word processor (as opposed to common functions such as those identified in Domain 1: Common Program Functions). Elements include paragraph formatting (including line spacing, indenting and creating bulleted or numbered lists), document formatting (including headers and footers), applying styles and other automatic formatting options, creating tables, applying borders and shading to text and tables, and inserting graphics into a document.*			
Objective 2.1	**Be able to format text and documents including the ability to use automatic formatting tools**			
IC^3-2 2.1.1	Change line spacing and paragraph spacing	yes	Lesson 4: 61, 62	4.2
IC^3-2 2.1.2	Indent text	yes	Lesson 4: 71, 72	4.9
IC^3-2 2.1.3	Create bulleted and numbered lists	yes	Lesson 4: 72, 73	SBS 4.10
IC^3-2 2.1.4	Insert symbols	yes	Lesson 6: 108	SBS 6.3
IC^3-2 2.1.5	Use, modify and delete tabs	yes	Lesson 4: 70, 71	SBS 4.8
IC^3-2 2.1.6	Insert a page break or section break	yes	Lesson 4: 73, 74	SBS 4.11
IC^3-2 2.1.7	Insert, modify and format page numbers	yes	Lesson 4: 73, 74	SBS 4.11
IC^3-2 2.1.8	Create, modify and format headers and footers	yes	Lesson 4: 73, 74	SBS 4.11
IC^3-2 2.1.9	Apply borders and shading to text paragraphs	yes	Lesson 6: 112, 113	SBS 6.7
IC^3-2 2.1.10	Create and apply styles	yes	Lesson 6: 122, 123	SBS 6.15

STANDARDIZED CODING NUMBER	OBJECTIVES & SKILL SETS	PERFORMANCE BASED	LESSON NUMBER & PAGE NUMBER	EXERCISE NUMBER
IC^3-2 2.1.11	Apply AutoFormats (themes)	yes	Lesson 6: 123, 124	SBS 6.16
IC^3-2 2.1.12	Use the Format Painter	yes	Lesson 4: 61, 77	PR 4-2
IC^3-2 2.1.13	Use AutoText	yes	Lesson 6: 124	SBS 6.17
Objective 2.2	**Be able to add tables and graphics to a document**			
IC^3-2 2.2.1	Create a table	yes	Lesson 5: 82, 90	SBS 5.9
IC^3-2 2.2.2	Select rows and columns	yes	Lesson 5: 85	SBS 5.3
IC^3-2 2.2.3	Insert rows and columns	yes	Lesson 5: 86	SBS 5.5
IC^3-2 2.2.4	Delete rows and columns	yes	Lesson 5: 86	SBS 5.5
IC^3-2 2.2.5	Split cells	yes	Lesson 5: 87	SBS 5.6
IC^3-2 2.2.6	Merge cells	yes	Lesson 5: 87	SBS 5.6
IC^3-2 2.2.7	Change column width and row height	yes	Lesson 5: 88, 89	SBS 5.7
IC^3-2 2.2.8	Split tables	yes	Lesson 5: 87, 89	SBS 5.7
IC^3-2 2.2.9	Format tables with borders and shading	yes	Lesson 5: 94, 95	SBS 5.11
IC^3-2 2.2.10	Automatically format tables with Table AutoFormat	yes	Lesson 5: 95, 96	SBS 5.12
IC^3-2 2.2.11	Insert pictures into a document	yes	Lesson 6: 105, 106, 108	SBS 6.2 SBS 6.3
IC^3-2 2.2.12	Modify pictures in a document	yes	Lesson 6: 109, 111	SBS 6.4 SBS 6.6
IC^3-2 2.2.13	Add drawn objects into a document	yes	Lesson 6: 116, 117, 119	SBS 6.9 SBS 6.11
IC^3-2 2.2.14	Manipulate drawn objects in a document	yes	Lesson 6: 116, 117	SBS 6.9

*Skill must be covered in "hands-on" exercise, lab, or assessment.
Key: SBS=Step-by-Step PR=Project CT=Critical Thinking

STANDARDIZED CODING NUMBER	OBJECTIVES & SKILL SETS	PERFORMANCE BASED *	LESSON NUMBER & PAGE NUMBER	EXERCISE NUMBER
Domain 3.0: Spreadsheet Functions	*This domain includes the knowledge and skills required to analyze information in an electronic worksheet and to format information using functions specific to spreadsheet formatting (as opposed to common formatting functions included in Domain 1). Elements include the ability to use formulas and functions, sort data, modify the structure of an electronic worksheet, and edit and format data in worksheet cells. Elements also include the ability to display information graphically using charts, and to analyze worksheet data as it appears in tables or graphs.*			
Objective 3.1	**Be able to modify worksheet data and structure**			
IC^3-2 3.1.1	Insert data into cells	yes	Lesson 10: 189, 190	SBS 10.2
IC^3-2 3.1.2	Modify data in cells	yes	Lesson 10: 189, 190, 194 Lesson 11: 208	SBS 10.2
IC^3-2 3.1.3	Fill cells	yes	Lesson 11: 210, 213	SBS 11.4 SBS 11.6
IC^3-2 3.1.4	Insert and delete cells	yes	Lesson 11: 207, 208	SBS 11.2
IC^3-2 3.1.5	Insert and delete rows and columns	yes	Lesson 11: 205, 206	SBS 11.1
IC^3-2 3.1.6	Insert and delete worksheets	yes	Lesson 11: 213, 214	SBS 11.7
IC^3-2 3.1.7	Adjust column width and row height	yes	Lesson 10: 193, 194	SBS 10.5
IC^3-2 3.1.8	Adjust column width using AutoFit	yes	Lesson 10: 194	SBS 10.5
IC^3-2 3.1.9	Hide and unhide rows and columns	yes	Lesson 11: 215	SBS 11.8
Objective 3.2	**Be able to sort data and manipulate data using formulas and functions**			
IC^3-2 3.2.1	Sort worksheet data based on one criteria	yes	Lesson 11: 216, 217	SBS 11.10
IC^3-2 3.2.2	Sort worksheet data based on multiple criteria	yes	Lesson 11: 217	SBS 11.10
IC^3-2 3.2.3	Insert arithmetic formulas into worksheet cells	yes	Lesson 12: 235, 236, 237, 238	SBS 12.1

STANDARDIZED CODING NUMBER	OBJECTIVES & SKILL SETS	PERFORMANCE BASED	LESSON NUMBER & PAGE NUMBER	EXERCISE NUMBER
IC^3-2 3.2.4	Identify frequently used worksheet functions	yes	Lesson 13: 253, 254, 255	SBS 13.1
IC^3-2 3.2.5	Insert formulas that include worksheet functions into cells	yes	Lesson 13: 263, 264	SBS 13.7
IC^3-2 3.2.6	Modify formulas and functions	yes	Lesson 12: 243	SBS 12.3
IC^3-2 3.2.7	Use AutoSum	yes	Lesson 12: 243, 244	SBS 12.4
IC^3-2 3.2.8	Identify common sources of errors in formulas and functions	no	Lesson 12: 239, 241	
IC^3-2 3.2.9	Draw logical conclusions based on worksheet data	no	Lesson 14: 284	
IC^3-2 3.2.10	Absolute vs. relative cell addresses	yes	Lesson 12: 245, 246	SBS 12.6
Objective 3.3	**Be able to format a worksheet**			
IC^3-2 3.3.1	Change number formats	yes	Lesson 10: 196	SBS 10.7
IC^3-2 3.3.2	Specify cell borders and shading	yes	Lesson 11: 224, 225	SBS 11.14
IC^3-2 3.3.3	Specify cell alignment (wrapping, rotation, etc.)	yes	Lesson 11: 227	SBS 11.16
IC^3-2 3.3.4	Create and apply styles	yes	Lesson 11: 226, 227	SBS 11.16
IC^3-2 3.3.5	Apply table AutoFormats	yes	Lesson 10: 200	SBS 10.10
IC^3-2 3.3.6	Use the Format Painter	yes	Lesson 10: 195, 197	SBS 10.7
IC^3-2 3.3.7	Insert a page break	yes	Lesson 11: 222, 223	SBS 11.13
IC^3-2 3.3.8	Create headers and footers	yes	Lesson 11: 220, 221	SBS 11.12
IC^3-2 3.3.9	Set a print area	yes	Lesson 11: 222, 223	SBS 11.13
IC^3-2 3.3.10	Specify scaling for printing	yes	Lesson 11: 218, 219	SBS 11.11
IC^3-2 3.3.11	Set gridlines to print	yes	Lesson 11: 225, 226	SBS 11.15

*Skill must be covered in "hands-on" exercise, lab, or assessment.
Key: SBS=Step-by-Step PR=Project CT=Critical Thinking

STANDARDIZED CODING NUMBER	OBJECTIVES & SKILL SETS	PERFORMANCE BASED *	LESSON NUMBER & PAGE NUMBER	EXERCISE NUMBER
IC^3-2 3.3.12	Specify repeating rows and columns	yes	Lesson 11: 228, 229	SBS 11.17
Objective 3.4	**Add pictures and charts to a worksheet**			
IC^3-2 3.4.1	Insert and modify pictures in a worksheet	yes	Lesson 14: 272, 274, 275	SBS 14.3 SBS 14.5
IC^3-2 3.4.2	Insert and manipulate drawn objects into a worksheet	yes	Lesson 14: 274, 275	SBS 14.4 SBS 14.5
IC^3-2 3.4.3	Create a chart based on worksheet data	yes	Lesson 14: 275, 276, 277	SBS 14.6
IC^3-2 3.4.4	Change chart type	yes	Lesson 14: 276, 277, 280, 282	SBS 14.6 SBS 14.8 SBS 14.10
IC^3-2 3.4.5	Modify chart elements	yes	Lesson 14: 276, 280, 281	SBS 14.8 SBS 14.9
IC^3-2 3.4.6	Be able to identify if a graph accurately represents worksheet data	no	Lesson 14: 284	

IC^3—Module 3: Living Online

STANDARDIZED CODING NUMBER	OBJECTIVES & SKILL SETS	PERFORMANCE BASED	LESSON NUMBER & PAGE NUMBER	EXERCISE NUMBER
Domain 1.0: Networks and the Internet	*This domain includes the knowledge and skills required to identify common terminology associated with computer networks and the Internet, components and benefits of networked computers, the difference between different types of networks (LAN and WAN), and how computer networks fit into other communications networks (like the telephone network).*			
Objective 1.1	**Identify network fundamentals and the benefits and risks of network computing**			
IC^3-3 1.1.1	Identify terminology relating to networks and the Internet (Local Area Network - LAN, Wide Area Network - WAN, server, client, node, Internet, Intranet, Extranet, electronic mail, World Wide Web, Web site, modem, switch, router, browser, bridge, firewall)	no	Lesson 1: 3, 4, 5, 11 Lesson 2: 22, 24, 26, 29 Lesson 6: 86	
IC^3-3 1.1.2	Identify how networks work	no	Lesson 1: 4, 5	

*Skill must be covered in "hands-on" exercise, lab or assessment
Key: SBS=Step-by-Step PR=Project CT=Critical Thinking

STANDARDIZED CODING NUMBER	OBJECTIVES & SKILL SETS	PERFORMANCE BASED *	LESSON NUMBER & PAGE NUMBER	EXERCISE NUMBER
IC^3-3 1.1.3	Identify the role of servers and clients in a network	no	Lesson 1: 4, 12	
IC^3-3 1.1.4	Identify how clients can connect to a network via dedicated connection or modem	no	Lesson 1: 5, 9	
IC^3-3 1.1.5	Identify benefits of networked computing (increased communications, sharing of files and other resources, enabling of workgroups, centralized control of computing resources, cost savings)	no	Lesson 1: 5	
IC^3-3 1.1.6	Identify the risks of networked computing (loss of autonomy, potential loss of privacy and security, potential for network-wide systems failure, virus attack, etc.)	no	Lesson 1: 13 Lesson 2: 26	
Objective 1.2	**Identify the relationship between computer networks, other communications networks (like the telephone network) and the Internet**			
IC^3-3 1.2.1	Identify the different ways the telephone system is used to transmit information (voice, fax, data)	no	Lesson 1: 5	
IC^3-3 1.2.2	Identify that the Internet is a "super network" of smaller computer networks	no	Lesson 2: 21, 22, 25	
IC^3-3 1.2.3	Identify that computers get onto the Internet via the "onramp" of a smaller computer network	no	Lesson 2: 23, 24	
IC^3-3 1.2.4	Identify how computers connect to the Internet (via a dedicated connection, via the phone lines, etc.)	no	Lesson 2: 24, 25	
IC^3-3 1.2.5	Identify Intranets, Extranets and how they relate to the Internet	no	Lesson 1: 14	

STANDARDIZED CODING NUMBER	OBJECTIVES & SKILL SETS	PERFORMANCE BASED	LESSON NUMBER & PAGE NUMBER	EXERCISE NUMBER
Domain 2.0: Electronic Mail	*This domain includes the knowledge and skills required to identify how electronic mail works and the makeup of an e-mail address. The domain also includes the ability to use an electronic mail software package and to identify the "rules of the road" (i.e., "netiquette") regarding the use of electronic mail.*			
Objective 2.1	**Identify how electronic mail works**			
IC^3-3 2.1.1	Identify how electronic mail works on a network	no	Lesson 3: 44	
IC^3-3 2.1.2	Identify how electronic mail works on the Internet	no	Lesson 3: 45	
IC?-3 2.1.3	Identify components of an e-mail message (address, subject line, body)	no	Lesson 3: 45	
IC^3-3 2.1.4	Identify the components of an electronic mail address	no	Lesson 3: 45	
IC^3-3 2.1.5	Identify when to use different e-mail options (reply, reply all, forward)	no	Lesson 3: 47, 49	
IC^3-3 2.1.6	Identify attachments	no	Lesson 3: 46	
Objective 2.2	**Identify how to use an electronic mail application**			
IC^3-3 2.2.1	Create an e-mail message	yes	Lesson 3: 46	SBS 3.5
IC^3-3 2.2.2	Fill out an e-mail message form correctly (inserting address, subject, body text, etc.)	yes	Lesson 3: 46	SBS 3.5
IC^3-3 2.2.3	Attach a file to an e-mail message	yes	Lesson 3: 46, 47, 48	SBS 3.5, 3.6
IC^3-3 2.2.4	Delete an attachment	yes	Lesson 3: 48	SBS 3.6
IC^3-3 2.2.5	Send mail	yes	Lesson 3: 46, 47	SBS 3.5
IC^3-3 2.2.5	View mail	yes	Lesson 3: 46	SBS 3.5, 3.6
IC^3-3 2.2.6	Search for mail	yes	Lesson 3: 48, 49	SBS 3.7
IC^3-3 2.2.7	Sort mail	yes	Lesson 3: 48, 49	SBS 3.7

*Skill must be covered in "hands-on" exercise, lab or assessment
Key: SBS=Step-by-Step PR=Project CT=Critical Thinking

STANDARDIZED CODING NUMBER	OBJECTIVES & SKILL SETS	PERFORMANCE BASED *	LESSON NUMBER & PAGE NUMBER	EXERCISE NUMBER
IC^3-3 2.2.8	Move and copy mail to different folders	yes	Lesson 3: 47, 49	SBS 3.7
IC^3-3 2.2.9	Select mail	yes	Lesson 3: 47, 49	SBS 3.7
IC^3-3 2.2.10	Save mail	yes	Lesson 3: 47, 48	SBS 3.6
IC^3-3 2.2.11	Delete mail	yes	Lesson 3: 47, 49	SBS 3.7
IC3-3 2.2.12	Reply to a mail message	yes	Lesson 3: 47, 48	SBS 3.6
IC^3-3 2.2.13	Reply to all	yes	Lesson 3: 48	SBS 3.6
IC^3-3 2.2.14	Forward a mail message	yes	Lesson 3: 47, 48	SBS 3.6
IC^3-3 2.2.15	Use an address book	yes	Lesson 3: 45, 46	SBS 3.5
IC^3-3 2.2.16	Select mail options	no	Lesson 3: 46	
Objective 2.3	**Identify the appropriate use of e-mail and e-mail related "netiquette"**			
IC^3-3 2.3.1	Identify the elements of a professional e-mail message (brevity, directness, correct spelling and grammar)		Lesson 3: 46	
IC^3-3 2.3.2	Identify when to include information from an original e-mail message in a response		Lesson 3: 47	
IC^3-3 2.3.3	Identify issues regarding unsolicited e-mail (Spam)		Lesson 4: 55	
IC^3-3 2.3.4	Identify the appropriate use of informal elements in an e-mail (such as emoticons or jokes)		Lesson 2: 30	
IC^3-3 2.3.5	Identify common problems associated with the widespread use of e-mail ("Inbox Overflow," hasty responses, blurring of the line between professional and informal communications, inappropriate use of reply options, junk mail, hoaxes, etc.)		Lesson 3: 46, 49	

STANDARDIZED CODING NUMBER	OBJECTIVES & SKILL SETS	PERFORMANCE BASED	LESSON NUMBER & PAGE NUMBER	EXERCISE NUMBER
Domain 3.0: Using the Internet	*This domain includes the knowledge and skills required to identify information and resources that are available on the Internet and use a Web browsing application. Elements include the ability to identify and know the difference between online resources (mailing lists, bulletin boards/newsgroups, Web pages, online databases, search engines, indexes, and commercial Web sites) and how to determine the quality of information found online. Elements also include the ability to use a Web browsing application such as Microsoft Internet Explorer® to browse the Internet.*			
Objective 3.1	**Identify different types of information sources on the Internet**			
IC^3-3 3.1.1	Identify mailing lists	no	Lesson 2: 30	
IC^3-3 3.1.2	Identify bulletin boards/newsgroups	no	Lesson 2: 32	
IC^3-3 3.1.3	Identify the difference between moderated and unmoderated mailing lists and bulletin boards/newsgroups	no	Lesson 2: 32	
IC^3-3 3.1.4	Identify different elements of a Web site	no	Lesson 2: 29 Lesson 4: 64	
IC^3-3 3.1.5	Identify different types of Web sites (commercial, academic and informational)	no	Lesson 2: 26	
IC^3-3 3.1.6	Identify online databases	no	Lesson 2: 26 Lesson 4: 56	
IC^3-3 3.2.1	Identify the make-up of a Web address/Uniform Resource Locator (URL)	no	Lesson 2: 27	
IC^3-3 3.2.2	Specify a URL in a Web browser	yes	Lesson 2: 29	SBS 2.1
IC^3-3 3.2.3	Go to a Web page by using links	yes	Lesson 2: 21, 29 Lesson 4: 65, 68	SBS 2.1 CT 4-1
IC^3-3 3.2.4	Go to or specify a home page	yes	Lesson 3: 40	SBS 3.1

*Skill must be covered in "hands-on" exercise, lab or assessment
Key: SBS=Step-by-Step PR=Project CT=Critical Thinking

STANDARDIZED CODING NUMBER	OBJECTIVES & SKILL SETS	PERFORMANCE BASED *	LESSON NUMBER & PAGE NUMBER	EXERCISE NUMBER
IC^3-3 3.2.5	Find specific information on a Web site	yes	Lesson 3: 40, 41	SBS 3.1
IC^3-3 3.2.6	Add a Web site to your list of Favorites/Bookmarks	yes	Lesson 3: 41, 42	SBS 3.2
IC^3-3 3.2.7	Manage personal lists of favorite Web sites/Bookmarks	yes	Lesson 3: 42	SBS 3.2
IC^3-3 3.2.8	Save the content of a Web site	yes	Lesson 3: 43	SBS 3.3
IC^3-3 3.2.9	Copy elements of a Web site	yes	Lesson 3: 43	SBS 3.4
IC^3-3 3.2.10	Print a Web page	yes	Lesson 3: 43, 44	SBS 3.4
Objective 3.3	**Be able to search the Internet for information**			
IC^3-3 3.3.1	Identify how online search engines and indexes work	no	Lesson 4: 54, 56	
IC^3-3 3.3.2	Identify the difference between different search engines	no	Lesson 4: 55, 56, 57	
IC^3-3 3.3.3	Search using specified keywords	yes	Lesson 4: 58	SBS 4.1
IC^3-3 3.3.4	Identify effective key words to use in a search	no	Lesson 4: 56	
IC^3-3 3.3.5	Search using Boolean search strings (using & or ^)	yes	Lesson 4: 63	SBS 4.2
IC^3-3 3.3.6	Identify effective Boolean search strategies	no	Lesson 4: 63	
IC^3-3 3.3.7	Identify how to evaluate the quality of information found on the Web (analyzing the source of a site, communicating with the creator of a site, analyzing internal links within a site, evaluating search engine results, comparing information found on the Internet with other "offline" sources such as professional journals, etc.)	no	Lesson 4: 57 Lesson 5: 69, 71, 72	

STANDARDIZED CODING NUMBER	OBJECTIVES & SKILL SETS	PERFORMANCE BASED	LESSON NUMBER & PAGE NUMBER	EXERCISE NUMBER
Domain 4.0: The Impact of Computing and the Internet on Society	*This domain includes the knowledge and skills required to identify the benefits and risks of computing and the Internet in many areas of society, from home and work to school and play. Elements include the ability to identify how computers and the Internet are used in different aspects of work, school, and home and how these areas of society are impacted by the availability of computer technology and online resources.*			
Objective 4.1	**Identify how computers are used in different areas of work, school and home**			
IC^3-3 4.1.1	Identify how computers and the Internet have changed the workplace (information management becoming part of nearly every job, etc.)	no	Lesson 2: 22	
IC^3-3 4.1.2	Identify the way computers and the Internet are used in education (e-learning, online collaborative projects, etc.)	no	Lesson 2: 22	
IC^3-3 4.1.3	Identify how computers and the Internet are used in the home (games, financial management, online shopping, etc.)	no	Lesson 2: 22	
IC^3-3 4.1.4	Identify the role of computers operating "behind the scenes" in everyday activities (ATMs, computers used to manage travel, credit card billing and other transactions, embedded computers in automobiles and household appliances, automated industrial processes)	no	Lesson 2: 22	
IC^3-3 4.1.5	Identify the benefits of computers and the Internet (increased productivity, communications, access to information, opportunities for the disabled and the disadvantaged, new methods of training and education)	no	Lesson 2: 23	

*Skill must be covered in "hands-on" exercise, lab or assessment
Key: SBS=Step-by-Step PR=Project CT=Critical Thinking

STANDARDIZED CODING NUMBER	OBJECTIVES & SKILL SETS	PERFORMANCE BASED *	LESSON NUMBER & PAGE NUMBER	EXERCISE NUMBER
Objective 4.2	**Identify the risks of using computer hardware and software**			
IC^3-3 4.2.1	Protecting computer hardware from theft or damage	no	Lesson 6: 82, 86	
IC^3-3 4.2.2	Protecting hardware from power irregularity or outages	no	Lesson 6: 81	
IC^3-3 4.2.3	Maintaining a safe working environment	no	Lesson 6: 89	
IC^3-3 4.2.4	Proper ergonomics (seating, lighting, etc.) when using computers/repetitive motion disorder	no	Lesson 6: 89	
IC^3-3 4.2.5	Securing your data	no	Lesson 6: 82, 86	
IC^3-3 4.2.6	Saving work in progress frequently	no	Lesson 6: 81	
IC^3-3 4.2.7	Data backup procedures and strategies	no	Lesson 6: 82	
IC^3-3 4.2.8	Proper use of passwords	no	Lesson 6: 88	
IC^3-3 4.2.9	Identify when information can or cannot be considered personal	no	Lesson 6: 85	
IC^3-3 4.2.10	Protecting against viruses, WORMS and other software threats	no	Lesson 6: 83	
IC^3-3 4.2.11	Protecting against hacking and unauthorized computer and network use	no	Lesson 6: 83, 86	
Objective 4.3	**Identify how to use the Internet safely and legally**			
IC^3-3 4.3.1	Restricting Internet access	no	Lesson 5: 70	
IC^3-3 4.3.2	Careful use of passwords	no	Lesson 6: 88	
IC^3-3 4.3.3	Careful use of credit card numbers	no	Lesson 3: 42 Lesson 6: 88	
IC^3-3 4.3.4	Copyright rules for online information	no	Lesson 5: 73, 74	
IC^3-3 4.3.5	Protecting your privacy online	no	Lesson 6: 88	
IC^3-3 4.3.6	Plagiarism, libel and other legal and ethical issues of creatingand using online information	no	Lesson 5: 76, 77	

GLOSSARY

8.3 alias Short filename that Windows assigns to files with long names so they can be used with programs that don't support long filenames.

A

Absolute cell reference A cell reference that does not change when the formula is copied or moved to a new location.

Active cell In Excel, a selected cell.

Active desktop A feature of Windows that allows you to add Web content to your desktop.

Active window The window or icon currently in use. The title bar of the active window is always highlighted (or displayed in a different color) to distinguish it from other open windows that may be visible in a tiled or cascaded screen.

Address bar The space in a window that displays the name of the open folder or object.

Address book Application that allows you to record e-mail and other contact information.

American Standard Code for Information Interchange (ASCII) Coding system that computers of all types and brands can translate.

Animation Special visual or sound effects added to text or an object on a PowerPoint slide.

Animation schemes Predesigned sets of visual effects added to text on PowerPoint slides.

Application file icon An icon that represents an application; double-clicking the icon starts the application.

Applications software Also called productivity software, it is designed for an end user. Some of the more commonly used application programs are word processors, database systems, presentation systems, spreadsheet programs, and desktop publishing programs.

Argument A value, cell reference, range, or text that acts as an operand in a function formula.

Arithmetic/logic unit (ALU) Section in the central processing unit that performs arithmetic computations and logical operations. The arithmetic operations include addition, subtraction, multiplication, and division. The logical operations involve comparisons.

Arrow keys Keys on the keyboard that you press to move the blinking insertion point on the screen.

Artificial intelligence Type of software that can process information on its own without human intervention.

Ascending order Sorts alphabetically from A to Z and numerically from the lowest to the highest number.

B

Background A pattern or a picture that can be used on the desktop.

Banner A full-width headline that spans across multiple newsletter-style columns, such as the title for a newsletter or report.

Biometric security measures Security tools that use a fingerprint, voice pattern, or the iris or retina of the eye to identify a person.

Bit A zero or one in computer code.

Boolean logic Method for searching databases. This works on a similar principle as search engine math, but has a little more power. Boolean logic consists of three logical operators: AND, NOT, OR.

Bot Type of robot used by search engines.

Browser Software program that you use to retrieve documents from the World Wide Web.

Bus topology Configuration in which all devices are connected to and share a master cable, referred to as the "bus" or "backbone."

Byte Made up of eight bits, a byte represents a single character, such as the letter *A*.

C

Cache memory High-speed random access memory that is used to increase the speed of the data processing cycle.

CD-R drives Disk drives on which you can write to a CD-ROM disk.

CD-ROM Disk that can store up to 680 MB of data; data can only be read from it.

Cell The intersection of a single row and a single column.

Cell comment A message that helps explain the information contained in the cell.

Cell reference Identifies the column letter and row number (for example, A1 or B4).

Central processing unit (CPU) Also called the microprocessor, the processor, or central processor, the CPU is the "brains" of the computer. The CPU is housed on a tiny silicon chip that contains millions of switches and pathways that help your computer make important decisions.

Channel Media, such as telephone wire, coaxial cable, microwave signal, or fiber-optic cable, that carries or transports data communication messages.

Chart A graphical representation of worksheet or table data.

Client A computer that uses the services of another program. The client program is used to contact and obtain data or request a service from the server.

Client/server network Computer configuration in which one or more computers on the networks act as a server.

Clicking Pressing and releasing the left (primary) mouse button.

Clip art Prepared pictures and other artwork you can insert into a document.

Clip Organizer A wide variety of pictures, photographs, sounds, and video clips that you can insert in your document.

Clipboard A temporary storage area for text and/or graphics that are to be cut or copied and then pasted to another location.

Command An instruction to perform an operation or execute a program. In Windows, commands are issued by making menu selections, by clicking on a toolbar button, or by clicking on a command button in a dialog box.

Command buttons Rectangular buttons in dialog boxes that execute an instruction. An ellipsis following a command button name (i.e. Browse...) indicates that another dialog box will appear if this command is chosen.

Communications channel Type of link through which data can be transmitted from one computer to another.

Computer Electronic device that receives, processes, and stores data, and produces a result (output).

Computer-based learning Using a computer for learning and instruction.

Computer crime A criminal act that is committed through the use of a computer, like getting into someone else's system and changing information or creating a computer virus and causing it to damage information on others' computers. It can also involve the theft of a computer and any equipment associated with the computer.

Computer fraud Conduct that involves the manipulation of a computer or computer data in order to dishonestly obtain money, property, or value or to cause loss. Examples of computer fraud include stealing money from bank accounts and stealing information from other persons' computers for gain.

Computer system Combination of hardware, software, and data working together.

Conditional formats Apply various formats to cell contents when certain conditions are met.

Contacts Persons with whom you communicate.

Contents pane The contents pane in the Explorer window gives a more detailed view of the structure by displaying all the folders and files contained in the drive or folder currently selected in the tree pane.

Control Panel Windows' central location for configuring or changing system hardware, software, and settings.

Control unit The "boss," so to speak, that coordinates all of the central processing unit's activities.

Controller Device that controls the transfer of data from the computer to a peripheral device and vice versa.

Copy Duplicate a selection so you can paste it in another position.

Copyright The exclusive right, granted by law for a certain number of years, to make and dispose of literary, musical, or artist work.

Crop To trim a graphic.

Currency On a Web page, this refers to the age of the information, how long it has been posted, and how often it is updated.

D

Data Information that is entered into the computer to be processed. Data consists of text, numbers, sounds, and images.

Data communications The technology that enables computers to communicate between each other. Data communications is defined as the transmission of text, numeric, voice, or video data from one machine to another. Popular examples are the Internet, electronic messages (e-mail), faxes, and electronic or online banking.

Data diddling Act of changing data before it is entered in the computer or after it has been entered.

Database A collection of related information organized for rapid search and retrieval.

Database software Software that makes it possible to create and maintain large collections of data.

Datasheet view A view in Access that displays the table data in columns and rows.

Default In any given set of choices, the choice that is preselected; the selection that is in effect when you open a program; the settings established during the installation process.

Dependent cells Worksheet formulas that reference a particular cell.

Descending order Sorts alphabetically from Z to A and numerically from the highest to the lowest number.

Design view A view in Access that displays field names and the types of values you can enter in each field. Use this view to define or modify the field formats.

Desktop The first screen you see when the operating system is launched and fully running. It is called the desktop because the icons are intended to represent the objects on a real desktop.

Desktop publishing The process of using a computer to combine text and graphics to create an attractive document.

Desktop shortcuts Icons you can create and place on the desktop to represent an application, folder, or file. When you click the shortcut icon, the application, folder, or file opens immediately.

Desktop theme A set of predefined elements such as icons, fonts, colors, and sounds that determine the look of your desktop.

Destination The location (folder or disk) where a copied file will reside.

Details A view in Windows that displays detailed information about a file, including the filename, size, its associated application, and the date and time it was last modified.

Dialog box An information-exchange window in which the user selects options, sets defaults, chooses items from lists, and otherwise provides information Windows needs before it can execute a command.

Digital cash Allows someone to pay by transmitting a number from one computer to another. The digital cash numbers are issued by a bank and represent a specified sum of real money; each number is unique.

Disk The magnetic medium on which data are stored.

Disk cleanup A program that enables you to clear your disk of unnecessary files.

Disk Defragmenter Rearranges disk files, storing each file in contiguous blocks.

Disk drive The hardware that finds, reads, and writes information to and from a disk.

Disk drive icons Identify (by letter and type) the disk drives that you can access on your system.

Distance learning Schooling concept in which students in remote locations receive instruction via telecommunications technology.

Document file icon An icon that shares the same distinctive feature, a piece of paper with a superimposed graphic, that helps create a link between a document and an application.

Domain name The portion of a Web site address that identifies the type of site. For example, the *.com* in *www.microsoft.com* is the domain name. The .com indicates that this is a commercial site.

Dot pitch Measurement of the distance between pixels.

Double-click Pressing the mouse button twice quickly.

Drag-and-drop Drag the mouse to move or copy selected text to a new location.

Dragging A special method of using a mouse to move a window or a graphic object across the screen—specifically, by (1) selecting the object to be moved and (2) pressing and holding down the mouse button while moving the mouse (and at the same time moving the object).

Drawing canvas An area upon which you can draw, arrange, and resize multiple shapes.

Drawing objects Artwork that you create using drawing tools.

E

Electronic commerce Also called e-commerce, it refers to business conducted via the Internet.

Electronic mail (e-mail) The capability to send a message from one person's computer to another person's computer where it is stored until read by the receiving person. E-mail messages can be sent to friends, family members and businesses locally or across the oceans.

Embedded chart A chart created on the same worksheet as the data.

Emphasis effect Controls the animation effects after the text or object appears on a PowerPoint slide.

Entrance effect Controls how the text or object animates as it appears on a PowerPoint slide.

Entry Data entered into a cell.

Ethernet LAN protocol that is based on the bus topology, but can work with the star topology as well. It supports data transfer rates of up to 10 megabits per second.

Event A scheduled item in the Outlook calendar that lasts 24 hours or longer.

Execution cycle Also called the E-cycle, it's the amount of time it takes the central processing unit to execute an instruction and store the results in RAM.

Exit effect Controls the animation effects at the end of the animation sequence on a PowerPoint slide.

Extended Binary Coded Decimal Interchange Code (EBCDIC) Standard computer code used mostly in very large computers.

Extension An extension of no longer than three characters is added to the file name following a period, called a "dot."

Extranet Network configuration that allows selected outside organizations to access internal information systems.

F

Field A single piece of information in a database. In Word, a special instruction that automatically inserts variable data. In Outlook, each piece of information in an Outlook form.

Field name A label to identify a field in a database.

Field properties Specifications that allow you to customize an Access field beyond choosing a data type.

Field selector A small box or bar that you click to select a column in a table in Datasheet view.

File A file may be the instructions the computer needs to operate (called program files or executable files), or a file may contain a text document that you can read (often referred to as a document file).

File allocation table (FAT) A special log on a disk where tracks are stored.

File transfer protocol (FTP) An Internet standard that allows users to download and upload files with other computers on the Internet.

Filename A name assigned to a file for identification.

Fill handle A small square in the bottom right corner of an active cell in a worksheet.

Filling A method of copying data in a worksheet.

Finder Program that displays the Macintosh desktop.

First line indent Only the first line of the paragraph is indented.

Floppy disk A small and portable kind of disk.

Folder A way to organize files into manageable groups.

Folders bar A hierarchical display of all objects on the desktop; also called the tree pane.

Font The general shape and style of a set of characters.

Footer Text and/or graphics appearing at the bottom of each page of a document.

Form In Outlook, a set of controls in which you enter a piece of information to be stored in an item.

Formatting Prepares a disk for use on a specific type of drive; imprints a disk with the information it needs to work in that particular kind of drive. Also, the ability to control the appearance and layout of data in a file.

Formula Equation used to calculate values in a spreadsheet cell.

Fragmented files Files that are not stored in contiguous clusters.

Function formula A special formula that names a function instead of using operators to calculate a result.

Function keys Keys on the keyboard that are used to give commands to the computer.

G

Graphical User Interface (GUI) Describes computer-user interaction in which the user relies on an easy-to-use visual setting—that is, familiar graphical images or icons (as in Windows)—rather than a difficult, word-based setting that requires memorization of complicated commands.

Graphics Items other than text, including photos, clip art, and drawing objects.

Graphics tablet Input device that has a flat drawing surface on which a user can draw figures or write something freehand.

Gridlines Nonprinting lines that display on the screen to show the boundary lines of a table.

H

Hacking Act of invading someone else's computer, usually for personal gain or just the satisfaction of being able to do it.

Hanging indent In a paragraph, all lines but the first "hang" (are indented) to the right of the first line.

Hard column break A manual column break.

Hard disk (also **hard disk drive**) A hard disk and a hard drive are one integrated unit that cannot easily be removed from the computer.

Hard page break A manual page break.

Hardware Tangible, physical computer equipment. Examples include the keyboard, processor, monitor, and printer.

Header Text and/or graphics appearing at the top of each page in a document.

Header row Labels at the top of columns in a worksheet.

Help Viewer Displayed when the Help option is selected in any Windows application. The information in each Help Viewer is relevant to that particular application.

Hits The results of a search on the Web.

Home page The first page that's displayed when you launch your browser.

Hyperlinks Objects on a Web page that, when clicked, take you to another location on the Web.

Hypertext markup language (HTML) This text-based program (language) is used to create documents for the WWW. HTML is a series of tags that are integrated into a text document. These tags describe how the text should be formatted when a Web browser displays it on the screen.

Hypertext transfer protocol (HTTP) Protocol that defines how messages are formatted and transmitted over the World Wide Web.

I

I-beam When positioned on text, the mouse pointer becomes an I-shaped pointer.

Icons Graphic images or symbols that represent applications (programs), files, disk drives, documents, embedded objects, or linked objects.

Impact printers Type of printer that uses a mechanism that actually strikes the paper to form images.

Ink-jet printers Type of printer in which the ink is sprayed onto the paper.

Input Data that is entered into the computer system via an input or storage device.

Input devices Enable you to input data and commands into the computer.

Insert mode In this default mode, new text is inserted between existing characters.

Instruction cycle Also called the I-cycle, it's the amount of time it takes the central processing unit to retrieve an instruction and complete the command.

Internet A global network connecting millions of computers, making it possible to exchange information.

Internet Explorer A Web browser used for communication on the Internet.

Intranet Internal network that uses protocols like that of the Internet.

Item A particular piece of information stored in an Outlook folder.

J

Jaz drives Type of disk capable of storing as much as 1 GB of data.

Joystick Pointing device that controls movement of objects on the screen.

K

Keyboard Common input device for entering numeric and alphabetic data into a computer.

Keyboarding Process of entering text by pressing keys on a keyboard.

Keywords Words you enter in a search engine to locate specified information on the Web.

L

Landscape orientation The document content is formatted with the long edge of the page at the top.

Laser printers Produce images using the same technology as copier machines.

Link Pointers in a hypertext document or Help window that connect with other hypertext documents or that jump you to other Help entries.

Linking A Windows feature that connects data in different documents or applications so that data changed in one document updates all other data that has been connected.

Local area network (LAN) A series of connected personal computers, workstations, and other devices such as printers or scanners within a confined space such as an office building.

Log off An option used to exit an account without turning off the computer so the name of a different user can log on at a later time.

Log on An option that identifies a person by user name and password so the user's personal settings and desktop will be loaded.

Logic bomb Computer virus that is triggered by the appearance or disappearance of specified data.

Logical functions Used to display text or values when certain conditions exist.

M

Magnetic tape drives Used for making backup copies of large volumes of data.

Main memory Also called random access memory or RAM, it is like short-term memory. It stores data while the computer is running. When the computer is turned off or if there is a loss of power, any data in the main memory disappears. The computer can read from and write to this type of memory.

Mainframe computers Large, powerful computers that are used for centralized storage, processing, and management of very large amounts of data.

Management information systems (MIS) Organized systems of processing and reporting information in an organization.

Math symbols Single-character symbols representing a word such as *and* or *or*, that you can use to narrow your search of information on the Web.

Mathematical functions Perform calculations that you could do using a scientific calculator.

Maximize To enlarge a window on the computer to fill the computer screen.

Memory On the computer's motherboard, it's where data is stored.

Menu List of commands or options grouped under specific headings or titles (File, Edit, etc.) on a window's menu bar.

Menu bar In every application window, a listing of menus directly under the title bar specifying the choices available in the current application.

Merge In Excel, combine multiple cells into a single cell.

Merging cells Converting two or more cells into a single cell.

Microcomputer Also called a personal or desktop computer, it's the type of computer designed for use by a single user.

Minicomputer Type of computer that is designed to serve multiple users and process significant amounts of data; larger than a microcomputer but smaller than a mainframe.

Minimize To reduce a window on the screen to a button on the taskbar.

Mixed cell reference A cell reference that contains both relative and absolute cell references.

Modem Communications hardware device that facilitates the transmission of data.

Modifier keys Keys on the keyboard that are used in conjunction with other keys to execute a command. The Shift, Ctrl, and Alt keys are examples of modifier keys.

Monitors Video display screens that can be either monochromatic (one color) or color.

Motherboard Circuit board in the computer that contains components such as the central processing unit, memory, basic controllers, and expansion ports and slots.

Mouse A pointing device that serves as a faster, more effective alternative to the keyboard in communicating instructions.

Mouse buttons Controls on a mouse that activate functions or call up menus when clicked.

Move To remove a selection from one position and paste it in another.

MS-DOS Microsoft Corporation's operating system designed for the personal computer.

Multitasking Running two or more distinct computer operations simultaneously—one in the foreground, the other(s) in the background.

My Computer A feature that displays the contents of your computer, provides information about different system resources, and allows you to perform tasks such as formatting disks and running applications.

My Documents A personal folder for storing files you have created or used.

My Network Places If connected to a network, it is used to display all connected computers and servers and to browse networked files.

N

Navigation Method by which you move through a Web site.

Network Connects one computer to other computers and peripheral devices. This connection enables the computers to share data and resources. If the computers are located relatively close to each other—in the same building or department— they are part of a local area network.

Network operating system System software that allows for a group of two or more microcomputers to be connected.

Newsgroup An online discussion group where participants exchange messages on a particular topic.

Non-impact printers Type of printer in which characters are formed without anything striking the paper.

Normal view In Word, the display of a document in a simple layout. In PowerPoint, a view of a presentation that shows the outline pane, the slide pane, and the notes pane.

Notebook computer Similar to a microcomputer; however, it is smaller and portable.

O

Operand Number or cell reference in a formula.

Operating systems Type of software that provides an interface between the user or application program and the computer hardware.

Operator A symbol that tells Excel what mathematical operation to perform in a worksheet formula.

Optical storage devices Use laser technology to read and write data on silver platters.

Option button Lets you choose one option from a group of options.

Order of evaluation The sequence used to calculate the value of a complex formula.

Orientation Determines whether your document will be printed lengthwise or crosswise on the sheet of paper. The default page orientation in all Office applications is portrait (taller than wide), but you can change it to landscape (wider than tall).

Output devices Enable the computer to give you the results of the processed data.

Overtype mode In this mode, new text replaces existing characters.

P

Parallel port Computer port that can transmit data eight bits at a time; usually used by the printer.

Parent folder The first level of folders on a disk. Subfolders are created within parent folders.

Path Identifies the disk and any folders relative to the location of the document.

Peer-to-peer Computer architecture in which all of the computers on a network are equal, and there is no computer designated as the server.

People Users of the computers who enter the data and use the output.

Personal digital assistant (PDA) Also called a palmtop computer, it's a small, portable type of computer.

Personal information management software (PIMS) Type of software designed to organize and manage personal tasks, appointments, and contacts.

PhotoCD Used to store digitized photographic images.

Placeholders Provide placement guides for adding text, pictures, tables, or charts.

Pointer (also **mouse pointer**) On-screen object (whose shape changes depending on the function) whose movement and function is controlled by the mouse.

Pointing device Device, such as a mouse or trackball, that allows the user to select objects on the screen.

Points A unit of measure for fonts. One inch equals approximately 72 points.

Pop-up An item in a Help screen displayed with a different color. Clicking the pop-up displays a box that defines the term.

Portrait orientation The document content is formatted with the short edge of the page at the top.

Precedent cells Worksheet cells that provide data to a formula.

Primary button The mouse button that is used for selecting and dragging. By default, the primary is the button on the left.

Primary key Uniquely identifies each record in an Access table.

Print Layout view The display of a document where the display shows the document as it will look when it is printed.

Printers Output devices that transfer data to a paper format.

Printhead Mechanism in a dot matrix printer that actually does the printing.

Problem solving Systematic approach of going from an initial situation to a desired situation that is subject to some resource constraints.

Protocols Standard formats for transferring data between two devices. TCP/IP is the agreed-upon international standard for transmitting data.

Public domain Information or content to which copyright protection does not apply and which is available for anyone to copy.

Q

Query Enables you to locate multiple records matching a specified criteria in a single action.

R

Radio button See *Option button*.

Range A selected group of cells.

Read only memory (ROM) A type of computer chip that stores specific instructions to manage the computer's operation. Unlike main memory, this type of memory is non-volatile—the instructions remain permanently on the chip.

Receiver Computer that receives a data transmission.

Record A group of fields in a database.

Record selector A small box or bar that you click to select a row in a table in Datasheet view.

Related search Preprogrammed queries or questions suggested by a Web search engine that are related to information on the current Web page.

Relative cell reference A cell reference that is adjusted when the formula is copied or moved to a new location.

Report A database object that allows you to organize, summarize, and print all or a portion of the data in a database.

Resolution The number of pixels or dots that a monitor can display.

Restore To return a maximized or minimized window to its previous size.

Right-clicking Pressing and quickly releasing the button on the right side of the mouse.

Ring topology Computer configuration in which the devices are connected in a circle, and each computer within the circle is connected to an adjoining device on either side.

S

Scanners Input devices that can change images into codes for input to the computer.

Screen size Diagonal measurement in inches from one corner of the computer monitor screen to the other.

Scroll To move (by way of scroll arrows) through a list, a block of text, or any other materials larger than the current window or screen.

Scroll bar Bar on the right side or bottom of a window that you click to bring different parts of a document into view.

Search engine Internet tool that helps you locate information on the Internet.

Search qualifiers Keywords that you can use to set search criteria in the Windows Help system.

Select (also highlight) To "select" an object, a block of text, or an icon and therefore identify it before issuing a command or an action that will affect the selected item.

Select text Identify text or blocks of text for editing or formatting.

Sender Computer that sends a data transmission.

Serial port Computer port that can transmit data one bit at a time; usually used by the modem and mouse.

Server A computer that handles requests for data, e-mail, file transfers, and other network services from other computers (clients).

Shareware Software you can use for free for a specified period of time. If you decide that you like it and it meets your needs, you are supposed to pay for it.

Shortcut A pointer to an application or document file.

Shortcut button A button in a Help entry that provides a shortcut for performing an action associated with the Help topic.

Shortcut key A combination of two or more keystrokes that, when pressed, carries out a specific action or function.

Shortcut menu A list of the most commonly performed options in the currently displayed menu.

Shortcut menu button Also called the secondary button, it's the button on the right of the mouse.

Simulations Models of real-world activities.

Size box Section of a window that you can drag to change the size of the window.

Sizing handles Small squares or circles surrounding a graphic or object, indicating that it is selected.

Slide design Specifies a color scheme, text format, backgrounds, bullet styles, and graphics for all the slides in a PowerPoint presentation.

Slide layout Arrangement of objects on a slide.

Slide Show view Allows you to view a PowerPoint slide in full view.

Slide Sorter view Displays PowerPoint slides as thumbnails.

Soft page break Page breaks that Word automatically formats as needed when text reaches the bottom margin.

Software Also called an application or a program, it is a set of instructions that tells the computer what to do. The two types of software are system software and application software.

Sound effect A recorded sound that can be added to animated text or objects on a PowerPoint slide.

Source A file to be copied.

Spam Junk mail sent via e-mail.

Special purpose keys Keys on the keyboard, such as the Esc or Num Lock keys, that perform a specialized function.

Spider A search engine robot that searches the Internet for keywords. It feeds the pages it finds to the search engine. It is called a spider because it crawls the Web continually, examining Web sites and finding and looking for links.

Splitting cells Converting a single cell into two or more cells.

Spreadsheet A grid of rows and columns containing numbers, text, and formats.

Spreadsheet software Software used to store, manipulate, and analyze numeric data.

Standard desktop In the opening Windows' screen, the entire background area where windows, icons, and dialog boxes represent your work area.

Standard toolbar The bar usually near the top of a window that contains buttons that instantly execute commands or access various functions.

Star topology Computer configuration in which all of the devices are connected to a central hub or computer.

Start button The button on the taskbar that will display options such as launching programs, opening documents, or other frequently needed tasks.

Statistical functions Describe large quantities of data.

Status bar A message or information area, usually located at the bottom of a window, that displays specific details about the currently selected object or the task being performed.

Style Set of formatting characteristics that you can apply to text, tables, and lists in your document.

Subfolder A way to further separate groups of files within a folder.

Subject directories Method for searching for information on the WWW.

Submenu The second menu. A submenu is indicated when there is a right-pointing arrow next to a menu option.

Supercomputer Largest and fastest computer, capable of storing and processing tremendous volumes of data.

Systems software A group of programs that coordinates and controls the resources and operations of a computer system. The three categories of systems software are operating systems, utilities, and language translators.

T

TCP/IP The acronym for Transmission Control Protocol/Internet Protocol, which is the protocol used by both LANs and WANs that has been adopted as a standard to connect hosts on the Internet.

Technology The application of scientific discoveries to the production of goods and services that improve the human environment.

Telecommunications Electronic transfer of data.

Teleconferencing Telecommunications service in which parties in remote locations can participate via telephone in a group meeting.

Template A file that contains formatting and text that you can customize to create a new document similar to, but slightly different from, the original.

Text boxes Boxes that contain text and can be resized and positioned like other drawing objects.

Theme A consistent design with elements such as fonts, graphics, colors, and backgrounds.

Thumbnails Miniature pictures of clip art and photos.

Time bomb Computer virus that does not cause its damage until a certain date or until the system has been booted a certain number of times.

Title bar Horizontal band in an application window, a document window, or a dialog box that displays the name of the application running in the window, the name of the data file in the window, or the name of the dialog box.

Toggle Turn an option on and off using the same procedure.

Token ring Widely used LAN protocol in which all of the computers are arranged in a circle and they communicate by passing and catching a special signal, called a token.

Topology The way or geometric arrangement of how the network is set up and connected. Example of topology are ring, star, or bus.

Touch display screen Input device where you use your fingers to "point" to an object on the screen.

Trackball Pointing device that works like a mouse turned upside down; it controls the movement of the on-screen pointer.

Tracks "Circles" on a disk where the magnetic read/write head stores data or retrieves it.

Transitions Determine the changes in the display that occur as you move from one PowerPoint slide to another in Slide Show view.

Transmission media The physical or wireless system used to move data from one location to another. Examples of transmission media are twisted pair wire, coaxial cable, or fiber optic cable.

Tree pane The left pane of the Explorer window; also called the folder bar.

Trigger Starts the animation on a PowerPoint slide.

Trigonometric functions Perform calculations that you could do using a scientific calculator.

Trojan horse Computer virus that does something different from what it is expected to do. It may look like it is doing one thing while in actuality it is doing something quite opposite (usually something disastrous).

U

Uniform Resource Locator (URL) An address for a resource or site on the World Wide Web. Web browsers use this address for locating files and other remote services.

Universal Serial Bus (USB) Standard that supports data transfer rates of up to 12 million bits per second.

UNIX Operating system developed by AT&T. It is considered portable, meaning it can run on just about any hardware platform.

Usenet Worldwide network of computers that facilitates the transmission of messages among the news servers.

User interface Part of the computer's operating system that users interact with.

V

Virtual reality An artificial environment that appears to feel like a real environment.

Virus Computer program that's written to cause corruption of data.

Voice recognition Input devices that are used to issue spoken or voice commands to the computer.

W

Web browser An interface to the World Wide Web that interprets hypertext links and lets you view sites and navigate from one Internet node to another.

Web server Displays Web pages and renders them into final form so that they can be viewed by anyone with an Internet connection and a Web browser. Every Web server has a unique Web address.

WebQuest Type of activity that uses the Internet for investigation and problem solving.

What's This? A dialog box Help feature that offers information about dialog box options.

Wide area network (WAN) A computer network that covers a large geographical area. Most WANs are made up of several connected LANs.

Wildcard character The asterisk (*) character used to represent characters you don't know in a search for words or terms.

Window On-screen area in which you view program folders, files, and icons.

Windows Name of the Microsoft operating system; also, the objects that characterize the Windows GUI.

Windows Explorer A program that lets you browse through, open, and manage your computer's disk drives, folders, and files (that is, move, copy, rename, and delete files).

Wizard A Windows feature that simplifies a task by guiding you through a series of prompts and questions.

Word-processing software Software you use to prepare text documents, such as letters, reports, flyers, brochures, and books.

Word wrap Text automatically moves to the next line when it reaches the right margin.

Workbook A collection of related worksheets.

Worksheet A grid of rows and columns containing numbers, text, and formulas.

World Wide Web (WWW) A collection of resources and interlinked documents that work together using a specific Internet protocol.

Worm Type of computer virus that makes many copies of itself resulting in the consumption of system resources, thus slowing down or actually halting tasks.

WORM disks Optical disk storage devices that use laser beams and optical technology to permanently store large volumes of data.

Z

Zip drives Type of disk capable of storing as much as 1 GB of data.

Zoom box Feature of Macintosh windows that you can click to reduce or enlarge the size of a window.

INDEX

Note: The prefix CF with page numbers indicates the Computing Fundamentals section of this book, KA indicates the Key Applications section, and LO indicates the Living Online section.

A

B

D

T

Z